THE LIFE

OF

THOMAS JEFFERSON.

BY

HENRY S. RANDALL, LL. D.

"THOMAS JEFFERSON STILL SURVIVES!"
The Last Words of John Adams.

IN THREE VOLUMES.

VOL. III.

NEW YORK:
DERBY & JACKSON, 119 NASSAU STREET.
1858.

Printing Statement:

Due to the very old age and scarcity of this book, many of the pages may be hard to read due to the blurring of the original text, possible missing pages, missing text, dark backgrounds and other issues beyond our control.

Because this is such an important and rare work, we believe it is best to reproduce this book regardless of its original condition.

Thank you for your understanding.

CONTENTS OF THE THIRD VOLUME.

[A complete Analytical Index will be found at the End of this Volume.]

CHAPTER I.

1802—1803.

CHAPTER II.

1803—1804.

CHAPTER III.

1804—1805.

CHAPTER IV.

1805—1806.

CHAPTER V.

1806—1807.

CHAPTER VI.

1807—1808.

CHAPTER VII.

1808—1809.

CHAPTER VIII.

1809.

CHAPTER IX.

1810—1813.

CHAPTER X.

1814—1816.

CHAPTER XI.

1817—1822.

CHAPTER XII.

1828—1825.

CHAPTER XIII.

1825—1826.

larly daring effort to beat the French Consul at a game he was himself very fond of playing towards other nations. The further chances of the game—the skill of the players—the end which tests the wisdom of the beginning—are to be hereafter recorded.

Before the close of Congress, General Hamilton resorted to his old practice of drawing up a plan, or programme of action, for his party. It was dated April, 1802, and addressed to Bayard. It is worth the study of those who feel interested in the inquiry whether he was a profound and wise statesman, understanding men, and especially understanding his own countrymen, and was borne down only by an overwhelming tide of circumstances which no sagacity could foresee or resist; or whether he was that visionary "projector" we have seen him so recently pronouncing the President—as much of an "exotic" in American affairs as he sometimes suspected himself of being[1] and as John Adams always declared him to be.

We present the material parts of the plan:

"Nothing is more fallacious than to expect to produce any valuable or permanent results in political projects by relying merely on the reason of men. Men are rather reasoning than reasonable animals, for the most part governed by the impulse of passion. This is a truth well understood by our adversaries, who have practised upon it with no small benefit to their cause, for at the very moment they are eulogizing the reason of men, and professing to appeal only to that faculty, they are courting the strongest and most active passion of the human heart—*vanity!*

"It is no less true, that the Federalists seem not to have attended to the fact sufficiently; and that they erred in relying so much on the rectitude and utility of their measures as to have neglected the cultivation of popular favor, by fair and justifiable expedients. The observation has been repeatedly made by me to individuals with whom I particularly conversed, and expedients suggested for gaining good will, which were never adopted. Unluckily, however, for us, in the competition for the passions of the people, our opponents have great advantages over us; for the plain reason that the vicious are far more active than the good passions; and that, to win the latter to our side, we must renounce our principles and our objects, and unite in corrupting public opinion, till it becomes fit for nothing but mischief. Yet, unless we can contrive to take hold of, and carry along with us, some strong feelings of the mind, we shall in vain calculate upon any substantial or durable results. Whatever plan we may adopt, to be successful, must be founded on the truth of this proposition. And perhaps it is not very easy for us to give it full effect; especially not without some deviations from what, on other occasions, we have maintained to be right. But in determining upon the propriety of the deviations, we must consider whether it be possible for us to succeed, without, in some degree,

[1] Letter to Morris, February 27th, 1802, already quoted.

employing the weapons which have been employed against us, and whether the actual state and future prospect of things be not such as to justify the reciprocal use of them. I need not tell you that I do not mean to countenance the imitation of things intrinsically unworthy, but only of such as may be denominated irregular; such as, in a sound and stable order of things, ought not to exist. Neither are you to infer that any revolutionary result is contemplated. In my opinion, the present Constitution is the standard to which we are to cling. Under its banners, *bond fide*, must we combat our political foes, rejecting all changes but through the channel itself provides for amendments. By these general views of the subject have my reflections been guided. I now offer you the outline of the plan which they have suggested. Let an association be formed to be denominated 'The Christian Constitutional Society.' Its objects to be—

" 1st. The support of the Christian religion.

" 2d. The support of the Constitution of the United States.

" *Its organization :*

" 1st. A council, consisting of a president and twelve members, of whom four and the president to be a quorum.

" 2d. A sub-directing council in each State, consisting of a vice-president and twelve members, of whom four, with the vice-president, to be a quorum; and

" 3d. As many branches in each State as local circumstances may permit to be formed by the sub-directing council.

" The meeting at Washington to nominate the president and vice, together with four members of each of the councils, who are to complete their own numbers respectively.

" *Its means :*

" 1st. The diffusion of information. For this purpose not only the newspapers but pamphlets must be largely employed; and to do this a fund must be created; five dollars annually, for eight years, to be contributed by each member who can really afford it (taking care not to burden the less able brethren), may afford a competent sum for a competent term. It is essential to be able to disseminate *gratis* useful publications. Wherever it can be done, and there is a press, clubs should be formed, to meet once a week, read the newspapers, and prepare essays, paragraphs, etc.

" 2d. The use of all lawful means in *concert* to promote the election of *fit* men ; a lively correspondence must be kept up between the different societies.

" 3d. The promoting of institutions of a charitable and useful nature in the management of Federalists. The populous cities ought particularly to be attended to ; perhaps it would be well to institute in such places—1st, societies for the relief of emigrants; 2d, academies, each with one professor, for instructing the different classes of mechanics in the principles of mechanics and the elements of chemistry. The cities have been employed by the Jacobins to give an impulse to the country; and it is believed to be an alarming fact, that while the question of Presidential election was pending in the House of Representatives, parties were organizing in several of the cities, in the event of there being no election, to cut off the leading Federalists and seize the government.

" The foregoing to be the principal engine, and in addition, let measures be adopted to bring as soon as possible the repeal of the judiciary law before the Supreme Court ; afterwards, if not before, let as many legislatures as can be prevailed upon, instruct their senators to endeavor to procure a repeal of the repealing law. The body of New England, speaking the same language, will give a powerful impulse. In Congress, our friends to *propose* little, to agree cordially to all good measures, and to resist and expose all bad. This is a general sketch of what has occurred to me. It is at the service of my friends for so much as it may be worth."

General Hamilton was even more unsuccessful when he attempted to secure the "sweet voices" of the multitude by caresses, than when he acted the natural and vigorous part of Coriolanus.

The passages in which he assures one of the most intimate and confidential of his political correspondents that *now* no "revolutionary result" is contemplated, that, "in his opinion," they must cling to the Constitution "*bonâ fide*," and reject "all changes but through the channel itself provided for amendments," are very suggestive.

This card-castle did not make a favorable impression on a man of equal ability and far greater shrewdness and knowledge of men. Bayard wrote back that "the plan was marked with great ingenuity, but he was not inclined to think that it was applicable to the state of things in this country." He said, "they had the greater number of political calculators," their opponents of "political fanatics;" that "an attempt at association, organized into clubs, on the part of the Federalists, would revive a thousand jealousies and suspicions which now began to slumber;" that they must "not be too impatient;" that two or three years, without any exertion on their part, "would render every honest man in the country their proselyte;" and finally, that he had "had an opportunity of learning the opinions of the Chief Justice," who "considered the late repealing act as operative in depriving the judges of all power derived under the act repealed," the office however still remaining, a "mere capacity, without a new appointment, to receive and exercise any new judicial powers which the legislature might confer."[1] And thus dropped the extinguisher on "The Christian Constitutional Society."

The President wrote Joel Barlow, May 3d, giving the political statistics of the United States at the time with great accuracy and force. The following sentences will show what he

[1] For letter, see Hamilton's Works, vol. vi. p. 543.

anticipated from Judge Marshall's then forthcoming biography of Washington:

" John Marshall is writing the life of General Washington from his papers. It is intended to come out just in time to influence the next Presidential election. It is written, therefore, principally with a view to electioneering purposes."

Congress adjourned on the 3d of May, and on the 5th the President set out on a flying visit home. He reached the capital again before the close of the month.

He wrote one of his usual highly respectful letters to Dr. Priestley, June 19th, repelling the praise of the latter for any exclusive agency in the great political revolution which had been effected—declaring that " no individual had a right to take any great share to himself" of its accomplishment—that " our people in a body were wise"—that " those they had assigned to the direction of their affairs had stood with a pretty even front—if any one of them had been withdrawn, many others, entirely equal, had been ready to fill his place with as good abilities." Few, probably, will quite concur in the accuracy of these modest expressions.

To MARIA JEFFERSON EPPES, BERMUDA HUNDRED.

WASHINGTON, *July 1st*, 1802.

MY DEAR MARIA:

Mr. Eppes's letter of May 11th is the last news I have heard of you. I wrote to him June 13. Your sister has been disappointed in her visit here by the measles breaking out in her family. It is therefore put off to October. I propose to leave this on the 21st inst., and shall be at Monticello on the 24th or 27th, according to the route I take; where I shall hope to find you on my arrival. I should very much apprehend that were you to continue at the Hundred till then, yourself, Mr. Eppes, or the little one, might be prevented by the diseases incident to the advancing season, from going up at all. It will therefore give me great pleasure to hear of your leaving the Hundred as soon as Mr. Eppes's affairs will permit. Mr. Trist and Dr. Bache will both set out within a few days for the Mississippi, with a view to remove their families thither in the fall; so we shall lose those two late accessions to our neighborhood. However, in the summer season, our complaint is not the want of society; and in the winter there can be little, even among neighbors. Dabney Carr was married on Monday (28), and set out yesterday (30) with his new wife for Albemarle, where he will join his mother, now keeping house at Dunlora, till he can fix himself in Charlottesville, which will be soon. Sam Carr returns decidedly to live at Dunlora; the marriage of the other sister to Dabney seems to have effected this. Peter and his wife are expected here daily on their way to Baltimore. From this sketch you may judge of the state of our neighborhood when we shall meet there. It will be infinitely joyful to me to be with you there, after the longest separation we have had for years. I count from one meeting to another as we do between port and port at sea ; and I long for the moment with the same earnestness. Present me affectionately to Mr. Eppes, and let me hear from you immediately. Be assured yourself of my tender and unchangeable affections.

TH. JEFFERSON.

———

To Maria Jefferson Eppes.

WASHINGTON, July 2, 1802.

MY DEAR MARIA:

My letter of yesterday had hardly got out of my hand when yours of June 21st and Mr. Eppes's of the 25th were delivered. I learn with extreme concern the state of your health and that of the child, and am happy to hear you have got from the Hundred to Eppington, the air of which will aid your convalescence, and will enable you to delay your journey to Monticello till you have recovered your strength to make the journey safe. With respect to the measles, they began in Mr. Randolph's family about the middle of June, and will probably be a month getting through the family ; so that you had better, when you go, pass on direct to Monticello, not calling at Edgehill. I will immediately write to your sister, and inform her I have advised you to this. I have not heard yet of the disease having got to Monticello, but the intercourse with Edgehill being hourly, it cannot have failed to have gone there immediately ; and as there are no young children there but Bet's and Sally's, and the disease is communicable before a person knows they have it, I have no doubt those children have passed through it. The children of the plantation, being a mile and a half off, can easily be guarded against. I will write to Monticello, and direct that should the nail boys or any others have it, they be removed to the plantation instantly on your arrival. Indeed, none of them but Bet's sons stay on the mountain : and they will be doubtless through it. I think, therefore, you may be there in perfect security. It had gone through the neighborhood chiefly when I was there in May ; so that it has probably disappeared. You should make inquiry on the road before you go into any house, as the disease is now universal throughout the State, and all the States. Present my most friendly attachment to Mr. and Mrs. Eppes. Tell the latter I have had her spectacles these 6 months, waiting for a direct conveyance. My best affections to Mr. Eppes, if with you, and the family, and tender and constant love to yourself.

TH. JEFFERSON.

P.S. I have always forgotten to answer your apologies about Critta, which were very unnecessary. I am happy she has been with you and useful to you. At Monticello there could be nothing for her to do ; so that her being with you is exactly as desirable to me as she can be useful to you.

———

To Maria Jefferson Eppes.

WASHINGTON, July 16, 1802.

MY DEAR MARIA:

Your sister informs me she has lately given you information of the health of the family. It seems her children have escaped the measles, though some of the negroes have had it. The following is an extract from her letter dated July 10th ·

" We are entirely free from the measles here now. Those of our people who had it are recovered. At Monticello, the last time I heard from there, three of the nail boys had it and others were complaining; but whether with the measles or not I could not learn. I will send over to Lilly immediately to let him know your orders on the subject." Those orders were to remove every person from the mountain who had or should have the measles. I have no doubt you may proceed with the utmost security. I shall be there before you, to wit, on Saturday the 24th, and will take care to have a clear stage, if anybody should still have it; but there can be no doubt it will have gone through all who were to have it before that date. I am satisfied Francis will have more to hope from the change of air, than to fear from the measles. And as to yourself, it is of great importance to get up into the country as soon as you are able, the liability to bilious diseases being exactly in proportion to the distance from the sea. I leave this on the 24th, and shall be in great hopes of receiving yourself and Mr. Eppes there immediately. I received two days ago his letter of the 8th, in which he gives me a poor account of your health, though he says you are recruiting. Make very short stages, be off always by daylight, and have your day's journey over by ten. In this way it is probable you may find the moderate exercise of the journey of service to yourself and Francis. Nothing is more frequent than to see a child reëstablished by a journey. Present my sincerest affections to the family at Eppington and to Mr. Eppes. Tell him the Tory newspapers are all attacking his publication, and urging it as a proof that Virginia has for object to change the Constitution of the United States, and to make it too impotent to curb the larger States. Accept yourself assurances of my constant and tenderest love.

TH. JEFFERSON.

On the 13th of July, the President addressed Mr. King, the American minister to England, on the subject of obtaining permission of the proper authorities for transporting the insurgent blacks of Virginia to the colony of Sierra Leone. The following was the closing paragraph of the letter, and it will become more interesting in the light of some subsequent circumstances :

" The request of the Legislature of Virginia having produced to me the occasion of addressing you, I avail myself of it to assure you of my perfect satisfaction with the manner in which you have conducted the several matters confided to you by us; and to express my hope that through your agency we may be able to remove everything inauspicious to a cordial friendship between this country and the one in which you are stationed; a friendship dictated by too many considerations not to be felt by the wise and the dispassionate of both nations. It is therefore with the sincerest pleasure I have observed on the part of the British Government various manifestations of just and friendly disposition towards us. We wish to cultivate peace and friendship with all nations, believing that course most conducive to the welfare of our own. It is natural that these friendships should bear some proportion to the common interests of the parties. The interesting relations between Great Britain and the United States, are certainly of the first order; and as such are estimated, and will be faithfully cultivated by us. These sentiments have been communicated to you from time to time in the official correspondence of the Secretary of State ; but I have thought it might not be unacceptable to be assured that they.perfectly concur with my own personal convictions, both in relation to yourself and the country in which you are. I pray you to accept assurances of my high consideration and respect."

The President's next two letters pertain to an affair which, at the time, was the theme of the most constant and offensive imputations against him by the opposition press ; and which has since been the subject of a good many historical misstatements. For these reasons, we prefer to give space for his own full explanations :

TO GOVERNOR MONROE.

WASHINGTON, *July* 16, 1802.

DEAR SIR :

Your favor of the 7th has been duly received. I am really mortified at the base ingratitude of Callender. It presents human nature in a hideous form. It gives me concern, because I perceive that relief, which was afforded him on mere motives of charity, may be viewed under the aspect of employing him as a writer. When the Political Progress of Britain first appeared in this country, it was in a periodical publication called the Bee, where I saw it. I was speaking of it in terms of strong approbation to a friend in Philadelphia, when he asked me if I knew that the author was then in the city, a fugitive from prosecution on account of that work, and in want of employ for his subsistence. This was the first of my learning that Callender was the author of the work. I considered him as a man of science fled from persecution, and assured my friend of my readiness to do whatever could serve him. It was long after this before I saw him; probably not till 1798. He had, in the meantime, written a second part of the Political Progress, much inferior to the first, and his History of the United States. In 1798, I think, I was applied to by Mr. Lieper to contribute to his relief. I did so. In 1799, I think, S. T. Mason applied for him. I contributed again. He had, by this time, paid me two or three personal visits. When he fled in a panic from Philadelphia to General Mason's, he wrote to me that he was a fugitive in want of employ, wished to know if he could get into a counting-house or a school, in my neighborhood or in that of Richmond ; that he had materials for a volume, and if he could get as much money as would buy the paper, the profit of the sale would be all his own. I availed myself of this pretext to cover a mere charity, by desiring him to consider me a subscriber for as many copies of his book as the money inclosed (fifty dollars) amounted to ; but to send me two copies only, as the others might lay till called for. But I discouraged his coming into my neighborhood. His first writings here had fallen far short of his original Political Progress, and the scurrilities of his subsequent ones began evidently to do mischief. As to myself, no man wished more to see his pen stopped ; but I considered him still as a proper object of benevolence. The succeeding year, he again wanted money to buy paper for another volume. I made his letter, as before, the occasion of giving him another fifty dollars. He considers these as proofs of my approbation of his writings, when they were mere charities, yielded under a strong conviction that he was injuring us by his writings. It is known to many that the sums given to him were such, and even smaller than I was in the habit of giving to others in distress, of the Federal as well as the Republican party, without attention to political principles. Soon after I was elected to the government, Callender came on here, wishing to be made postmaster at Richmond. I knew him to be totally unfit for it; and however ready I was to aid him with my own charities (and I then gave him fifty dollars), I did not think the public offices confided to me to give away as charities. He took it in mortal offence, and from that moment has been hauling off to his former enemies, the Federalists. Besides the letter I wrote him in answer to the one from General Mason's, I wrote him another, containing answers to two questions he addressed to me. 1. Whether Mr. Jay received salary as Chief Justice and Envoy at the same time; and 2, something relative to the expenses of an embassy to Constantinople. I think these were the only letters I ever wrote him in answer to volumes he was perpetually writing to me. This is the true state of what has passed between him and me. I do not know that it can be used without committing me in controversy, as it were, with one too little respected by the public to merit that notice. I leave to your judgment what use can be made of these facts. Perhaps it will be better judged of, when we see what use the Tories will endeavor to make of their new friend. I shall leave this on the 21st, and be at Monticello probably on the 24th, or within two or three days of that, and shall hope, ere long, to see you there.

Accept assurances of my affectionate attachment.

To Governor Monroe.

Washington, *July* 17, 1802.

DEAR SIR:

After writing you on the 15th, I turned to my letter file to see what letters I had written to Callender, and found them to have been of the dates of 1798, October the 11th, and 1799, September the 6th, and October the 6th; but on looking for the letters, they were not in their places, nor to be found. On recollection, I believe I sent them to you a year or two ago. If you have them, I shall be glad to receive them at Monticello, where I shall be on this day se'nnight. I inclose you a paper, which shows the Tories mean to pervert these charities to Callender as much as they can. They will probably first represent me as the patron and support of the Prospect before Us, and other things of Callender's; and then picking out all the scurrilities of the author against General Washington, Mr. Adams, and others, impute them to me. I, as well as most other Republicans who were in the way of doing it, contributed what I could afford to the support of the Republican papers and printers, paid sums of money for the Bee, the Albany Register, etc., when they were staggering under the sedition law; contributed to the fines of Callender himself, of Holt, Brown, and others, suffering under that law. I discharged, when I came into office, such as were under the persecution of our enemies, without instituting any prosecutions in retaliation. They may, therefore, with the same justice, impute to me, or to every Republican contributor, everything which was ever published in those papers or by those persons. I must correct a fact in mine of the 15th. I find I did not inclose the fifty dollars to Callender himself while at General Mason's, but authorized the General to draw on my correspondent at Richmond, and to give the money to Callender. So that the other fifty dollars of which he speaks were by order on my correspondent at Richmond.[1]

Accept assurances of my affectionate esteem and respect.

James Thompson Callender was a Scotchman by birth; was well educated; and possessed much coarse, vigorous ability. His talents and his previous history attracted a good deal of notice and sympathy from the party in the United States whose interests he so warmly espoused; but his course was steadily downward, owing to habits of inebriety and of consorting with vicious and degraded men. Even his mind seemed to fail rapidly with every succeeding effort, and as he sunk into the brutality he also sunk into the impotence of a common blackguard. He had been made the victim of an oppressive law—his private conduct was unknown to Mr. Jefferson—his increasing newspaper virulence was still of a milder type than that of a host of writers on the other side—and he was one of those pertinacious mendicants who having fastened themselves, by successful appeals to sympathy, on a respectable man, can only be shaken off at the expense of some disgusting quarrel.

A picture of this transaction, which has been rendered familiar to all American readers, exhibits Mr. Jefferson as continuing to confer the gratuities we have recorded, on a writer who was indecently attacking the personal character of a rival candi-

---

[1] The account book has the following entries:

1797.	Dec. 14.	Paid Callender for pamphlets, . . .	.	$4 33
"	" 23.	Paid Callender for books and pamphlets, . .	.	5 00
1798.	Feb. 9.	Paid T. Lieper for Callender, for five copies of his Sketches, ...	.	5 00
"	March 23.	Gave Lieper order on Barnes for Callender,	.	16 00
"	May 23.	Paid Callender for books, ...	.	3 00
"	" 28.	Paid Callender for books, . . .	.	5 00
"	June 26.	Paid Callender for his next book, . .	.	5 00
1799.	Sept. 6.	Wrote to G. Jefferson & Co. to pay to J. T. Callender,		50 00
1800.	Oct. 23.	Directed G. Jefferson to pay Callender, .	.	50 00
1801.	May 28.	Gave in charity to J. T. Callender, .	.	50 00

These are all the entries where Callender's name occurs excepting two, which are memoranda of sums of money paid him for other persons, of less than five dollars each. Mr. Jefferson states that he was in the habit of giving to others in distress, " without attention to political principles." Our eye now rests on an entry, near one of the preceding, of $50 sent to a superannuated Virginia officer, who we believe to have been an ardent Federalist. Entries of gratuities of equal amount to other individuals occur on several occasions, where we have no means of tracing the politics of the individual. The sums contributed by him to newspapers, and to aid in paying the fines under the Sedition Law, cannot be traced, because in some cases, probably, they were paid to third persons, and in others we are not acquainted with the names of the publishers. In 1799, he paid $25 to Senator Mason for " Lyon," and the same year sent " Lyon " $25 for " Staunton Gazettes." These are interspersed with entries (among the first that catches our eye) of $100 to an academy; $15 to an Episcopalian clergyman; $7.50 contribution at a sermon, etc., etc.; and daily ones, ranging from $1 to $20, to the old, the lame, the blind, etc

date. This is believed to be a purely gratuitous assumption. We confess we never have found our curiosity strong enough to vanquish our disinclination to go back and examine the writings of this man. But it is certain that Mr. Adams, afterwards, so far from complaining of personal attacks on himself, in his two Presidential contests with Jefferson, admitted that he was most handsomely used in this particular; and declared that his own party friends had specially contributed to the ruin of their cause by their entirely different conduct towards Mr. Jefferson. And nowhere have we, in our political investigations, found an allusion to any insulting imputations on Mr. Adams's private character, tracing back to or repeated by Callender. This lower deep of his infamy was undoubtedly reserved for new associations and new victims.

But if these are erroneous conjectures, it will be very easy to demonstrate the mistake from printed records. If it should be proved that Callender was in the habit of denouncing Mr. Adams as a man destitute of personal veracity, as a suborner of perjury, as a foreign ambassador who attempted to procure a deliberate pecuniary fraud on a class of public creditors, as a man of wealth who obtained his property by cheating a widowed sister and her orphaned children out of their patrimony, as an atheist, as an open scorner of the Sabbath and all religious rites, as an indecent reviler of the Saviour,[1] as a parent who had brought shame and agony on his daughters, by converting his house into an African brothel[2]—or of bringing kindred or analogous charges—then we shall blush to find that any considerations induced Mr. Jefferson to continue even that degree of countenance to the author implied by making him an object of charity;—though the "gentle quality" of a kind man's mercy will often induce him to drop a pittance into the hand of avowed infamy sooner than see anything of man or woman kind suffering for food or shelter. To such, even such straits, the improvidence of Callender had exposed him.

---

[1] Saying that an old dilapidated church "was good enough for him who was born in a manger," etc.!

[2] We have at this moment lying before us some pretty well written lines, copied from a Philadelphia paper, and originally published in a Boston paper—(both of which received the personal and official patronage of the Federal party)—which represents Mr. Jefferson's daughters weeping to see a *negress* installed in the place of their mother. We hope to be excused these details, but it seems to us about time when such traditions as the story of Jefferson's connection with Callender are beginning to pass into pseudo "history," to call back attention to some of the facts.

Mr. Jefferson did not explain another charge connected with his treatment of this man, which was also included by the political writers of the day among the "rewards" he had conferred on him for "libelling Mr. Adams"—namely, that he had pardoned him from prison and remitted his fine, as a victim of the Sedition Law. He probably supposed no such explanations were necessary to a friend, who knew that he took the same course towards all who had been condemned under what he regarded, and was determined in all cases to treat officially, as a wholly unconstitutional act.

The post-office at Richmond (worth about $1,500 a year) refused to Callender, was held by a Federal editor. On receiving this refusal, the former thereupon connected himself with the Richmond Recorder, and commenced a foul outpouring of personal calumnies on the President. Every enemy the latter had in Virginia ready to descend to such employment, emptied into this ready conduit all the old gossip, exploded calumnies and base suspicions which can be picked up among low neighbors and unscrupulous enemies in regard to any prominent man; and they swelled the putrid stream with such new and monstrous fabrications as they chose—for the fear of libel prosecutions was no longer a "hangman's whip" to "haud" this class of persons "in order."

Nearly every people have had a class who subsist by levying "black mail" on those ready to buy exemption for themselves or their families from dirty slanders, and by catering to the appetite for scandal in those who are beneath attack. The assailant is below contradiction; he is below the punishment of law. Personal chastisement he would delight in, because it would advertise him in his trade, and because he would gladly take kicks which could be coined into pence in an action for "assault and battery." Callender sunk into this avocation. When he demanded the Richmond post-office, the President acted the part of Charicles instead of Nicias,[1] and he took the consequences.

Shall we declare the fact that the Richmond Recorder,

---

[1] Plutarch quotes one of the comic poets of his day as saying: "Charicles would not give one mina to prevent my declaring that he was the first fruits of his mother's amours: but Nicias, the son of Niceratus, gave me four. Why he did it I shall not say, though I know it perfectly well. For Nicias is my friend, a very wise man besides, in my opinion."

which before was an obscure paper, scarcely known out of the city, rapidly attained a circulation throughout the United States !

Callender, elated by his success and provided with new means, plunged deeper in debauchery. Bloated and noisome, he reeled from one den of infamy to another when not engaged in collating or concocting attacks on Mr. Jefferson. This continued until he was drowned in the James River, into which he had gone to bathe in a state of intoxication.

The President arrived at Monticello July 25th, on his usual visit during the unhealthy season. He was made happy by the conditions so fondly anticipated in his letters to Mrs. Eppes—the presence of his dearly loved children and grandchildren.

The domestic details of the period are not specially interesting. His income for his first Presidential year did not meet his expenditures. We are tempted to give the heads of both of these as we find them analyzed in the account-book. The reader will not forget that the items of an unmarried man's establishment must necessarily considerably vary in kind from those of one surrounded by a family of both sexes :

Analysis of Expenditures from March 4, 1801, to March 4, 1802.

Secretary	$450 00	
Provisions	4,504 84	
Fuel	690 88	
Miscellaneous	295 82	
Servants	2,675 84	
Groceries (not wine)	2,003 71	
Wines	2,797 28	
Stable	884 45	
Dress, Saddlery, etc.	567 36	
Charities [in cash]	978 20	
Contingencies	557 81	
Books and Stationery	391 30	$16,797 59
Debts prior to March 4, 1801, paid	3,917 59	
Loans	170 00	
Acquisitions (lands, horses and carriages)	4,712 74	
Building (at Monticello)	2,076 29	
Furniture	545 48	11,422 10
Household Expenses at Monticello	652 82	
Plantation Expenses at do.	3,732 23	4,385 05
Family Aids	1,030 10	1,030 10
	$33,634 84	$33,634 84

CR.

By Salary	. $25,000 00
Tobacco	. 2,974 00
Profits of Nailery supposed about . . .	. 533 33
A debt contracted with J. Barnes . .	. 4,361 00
	$32,868 33
Error	. 766 51
	$33,634 84

He supposes the error to have proceeded from having in some cases set down the same article of expense twice; but he says the above " is exact enough to give general ideas."

The President returned to the capital on the 5th of October.

To MARIA JEFFERSON EPPES.

MY DEAR MARIA: WASHINGTON, *Oct.* 7, 1802.

I arrived here on the fourth day of my journey without accident. On the day and next day after my arrival I was much indisposed with a general soreness all over, a ringing in the head and deafness. It is wearing off slowly, and was probably produced by travelling very early two mornings in the fog. I have desired Mr. Jefferson to furnish you with whatever you may call for on my account; and I insist on your calling freely. It never was my intention that a visit for my gratification should be at your expense. It will be absolutely necessary for me to send fresh horses to meet you, as no horses, after the three first days' journey, can encounter the fourth, which is hilly beyond anything you have ever seen. I shall expect to learn from you soon the day of your departure, that I may make proper arrangements. Present me affectionately to Mr. Eppes, and accept yourself my tenderest love.

TH. JEFFERSON.

Receiving a letter from Livingston (who had not yet got the President's of April 18th), mentioning the alienation from the United States which pervaded all the prominent circles of France, the President did not in the least unbend from his previous attitude. He replied October 10th:

"The departure of Madame Brugnard for France furnishes me a safe conveyance of a letter, which I cannot avoid embracing, although I have nothing particular for the subject of it. It is well, however, to be able to inform you, generally, through a safe channel, that we stand completely corrected of the error, that either the Government or the nation of France has any remains of friendship for us. The portion of that country which forms an exception, though respectable in weight, is weak in numbers. On the contrary, it appears evident, that an unfriendly spirit prevails in the most important individuals of the Government towards us. In this state of things, we shall so take our distance between the two rival nations, as, remaining disengaged till necessity compels us, we may haul finally to the enemy of that which shall make it necessary. We see all the disadvantageous consequences of taking a side, and shall be forced into it only by a more disagreeable alternative ; in which event, we must countervail the disadvantages by measures which will give us splendor and power, but not as much happiness as our present system. We wish, therefore, to remain well with France. But we see that no consequences, however ruinous to them, can secure us with certainty against the extravagance of her present rulers. I think, therefore, that while we do nothing which the first nation on earth would deem crouching, we had better give to all our communications with them a very mild, complaisant, and even friendly complexion, but always independent. Ask no favors, leave small and irritating things to be conducted by the individuals interested in them, interfere ourselves but in the greatest cases, and then not push them to irritation. No matter at present existing between them and us is important enough to risk a breach of peace ; peace being indeed the most important of all things for us, except the preserving an erect and independent attitude. Although I know your own judgment leads you to pursue this line identically, yet I thought it just to strengthen it by the concurrence of my own."

He wrote Mr. Gallatin on the 13th, expressing the opinion that the act for building piers in the Delaware was unconstitutional, so far as it was based on the right of Congress to regulate commerce, and that " it would lead to a bottomless expense, and to the greatest abuses." He thought, however, it might be brought within the Constitution under the head of providing and maintaining a navy, as it " provided receptacles for it and places to cover and preserve it ;" and we, he says " ought always to presume that the real intention which is alone consistent with the Constitution." He thought the same objection existed to the construction of lighthouses as a regulation of commerce ; but that " the utility of the thing had sanctioned the infraction." " But if on that infraction we built a second, on that second a third, etc., any one of the powers in the Constitution might be made to comprehend every power of government."

He wrote the Attorney-General on the 23d, congratulating him on the fact that the Republicans had gained ground generally in the recent elections, and that they " had lost ground in not a single district of the United States, excepting Kent county in Delaware, where a religious dissension occasioned it." His magnanimity towards the Federalists—still the incumbents of much the largest portion of the best offices within his gift—while nearly every Federal press in the United States was reeking with the filthy scurrilities of Callender, is manifested in the following passages :

"Their bitterness increases with their desperation. They are trying slanders now which nothing could prompt but a gall which blinds their judgments as well as their consciences. I shall take no other revenge than, by a steady pursuit of economy and peace, and by the establishment of Republican principles in substance and in form, to sink Federalism into an abyss from which there shall be no resurrection for it. I still think our original idea as to office is best: that is, to depend for the obtaining a just participation, on deaths, resignations, and delinquencies. This will least affect the tranquillity of the people, and prevent their giving into the suggestion of our enemies, that ours has been a contest for office, not for principle. This is rather a slow operation, but it is sure if we pursue it steadily, which, however, has not been done with the undeviating resolution I could have wished. To these means of obtaining a just share in the transaction of the public business shall be added one other, to wit, removal for electioneering activity, or open and industrious opposition to the principles of the present Government, legislative and executive. Every officer of the Government may vote at elections according to his conscience; but we should betray the cause committed to our care, were we to permit the influence of official patronage to be used to overthrow that cause. Your present situation will enable you to judge of prominent offenders in your State, in the case of the present election. I pray you to seek them, to mark them, to be quite sure of your ground, that we may commit no error or wrong, and leave the rest to me. I have been urged to remove Mr. Whittemore, the surveyor of Gloucester, on grounds of neglect of duty and industrious opposition. Yet no facts are so distinctly charged as to make the step sure which we should take in this. Will you take the trouble to satisfy yourself on this point? I think it not amiss that it should be known that we are determined to remove officers who are active or open mouthed against the Government, by which I mean the legislature as well as the Executive."

On the 16th of October, Morales, the Spanish Intendant of Louisiana, issued a proclamation withdrawing the privilege of deposit at New Orleans, which had been granted to citizens of the United States by the treaty of 1795 for three years, with a stipulation that it should not be taken away without conceding "an equivalent on another part of the bank of the Mississippi." The last condition was wholly overlooked or disregarded. This procedure produced a great excitement in our western States. The Governor of Kentucky transmitted information of it to the President on the 30th of November. On the 1st of December, the Legislature of that State memorialized Congress, complaining of the infraction of the treaty. But the facts did not reach the President in time to be communicated in his opening message to Congress. That body had stood adjourned to the 6th of December, but a quorum of the Senate did not convene until the 14th.

The President's message, after enumerating those pleasing circumstances in our national affairs "which marked the good.

ness of that being from whose favor they flowed"—"peace and friendship abroad, law, order, and religion at home; good affection and harmony with our Indian neighbors; our burdens lightened, yet our income sufficient for the public wants, and the produce of the year great beyond example," proceeded to state, that on the return of peace to Europe, it was to be expected that our carrying trade would be diminished; but that it had been further seriously injured by the "monopolizing discriminations" of some powers. Where the relinquishment of these could not be brought about by friendly discussion, he said it would be for the legislature to decide whether they were to be met with countervailing discriminations, or whether the evil was to be provided for some other way. He laid before the House "with satisfaction" an act of the British Parliament authorizing a mutual abolition of the duties and countervailing duties permitted under the treaty of 1794. He declared "it showed on their part a spirit of justice and friendly accommodation which it was our duty and our interest to cultivate with all nations." He recommended more stringent laws providing for the return of our seamen discharged in foreign ports.

The cession of Louisiana to France was only alluded to. He said it "would make a change in our foreign relations which would doubtless have a just weight in any deliberations of the legislature connected with that subject."

He stated that our fleet before Tripoli had been reinforced, under the apprehension that the other Barbary powers might take part in the war; but this apprehension had proved unfounded for the present. Tripoli had been so closely watched that but one American merchant vessel had fallen a prey to its cruisers.

He communicated for ratification the convention with Georgia for the cession of the territory lying west of her; informed the House how far he had proceeded in settling boundaries with the Indians; suggested the expediency of encouraging the settlement of the relinquished Choctaw territory "as an outpost of the United States, surrounded by strong neighbors and distant from its support," and that a monopoly which would prevent its becoming populated should be guarded against by making actual habitation a condition of the continuance of title.

In the department of finance he informed Congress that the external duties had rapidly increased; that besides answering all the regular exigencies of government, upwards of nine millions (including one million raised by the sale of bank stock) had been paid from the Treasury in one year towards the principal and interest of the public debt, making a reduction of nearly five millions and a half in its principal; and that four millions and a half remained in the Treasury, in a course of application to a further discharge of debt and current demands. But he said, " as the effect of peace on the amount of duties was not yet fully ascertained, it was the more necessary to practice every useful economy, and to incur no expense which might be avoided without prejudice."

After mentioning some facts in regard to the cessation of internal taxes, and in regard to certain fiscal operations, he proceeded to say :

" When effects so salutary result from the plans you have already sanctioned, when merely by avoiding false objects of expense we are able, without a direct tax, without internal taxes, and without borrowing, to make large and effectual payments towards the discharge of our public debt, and the emancipation of our posterity from that moral canker, it is an encouragement, fellow citizens, of the highest order to proceed as we have begun, in substituting economy for taxation, and in pursuing what is useful for a nation placed as we are, rather than what is practised by others under different circumstances. And whensoever we are destined to meet events which shall call forth all the energies of our countrymen, we have the firmest reliance on those energies, and the comfort of leaving for calls like these the extraordinary resources of loans and internal taxes. In the meantime, by payments of the principal of our debt, we are liberating, annually, portions of the external taxes, and forming from them a growing fund still further to lessen the necessity of recurring to extraordinary resources."

No change was recommended in the military establishment. A review of the militia law was urged. The only change proposed for the navy was the procuring some smaller vessels for Barbary service in the place of those larger ones which were not sufficiently available on so shallow a coast. It was recommended that the first further annual appropriations for naval defences should be expended in saving those already possessed. As no care or attention could preserve vessels lying in the water and exposed to the sun, from rapid decay, he suggested that those not in use be laid up in dry docks under cover from the sun, to be constructed at Washington. He stated that an abundance of running water could there be obtained, at heights far enough above the level of the tide to be employed, as was practised in lock navigation, as a means for raising the vessels to the desired beds.

The message closed thus:

" To cultivate peace and maintain commerce and navigation in all their lawful enterprises; to foster our fisheries and nurseries of navigation and for the nurture of man, and protect the manufactures adapted to our circumstances; to preserve the faith of the nation by an exact discharge of its debts and contracts, expend the public money with the same care and economy we would practise with our own, and impose on our citizens no unnecessary burden; to keep in all things within the pale of our constitutional powers, and cherish the federal Union as the only rock of safety—these, fellow citizens, are the landmarks by which we are to guide ourselves in all our proceedings. By continuing to make these our rule of action, we shall endear to our countrymen the true principles of their Constitution, and promote a union of sentiment and of action equally auspicious to their happiness and safety. On my part you may count on a cordial concurrence in every measure for the public good, and on all the information I possess which may enable you to discharge to advantage the high functions with which you are invested by your country."

The message gave great satisfaction to the Republicans, and even to many of the moderate Federalists. But it was not to the taste of a portion of the latter party. Hamilton represented the views of this class in a letter to General C. C. Pinckney, December 29th:

" Amidst the triumphant reign of democracy, do you retain sufficient interest in public affairs to feel any curiosity about what is going on? In my opinion, the follies and vices of the Administration have as yet made no material impression to their disadvantage. On the contrary, I think the malady is rather progressive than upon the decline in our northern quarter. The last *lullaby* message, instead of inspiring contempt, attracts praise. Mankind are forever destined to be the dupes of bold or cunning imposture. But a difficult knot has been twisted by the incidents of the cession of Louisiana, and the interruption of the deposit of New Orleans. You have seen the soft turn given to this in the message. Yet we are told that the President, in conversation, is very stout. The great embarrassment must be how to carry on the war without taxes. The pretty scheme of substituting economy to taxation will not do here. And a war would be a terrible comment upon the abandonment of the internal revenue. Yet how is popularity to be preserved with the western partisans, if their interests are tamely sacrificed? Will the artifice be for the chief to hold a bold language, and the subalterns to act a feeble part? Time must explain. You know my general theory as to our western affairs. I have always held that the unity of our empire, and the best interests of our nation, require that we shall annex to the United States all the territory east of the Mississippi, New Orleans included. Of course, I infer that, on an emergency like the present, energy is wisdom."[1]

Pinckney replied a few weeks afterwards:

"Does there not appear to be a great want of nerve and energy in the measures our rulers are adopting? They are not calculated to avoid war, and we shall have to encounter it in a shameful state of unpreparedness. Yet such is the infatuation of the people, that anti-Federalism certainly gains ground in this State, which can only exist by a strong union and firm government."[2]

Sedgwick was a little more hopeful. "There was one consolation under all the humiliation which we endured from a sense of the degradation of our national character. This state of things could not long exist."[3]

Morris wrote an English friend:

"In truth, there is just now so much of what we call philosophy among our rulers, that we must not be surprised at the charge of pusillanimity. And our people have so much mercantile spirit, that, if other nations will keep their hands out of our pockets, it is not a trifling insult that will rouse us. Indeed, it is the fashion to say, that when injured it is more honorable to wait in patience the uncertain issue of negotiation, than promptly to do ourselves right by an act of hostility.

*   *   *   *   *   *

"It is the fashion with those discontented creatures, called Federalists, to say, that our President is not a Christian; yet they must acknowledge that in true Christian meekness, when smitten on one cheek he turns the other, and by his late appointment of Monroe, has taken special care that a stone, which the builders rejected, should be made first of the corner. These are his *works;* and for his *faith,* it is not as a grain of mustard, but the full size of a pumpkin, so that while the men of mustard-seed faith can only move mountains, he finds no difficulty in swallowing them. He believes, for instance, in the perfectibility of man, the wisdom of mobs, and moderation of Jacobins. He believes in payment of debts by diminution of revenue, in defence of territory by reduction of armies, and in vindication of rights by the appointment of ambassadors."[4]

A groan broke from the uneasy retirement of Quincy. In answer to an invitation of citizens of Plymouth to attend a public festival, Mr. Adams wrote:

"I feel a well-grounded conviction that the best principles of our great and glorious ancestors are inherited by a large portion of the American people. And if the talents, the policy, the address, the power, the bigotry and tyranny of Archbishop Laud and the court of Charles the First were not able to destroy or discredit

¹ Hamilton's Works, vol. vi. p. 551.   Ib. p. 554.   ² Ib. p. 552.
³ Morris's Works, vol. iii. p. 176. The letter is dated January 14th, immediately after the nomination of Monroe as Minister Extraordinary to France and Spain.

em in 1630 or 1635, there is little cause of apprehension for them from the
eble efforts of the frivolous libertines who are combining, conspiring, and intriguing
gainst them in 1802."

The important business in Congress opened with proceedings
n respect to the Spanish violation of treaty at New Orleans.
Randolph, chairman of the Committee of Ways and Means, on
he 17th of December, moved to call on the President for infor-
nation; and the latter communicated a copy of the order of the
panish Intendant, and some other official papers as they were
eceived.

The Federalists determined to drive the Administration from
ts policy, and vindicate their own former one, by blowing up
war excitement against Spain and France. Griswold moved,
anuary 4th (1803), for the official documents in relation to the
ession of Louisiana from Spain to France, and a report of all
he circumstances, "unless such documents and report would, in
he opinion of the President, divulge to the House particular
ransactions not proper at this time to be communicated." On
he question of reference, a sharp skirmish took place, involving
he point whether the debate should be public or private. The
'ederalists insisted that it should be public—that the question
nvolved no secret—that the Government had exhibited remiss-
ess—that it was time for the House to act, etc. The call
or more papers was voted down, and on the House being
leared, Randolph submitted the following resolution:

Resolved, That the House receive, with great sensibility, the information of a
isposition in certain officers of the Spanish Government at New Orleans to obstruct
e navigation of the river Mississippi, as secured to the United States by the most
lemn stipulations. That, adhering to the humane and wise policy which ought
rer to characterize a free people, and by which the United States have always pro-
sed to be governed, willing, at the same time, to ascribe this breach of compact
 the unauthorized misconduct of certain individuals, rather than to a want of good
ith on the part of his Catholic Majesty, and relying with perfect confidence on the
igilance and wisdom of the Executive, they will wait the issue of such measures as
lat department of the Government shall have pursued for asserting the rights and
indicating the injuries of the United States; holding it to be their duty, at the
me time, to express their unalterable determination to maintain the boundaries,
nd the rights of navigation and commerce through the river Mississippi, as esta-
lished by existing treaties.

Griswold the next day, in the House, submitted and pro-
ceded to debate a motion in regard to the reference of his re

lution—which was already disposed of—saying, " if gentlemen were disposed to deny this information, let the denial be public." On his motion being voted down he submitted the following resolutions:

Resolved, That the people of the United States are entitled to the free navigation of the river Mississippi.

Resolved, That the navigation of the river Mississippi has been obstructed by the regulations recently carried into effect at New Orleans.

Resolved, That a committee be appointed to inquire whether any, and, if any, what legislative measures are necessary to secure to the people of the United States the free navigation of the river Mississippi.

The House refused to take these up for present consideration by a vote of fifty to thirty-two. The committee to which Randolph's resolution was referred, passed it January 7th. On its being reported to the House, it was moved to strike out the clauses avowing confidence in the Executive and a determination to await the issue of its measures. This failed—yeas thirty, nays fifty-three—and after some other divisions the original resolution passed, yeas fifty, nays twenty-five.

A bill passed, February 26th, appropriating two millions of dollars " to defray the expenses which might be incurred in relation to the intercourse between the United States and foreign nations." The report on which this was founded, avowed the object of the appropriation to be " to enable the Executive to commence with more effect a negotiation with the French and Spanish Governments relative to the purchase from them of the island of New Orleans and the provinces of East and West Florida."

On the 11th of February the President had nominated a Minister Extraordinary for the purpose of attempting to effect these objects. The next day the Senate confirmed the appointment. Yet on the 14th, Ross, of Pennsylvania, commenced in the latter body a very inflammatory speech, accusing the government of tamely sacrificing the interests of our western States. On denouncing the attempt to purchase the territory " by giving two millions of dollars to certain influential persons about court"—he was called to order by Wright, of Maryland, for publicly debating upon confidential information. Vice-President Burr " perceived nothing improper or out of order in what had been said." Nicholas " hoped the galleries would be cleared." Ross vociferated: "I will never speak on this subject with closed doors. The moment you shut your doors I cease; and when they are opened I will proceed. There is nothing of a secret or confidential nature in what I have to say."

On the 16th, he resumed and finished his remarks, in the Senate, in a similar vein; and in conclusion moved the following resolutions:

Resolved, That the United States have an indisputable right to the free navigation of the river Mississippi, and a convenient place of deposit for their produce and merchandise in the island of New Orleans.

That the late infraction of such, their unquestionable right, is an aggression hostile to their honor and interest.

That it does not consist with the dignity or safety of this Union to hold a right so important by a tenure so uncertain.

That it materially concerns such of the American citizens as dwell on the western waters, and is essential to the union, strength, and prosperity of these States, that they obtain complete security for the full and peaceable enjoyment of such their absolute right.

That the President be authorized to take immediate possession of such place or places, in the said island, or the adjacent territories, as he may deem fit and convenient for the purposes aforesaid; and to adopt such other measures for obtaining that complete security as to him in his wisdom shall seem meet.

That he be authorized to call into actual service any number of the militia of the States of South Carolina, Georgia, Ohio, Kentucky, Tennessee, or the Mississippi Territory, which he may think proper, not exceeding fifty thousand, and to employ them, together with the military and naval forces of the Union, for effecting the objects above mentioned.

That the sum of five millions of dollars be appropriated to the carrying into effect the foregoing resolutions, and that the whole or any part of that sum be paid or applied, on warrants drawn in pursuance of such directions as the President may, from time to time, think proper to give to the Secretary of the Treasury.

On the 23d of February, Breckenridge moved to strike out all after the word "Resolved," in Ross's resolutions, and to substitute provisions authorizing the President, whenever he should deem it expedient, to require the Executives of the several States to arm and call out eighty thousand effective militia, or to accept volunteers in the place of a portion of the detachment; to appropriate ———— sums for defraying expenses and erecting one or more arsenals, at such places as the President should judge proper, on the "western waters." The last words were all that gave any indication whatever of the object of the force.

De Witt Clinton, of New York, made his first elaborate speech in the Senate, February 23d; and it was on the preceding question. He was then within a few weeks of his thirty-fourth birth-day. He exhibited that legal research, that profound statistical and historical knowledge, that lofty and severe tone towards opponents, and we need not add, that talent which distinguished him through life. As a specimen both of the man, and of the manner of handling, on the Republican side, one of the incessant allusions of the Federalists, we select the following passages :

"We have heard much of the policy of Washington; it has been sounded in our ears from all quarters, and an honorable gentleman from Delaware (Mr. White) has triumphantly contrasted it with that adopted by the present Administration. I am not disposed to censure it in this case; on the contrary, I think it a high and respectable authority; but let it be properly understood in order to be rightly appreciated, and it will be found that the United States under his Administration, and that of his successor, have received injuries more deleterious, insults more atrocious, and indignities more pointed than the present, and that the pacific measure of negotiation was preferred. If our national honor has survived the severe wounds it then received, it may surely outlive the comparatively slight attack now made upon it; but if its ghost only now remains to haunt the consciences of the honorable gentlemen who were then in power, and who polluted their hands with the foul murder, let them not attempt to transfer the odium and the crime to those who had no hand in the guilty deed. The reins of Government were in their hands, and if the course they at that time pursued was diametrically opposite to that they now urge for our adoption, what shall we say of their consistency? What will they say of it themselves? What will their country say of it? Will it be believed that the tinkling sounds and professions of patriotism which have been so vehemently pressed upon us, are the emanations of sincerity, or will they be set down to the account of juggling imposture?"

After mentioning the injuries inflicted on us by England since the treaty of peace, and among them one perhaps not generally known, that in addition to detaining the American posts, she for a time added the insult of making Niagara, in the State of New York, the seat of government for Upper Canada, Mr. Clinton continued :

"It is well known we were engaged in a bloody and expensive war with several of the Indian tribes; that two of our armies had been routed by them, and that we were finally compelled to make great efforts to turn the tide of victory. These Indians were encouraged and aided by the emissaries of Great Britain—British subjects were seen disguised fighting in their ranks, and British agents were known to furnish them with provisions and the implements of war. The Governor-General of Canada, a highly confidential and distinguished officer, delivered a speech to the seven nations of Lower Canada, exciting them to enmity against this country; but in order to furnish the savages at war with sufficient aid, a detachment of British troops penetrated into our territory, and erected a fort on the Miami River. Here the Indians, dispersed and defeated by Wayne, took refuge, and were protected under the muzzle of British cannon. A violation of territory is one of the most flagrant injuries which can be offered to a nation, and would in most cases justify an immediate resort to arms, because, in most cases, essential to self-defence. Not content with exciting the savages of America against us, Great Britain extended her hostility to the eastern hemisphere, and let loose the barbarians of Africa upon us. A war existed at that time between Portugal and Algiers; the former blocked up the mouth of the Straits, by her superior naval force, and prevented the pirates from a communication with the Atlantic. Portugal has been for a long time subservient to the views of Great Britain; a peace was effected through the mediation of the latter; our unprotected merchantmen were then exposed without defence to the piracies of Algiers. Thus in three quarters of the globe we at one time felt the effects of British enmity. In the meantime, our commerce in every sea was exposed to her rapacity. All France was declared in a state of siege, and the conveyance of provisions expressly interdicted to neutrals. Paper blockades were substituted for actual ones, and the staple commodities of our country lay perishing in our storehouses, or were captured on the ocean, and diverted from the lawful proprietors. Our seamen were pressed wherever found; our protections were a subject of derision, and opposition to the imperious mandates of their haughty tyrants was punished by famine or by stripes, by imprisonment or by the gibbet. To complete the full measure of our wrongs, the November orders of 1793 were issued; our ships were swept from the ocean as by the operation of enchantment; hundreds of them were captured; almost all our merchants were greatly injured, and many of them reduced to extreme poverty.

" These proceedings, without even a pretext, without the forms of justice, without the semblance of equity, were calculated to inflame every American feeling, and to nerve every American arm. Negotiation was, however, pursued; an envoy *extraordinary*, in every sense of the word, was sent to demand redress, and a treaty of amity, commerce, and navigation was formed and ratified. These events took place under the administration of Washington."[1]

He next described, in as animated a vein, the aggressions of France, and Mr. Adams's persisting in sending ministers until peace was secured with that power.

Wright of Maryland also pungently exposed the hypocrisy of appealing to the example of Washington for precipitating the country into war before resorting to negotiation. It would now, indeed, appear incredible that men who supported the

---

[1] In a second speech, Mr. Clinton was particularly severe on Jay, speaking of his treaty as a " bad and disgraceful " one—" neither honorable nor advantageous to this country "—a " pernicious instrument " signed without " expunging one of its most degrading provisions," because " General Washington was prevailed upon by the circumstances of the times" and " elected it as only a lesser evil than war." He declared that if the contents of the treaty had been known in New York, Mr. Jay's chance of success in the Governor election " would have been forlorn," and that " at the subsequent election he was withdrawn "—that Chancellor Livingston was " as much superior to him as Hyperion to a satyr "—that " his incompetency [as Governor] became notorious," and that " he was found unqualified to hold the reins of state "—that " the men of his own party knew it and lamented it," and that " he fell like Lucifer, never to rise again." The debate, strange to say, closed without any answer to this attack on Mr. Jay.

first President's foreign policy in 1794–5, should in 1803 urge avowed war measures towards Spain, which also were expected to involve a war with France, for the single act of a remote colonial officer, and before ascertaining whether his Government would either sanction or refuse to make reparation for his conduct. But it would appear still more incredible that a party thus circumstanced should voluntarily invite comparisons between their conduct on the two occasions, did we not consider men's blindness under partisan excitement, and did we not remember how sytematically Cabot's plan of impressing the name of Washington into the service of Federalism, in the face of any facts, and by mere force of reiteration, was carried out by that party.

Mr. Clinton might have instructively extended his contrast in the action of the Federalists towards foreign powers, on the different occasions mentioned, to their deportment towards our own Executive.

In 1795, they pronounced it unconstitutional and indecorous for the House to call on the Executive for diplomatic papers, to throw light on topics on which it was called upon by the Executive to legislate, after the constitutional functions of the latter in the premises were exhausted, and after the diplomatic arrangements were complete and not liable to be defeated or disturbed, so far as other powers were concerned, by making them subjects of legislative examination. In 1803, they claimed that the House could properly call for papers which were the subjects of pending and unfinished negotiation—that it could at this stage properly discuss the contents of such papers publicly, making them the topics of inflammatory denunciation against our own Executive, and of the most irritating strictures upon and menaces against the powers with whom it was negotiating—and that to deny these claims was to withhold information to which the legal rights and most important interests of the people entitled them. And these pretensions were set up by a party who had just resisted the admission of independent reporters of ordinary congressional proceedings for the use of the people!

In 1795, the Federalists considered the treaty-making power so paramount and absolute in its province, that it had not only a right to form treaties and proclaim them supreme laws of the land without interference or coöperation from, or consultation with, the House of Representatives, but that the latter had not a particle of discretion in respect to enacting laws for their execution—that it was constitutionally bound, under any circumstances, to carry out the agreements of the treaty-making power. In 1803, the same party insisted that the House could of right interfere in advance to prejudge, condemn, forestall, control or defeat the measures of the treaty-making power; and that when this action was stopped by the regular and binding decision of the legislative body, it was morally proper and decorous in members of the minority to resort to evasions, and even to irregularity to continue it, in order to inflame and exasperate the public mind against the anticipated action of the President and Senate.

It has been said that, in the policies pursued at these two epochs, the parties but changed places. This is true only to a comparatively slight extent. There is no real general analogy between the positions of the Republicans in 1795 and the Federalists in 1803—no substantial similarity in their conduct. It was the latter party alone which had completely changed its attitude.

This violent and irregular conduct of the Federalists came with less grace, too, from a party which had uniformly affected to be peculiarly and almost exclusively the conservative one of the country. It had assumed to possess nearly all the education and intelligence of the nation, and their natural concomitants—love of order, respect for constituted authority, and disposition to preserve intact the established organs and powers of civil government. It had been one of its cardinal, avowed theories as a party, that the federal Executive should not only be retained in complete possession of all the official powers with which he was vested by the Constitution, but that in all cases where construction was resorted to, it should tend to enhance instead of diminishing his authority. It had contended this was essentially necessary to preserve national order, unity and obedience to law. It had been the constant burden of its complaints against the opposite party that its doctrines tended to opposite results.

But, as usual, the Federalists wholly overacted, and made a most bungling exhibition of ignorance and awkwardness in a new situation, when they attempted to play a popular part.

The suddenness of the change, and the nakedness of the motive, not only proved the want of sincerity, but it demonstrated even more effectually than their natural conduct, their contempt for the popular understanding and integrity. That chastity must be thought prurient which is expected to surrender at the first summons of those who have always previously exhibited aversion and scorn. That understanding and moral fidelity must be thought at a low ebb which is supposed capable of deserting old and tried friends to follow old and known opponents at the first leer of invitation.

The Congressional representatives of those western States, for the people of which the Federalists had suddenly conceived so vehement an affection, do not appear to have been at all alarmed by the apprehension that the latter would get between them and their constituents. Led by the calm, discreet, and able Breckenridge, they stood by the Administration and awaited results. Breckenridge's motion to strike out Ross's resolutions and insert his own, passed February 25th.

Another question of this session, which called out a strong display of party feeling, rose on a memorial of the Supreme Court judges, who had been legislated out of office the preceding session. They urged that "rights secured to them by the Constitution as members of the judicial department had been impaired;" and they asked Congress to assign them their judicial duties and provide for their compensation. They offered to submit their right to the latter to judicial decision. The House decided (January 27th) by a vote of sixty-one to thirty-seven, that the prayer of the petitioners ought not to be granted; and the Senate a few days after, by a vote of fifteen to thirteen, took equivalent action.

It will be remembered that Mr. Jefferson, when Minister to France, suggested to the celebrated traveller, Ledyard, an exploration of western America. In 1792, he proposed to the American Philosophical Society to procure such an exploration, with funds raised by subscription; and it was under the auspices of this Society, and under instructions prepared by Mr. Jefferson,[1] that Michaux, the celebrated French traveller and botanist, proceeded on his exploration westward, until recalled by

---

[1] For which see Jefferson's Works, Cong. Ed., vol. ix., p. 434.

the French Minister.[1] The utility of ascertaining the character
of the interior of Louisiana at this juncture, was pressed by far
weightier considerations than the mere extension of science.
He, therefore, in a confidential message to the House, on the 18th
of January, recommended sending an exploring party to trace
the Missouri to its source, cross the mountains, and follow the
best water communication which offered itself from thence to
the Pacific. Congress approved the recommendation, and made
an appropriation to defray the expense.[2]

Leib, of Pennsylvania, moved, January 3d, to submit to the
State Legislatures an amendment of the Constitution, which had
passed the House the preceding session, but been rejected in the
Senate, to the effect that in all future elections of President and
Vice-President, the office for which each was intended should
be designated on the ballot. Huger, of South Carolina, subsequently moved an additional amendment, requiring the electors
to be uniformly chosen by the single district system. The House
took no definite action on either proposition.

Ohio was admitted this session as a State into the Union,
with a population (by the last preceding census) of 45,365.

A law passed (February 28th) prohibiting the importation of
" any negro, mulatto, or other person of color," not a native or
inhabitant, into any State "where by the laws thereof their admission was prohibited," under the penalty of one thousand dollars
for every person thus imported, and forfeiture of the vessel.

The President was authorized (February 28th) to cause
to be built or purchased four vessels of war of not exceeding
sixteen guns each, for the Mediterranean service, and fifteen
gunboats for the Mississippi.

One of the most important questions of the session arose on
what was termed the " Yazoo Claims"—the claims of a com-

[1] Sketch of Merriwether Lewis, Jefferson's Works, Cong. Ed., vol. viii., p. 484.

[2] This was the origin of the well-known Expedition of Lewis and Clarke. Captain
Merriwether Lewis was the private secretary of the President. For the President's high
estimate of his character and abilities, see " Biographical Sketch of Merriwether Lewis,"
Jefferson's Works. Cong. Ed., vol. viii., pp. 480–494. With him was associated William
Clarke, brother of George Rogers Clarke, " the Hannibal of the West." Professor Tucker
says William Clarke partook of his brother's " capacity to endure hardship and encounter danger, as well as his practical good sense." In April, 1803, the President communicated his instructions to Captain Lewis. (See Jefferson's Works, Cong. Ed., vol. viii.,
pp. 485–491.) Delays occurred. and it was not until the 14th of May, 1804, that the party
left the banks of the Mississippi and commenced ascending the Missouri. Capt. Lewis
and his companion Clarke reached Washington on their return, February, 1807. The
results of the Exploration have been published.

pany to lands which the United States had received from Georgia with a stipulation to respect certain enumerated classes of private claims. Nothing important resulting from the present action of Congress on the subject, we have, on second thought, cast aside as irrelevant a somewhat detailed account we had prepared of one of the most enormous swindling operations recorded in American, or perhaps any other history. It was claimed that, notwithstanding the fraud, equitable rights had inured to innocent third persons, pending the operations, which the United States ought, in the display of a liberal justice, to recognize; and on this point arose a contest in Congress which continued many years. It was not made a party question, but was conducted with all the acerbity of partisan violence in and out of Congress. Our older citizens retain vivid recollections of the heat exhibited in the newspapers on this exciting topic. Those desiring an account of the affair will find it in the Annals of Congress, and in nearly all the detailed histories of the period. The subject occupies considerable space in Garland's Life of Randolph. The latter, unsparing towards even an equity which sprouted from corruption, was one of the strongest opponents of the claims; and as sourness and misanthropy gradually deepened their shadows over his mind, his hostility rose to the vengefulness of personal hate. His philippics on this subject against the actors in the transactions, and against others whom he accused (in many instances no doubt erroneously) of being actors, rival in acrimony the celebrated productions from which the term philippic is derived.

We are not aware that the President ever took any avowed side in the controversy. Both of his sons-in-law, however, were members of Congress before it was disposed of, and voted with the opponents of the claims.

During this session, the President was strongly pressed by the Georgia authorities to obtain the cession of certain Indian lands within the limits of that State, which the United States had stipulated to obtain as soon as they could do so peaceably and for a reasonable price. The Georgians also claimed that Colonel Hawkins, the United States Indian Agent, dissuaded the Indians from selling. The President's reply to General Jackson, of Georgia, a letter from him to Hawkins, two others not long afterwards to Governors Harrison and Claiborne, and his various addresses to Indian deputations, fully develop his views of Indian policy. He acted fully and fairly on the hypothesis, in all cases, that the Indians were as much the real owners of not only their sparsedly inhabited territories, but of the vast hunting-grounds over which they were accustomed to rove, as were white men holding legal title-deeds of their land—with the only difference that territories belonging to Indians (and there could be no more beneficent provision for them) could only be alienated to or by consent of the United States. The President was firmly opposed to procuring any cessions of their territory excepting peaceably and for a fair equivalent—in other words, for what was considered at the time fully equal in value, by the Indians, to their unused lands.[1] The agents the President instrusted with these negotiations were such men as Hawkins (accused by some of the impatient Georgians of being "more attached to the interests of the Indians than of the United States"), Harrison,[2] Claiborne, and others of equal character. And he required that all cessions of Indian territory should be not only nominally, but in point of fact voluntary. He made the following declarations (November 3d, 1802), to "Handsome Lake," an Indian chief, who came to complain of certain sales made by his nation to the State of New York:

"You remind me, brother, of what I have said to you, when you visited me the last winter, that the lands you then held would remain yours, and should never go from you but when you should be disposed to sell. This I now repeat, and will ever abide by. We, indeed, are always ready to buy land; but we will never ask but when you wish to sell; and our laws, in order to protect you against imposition, have forbidden individuals to purchase lands from you; and have rendered it necessary, when you desire to sell, even to a State, that an agent from the United States should attend the sale, see that your consent is freely given, a satisfactory price paid, and report to us what has been done, for our approbation. This was done in the late case of which you complain.

* * * * *

"Nor do I think, brother, that the sale of lands is, under all circumstances, injurious to your people. While they depended on hunting, the more extensive the forest around them, the more game they would yield. But going into a state of agri-

[1] The apparent equivalent, would now, in many cases, perhaps, appear but little more than nominal. But we believe we have fairly represented the intention of the President. In many cases, the lands sold by them were of no use to them whatever, and were not even used for hunting. And the President believed that if the arts of civilized industry could be introduced among them—a constant end of all his Indian policies—they would be better off without these vast unoccupied possessions to seduce them back into the habits of savage life. But his views will speak better for themselves in some; quotations we propose to make from his addresses to the Indian tribes.

[2] William Henry Harrison, afterwards President of the United States.

culture, it may be as advantageous to a society, as it is to an individual, who has more land than he can improve, to sell a part, and lay out the money in stock and implements of agriculture, for the better improvement of the residue. A little land well stocked and improved, will yield more than a great deal without stock or improvement. I hope, therefore, that on further reflection, you will see this transaction in a more favorable light, both as it concerns the interest of your nation, and the exercise of that superintending care which I am sincerely anxious to employ for their subsistence and happiness. Go on then, brother, in the great reformation you have undertaken. Persuade our red brethren then to be sober, and to cultivate their lands ; and their women to spin and weave for their families. You will soon see your women and children well fed and clothed, your men living happily in peace and plenty, and your numbers increasing from year to year. It will be a great glory to you to have been the instrument of so happy a change, and your children's children, from generation to generation, will repeat your name with love and gratitude forever. In all your enterprises for the good of your people, you may count with confidence on the aid and protection of the United States, and on the sincerity and zeal with which I am myself animated in the furthering of this humane work. You are our brethren of the same land ; we wish your prosperity as brethren should do. Farewell."

To a delegation of the Miamis and Delawares, he declared (January 8th, 1803), that Governor Harrison had, by his directions, agreed to accept a breadth of twenty-four leagues, extending from Point Coupee to the mouth of White River, where a breadth of seventy leagues had been bought of the tribes occupying it, and paid for ; and this had been done from " the desire of peace and friendship " with the Indians, "and of doing nothing which should distress" them. He continued :

" You complain that our people buy your lands individually, and settle and hunt on them without leave. To convince you of the care we have taken to guard you against the injuries and arts of interested individuals, I now will give you a copy of a law, of our great council the Congress, forbidding individuals to buy lands from you, or to settle or hunt on your lands ; and making them liable to severe punishment. And if you will at any time seize such individuals, and deliver them to any officer of the United States, they will be punished according to law.

" We have long been sensible, brothers, of the great injury you receive from an immoderate use of spirituous liquors ; and although it be profitable to us to make and sell these liquors, yet we value more the preservation of your health and happiness. Heretofore we apprehended you would be displeased, were we to withhold them from you. But believing it to be your desire, we have taken measures to prevent their being carried into your country ; and we sincerely rejoice at this proof of your wisdom. Instead of spending the produce of your hunting in purchasing this pernicious drink, which produces poverty, broils and murders, it will now be employed in procuring food and clothing for your families, and increasing instead of diminishing your numbers.

" You have proposed, brothers, that we should deduct from your next year's annuity, the expenses of your journey here ; but this would be an exactness we do not practise with our red brethren. We will bear with satisfaction the expenses of your journey, and of whatever is necessary for your personal comfort; and will not, by deducting them, lessen the amount of the necessaries which your women and children are to receive the next year."

He informed them also that, at their request, smiths had been provided them; and that the United States agent would furnish them implements of husbandry and manufacture whenever they would use them.

The President's favorite plan in regard to the ultimate disposition of the Indian race is sketched in a letter to Hawkins; and it will now sound to most persons more like a dream of philanthropy than a serious proposition. He wrote:

"I consider the business of hunting as already become insufficient to furnish clothing and subsistence to the Indians. The promotion of agriculture, therefore, and household manufacture, are essential in their preservation, and I am disposed to aid and encourage it liberally. This will enable them to live on much smaller portions of land, and indeed will render their vast forests useless but for the range of cattle; for which purpose, also, as they become better farmers, they will be found useless, and even disadvantageous. While they are learning to do better on less land, our increasing numbers will be calling for more land, and thus a coincidence of interests will be produced between those who have lands to spare, and want other necessaries, and those who have such necessaries to spare, and want lands. This commerce, then, will be for the good of both, and those who are friends to both ought to encourage it. You are in the station peculiarly charged with this interchange, and who have it peculiarly in your power to promote among the Indians a sense of the superior value of a little land, well cultivated, over a great deal, unimproved, and to encourage them to make this estimate truly. The wisdom of the animal which amputates and abandons to the hunter the parts for which he is pursued should be theirs, with this difference, that the former sacrifices what is useful, the latter what is not. In truth, the ultimate point of rest and happiness for them is to let our settlements and theirs meet and blend together, to intermix and become one people. Incorporating themselves with us as citizens of the United States, this is what the natural progress of things will of course bring on, and it will be better to promote than to retard it. Surely it will be better for them to be identified with us, and preserved in the occupation of their lands, than be exposed to the many casualties which may endanger them while a separate people."

If the Indians did not come into this view, the President's next choice was to induce them all to emigrate beyond the Mississippi, supplying them with everything essential to their comfort and happiness—and give them a home where the conflicting interests of white settlers would not pursue them. His present anxiety was to secure a belt of territory of the Indians on the east bank of the Mississippi throughout its whole length, for the

purpose of planting upon it a population of whites, both to defend the frontier and to be prepared for other emergencies which
might arise—in plain English, to rush upon Louisiana, and especially upon New Orleans, if that alternative should be forced
upon us.

But to return to the events of the session.

The recommendation in the message to repeal the discrimi-
nating duties was not carried out. The navigating interests of
the North remonstrated warmly against it, and it was suffered
to drop without any decisive action.

A proposition to discontinue the mint, urged by some of the
ultra advocates of retrenchment, fortunately failed.

The President's recommendations to construct a dry dock at
the city of Washington had been referred to a select committee,
of which the chairman was the learned Dr. Mitchell of New
York. It reported the following resolution:

Resolved—That for preventing rottenness and decay in the ships of the navy,
the President of the United States be, and hereby is, authorized to cause a dry-dock,
with convenient canals, locks, machinery, and water-courses, to be constructed at or
near the public Navy Yard in the city of Washington, which dock shall be capable
of containing twelve frigates, or ships-of-war, and of preserving them dry, and
safely sheltered from sunshine and rain; and that, for carrying the same into effect,
—— dollars be, and the same hereby are, appropriated, to be paid out of any
moneys in the Treasury not otherwise appropriated.

Dr. Mitchell stated that there had been placed before the
committee, drawings, surveys and estimates by engineers, which
made the project appear so plausible, that there was a unanimous vote in its favor. He had been informed that Sweden and
Venice[1] had done something of the same kind. The object, he
said, was thus to preserve a number of new ships not launched
nor wetted in service, and "there could be no doubt they might
be so covered and protected as to keep as well as furniture in a
house." He proceeded to explain that this would not apply to
ships that "had grown foul and water soaken" in the ocean.

Dr. Eustis, of Massachusetts, opposed the resolution on the
ground of the inappropriateness of the locality—that there was
danger that the ships, "resting for a long time on comparatively

[1] Mr. Jefferson remarked in a letter (to the date of which we cannot now refer) in
after years, that he derived his idea from an account of something of a similar kind in
Venice.

small resting points, might be racked and injured in their frames"—that he doubted the practicability of proper ventilation—that it "was not known to him that any of the European nations had adopted this plan"—that they "had incurred immense expense in building, and it was to be presumed had fallen on the best means of preserving their ships"—that he thought, in works of such magnitude, it was more prudent to follow than to lead older and more experienced nations. General S. Smith answered several of Eustis's objections. He thought the place practicable and suitable, and that there was no more danger of the ships hogging when lowered on their blocks than when on the stocks. On the subject of ventilation he doubted; but he thought it might be accomplished by taking off the garboard streaks of each ship, and streaks from their ceiling at proper intervals. He said:

> "He had seen at Venice, above twenty ships-of-war in the arsenal, completely under cover, each lying afloat in its own dock, with stores on each side, in which their materials were deposited. He was told the whole number could be put to sea in twenty or thirty days' notice."

Griswold said: "He must confess that the project appeared to him a visionary scheme, originating in the philosophy of the present day."

The Republicans representing those seaport and other local interests which were averse to making Washington the principal naval station of the country, joined the Federalists in a vote to refuse the Committee leave to sit again, and here the thing dropped.

Eustis's arguments were legitimate ones, and presented fair subjects of doubt, though he did not attempt to disguise a degree of local feeling in the matter. But Griswold threw out the Federal text-word. It was a scheme of the modern " philosophy !"

The speculations on the causes of animal color, in the Notes on Virginia, the "horned toads," and the " salt mountains " of " Philosopher Jefferson " did not furnish topics of such exquisite and inexhaustible merriment to his opponents as the unlucky dry-docks !

It is probable that the fact that Dr. Mitchell reported the resolution increased the zest of the entertainment. It was claimed that this learned man was singularly ignorant in practical affairs, and traditionary anecdotes without number are handed down of amusing pranks played on his credulity by wags who had not the fear of "philosophy" before their eyes. Some of these may possibly be true ; but if most of them are, it is a remarkable coincidence that such a host of things should have happened to one man, recorded previously of real or imaginary personages, from the days of the comic poets of Greece down to those of Rabelais, Le Sage, and Joe Miller. But, at all events, Dr. Mitchell has furnished a prime brilliant in the colloquial setting round "Philosopher Jefferson."

The French have a not bad maxim that "he laughs best that laughs latest." To be ignorant is not certainly to be "practical." To be learned is not always to be a fool!

> "Leaden Ignorance rears her head and laughs,
> And fat Stupidity shakes his jolly sides"

sometimes at "philosophic vagaries" which turn out to be substantive things. The "horned toads" and "salt mountains" still flourish! The essential principle of the dry-dock[1] has since been introduced with perfect success and preëminent advantage into the American navy.

The seventh Congress terminated on the 3d of March, 1803. The following letter alludes to the loss in future of a distinguished member from that body, and the accession of a new one nearly connected with the family of the President:

TO MARIA JEFFERSON EPPES.

WASHINGTON, Jan. 18, 1803.

MY DEAR MARIA:

Yours by John came safely to hand, and informed me of your ultimate arrival at Edgehill. Mr. Randolph's letter from Gordon's, received the night before, gave me the first certain intelligence I had received since your departure. A rumor had come here of your having been stopped two or three days at Ball Run, and in a miserable hovel; so that I had passed ten days in anxious uncertainty about you. Your apologies, my dear Maria, on the article of expense, are quite without necessity. You did not here indulge yourselves as much as I wished, and nothing prevented my supplying your backwardness but my total ignorance in articles which might suit you. Mr. Eppes's election will, I am in hopes, secure me your

---

[1] That is, fitting vessels into a good state of forwardness for sea, and keeping them high and dry under cover, to protect them from the sun and rain, until they are wanted for public use.

musing; but the receipts are valuable. Present my tender love to
ses to the young ones, and my affections to Mr. Randolph and Mr.
suppose you will see soon. Be assured of my unceasing and anxious
lf.

TH. JEFFERSON.

———

To MARIA JEFFERSON EPPES, BERMUDA HUNDRED.

WASHINGTON, April 25, 1803.

lA:

er from Mr. Eppes, dated at the Hundred April 14th, he informed
1 had got well through his measles; but he does not say what your
to be. My chief anxiety is that you should be back to Monticello
June. I shall advise Martha to get back from here by the middle of
he sickly season really commences here by that time, although the
e Government venture to remain till the last week of that month.
. Carr stayed with me five or six days on their way to Baltimore. I
>ose to return in June. Nelly Carr continues in ill health; I believe
out the same time to get back to Dunlora. I wrote to Mr. Eppes
assured of my most affectionate and tender love to yourself and
· me. My cordial salutations to the family at Eppington when you
eu.

TH. JEFFERSON.

owing letter will be read with unusual interest, as it
obably the strongest written expression ever made
erson to one of his family on the subject of his reli-
ns. The circumstances that drew it out are stated in

To MARTHA JEFFERSON RANDOLPH.

WASHINGTON, April 25, 1803.

THA:

I have not had a line from Monticello or Edgehill since I parted with you. Peter Carr and Mrs. Carr, who stayed with me five or six days, told me Cornelia had got happily through her measles, and that Ellen had not taken them. But what has become of Anne? I thought I had her promise to write once a week, at least the words "all's well." It is now time for you to let me know when you expect .to be able to set out for Washington, and whether your own carriage can bring you half way. I think my Chickasaws, if drove moderately, will bring you well that far. Mr. Lilly knows you will want them and can add a fourth. I think that by changing horses half way you will come with more comfort. I have no gentleman to send for your escort. Finding here a beautiful blue Casimir, water proof, and thinking it will be particularly à propos for Mr. Randolph as a travelling coat for his journey, I have taken enough for that purpose, and will send it to Mr. Benson, postmaster at Fredericksburg, to be forwarded by Abrahams, and hope it will be received in time.

Mr. and Mrs. Madison will set out for Orange about the last day of the month. They will stay there but a week. I write to Maria to-day; but supposing her at the Hundred, according to what she told me of her movements, I send my letter there. I wish you to come on as early as possible, because though the members of the Government remain here to the last week in July, yet the sickly season commences in fact by the middle of that month, and it would not be safe for you to keep the children here longer than that, lest any one of them, being taken sick early, might detain the whole here till the season of general danger, and perhaps through it. Kiss the children for me. Present me affectionately to Mr. Randolph, and accept yourself assurances of my constant and tenderest love.

TH. JEFFERSON.

The religious creed here mentioned as having been placed on paper is contained in a letter to which attention will be hereafter called.

CHAPTER II.

1803—1804.

CHANCELLOR LIVINGSTON, on reaching the Court of France, had found himself coolly received. Jacobinism had go̶ne̶ ̶o̶u̶t̶ ̶o̶f̶ fashion there. But he soon showed that his repub̶l̶i̶c̶ unaggressive and unmeddling. His personal tastes and habits were as far removed as possible from the Jacobin standards. He had as few of the arts or airs of the demagogue or *sans-culotte* as the other great leaders of American Republicanism.[1] Few of Bonaparte's courtiers, aspiring to the dignity of *ancien régime*, approached the long-occupied social plane of the stately American Patroon; and most of them were upstarts compared with him in personal and family pretensions. His wealth was reputed ducal. His hereditary possessions were greater than half a dozen French marquisates in the days of the Bourbons. He had sat in Revolutionary and pre-Revolutionary Congresses. He had been one of the committee appointed to draft the Declaration of Independence; and though not in Congress to sign the instrument, the name of a near kinsman was on this more than Battle Abbey roll. He had conducted with distinguished capacity the foreign bureau of his country. A full score of his family of the existing generation, and more than twice that number of his kinsmen, had borne high civic and military commissions. His own whole life had been spent in the highest ranks of office.

But Mr. Livingston wore his pretensions with affability and grace. Without coming under Sir Henry Wotton's punning definition of an ambassador—"an honest gentleman sent to *lie* abroad for his country"[2]—he was a man of the world, possessed

[1] Never was there a class of men who less put on the personal arts of demagogues than the Jeffersons, Samuel Adamses, Clintons, Livingstons, Dickinsons, McKeans, Macons, Pendletons, Madisons, Monroes, Masons, Nicholases, Randolphs, Breckenridges, Rodneys, etc., etc., *before or after election!* In this respect they (if we may credit English accounts) formed a most marked contrast with the manners of the English nobility of the same period, when they or their family cadets, or friends, were candidates for contested seats in the House of Commons. It is matter of record that the fortunes of even noble families were wrecked in these contests. One of Wilberforce's elections cost more than the annual expenses of one of our *then* American State Governments. Noblemen went about shaking hands and personally soliciting votes. Duchesses and Countesses did the same; and tradition says that the magnificent Duchess of Devonshire (the same, we believe, so nobly immortalized as "free Nature's uncorrupted child," in a lyric of Coleridge), on being offered a vote by a greasy clown—for Fox, if we remember aright —in exchange for a kiss, promptly *sealed* the contract and won the vote!

An American statesman of that day could address the people at the polls, explaining his views—but he could not stoop to individual solicitation, and much less to some other English appliances. And his wife or his daughter would as soon have thought of emulating the exploit of Godiva (of Coventry) as of the Duchess Georgiana.

The American "Jacobins" of 1796, 1800, and thence along through the third Presidency, are not to be mistaken by *young* historical students for the pure French article! If democracy is Jacobinism *per se*, they were Jacobins. But in all the practical applications, and in the externals, they were about as near the French standard as were Aristides, Fabricius, and William Tell.

[2] Dr. Dunglison, of Philadelphia, gave us a new turn to this witticism by Mr. Madison. The latter was on his back on a sofa, at Montpellier, complaining of considerable indisposition, but talking with great volubility to some guests. The Doctor suggested that he would not benefit himself by speaking so much in that position. "Oh, Doctor, I always talk easiest when I *lie*," was the reply.

social tact and business experience, was remarkably well informed, was broad and liberal in his views, and on all classes of
subjects displayed uncommon abilities. When such a man
sought to please, he could not fail. He was soon a favorite with
the First Consul, and with the more liberal and intelligent of
the statesmen who surrounded him.

Livingston's powers, we are inclined to think, were more remarkable for their range than for their intensity in any one department. He was scarcely an originator, though he caught a
new idea promptly; and the history of his life—his munificent
assistance of Fulton—his introduction of fine-wooled sheep into
his country—and his patronage of all proposed undertakings of
value, show how readily and liberally he entered upon new lines
of thought and new practices. And having adopted an idea he
pushed it with vigor and talent. Such a man was well adapted
to be an ambassador of a republic, the path of which was plain
and straight-forward—which had few diplomatic secrets and
cared very little for those of other governments.

The French Government, however, studiously avoided giving
our minister any information of its purchase of Louisiana or its
non-purchase of Florida. The reason will presently appear in a
dispatch of Livingston.

The latter, according to his instructions, attempted as a primary object to prevent the French continental acquisitions, and
next, if they took place, to attempt to obtain that portion of
them east of the Mississippi, and particularly West Florida, in
order to secure the outlets to the Gulf of Mexico furnished by its
rivers, especially the Mobile. In this Livingston met with no
encouragement. On his hinting at a purchase, the minister told
him " none but spendthrifts satisfied their debts by selling their
lands." [1] De Marbois (a steady friend of the United States)
informed him that the French government considered the
acquired possessions an excellent " outlet for their turbulent
spirits." [2] He soon learned that their colonization was a favorite
scheme of the First Consul.[3] Some passages in a dispatch of
Livingston, of January 13th, 1802, deserve particular attention:

" By the secrecy and duplicity practised relative to this object, it is clear to me
that they apprehend some opposition on the part of America to their plans. I have,

[1] See Livingston's dispatches of December 10th and 12th, 1801.
[2] Ib. December 31.   [3] Ib. February 26, 1802.

however, on all occasions declared that as long as France conforms to the existing treaty between us and Spain, the Government of the United States does not consider herself as having any interest in opposing the exchange. The evil our country has suffered by their rupture with France is not to be calculated. We have become an object of jealousy both to the Government and people.

"The reluctance we have shown to a renewal of the treaty of 1778, has created many suspicions. Among other absurd ones, they believe seriously that we have an eye to the conquest of their islands.[1] The business of Louisiana also originated in that; and they say expressly that they could have no pretence, so far as related to the Floridas, to make this exchange, had the treaty been renewed, since by the sixth article they were expressly prohibited from touching the Floridas. I own I have always considered this article, and the guaranty of our independence, as more important to us than the guaranty of the islands was to France: and the sacrifices we have made of an immense claim to get rid of it, as a dead loss."

By comparing this with Jefferson's letter of April 18th, 1802, given in our preceding chapter, it will be seen·how completely the President's views differed from Mr. Livingston's in regard to the consequences of a French colonization of Louisiana, and in regard to the proper policy to be adopted by the United States if it was attempted. And the further dispatches show that no change took place in the minister's views until he received the letter of the President. The policy which secured the purchase of Louisiana was purely original with the latter. Not a distant hint—not even an analogous idea was received from any other quarter.

The minister again wrote home, March 24th, that the colonization of New Orleans was "a darling object of the First Consul"—that he "saw in it a mean to gratify his friends and dispose of his armies"—that it was thought "that New Orleans must command the trade of our whole western country"—that the French had been persuaded "that the Indians were attached to France and hated the Americans"—that "the country was a paradise," etc. The minister then proposed that the United States establish a port at Natchez, or elsewhere, and give it such advantages "as would bring our vessels to it without touching at New Orleans."

He wrote, April 24th, that the French minister "would give no answer to any inquiries he made" on the subject of Louisiana; that the government was "at that moment fitting out an armament" to take possession, consisting of "between five and

---

[1] Had there not been a *foundation* for this suspicion? Had not the French Minister in the United States penetrated the projects of the Miranda schemers?

seven thousand men, under the command of General Berna-
dotte," who would shortly sail for New Orleans, "unless the
state of affairs in St. Domingo should change their destination."
He declared his information certain, and again pressed his Government " immediately to take measures to enable the Natchez
to rival New Orleans."

Some other letters passed which are not necessary to be men-
tioned.   On the 30th of July, Livingston wrote the Secretary of
State that he had received his dispatches of May 1st and 11th, the
President's letter through Dupont de Nemours, of the preceding
April 18th (1802), and that he was preparing a Memoir to the
French Government.

The formal instructions of May 1st and 11th fell far short of
the scope or decision of the President's private letter which he
had sent to Dupont de Nemours open, expressly and avowedly
to have its contents made known to the French Government.   The former, however, directed the minister to urge upon
France " an abandonment of her present purpose."   Those of
the 1st directed him to endeavor to ascertain at what *price* she
would relinquish the Floridas—those of the 11th, to employ
" every effort and address" to procure the cession of all territory
east of the Mississippi, including New Orleans—and he was authorized, should it become absolutely necessary in order to
secure this, to guarantee the French possessions west of the
river.

The discrepancy between the instructions and private letter
admits of a ready explanation.   The one exhibited the official attitude which it was considered prudent to take—the other gave
warning of the inner and entire feelings and purposes, in a form
which would have its full effect, but which could not be officially recognized and therefore construed into a menace, or
made the subject of official discussion and disclosure.   The inofficial letter, in effect, converted the propositions of the official
ones into ultimata.   If France would cede to the United States
New Orleans, and all the territory east of the Mississippi, for
an equivalent in money, then the " marrying" with England
would not take place, and France could have the benefit of another American guaranty.   But what was a guaranty worth
which would fall with the first collision of the parties between
whom the predicted " friction" would not be in the least reduced

by the proposed arrangement? What would the remaining territory be worth to France (never worth a thousandth part as much to her as to the United States), in the then situation of the world, without any navigable approach to the greater portion of it, except through a river of which the United States would hold the absolute control?

To accept the President's offer would be to give up the most valuable part of the possession and the key to all the remainder for the purpose of having the remainder secured from England. Yet, if the reasoning in the President's letter was sound (which enforced the first cession), the rest would inevitably soon follow that cession. In fact, the first cession would render the second more inevitable, and a thousand times less capable of being forcibly prevented. The President's idea, then, amounted practically to this: that if France would sell us all we then needed of her territory, for either commercial, military, or any other purposes, we would help her (or rather allow her to help us) keep the other part from a more dangerous occupant, until we also had need for that other part. Precisely in this light the French government viewed this offer. Talleyrand emphatically declared that if the French Government gave up what we then asked, what was left was worthless to France.

We neither accuse nor suspect Mr. Jefferson of insincerity. There is no doubt he would have respected his guaranty; and that he would have remained adverse to taking any unjust advantage. But he foresaw, and clearly and warningly pointed to the train of causes which must inevitably end, sooner or later, in the overthrow of any French power on the Mississippi. Having done this, he took middle ground—ground that would neither disgust France nor mankind by its rapacity—and awaited the result. We have no doubt that having such intellects as Bonaparte's and Talleyrand's to deal with, he very strongly anticipated the result which finally took place. It was to be ready for this, or some other equivalent or similar proposition, that he sent Monroe to France, with verbal instructions extending to any contingency.

The President's views produced no immediate visible change in Bonaparte's plans. Livingston informed his Government, November 11th, that the military expedition to New Orleans was about embarking, and he feared "no prudence would prevent hostilities ere long." Some of his later dispatches were rather more hopeful in their tenor, but no marked change occurred in the open aspect of things until the news reached France of the war flame that was burning in Congress, on account of the proceedings of Morales at New Orleans. The Federalists, who were so vehemently laboring to overthrow the Administration on that question, were unconsciously playing into its hands, and as effectually serving one of its great objects —the greatest object of its foreign policy—as if they had been employed expressly for that purpose.

When intelligence of war resolutions, vehement speeches in Congress, and of every other apparent indication of a popular ferment and of a national explosion in the United States, was wafted across the Atlantic, the French Consul—used to the fiery energy of democratic legislatures—unable to discern distinctly at such a distance between parties—finding one set openly talking war and the other only asking for privacy in the deliberations on the question—observing that all were in favor of firm declarations and provisional warlike preparations—fancied he saw the American scenes of 1798 about to be reënacted. He saw the United States again preparing with the prodigal bravery which distinguishes an aroused democracy, to tauntingly defy France to the combat; and he doubtless believed this was the first act in the drama which the President's letter had foreshadowed.

It would be something worse than ridiculous to suppose that Bonaparte was intimidated, or that the Directory were intimidated in 1798. But the question was, in commercial phrase, would the contest "pay?" Was it worth while to wage a war with so distant a power while the marine of France was so inferior to that of England, the sure ally of the enemies of France? Was it worth while to attempt to garrison a wilderness, destitute even of provisions, against five millions of contiguous people, who could reach it by a large number of navigable rivers? Was it worth while to expose the French West India possessions to the attacks of such a neighbor? Was it worth while to tempt a partition of all the colonial possessions of France between the United States and England? Was it worth while to "marry" these powers in the bonds of a common interest, and induce their allied maritime flags to "maintain exclusive possession of the ocean," and fix "the sentence which was to restrain France forever within her low-water mark?"

The shattered ships of France bore good testimony whether the menaces of the President in the last particular would prove bagatelles, if the policy he threatened was entered upon.

The victor of Lodi, Aboukir, and Marengo—the Dictator of southern Europe—could have laughed at the President's threats if nothing but the Rhine or the Pyrenees had separated the domains over which they ruled. But circumstances sometimes more than counterbalance strength. A mountaineer in a pass is more formidable than a battalion on a plain. The United States held the unapproached maritime supremacy of the western hemisphere. She held more. Maritime skill and maritime victory were hers by birthright. Never man for man and gun for gun had her flag been struck to Christian or Corsair; and now the Levantine seas were witnessing her avenging chastisement of those to whom Europe paid tribute. United with England, and only given time to build (in the mechanical sense of the term) fleets, and no ocean or sea could float a sail which was not under the protection of their associated flags.

But independently of such future results, and looking only to existing facts, Bonaparte was not weak enough in military capacity to suppose for a moment he could hold a level and comparatively unfortified mud bank, inhabited by a few thousand Creoles, and a vast wilderness occupied only by savages, with the Atlantic between it and France, against the fighting men of five millions of people, and with England joyfully and eagerly ready to intercept every succor he could send, so that not a regiment would reach America without in part owing it to favoring accidents.

The moment, therefore, he believed the President's avowals had been made in earnest, and that the American people were ready to uphold them—ready to fight for the territory—(and what could he expect if the American Republicans, the only party that could ever tolerate France, should lead in the war feeling?) his strong sagacity at once foresaw that his colonization projects were at an end; that these new domains were worthless to France, and must soon pass entirely from its grasp. Measuring as he always did the sentiment of America towards France by the Federal standard, he probably considered any guaranty the latter could receive from the former as a far weaker and more ephemeral engagement than it would actually have proved. Necessity would have broken it. But he believed the merest pretext would suffice. It was both for his advantage and credit, then, to get rid of it for the best equivalent he could obtain, before another war should break out between France and England.

We have stated the object the President had in view in sending Monroe to France, and clothed with a still higher grade of ministerial functions than Livingston. Let the reader carefully examine the following letter and judge:

To Governor Monroe.

Washington, *January* 18, 1808.

DEAR SIR:

I dropped you a line on the 10th, informing you of a nomination I had made of you to the Senate, and yesterday I inclosed you their approbation, not then having time to write. The agitation of the public mind on occasion of the late suspension of our right of deposit at New Orleans is extreme. In the western country it is natural, and grounded on honest motives. In the seaports it proceeds from a desire for war, which increases the mercantile lottery: in the Federalists, generally, and especially those of Congress, the object is to force us into war if possible, in order to derange our finances, or if this cannot be done, to attach the western country to them, as their best friends, and thus get again into power. Remonstrances, memorials, etc., are now circulating through the whole of the western country, and signed by the body of the people. The measures we have been pursuing, being invisible, do not satisfy their minds. Something sensible, therefore, has become necessary; *and indeed our object of purchasing New Orleans and the Floridas is a measure liable to assume so many shapes, that no instructions could be squared to fit them.* It was essential, then, to send a minister extraordinary, to be joined with the ordinary one, *with discretionary powers; first, however, well impressed with all our views, and therefore qualified to meet and modify to these every form of proposition which could come from the other party. This could be done only in full and frequent oral communications.* Having determined on this, there could not be two opinions among the Republicans as to the person. You possessed the unlimited confidence of the Administration and of the western people; and generally of the Republicans everywhere; and were you to refuse to go, no other man can be found who does this. The measure has already silenced the Federalists here. Congress will no longer be agitated by them: and the country will become calm as fast as the information extends over it. All eyes, all hopes are now fixed on you; and were you to decline, the chagrin would be universal, and would shake under your feet the high ground on which you stand with the public. Indeed, I know nothing which would produce such a shock. For on the event of this mission depend the future destinies of this Republic. If we cannot, by a purchase of the country, insure to ourselves a course of perpetual peace and friendship with all nations, then as war cannot be distant, it behoves us immediately to be preparing for that course, without, however, hastening it; and it may be necessary (on your failure on the Continent) to cross the Channel. We shall get entangled in European politics, and

figuring more, be much less happy and prosperous. This can only be prevented by a successful issue to your present mission. I am sensible, after the measures you have taken for getting into a different line of business, that it will be a great sacrifice on your part, and presents from the season and other circumstances serious difficulties. But some men are born for the public. Nature, by fitting them for the service of the human race on a broad scale, has stamped them with the evidences of her destination and their duty.

But I am particularly concerned that, in the present case, you have more than one sacrifice to make. To reform the prodigalities of our predecessors is understood to be peculiarly our duty, and to bring the Government to a simple and economical course. They, in order to increase expense, debt, taxation and patronage, tried always how much they could give. The outfit given to ministers resident to enable them to furnish their house, but given by no nation to a temporary minister, who is never expected to take a house or to entertain, but considered on the footing of a *voyageur*, they gave to their extraordinary missionaries by wholesale. In the beginning of our Administration, among other articles of reformation in expense, it was determined not to give an outfit to ministers extraordinary, and not to incur the expense with any minister of sending a frigate to carry or bring him. The Boston happened to be going to the Mediterranean, and was permitted, therefore, to take up Mr. Livingston and touch in a port of France. A frigate was denied to Charles Pinckney, and has been refused to Mr. King for his return. Mr. Madison's friendship and mine to you being so well known, the public will have eagle eyes to watch if we grant you any indulgences out of the general rule; and on the other hand, the example set in your case will be more cogent on future ones, and produce greater approbation to our conduct. The allowance, therefore, will be in this, and all similar cases, all the expenses of your journey and voyage, taking a ship's cabin to yourself, nine thousand dollars a year from your leaving home till the proceedings of your mission are terminated, and then the quarter's salary for the expenses of your return, as prescribed by law. As to the time of your going, you cannot too much hasten it, as the moment in France is critical. St. Domingo delays their taking possession of Louisiana, and they are in the last distress for money for current purposes. You should arrange your affairs for an absence of a year at least, perhaps for a long one. It will be necessary for you to stay here some days on your way to New York. You will receive here what advance you choose.[1]

Accept assurances of my constant and affectionate attachment.

TH. JEFFERSON.

Mr. Livingston, meanwhile, had continued vigorously to press his applications to the French Government, and he had succeeded in obtaining a direct access for his memorials to Bonaparte, without the intervention of a minister. He procured some concessions on incidental questions, but nothing looking towards a sale of the Floridas, or of another province which it has been assumed that nobody in America had yet

[1] The vote in the Senate on confirming Monroe's appointment stood fifteen to twelve —a strict party division.

thought of purchasing! He again wrote the Secretary of State, March 11 (1803), that Talleyrand "had assured him no sale would be heard of," and on the 12th as follows:

> "With respect to a *negotiation for Louisiana*, I think nothing will be effected here. I have done everything I can, through the Spanish Ambassador, to obstruct the bargain [between France and Spain] for the Floridas, and I have great hope that it will not be soon concluded."

The Consul had not yet spoken. Talleyrand had not reached this point in the negotiation. A better offer was hoped for. But Bonaparte would soon be obliged either to speak—to give up a great European measure matured in his mind—or to undertake that measure under circumstances which would strip him of Louisiana, and possibly the French West Indies in addition, without any equivalent. The "first cannon fired in Europe" was about to roar the knell of the Peace of Amiens, and it was for Bonaparte to say whether it should be the "signal" also for "holding the two continents of America in sequestration for the common purposes of the united British and American nations." There is little doubt that his mind was fully made up which was the preferable alternative long before Mr. Livingston was apprised of the fact.

In Livingston's dispatch of March 12th he mentioned an interview between the Consul and Lord Whitmouth, the English ambassador, in the drawing-rooms of Madame Bonaparte, in which the former assumed that vehemently angry and menacing tone with which he was accustomed to overwhelm the ministers of hostile powers, on the eve of war. The nerves of the stout Englishman did not shiver. None of Bonaparte's rage on this occasion, however, was affected. He had been deeply incensed by the bitter denunciations heaped upon him in the British Parliament, and by a stream of English publications, which represented him in the most odious light.[1] Causes of dissatisfaction had been constantly accumulating between the nations. England, indeed, wanted war. France was gaining a rapid ascendency on the Continent. The war was, therefore, inevitable. Its approach was announced by Bonaparte on the 13th of March, in an

---

[1] Bonaparte took particular offence at Sir Robert Wilson's narrative of the English Expedition to Egypt, dedicated by permission to the Duke of York, and publicly presented by the author to George III. and accepted at a levee.

audience of foreign ministers. It soon broke out on both sides
with peculiar vindictiveness, and with mutual outrage.[1]

On the 11th of April, Livingston wrote his government that
Talleyrand had that day asked him whether the United States
" wished to have the whole of Louisiana "—that he " told him
no ; that our wishes extended only to New Orleans and the Floridas." Talleyrand replied, if the French " gave New Orleans,
the rest would be of little value, and that he would wish to
know what we would give for the whole." Livingston says:

> " I told him it was a subject I had not thought of ; but I supposed we should
> not object to twenty millions, provided our citizens were paid. He told me this was
> too low an offer ; and that he would be glad if I would reflect upon it, and tell him
> to-morrow. I told him that as Mr. Monroe would be in town in two days, I would
> delay my further offer until I had the pleasure of introducing him. He added, that
> he did not speak from authority, but that the idea had struck him. I have reason,
> however, to think that this resolution was taken in council on Saturday."

On Friday, Livingston had received Ross's motion in the
United States Senate, and given copies to Talleyrand and Marbois. Other news of the same tenor had been for some time
reaching the French Government.

Monroe arrived on the 12th. On the 13th, Marbois (into
whose hands Bonaparte had put the negotiations, on hearing
through the English press that the United States had appropriated two millions of dollars to bribe the persons about him), informed Mr. Livingston that Bonaparte said to him on Sunday :
" You have charge of the treasury ; let them [the Americans]
give you one hundred millions of francs, and pay their own
claims and take the whole country." Livingston declined to
answer this proposition without consulting Monroe. The ministers, on the 15th, offered fifty millions, including the claims ;
and then shrewdly " resolved to rest a few days on their oars."
War was swiftly coming ; additional funds were more desirable
to France than additional enemies !

On the 30th of April—just eleven days before Lord Whitmouth received his passports and left France—a treaty and two
conventions were entered into between the American and
French ministers, by which France ceded the entire province of

---

[1] England, before declaring war, seized two hundred French vessels, worth, with
their cargoes, three millions sterling. France retaliated by ordering the arrest of about
ten thousand English in France and treating them as prisoners of war.

Louisiana to the United States, for the sum of sixty millions of francs,[1] to be paid to France—twenty millions to be paid to citizens of the United States due from France (for supplies, embargoes, and prizes made at sea)—and in further consideration of certain stipulations in favor of the inhabitants of the ceded territory, and certain commercial privileges secured to France.

It was provided that the inhabitants of Louisiana should "be incorporated into the Union of the United States, and admitted as soon as possible, according to the principles of the Federal Constitution, to the enjoyment of all the rights, advantages, and immunities of citizens of the United States ; and, in the mean time, they should be maintained and protected in the free enjoyment of their liberty, property, and the religion which they professed."

It was provided that French or Spanish ships coming directly from their own country, or any of their colonies, and loaded only with the produce or manufactures thereof, should for the space of twelve years be admitted to any port within the ceded territory, in the same manner and on the same terms with American vessels coming from those places.   And for that period no other nation was to have a right to the same privileges in the ports of the ceded territory.   But this was not to affect the regulations the United States might make concerning the exportation of their own produce and merchandise, or any right they might have to make such regulations.   After the expiration of the twelve years, and forever, the ships of France were to be treated upon the footing of the most favored nations in the ports of the ceded territory.

The financial arrangements were included in the " Conventions," as France exhibited a sensitive disinclination to have this territorial transfer formally assume its real character of a sale for money.   But a careful inspection of the treaties will show that she had much less reason to blush for her conduct on this occasion than nations commonly have which either cede or acquire territory.   Her stipulations in behalf of the existing and future population of Louisiana were most humane and noble, and those which affected her American creditors were conceived in the highest spirit of magnanimity and honor.   It is curious to

---

[1] It was stipulated that, in this convention, five franc 3333-10000 (or five livres eight sous tournois) should equal the dollar of the United States.

speculate what a different air this international compact might have been made to wear, had the superseded Talleyrand been the negotiator instead of the austerely virtuous Marbois. And let us not withhold from the Consul of France the credit which is due him for appointing, and approving the proceedings of such a minister.

We think it was Napoleon who said he had noticed that Providence generally favored the heaviest and best disciplined battalions. Fortune wafts on those who seize her at the ebb. The "good luck," to which it gave the opposition so much consolation to attribute the President's success in the purchase of Louisiana, continued. The house of Baring, in London, offered for a moderate commission at once to take the American stocks which were created for the purchase money of Louisiana, at their current value in England, and to meet our engagements to France by stipulated monthly installments. It is not at all probable that this offer to furnish so large a sum to an enemy could have been made without understanding with the British Government. Nay, the latter had projected an expedition to capture New Orleans as soon as her war with France should break out, but on being apprised by Mr. King of the measures of the United States towards a purchase, evinced apparent satisfaction with such an arrangement. And on learning the terms of the cession, even George III., if the well-turned diplomatic language of Lord Hawkesbury may be credited, grew gracious, and expressed high approbation of their tenor.[1]

England had every right to feel gratified. No alliance against her power, no special guaranties against her arms, no injurious discriminations against her navigation had been inserted in the treaties. France was stripped of her American continental possessions, and crippled from ever becoming the rival of England in colonial establishments. The ceded territory had gone into the hands of the only power which could hold it safely from all European rivals, and against which it would have been in vain for England herself to contend for its posses-

---

[1] Lord Hawkesbury wrote Mr. King (May 19th, 1803), that his Majesty expressed his satisfaction that the treaty had been so framed "as not to infringe any right of Great Britain in the navigation of the Mississippi;" and that he regarded it as "the most satisfactory evidence of a disposition on the part of the Government of the United States—correspondent to that which his Majesty entertained—to promote and improve that harmony and good understanding which so happily subsisted between the two countries, and which was so conducive to their mutual benefit!"

sion. The sum paid into the coffers of France would not approach that which England would save in sending fleets against and in maintaining possession of Louisiana against both France and the United States, without any hope that possession would be permanent. And finally, England could now concentrate all her force without reference to transatlantic efforts or interruptions, in her death-struggle with that modern Alexander against whom it might soon be necessary to defend even her own shores from invasion.

Livingston and Monroe communicated the result of their negotiations to the American Government, May 13th. It is to be presumed the paper was drawn up by Livingston, and was acquiesced in by Monroe, to escape an eclaircissement which would add to existing irritations.[1] It said that they (the ministers) " well knew " that " an acquisition of so great extent was not contemplated by their appointment," but " they were persuaded that the circumstances and considerations which induced them to make it, would justify them in the measure to their Government and country."

So far as official written instructions were concerned, this was true; but both Livingston's official and Jefferson's inofficial letters show that it was an erroneous view—show that procuring Louisiana had been " contemplated " and made the subject of diplomatic correspondence—show that Jefferson had meditated and resolved on obtaining, if practicable, every foot of the American continental possessions of France, the moment he learned that France had obtained them—show that he had communicated these views to Livingston, while that minister was expressing to the French Government, and no doubt honestly entertaining, a wholly different class of ideas. And there is not a particle of doubt that it was precisely to seize upon a favora-

---

[1] Livingston expressed considerable feeling at Monroe's appointment, and at his superiority of official grade. He believed " it was important that he [Livingston] be thought to stand as well with his government as any other person." He thought " his age, and the stations he had held, entitled him not to have any person placed above him in the line he had filled," etc. (See his dispatch to Madison, April 17th.) There were not wanting persons who were earnestly attempting to convince Livingston that the Administration were secretly hostile to him, and who communicated to him all sorts of tattle and gossip to prove their assertions. We are ashamed to say that as high bred a man as Gouverneur Morris rivalled a chambermaid's industry in the latter particular. (See his correspondence, edited by Sparks.) A jest of Bonaparte, in regard to Livingston's deafness, was repeated by " beau Dawson" at the capital, and therefore was represented to him as a Government insult, etc., etc.!

blo crisis, should it occur, to do exactly what was done, that Monroe was sent charged with his *verbal* instructions.[1]

Mr. Madison's reply[2] (as Secretary of State) to the communication of May 13th, was worded with peculiar care, its object being, without giving offence to Mr. Livingston, to dissent from the statement that the ministers had acted contrary to any previous views or wishes of their Government, or had taken a step which had not been "contemplated" by their Government, or one which they had not been expected to promptly and eagerly adopt if available. After expressing the unequivocal approbation of the Government for the proceedings of the ministers, he said :

"This approbation is in no respect precluded by the silence of your commission and instructions. When these were made out, the object of the most sanguine was limited to the establishment of the Mississippi as our boundary. It was not presumed that more could be sought by the United States, either with a chance of success, or perhaps without being suspected of a greedy ambition, than the island of New Orleans and the two Floridas ; It being little doubted that the latter was, or would be comprehended in the cession from Spain to France. To the acquisition of New Orleans and the Floridas, the provision was, therefore, accommodated. Nor was it to be supposed that in case the French government should be willing to part with more than the territory on one side of the Mississippi, an arrangement with Spain for restoring to her the territory on the other side, would not be preferred to a sale of it to the United States. It might be added, that the ample views of the subject carried with him by Mr. Monroe, and the confidence felt that your judicious management would make the most [of?] favorable occurrences, lessened the neces-

---

[1] We could, had we esteemed it in the least degree necessary, have brought an abundance of other proofs that Jefferson's eye was steadily on Louisiana. And how accurately he foresaw the approaching crisis which would place the game in our hands, will appear by the following letter, written before the intelligence of a warlike move in Europe had reached the United States. It also derives much additional significance from the fact that it was addressed to Claiborne, the Governor of the Territory (Mississippi) adjoining the French possessions. It was intended to prepare that officer's mind, and through him the minds of the American borderers, for the issue of swift-coming war, if negotiations failed. He wrote (May 24th, 1803) :

"I consider war between France and England as unavoidable. The former is much averse to it, but the latter sees her own existence to depend on a remodification of the face of Europe, over which France has extended its sway much farther since than before the treaty of Amiens. That instrument is therefore considered as insufficient for the general security ; in fact, as virtually subverted, by the subsequent usurpations of Bonaparte on the powers of Europe. A remodification is therefore required by England, and evidently cannot be agreed to by Bonaparte, whose power, resting on the transcendent opinion entertained of him, would sink with that on any retrograde movement. In this conflict, our neutrality will be cheaply purchased by a cession of the island of New Orleans and the Floridas : because taking part in the war, we could so certainly seize and securely hold them *and more.* And although it would be unwise in us to let such an opportunity pass by of obtaining the necessary accession to our territory even by force, if not obtainable otherwise, yet it is infinitely more desirable to obtain it with the blessing of neutrality rather than the curse of war."

[2] July 29th.

sity of multiplying provisions for every turn which your negotiations might possibly take."

He then very quietly mentioned that it was the tenor of Mr. Livingston's own dispatches which had " left no expectation of any arrangement with France, by which an extensive acquisition was to be made, *unless in a favorable crisis of which advantage should be taken.*"

Is it asked if we entertain any doubt that Monroe, with his verbal instructions, would have concurred readily in a treaty based on the President's formal and official offer, that is, on the separate acquisition of the Floridas and New Orleans? No such doubt is entertained. No question is made that the President and the American people would have rested satisfied with that acquisition for a generation to come. But it is not probable that the President expected his official demand would be complied with, and no more. If so, he sent Monroe to France for nothing, and much of his letter to him of January 13th, 1803, is wholly unmeaning gibberish. Undoubtedly he hoped for a more favorable arrangement. Undoubtedly he verbally instructed Monroe to acquire as much territory as practicable. Undoubtedly Monroe would never have signed a treaty which did not obtain more than New Orleans—and France did not, as it proved, own the Floridas. After reading the President's letter to Livingston, of April 18th, 1802, it would be absurd to declare that he did not " contemplate" the acquisition of Louisiana, that he did not solely originate the idea, that he did not originate and put in motion the train of causes by which it was accomplished.

Monroe, with his customary steady discretion and modesty, kept silent as to his share of the merit of this negotiation. Jefferson's temptation to speak was stronger. The opposition, with its usual variety and diversity of grounds of attack, insisted—first, that the purchase was inexpedient, unconstitutional, and disgraceful in its character; secondly, that it was the result of " good luck," and was wholly unforeseen and unthought of; thirdly, that Livingston's energy and tact had broken away from instructions to rescue a feeble and irresolute Administration. The President did once or twice hint to very confidential correspondents that if all the facts were before the public, it would be shown that the ministers had not been compelled to take any unauthorized or unexpected responsibility; and he also hinted that Monroe was entitled to a full share of credit for what had been accomplished.[1] Beyond this he coolly let the newspaper trumpet blare on and reduce him to a secondary attitude to those who, if they had executed well, had acted only as his instruments. He had conceived the design—he had foreseen the occasion—he had even given the signal to strike when the occasion came.

It was no ordinary triumph of which he omitted to claim the glory. When from the bema of the Pnyx the flashing eye of Demosthenes glanced from the upturned faces of the people of Athens to the scenes of those heroic achievements which he invoked them to emulate, it looked beyond the Gulf of Salamis and the plain of Marathon. Parnes, in whose rocky gorge stood Phyle, towered before him in the north, and in the south the heights on whose southern bases broke the waves of the Ægean. Almost the whole land of Attica lay under his vision, and near enough to have its great outlines distinguishable. What a world was clustered within that compass!

The land of Attica, whose sword shook and whose civilization conquered the world, had the superficial area and about one third the agricultural productiveness of a moderate sized county in any of the American States which have been erected in the province of French Louisiana.[2]

No conqueror who has trod the earth to fill it with desolation and mourning, ever conquered and permanently amalgamated with his native kingdom, a remote approach to the same extent of territory.

But one kingdom in Europe equals the extent of one of its present States.[3] Germany supports a population of thirty-seven millions of people. All Germany has a little more than the area of two-thirds of Nebraska; and, acre for acre, less tillable

[1] For example, the President wrote General Gates. July 14th, 1803: "I find our opposition is very willing to pluck feathers from Monroe, although not fond of sticking them into Livingston's coat. The truth is, both have a just portion of merit; and were it necessary or proper, it would be shown that each has rendered peculiar services, and of important value. These grumblers, too, are very uneasy lest the Administration should share some little credit for the acquisition, the whole of which they ascribe to the accident of war. They would be cruelly mortified could they see our files from May, 1801, the first organization of the Administration, but more especially from April, 1802. They would see, that though we could not say when war would arise, yet we said with energy what would take place when it should arise. We did not, by our intrigues, produce the war; but we availed ourselves of it when it happened."

[2] Attica contains not to exceed seven hundred square miles. This is below the average size of counties in most of the American States.

[3] The State of Nebraska contains 335,882 square miles.

land. Louisiana, as densely populated in proportion to its natural materials of sustentation as parts of Europe, would be capable of supporting somewhere from four to five hundred millions of people.[1] The whole United States became capable, by this acquisition, of sustaining a larger population than ever occupied Europe.

The purchase secured, independently of territory, several prime national objects. It gave us that homogeneousness, unity and independence which is derived from the absolute control and disposition of our commerce, trade and industry in every department, without the hindrance or meddling of any intervening nation between us and any natural element of industry, between us and the sea, or between us and the open market of the world. It gave us ocean boundaries on all exposed sides, for it left Canada exposed to us and not us to Canada. It made us indisputably and forever (if our own Union is preserved) the controllers of the western hemisphere. It placed our national course, character, civilization and destiny solely in our own hands. It gave us the certain sources of a not distant numerical strength to which that of the mightiest empires of the past or present is insignificant.

A Gallic Cæsar was leading his armies over shattered kingdoms. His armed foot shook the world. He decimated Europe. Millions on millions of mankind perished, and there was scarcely a human habitation from the Polar Seas to the Mediterranean, where the voice of lamentation was not heard over slaughtered kindred, to swell the conqueror's strength and "glory!" And the carnage and rapine of war are trifling evils compared with its demoralizations. The rolling tide of conquest subsided. France shrunk back to her ancient limits. Napoleon died a repining captive on a rock of the ocean. The stupendous tragedy was played out; and no physical results were left behind but decrease, depopulation and universal loss.

A republican President, on a distant continent, was also seeking to aggrandize his country. He led no armies. He shed not a solitary drop of human blood. He caused not a tear

---

[1] Its area, not including Texas (afterwards improperly surrendered from the purchase) and the region west of the Rocky Mountains, is not far, probably, from a million of square miles. But for all practical purposes and results, the purchase extended beyond the Rocky Mountains to the Pacific; and Texas should have been ours without a reannexation.

of human woe. He bent not one toiling back lower by governmental burdens. Strangest of political anomalies (and ludicrous as strange to the representatives of the ideas of the tyrannical and bloody past), he lightened the taxes while he was lightening the debts of a nation. And without interrupting either of these meliorations for an instant—without imposing a single new exaction on his people—he acquired, peaceably and permanently for his country, more extensive and fertile domains than ever for a moment owned the sway of Napoleon—more extensive ones than his gory plume ever floated over.

Which of these victors deserves to be termed " glorious?"

Yet, with that serene and unselfish equanimity, which ever preferred his cause to his vanity, this more than conqueror allowed his real agency in this great achievement to go unexplained to the day of his death, and to be in a good measure attributed to mere accident, taken advantage of quite as much by others as by himself. He wrote no laurelled letter.[1] He asked no Triumph.

An erroneous expression of Mr. Livingston, or one at least which has conveyed erroneous impressions, has been pointed out. What were the precise ideas which possessed his mind at the moment we cannot undertake to say. It is probable the dispatch was hastily written amidst the excitement of great events. The particular remark under notice must have been uttered without special consideration. We are not aware that he ever reiterated the statement. We suppose him to have been laboring possibly under a little pique, and like other men to have been disposed to claim his full share of credit where he momentarily felt that his capacity had been questioned. He is conceded to have been an able man, who discharged his assigned duty well. He, beyond all question, was an upright man, who would have uttered no intentional misrepresentation to benefit himself or injure another. No blame is affixed to him for a casual mistake. We could not possibly suppose it was deliberate had it come from a vastly inferior man, because a moment's recollection would have told him he was writing for the eyes of

---

[1] The Roman generals affixed laurel to their dispatches, and also to the spears and javelins of their soldiery on winning a victory. " Laurus Romanis praecipuè laetitiæ victoriarumque nuntia additur literis, et militiam lanceis pilisque."—(Pliny, lib. xv. s. 30.)

those who must have documentary proof that they had "contemplated" *all* that had been accomplished.

The delicacy with which Mr. Livingston was treated probably saved the Administration from a serious New York feud, and the next Administration the vote of that State. It required the firm support of the Livingston family and interest to give Mr. Madison the victory he there achieved over another and Republican candidate.

Monroe had been directed, if the negotiations with France failed, to cross the Channel and make preparations for resorting to the policy which Jefferson had informed the French Government, through Dupont de Nemours, would be the alternative in the event of that failure. In the meantime, the President had held out a signal to England, in a letter which will become more noticeable in the light of some future facts. He wrote Sir John Sinclair, June 30th, 1803:

"We are still uninformed here whether you are again at war. Bonaparte has produced such a state of things in Europe as it would seem difficult for him to relinquish in any sensible degree, and equally dangerous for Great Britain to suffer to go on, especially if accompanied by maritime preparations on his part. The events which have taken place in France have lessened in the American mind the motives of interest which it felt in that revolution, and its amity towards that country now rests on its love of peace and commerce. We see, at the same time, with great concern, the position in which Great Britain is placed, and should be sincerely afflicted were any disaster to deprive mankind of the benefit of such a bulwark against the torrent which has for some time been bearing down all before it. But her power and powers at sea seem to render everything safe in the end. Peace is our passion, and the wrongs might drive us from it. We prefer trying *ever* other just principles, right and safety, before we would recur to war."

The last three sentences are a jumble of typographical errors. Mr. Jefferson's copy of the letter is (or should be) locked up in the State Department at Washington, and therefore we cannot correct these sentences authoritatively. They perhaps carry a sufficient inkling of the sense to render it unnecessary.

Such a letter, addressed to such a man, and containing no restrictions on the communication of its contents, was of course intended for the eye of Government. It was accordingly immediately communicated to the British Cabinet, and produced most marked and favorable changes in the relations of the two countries.

Ten days afterwards, the President wrote a letter of similar import to the Earl of Buchan, who had previously addressed him as he had Washington; and who, as the older brother of two such men as Thomas and Henry Erskine, was probably supposed by both Presidents to be a man of consequence and sense.[1]

In the spring of 1803, audible murmurs were heard among the Republicans at the President's continued refusal to make a more general removal of the Federalists from office. In Pennsylvania, where a contrary rule had been practised by the State-appointing power, the dissatisfaction threatened to assume the form of a serious schism. To Mr. Nicholson, who had communicated particulars on the subject, the President wrote, May 13th, making excuses for the conduct of the malcontents, mentioning the number of removals he had made, and calmly announcing his unshaken determination to adhere to his policy. He said :

"We laid down our line of proceedings on mature inquiry and consideration in 1801, and have not departed from it. Some removals, to wit, sixteen to the end of our first session of Congress, were made on political principles alone, in very urgent cases; and we determined to make no more but for delinquency, or active and bitter opposition to the order of things which the public will had established. On this last ground nine were removed from the end of the first to the end of the second session of Congress; and one since that. So that sixteen only have been removed in the whole for political principles, that is to say, to make room for some participation for the Republicans. These were a mere fraud not suffered to go into effect. Pursuing our object of harmonizing all good people of whatever description, we shall steadily adhere to our rule, and it is with sincere pleasure I learn that it is approved by the more moderate part of our friends."

He thus gave the result of the spring elections of 1803, in a letter to Governor Claiborne (May 24):

"The elections which have taken place this spring, prove that the spirit of Republicanism has repossessed the whole mass of our country from Connecticut southwardly and westwardly. The three New England States of New Hampshire, Massachusetts and Connecticut alone hold out. In these, though we have not gained the last year as much as we had expected, yet we are gaining steadily and sensibly. In Massachusetts we have gained three senators more than we had the last year,

---

[1] This "bustling, old, intermeddling coxcomb"—this "silliest and vainest of busy-bodies"—as Lockhart terms him (Life of Scott, vol. iv. chap. viii.), if not something still more contemptible—as a story told of him by Allan Cunningham, in his life of the painter Barry (near the close) would lead us to suspect—was the laughingstock of his contemporaries. He appears to have been fond of patronizing American as well as domestic celebrities. The Wallace box and the consequent mention of his lordship in the will of General Washington, are familiar to our readers.

and it is believed our gain in the lower house will be in proportion. In Connecticut we have rather lost in the Legislature, but in the mass of the people, where we had, on the election of Governor the last year, but twenty-nine Republican out of every hundred votes, we this year have thirty-five out of every hundred; with the phalanx of priests and lawyers against us, Republicanism works up slowly in that quarter; but in a year or two more we shall have a majority even there. In the next House of Representatives there will be about forty-two Federal and a hundred Republican members. Be assured that, excepting in this northeastern and your southwestern corner of the Union, monarchism, which has been so falsely miscalled Federalism, is dead and buried, and no day of resurrection will ever dawn upon that; that it has retired to the two extreme and opposite angles of our land, from whence it will have ultimately and shortly to take its final flight."

The President set out for home on the 19th of August, and reached the capital again on the 25th of September.

He addressed a letter to Senator Breckenridge, August 12th, which deserves a careful perusal:

"Objections are raising to the eastward against the vast extent of our boundaries, and propositions are made to exchange Louisiana, or a part of it, for the Floridas. But, as I have said, we shall get the Floridas without, and I would not give one inch of the waters of the Mississippi to any nation, because I see in a light very important to our peace the exclusive right to its navigation, and the admission of no nation into it, but as into the Potomac or Delaware, with our consent and under our police. These Federalists see in this acquisition the formation of a new confederacy, embracing all the waters of the Mississippi, on both sides of it, and a separation of its eastern waters from us. These combinations depend on so many circumstances which we cannot foresee, that I place little reliance on them. We have seldom seen neighborhood produce affection among nations. The reverse is almost the universal truth. Besides, if it should become the great interest of those nations to separate from this, if their happiness should depend on it so strongly as to induce them to go through that convulsion, why should the Atlantic States dread it? But especially why should we, their present inhabitants, take side in such a question? When I view the Atlantic States, procuring for those on the eastern waters of the Mississippi friendly instead of hostile neighbors on its western waters, I do not view it as an Englishman would the procuring future blessings for the French nation, with whom he has no relations of blood or affection. The future inhabitants of the Atlantic and Mississippi States will be our sons. We leave them in distinct but bordering establishments. We think we see their happiness in their union, and we wish it. Events may prove it otherwise; and if they see their interest in separation, why should we take side with our Atlantic rather than our Mississippi descendants? It is the elder and the younger son differing. God bless them both, and keep them in union, if it be for their good, but separate them, if it be better. The inhabited part of Louisiana, from Point Coupée to the sea, will of course be immediately a territorial government, and soon a State. But above that, the best use we can make of the country for some time, will be to give establishments in it to the Indians on the east side of the Mississippi, in exchange for their present country, and open land offices in the last, and thus make this acquisition the means of filling up the eastern side, instead of drawing off its population. When we shall be full on this side, we may .ay off a range of States on the western bank from the head to the mouth, and so, range after range, advancing compactly as we multiply.

"This treaty must of course be laid before both houses, because both have important functions to exercise respecting it. They, I presume, will see their duty to their country in ratifying and paying for it, so as to secure a good which would otherwise probably be never again in their power. But I suppose they must then appeal to the nation for an additional article to the Constitution, approving and confirming an act which the nation had not previously authorized. The Constitution has made no provision for our holding foreign territory, still less for incorporating foreign nations into our Union. The Executive, in seizing the fugitive occurrence which so much advances the good of their country, have done an act beyond the Constitution. The Legislature, in casting behind them metaphysical subtleties, and risking themselves like faithful servants, must ratify and pay for it, and throw themselves on their country for doing for them unauthorized what we know they would have done for themselves had they been in a situation to do it. It is the case of a guardian, investing the money of his ward in purchasing an important adjacent territory; and saying to him when of age, I did this for your good; I pretend to no right to bind you: you may disavow me, and I must get out of the scrape as I can: I thought it my duty to risk myself for you. But we shall not be disavowed by the nation, and their act of indemnity will confirm and not weaken the Constitution, by more strongly marking out its lines.

"We have nothing later from Europe than the public papers give. I hope yourself and all the western members will make a sacred point of being at the first day of the meeting of Congress; for *vestra res regitur*.

"Accept my affectionate salutations and assurances of esteem and respect."

In a letter to the Attorney-General (August 30th), the President made him the bearer of his refusal to citizens of Boston to communicate his birth-day, which they had desired to ascertain for the purpose of observing it as an anniversary. He said:

"With respect to the day on which they wish to fix their anniversary, they may be told, that disapproving myself of transferring the honors and veneration for the great birthday of our Republic to any individual, or of dividing them with individuals, I have declined letting my own birthday be known, and have engaged my family not to communicate it. This has been the uniform answer to every application of the kind."

Accordingly, his birthday was never publicly known until after his death.

In the same letter, he drew up something like the form of an amendment, which he wished to see made to the Constitution, to sanction retrospectively the acquisition of Louisiana on the terms of the treaty, and to cover the future annexation of Florida. But he expressed his entire views on the subject much more fully in a letter to Senator Nicholas of Virginia, as well as new reasons for the speedy action of both Houses of Congress

—the one for ratifying the treaty, the other in carrying it into effect:

To WILSON C. NICHOLAS.

MONTICELLO, *September 7*, 1808.

DEAR SIR:

Your favor of the 3d was delivered me at court; but we were much disappointed in not seeing you, Mr. Madison and the Governor[1] being here at the time. I inclose you a letter of Monroe on the subject of the late treaty. You will observe a hint in it, to do without delay what we are bound to do. There is reason, in the opinion of our ministers, to believe, that if the thing were to do over again, it could not be obtained, and that if we give the least opening, they will declare the treaty void. A warning amounting to that has been given to them, and an unusual kind of letter written by their minister to our Secretary of State direct.

Whatever Congress shall think it necessary to do, should be done with as little debate as possible, and particularly so far as respects the constitutional difficulty. I am aware of the force of the observations you make on the power given by the Constitution to Congress to admit new States into the Union, without restraining the subject to the territory then constituting the United States. But when I consider that the limits of the United States are precisely fixed by the treaty of 1783, that the Constitution expressly declares itself to be made for the United States, I cannot help believing the intention was not to permit Congress to admit into the Union new States, which should be formed out of the territory for which, and under whose authority alone, they were then acting. I do not believe it was meant that they might receive England, Ireland, Holland, etc., into it, which would be the case on your construction. When an instrument admits two constructions, the one safe, the other dangerous, the one precise, the other indefinite, I prefer that which is safe and precise. I had rather ask an enlargement of power from the nation, where it is found necessary, than to assume it by a construction which would make our powers boundless. Our peculiar security is in the possession of a written Constitution. Let us not make it a blank paper by construction.

I say the same as to the opinion of those who consider the grant of the treaty-making power as boundless. If it is, then we have no Constitution. If it has bounds, they can be no others than the definitions of the powers which that instrument gives. It specifies and delineates the operations permitted to the federal Government, and gives all the powers necessary to carry these into execution. Whatever of these enumerated objects is proper for a law, Congress may make the law; whatever is proper to be executed by way of a treaty, the President and Senate may enter into the treaty; whatever is to be done by a judicial sentence, the judges may pass the sentence. Nothing is more likely than that their enumeration of powers is defective. This is the ordinary case of all human works. Let us go on then perfecting it, by adding, by way of amendment to the Constitution, those powers which time and trial show are still wanting. But it has been taken too much for granted, that by this rigorous construction the treaty power would be reduced to nothing. I had occasion once to examine its effect on the French treaty, made by the old Congress, and found that out of thirty odd articles which that contained, there were one, two, or three only which could not now be stipulated under our ·

---

[1] John Page, Mr. Jefferson's schoolboy friend, was now Governor of Virginia.

present Constitution. I confess, then, I think it important, in the present case, to set an example against broad construction, by appealing for new power to the people. If, however, our friends shall think differently, certainly I shall acquiesce with satisfaction; confiding, that the good sense of our country will correct the evil of construction when it shall produce ill effects.

Congress had been called by an executive proclamation to meet on the 17th of October, for the purpose of acting in time on the treaty, and a quorum was present at the appointed day.

Various new members appeared in the Senate. From Vermont, Israel Smith, in the place of Chipman; from Massachusetts (elected by an arrangement between the two Federal wings), Timothy Pickering in the place of D. Foster, and John Quincy Adams in the place of J. Mason; from Rhode Island, Samuel I. Potter in the place of T. Foster; from New York,[1] Theodorus Baily in the place of Governeur Morris; from Pennsylvania, Samuel Maclay in the place of Ross; from New Jersey, John Condit in the place of Ogden; from Virginia, John Taylor in the place of S. T. Mason, deceased; from Maryland, Samuel Smith in the place of Howard; from South Carolina, Pierce Butler in the place of Calhoun, deceased; and from the new State of Ohio, John Smith and Thomas Worthington. The gains were all Republican; and of the thirty-four members but nine were Federalists.

In the House of Representatives the Republicans consisted of over one hundred members, while the Federalists had less than forty. Several of the prominent leaders of the latter had been beaten in the canvass. Bayard had been defeated in his district by Cæsar A. Rodney, son of that Rodney who signed the Declaration of Independence. Both Adams and Pickering the new Massachusetts senators, had, before their election to the Senate, run for Congress and been defeated, the first by Dr. Eustis, and the second by Crowninshield.

The Republicans had lost two conspicuous members 'n the House—Giles by illness, and General Samuel Smith by his election to the Senate. Among the prominent old Republican members were Macon and Alston of North Carolina, John Randolph and Clopton from Virginia, Eustis and Varnum from Massachusetts, Mitchell and Van Cortlandt from New York,

---

[1] De Witt Clinton resigned, and General John Armstrong (who had preceded Clinton) was appointed by the Governor to fill the vacancy, November 10, 1803.

Leib, Gregg, Smilie and Findley from Pennsylvania, and Nicholson from Maryland. Among the prominent new Republican members were Rodney of Delaware, Crowninshield of Massachusetts, Root of New York, Clay of Pennsylvania, Jones, T. M. Randolph and Eppes[1] of Virginia, and Campbell of Tennessee.

Connecticut had returned its former Federal delegation, Griswold, Goddard, Dana, Smith and Davenport; and these, with Huger of South Carolina, and Thatcher of Massachusetts, old members, and Gaylord Griswold of New York, a new member, were the leading representatives on that side.

Mr. Macon was reëlected speaker.

The President's Message, after stating the acquisition of Louisiana, recommended, after the treaty should receive the constitutional sanction of the Senate, that measures be taken for the immediate occupation and temporary government of the territory, for " rendering the change of government a blessing to our newly adopted brethren "—" and for confirming to the Indian inhabitants their occupancy and self-government, establishing friendly and commercial relations with them." The constitutional difficulty was not mentioned.

" Another important acquisition of territory " was communicated. This was the purchase from the Kaskaskia Indians, of a broad belt of territory, extending from the mouth of the Illinois river, " to and up the Ohio "—comprising that part of the present State of Illinois lying south of the mouth of the Illinois river, and perhaps some part of Indiana. The Kaskaskia tribe had no difficulties with the United States, but the wars and casualties of savage life had reduced them to a few persons, wholly unable to defend themselves from the adjacent tribes. The United States left them lands sufficient for their maintenance, and, in exchange for the remainder, stipulated to protect them, and to pay them an annuity in money, agricultural implements, and such other articles as they might desire. Though the President did not regard this territory "so necessary as a barrier since the acquisition of the other bank," still he thought it should be laid open to immediate settlement, that " its inhabitants might descend with rapidity in support of the lower country, should future circumstances expose that to foreign enterprise."

[1] The two last, sons-in-law of the President.

He stated that the smaller vessels, authorized by Congress, had been dispatched to the Mediterranean.

An account of the receipts and expenditures of the year ending 30th of September preceding, he said showed that between eleven and twelve millions had been paid into the treasury. The amount of debt paid for the same year, was about three million one hundred thousand dollars, exclusive of interest, making, with the payment of the preceding year, a discharge of more than eight millions and a half of dollars of the principal of that debt, besides the interest which had accrued. And there was left in the treasury a balance of nearly six millions of dollars.

He contemplated the extinguishment of all preceding debts, before the stocks issued for the purchase of Louisiana would become redeemable; and he " could not but hope " that Congress would find means to meet the accruing interest on those stocks in the " progression of our revenue," without recurring to new taxes.

He stated that the sums appropriated for gun-boats on the Mississippi, and for other belligerent objects, had not been made use of.

The following are passages from the Message :

"We have seen with sincere concern the flames of war lighted up again in Europe, and nations with whom we have the most friendly and useful relations engaged in mutual destruction. While we regret the miseries in which we see others involved, let us bow with gratitude to that kind Providence which, inspiring with wisdom and moderation our late legislative councils while placed under the urgency of the greatest wrongs, guarded us from hastily entering into the sanguinary contest, and left us only to look on and to pity its ravages. These will be heaviest on those immediately engaged. Yet the nations pursuing peace will not be exempt from all evil. In the course of this conflict, let it be our endeavor, as it is our interest and desire, to cultivate the friendship of the belligerent nations by every act of justice and of incessant kindness; to receive their armed vessels with hospitality from the distresses of the sea, but to administer the means of annoyance to none; to establish in our harbors such a police as may maintain law and order; to restrain our citizens from embarking individually in a war in which their country takes no part; to punish severely those persons, citizen or alien, who shall usurp the cover of our flag for vessels not entitled to it, infecting thereby with suspicion those of real Americans, and committing us into controversies for the redress of wrongs not our own; to exact from every nation the observance toward our vessels and citizens, of those principles and practices which all civilized people acknowledge; to merit the character of a just nation, and maintain that of an independent one, preferring every consequence to insult and habitual wrong.

*   *   *   *   *   *   *   *   *

"Some contraventions of right have already taken place, both within our juris-
dictional limits and on the high seas. The friendly disposition of the governments
from whose agents they have proceeded, as well as their wisdom and regard for justice, leaves us in reasonable expectation that they will be rectified and prevented in
future; and that no act will be countenanced by them which threatens to disturb
our friendly intercourse. Separated by a wide ocean from the nations of Europe,
and from the political interests which entangle them together, with productions
and wants which render our commerce and friendship useful to them and theirs to
us, it cannot be the interest of any to assail us, nor ours to disturb them. We
should be most unwise, indeed, were we to cast away the singular blessings of the
position in which nature has placed us, the opportunity she has endowed us with
of pursuing, at a distance from foreign contentions, the paths of industry, peace,
and happiness; of cultivating general friendship, and of bringing collisions of interest to the umpirage of reason rather than of force. How desirable then must it be,
in a Government like ours, to see its citizens adopt individually the views, the interests, and the conduct which their country should pursue, divesting themselves
of those passions and partialities which tend to lessen useful friendships, and to embarrass and embroil us in the calamitous scenes of Europe."

The Senate ratified the treaty and conventions with France
October 20th, after two days' discussion, every Federal member
present, except Dayton, voting in the negative. The noes were
Olcott and Plumer of New Hampshire, Pickering of Massachusetts, Hillhouse and Tracy of Connecticut, Wells and White
of Delaware. John Q. Adams of Massachusetts had not yet
taken his seat.

On the 22d day of October, John Randolph moved, in the
House of Representatives, "that provision ought to be made for
carrying into effect the treaty and conventions concluded at
Paris on the 30th of April, 1803, between the United States of
America and the French Republic."

On the 24th (Monday), Roger Griswold, of Connecticut,
moved a call on the President for copies of the treaty between
the French Republic and Spain of the 1st of October, 1800
(the treaty of Ildefonso, by which Spain ceded Louisiana to
France)—of the deed of the cession of Louisiana from Spain
to France, if any such existed—of such correspondence between
our Government and the Spanish minister " as would show the
assent or dissent of Spain to the purchase of Louisiana by the
United States"—and of all papers in possession of Government
going to show whether it had acquired a title to the province.

Under cover of urging the passage of the last resolution, the
great body of Federalists took a determined stand against the

execution of the treaty.   Their grounds of opposition were various, and often inconsistent with each other.   They very generally avowed a distrust of the validity of the French title to the province; and some directly questioned the good faith of France in the ostensible sale.   All appeared to think that, at best, we were giving a large sum of money to purchase a mere quit-claim title; and several insisted that we were only buying a future war with Spain, and that Spain might at some later day be in a condition to effectually reclaim her lost province.

Griswold, of Connecticut, urged that by the showing of the treaty of Ildefonso, as recited in the French treaty of cession to us, Spain had really made no cession to France, but only promised to cede on certain conditions; and that Congress was in possession of no proof that those conditions had been complied with.

Some Federal gentlemen complained bitterly that the Government had not "manifested that firm, dignified, manly tone of virtue and spirit," it had done in Washington's day; that the President had not "appeared like the veteran chief ready to gird his loins in defence of his country's rights;" that instead of "maintaining our national independence" by "men," he had done it by "money;" that he had humiliatingly purchased the friendship of France; that "if we purchased this friendship once, we should be compelled to make annual contributions to their avarice;"[1] and much more in this "days of chivalry are past" tone!

The Federal party again, by demanding diplomatic papers in the House of Representatives pending legislation to execute a treaty, and by assuming a right in the House to exercise an option in regard to such legislation, exhibited their inconsistency with views, which they claimed it was a gross and Jacobinical

---

[1] And a fervid orator continued;

"Repeated concessions would only produce a repetition of injury, and, at last, when we had completely compromitted our national dignity, and offered up our last cent as an oblation to Gallic rapacity, we would be further from conciliation than ever. The spirit of universal domination, instead of being allayed by those measures which have been intended for its abatement, would rage with redoubled fury. Elated by those sacrifices which had been intended to appease it, it would still grow more fierce; it would soon stride across the Mississippi, and every encroachment which conquest or cunning could effect might be expected. The tomahawk of the savage and the knife of the negro would confederate in the league, and there would be no interval of peace, until we should either be able to drive them from their location altogether, or else offer up our sovereignty as a homage of our respect, and permit our country to be blotted out of the list of nations forever."

outrage on the Constitution to question in 1795.[1] And they made as luminous an exhibition of the same quality, in now vehemently and persistently opposing a peaceful acquisition, at half the expense of a single active campaign, of that very territory which a year before they had urged the forcible seizure of at the cost of a war with Spain and Napoleon! Now many declared it worthless, and all insisted it had been entirely overpaid for, in consequence of the fear and the partiality which the Administration entertained for France!

Griswold of New York made perhaps the ablest speech on the Federal side, or at least he first took the strong positions of that side. He raised the constitutional questions which we have seen advanced by the President, with clearness and force, and an additional one that the seventh article of the treaty (prescribing that French and Spanish vessels should enter the ports of Louisiana as mentioned in our summary of the treaty) granted a favor to the port of New Orleans over other ports and hence was in conflict with the clause in the ninth section of the first article of the Constitution, in the following words: "no preference shall be given by any regulation of commerce or revenue to the ports of one State over those of another."

The Federal imputations and suspicions in respect to the validity of the French title to Louisiana, and its consequent ability to convey a good title to the United States, were met, on the other side of the chamber, by the undeniable fact that by a royal order of the King of Spain, the province had already been publicly and formally delivered over to France; thus, if the treaty of Ildefonso was but a promise to cede, acknowledging a satisfaction of the preliminary conditions, and making the cession complete.

All the Republican members who spoke on that question contended that the provisions of the treaty could be carried out without an infraction of the Constitution. This unity of expression leads to the inference that the point had been discussed and decided in a preliminary caucus; or else we must suppose the President stood alone in his party in the views recently expressed to Mr. Nicholas.

John Randolph—still chairman of the Committee of Ways

---

[1] Some of the same Federal members were in the House on both occasions. Griswold of Connecticut, who *moved* for the papers in 1803, *voted* against the call in 1795.

and Means and floor leader of the Republicans—very plainly
proved in this debate how much less adapted he was to a comprehensive discussion of principles, than to brilliant declamation
spiced with shrewd turns and personal applications. He met
G. Griswold's argument by attempting to prove that the Constitution could not have been made for and in reference to any
fixed limits, for the peace of Paris prescribed our northwestern
boundaries to be the extension of a line due west from the Lake
of the Woods to its intersection with the Mississippi; but inasmuch as a line so extended would not touch the Mississippi, it
followed that the United States were without limits in that direction.

The strong grounds of those who argued in favor of the constitutionality of the treaty were first presented connectedly and
succinctly by Mr. Nicholson; and as we have given the President's views, it may be satisfactory to show an outline of those
which induced a majority of his party to adopt a different line of
action from that he proposed.

"Had I [said Mr. Nicholson] been asked anywhere but in this House, whether a
sovereign nation had a right to acquire new territory, I should have thought the
question an absurd one. It appears to me too plain and undeniable to admit of
demonstration. Is it necessary to resort to ancient authorities to establish a position which is proved by the conduct pursued by all nations, from the earliest periods
of the world, and which arises from the very nature of society? Can it be doubted,
that when a State is attacked, it has the right to assail its enemy in turn, and weaken
the aggressor by dispossessing him of a part of his territory. Surely the opinions of
all writers, both ancient and modern, and the examples of all nations, in all ages, can
leave no reason to doubt on this subject.

*　*　*　*　*　*　*　*　*　*　*　*

Let the Constitution, however, be examined, let the principles on which it was
formed be taken into view, and it will be found that, instead of forbidding, the Constitution recognizes the authority to acquire territory. In the year 1776, when the
United States absolved their allegiance to Great Britain, each State became a separate and independent sovereignty. As independent sovereignties, they had full
power, in the language of the Declaration of Independence, 'to levy war, conclude
peace, contract alliances, establish commerce, and do all other acts and things which
independent States might of right do.' Each State, separately and for itself, had
all the attributes of sovereignty, and no man can be hardy enough to deny, that,
at that time, any of the respective States had the capacity to extend its limits,
either by conquest or by purchase. These are the only two methods, indeed, by
which territory may be acquired; and there have been very few wars in which the
subjects of one nation or another have not been compelled to change masters. In
the year 1781, the articles of Confederation were finally agreed to, and each State
surrendered a portion of its sovereignty for the common benefit of the whole.

.. was given up. The management of external concerns
...ress alone had the power to levy war, conclude
...pacity of the individual States to acquire new
It was surrendered to the General Govern-
... the year 1788, the States again return-
...e. Their sovereignty was once more
...as of a more permanent Union, to secure
blessings of liberty. The present Constitu-
.. portion of individual sovereignty was surren-
was given to Congress, the right to make treaties
.. onquest and purchase alone are the means by which
The one can only be effected by war, the other by treaty,
...ted themselves of these powers, and gave them to the Gene-
.. gave, at the same time, that right to acquire territory, which
...ginally had. The right must exist somewhere. It is essential to
...ereignty. The tenth section of the first article of the Constitution
.. ohibits the States from entering into treaties, or levying war, and even
.. ...ng any compact or agreement with another State, or a foreign Power
.. .t the consent of Congress. All the rights which the States originally enjoyed,
... either reserved to the States, or are vested in the General Government. If they
once had the power individually to acquire territory, and this is now prohibited to them
by the Constitution, it follows, of course, that the power is vested in the United States.[1]

In support of this same view, Dr. Mitchell, of New York,
asked if " by any force of the currents of the ocean, or any conflicts of the winds and the waves, a new surface of earth should
emerge from the neighborhood of Cape Hatteras, it would be
unconstitutional to take possession of it?" He, and some other
speakers, contended that every purchase of lands by the United
States from Indian nations was as much a real extension of their
existing territory as this. He claimed that the cession by
Great Britain to the United States, by the peace of Paris, of
domains which were in the possession of the original inhabitants,
was merely a quit-claim; but that the paramount title of the
original inhabitants was not thereby affected, and to acquire it,
was to acquire foreign territory.

In reply to G. Griswold's second constitutional objection,
several positions were taken. Perhaps as many rested their

[1] A spark of light falls on the Constitutional question in a letter from Gouverneur Morris
(the *draftsman* of the Constitution), in a letter to Henry W. Livingston, December 4th,
1803.
" I always thought that when we should acquire Canada and Louisiana, it would be
proper to govern them as provinces and allow them no voice in our councils. In word-
ing the third section of the fourth article I went as far as circumstances would permit
to establish the exclusion. Candor obliges me to add my belief, that, had it been more
pointedly expressed, a strong opposition would have been made." (Morris's Life and
Works, vol. iii. p. 192.)

action on the view set forth in the following remarks of Rodney, as on any other :

"This is property ceded to us [he said] by the Power ceding it, with a particular reservation. I am not for quibbling about words, or distorting terms. Taking the seventh article and fairly considering it, it amounts to nothing more than a particular reservation—upon delivering possession of the territory, which I take to be the true meaning of the language which is used ; and will any gentleman say that accepting the treaty, under this stipulation, will not be most advantageous to us? What individual State will be affected by it more than any other? Does it give the State of Massachusetts an advantage over New York? I would be glad to know what State it particularly affects, and in what way. 'No preference,' says the Constitution, 'shall be given by any regulation of commerce or revenue to the ports of one State over those of another.' In what way, under this treaty, is there any preference of one port over another? I would be glad to see it pointed out, and to be shown whether there is any preference of Delaware over Massachusetts, or of Virginia over Georgia. No. The Constitution adverts to States themselves ; and that the distinction between States and Territories is bottomed upon reason. Whence the necessity of the distinction? When Territories grow into States, and become represented in the public councils, a majority of them may league together, and carry into effect regulations prejudicial to other States. Hence the Constitution provides that in all commercial regulations all the States shall be equally affected. But such a league cannot be affected by Territories, which have no senators in the other branch, and in this only the voice, without the vote, of a single delegate. Independent of this consideration is this : if by any particular territorial regulation the territory of the United States is benefited, that territory being the common property of the United States, a public stock in which they all share, every State in the Union reaps alike the benefit."

There was much partisan recrimination throughout the debate. The Federalists had their action in 1795 often cast in their teeth ; and they were as often tauntingly told that they had no constitutional scruples about acquiring territory no further back than the preceding session of Congress.

On the first point they still affected to adhere to their former position that the treaty-making power was absolute within its constitutional province—but they claimed that if a treaty was unconstitutional, it was a nullity, and that the House was authorized to treat it as such. If the House was entitled to decide whether the treaty-making power acted constitutionally, when could it not interfere in the action of the latter?[1]

To escape the second ground of attack, they admitted that

---

[1] And in 1795, the Federalists had justified the assumption that the President was authorized to declare a treaty a supreme law of the land, by proclamation, even before its contents were made known to the House !

by conquest, and even by pur-
could not be admitted to the
of Connecticut said :

may undonbtedly be obtained by conquest
juest nor the purchase can incorporate them
.1 the condition of colonies, and be governed
iird article is not that the province of Louisiana
that neither this nor any other foreign nation
i by treaty or by a law ; and as this country has
only under the condition of an incorporation, it
.onstitutional or impossible, the cession itself falls

i taken as the debate progressed by near-
.eralists. It involved the admission of a
rogative of sovereignty in the Federal
ressed in the Constitution. If this extend-
i of territory, it would seem to be a curious
i that it did not also extend to putting the
.ooting of citizens. It would involve a strange
.ernment professing that legal equality among
natural right, and offering citizenship within
. all foreigners of the Caucasian race, should be
.ever treat and govern its own children who had
-s a river into another portion of its own territories,

.ction appears to us too frivolous to have been sin-
.ere was a strong motive for maintaining its validity.
.igland members, partly on sectional and partly on
.nsiderations, were deeply averse to adding new
.ic Union west of the Mississippi. The affiliations
.riates would naturally be stronger with those which
.iguous, and whose physical interests were the same.
.uld not be tied to either the maritime interests or the
.-m of New England. Their admission therefore would
introduction of new partners into the body corporate
would reduce the relative importance and power of the
.i States. Therefore it was held necessary by the latter to
. forever in colonial vassalage a territory more than thirty
... larger than New England—a territory containing more
.:i a hundred millions of square miles, the average fertility of

which was probably equal to that of the natural fertility of the best square mile of land in New England—a territory to be inhabited at some future day by more than thirty times the existing population of the original States, and by a population in equal proportion to that of the original States, the descendants of those whose arms and sufferings secured the independence of the American Union!

So, too, individually the power of all the other corporators would be diminished by the increase of the number; and the material interests of New England would really be more benefited by this addition of States than those of the contiguous western ones. Agriculture could never be the leading interest among the sterile rocks and the keenly enterprising people of New England. In proportion to population or territory, she excelled in the maritime branch of national industry. She would soon be inevitably called upon to take the lead in the manufacturing branch, for she had the best natural facilities therefor, and the greatest need of employments extraneous of agriculture. The incorporation of New States would widen her markets, and at the same time increase and cheapen the products she required in exchange. To the agricultural States, the addition of new ones raising the same products opened no new markets, and it increased the competitors desirous to supply those already existing, or which were to spring up with new interests in the less fertile Atlantic States.

If the addition would disturb the partisan *statu-quo*, one would think the Federalists were reduced to a condition too depressed to ask to have a territory larger than all the original territory of the Union kept in perpetual colonial subserviency, for the sake of leaving them a chance for recovering their political ascendency. Besides, those who profess any grade of republican principles, are bound to recognize the propriety as well as the right of self-government in those who are as capable as themselves of its exercise. If they believe their own doctrines, they are also bound to believe they will prevail in the minds of such persons.

No Federal statesman of that day besides Governeur Morris, foresaw the natural and legitimate consequences which ought to inure to New England from the erection of trans-Mississippian States. His views were tinged with some of his customary refinements, and he imagined motives which would probably never have operated; but he caught the main idea, that New England ought to be the section of the Union more than all others, benefited by the purchase of Louisiana.

Not so thought the class of statesmen who then represented New England Federalism. Plunging forward from one transparent inconsistency to another—acrid, pharasaical, and controlled by a narrow and selfish partisanship—they resisted the acquisition desperately to the last; and when it took place, immediately entered upon a course as well calculated to drive off every resulting benefit to New England, as if it had been devised for that especial purpose.

It is not necessary here to recount all the partisan manœuvres which took place in the House of Representatives, pending its action on the treaty.

The resolution, that provision ought to be made for carrying it into effect, passed October 25th, yeas ninety, nays twenty-five.

On the act authorizing a creation of stocks to raise money for the stipulated payments to France, the Federal senators were enabled to relieve their feelings, also, before a public audience; and the whole range of the debate in the House was again travelled over, and with increased violence, because their talking increased their excitement.

White, of Delaware, declared it was only "buying of France an authority to make war on Spain," and he asked if gentlemen would "submit to the degradation" "at so inconvénient a price?" Admitting that we must have New Orleans and some other positions on the river, necessary to secure its navigation, he believed the possession of Louisiana "would be the greatest curse that could at present befall us;" "he would rather see it given to France or Spain." But if "this extent of territory was a desirable acquisition, fifteen millions of dollars was a most enormous sum to give." Our ministers at Paris ought to have taken advantage of circumstances to "lessen the consideration."

Pickering, of Massachusetts, did not believe the third article of the treaty could be rendered legal by even an amendment of the Constitution made in the ordinary way. He believed the assent of every State would be requisite. He took the usual ground that the Government could acquire new territory by purchase or conquest, and govern it "as a dependent province."

This recent Secretary of State contemptuously repudiated any reliance on the honor and justice of France, declaring that "for ten or fifteen years past we had known too well what they were."

John Q. Adams, of Massachusetts, who had voted against the bill which had passed the Senate (October 26th) to enable the President to take possession of the ceded territory, declared himself in favor of the present bill. He said he "was free to confess that the third article [of the treaty] and more especially the seventh, contained engagements placing us in a dilemma, from which he saw no possible mode of extricating ourselves but by an amendment, *or rather an addition* to the Constitution." But this was only saying that the President and Senate had bound the nation to engagements which required the coöperation of more extensive powers than theirs, to carry them into execution. He continued:

"This is what your ministers, in the very case before you, have confessedly done. It is well known that their powers did not authorize them to conclude this treaty; but they acted for the benefit of their country, and this House by a large majority has advised to the ratification of their proceedings. Suppose, then, not only that tne ministers who signed, but the President and Senate who ratified this compact, have exceeded their powers. Suppose that the other House of Congress, who have given their assent by passing this and other bills for the fulfillment of the obligations it imposes on us, have exceeded their powers. Nay, suppose even that the majority of States competent to amend the Constitution in other cases, could not amend it in this, without exceeding their powers—and this is the extremest point to which any gentlemen on this floor has extended his scruples—suppose all this, and there still remains in the country a power competent to adopt and sanction every part of our engagements, and to carry them entirely into execution. For notwithstanding the objections and apprehensions of many individuals, of many wise, able and excellent men, in various parts of the Union, yet such is the public favor attending the transaction which commenced by the negotiation of this treaty, and which I hope will terminate in our full, undisturbed, and undisputed possession of the ceded territory, that I firmly believe if an amendment to the Constitution, amply sufficient for the accomplishment of everything for which we have contracted, shall be proposed, as I think it ought, it will be adopted by the legislature of every State in the Union. We can therefore fulfill our part of the conventions, and this is all that France has a right to require of us.

Dayton, of New Jersey, favored the bill in a vigorous speech, and he properly condemned the "allusions artfully made" in public debate by some of his political friends, and particularly White of Delaware, to "documents communicated under the injunction of secrecy."

Tracy, of Connecticut, took the same ground with Pickering in regard to the necessity of obtaining the unanimous consent of the States to sanction the incorporation of territory into the Union, and in regard to the constitutional right of acquiring and governing foreign territory.

On the Republican side, Jackson of Georgia, Wright of Maryland, Taylor of Virginia, Butler of South Carolina, Breckenridge of Kentucky, Nicholas of Virginia, and Cocke of Tennessee, spoke in favor of the bill.

The question was taken, November 3d, and the vote stood yeas twenty-six, nays five. All the Republicans voted for it, and also Adams, Dayton, Olcott, and Plumer (the two last from New Hampshire), Federalists.

The reputation acquired by the Administration from the Louisiana purchase would have been great under any circumstances. But the bitter opposition of its opponents added to the effect. They drew attention to the subject. They set the nation to contemplating the results likely to flow from the acquisition. They prevented the people from tacitly settling down into the idea that it was a sort of matter of course under the circumstances, and that any set of rulers would have taken the same steps, and secured the same advantages. They by these means taught candid and reflecting men, even among the Federalists, that a great and vigorous statesman guided the helm of public affairs, instead of the philosophical and visionary theorist who had been described to them. And when liberal men discover that they have been mistaken in estimating an opponent in one important particular, they are prone to push their investigations further.

There was much which was calculated to make a fair scrutiny redound to the further credit of the Administration. The standing army had been reduced to a handful, and our great naval preparations were stopped, yet our foreign relations, beyond the speck of war in the Mediterranean, were strictly peaceful; we had not been so free from foreign aggressions since the origin of the government; and internally not a county, or town, or hamlet of the United States was menacing " insurrection," or even expressing discontent. The taxes were abolished, yet public debt was visibly and rapidly decreasing. Great treasury schemes were extinct, yet industry prospered. The press and tongue were free, yet the Government gained daily in popularity.

Democracy was everywhere triumphant, yet law, order, and religion maintained their ascendency. Great and expensive judicial "engines of government" had fallen, yet every man sat under his own vine and fig tree, and enjoyed his own in security. Never since the dawn of time was there a government which met all the ends of its institution better, or with less burden to the governed.

The Federalists, since the Administration of Washington, had not only seized nearly every practicable occasion to legislate unwisely, but they had exhibited an infatuation—what almost seemed an infatuated desire—to seize occasions to take a violent issue with the settled feelings and opinions of the American people. They had, in the election of 1801, alienated the body of the people. Yet many a man of character lingered with them, ashamed to abandon his colors. The desertion of leaders at that time bore no proportion to the popular desertion. But their conduct on the Louisiana question sent off to their enemy's camp a large body of their principal men. That a little handful in Congress, scarcely numerous enough to make a serious parliamentary opposition, should, on this question, where the Government had almost the entire mass of the nation on its side, so furiously and acrimoniously contest every inch, was something more than a common party error. It betrayed an extent of political folly for which there could be neither cure nor hope. It was no shame to leave men to their own labors, who, like Sydney Smith's Mrs. Partington, chose to employ themselves in mopping back the Atlantic! The vote in the Senate foreshadowed that thenceforth the Federal ascendency would be found tottering even in New England.

But the ultra-Federalist leaders were predestined to learn nothing by experience. They were pure "exotics" amidst the mass of American mind. They could neither see nor hear anything but their favorite idea. They groped about like foreigners, never understanding the character of their countrymen, nor the system of things in which they were placed. They were the shadows of an old *régime*, having no commixture or sympathy with the generation about them. They were political Quixotes, dreaming over the dreams, and, in imagination, fighting over the battles of a bygone age.

Fisher Ames wrote Thomas Dwight, October 31, 1803·

"Having bought an empire, who is to be the emperor? The sovereign people? all, or only the people of the dominant States, and the dominant demagogues in those States, who call themselves the people? As in old Rome, Marius, or Sylla, or Cæsar, Pompey, Antony, or Lepidus will vote themselves provinces and triumphs. . . . . . Never before was it attempted to play the fool on so great a scale. The game, however, will not be half played; nay, it will not be begun, before it is changed into another, where the knave will turn up trump and win the odd trick. . . . . .

"But what say you wise ones? Is the payment of so many millions to a belligerent no breach of neutrality, especially under the existing circumstances of the case, when Great Britain is fighting our battles and the battles of mankind, and France is combating for the power to enslave and plunder us and all the world?"[1]

It was about a fortnight after this that he wrote the declaration that in "England he beheld a real people," and "patriotism broad awake," quoted in an earlier portion of this work; and he was peculiarly liberal at this period in applying his customary savory "free negro" comparisons to our Government and people.

Morris wrote Roger Griswold, November 25th, 1803:

"When the people have been long enough drunk, they will get sober; but while the frolic lasts, to reason with them is useless. Their present leaders take advantage of their besotted condition, and tie their hands and feet; but if this prevents them from running into the fire, why should we, who are their friends, complain?"[2]

Whether Hamilton wrote in respect to the accession of Louisiana, and his letters have not been preserved, we are unable to say. We find nothing on the topic in his published correspondence.

Some other events of the Congressional session demand our notice.

The bankrupt law passed during Mr. Adams's Administration was repealed, with the hearty concurrence of the President. This sent another large batch of Government appointees out of office.

Louisiana was erected into two territories, that portion of it south of a line running west from the Mississippi, at 33° of north latitude, called Orleans, and that north retaining the name of Louisiana. A temporary government was framed for each.

[1] Ames's Works, vol. i. p. 329. It is probable that Mr. Ames's habitual solicitude for the rights of England would not have so far outran those of George III. and Lord Hawkesbury had he seen Mr. King's dispatches.
[2] Morris's Life and Works, vol. iii. p. 184.

A bill passed by the requisite majority of two-thirds, though warmly resisted by the Federalists, for submitting an amendment of the Constitution, requiring the President and Vice-President to be separately voted for.

On the 5th of December the President had announced the cessation of difficulties with Morocco, and he awarded great praise to the officers who had commanded in the operations against that power, Preble, Rogers, Campbell and Bainbridge.

On the 20th of March a private message communicated the intelligence that Captain Bainbridge had been wrecked in the Philadelphia frigate, on the coast of Tripoli, and that its entire crew had fallen into the hands of the Tripolitans.

On the 26th of March a bill passed, imposing, after the 30th of June following, an additional duty of two and a half per centum *ad valorem* on all imports paying *ad valorem* duties, and increasing it to ten per centum on imports in foreign vessels. The proceeds of this tariff were to be termed the " Mediterranean Fund," and exclusively applied to carrying on the warlike operations necessary for the protection of commerce in that sea.

An indication of the height to which party spirit ran this session is presented by the circumstance that a resolution, introduced into the Senate, that the members wear crape on their arms for a month, " in testimony of the national gratitude and reverence " to the memories of Samuel Adams and Edmund Pendleton, recently deceased, was made a party question, every Federalist but White of Delaware voting against it.[1] The House had unanimously decided to wear this badge of mourning for Samuel Adams. On learning the death of Pendleton, a similar resolution passed without any dissenting votes.[2]

John Pickering, Judge of the United States District Court of New Hampshire, was put on his trial before the Senate, for impeachment, on charges preferred the preceding session. His son petitioned for a delay, on the ground that his father had been insane for upwards of two years, and still continued so, and that he was too feeble to be brought to Washington. He had exercised judicial duties during this alleged derangement. He had been given the whole period since the last session to

[1] Bradley of Vermont, and John Smith of Ohio, Republicans, voted with the Federalists.

[2] Ayes, seventy-seven.

prepare for trial. No overture was made looking towards his vacation of the office. The Senate, therefore, decided the trial must proceed.

Though there was some respectable testimony in proof of his insanity prior to his intemperance, it was made abundantly apparent that he was a gross, habitual and notorious drunkard; and that, if the wild, indecorous and illegal proceedings[1] of which he was guilty were not the sole results of actual and ordinary drunkenness, the insanity he manifested was the concomitant and reciprocal effect of his wholly unrestrained inebriety.

After two ineffectual attempts to suspend proceedings, decided by nearly strict party votes (the Federalists voting for, and the Republicans against the suspension), the trial was pushed to a close, and Pickering was pronounced guilty on the articles of impeachment by a vote of nineteen to seven. The nays were all Federalists. The vote for removal stood twenty to six, Wells of Delaware now voting with the majority.

An effort was made throughout the trial, and afterwards, to represent this unfortunate officer as the victim of Republican and Executive persecution. But the real features of the case were too broad and apparent to be mistaken by any one.

The House ordered articles of impeachment to be prepared against Samuel Chase, one of the Associate Justices of the Supreme Court of the United States, but his trial was deferred to the next session.

Congress adjourned on the 27th of March.

[1] He raved and blasphemed on the bench in open court—cursed the parties—called people (sometimes perfect strangers) to come up and sit beside him on the bench, threatening to cane them if they refused. He had wholly refused to perform his duties in a case where he was called upon to enforce the revenue laws of the United States.

CHAPTER III.

1804—1805.

DURING the late session of Congress, a Republican caucus had been held to nominate candidates for the Presidency and

90

Vice-Presidency. Mr. Jefferson was unanimously renominated. Colonel Burr was so completely stripped of the confidence of his party that there was not a faction in Congress in favor of his reelection; and the vote for the Vice-Presidential candidate stood for George Clinton, sixty-seven; for John Breckenridge, twenty; for Levi Lincoln, nine; for John Langdon, seven; for Gideon Granger, four; for Samuel Maclay, one.

Mr. Clinton had been Governor of New York throughout the Revolution and for a considerable subsequent period. He had been the leader of the party in that State which so long and pertinaciously opposed the adoption of the Federal Constitution; and he became the leader of the Republicans when that party was organized. Without any of that brilliancy of talent possessed by his celebrated nephew, De Witt Clinton, he was nevertheless a man of solid parts, firm good sense, and invincible determination. His decided executive ability had been tested by a long and successful career in civil and military positions. His integrity was undisputed, his private character irreproachable. He was four years older than the President. All things considered, his nomination was an eminently fit one, and it was greatly to be regretted that it had not been made four years earlier, in the place of that of a corrupt intriguer who had never really approached Mr. Clinton in the estimation of the people of his State.[1]

We shall glance rapidly over such of the President's correspondence during the late session, as has not been adverted to, and which presents interesting ideas or facts not already given.

In a letter to David Williams, November 14th (1803), he complained that certain causes, which he enumerated, had "long since produced an overcharge in the class of competitors for learned occupations, and great distress among the supernumerary candidates; and the more, as their habits of life had disqualified them for reëntering into the laborious class." In other words, Mr. Jefferson meant to say that the legal and medical professions were overstocked, including teachers in the higher departments of science.[2] The remedy he proposed was to make

---

[1] Those who desire to know the causes and means of Burr's first nomination, and why Mr. Clinton was passed over on that occasion, will find them explained in Hammond's Political History of New York.

[2] The disturbed political relations of Europe had driven many learned men to our shores, who being unacquainted with American modes of living, suffered, in some in

agriculture a scientific profession or avocation, and thus lure the "supernumeraries" into an employment where they would find occupation both for the body and mind. He said:

"The evil cannot be suddenly, nor perhaps ever entirely cured: nor should I presume to say by what means it may be cured. Doubtless there are many engines which the nation might bring to bear on this object. Public opinion, and public encouragement are among these. The class principally defective is that of agriculture. It is the first in utility, and ought to be the first in respect. The same artificial means which have been used to produce a competition in learning, may be equally successful in restoring agriculture to its primary dignity in the eyes of men. It is a science of the very first order. It counts among its handmaids the most respectable sciences, such as Chemistry, Natural Philosophy, Mechanics, Mathematics generally, Natural History, Botany. In every College and University, a professorship of agriculture, and the class of its students, might be honored as the first. Young men closing their academical education with this, as the crown of all other sciences, fascinated with its solid charms, and at a time when they are to choose an occupation, instead of crowding the other classes, would return to the farms of their fathers, their own, or those of others, and replenish and invigorate a calling, now languishing under contempt and oppression. The charitable schools, instead of storing their pupils with a lore which the present state of society does not call for, converted into schools of agriculture, might restore them to that branch qualified to enrich and honor themselves, and to increase the productions of the nation instead of consuming them. A gradual abolition of the useless offices, so much accumulated in all governments, might close this drain also from the labors of the field, and lessen the burdens imposed on them. By these, and the better means which will occur to others, the surcharge of the learned, might in time be drawn off to recruit the laboring class of citizens, the sum of industry be increased, and that of misery diminished.

* * * * *

"The general desire of men to live by their heads rather than their hands, and the strong allurements of great cities to those who have any turn for dissipation, threaten to make them here, as in Europe, the sinks of voluntary misery."

Views according with the above were often expressed by the President in his family. His grandson, Colonel T. J. Randolph, writes us:

"He held in little esteem the education that made men ignorant and helpless as to the common necessities of life; and he exemplified it by an incident which occurred to a young gentleman returned from Europe, where he had been educated. On riding out with his companions, the strap of his saddle-girth broke at the hole of the buckle; and they, perceiving it an accident easily remedied, rode on and left him. A plain man coming up, and seeing that his horse had made a circular path in the road

stances, a good deal of distress. Mr. Jefferson remarked, in the letter from which we are quoting: "Many, who cannot find employment in Europe, accordingly come here. Those who can labor do well, for the most part. Of the learned class of emigrants, a small portion find employments analogous to their talents. But many fail, and return to complete their course of misery in the scenes where it began."

in his impatience to get on, asked if he could aid him? 'Oh, sir,' replied the young man, 'if you could only assist me to get it up to the next hole?' 'Suppose you let it out a hole or two on the other side,' said the man."

In a letter to Mr. Gallatin, of December 13th, the President advised him that he should consider it inexpedient for the former to give any opinion in reply to a question from the president of the United States Bank, whether it would be proper to change the manner of electing the officers of the branch institutions; and this on the ground that the Government ought not, by volunteering its sanction, to disarm itself "of any fair right of animadversion, whenever that institution should be a legitimate subject of consideration." What follows, shows that his hostility to the Bank was quite as decided as on the first presentation of the question during General Washington's Administration— that, indeed, it had rather gained than lost in intensity. He wrote:

"From a passage in the letter of the President, I observe an idea of establishing a branch bank of the United States in New Orleans. This institution is one of the most deadly hostility existing, against the principles and form of our Constitution. The nation is, at this time, so strong and united in its sentiments, that it cannot be shaken at this moment. But suppose a series of untoward events should occur, sufficient to bring into doubt the competency of a republican government to meet a crisis of great danger, or to unhinge the confidence of the people in the public functionaries; an institution like this, penetrating by its branches every part of the Union, acting by command and in phalanx, may, in a critical moment, upset the government. I deem no government safe which is under the vassalage of any self-constituted authorities, or any other authority than that of the nation, or its regular functionaries. What an obstruction could not this bank of the United States, with all its branch banks, be in time of war? It might dictate to us the peace we should accept, or withdraw its aids. Ought we then to give further growth to an institution so powerful, so hostile? That it is so hostile we know, 1, from a knowledge of the principles of the persons composing the body of directors in every bank, principal or branch; and those of most of the stockholders: 2, from their opposition to the measures and principles of the Government, and to the election of those friendly to them: and 3, from the sentiments of the newspapers they support. Now, while we are strong, it is the greatest duty we owe to the safety of our Constitution, to bring this powerful enemy to a perfect subordination under its authorities. The first measure would be to reduce them to an equal footing only with other banks, as to the favors of the Government. But, in order to be able to meet a general combination of the banks against us, in a critical emergency, could we not make a beginning towards an independent use of our own money, towards holding our own bank in all the deposits where it is received, and letting the treasurer give his draft or note, for payment at any particular place, which, in a well conducted government, ought to have as much credit as any private draft, or bank note, or bill, and would give us the same facilities which we derive from the banks? I pray you to turn this subject in your mind, and to give it the benefit of your knowledge of details; whereas, I have only very general views of the subject. Affectionate salutations."

A remark in a letter to Timothy Bloodworth, January 29th (1804), gives the substance of one frequently made by him, smilingly, in his family. After reciting some of the measures of his Administration, he said:

"I think [these] must reconcile the great body of those who thought themselves our enemies, but were in truth only the enemies of certain Jacobinical, atheistical, anarchical, imaginary caricatures, which existed only in the land of the Raw-head and Bloody-bones, beings created to frighten the credulous."

Colonel Randolph writes us:

"In speaking of the calumnies which had been uttered against his public and private character with such unmitigated and untiring bitterness, he said that he had not considered them as abusing him; they had never known him. They had created an imaginary being clothed with odious attributes, to whom they gave his name; and it was against that creature of their imaginations they had levelled their anathemas."

Mr. Jefferson wrote Dr. Priestley, January 29th:

"Have you seen the new work of Malthus on population? It is one of the ablest I have ever seen. Although his main object is to delineate the effects of redundancy of population, and to test the poor laws of England, and other palliations for that evil, several important questions in political economy, allied to his subject incidentally, are treated with a masterly hand. It is a single octavo volume, and I have been only able to read a borrowed copy, the only one I have yet heard of."

On the 1st of February, he thanked M. Say, the distinguished French writer on Political Economy, for a copy of his work on that subject, which he had just forwarded to the President. He again spoke well of Malthus's work. He advanced, or rather suggested the idea, that the distribution of labor supposed to be the best in Europe—namely, placing manufacturing hands alongside the agricultural, "so that the one part shall feed both, and the other part furnish both with clothes and other comforts"—might not be the one best applicable to the United States. As Europe had as much population as her products could sustain (or as the increase in each must be limited and slow), and as America had land enough to keep up the most rapid possible advance of population, and at the same time produce an enormous surplus of food, he suggested whether it would not be better for America to raise food " to nourish the now perishing births of Europe" (an allusion to Malthus's theory of the fatal necessity of starvation, where human fecundity outruns the means of subsistence), and that Europe in return should send us " our clothes and other comforts."   He said "morality" favored this idea ; and "so invariably did the laws of nature create our duties and interests, that when they seem to be at variance, we ought to suspect some fallacy in our reasonings."

In a letter to Mr. Gerry, of March 3d, the President, after stating the general prospects of the two political parties, thus alluded to his feelings in respect to his own renomination :

"I sincerely regret that the unbounded calumnies of the Federal party have obliged me to throw myself on the verdict of my country for trial, my great desire having been to retire, at the end of the present term, to a life of tranquillity ; and it was my decided purpose when I entered into office. They force my continuance. If we can keep the vessel of State as steadily in her course for another four years, my earthly purposes will be accomplished, and I shall be free to enjoy, as you are doing, my family, my farm, and my books."

On the 16th of April he wrote (from Monticello) to the Postmaster General, commenting on a statement of the latter that there was a Federal scheme on foot for forming a coalition between the Federalists and Republicans, " of what they called the seven eastern States."   The commentary is far too good to be omitted :

"The Federalists know, that, *eo nomine*, they are gone forever. Their object, therefore, is how to return into power under some other form. Undoubtedly they have but one means, which is to divide the Republicans, join the minority, and barter with them for the cloak of their name. I say, *join the minority;* because the majority of the Republicans, not needing them, will not buy them. The minority, having no other means of ruling the majority, will give a price for auxiliaries, and that price must be principle. It is true that the Federalists, needing their numbers also, must also give a price, and principle is the coin they must pay in. Thus a bastard system of Federo-Republicanism will rise on the ruins of the true principles of our Revolution. And when this party is formed, who will constitute the majority of it, which majority is then to dictate? Certainly the Federalists. Thus their proposition of putting themselves into gear with the Republican minority, is exactly like Roger Sherman's proposition to add Connecticut to Rhode Island. The idea of forming seven eastern States is moreover clearly to form the basis of a separation of the Union. Is it possible that real Republicans can be gulled by such a bait? And for what? What do they wish that they have not? Federal measures? That is impossible? Republican measures? Have they them not? Can any one deny, that in all important questions of principle, Republicanism prevails? But do they not want that their individual will shall govern the majority? They may purchase the gratification of this unjust wish, for a little time, at a great price; but the Federalists must not have the passions of other men, if, after getting thus into the seat of power, they suffer themselves to be governed by their minority. This minority may say, that whenever they relapse into their own principles, they will quit them and draw the seat from under them. They may quit them, indeed, but in the meantime, all the venal will have become associated with them, and will give them a majority sufficient to keep them in place, and to enable them to eject the heterogeneous friends by whose aid they get again into power. I cannot believe any portion of real Republicans will enter into this trap; and if they do, I do not believe they can carry with them the mass of their States, advancing so steadily as we see them, to a union of principle with their brethren. It will be found in this, as in all other similar cases, that crooked schemes will end by overwhelming their authors and coadjutors in disgrace, and that he alone who walks strict and upright, and who, in matters of opinion, will be contented that others should be as free as himself, and acquiesce when his opionion is fairly overruled, will attain his object in the end. And that this may be the conduct of us all, I offer my sincere prayers, as well as for your health and happiness."

The following family letters, though scattered over a wide space, we prefer, for obvious reasons, to present connectedly.

TO MARIA JEFFERSON EPPES, EDGEHILL.

WASHINGTON, *Nov.* 27, 1903.

It is rare, my ever dear Maria, during a session of Congress that I can get time to write anything but letters of business, and this, though a day of rest to others, is not all so to me. We are all well here, and hope the post of this evening will bring us information of the health of all at Edgehill, and particularly that Martha and the new bantling are both well; and that her example gives you good spirits. When Congress will rise no mortal can tell: not from the quantity, but the dilatoriness of business. Mr. Lilly having finished the mill, is now, I suppose, engaged in the road which we have been so long wanting; and that done, the next job will be the levelling of Pantops. I anxiously long to see under way the work necessary to fix you there, that we may one day be all together. Mr. Stewart is now here on his way back to his family, whom he will probably join Thursday or Friday. Will you tell your sister that the pair of stockings she sent me by Mr. Randolph are quite large enough, and also have fur enough in them. I inclose some papers for Anne; and must continue in debt to Jefferson a letter for a while longer. Take care of yourself, my dearest Maria, have good spirits, and know that courage is as essential to triumph in your case as in that of a soldier. Keep us all, therefore, in heart of being so yourself; give my tender affections to your sister, and receive them for yourself also, with assurances that I live in your love only, and in that of your sister.

Adieu, my dear daughter.

TH. JEFFERSON.

To Maria Jefferson Eppes, Edgehill.

Washington, *Dec.* 26, 1803.

I now return, my dearest Maria, the paper which you lent me for Mr. Page, and which he has returned some days since. I have prevailed on Dr. Priestley to undertake the work of which this is only the syllabus or plan. He says he can accomplish it in the course of a year. But, in truth, his health is so much impaired and his body become so feeble, that there is reason to fear he will not live out even the short term he has asked for it. You may inform Mr. Eppes and Mr. Randolph that no mail arrived the last night from the Natchez. I presume the great rains which have fallen have rendered some of the water courses impassable. On new-year's day, however, we shall hear of the delivery of New Orleans to us. Till then the Legislature seem disposed to do nothing but meet and adjourn. Mrs. Livingston, formerly the younger Miss Allen, made kind inquiries after you the other day. She said she was at school with you at Mrs. Pine's. Not knowing the time destined for your expected indisposition, I am anxious on your account. You are prepared to meet it with courage, I hope. Some female friend of your mamma's (I forget whom) used to say it was no more than a jog of the elbow. The material thing is, to have scientific aid in readiness, that if anything uncommon takes place it may be redressed on the spot, and not be made serious by delay. It is a case which least of all will wait for doctors to be sent for, therefore with this single precaution nothing is ever to be feared. I was in hopes to have heard from Edgehill last night, but I suppose your post has failed.

I shall expect to see the gentlemen here next Sunday night to take part in the gala of Monday. Give my tenderest love to your sister, of whom I have not heard for a fortnight, and my affectionate salutations to the gentlemen and young ones, and continue to love me yourself, and be assured of my warmest affections.

Th. Jefferson.

To Maria Jefferson Eppes, Edgehill.

Washington, *Jan.* 29, 1804.

My dearest Maria:

This evening ought to have brought in the western mail, but it is not arrived, consequently we hear nothing from our neighborhood. I rejoice that this is the last time our Milton mail will be embarrassed with that from New Orleans; the rapidity of which occasioned our letters often to be left in the post-offices—it now returns to its former establishment of twice a week, so that we may hear oftener from you; and in communicating to us frequently of the state of things, I hope you will not be sparing if it be only by saying that "all is well." I think Congress will rise the 2d week in March, when we shall join you—perhaps Mr. Eppes may sooner. On this I presume he writes you. It would have been the most desirable of all things could we have got away by this time. However, I hope you will let us all see that you have within yourself the resource of a courage not requiring the presence of anybody. Since proposing to Anne the undertaking to raise bantams, I have received from Algiers two pair of beautiful fowls, something larger than our common fowls, with fine aigrettes. They are not so large nor valuable as the East India fowl, but both kinds, as well as the bantams, are well worthy of being raised. We must, therefore, distribute them among us, and raise them clear of mixture of any kind.

All this we will settle together in March, and soon after we will begin the levelling and establishment of your hen-house at Pantops. Give my tenderest love to your sister; to all the young ones kisses; to yourself everything affectionate.

Th. Jefferson.

To Maria Jefferson Eppes, Edgehill.

Washington, Feb. 26, 1804.

A thousand joys to you, my dear Maria, on the happy accession to your family. A letter from our dear Martha by last post gave me the happy news that your crisis was happily over and all well. I had supposed that if you were a little later than your calculation, and the rising of Congress as early as we expected, we might have been with you at the moment when it would have been so encouraging to have had your friends around you. I rejoice, indeed, that all is so well. Congress talk of rising the 12th of March, but they will probably be some days later. You will doubtless see see Mr. Eppes and Mr. Randolph immediately on the rising of Congress. I shall hardly be able to get away till some days after them. By that time I hope you will be able to go with us to Monticello, and that we shall *all* be there together for a month: and the interval between that and the autumnal visit will not be long. Will you desire your sister to send for Mr. Lilly, and to advise him what orders to give Goliah for providing those vegetables which may come into use for the months of April, August, and September—deliver her also my affectionate love. I will write to her the next week. Kiss all the little ones, and be assured yourself of my tender and unchangeable affection.

Th. Jefferson.

To Maria Jefferson Eppes, Edgehill.

Washington, Mar. 8, 1804.

The account of your illness, my dearest Maria, was known to me only this morning.. Nothing but the impossibility of Congress proceeding a single step in my absence presents an insuperable bar. Mr. Eppes goes off, and I hope will find you in a convalescent state. Next to the desire that it may be so, is that of being speedily informed and of being relieved from the terrible anxiety in which I shall be till I hear from you. God bless you, my ever dear daughter, and preserve you safe to the blessing of us all.

Th. Jefferson.

To John W. Eppes, Edgehill.

Washington, March 15, 1804.

Dear Sir:

Your letter of the 9th has at length relieved my spirits; still the debility of Maria will need attention, lest a recurrence of fever should degenerate into typhus. I should suppose the system of wine and food as effectual to prevent as to cure that fever, and think she should use both, as freely as she finds she can bear them, light food and cordial wines. The sherry at Monticello is old and genuine, and the Pedro Ximenes much older still and stomachic. Her palate and stomach will be the best arbiters between them. Congress have deferred their adjournment a week, to wit, to the 26th, consequently we return a week later. I presume I can be with you by the first of April. I hope Maria will by that time be well enough to go over to Monticello with us, and I hope you will thereafter take up your residence there. The house, its contents, and appendages and servants, are as freely subjected to you as to myself and I hope you will make it your home till we can get you fixed at Pantops. I do not think Maria should be ventured below after this date. I will endeavor to forward to Mr. Benson, postmaster at Fredericksburg, a small parcel of the oats for you. The only difficulty is to find some gentleman going on in the stage who will take charge of them by the way. My tenderest love to Maria and Patsy,[1] and all the young ones; affectionate salutations to yourself.

                                                                TH. JEFFERSON.

——

TO JOHN W. EPPES.
                                                    WASHINGTON, *June* 4, 1804.
DEAR SIR:

I should much sooner have written to you but for the press of business which had accumulated at my return, and which is not yet entirely got under. We lamented much that you had not staid a day longer at Monticello, as on the evening of your departure the Eppington family arrived, and it would have added much to our pleasure to have been all together, the four or five days that the weather detained me at home. We consented to consign little Maria to the entreaties of Mrs. Eppes, until August, when she promised to bring her back herself. Nature's laws will in time deprive her of all her older connections; it will then be a great comfort to have been brought up with those of her own age, as sisters and brothers of the same house, knowing each other in no other relation, and ready to become the parents of each other's orphan children. While I live, both of the children will be to me the dearest of all pledges: and I should consider it as increasing our misfortune, should we have the less of your society. It will in no wise change my views at Pantops, and should considerations which ought not to be opposed by me in the actual state of things induce you to change the purpose of your residence at Pantops, I shall still do there what I had always proposed to you, expecting it will some day become the residence of Francis. I may only take more time for it. After Lilly shall have done at the mill, which I suppose will be by the time of my return home, there are then three jobs for him, the levelling at Pantops, the road along the river, and the levelling of the garden at Monticello. Which of these be first enters on, will depend on your views. If they be to get to Pantops as soon as you can, he shall first do that levelling, that it may be in readiness to begin a house the next season. In any other case I should set him about the road first, but I should be happier did the other order of things coincide more with your happiness. But I press nothing, because my own feelings as a parent teach me how to estimate and respect the feelings of parents. On this subject you must give me your wishes with frankness, as mine will be most gratified in taking the direction of yours.

I inclose you a letter I received lately from Mrs. Adams. The sentiments ex-

———
[1] Mrs. Randolph.

pressed in it are sincere. Her attachment was constant. Although all of them point to another object directly, yet the expressing them to me is a proof that our friendship is unbroken on her part. It has been a strong one, and has gone through trying circumstances on both sides, yet I retain it strongly both for herself and Mr. Adams. He and myself have gone through so many scenes together, that all his qualities have been proved to me, and I know him to possess so many good ones, as that I have never withdrawn my esteem, and I am happy that this letter gives me opportunity of expressing it to both of them. I shall do it with a frank declaration that one act of his life, and never but one, gave me personal displeasure, his midnight appointments. If respect for him will not permit me to ascribe that altogether to the influence of others, it will leave something for friendship to forgive. If Patsy is with you, communicate the letter to her, and be so good as to reinclose it to me. I think I shall leave this about the 22d of July, and shall hope to find you in Albemarle, and that you will soon be followed there by the Eppington family. I shall take my trip to Bedford soon after my arrival. Present me affectionately to the family at Eppington. Keep Francis mindful of me, and give both of them my kisses.

Affectionately adieu,
TH. JEFFERSON.

To JOHN W. EPPES, EPPINGTON.

MONTICELLO, *August* 7, 1804.

DEAR SIR:

Your letters of July 16th and 29th both came to me on the 2d instant. I receive with great delight the information of the perfect health of our dear infants, and hope to see yourself, the family and them, as soon as circumstances admit. With respect to Melinda, I have too many already to leave here in idleness when I go away; and at Washington I prefer white servants, who, when they mis-behave, can be exchanged. John knew he was not to expect her society, but when he should be at Monticello, and then subject to the casualty of her being here or not. You mention a horse to be had, of a *fine* bay, and again that he is of the color of your horse. I do not well recollect the shade of yours, but if you think this one would do with Castor or Fitzpartner, I would take him at the price you mention, but should be glad to have as much breadth for the payment as the seller could admit, and at any rate not less than ninety-days. I know no finer horse than yours, but he is much too fiery to be trusted in a carriage; the only use I have for him while Arcturus remains. He is also too small. I write this letter in the hope you will be here before you can receive it, but on the possibility that the cause which detained you at the date of yours may continue. My affectionate salutations and esteem attend the family at Eppington and yourself.

TH. JEFFERSON.

P. S. By your mentioning that Francis will be your constant companion, I am in hopes I shall have him here with you during the session of Congress.

In Mr. Jefferson's family register, is the following entry:

"Mary Jefferson, born Aug. 1, 1778, 1 h. 30 m, A.M. Died April 17, 1804, between 8 and 9 A.M.

The following letter, from a niece of the deceased, was not written with a thought to publication; but we trust we shall be pardoned for transcribing it. It contains some particulars already given—but the motive for presenting the narrative unbroken, will be apparent.

To HENRY S. RANDALL.

BOSTON, 15 *January*, 1856.

MY DEAR MR. RANDALL.
*   *   *   *   *   *   *

I find an old memorandum, made many years ago, I know not when nor under what circumstances, but by my own hand, in the fly leaf of a Bible. It is to this effect: "Maria Jefferson was born in 1778, and married in 1797, John Wayles Eppes, son of Francis Eppes and Elizabeth Wayles, second daughter of John Wayles. Maria Jefferson died April, 1804, leaving two children, Francis born in 1801, and Maria who died an infant."

I have no recollection of the time when I made this memorandum, but I have no doubt of its accuracy.

Mrs. Eppes was never well after the birth of her last child. She lingered a while, but never recovered. My grandfather was in Washington, and my aunt passed the winter at Edgehill where she was confined. I remember the tender and devoted care of my mother, how she watched over her sister, and with what anxious affection she anticipated her every want. I remember, at one time, that she left her chamber and her own infant, that she might sleep in my aunt's room, to assist in taking care of her and her child. I well recollect my poor aunt's pale, faded, and feeble look. My grandfather, during his Presidency, made two visits every year to Monticello, a short one in early spring, and a longer one the latter part of the summer. He always stopped at Edgehill, where my mother was then living, to take her and her whole family to Monticello with him. He came this year as usual, anxious about the health of his youngest daughter, whose situation, though such as to excite the apprehension of her friends, was not deemed one of immediate danger. She had been delicate and something of an invalid, if I remember right, for some years. She was carried to Monticello in a litter borne by men. The distance was perhaps four miles, and she bore the removal well. After this, however, she continued as before, steadily to decline. She was taken out when the weather permitted, and carried around the lawn in a carriage, I think drawn by men, and I remember following the carriage over the smooth green turf. How long she lived I do not recollect, but it could have been but a short time. One morning I heard that my aunt was dying; I crept softly from my nursery to her chamber door, and being alarmed by her short, hard breathing, ran away again. I have a distinct recollection of confusion and dismay in the household. I did not see my mother. By and by one of the female servants came running in where I was with other persons, to say that Mrs. Eppes was dead. The day passed I do not know how. Late in the afternoon I was taken to the death-chamber. The body was covered with a white cloth, over which had been strewed a profusion of flowers. A day or two after, I followed the coffin to the burying-ground on the mountain side, and saw it consigned to the earth, where it has lain undisturbed for more than fifty years.

My mother has told me that on the day of her sister's death, she left her father alone for some hours. He then sent for her, and she found him with the Bible in his hands. He who has been so often and so harshly accused of unbelief, he, in his hour of intense affliction, sought and found consolation in the sacred volume. The comforter was there for his true heart and devout spirit, even though his faith might not be what the world calls orthodox.

There was something very touching in the sight of this once beautiful and still lovely young woman, fading away just as the spring was coming on with its buds and blossoms—nature reviving as she was sinking and closing her eyes on all that she loved best in life. She perished not in autumn with the flowers, but as they were opening to the sun and air in all the freshness of spring. I think the weather was fine, for over my own recollection of these times there is a soft, dreamy sort of haze, such as wraps the earth in warm dewy spring-time.

You know enough of my aunt's early history to be aware that she did not accompany her father, as my mother did, when he first went to France. She joined him, I think, only about two years before his return, and was placed in the same convent where my mother received her education. Here she went by the name of Mademoiselle *Polie*. As a child she was called Polly by her friends. It was on her way to Paris that she staid awhile in London with Mrs. Adams, and there is a pleasing mention of her in that lady's published letters.

I think the visit (not a very long one) made by my mother and aunt to their father in Washington, must have been in the winter of 1802-3. My aunt, I believe, was never there again; but after her death, about the winter of 1805-6, my mother, with all her children, passed some time at the President's house. I remember that both my father and Uncle Eppes were *then* in Congress, but cannot say whether this was the case in 1802-3.

My aunt, Mrs. Eppes, was singularly beautiful. She was high principled, just, and generous. Her temper, naturally mild, became I think, saddened by ill-health, in the latter part of her life. In that respect she differed from my mother, whose disposition seemed to have the sunshine of heaven in it. Nothing ever wearied my mother's patience, or exhausted, what was inexhaustible, her sweetness, her kindness, indulgence, and self-devotion. She was intellectually somewhat superior to her sister, who was sensible of the difference, though she was of too noble a nature for her feelings ever to assume an ignoble character. There was between the sisters the strongest and warmest attachment, the most perfect confidence and affection.

My aunt utterly undervalued and disregarded her own beauty, remarkable as it was. She was never fond of dress or ornament, and was always careless of admiration. She was even vexed by allusions to her beauty, saying that people only praised her for that, because they could not praise her for better things. If my mother inadvertently exclaimed, half sportively, " Maria, if I only had your beauty," my aunt would resent it as far as she could resent anything said or done by her sister. It may be said that the extraordinary value she attached to talent, was mainly founded in her idea that by the possession of it, she would become a more suitable companion for her father. Both daughters considered his affection as the great good of their lives, and both loved him with all the devotion of their most loving hearts. My aunt sometimes mourned over the fear that her father *must* prefer her sister's society, and *could* not take the same pleasure in hers. This very humility in one so lovely was a charm the more in her character. She was greatly loved and esteemed by all her friends. She was on a footing of the most intimate friendship with my father's sister, Mrs. T. Eston Randolph, herself a most exemplary and admirable woman, whose daughter, long years after, married Francis, Mrs. Eppes's son.

I know not, my dear Mr. Randall, whether this letter will add anything to the knowledge you already possess of this one of my grandfather's family. Should it not, you must take the will for the deed, and as I am somewhat wearied by the rapidity with which I have written, in order to avoid delay, I will bid you adieu with my very best wishes for your entire success in your arduous undertaking.

Very truly yours.

Mr. Jefferson felt this blow with terrible keenness. Letters of condolence poured in upon him from his early friends. To none did he unbosom himself more fully than to his old classmate and boyish confidant, Governor Page. He wrote him, June 25th:

"Your letter, my dear friend, of the 25th ultimo, is a new proof of the goodness of your heart, and the part you take in my loss marks an affectionate concern for the greatness of it. It is great indeed. Others may lose of their abundance, but I, of my want, have lost even the half of all I had. My evening prospects now hang on the slender thread of a single life. Perhaps I may be destined to see even this last cord of parental affection broken! The hope with which I had looked forward to the moment, when, resigning public cares to younger hands, I was to retire to that domestic comfort from which the last great step is to be taken, is fearfully blighted. When you and I look back on the country over which we have passed, what a field of slaughter does it exhibit! Where are all the friends who entered it with us, under all the inspiring energies of health and hope? As if pursued by the havoc of war, they are strewed by the way, some earlier, some later, and scarce a few stragglers remain to count the numbers fallen, and to mark yet, by their own fall, the last footsteps of their party. Is it a desirable thing to bear up through the heat of the action, to witness the death of all our companions, and merely be the last victim? I doubt it. We have, however, the traveller's consolation. Every step shortens the distance we have to go; the end of our journey is in sight, the bed wherein we are to rest, and to rise in the midst of the friends we have lost. ' We sorrow not then as others who have no hope;' but look forward to the day which 'joins us to the great majority.' But whatever is to be our destiny, wisdom, as well as duty, dictates that we should acquiesce in the will of him whose it is to give and take away, and be contented in the enjoyment of those who are still permitted to be with us. Of those connected by blood, the number does not depend on us. But friends we have, if we have merited them. Those of our earliest years stand nearest in our affections. But in this, too, you and I have been unlucky. Of our college friends (and they are the dearest) how few have stood with us in the great political questions which have agitated our country: and these were of a nature to justify agitation. I did not believe the Lilliputian fetters of that day strong enough to have bound so many. Will not Mrs. Page, yourself and family, think it prudent to seek a healthier region for the months of August and September? And may we not flatter ourselves that you will cast your eye on Monticello? We have not many summers to live. While fortune places us then within striking distance, let us avail ourselves of it, to meet and talk over the tales of other times.

"Present me respectfully to Mrs. Page, and accept yourself my friendly salutations and assurances of constant affection."

Three days after, he wrote Judge Tyler :[1]

"I lament to learn that a like misfortune has enabled you to estimate the afflictions of a father on the loss of a beloved child. However terrible the possibility of such another accident, it is still a blessing for you of inestimable value that you would not even then descend childless to the grave. Three sons, and hopeful ones too, are a rich treasure. I rejoice when I hear of young men of virtue and talents, worthy to receive, and likely to preserve the splendid inheritance of self-government, which we have acquired and shaped for them."

The letter of condolence from Mrs. Adams, alluded to and inclosed in Mr. Jefferson's letter to Mr. Eppes (of June 4th), was as follows :

To Thomas Jefferson.

Sir :   QUINCY, 20th May, 1804.

Had you been no other than the private inhabitant of Monticello, I should, ere this time, have addressed you with that sympathy which a recent event has awakened in my bosom; but reasons of various kinds withheld my pen, until the powerful feelings of my heart burst through the restraint, and called upon me to shed the tear of sorrow over the departed remains of your beloved and deserving daughter. An event which I most sincerely mourn.

The attachment which I formed for her when you committed her to my care upon her arrival in a foreign land, under circumstances peculiarly interesting, has remained with me to this hour; and the account of her death, which I read in a late paper, recalled to my recollection the tender scene of her separation from me, when, with the strongest sensibility, she clung around my neck, and wet my bosom with her tears, saying, "Oh, now I have learned to love you, why will they take me from you."

It has been some time since I conceived that any event in this life could call forth feelings of mutual sympathy. But I know how closely entwined around a parent's heart are those cords which bind the parental to the filial bosom ; and when snapped asunder, how agonizing the pangs. I have tasted of the bitter cup, and bow with reverence and submission before the great Dispenser of it, without whose permission and over-ruling providence not a sparrow falls to the ground. That you may derive comfort and consolation in this day of your sorrow and affliction from that only source calculated to heal the broken heart, a firm belief in the being, perfections and attributes of God, is the sincere and ardent wish of her who once took pleasure in subscribing herself your friend.

ABIGAIL ADAMS.

This letter, from one whose bosom had so often pillowed the head of his dead daughter, was well calculated to call back the

---

[1] Afterwards Governor of Virginia, and father of President John Tyler.

recollections mentioned to Mr. Eppes; and it will be seen, on reverting to that letter, with what delicacy Mr. Jefferson overlooked and sought to cover up the omission of all kindly expressions to himself. He carried out the intention avowed to his son-in-law, of making an overture to a renewal of former friendship, in the following letter:

TO MRS. ADAMS.

WASHINGTON, June 13, 1804.

DEAR MADAM:

The affectionate sentiments which you have had the goodness to express in your letter of May the 20th, towards my dear departed daughter, have awakened in me sensibilities natural to the occasion, and recalled your kindnesses to her, which I shall ever remember with gratitude and friendship. I can assure you with truth, they had made an indelible impression on her mind, and that to the last, on our meetings after long separations, whether I had heard lately of you, and how you did, were among the earliest of her inquiries. In giving you this assurance I perform a sacred duty for her, and, at the same time, am thankful for the occasion furnished me, of expressing my regret that circumstances should have arisen, which have seemed to draw a line of separation between us. The friendship with which you honored me has ever been valued, and fully reciprocated; and although events have been passing which might be trying to some minds, I never believed yours to be of that kind, nor felt that my own was. Neither my estimate of your character, nor the esteem founded in that, has ever been lessened for a single moment, although doubts whether it would be acceptable may have forbidden manifestations of it.

Mr. Adams's friendship and mine began at an earlier date. It accompanied us through long and important scenes. The different conclusions we had drawn from our political reading and reflections, were not permitted to lessen personal esteem; each party being conscious they were the result of an honest conviction in the other. Like differences of opinion existing among our fellow-citizens, attached them to one or the other of us, and produced a rivalship in their minds which did not exist in ours. We never stood in one another's way; but if either had been withdrawn at any time, his favorers would not have gone over to the other, but would have sought for some one of homogeneous opinions. This consideration was sufficient to keep down all jealousy between us, and to guard our friendship from any disturbance by sentiments of rivalship; and I can say with truth, that one act of Mr. Adams's life, and one only, ever gave me a moment's personal displeasure. I did consider his last appointments to office as personally unkind. They were from among my most ardent political enemies, from whom no faithful coöperation could ever be expected; and laid me under the embarrassment of acting through men whose views were to defeat mine, or to encounter the odium of putting others in their places. It seems but common justice to leave a successor free to act by instruments of his own choice. If my respect for him did not permit me to ascribe the whole blame to the influence of others, it left something for friendship to forgive, and after brooding over it for some little time, and not always resisting the expression of it, I forgave it cordially, and returned to the same state of esteem and respect for him which had so long subsisted. Having come into life a little later than Mr. Adams, his career has preceded mine, as mine is followed by some other; and it will probably be closed at the same distance after him which time originally placed between us. I maintain for him, and shall carry into private life, an uniform and high measure of respect and good will, and for yourself a sincere attachment.

I have thus, my dear madam, opened myself to you without reserve, which I have long wished an opportunity of doing; and without knowing how it will be received, I feel relief from being unbosomed. And I have now only to entreat your forgiveness for this transition from a subject of domestic affliction, to one which seems of a different aspect. But though connected with political events, it has been viewed by me most strongly in its unfortunate bearings on my private friendships. The injury these have sustained has been a heavy price for what has never given me equal pleasure. That you may both be favored with health, tranquillity and long life, is the prayer of one who tenders you the assurance of his highest consideration and esteem.

Mrs. Adams replied, and having repelled the imputation of "personal unkindness" in Mr. Adams's late official appointments, proceeded in pointed language to arraign the President's conduct in liberating Callender; and she spoke of the President's having given him a " reward of fifty dollars "—of having " cherished and warmed" the serpent, etc. She said, " there was one other act of his administration which she considered as personally unkind, and which his own mind would easily suggest to him, but as it neither affected character nor reputation, she forbore to state it."

The President, in answer, explained his gratuities to Callender substantially as he had done to Monroe; declared he released him, as he did all the other victims of the Sedition Law, because he considered that law a nullity under the Constitution "as absolute and palpable as if Congress had ordered us to fall down and worship a graven image." He declared, " on his honor," that he had not the remotest idea to what other act Mrs. Adams alluded, as personally unkind, as " he never did a single one with an unkind intention."

Mrs. Adams was not mollified. She thought it devolved on the " supreme judges of the nation " to say what laws were constitutional. She specified the act of personal unkindness to have been the removal by the President of her oldest son from an office to which he had been appointed soon after his return from Europe.

A "press of business" delayed the President's reply. " With those who wished to think amiss of him," he said, " he had learned to be perfectly indifferent; but when he knew a mind to be ingenuous, and to need only truth to set it to rights, he could not be passive." He informed Mrs. Adams that he had not even been aware that Mr. J. Q. Adams had held the office indicated; explained how the removal occurred; and declared that it would have given him real pleasure to prefer her son to some other Federalists retained in the same office in Boston, both on account of his knowledge of J. Q. Adams's integrity and his own "sincere dispositions towards herself and Mr. Adams." After an argument to show that the President was as much the judge of the Constitution, in the execution of his own official duties, as were the Supreme Court in theirs, he concluded thus:

"The candor manifested in your letter, and which I ever believed you to possess, has alone inspired the desire of calling your attention, once more, to those circumstances of fact and motive by which I claim to be judged. I hope you will see these intrusions on your time to be, what they really are, proofs of my great respect for you. I tolerate with the utmost latitude the right of others to differ from me in opinion without imputing to them criminality. I know too well the weakness and uncertainty of human reason to wonder at its different results. Both of our political parties, at least the honest part of them, agree conscientiously in the same object—the public good; but they differ essentially in what they deem the means of promoting that good. One side believes it best done by one composition of the governing powers; the other, by a different one. One fears most the ignorance of the people; the other, the selfishness of rulers independent of them. Which is right, time and experience will prove. We think that one side of this experiment has been long enough tried, and proved not to promote the good of the many; and that the other has not been fairly and sufficiently tried. Our opponents think the reverse. With whichever opinion the body of the nation concurs, that must prevail. My anxieties on this subject will never carry me beyond the use of fair and honorable means, of truth and reason; nor have they ever lessened my esteem for moral worth, nor alienated my affections from a single friend, who did not first withdraw himself. Whenever this has happened, I confess I have not been insensible to it; yet have ever kept myself open to a return of their justice. I conclude with sincere prayers for your health and happiness, that yourself and Mr. Adams may long enjoy the tranquillity you desire and merit, and see in the prosperity of your family what is the consummation of the last and warmest of human wishes."

It would be difficult to indicate the precise tone of Mrs. Adams's answer without giving the letter entire, and this we have no wish to do. Suffice it to say, she "closed the correspondence" with her feelings apparently as unappeased as when it was opened.

Subjoined to the copy of her last letter, says Mr. Adams's

family biographer, was found the following memorandum in the handwriting of her husband:

QUINCY, *19th November,* 1904.

The whole of this correspondence was begun and conducted without my knowledge or suspicion. Last evening and this morning, at the desire of Mrs. Adams, I read the whole. I have no remarks to make upon it, at this time and in this place.

J. ADAMS.

The spectacle of a man at the summit of power and popularity in his country, so kindly, and so calmly defending himself from imputations, which, it must be confessed, were not invariably put in precisely those forms of expression which gentlemen are accustomed to receive without offence from gentlemen—so repeatedly renewing his unaccepted overtures—and this to those, who, crushed under the load of an enormous unpopularity, had no power to benefit or harm him, or at such a distance, either to increase or diminish his social enjoyments, was a good exemplification of Martha Jefferson's often repeated remark : " My father never gave up a friend or an opinion."

While we survey with pleasure the triumphant, yet desolate, victor, making such concessions to ancient friendship and to a woman—and making these concessions to a woman on precisely the same rational grounds that he would have made them to one of the other sex, without any apologizing parade of mawkish or chivalresque sentiment—we must not judge too harshly of Mrs. Adams, or pronounce her destitute of womanly amiability. Her lofty lineaments carried a trace of the Puritan severity. They were those of the helmed Minerva, and not of the cestus-girdled Venus. Her correspondence uniformly exhibits a didactic personage—a little inclined to assume a sermonizing attitude, as befitted the well-trained and self-reliant daughter of a New England country clergyman—and a little inclined, after the custom of her people, to return thanks that she had not lot or part in anything that was not of Massachusetts. Perhaps the masculineness of her understanding extended somewhat to the firmness of her temper. But towering above and obscuring these minor angularities, she possessed a strength of intellectual and moral character, which commands our unqualified admiration. Her decision would have manifested itself for her friend or her cause, when softer spirits would have shrunk away, or been paralyzed with terror. When her New England frigidness gave way and kindled into enthusiasm, it was not the burning straw, but the red hot steel.[1] On the stranding deck, at the gibbet's foot, in any other deadly pass where undaunted moral courage can light up the coming gloom of "the valley and shadow of death," Mrs. Adams would have stood by the side of those she loved uttering words of encouragement: and in that more desperate pass where death or overthrow are balanced against dishonor, she would have firmly bade the most loved friend on earth embrace the former like a bride.

Mr. Jefferson, there is no doubt, judged her feelings truly when he inclosed her letter to his bereaved son-in-law. Why did she write him, if this "chosen one of the earth," was not struggling for his ancient place in her warm friendship? Could her letter carry feelings of kindness to the ear of death? Is there such a thing as hostile condolences? Would Mrs. Adams have gratuitously entered the house of mourning to insult its inmates with such a communication? The very fact that she could not conceal her wound proved the existence of that deep, ancient regard, which could alone give it this festering soreness —this irrepressible sting. To adopt any other solution would be to assign motives to her which were unwomanly, and for which the epithet petty would be quite too mild. Had Mr. Adams been the victor, and Mr. Jefferson the vanquished, half the advances made by the latter would have sufficed. But in high natures the pride of defeat is greater and more exacting than that of victory. The overthrow of a President had not then been made a common occurrence. There were circumstances which rendered the downfall of Mr. Adams personally humiliating and irritating. Mrs. Adams felt morbidly for her husband; and in 1804 the wound was too recent to be "medicined."

But she was afterwards to do herself justice by spontaneously making advances to the now repulsed friend; and we need not say her first overture was met. The sunlight of restored friendship was yet to shed a golden radiance over the de-

[1] The young man's wrath is like light straw on fire,
Heard ye so merry the little bird sing?
But like red-hot steel is the old man's ire,
And the throstle-cock's head is under his wing. *Old Ballad.*

clining days of the Tongue and the Pen of the Revolution.
The next letter of condolence was to go from Monticello to
Quincy; and, alas! its occasion was to be Mrs. Adams's own
decease. The English language does not contain a more
touching expression of sympathy than that which Mr. Jefferson sent to her aged and stricken partner, when this high-souled
and noble woman sunk into the tomb.

We resume the President's correspondence in its regular order. In a letter to Gallatin, of May 20th, he directed a public
avowal of a rule he had established in regard to removals from
office:

"Although I know that it is best generally to assign no reason for a removal
from office, yet there are also times when the declaration of a principle is advantageous. Such was the moment at which the New Haven letter appeared. It explained our principles to our friends, and they rallied to them. The public sentiment has taken a considerable stride since that, and seems to require that they
should know again where we stand. I suggest therefore for your consideration, instead of the following passage in your letter to Bowen, 'I think it due to candor
at the same time to inform you, that I had been for some time been determined to
remove you from office, although a successor has not yet been appointed by the
President, nor the precise time fixed for that purpose communicated to me;' to
substitute this, 'I think it due candor at the same time to inform you, that the
President considering that the patronage of public office should no longer be confided to one who uses it for active opposition to the national will, had some time
since determined to place your office in other hands. But a successor not being
yet fixed on, I am not able to name the precise time when it will take place.'

"My own opinion is, that the declaration of this principle will meet the entire
approbation of all moderate republicans, and will extort indulgence from all
warmer ones. Seeing that we do not mean to leave arms in the hands of active
enemies, they will care the less at our tolerance of the inactive. Nevertheless, if
you are strongly of opinion against such a declaration, let the letter go as you
had written it."

He wrote the Secretary of State, July 5th, in respect to a recent Cabinet conference, on the subject of the boundaries of
Louisiana:

"We did not collect the sense of our brethren the other day by regular questions, but as far as I could understand from what was said, it appeared to be,—
1. That an acknowledgment of our right to the Perdido, is a *sine quâ non*, and no
price to be given for it. 2. No absolute and perpetual relinquishment of right is
to be made of the country east of Rio Bravo del Norte, even in exchange for
Florida. [I am not quite sure that this was the opinion of all.] 3. That a country
may be laid off within which no further settlement shall be made by either party
for a given time, say thirty years. This country to be from the North River east-

wardly towards the Colorado, or even to, but not beyond the Mexican or Sabine river. To whatever river it be extended, it might from its source run northwest, as the most eligible direction; but a due north line would produce no restraint that we should feel in twenty years. This relinquishment, and two millions of dollars, to be the price of all the Floridas east of the Perdido, or to be apportioned to whatever part they will cede."

But he declared that during the conferences neither party ought to strengthen their position north of the Iberville, between the Mississippi and Perdido (the disputed territory), or interrupt the navigation of the rivers therein; and that Spain should be immediately told that if she would not accede to this, the United States would at once exercise and protect her right to navigate the Mobile, and increase her forces as fast as Spain did.

The appointment of a Governor and Legislative Council in the temporary government formed in the new Territory of Orleans had been conferred on the President. Claiborne, late Governor of Mississippi, had been appointed Governor of the Territory. On the 4th of July the President wrote him to forward the names of suitable persons to comprise the Council. He desired them to be "men of integrity, of understanding, of clear property, and influence among the people, well acquainted with the laws, customs and habits of the country, and drawn from the different parts of the Territory, whose population was considerable." He said "a majority should be of sound American characters, long established and esteemed there, and the rest of French or Spaniards, the most estimable and well affected." He wished "short sketches of the material outlines for estimating them;" and he gave Claiborne to understand that he himself meant to exercise really as well as nominally the appointing power, by requesting him to write early, as "he might perhaps have occasion to consult him again before a final determination." He inclosed a blank commission to be filled with the name of a Surveyor and Inspector of the port of Bayou St. John, saying he would "prefer a native Frenchman," if one could be found disposed to coöperate in extirpating the corruption which prevailed under the former Government," and [which] had so familiarized itself, as that men, otherwise honest, could look on [it] without horror." He concluded: "I pray you be alive to the suppression of this odious practice, and that you bring to punishment and brand with eternal disgrace every man guilty of it, whatever be his station."

A few days after, he forwarded to Claiborne his commission; but he desired " to enter into frank explanations," by informing the latter, that he had originally designed the office for another person—General Lafayette. But circumstances existed which did not then permit, and might not perhaps afterwards permit the nomination.

He wrote Mazzei, July 18th, and this time he cautioned him against injudicious publications, by hinting that " every word of his which they [" a phalanx of old tories and monarchists, more envenomed, as all their hopes became more desperate "] could get hold of, however innocent, however orthodox, even, was twisted, tormented, perverted, and, like the words of holy writ, was made to mean everything but what they were intended to mean." He informed him that the United States had dropped the system of making commercial treaties with other nations so far as it could be avoided; that the one with England had not been renewed, and all other overtures declined; that he " believed that with nations, as with individuals, dealings might be carried on as advantageously, perhaps more so, while their continuance depended on a voluntary good treatment, as if fixed by a contract, which, when it became injurious to either, was made by forced constructions to mean what suited them, and became a cause of war, instead of a bond of peace." It was not from a want of friendship then (and here shines out probably the principal object of the letter) that we did not propose a treaty with Naples, with whom we had so many common interests, and with whom we should be so glad to exchange every favor, but " because it was against our system to embarrass ourselves with treaties, or entangle ourselves at all with the affairs of Europe." He mentioned that five fine frigates had been sent to the Mediterranean to " to recover the credit which Commodore Morris's two years sleep lost us, and for which he had been broke."[1] The President stated the excellent condition of the finances, notwithstanding the " little diversion " of the Tripolitan

---

[1] Morris reached home in November, 1803, and his explanations of his conduct not proving satisfactory, a Court of Inquiry was convened March 10th, 1804, which found that he had not exercised due diligence and activity in annoying the enemy on various occasions. Thereupon, the President dismissed him from the navy.

war ; that the "spirit of republicanism was now in almost all its ancient vigor, five-sixths of the people being with us ;" that " fourteen of the seventeen States were completely with us, and two of the other three will be in one year." In regard to his own renomination, he said :

" I should have retired at the end of the first four years, but that the immense load of tory calumnies which have been manufactured respecting me, and have filled the European market, have obliged me to appeal once more to my country for a justification. I have no fear but that I shall receive honorable testimony by their verdict on those calumnies. At the end of the next four years I shall certainly retire. Age, inclination, and principle all dictate this. My health, which at one time threatened an unfavorable turn, is now firm."

And here is an interesting word in regard to Lafayette, and to some other other matters :

" The acquisition of Louisiana, besides doubling our extent, and trebling our quantity of fertile country, is of incalculable value, as relieving us from the danger of war. It has enabled us to do a handsome thing for Fayette. He had received a grant of between eleven and twelve thousand acres north of Ohio, worth, perhaps, a dollar an acre. We have obtained permission of Congress to locate it in Louisiana. Locations can be found adjacent to the city of New Orleans, in the island of New Orleans and in its vicinity, the value of which cannot be calculated. I hope it will induce him to come over and settle there with his family. Mr. Livingston having asked leave to return, General Armstrong, his brother-in-law, goes in his place : he is of the first order of talents.

* * * * * * *

" Remarkable deaths lately, are, Samuel Adams, Edmund Pendleton, Alexander Hamilton, Stephens Thompson Mason, Mann Page, Bellini, and Parson Andrews. To these I have the inexpressible grief of adding the name of my youngest daughter, who had married a son of Mr. Eppes, and has left two children. My eldest daughter alone remains to me, and has six children. This loss has increased my anxiety to retire, while it has dreadfully lessened the comfort of doing it. Wythe, Dickinson, and Charles Thompson are all living, and are firm republicans."

The President made his usual visit to Monticello during the " unhealthy season " at Washington. His building and improvements went on as usual, and there is nothing connected with his stay which needs a record.

In a letter to Madison, of August 15th, after ironically mentioning some news of an " awful complexion " received of combined French and English designs on the United States, he added seriously that he wished Congress, as soon as it assembled, to complete the incorporation of Louisiana, in order to cut off all further pretence for France " to patronize the rights of Louisiana." He thought, too, the British insults again commencing in our harbors ought to be summarily arrested. " We could not," he said, " be respected by France as a neutral nation, nor by the world or ourselves as an independent one, if we did not take effectual measures to support, at every risk, our authority in our own harbors."

The Presidential election was now approaching, and it would appear that the Republican collectors, marshals, and other appointees of the President, had supposed that the Executive objection to the active and official partisanship of their class extended only to opponents; for we find the President writing Gallatin, Sept. 8th : " I think the officers of the Federal Government are meddling too much with the public elections. Will it be best to admonish them privately or by proclamation ? This for consideration till we meet. I shall be at Washington by the last day of the month." This was not the only nor the strongest expression of the same tenor made by him during the canvass. It is amusing to speculate on the conclusions which would be formed of a Chief Magistrate's sanity, who should display such scruples as these in the present " age of advancement !"

On the 11th of July, on the same spot, we believe, where, at no long period before, a loved son had fallen in a conflict of the same kind, General Hamilton was mortally wounded by the Vice-President of the United States, Aaron Burr, in a duel ; and he died the next day. All the preliminaries and incidents of the tragedy are too well known to call for any notice here.

Let us in justice record that the last public letter ever written by this statesman (addressed to Theodore Sedgwick, July 10th, 1804) was to discourage a New England project for a "dismemberment of our empire," which sprung up on the acquisition of Louisiana. We shall have more to say of this project hereafter. And if the last thought of that letter is a denunciation of democracy, we have no doubt it was a sincere one.[1]

---

[1] At the time of General Hamilton's death his political influence was prostrated. He was unable to prevent the body of his party in New York from supporting Burr for Governor in 1804. Gaylord Griswold, the ablest Federal member from New York in the late Congress, published a letter, February 27th, 1804, in which he urged his party to support Burr, openly imputing Hamilton's opposition to " personal resentment." It was in unavailingly resisting this tide that the latter uttered the words that cost him his life.

The constitutional amendment requiring the President and Vice-President to be separately voted for, was adopted before the election of 1804; and that election resulted as follows:

NAMES OF STATES.	FOR PRESIDENT.		FOR VICE-PRESIDENT.	
	Thomas Jefferson.	Charles C. Pinckney.	George Clinton.	Rufus King.
New Hampshire...............	7	—	7	—
Massachusetts.................	19	—	19	—
Rhode Island.................	4	—	4	—
Connecticut,.................	—	9	—	9
Vermont....................	6	—	6	—
New York...................	19	—	19	—
New Jersey..................	8	—	8	—
Pennsylvania................	20	—	20	—
Delaware....................	—	3	—	3
Maryland...................	9	2	9	2
Virginia....................	24	—	24	—
North Carolina..............	14	—	14	—
South Carolina..............	10	—	10	—
Georgia....................	6	—	6	—
Tennessee...................	5	—	5	—
Kentucky...................	8	—	8	—
Ohio......................	3	—	3	—
	162	14	162	14

For a seriously contested Presidential election, this was by far the most unanimous one in the result that ever has taken place, or that perhaps ever will take place in our country.

The Federalists fought with the rage of despair. Newspaper, bar-room, and the political pulpit, rung with more numerous and more indecent charges against Mr. Jefferson, than in 1801. It here occurs to us, that we have omitted to mention a circumstance which afforded the subject of much new Federal indignation. We will let Mr. Thomas Moore, the Irish poet, preface it in a passage taken from a letter he wrote to his mother from Baltimore, June 13th, 1804, which is published in Lord John Russell's Memoirs, Journal and Correspondence of Moore.[1]

"I [writes Moore] stopped at Washington with Mr. and Mrs. Merry for near a week; they have been treated with the most pointed incivility by the present democratic President, Mr. Jefferson; and it is only the precarious situation of Great Britain which could possibly induce it to overlook such indecent, though at

[1] Q. r., vol. i. p. 162.

the same time, petty hostility. I was presented by Mr. Merry to both the Secretary of State and the President." . . . .

The "indecent and petty hostility" to Mr. and Mrs. Merry was manifested in this wise. They were invited to dine at the President's. When dinner was announced Mr. Jefferson chanced to be standing by and talking with Mrs. Madison at some distance from Mrs. Merry, and he accompanied the former to the table. Mr. Merry regarded this as almost an insult.

Such a stir was made by the angry ambassador, that Madison wrote Monroe (who had succeeded Mr. King as our minister to England), apprising him of the facts to enable him to answer an expected call of the British Government for official explanations. Monroe, however, got his first information from a friendly British under-secretary, who intimated that he would soon probably hear of the matter through a different channel. The minister was delighted. Within a very short period the wife of an English under-secretary had been accorded precedence over his own, under analogous circumstances. He had no great fund of humor, but the absurdity of the whole affair, and the excellent materials in his possession for a reply to a call for explanations, struck him in a most amusing light. Shaking with merriment, he hinted to his informant the satisfaction the call would give him. He never afterwards heard a lisp on the subject.[1]

Mrs. Merry tossed her head without shaking the peace of two nations, and poor Mrs. Madison was saved from involuntarily "firing another Troy." But Merry never forgot this "pointed incivility"—though he and his friends knew that, by an express regulation at the White House, all etiquette in respect to official precedence was formally abolished, and though with the most stringent etiquette of the Celestial Empire in force, it would seem an amusing specimen of impertinence in him to claim priority over the Secretary of State of the United States.

---

[1] We have the facts from an intimate friend of Monroe, who often heard him tell the story. He as often told a much better one of some laughable circumstances, which took place at an official dinner where he was ranked below the ministers of sundry German States "about half as big," Monroe would exclaim in his narration—"about half as big, by the lord! sir, as our county of Albemarle." and where the attentions of the Russian minister, and a certain ludicrous blunder of his own at the expense of the representatives of "the little German principalities," gave him ample revenge. and lasting diversion The story would carry us too much out of the record. Monroe had no wit, but infinite bonhomie. Among familiar friends he was an unreserved and delightful companion.

But the farce was not ended. Mrs. Merry thenceforth eschewed the Presidential mansion, and if her husband went there it was only officially. After the clamor subsided, the President felt a good natured desire to put an end to this frivolous matter, and to relieve the offended dignitaries from the awkwardness of their position. Accordingly he made inquiry through a common friend (the representative, we think, of the Swedish Government), whether Mr. and Mrs. Merry would accept an invitation to a family dinner. The former was understood to give an affirmative answer, and the invitation was sent, written in the President's own hand. The minister replied by addressing the Secretary of State to know whether he was invited in his private or his official capacity: if in the one, he must obtain the permission of his sovereign; if in the other, he must receive an assurance in advance that he would be treated as became his position. The "Secretary of State" put an end to the correspondence in a very dry note; and here the affair ended.

Mr. Thomas Moore had an individual cause of complaint against the President, the history and consequences of which would be in no way worth repeating except for a characteristic anecdote they chance to furnish of the latter. Moore was, as he remarks, presented to the President by Mr. Merry. He had then published nothing which had crossed the Atlantic but

—— " gentle Little's moral song
To soothe the mania of the amorous throng."

Mr. Jefferson knew not the "young Catullus of his day:" and had no conception that he stood in the dangerous presence of the hero of Chalk-Farm, or of the wielder of the better-loaded weapons of a clever lampooner. Accordingly, standing stark six feet two inches and a half, and with that cold first look he always cast upon a stranger, the President gazed down on the perfumed little Adonis, spoke to him, and being occupied, gave him no more attention. Moore (then twenty-four) had crossed the Atlantic in the same vessel with Mr. and Mrs. Merry, in October, 1803, and had hardly set foot in the United States before he began to write home his own and Mrs. Merry's intense disgust at everything in the United States. He repaired to Bermuda, where he spent the winter; made his appearance in

Washington in June, 1804 ; met with the undistinguished reception mentioned; was flattered by Mrs. Merry's sympathizers, and fell to lampooning the President and everything American except a few attentive Federal gentlemen and ladies.[1]

When his scurrilous attacks on the President were published, they soon fell into the hands of Hon. William A. Burwell, member of Congress from Virginia, the President's former private secretary, and the intimate and devoted friend of himself and his family. Burwell carried the matter to Mrs. Randolph, and even the gentle Martha was roused at these insults coming from a man who had been introduced into society and patronized by the British minister. They talked themselves into a towering indignation, and then agreed that it was proper to place the subject before the President. This took place at Monticello,

---

[1] We will present the curious in such matters with some specimens selected from a rapid inspection of a few pages, preserving such italicization as we find. Moore wrote his mother, November 7th, 1803:

"This Norfolk, the capital [!] of Virginia, is a most strange place ; nothing to be seen in the streets but dogs and negroes, and the few ladies that *pass for white* are to be sure the most unlovely pieces of crockery I ever set my eyes on. . . . . . Poor Mrs. Merry has been as ill treated by the mosquitoes as she has been by every one else. They have bit her into a fever."

In his letter already quoted in the text (June 13th, 1804), he said:

"I have passed the Potomac, the Rappahannock, the Occoquan, the Potapsio, and many other rivers, with names as barbarous as the inhabitants: every step I *take* not only *reconciles*, but *endears* to me, not only the excellences but even the errors of Old England. Such a road as I have come! and in such a conveyance! The mail takes twelve passengers, which generally consist of squalling children, stinking negroes, and republicans smoking cigars! How often it has occurred to me that nothing can be more emblematical of the *government* of this country than its *stages*, filled with a motley mixture, all 'hail-fellows-well-met,' driving through mud and filth, which *bespatters* them as they *raise* it, and risking an *upset* at every step. God comfort their capacities! As soon as I am away from them, both the stages and the government may have the same fate for what *I* care."

He wrote his mother, June 26th, 1804:

"My reception at Philadelphia was extremely flattering : and it is the only place in America which can boast any literary society, and my name had prepossessed them more strongly than I deserve. But their affectionate attentions went far beyond this deference to reputation; I was quite caressed while there ; and their anxiety to make me known by introductory letters to all their friends on my way, and two or three little poems of a very flattering kind, which some of their choicest men addressed to me, all went so warmly to my heart, that I felt quite a regret in leaving them," etc.

Great was Mr. Moore's disgust at the "philosophic humility" of the American President. He did not like his style of living. The President only occupied "a corner" of his mansion. The "grand edifice" was "encircled by a very rude pale, through which a common rustic stile introduced visitors," etc., etc. The admirer of freedom in his own land was especially disgusted with the President's politics. Here is a moderate specimen from his "Epistles, Odes, and other Poems" :

> "If thou hast got within thy freeborn breast,
> One pulse that beats more proudly than the rest,
> With honest scorn for that inglorious soul,
> Which creeps and winds beneath a mob's control,
> Which courts the rabble's smile, the rabble's nod,
> And makes, like Egypt, every beast its God !
> There in those walls—but burning tongue forbear !
> Rank must be reverenced, even the rank that's there:
> So here I pause "——

Mr. Moore did not always "pause" even at this point.

and the latter was sitting reading in his library, serenely unconscious of calamity. Burwell pointed out the obnoxious passages.
The victim glanced through them, looked at one angry interlocu-
tor and then the other. It was amusing enough to see Burwell so
exasperated; but the calm, gentle Martha's passion-gust was irresistible. Mr. Jefferson broke into a hearty, clear laugh. There
was more than argument—there was conviction in that laugh.
The indignant pair retreated, looking a little crest-fallen, but as
soon as the library door closed, joined heartily in the merriment.

Finally (about 1814 we should say), Moore's Irish Melodies
appeared in the United States. Our informant in all these particulars, with some curiosity, put the book into her grandfather's
hands. "Why," said he, "this is the little man who satirized
me so!" He read along. He had always sympathized keenly
with the Irish patriots. The delightful rhythm fell like music on
a susceptible ear. He presently exclaimed: "Why, he *is* a
poet after all!" Henceforth the Bard of Erin shared with
Burns the honor of being familiarly read by the retired statesman, when Byron, Wordsworth, Southey, Coleridge, Campbell,
etc., never could (or at least never did) break through the bar-
riers of his early habits and tastes.[1]

Some of Moore's songs, like those commencing, "Oh, breathe
not his name," "When he who adores thee," and "Oh, blame
not the bard," were special favorites; and the last page which
Mr. Jefferson's dying hand traced, his farewell to his daughter,
contained a quotation of several lines from the one commencing
"It is not the tear at this moment shed."[2]

[1] Mr. Jefferson was fond of Allan Ramsay, Tannahill, and, indeed, nearly all the Scotch
song writers, and of both the lyrical and pastoral ballads of every land. This shows that
he loved *poetry*; and was not tied to its earlier schools, with merely such exceptions as
we have named in the text. We could point out things in the writings of every one of
the poets we have mentioned as rejected by him, which we feel certain, by analogy,
he would have admired if he could have been persuaded to read them. But old men learn
to disrelish making new literary as well as new personal acquaintances. And we doubt
whether there was ever a genuine admirer of Pope, who afterwards fell cordially into
the modern school.

[2] He apparently never bestowed a second thought on Moore's pasquinades on himself
and the United States. Others did not share in this "philosophic" indifference. The
American Eagle has always been a rather thin-skinned bird. John Quincy Adams,
writing (in 1809) of some British accusations against us, said: "It is one of those scandalous calumnies which a number of starveling vagabonds in England, which Cobbett,
and Moore the minstrel of the brothels, have been for some years administering to the
malignant passions of the country." The younger Adams never forgot a grudge. In
1821, when Secretary of State, in a Fourth of July oration delivered at Washington, he
exclaimed: "Stand forth, ye champions of Britannia, ... ye spawners of fustian
romance and lascivious lyrics." Most will probably consider the "philosophic" taste
best. Mr. Moore grew to be a man—but never one to be converted into the antagonist
of a nation.

The second session of the eighth Congress convened on the 5th of November. The President's message announced that the commerce of neutral nations on the ocean had suffered less than on former occasions of European war, but that owing to peculiar causes, commerce in the American seas had suffered more ; and that infringements on our jurisdiction and laws had even taken place in our own harbors. But the friendly conduct, elsewhere, of the governments from whom these acts proceeded, gave confidence, he declared, that our representations on the subject would be properly regarded.

He said that while noticing the irregularities of others on the ocean, our own ought not to be overlooked or "left unprovided for." Complaints had been received that armed American merchant vessels had attempted to force a commerce into certain ports in defiance of their laws. He continued :

"That individuals should undertake to wage private war, independently of the authority of their country, cannot be permitted in a well ordered society. Its tendency to produce aggression on the laws and rights of other nations, and to endanger the peace of our own, is so obvious, that I doubt not you will adopt measures for restraining it effectually in future."

He explained that Spain had misunderstood the object of the act of the last session, establishing a district and port of entry on the waters of the Mobile, in consequence of which it had suspended the ratification of the treaty of 1802 ; but explanations of our pacific and unaggressive intentions having been given, that Government had gone so far as to withdraw its objections to the validity of our title to Louisiana—the boundaries, however, yet remaining to be settled.

Having stated the condition of our affairs with the Barbary powers (containing nothing of particular interest), he informed Congress of the steps which had been taken to organize the territories of Orleans, Louisiana, and Indiana.

After speaking of the apparently friendly feelings of the Indians in the newly acquired territory, he remarked :

"By pursuing a uniform course of justice towards them, by aiding them in all the improvements which may better their condition, and especially by establishing a commerce on terms which shall be advantageous to them and only not losing to us, and so regulated as that no incendiaries of our own or any other nation may be permitted to disturb the natural effects of our just and friendly offices, we may render ourselves so necessary to their comfort and prosperity, that the protection of citizens from their disorderly members will become their interest and their voluntary care. Instead, therefore, of an augmentation of military force proportioned to our extension of frontier, I proposed a moderate enlargement of the capital employed in that commerce, as a more effectual, economical, and humane instrument for preserving peace and good neighborhood with them."

He announced that all the country between the Wabash and the Ohio, south of the road from the rapids towards Vincennes, had been purchased of the Delawares, and also, a claim to the same territory of the Piankeshaws, which it had been thought best to "quiet by fair purchase." This territory fronted three hundred miles on the Ohio, and nearly half that length on the Wabash, and with the cession before made by the Kaskaskias, "nearly consolidated our possessions north of the Ohio, in a very respectable breadth, from Lake Erie to the Mississippi."

With a view to preserve our rights as a neutral power, and enforce our jurisdiction within our own waters, the following recommendation was made:

"The act of Congress of February 28th, 1803, for building and employing a number of gunboats, is now in a course of execution to the extent there provided for. The obstacles to naval enterprise which vessels of this construction offer for our seaport towns—their utility towards supporting within our waters the authority of the laws—the promptness with which they will be manned by the seamen and militia of the place the moment they are wanting—the facility of their assembling from different parts of the coast to any point where they are required in greater force than ordinary—the economy of their maintenance and preservation from decay when not in actual service—and the competence of our finances to this defensive provision, without any new burden, are considerations which will have due weight with Congress in deciding on the expediency of adding to their number from year to year, as experience shall test their utility, until all our important harbors, by these and auxiliary means shall be ensured against insult and opposition to the laws."

He declared that no augmentation of the army was required —but that improvements in the militia " would be always seasonable."

Lastly, in regard to the finances, he said that the receipt of eleven millions and a half of dollars during the last fiscal year, has enabled the Government, after meeting ordinary expenses, to pay upwards of $3,600,000 of the public debt exclusive of interest—making, with the two preceding years, a diminution of $12,000,000 of principal, and the payment of a still larger sum in interest. After presenting some estimates for the ensuing year, he thus closed:

" Whether the great interests of agriculture, manufactures, commerce, or navigation, can, within the pale of your constitutional powers, be aided in any of their relations ; whether laws are provided in all cases where they are wanting ; whether those provided are exactly what they should be ; whether any abuses take place in their administration, or in that of the public revenues ; whether the organization of the public agents or of the public force is perfect in all its parts ; in fine, whether anything can be done to advance the general good, are questions within the limits of your functions which will necessary occupy your attention. In these and other matters which you in your wisdom may propose for the good of our country, you may count with assurance on my hearty coöperation and faithful execution."

Several changes had taken place in the Senate since the preceding session. From Virginia, William B. Giles, now improved in his health, took the place of Venable, resigned ; and Andrew Moore of the same State, that of Nicholas, resigned. From Delaware, James A. Bayard succeeded Wells, resigned. From New York, Dr. S. L. Mitchell succeeded Armstrong, whose seat had been vacated by his appointment to the French mission.[1] Benjamin Howland, of Rhode Island, succeeded Potter, deceased. These personal changes involved no political ones.

The great event of the session was the trial of Samuel Chase, one of the associate Justices of the Supreme Court of the United States, impeached by the House of Representatives before the Senate. The articles of impeachment charged Chase with arbitrary, oppressive, unjust, and intemperate conduct on various occasions.

The managers chosen by the House were J. Randolph, Rodney, Nicholson, Early, Boyle, Nelson, and G. W. Campbell. On Nelson's declining, Clarke was chosen in his place. The counsel for Judge Chase were Harper, Martin, Hopkinson, and Key ; and Charles Lee was subsequently added. The respondent asked a delay until the next session. This was refused, on the ground that he had already had ample time for preparation ; but a delay of a month was granted.

Arbitrary, indecorous, and unquestionably illegal conduct— conduct that now would be no more likely to be ventured upon or tolerated in the same office in the United States than the reënactment of the Alien and Sedition laws by Congress—was clearly proved upon this openly and officially partisan judge. But on the question addressed to each senator, " is the respondent guilty or not guilty, of a high crime or misdemeanor as charged in ——

[1] In place of his brother-in-law, R. R. Livingston, resigned.

article of impeachment?—the constitutional majority of two-thirds in no case voted for his conviction. A majority, however, in several instances so voted. For example, on article fourth, charging that the conduct of the respondent in Callender's case "was marked during the whole course of the said trial, by manifest injustice, partiality and intemperance," in refusing a postponement, "in the use of unusual, rude, and contemptuous expressions towards the prisoner's counsel," "in repeated and vexatious interruptions," and in "an indecent solicitude" for the conviction of the accused, the number who pronounced guilty were eighteen—not guilty, sixteen: and on article eighth, charging that at the Circuit Court at Baltimore, May, 1803, the respondent in his charge to the grand jury delivered "an intemperate and inflammatory political harangue," exhibited conduct "indecent and unbecoming a judge of the United States," made an unwarrantable interference with the legislature of a State, etc., the number who pronounced guilty were nineteen—not guilty, fifteen.

There was not, it is probable, a senator (beyond possibly two or three political monomaniacs) who doubted either the impropriety or the illegality of Judge Chase's conduct; but whether he had committed a high crime, deserving not only deprivation of office, but the attending lasting disgrace, was a question which admitted of a greater diversity of honest judgment. The feeling of conservatism, the consciousness of the deep danger of interfering with the independence of the national judiciary, and especially of having its tenures made the sport of partisan majorities in Congress—a subject to which recent incidents in some of the States were calling much attention [1]—interfered most powerfully to save him.

And another consideration plead still more strongly for him. The grey-haired old man who sat awaiting his doom had been a member of the Congress of 1776. He had been among the foremost of those who had offered their necks to the cord and their property to the flames for their country. His signature was attached at the head of the delegation of his State to the Declaration of Independence. Few doubted that the fiery and characteristic vehemence he had manifested in hunting down

---

[1] The Republicans of Pennsylvania had nearly or quite all the Federal judges of the Supreme Court of that State on trial for impeachment.

and persecuting from city to city the advocates of democracy, was as sincere as that which urged him undaunted against the power of Britain. And some other incidental circumstances befriended him.[1] But his acquittal produced deep temporary irritation. John Randolph, the same day, moved to submit to the State Legislatures an amendment of the Constitution to the following effect:

"The judges of the Supreme Court, and of all other courts of the United States, shall be removed by the President on the joint address of both Houses of Congress requesting the same, anything in the Constitution of the United States to the contrary notwithstanding."

This was referred to the consideration of a committee of the whole House—yeas, sixty-eight; nays, thirty-three. It was then made the order of the day for the first Monday in December ensuing.[2]

Nicholson offered another constitutional amendment:

"That the Legislature of any State may, when the said Legislature shall think proper, recall, at any period whatever, any senator of the United States who may have been elected by them; and whenever a vote of the Legislature of any State, vacating the seat of any senator of the United States, who may have been elected by the said State, shall be made known to the Senate of the United States, the seat of such senator shall thenceforth be vacated."

This was referred to a committee of the whole House by a vote of fifty-three to forty-six, and then was made the order of the day for the first Monday in December, by a vote of seventy to twenty-eight. The divisions of the House on this and on Randolph's proposition must undoubtedly be understood as showing that a large majority of that body were disposed, at the moment, to pointedly condemn the Senate's action

One of the first proceedings of Congress, this session, was to pass a joint resolution bestowing a sword on Captain Stephen Decatur, and on each of the officers and crew of the ketch "Intrepid" two months' pay, as a testimonial to their gallantry

[1] In our judgment, the articles of impeachment were not skillfully drawn to procure a conviction. They showed more of John Randolph's spirit and tone (he took the lead in the whole affair) than those of a wary, discreet, experienced prosecutor. Mr. Randolph, too, took a very leading part on the trial. He evinced singular abilities perhaps for a layman. But, it is not denied that he was overmatched by the professional skill of the defence: and his colleagues could not act very independently for themselves under his dictatorial and irascible leadership.

[2] Congress had but two more days to sit.

in attacking and destroying, in the harbor of Tripoli, a Tripolitan frigate of forty-four guns. This was the former " Philadelphia," lying filled with men under the guns of that city, and almost surrounded by other armed Moorish vessels. Her destruction (February 14th, 1804), by the crew of a vessel of three or four hundred tons, the manner in which it was accomplished, and the escape of Decatur and his men from the conflagration and the tempest of shot which that conflagration directed upon the assailants, reads more like a narrative of romance than a sober incident of reality.

The President's recommendation of the extension of the gunboat system for the defence of our harbors and seaport towns,[1]

---

[1] His scheme was more fully developed and his general reasons for it given in answer to inquiries from Nicholson, chairman of the committee to whom the subject was referred in the House of Representatives. This letter demands the perusal of those who would fairly understand the celebrated gunboat project which has drawn so many sneers on the head of its proposer:

" WASHINGTON, Dec. 14, 1805.

"DEAR SIR:
    " Mr. Eppes has this moment put into my hands your letter of yesterday, asking information on the subject of the gunboats proposed to be built. I lose no time in communicating to you fully my whole views respecting them, premising a few words on the system of fortifications. Considering the harbors which, from their situation and importance, are entitled to defence, and the estimates we have seen of the fortifications planned for some of them, this system cannot be completed on a moderate scale for less than fifty millions of dollars, nor manned, in time of war, with less than fifty thousand men, and in peace, two thousand. And when done they avail little ; because all military men agree, that wherever a vessel may pass a fort without tacking under her guns, which is the case in all our seaport towns, she may be annoyed more or less, according to the advantages of the position, but can never be prevented. Our own experience during the war proved this on different occasions. Our predecessors have, nevertheless, proposed to go into this system, and had commenced it. But no law requiring us to proceed, we have suspended it.
    " If we cannot hinder vessels from entering our harbors, we should turn our attention to putting it out of their power to lie, or come to, before a town, to injure it. Two means of doing this may be adopted in aid of each other. 1. Heavy cannon on travelling carriages, which may be moved to any point on the bank or beach most convenient for dislodging the vessel. A sufficient number of these should be lent to each seaport town, and their militia trained to them. The Executive is authorized to do this ; it has been done in a smaller degree, and will now be done more competently.
    " 2. Having cannon on floating batteries or boats, which may be so stationed as to prevent a vessel entering the harbor, or force her after entering to depart. There are about fifteen harbors in the United States which ought to be in a state of substantial defence. The whole of these would require, according to the best opinions, two hundred and forty gunboats. Their cost was estimated by Captain Rogers at two thousand dollars each ; but we had better say four thousand dollars. The whole would cost one million of dollars. But we should allow ourselves ten years to complete it, unless circumstances should force it sooner. There are three situations in which the gunboat may be. 1. Hauled up under a shed, in readiness to be launched and manned by the seamen and militia of the town on short notice. In this situation she costs nothing but an inclosure, or a sentinel to see that no mischief is done to her. 2. Afloat, and with men enough to navigate her in harbor, and take care of her, but depending on receiving her crew from the town on short warning. In this situation, her annual expense is about two thousand dollars, as by an official estimate at the end of this letter. 3. Fully manned for action. Her annual expense in this situation is about eight thousand dollars, as per estimate subjoined. When there is general peace, we should probably keep about six or seven afloat in the second situation: their annual expense twelve to fourteen thousand dollars ; the rest all hauled up. When France and England are at war, we should keep, at the utmost,

encountered a great amount of invective and ridicule; and many of the officers of the navy joined heartily in this feeling. An English view of navy life then prevailed extensively in our country. Our eye rests on a published letter of Colonel Burr to Charles Biddle (July 20th, 1803), wherein, speaking of the two young Biddles' going the day before on board the frigate President, he said: "The more I reflect on the destination of these young men, the more I am pleased with it; and if I had but one son, I think I should place him in the navy. If the object be ambition, our navy presents the best prospect of honor and advancement. A young man of merit may be sure of rapid promotion and opportunities of distinction. If the pursuit be wealth, still the navy offers the fairest and most honorable means of acquiring it."

This reflects the public sentiment of the day. The President's plan, so far as it extended, would overturn this whole system at once—shut up these convenient avenues to fame and wealth for the sons of influential families—and for the quarter-deck, the high command, the fierce conflict of great squadrons, the prize-money where whole convoys of merchantmen were swooped up by the victor, the pomp of armadas sweeping over the ocean to wage and provoke wars, substitute a mere defensive system, carried on in boats of one or two guns, temporarily manned in part by a sort of marine militia, and when out of service, hauled up high and dry, like a farmer's cart "under a shed." A change like this would not be expected to be relished by the officers, or by persons anxious to obtain commissions. Mr. Cooper, indeed, we believe, says that the gunboats were popular, at least for a time, among the younger officers. But it is probable this was rather among the class of young men, who expected nothing but as the reward of hard work and

twenty-five in the second situation, their annual expense fifty thousand dollars. When we should be at war ourselves, some of them would probably be kept in the third situation, at an annual expense of eight thousand dollars; but how many, must depend on the circumstances of the war. We now possess ten, built and building. It is the opinion of those consulted, that fifteen more would enable us to put every harbor under our view into a respectable condition; and that this should limit the views of the present year. This would require that an appropriation of sixty thousand dollars, and I suppose *that* the best way of limiting it, without declaring the number, as perhaps that sum would build more. I should think it best not to give a detailed report, which exposes our policy too much. A bill, with verbal explanations, will suffice for the information of the House. I do not know whether General Wilkinson would approve the printing his paper. If he would, it would be useful.

"Accept affectionate and respectful salutations.

                                    TH. JEFFERSON."

distinguished gallantry. The gunboats would give them separate commands and a chance to exhibit individual merit. But the influential class, who looked upon the navy as an institution designed to afford aristocratic and profitable employment to the younger sons of prominent Government supporters, were of a different opinion.

For the genuine admirers of England it was sufficient, because an insular and manufacturing nation, with great colonial establishments, placed her principal dependence for offensive and defensive war on a navy, that we, a continental and agricultural power, with vast territory and without any colonial establishments, should do precisely the same. And next, we had a section of country specially commercial and maritime in its pursuits. Its navigators were anxious to penetrate every ocean in the eager pursuit of wealth. To protect them efficiently and securely in every sea would require a great navy. Consequently the interests of twelve or thirteen of the partners of a national and industrial brotherhood should be made to give way to those of four or five partners. England rendered all other interests subservient to commerce; why should not we? Why should not ninety-five husbandmen, in addition to paying to five merchants a higher scale of profits than they ever received on their own industry, also agree to pay taxes or duties forever, to insure the ventures of the latter against all losses from enemies? Could any English theory of political economy be wrong in itself, or not applicable to all countries and under all circumstances?

We are met on every page of a class of histories with the declaration that, if instead of arresting the growth of the navy and recommending gunboats and other defensive preparations, President Jefferson had carried out the building of the vessels authorized during Mr. Adams's Administration, and made a proportional increase, we should not, when the war with England in 1812 finally came, have been subject to invasion wherever a British army chose to disembark; in a word, that we should have been able to confine the contest principally to the ocean, and wage it there successfully. Even Mr. Cooper talks a little in this vein in his Naval History.

England had in 1803, says a very accurate British writer, "no less than five hundred ships of war."[1] She was steadily

---

[1] Lockhart, in Life of Napoleon.

and even rapidly increasing this force. In 1805 she annihilated all European naval opposition at Trafalgar. The combined fleets of Christendom thenceforth were not a match for hers.

When President Adams's "quasi-war" with France closed, we had, including all descriptions and grades, thirty-four public vessels. On Jefferson's accession, some of the lighter and less valuable ones were sold, but Mr. Cooper concedes that "perhaps four-fifths" of the real strength of the navy "was preserved."[1] The ships retained were fourteen in number, consisting of three of forty-four guns, four of thirty-eight, one of thirty-six, one of thirty-two, four of twenty-eight, and one of twelve. Mr. Jefferson found materials partly collected for half a dozen first-class vessels, authorized to be constructed during our maritime war with France. To subserve a special purpose, he recommended four small vessels in 1803, and they were completed, carrying in all thirty-five guns.

Let us suppose that the materials left by Mr. Adams had been promptly used, and that the Government had gone on devoting every farthing which was paid on the national debt, and which could have been safely raised by internal taxes, to building, fitting out, supporting and disciplining a navy, down to the year 1812—and all this in the bare anticipation of a war which might never take place. What then would have been our naval force compared with that of England? Our increase would not in the meantime have actually kept pace with her increase! Mr. Cooper states that in 1812 England had a thousand and sixty ships of war, and that between seven and eight hundred of them (probably as large a proportion of the whole number as in 1801) were efficient cruising vessels. The increase of the British navy, then, during nine years, had been upwards of five hundred vessels of war. We have been threatened with maritime wars—wars with the same power—since that of 1812. We never, it will probably be conceded, have shown any cowardly reluctance for the contest. Yet with a population more than five times doubled—with available wealth ten times doubled—we have not at this day (1857) an approach to the number of public ships which England added to her navy

---

[1] Notwithstanding the outcry raised about reducing the navy, but one *frigate* was sold —the Washington; a ship, Mr. Cooper says, not built for or fit to be retained in the public service.

within those nine years! And be it remembered, we have not at this day a stronger navy, in proportion to our national population and wealth, than we had at the close of Jefferson's Administration. If his non-preparation was a curse, the curse follows and rests on us still.

Our population during that Administration did not exceed about one-fifth that of Great Britain. She was by far the richest nation, in money, on the globe. We had, probably, as little of the pecuniary "sinew of war" as any other nation of equal numbers.

How utterly absurd, then, is it to say that it was the duty of our Government, instead of going on paying our debts and leaving our people to grow in numbers and wealth, to suffer our debt to increase beyond the power of subsequent extinction, and additionally cripple the nation with taxes, in the attempt to build up a maritime strength capable of coping with that of Great Britain!

Our little navy, it is true, accomplished all but miracles in the second war with England. It covered itself and our national name with glory. But its weakness was one of its principal protections. England could not afford to send her vast armadas to chase our single frigates, darting like ospreys over the ocean. Could we have sent out such fleets as France and Spain sent to Aboukir and Trafalgar, battles like those of Aboukir and Trafalgar would again have been fought; and whatever we may claim for ourselves on equal terms, we should not have had one against ten, not one against twenty ships, guns or men, to oppose hers. And in what condition would we have been, yet a comparatively moneyless and agricultural people, strained up to the last effort—with compound interest accumulating on former national debts, and not enough current revenue to support our navy, to say nothing of other expenses—in what condition would we have been to lose a naval action or two like that of Trafalgar? Yet if we had won a Trafalgar one day, the next we should have had to fight it over again, and against overwhelming odds, with the mistress of the seas.

It was to be expected that a political opposition would prate, and it afforded excellent occasion for "Buncombe" speakers in Congress to talk of what we should have accomplished had we devoted ourselves thus "energetically" to the erection of a navy during Mr. Jefferson's Administration; and we see not why, by the same reasoning, General Washington's and a considerable share of Mr. Adams's should not also be included. But, it is very hard to credit that any well-informed and reflecting American, could ever, in the hottest frenzy of political excitement, have persuaded himself for a moment that this course would have been for the true interest of his country.

We built no great navy. We bore the brunt of subsequent war as best we might. We suffered calamities, and what some esteemed disgraces. Nearly all the European kingdoms, including those which have ground their own people into the dust for ages to prepare them to defend themselves against other nations, have been invaded, and their capitals have been in possession of an enemy within the present century. We, a comparative handful of population scattered over a surface equalling half Europe, suffered the same "disgrace."

But after attaching all possible importance to the real and the imaginary inflictions of the war of 1812, does any intelligent person doubt that we are stronger to-day by the mere force of increased growth, than we should have been had we steadily pursued the policy of preparing for war, and especially the policy of preparing to cope with England on the seas? Preparation for war requires expenditure, and renders all the capital it absorbs unproductive for other objects. To the extent of that absorption, means of development and improvement are sacrificed. These effects extend even to populational increase. Where means to open the road, bridge the river, and repel the savage are wanting, population does not spread so rapidly over territorial surfaces. Where governmental exactions fall heavily and chillingly on industry, early marriage and rapid and healthy increase are materially checked, even though actual physical want is not produced. Population only springs lush and vigorous to the maximum of increase where plenty, and free and smiling plenty, abounds.

We are now proportionably as unarmed on sea and land as in 1804. "Jefferson's peace policy" as it was contemptuously styled by that party who remained intellectually and politically European colonists—Jefferson's policy of GROWING instead of ARMING—prevailed until it became thoroughly incorporated into and the very corner-stone of our national policy. It may be properly called the American system. And what has been the result? We will not ask the fields of Mexico to answer. We will not ask the colonized and blossoming wilderness—the farm-homes within the shadows of the Rocky Mountains—our banner floating on the shores of the Pacific—to make answer. But we will ask any occasional representative and remnant of the old European colonial party, if there is at this day a power on earth that has spent centuries in arming, that we either fear, or that could be induced, on any slight occasion, to provoke a war with the United States?

We resume our historic narrative. The gunboat bill passed Congress in the session of 1804-5. A stringent law was enacted for the apprehension by civil process (supported if necessary by military force) of violators of our neutrality, on board foreign armed vessels. If resistance took place and death ensued, it was made punishable as felonious homicide. The President was authorized to permit or interdict the entrance of foreign vessels into our waters, to prohibit supplies to them, and to remove them by force if necessary. Stringent enactments were made, at the President's suggestion, to prevent armed American merchant ships from forcing a contraband trade, as they were officially charged with doing, in the West Indies. A new territorial act was passed for Orleans, conforming its government generally to that of Mississippi, and preparing for its admission as a State when it should contain sixty thousand free inhabitants. Louisiana was erected into a territorial government of the second class. Michigan was detached from Indiana and also erected into a territorial government of the second class.

The President's correspondence, during the session, embraced few topics of present interest. In quoting some of his former remarks about the degradation of morals among mechanical operatives, we stated that he lived to retract those opinions. A letter to Mr. Lithson, January 4th, 1805, contains that retraction in the most ample terms.[1]

[1] We will make room for the directly pertinent part of this letter, and the reader will doubtless keep in mind that it was not written during an election contest, but after its author had received the last office he would accept from the hands of his countrymen.
"Your letter of December 4th [he wrote Mr. Lithson] has been duly received. Mr. ____ informed me that he meant to publish a new edition of the notes on Virginia, and I had in contemplation some particular alterations which would require little time to make. My occupations by no means permit me at this time to revise the text, and make those changes in it which I should now do. I should in that case certainly qualify several expressions in the nineteenth chapter, which have been construed differently from what they were intended. I had under my eye, when writing, the manufacturers of the great cities in the old countries, at the time present, with whom the want of food and clothing

The following letter to Colonel John Taylor of Caroline (January 6th) shows the firm determination of the President to retire at the close of his second term, though the importunate entreaties of friends had thus far prevented any public announcement of that fact.

"My opinion originally was that the President of the United States should have been elected for seven years, and forever ineligible afterwards. I have since become sensible that seven years is too long to be irremovable, and that there should be a peaceable way of withdrawing a man in midway who is doing wrong. The service for eight years, with a power to remove at the end of the first four, comes nearly to my principle as corrected by experience; and it is in adherence to that, that I determine to withdraw at the end of my second term. The danger is that the indulgence and attachments of the people will keep a man in the chair after he becomes a dotard, that reëlection through life shall become habitual, and election for life follow that. General Washington set the example of voluntary retirement after eight years. I shall follow it. And a few more precedents will oppose the obstacle of habit to any one after awhile who shall endeavor to extend his term. Perhaps it may beget a disposition to establish it by an amendment of the Constitution. I believe I am doing right therefore in pursuing my principle. I had determined to declare my intention, but I have consented to be silent on the opinion of friends, who think it best not to put a continuance out of my power in defiance of all circumstances. There is, however, but one circumstance which could engage my acquiescence in another election; to wit, such a division about a successor, as might bring in a monarchist. But that circumstance is impossible. While, therefore, I shall make no formal declaration to the public of my purpose, I have freely let it be understood in private conversation. In this I am persuaded yourself and my friends generally will approve of my views. And should I, at the end of a second term, carry into retirement all the favor which the first has acquired, I shall feel the consolation of having done all the good in my power, and expect with more than composure the termination of a life no longer valuable to others or of importance to myself."

The President's second inauguration took place on the 4th of March, 1805, in the sixty-second year of his age.

His speech on the occasion was longer than his former one, and much less ornately written. He declared that "his conscience told him that he had, on every occasion, acted up to" the declaration of his first inaugural address, "according to its obvious import and to the understanding of every candid mind" Allud-

necessary to sustain life, has begotten a depravity of morals, a dependence and corruption, which renders them an undesirable accession to a country whose morals are sound. My expressions looked forward to the time when our own great cities would get into the same state. But they have been quoted as if meant for the present time here. As yet our manufacturers are as much at their ease, as independent and moral, as our agricultural inhabitants, and they will continue so as long as there are vacant lands for them to resort to: because whenever it shall be attempted by the other classes to reduce them to the minimum of subsistence, they will quit their trades and go to laboring the earth."

ing to the fortunate state of our foreign relations, he said: "We are firmly convinced, and we act on that conviction, that with nations as with individuals, our interests soundly calculated, will ever be found inseparable from our moral duties; and history bears witness to the fact, that a just nation is taken on its word, when recourse is had to armaments and wars to bridle others."

After stating our overflowing income, he, in suggesting what applications might be made of it, after extinguishing the public debt and meeting all other necessary objects, mentioned that it might be disposed of by "a just repartition among the States, and [by] a corresponding amendment of the Constitution, be applied, in time of peace, to rivers, canals, roads, arts, manufactures, education, and other objects within each State." In time of war, it might be made to meet all the expenses of war, "without encroaching on the rights of future generations, by burdening them with the debts of the past."

In regard to the acquisition of Louisiana, he said:

"I know that the acquisition of Louisiana has been disapproved of by some, from a candid apprehension that the enlargement of our territory would endanger its Union. But who can limit the extent to which the federative principle may operate effectively? The larger our association, the less will it be shaken by local passions; and, in any view, is it not better that the opposite bank of the Mississippi should be settled by our own brethren and children, than by strangers of another family? With which shall we be most likely to live in harmony and friendly intercourse?"

Two clauses in the address pertain to the Indians. The first exhibits his deep humanity for that unfortunate race. The second, while exposing some of the most prominent causes of their continuous decline, is evidently intended as a hit at a class of white men. It is as follows:

"But the endeavors to enlighten them on the fate which awaits their present course of life, to induce them to exercise their reason, follow its dictates, and change their pursuits with the change of circumstances, have powerful obstacles to encounter; they are combated by the habits of their bodies, prejudice of their minds, ignorance, pride, and the influence of interested and crafty individuals among them, who feel themselves something in the present order of things, and fear to become nothing in any other. These persons inculcate a sanctimonious reverence for the customs of their ancestors; that whatsoever they did, must be done through all time; that reason is a false guide, and to advance under its counsel, in their physical, moral, or political condition, is perilous innovation; that their duty is to remain as their Creator made them, ignorance being safety, and knowledge full of danger; in short, my friends, among them is seen the action and counteraction of good sense and bigotry; they, too, have their *anti-philosophers*,[1] who find an interest in keeping things in their present state, who dread reformation, and exert all their faculties to maintain the ascendency of habit over the duty of improving our reason, and obeying its mandates."

He stated that "the artillery of the press had been levelled against" the Administration, "charged with whatever its licentiousness could devise or dare." These abuses might have been corrected and punished under State laws. But he considered it important to know "whether freedom of discussion, unaided by power, was not sufficient for the propagation and protection of truth—whether a Government conducting itself in the true spirit of its Constitution, with zeal and purity, and doing no act which it would be unwilling the whole world should witness, can be written down by falsehood and defamation." The experiment, he said, had been tried: the verdict of the people "had been honorable to those who served them, and consolatory to the friend of man, who believed he might be intrusted with his own affairs."

He contemplated " the union of sentiment now manifested so generally, as auguring harmony and happiness to our future course :" correct principles were extending; a kindly and patient toleration should be shown to the dissentients.

The following is the concluding paragraph:

" I shall now enter on the duties to which my fellow citizens have again called me, and shall proceed in the spirit of those principles which they have approved. I fear not that any motives of interest may lead me astray; I am sensible of no passion which could seduce me knowingly from the path of justice; but the weakness of human nature, and the limits of my own understanding, will produce errors of judgment sometimes injurious to your interests. I shall need, therefore, all the indulgence I have heretofore experienced—the want of it will certainly not lessen with increasing years. I shall need, too, the favor of that Being in whose hands we are, who led our forefathers, as Israel of old, from their native land, and planted them in a country flowing with all the necessaries and comforts of life; who has covered our infancy with his providence, and our riper years with his wisdom and power; and to whose goodness I ask you to join with me in supplications, that he will so enlighten the minds of your servants, guide their councils, and prosper their measures, that whatsoever they do, shall result in your good, and shall secure to you the peace, friendship, and approbation of all nations."

Some changes in the Cabinet took place at the period of the President's entrance on his second term. Mr. Lincoln, the At-

---

[1] The italicization of this word is, of course, ours.

torney-General, resigned, and on the second of March, Robert Smith, the Secretary of the Navy, was appointed in his place. Jacob Crowninshield, of Massachusetts, was the same day appointed to the Navy department. But Mr. Crowninshield, very extensively engaged in commerce, could not accept the office. Smith returned to his former place, and John Breckenridge, of Kentucky, was appointed Attorney-General on the 23d of the ensuing December.

The "union of sentiment" spoken of in the President's inaugural address, though it did not soon diminish in regard to national affairs, was broken in upon by severe local schisms in several of the States. There were not enough Federalists left in some of them to form the outside pressure necessary to keep the Republicans together; and, as generally happens in such cases, personal ambition and personal preferences and dislikes led to speedy disruptions. The Burr faction in New York, consisting of a few Democrats aided by the main body of the Federalists, was scarcely swept away, before a division took place between the Clintons and Livingstons, and raged with proscriptive fury. In Pennsylvania, a bitter feud sprung up between the ultra Democrats, who desired to introduce more radical features into the State Constitution (such as a limitation of the term of judges, the annual election of senators, and the reduction of the Execuitve patronage), and the more conservative branch, who opposed these innovations. The former took the name of the "Friends of the People," the latter of "Constitutionalists." McKean having vetoed some legislative measures of the "Friends of the People," that party denounced him, and nominated Simon Snyder for Governor. McKean was supported by the "Constitutionalists" and Federalists at the fall election, and was elected by a considerable majority. The Aurora took part, with its usual vehemence, with the radicals. Leib supported the same side; and Thomas Paine—now settled down on a farm given him by the State of New York—wrote articles in its favor. Dallas and Logan sided with McKean. Some difficulties had also broken out among the Kentucky Republicans—which it is not important here to describe.

In a letter to Dr. Logan, May 11th, the President, without favoring either of the Pennsylvania factions, lamented the division, declaring that "the minority, whichever section should be the minority, would end in a coalition with the Federalists, and some compromise of principle ; because these would not sell their aid for nothing."

The collection of Mr. Jefferson's letters to his daughters, in our possession, mostly closed with the death of Mrs. Eppes. From that period we have scattering family letters addressed to his son-in-law, Mr. Eppes, and after some period, to several of his grandchildren.

To John W. Eppes, Eppington.

Washington, *May 27th, 1805.*

Dear Sir :

Not understanding the conveyance to you by post beyond Richmond, I have thought it safest to remit the 100 D. for you to Gibson & Jefferson, subject to your order, which is done this day. I was never better pleased with a riding-horse than with Jacobin. It is now really a luxury to me to ride. The early prevalence of sickness for this season will probably drive us hence earlier than usual, perhaps by the middle of July. I shall proceed almost directly to Bedford, and will there take to my assistance Mr. Clay and Mr. Clark, and lay off at the east end of the tract so much as shall, taking quality and quantity into consideration, be equal to the average value of 1000 acres of the whole tract generally. The tenderest considerations ensure a conscientious performance of this duty, and to be governed by the judgment of those who, knowing the tract well, will have no motive but to do what is right. I shall hope on my return from Bedford to find you at Monticello with the beloved children, objects of my tenderest solicitudes. I shall not be without a hope of seeing Mr. and Mrs. Eppes also at Monticello. Though I cannot now repay their visits, if they will trust me four years I will overgo the measure. You will see in the papers an extra letter of Elliot's of extraordinary aspect. It contains some absolute untruths, but what is most remarkable is, that expressions are so put together as to be literally true when strictly considered and analyzed, and yet to convey to ninety-nine readers out of one hundred the most absolute and mischievous falsehoods. It is a most insidious attempt to cover his own opinions and passions under the mantle of the Executive, and to fill with inquietude the Republicans who have not the means of good information. Present me to Mr. and Mrs. Eppes and family, and accept my affectionate salutations.

Th. Jefferson.

CHAPTER IV.

1805—1806.

On the 29th of March (1805), in a letter to Judge Tyler of Virginia, the President thus alluded to the Tripolitan war:

187

" Our intention in sending Morris with a respectable force, was to try whether peace could be forced by a coercive enterprise on their town. His inexecution of orders baffled that effort. Having broke him, we try the same experiment under a better commander. If in the course of the summer they cannot produce peace, we shall recall our force, except one frigate and two small vessels, which will keep up a perpetual blockade. Such a blockade will cost us no more than a state of peace, and will save us from increased tributes, and the disgrace attached to them. There is reason to believe the example we have set begins already to work on the dispositions of the powers of Europe to emancipate themselves from that degrading yoke. Should we produce such a revolution there, we shall be amply rewarded for what we have done." .

Early in 1804, before information of Commodore Preble's energetic proceedings had reached the United States, and when it was strongly suspected that Morocco was preparing to join Tripoli, the President had strengthened our naval force in the Mediterranean by sending out the following frigates: President, 44; Congress, 38; Constellation, 38; and Essex, 32. There being but three captains in the navy junior to Preble (and one of these, Bainbridge, being a prisoner to the Tripolitans) it was necessary to send out officers who were his seniors in rank. Decatur was promoted to a captaincy for his conduct at Tripoli, and the ranks of masters and commanders, dropped at the reduction of 1801, were revived.

Before the arrival of the new squadron, Preble had made various captures. On the 3d of August (1804) he bombarded Tripoli, and several of the enemy's strong gunboats, lying in the harbor, were carried by boarding against tremendous odds. The John Adams, 32, soon after arrived from home, announcing the approach of the additional fleet; but their coming being delayed, Preble again bombarded the enemy's capital on the 24th and 29th, the last time with serious effect. A sharp engagement also took place on the 3d of September.

On the evening of the next day, a most tragical event occurred. The ketch Intrepid, which had been used by Decatur in the destruction of the Philadelphia, having been fitted as a floating mine, with a hundred barrels of gunpowder in her magazine, and her deck loaded with shot, shells and kentledge, was sent into the harbor at night to be exploded in the midst of the enemy's cruisers. Captain Somers and Lieutenant Wadsworth, selected from a list of volunteers, were the only officers (except young Israel, who, having been refused permission, sprung on board at the last moment) permitted to take part in the desperate service; and they had a volunteer crew as determined as themselves. It was said that Preble felt unutterable anxiety as the "Infernal" and the accompanying boats, which were to lie at the harbor's mouth, to aid in bringing off her crew, put off into the dense haze of a summer night, through which the stars were dimly discernible. Several Moorish gunboats lay near the harbor's mouth; the vessel was filled with combustibles which a spark would ignite; and a shot from a boat or the batteries was liable to explode her with the suddenness of a bomb. But above all, whispers had stolen through the squadron that the crew had generally declared they would neither retreat until their object was accomplished nor be taken alive.

In trying a port-fire in the cabin of the Constitution a day or two before the ketch was ready to proceed, Commodore Preble had remarked that he thought it burned a few seconds too long, and that an enemy might possibly reach the vessel and extinguish it before the train was fired. "I ask for no port-fire at all," was Captain Somers's ominous reply. The deeds of Decatur and others had begotten among our young officers in the Mediterranean a spirit of gallantry too wild and daring for the dictates of sober reason, if not for the ultimate good of the service itself.

When last seen by the straining eyes of those left behind, the Intrepid was moving slowly (she was a dull sailer) but steadily into the gloom, and her shadowy outline was discovered within a musket-shot of the mole, standing directly for the harbor. After a few moments of breathless anxiety, the silence was suddenly broken by the opening roar of the enemy's guns, and a storm of shot lashed the passages of the bay. Presently, a glare of lurid light shot to the heavens, followed by an explosion which shook sea and land. This was the last ever certainly known of the fate of the fire-ship or any of its crew. Mangled forms were afterwards found among the rocks of the harbor, but so blackened and mutilated, so

"Scorched and shrivell'd to a span,"

that none could discern whether they were the corpses of

Christians or Moors. Certain circumstances led the officers of the American fleet to conjecture that the Intrepid was prematurely discovered and boarded by the enemy—perhaps from the gunboats lying near the harbor's mouth—and that Somers fired the train, and sent all to destruction together.[1] But the mystery never has been in the least cleared up, and now never can be until that day when all mysteries shall be cleared up.

The season and the condition of the American squadron made it necessary to suspend active operations; and leaving a sufficient detachment to enforce the blockade, Commodore Preble sailed for Syracuse in the island of Sicily. On the 10th of September, the President—the flag-ship of Commodore Barron, thenceforth the senior captain in command—and the Constellation arrived. Preble returned home in the John Adams to receive the hearty applause of the Government and people of his country. Congress voted him thanks and a gold medal.

We will here take occasion to remark that one of the recommendations of this fine officer to his Government, as the result of his Mediterranean experience, was to provide bomb-ketches and gunboats for the assault of such places as Tripoli. He had not discovered, like a good many landsmen in and out of Congress, that this economical species of marine force was wholly inefficient. His fierce combats with the gunboats which defended the harbor of Tripoli, had impressed a very different conviction on his mind.

The force left in the Mediterranean under the orders of Barron consisted of the President, 44; Constitution, 44; Congress, 38; Constellation, 38; Essex, 32; Siren, 16; Argus, 16; Vixen, 12; Enterprise, 12; Nautilus, 12. The John Adams, 28, and Hornet, 12, were afterwards added to the squadron; and as soon as they could be prepared, two bomb-ketches, the Vengeance and Spitfire, and ten gunboats (seven of two guns and three of one gun) were sent out. This did not look very much like a disposition on the part of our Government to leave the national vessels "rotting out of commission," when there was an occasion for their services. It did not look much like meeting actual enemies with " moral philosophy and commercial restrictions, with dry-docks and gunboats, with non-intercourse and embar-

---

[1] This was Commodore Preble's impression; but Mr. Cooper takes a different view of the probabilities.

goes, till the American nation were told that they could not be kicked into a war."[1]

The spring of 1805 opened with an adventure in our Barbary war bordering on the romantic. The reigning bashaw of Tripoli, Jussuf Caramalli, was a usurper, having driven his older brother, Hamet, from the throne. The latter had taken refuge among the Mamelukes of Egypt. It had been suggested to the American officers that the name and services of the exiled prince might be advantageously used in this war. Captain Eaton, our consul at Tunis, formed a project of this kind, and returned home to obtain permission to carry it into execution. He so far obtained this, that Commodore Barron was instructed to aid the execution of his plans to such extent as he should deem prudent. The commodore sent Eaton to Alexandria in the Argus. He arrived late in November (1804), and proceeded to Cairo, where he was received favorably by the Viceroy of Egypt, and Hamet Caramalli entered at once into his views.

They assembled a force of about five hundred men, composed, it was said, of twelve different nations, and then advanced across the Lybian Desert in the direction of Derne. The distance, six hundred miles, was accomplished in fifty days, and on the 26th of April (1805) they encamped in the rear of that town, the capital of one of the Tripolitan provinces. The city contained about fifteen thousand inhabitants, and was defended by some military works and a garrison. The Argus, Captain Hull, the Hornet, Lieutenant-Commandant Evans, and the Nautilus, Lieutenant-Commandant Dent, which had been on the look-out for Eaton and his forces, arrived at the same time before the town. Some marines, and arms for Eaton's troops, (now swelled to a considerable body by the accession of Arabs) were landed; and on the 27th of April, this motley force rushed to the assault, the vessels firing on the batteries of the town at such short range that the Hornet was anchored within pistol-shot of one of the latter. The defence was spirited, but the city was captured in less than two hours. An army sent by

---

[1] This sentence is from John Quincy Adams's eulogy on Madison, 1836. The remark, indeed, was intended to specially apply to a later period and state of things; but he leads to the inference that the kinds of preparation he names were the only ones Mr. Jefferson ever approved of or made for war. And we think, while indulging in this strain of remark, he forgot to make any reference to the Tripolitan war. We may have occasion hereafter to call attention to Mr. J. Q. Adams's consistency on this subject.

Jussuf was defeated on the 13th of May, and more effectually so on the 10th of June.

Eaton's hopes now soared high that with proper supplies and reinforcements from Commodore Barron, Tripoli itself would soon be at his feet. To his applications, however, the commodore made answer, that Hamet was now in possession of the second province of the regency, and that if he had the influence to which he laid claim, he ought to be able to effect his purpose by the ordinary coöperation of the fleet. Barron (wasted to great debility by illness) possibly had not too much confidence in the discretion of Eaton, and none whatever in that of Hamet Caramalli, who, he wrote Colonel Lear, had neither energy, military talents, nor resources of any kind. He believed that a powerful impression had been produced on the mind of the reigning bashaw, and that then was the time to treat favorably with him and recover Commodore Bainbridge and the crew of the Philadelphia[1] "from the bondage of a bigoted and unfeeling tyrant."

The Danish consul, Nissen, communicated overtures from the bashaw's prime minister—evidently supposing that a peace would be desirable, under the circumstances, to the United States. Bainbridge himself wrote Barron from his captivity:

"I have not the least doubt that was a person to come here to negotiate before an attack is made, that peace would be effected for one hundred and twenty thousand dollars, and if the attack should not prove very successful, it is very probable that such a sum would not release us from captivity, at least for some time. Apprehension is often worse than realization. I sincerely hope that a person will come, because I think it the most favorable moment."

Acting under the advice of Barron, Colonel Lear opened a communication with the bashaw. The latter demanded $200,000 dollars for peace and ransom. Lear rejected the proposition at once, and proposed as his ultimatum that a mutual delivery of prisoners should take place, and as the bashaw had more than two hundred the most, he offered to "give him $60,000 for them, but not a cent for peace." These terms were agreed upon.

Both Barron's and Lear's conduct on this occasion has been often criticised. A life of Eaton has appeared, in which Lear

[1] This consisted of about three hundred men, including twenty-two quarter-deck officers.

is loaded with accusations for arresting by a dishonorable peace the splendid career of the former to a great national conquest. And when a son of Hamet Caramalli was recently in the United States, soliciting compensation for the injustice done to his father, several romantic tales on the subject appeared in our periodical publications.

Commodore Rodgers, who succeeded to Barron in the command before the treaty was concluded,[1] and who certainly was never accused of preferring other arguments where powder and ball were the best ones, decidedly approved of his predecessor's measures and of the treaty. He wrote the Secretary of the Navy to that effect (June 8th) and then sailed to Tunis, and under the muzzles of his cannon, dictated a peace to its Bey.

Eaton's light-armed force had done well against a town whose principal batteries could be engaged on equal terms by two or three little vessels close in upon land. Tripoli was quite another affair. It had more than once repulsed our entire squadron. It had a wall and strong landward defences, against which a riffraff of two or three thousand Arabs (about as good soldiers as American Indians, and indeed very similar ones) could effect no more than a swarm of hornets. It would not have been in the power of a much better trained and more systematic soldier than Eaton to suddenly convert such materials into proper ones for conducting siege-trains and regular approaches. A perusal of not only the earlier but the subsequent history of the Barbary States will serve to dispel many fanciful impressions on this subject. It is probable that if we had attempted dynasty-founding and protectorates in Africa, we should have been compelled to engage in a land war with all the Barbary States. The degree of material necessary for such an enterprise has since been shown by the experience of the French in Algeria.

But what would have been the special objects (so long as we attained the general ones of the war) of capturing Tripoli? The ones alleged are that we should have thus avoided the degradation of paying $60,000, and that we should have discharged an obligation to Hamet.

It was not a very sore disgrace for a transatlantic power to

---

[1] Barron resigned on account of ill health, and was succeeded by Rodgers, May 22d.

pay that sum for the greater number of prisoners, when the oldest and strongest nations of Europe continued not only to pay ransom for prisoners, but large sums avowedly for peace. When all the ends of equity and convenience are answered, the point of ceremonial honor does not rise very high in treating with barbarians.

But the other question, it must be admitted, was an important one. If we lured Hamet Caramalli from a distant retreat—if we took his contribution to our force, though it should amount to no more than five hungry Arabs, whose services were not worth their rations—and if we stipulated, in consideration of his force, his name, or on any other ground, to do our best before concluding any peace to place him on the throne which perhaps *his* father usurped—then Lear, and Barron, and Rogers voluntarily tarnished the good faith of their country. They could not pretend they had made all reasonable effort to redeem such a stipulation till at least a bloody assault by sea and land on Tripoli had left them victors, or sent them (as it probably would) shattered and broken from the onset. And, under the same supposition, the President disgraced himself by approving of the treachery of his instruments; the Senate disgraced itself by approving the treaty; and the House of Representatives (admitting it had some option in legislating to execute treaties) disgraced itself by making any provisions for its execution. Moreover, the American Congress and people lately doubly disgraced themselves (for now neither poverty nor ignorance of facts could be properly pleaded) by turning a deaf ear to the application of the son of a martyr to their forefathers' treachery.

But this entire hypothesis, fortunately, rests on the imagination of tale writers. Eaton was deeply chagrined at a result which he believed arrested him on the high road to victory and renown. But he never was able to show that Hamet had been, to the least degree, deceived by our Government. He wrote Commodore Rodgers (June 30th) that "our peace with Tripoli was certainly more favorable, and, considered separately, more honorable, than any peace obtained by any Christian nation with a Barbary regency, at any period within a hundred years."

In fact, Eaton was never vested with power to pledge our Government, if such had been his own wish, to an agreement to effect the restoration of Hamet. Barron, in supreme command, expressly instructed him to make no such stipulations. He wrote to him March 22d, 1805:

"I feel it my duty to state explicitly that I must withhold my sanction to any convention or agreement committing the United States, or tending to impress on Hamet Bashaw [Hamet Caramalli] a conviction that we have bound ourselves to place him upon the throne. The consequences involved in such an engagement cannot but strike you forcibly, and a general view of our situation, in relation to the reigning bashaw and our unfortunate countrymen in Tripoli, will be sufficient to mark its inexpediency."

In Eaton's reply (May 30), he urged that it would be impolitic and unjust to make peace without restoring Hamet, but he did not hint that he had entered into a *stipulation* to do so. He admitted that nothing could be accomplished without more "military talent and firmness" than was possessed by that prince and his followers. He described the latter as " rather a rabble than an army." His " convention " with Hamet stipulated that the United States " should use their utmost exertions " for the restoration of the latter, " so far as comported with their own honor and interest," and this convention was to be submitted to the President for ratification. After the treaty of peace was concluded with Jussuf, Hamet wrote to General Eaton (June 29th, 1805):

"On returning to your happy country, to which I wish you a safe passage, I request you will express to your sovereign my cordial thanks for his manifestations of friendship towards me. Had it been ordained that measures might have been carried forward to the attainment of my wishes, the restoration of my rightful domains to me, it would certainly have been cause of eternal gratitude. But, it is true, my own means were small. I know, indeed, that they did not answer your reasonable expectations. And this, I am ready to admit, is a good reason why you should not choose to persevere in an enterprise hazardous in itself and perhaps doubtful in its issue. I submit to the will of God, and thank the king of America, and all his servants, for their kind dispositions towards me."

Two months later, Hamet claimed that the restoration of his throne was guaranteed by the convention and by the verbal assurances of Eaton. The latter vaguely countenanced his pretensions, without, however, making any direct admission in regard to his own alleged personal promises, or attempting to show that he either had the right to make, or had made, such an official stipulation. If Hamet was misled (which is very doubtful), he owed it entirely to the indiscretion of Eaton, who equally exceeded the letter and spirit of his instructions.

No foreign undertaking of the same magnitude in which the United States have ever been engaged, has been more proper, more useful, more creditably conducted, more brilliantly terminated, more pregnant with direct and incidental advantages to our country, than our war with the Barbary States during Mr. Jefferson's Administration. And it was no infringement of his peace policy. His peace policy did not extend to tolerating piracy or paying tribute.

The purchase of Louisiana had roused the old jealousies of Spain towards the United States. She had made and withdrawn a protest against the transfer; but the arrangement of boundaries stirred up new irritations. Her tone grew haughtier; and on the 7th of August (1805) the President wrote the Secretary of State, from Monticello, that "from the papers already received, he inferred a confident reliance, on the part of Spain, on the omnipotence of Bonaparte, but a desire of procrastination till peace in Europe should leave us without an ally." The Emperor Napoleon (he assumed the imperial title and dignity May 18th, 1804), had, indeed, adopted a very dictatorial tone towards us, and evinced a disposition to interfere directly in our disputes with Spain. Our contraband trade in the West Indies undoubtedly irritated him to some extent, but we had committed a greater sin than this. We had balked one of his projects; we had compelled him to do what he did not desire to do; the laugh of the world was against him in the affair. Since that period his fortunes had been successful; crowns had rained on his family. And he now was in close alliance with Spain.

The President had without hesitation resolved to repel Napoleon's dangerous interference, and if this course would provoke war, to invite it at once, instead of waiting for a European peace. He wrote from home (August 7th) proposing to the Cabinet a provisional alliance with England. On receiving from the Secretary of State a letter of the French minister, undertaking to say how our Government must treat General Moreau, then an exile in the United States, he said "he confessed" it "excited in him both jealousy and offence," and he added:

"The style of that Government, in the Spanish business, was calculated to excite indignation; but it was a case in which that might have done injury. But the pro-sent is a case which would justify some notice in order to let them understand we are not of those powers who will receive and execute mandates. I think the answer should show independence as well as friendship. I am anxious to receive the opinions of our brethren after their review and consideration of the Spanish papers. I am strongly impressed with a belief of hostile and treacherous intentions against us on the part of France, and that we should lose no time in securing something more than a mutual friendship with England."

Two days later (August 27th) he made this full exposition of his views to the Secretary of State :

. . . "Considering the character of Bonaparte, I think it material at once to let him see that we are not of the powers who will receive his orders.

"I think you have misconceived the nature of the treaty I thought we should propose to England. I have no idea of committing ourselves immediately or independently of our further will to the war. The treaty should be provisional only, to come into force on the event of our being engaged in war with either France or Spain during the present war in Europe. In that event we should make common cause, and England should stipulate not to make peace without our obtaining the objects for which we go to war, to wit : the acknowledgment by Spain of the rightful boundaries of Louisiana (which we should reduce to our minimum by a secret article); and 2, indemnification for spoliations, for which purpose we should be allowed to make reprisals on the Floridas, and *retain them* as an indemnification. Our coöperation in the war (if we should actually enter into it) would be sufficient consideration for Great Britain to engage for its object ; and it being generally known to France and Spain that we had entered into treaty with England, would probably ensure us a peaceful and immediate settlement of both points. But another motive, much more powerful, would indubitably induce England to go much further. Whatever ill-humor may at times have been expressed against us by individuals of that country, the first wish of every Englishman's heart is to see us once more fighting by their sides against France ; nor could the king or his ministers do an act so popular as to enter into an alliance with us. The nation would not weigh the consideration by grains and scruples. They would consider it as the price and pledge of an indissoluble friendship. I think it possible that for such a provisional treaty their general guarantee of ☐ Louisiana and the Floridas. At any rate, we might try them. A failure would not make our situation worse. If such a one could be obtained, we might await our own convenience for calling up the *casus fœderis.* I think it important that England should receive an overture as early as possible, as it might prevent her listening to terms of peace."

The following, to same (September 16th), discloses all that is further necessary to exhibit the President's policy towards the powers named :

"The inclosed letter from General Armstrong furnishes matter for consideration. You know the French considered themselves entitled to the Rio Bravo, and that Laussa declared his orders to be to receive possession to that limit, but not to Perdido ; and that France has to us been always silent as to the western boundary, while she spoke decisively as to the eastern. You know Turreau agreed with us

that neither party should strengthen themselves in the disputed country during negotiation ; and Armstrong, who says Monroe concurs with him, is of opinion, from
the character of the Emperor, that were we to restrict ourselves to taking the posts
on the west side of the Mississippi, and threaten a cessation of intercourse with
Spain, Bonaparte would interpose efficiently to prevent the quarrel from going further. Add to these things the fact that Spain has sent five hundred colonists to St.
Antonio, and one hundred troops to Nacogdoches, and probably has fixed or prepared a post at the Bay of St. Bernard, at Matagordo. Supposing, then, a previous
alliance with England to guard us in the worst event, I should propose that Congress should pass acts, 1, authorizing the Executive to suspend intercourse with
Spain at discretion ; 2, to dislodge the new establishments of Spain between the
Mississippi and Bravo ; and 3, to appoint commissioners to examine and ascertain all
claims for spoliation that they might be preserved for future indemnification. I commit these ideas merely for consideration, and that the subject may be matured by
the time of our meeting at Washington, where I shall be myself on the 2d of October."

But new events were suddenly to change the current of our
foreign relations. The battle of Trafalgar was fought October
21st, 1805. This left Napoleon in no condition to dictate terms
to trans-oceanic powers. England had formed a close alliance
with Russia, and the "conquest"[1] of Trafalgar made her absolute
and undisputed on the seas. She now less needed the kind of
assistance the United States could render her, and had no apprehension of any injury they could inflict upon her. Nor
could an alliance or coöperation of the United States with
France and Spain thenceforth in the least either endanger, or
hold in check, her overwhelming naval supremacy.

Since the peace of Amiens, American commerce had rapidly
increased. The recent European war had enormously swelled
our carrying trade. The last was at the expense of English
shipping interests. England, therefore, had two inducements to
fall on our commerce—the one, to gather the harvest of present plunder, the other to destroy competition then and in
future. To secure these objects was more important to her than
our friendship or our enmity, and therefore it was unhesitatingly determined upon.

Henceforth Spain was comparatively powerless against the
United States ; Napoleon could not reach us with his arms ; and
England assumed the position of our most encroaching and dread-
ed enemy. The former posture of things was exactly reversed.

Even before the battle of Trafalgar, Great Britain had be-

[1] Lord Nelson was wont to thus term his far less decisive victory of the Nile.

gun to revive old pretensions—those she had set up in the Seven Years' war—against neutral commerce. A number of our vessels had been condemned in her Admiralty courts on strained constructions of maritime law. If we had been compelled to ask her alliance against Napoleon, it may be regarded as doubtful whether we could then have secured it without the most injurious maritime concessions.

Our commerce had suffered annoyances, during 1805, from other quarters besides England. The character and extent of these will be found sufficiently adverted to in the President's message at the meeting of Congress. But towards the close of that year, we had no further serious maritime difficulties to apprehend from any power but the haughty and now undisputed mistress of the seas.

The ninth Congress assembled on the 2d of December, 1805. In the Senate, Nicholas Gilman became the successor of Olcott from New Hampshire; James Fenner of Ellery, from Rhode Island; Aaron Kitchell of Dayton, from New Jersey; James Turner of Franklin, from North Carolina; Buckner Thurston of Brown, and John Adair of Breckenridge, from Kentucky; and Daniel Smith of Cocke, from Tennessee. All the new members were Republicans, and two of them, Gilman and Kitchell, succeeded Federal incumbents, so that the latter party retained but seven representatives in the Senate.

Nearly all the leading Republican members of the late Congress had been reëlected. Among the new ones on the same side, were Daniel D. Tompkins, afterwards Governor of New York and Vice-President of the United States; George Clinton, Jr., a nephew of the Vice-President; and Gurdon S. Mumford, all of New York. Tompkins did not, however, take his seat, having been appointed a judge of the Supreme Court of his State. The Federalists had not more than twenty-five members, and these were mostly from New England. But they had suffered material losses in New England—ten of the seventeen Massachusetts representatives now belonging to their opponents. They had, however, again carried the Boston district, and elected Josiah Quincy as the successor of Doctor Eustis. Dana, John Cotton Smith, and Davenport appeared from Connecticut; and these, with Quincy, were the most prominent Federalists in the House.

Macon was again elected speaker, after a close contest, over Varnum. The Federalists supported John Cotton Smith.

The President's Message, after alluding to the recent ravages of the yellow fever in two of our cities, and making some suggestions in relation to the quarantine regulations, proceeded to unfold the state of our foreign relations. He thus alluded to the recent depredations on our commerce:

"Since our last meeting, the aspect of our foreign relations has considerably changed. Our coasts have been infested and our harbors watched by private armed vessels, some of them without commissions, some with illegal commissions, others with those of legal form, but committing piratical acts beyond the authority of their commissions. They have captured in the very entrance of our harbors, as well as on the high seas, not only the vessels of our friends coming to trade with us, but our own also. They have carried them off under pretence of legal adjudication, but not daring to approach a court of justice, they have plundered and sunk them by the way, or in obscure places where no evidence could arise against them; maltreated the crews, and abandoned them in boats in the open sea or on desert shores without food or covering. These enormities appearing to be unreached by any control of their sovereigns, I found it necessary to equip a force to cruise within our own seas, to arrest all vessels of these descriptions found hovering on our coast within the limits of the Gulf Stream, and to bring the offenders in for trial as pirates."

He added that " the same system of hovering on our coasts and harbors under color of seeking enemies," had been carried on also by public armed ships; and that new principles had been interpolated into the laws of nations by which " a belligerent took to itself a commerce with its own enemy which it denied to a neutral." He declared that reason revolted at this inconsistency, and that our interests " imposed on us the obligation of providing an effectual and determined opposition to a doctrine so injurious to the rights of peaceable nations."

He stated that Spain had refused to pay for old admitted spoliations, and continued to commit new ones—that she obstructed our commerce in the Mobile—refused to accede to propositions for amicably adjusting the boundaries of Louisiana—and had recently made inroads into and seized and plundered some of our citizens in portions of the territory which she had before delivered up. He had therefore ordered our troops on that frontier to protect our citizens and "repel by arms any similar aggression in future."

He thought, in the case of all the offending powers, we ought still to hope for peace, but " he could not but recommend such preparations as circumstances called for." He proceeded to enumerate these:

"The first object is to place our seaport towns out of the danger of insult. Measures have been already taken for furnishing them with heavy cannon for the service of such land batteries as may make a part of their defence against armed vessels approaching them. In aid of these it is desirable that we should have a competent number of gunboats; and the number to be competent must be considerable. If immediately begun, they may be in readiness for service at the opening of the next season. Whether it will be necessary to augment our land forces will be decided by occurrences probably in the course of your session. In the meantime, you will consider whether it would not be expedient, for a state of peace as well as of war, so to organize or class the militia as would enable us, on a sudden emergency, to call for the services of the younger portions, unencumbered with the old and those having families. Upward of three hundred thousand able-bodied men, between the ages of eighteen and twenty-six years, which the last census shows we may now count within our limits, will furnish a competent number for offence or defence in any point where they may be wanted, and will give time for raising regular forces after the necessity of them shall become certain; and the reducing to the early period of life all its active service cannot but be desirable to our younger citizens, of the present as well as future times, inasmuch as it engages to them in more advanced age a quiet and undisturbed repose in the bosom of their families. I cannot, then, but earnestly recommend to your early consideration the expediency of so modifying our militia system as, by a separation of the more active part from that which is less so, we may draw from it, when necessary, an efficient corps fit for real and active service, and to be called to it in regular rotation.

"Considerable provision has been made, under former authorities from Congress, of materials for the construction of ships of war of seventy-four guns. These materials are on hand subject to the further will of the legislature.

"An immediate prohibition of the exportation of arms and ammunition is also submitted to your determination."

He alluded to the successful termination of the war with Tripoli—praising the conduct of Eaton; and to the apparently favorable condition of our negotiation with Tunis.

He recommended that the existing limitation of the number of frigates to be kept in service in time of peace, and of their crews (to two-thirds their regular complement), be changed to a limitation of the number of seamen employed in the whole service, so that the ships in commission could be fully manned if the occasion should require.

After adverting to the favorable situation of our Indian relations and to certain new treaties of purchase, he took up the subject of the finances, and stated that after meeting all other demands, about two millions had been paid during the current year, on the debt contracted under the British treaty, and convention—and upwards of four millions of principal and four millions of interest on the public debt. Besides this, four millions and a half remained in the Treasury on the 30th day of September; and it had not been necessary to borrow the money as authorized by the act of 1803, to meet the claims of our citizens assumed by the convention with France.

On the 6th of December, the President sent in a confidential message entering more fully upon our affairs with Spain. He stated the aggressive conduct of that power—that our special minister, Mr. Monroe, and our resident minister, Mr. Pinckney, had long been fruitlessly employed in attempting to procure some adjustment—that Spain claimed that our Louisiana boundaries did not extend east of the Iberville, and that "our line to the west was one which would have left us but a string of land on that bank of the Mississippi." The conduct of France in this controversy was then alluded to. He said, "she was prompt and decided in her declarations, that her demands on Spain for French spoliations carried into Spanish ports, were included in the settlement between the United States and France; that she took at once the ground, that she had acquired no right from Spain, and had meant to deliver us none, eastward of the Iberville." He concluded:

"The present crisis in Europe is favorable for pressing a settlement, and not a moment should be lost in availing ourselves of it. Should it pass unimproved, our situation would become much more difficult. Formal war is not necessary; it is not probable it will follow; but the protection of our citizens, the spirit and honor of our country require, that force should be interposed to a certain degree; it will probably contribute to advance the object of peace. *But the course to be pursued will require the command of means which it belongs to Congress exclusively to deny or to yield.* To them I communicate every fact material for their information, and the documents necessary to enable them to judge for themselves. To their wisdom, then, I look for the course I am to pursue, and will pursue with sincere zeal that which they shall approve."

The above message was referred to a committee of which John Randolph was chairman. It reported January 3rd (the doors being closed) denouncing the conduct of Spain in severe terms, and declaring that she had given "ample cause for a formal declaration of war;" but by reason of our debts and other circumstances, peace was recommended if it could be main tained compatibly with the honor and interests of the country. The report concluded with the following resolution:

"*Resolved,* That such number of troops (not exceeding ———) as the President of the United States shall deem sufficient to protect the Southern frontiers of the United States from Spanish inroad and insult, and to chastise the same, be immediately raised."

Bidwell, a member of the committee, moved as a substitute for this resolution, that an appropriation be made to enable the President to defray any extraordinary expenses which might arise in our intercourse with foreign nations. The object of this, which was not concealed, was to enable the President to purchase Florida, a solution hinted at in his special message, and which he and his Cabinet were known to favor. Both the resolutions were warmly debated, with closed doors, until the 11th of January, when the question was taken on the original resolution (Randolph's), and it was defeated by a vote of seventy-two to fifty-eight. The Federalists voted in the minority. Bidwell's resolution passed, after a protracted contest in regard to its phraseology, and the sum of two millions of dollars was appropriated.

Randolph led the opposition, and he made an open quarrel with the Administration. The burden of his grievance was that the President had not directly explained his objects and asked for a specific sum, thereby (insisted this modest gentleman) shifting off the responsibility which the Executive ought to have assumed, somewhat on the House, but specially and particularly on the shoulders of Mr. John Randolph, chairman of the committee of Ways and Means.

Mr. Randolph had been for some time uneasy in his position. His taste was not for that grave, argumentative, and laborious exposition, which is the province of a majority leader. He delighted more in brilliant declamation, fierce personal retorts, and burning invective. His mind, like his education, was desultory—rather cultivated at points which enabled him to make a brilliant display, than comprehensive or profound. Even his knowledge was picked out of a mass of promiscuous reading rather than attained by systematic investigation, or by a broad and thorough culture on the given topic. He was like those diligent review readers, who gather a collection of pithy quotations from every book, without troubling themselves to wade through the original.   He had a most retentive memory, which culled and laid aside for future use everything which could be introduced into a speech with particular effect.   Perhaps it would not be just to say that, like Sheridan, he manufactured his finest rhetoric, and laid in wait for some occasion when he could palm it off as impromptu ; but still his fine sayings, as a class, are those which are as likely to borrow the raw material or the groundwork from recollection as from the original conceptions of the moment.

Both nature and cultivation had made him the master of one kind of wit.   It was not the genial variety which delights all hearers, enlivens with a refreshing laugh the humdrum of ordinary parliamentary routine, or adds zest to social intercourse. It was bitter, cynical, and often appeared malignant, because it came in the form of attack without any reasonable provocation, and on the heads of those who could not make any effective defence.   If, for example, an obscure and particularly if a new and plain member presumed to appear in debate on a different side of the question from the overbearing lord " of Roanoke," and if that member had anything in his appearance, manners, diction, or the like, which could be made the subject of an insulting sarcasm, it generally came ; and there was always enough of real or supposed application to inflict personal mortification and pain ; and sometimes enough to make its victim the butt of an undying joke.   Nor did Mr. Randolph save all these javelins for opponents.   He did not at all like to have later and common men in his own party claim equality or right of judgment.   He treated them with intolerable hauteur.   If they followed him, it was through fear, and the force of party obligations.   They could have no affection for him.   Such leadership would have been fatal to a political organization, the situation of which demanded skill or good judgment.

In looking back at his speeches, it is difficult to resist the impression that his talents, even in his own line, were considerably exaggerated.   One is inclined to suspect that he was often admired because it had become the fashion to admire him— that, as in the case of established wits and beauties, people cried bravo to prove their own cleverness.   At least, most of the scathing bolts seem rather harmless now ; and this is not the case with some of those which Fox and Burke and Pitt hurled at each other's heads during parallel parliamentary epochs. Specimens of Franklin's retorts are preserved which are as fresh and keen as when they originally went whizzing to their mark.

It is probable, too, that Randolph's peculiarities heightened and gave a degree of extraneous and scenic effect to what he uttered. His pride, his isolation, his rich appointments, his claims to a baronial family consequence, his aristocratic assumption of superiority, his capricious and dangerous temper, all set him apart, and made him a popular marvel. His personal appearance, also, was unusual and striking. He was tall and excessively meagre; his face cadaverous and beardless. There was something in his general aspect which reminded one of his lineage from the royal Powhattan. His eye was piercingly brilliant; and had the power of freezing or burning as it reflected the passion-torrent within. The shrill key of his voice approached that of those victims of jealous barbarity who watch Eastern harems, and its least whisper smote on the ear like the ringing clink of metal. Each word seemed vitalized into a substantive thing—an impinging material body—by the intensity of his mental action, and the vehemence of his feelings. His modes of thought were so eccentric and took such unexpected turns—his attacks were so capriciously made or withheld, that curiosity always stood tiptoe awaiting some wonder. Lastly, strange gleams of approaching or actual insanity came to increase the feverish interest of the spectacle.

He did not lack genius. His declamation was often splendid. In some respects he had great penetration. None could so skillfully appeal to the feelings and prejudices of his own class in Virginia and elsewhere. He well understood the pulse of a deliberative body. We shall soon find Mr. Jefferson speaking of his "popular eloquence." This does not seem to accurately define his kind of oratory. It certainly was neither profound nor philosophic. It never exhausted the facts of the topic. It rarely even instructed. It piquantly seized upon some striking analogy, or some overlooked flaw, and coruscated about it with a medley of historic and semi-poetical illustration, uttered in a unique way, by a most unique man. And having roused a train of feeling, he could keep it up and urge it along with much apparent effect. But there was no depth in the current thus set flowing. Men listened as in a good dramatic exhibition. They laughed, they almost wept. When it was over, they drew one long breath, and then fell back into common life, as if nothing had happened. No stern resolves were planted in the bosom, as if the hearer had been listening to Otis or John Adams. Men gazed not aslant for arms or firebrands, as if Henry's fiery invocations had been ringing in their ears. It would be easy to descend two or three grades lower among American "popular" orators, and still find those superior to John Randolph.

Before wonder and adulation, or the fever-fire of excitement, had turned his brain, Randolph did not lack considerable judgment in political affairs. His integrity was unquestionable. He scorned meanness, duplicity, or cowardice. His loves, like his hates, were sincere and vehement. He could be a captivating companion, and the pure and noble Macon loved him like a brother to the end of his life.

But every good gift had a concomitant bad one. He was a bundle of opposite extremes, curiously bound together in one incongruous and diseased human frame. He was a living antithesis. We have mentioned some of his parliamentary and other contradictions. His private ones were not less marked. His integrity, for example, did not place him above the most paltry suspicions of other men, whose standards were notoriously as high as his own; and the virulence and egotism of his temper made him ready to pour out these suspicions at once, and if chafed by opposition, to swell them to a torrent of invective. His courage was combined with quarrelsomeness. He was more than ready to put every dispute on the footing of personal offence. He fought a number of duels for words which were uttered in parliamentary debate, and which were characterized by less than his own habitual personalities. If not truculent by disposition (and we do not believe he was) his overstrained pride and punctiliousness generally left no other escape from a controversy with those who acknowledged what is termed the "code of honor." Even his friendships and hates, deep though they were for the time being, rarely survived an important difference of opinion. Or rather, love of opposition and change was a disease of his organization. He followed Jefferson devotedly for years, and then broke off on the provocation, or pretence, we have seen. He loved Mr. Madison, and soon fiercely hated and denounced him. He was enthusiastic in his admiration of Monroe, and afterwards poured out on him epithets implying contempt. He was one of the earliest supporters of General Jackson, and one of the first to abandon him. He insulted Mr. Clay in the Senate, fought with him, and then rushed in a dying state across the country, as fast as his horses could be driven, to be reconciled to him. He clung to Macon, Tazewell, and a little knot of friends through all; but had one of these been elected President, Randolph would probably have denounced him within six months of his inauguration.

Jefferson was his first and longest official love. His character during the first Presidency of the former was sounder and more even than ever afterwards. Admiration and wonder had not fostered his worse qualities into full bloom. He had not, since the full development of his powers, tasted the acid luxury of opposition.[1] Disappointment in love (to adopt a hypothesis hinted at by Mr. Garland) and long physical disease, had not reached that acme which unhinged him. The coming madness had not touched his brain.[2]

---

[1] Professor Tucker states that in an early period of Mr. Jefferson's Administration, Randolph once read to him (Tucker) and George Hay, of Richmond, a passage from one of Godwin's novels, in which "the excitements and the triumphs of a leader of the opposition are very forcibly depicted," and the "remarks that he made and the emotion he exhibited" conveyed the impression to his hearers that he felt "a painful contrast between his then position in Congress and that which he had held in the preceding Administration."—*Tucker's Jefferson*, vol. ii. p. 189.

[2] The President's estimate of John Randolph has been the theme of some speculation. (See Benton's Thirty Years' View, vol. i. p. 473.) He undoubtedly treated him with all the respect and confidence with which he would have treated any person to whom his party in the House of Representatives assigned the position of leader: and it is not probable that Randolph's punctilious and exacting temper suggested the omission of any of the mere forms of attention. But we find no confidential personal or political correspondence between them. We do not believe any really confidential relations ever existed between them. Jefferson was too penetrating not to fully understand the want of balance and reliability in his character. We soon shall see hints enough of this in a letter to Monroe, where good taste and tact required him, under the particular circumstances, to award to Randolph all the credit to which he was entitled. In reality, there were few points of temper, disposition, judgment, or even political views, where there was much room for congeniality between the two men. The last portion of this remark may sound strangely, as Randolph was an ultra State-rights man, and was as austerely as Jefferson in favor of simple, pure, and republican forms. But his democracy was mostly theoretical. Indeed, it ceased to be even his theory. Burke became his political idol, and this early and fiery champion of republicanism spent his last days in raving and gibbering through his desolate ancestral halls against the overthrow of entails and aristocracy in Virginia; and he justly held Jefferson accountable as their overthrower. We should not quite tell the whole story if we should omit to mention that there was an imputed proximate cause for Randolph's defection from the Administration. Christopher Clark, his colleague and warm admirer, having heard him often speak of making a voyage to Europe at this period, applied to the President and Secretary of State to give him the English mission. Mr. Clark pushed his point far enough to discover that neither Jefferson nor Madison considered Mr. Randolph fitted for that position. It was not

The breach having been effected, Randolph soon threw off the restraints of moderation. Varnum, Bidwell, and other Republican leaders, who continued to be treated exactly as he himself had been treated by the President, and who made no more sacrifices of personal independence than he had done, were "Charles Jenkinsons"—"backstairs favorites" to "carry down secret messages to the House"—and, as if venom was not perfect without scurrility, he has the credit on one occasion of having stigmatized them as "the pages of the Presidential water-closet!" It is not necessary to enlarge on this class of details.

Such was the origin of the "Quids;" for the little handful that followed Mr. Randolph subsequently took that name. One of their earliest measures was to concert an opposition to Madison for the succession, and for that object they made themselves clamorous advocates of Monroe. In a letter to the latter, soon after the close of the session (May 4th) the President thus characteristically gave his impressions of Randolph's defection, and the history of its result:

"Our old friend, Mercer, broke off from us some time ago; at first professing to disdain joining the Federalists, yet, from the habit of voting together, becoming soon identified with them. Without carrying over with him one single person, he is now in a state of as perfect obscurity as if his name had never been known. Mr. J. Randolph is in the same track, and will end in the same way. His course has excited considerable alarm. Timid men consider it as a proof of the weakness of our Government, and that it is to be rent into pieces by demagogues, and to end in anarchy. I survey the scene with a different eye, and draw a different augury from it. In a House of Representatives of a great mass of good sense, Mr. Randolph's popular eloquence gave him such advantages as to place him unrivalled as the leader of the House; and, although not conciliatory to those whom he led, principles of duty and patriotism induced many of them to swallow humiliations he subjected them to, and to vote as was right, as long as he kept the path of right himself. The sudden defection of such a man could not but produce a momentary astonishment, and even dismay; but for a moment only. The good sense of the House rallied around its principles, and without any leader pursued steadily the business of the session, did it well, and by a strength of vote which has never before been seen. Upon all trying questions, exclusive of the Federalists, the minority of Republicans voting with him has been from four to six or eight, against from ninety to one hundred; and although he yet treats the Federalists with ineffable contempt, yet, having declared eternal opposition to this Administration, and consequently associated with them in his votes, he will, like Mercer, end with them. The augury I draw

believed that the latter had prompted the application, but it was believed that he resented the refusal as much as if it had been made to himself. A later Administration pursued a different course, but with no different ultimate result.

from this is, that there is a steady, good sense in the Legislature, and in the body of the nation, joined with good intentions, which will lead them to discern and to pursue the public good under all circumstances which can arise, and that no *ignis fatuus* will be able to lead them long astray. In the present case, the public sentiment, as far as declarations of it have yet come in, is, without a single exception, in firm adherence to the Administration.

*   *   *   *   *   *   *   *

"The great body of your friends are among the firmest adherents to the Administration, and in their support of you will suffer Mr. Randolph to have no communications with them. My former letter told you the line which both duty and inclination would lead me sacredly to pursue. But it is unfortunate for you, to be embarrassed with such a *soi-disant* friend. You must not commit yourself to him."

We will resume our account of the proceedings of the first session of the ninth Congress. On the 17th of January (1806), the President communicated a special message in regard to British captures, which were calling out memorials from the merchants of all our seaport towns. He declared that the principle now sought to be overthrown by British authorities (the right of neutrals to trade with belligerents in ports not blockaded and in articles not contraband) was supposed to have been settled in our favor by the joint Commission—and that Great Britain had actually paid us damages, under the awards of that Commission, for infractions of this right. He stated that our minister had made unavailing representations on the subject, and also in regard to impressment, concerning which latter a hope had existed of satisfactory arrangement, but which now had passed away.

The message being referred to a Committee of the Whole, various propositions for retaliatory action rapidly followed. Gregg, of Pennsylvania, moved to suspend all further importations from Great Britain until satisfactory arrangements were made in regard to captures and impressments.[1] Clay (of the same State) proposed a retaliation in kind for interdictions against American vessels; that foreign vessels should not carry merchandise from the United States to their own ports, or bring their own merchandise to our ports where the same privilege was not extended to American vessels; and that no foreign vessel should import any merchandise into the United States not the product of the nation to which the ship belonged, unless expressly per-

[1] January 29th.

mitted by treaty, or unless during a war to which the United States were parties.[1] Nicholson, of Maryland, moved to exclude various specific articles of the growth or manufacture of Great Britain.[2] Crowninshield, of Massachusetts, moved to cut off all intercourse with European colonies in America, unless American vessels were allowed to share in the export and import trade. Sloan, of New Jersey, moved that all intercourse with the British dominions should cease within a specified time, unless she restored our impressed seamen and discharged and made reparation for detaining our vessels contrary to the law of nations.[3]

Gregg's resolution was the principal one discussed. The opposition attacked it on the ground that it was a war measure in disguise. Its friends " say, it is true," exclaimed Randolph, "that it is not a war measure, but they defend it on principles that would justify none but war measures, and seem pleased with the idea that it may prove the forerunner of war." He denounced our carrying trade as most fraudulently conducted— that " whilst we boasted of our honor on this floor, our name had become a by-word among the nations,"—that it was the " spirit of an avaricious traffic [which] would plunge us in war "—and he said " if this great agricultural nation is to be governed by Salem and Boston, New York and Philadelphia, and Baltimore, and Norfolk, and Charleston, let gentlemen come out and say so."

This narrow argument was not a very palatable one to the Federalists of New England; but they were willing to take Mr. Randolph's spurning help, on any terms. His " independence " was warmly eulogized; and thenceforth these remote extremes were generally found practically acting together against the Administration.

On the 13th of March, the House divided on a motion to discharge the Committee of the Whole from the further consideration of Gregg's resolution, and the vote stood yeas, twenty-four —nays, one hundred and one ; and on a like motion in regard to Sloan's resolution, the vote stood yeas, twenty-six—nays, ninety-eight.

On the 26th of March, the question was taken on the bill which reflected the wishes of the President. It provided that after the 15th day of the ensuing November—nearly eight months in advance—certain specified articles should no longer be imported from the British dominions, or from elsewhere, if of British production. This partial prohibition would be much less offensive to England—would incidentally favor branches of our own industry—and the delay would give ample time for adjustment with that power, and a consequent repeal of the law before it should go into operation. The vote on its passage stood, yeas, ninety-three—nays, thirty-two. The entire body of the Federalists voted in the negative, and with them John Randolph and his friends. The bill passed the Senate, April 15th, by a vote of nineteen to nine, J. Q. Adams voting with the majority, and Adair, Logan, Stone, and Sumpter, Republican senators, voting with the Federal minority.

The precautionary regulations made at the last session, against a contraband trade between our merchants and St. Domingo, had not proved effectual, and an act was passed to entirely prohibit all intercourse with the revolted provinces, for a year, unless the prohibition should be sooner removed by the President.

Congress appropriated one hundred and fifty thousand dollars to enable the President to cause the ports and harbors of the United States to be better fortified and protected—two hundred and fifty thousand dollars to enable him to cause fifty gunboats to be constructed—twenty thousand dollars to enable him to man and equip them—and he was authorized to direct any of the armed vessels of the United States to be sold, whenever he judged them too much out of repair to be profitably refitted. He was empowered to call as many of the public vessels as he should deem proper into service, the only restriction being on the number of seamen employed. He was authorized to require the State Executives to organize, equip, and hold in readiness to march at a moment's warning, one hundred thousand militia, and to call this force into service " when he should judge the exigencies of the United States required it."

The slenderness of the military appropriations shows probably two or three things—that there was a strong expectation of averting war—that if it ultimately came, the Government expected to rely mainly on citizen soldiery—and lastly, that, in those days, money was a scarce commodity.

A law was enacted to appoint commissioners to lay out a road from Cumberland, in Maryland, to the State of Ohio, their report to be subject to the approval of the President. If he approved, he was to obtain the consent of the States through which the road was to pass, and cause it to be constructed.

This bill passed without much discussion, and in glancing through the debates, we have not noticed that any question was then raised as to its constitutionality.[1] In the act of Congress of April 30th, 1802, to enable the people of Ohio to form a State government, it had been provided that in consideration the lands within the State sold by the General Government should be exempted by an irrevocable ordinance from all kinds of State taxes for five years, after such sale (a measure, designed to favor emigration to this frontier territory at a time esteemed critical), one twentieth part of the net proceeds of the government lands sold in the State " should be applied to the laying out and making public roads, leading from the navigable waters emptying into the Atlantic, to the Ohio, to the said State, and through the same ; such roads to be laid out under the authority of Congress, with the consent of the several States through which the road should pass."

By the act of Congress of March 3d, 1803, it was further provided that three per cent. of the net proceeds of the public lands therein should be paid to the State, to be applied to opening and making roads, "and to no other purpose whatever." A committee reported in the Senate, December 18th, 1805, that the net proceeds of the sales of the public lands in the State from July 1, 1803, to September 30, 1805, amounted to $632,604 27, and that the sum then subject to the uses directed by the law of 1802 amounted to $12,652, and was steadily accumulating. It was under these circumstances that the bill for the construction of the " National road," as it was termed, passed.

It is apparent that this law did not stand on the same footing with one which should assume to the General Government the right of constructing post-roads promiscuously, and from any funds in the Treasury, even with the consent of the States. Ohio was allowed, for a valuable consideration, to reap the incidental advantage of an avenue between the sea-board and the Mississippi, which (when the act of 1802 was passed) equally had the military protection of our frontiers in view. In 1806, Congress

---

[1] But we may have overlooked some thing of this kind.

also had the military as well as other national connections of the East and West distinctly in view, and it was too late, in the latter year, to raise constitutional objections, unless the Government desired, under that plea, to break its faith with the State of Ohio. It would not have redeemed that faith merely to grant the money to the State. She could not make provisions to disburse moneys in road-building in other States. The United States had as much contracted to supervise the construction of the road, as to appropriate the specified funds. And it was not generally thought, in 1806, that the bond of connection between the eastern and western States was so perfectly solid and permanent in its texture that all additions to its strength were supererogatory, or that it was best to test that strength by a breach of faith based on a scruple which was not allowed to weigh when a contract important to the interests of the West was deliberately entered into by our Government. On the final passage of the bill the vote stood, in the House, yeas sixty-six, nays fifty. In the Senate, no vote by yeas and nays appears to have been taken. The objections of the minority seem to have been to the time of action, or to the particular location of the road. The division was not a party one, and perhaps as many "strict constructionists" of the Constitution voted in the affirmative as the negative. Such was the origin of a measure which ultimately grew so far beyond its original and constitutional objects, and led to such an abyss of Congressional "log-rolling" and corruption, that its progress was happily arrested by an Executive veto.

The United States coast survey originated at this session, in an appropriation of five thousand dollars, to be expended by the Secretary of the Treasury in causing the coast of North Carolina, between Cape Hatteras and Cape Fear, to be surveyed.

An act was passed (after severe opposition from the Federalists, aided by Randolph and his followers), continuing the collection of the "Mediterranean Fund," to the end of the next session of Congress.

Among the important measures that failed during the session was one to complete six ships of the line, the materials for which had been mostly collected during Mr. Adams's Administration. A bill was introduced to tax the importation of slaves ten dollars a head, the Constitution having prevented an entire inhi bition of that importation before 1808. After the consumption of much time, and the usual bandying of recriminations between, in commercial phrase, the "importers and consumers" of the article, the subject was allowed to go over to the next session. Congress adjourned on the 21st of April.

The Administration had passed a severe ordeal, and passed it with its strength essentially unbroken. Reports had been industriously circulated that the President gave his ear entirely to the eastern Republicans, that he was estranged from those of the South, and that alarming dissensions existed in the Cabinet proper. The last of these allegations was without a shadow of foundation.[1] The two first were believed by nobody, unless by Randolph and his little faction of Quids, in the House, and by such Republican senators as Bradley, of Vermont. And the splintering off of this fragment, so far from weakening, actually strengthened the Administration. It is said a crushed insurrection gives solidity to a government. A party insurrection commenced under such imposing auspices, urged with a vindictiveness exceeding that of former enemies, and resulting in so trifling a loss, was well calculated to increase popular confidence in the strength of the Administration, and to teach uneasy coteries and individuals that their opposition would prove dangerous only to themselves.

A circumstance occurred in the closing hours of the late session, which is so inaccurately, not to say fantastically, described in Garland's Life of John Randolph, and which so nearly concerns those connected with the subject of this biography, and indirectly, Mr. Jefferson himself, that we cannot pass it over in silence. Randoph, who had for months been in open and avowed hostility to the Administration, is represented by his biographer as its friend, but as a friend whom, on account of his independence and honesty, it was necessary to "silence or drive into the ranks of the Federalists." Mr. Garland melodramatically says:

"The plot was now ripe for execution: like Cæsar, he was to fall on the floor of the Senate by the hands of his treacherous friends. The evening of the 21st of April, on the final adjournment of the House, was selected as the time—that parting hour, usually given up to hilarity, to friendship, and an oblivious forgetfulness of all

---

[1] See President's letter to Duane, of March 22d, 1806; and to Gallatin, October 12th, 1806.

past animosities, was chosen as the fit occasion to stab to the heart one who should have been their pride and their ornament. . . . . . As the dim shades of night were gathering over the legislative hall, while the dim light of the taper served only to make darkness visible, the conspirators, each with his part well conned and prepared, commenced the assault on their unsuspecting victim, who sat as a confiding friend in their midst."

He proceeds to narrate what took place, in about an equal vein of truthfulness and consistency. Those who wish to read his account in full, must turn to his Life of Randolph (vol. i., p. 247). The substance of it, and all of it that is of any importance, in this connection, will be found mentioned, and most effectually answered, in the following letter, from one of the sons of Thomas Mann Randolph:

To HENRY S. RANDALL.

RICHMOND, *Feb. 8th,* 1856.

DEAR SIR:

You ask me to give a correct account of the personal difficulty between John Randolph of Roanoke and my father, Thomas Mann Randolph, which has been introduced into the biography of the former, written by Hugh A. Garland. As you may well suppose from your knowledge of my father's character, Mr. Garland's story is thoroughly inaccurate.

He attributes the collision to a supposed conspiracy planned by Messrs. Findley, Sloane and T. M. Randolph, the object of which was to crush Mr. John Randolph. Mr. Garland's sole authority for this alleged conspiracy is an anonymous letter in the Aurora, signed " A Citizen," and manifestly the production of a warm partisan. This letter has been incorporated literally in Mr. Garland's book, although it was publicly contradicted in the Intelligencer at the time of its publication, and betrays its want of truth on its face. The conspirators are said to have been prepared each " with his part well conned," and are then introduced in a condition indicating anything else rather than cool preparation. Mr. Findlay we are told was " very much intoxicated;" Mr. T. M. Randolph was boiling with " rage and defiance ;" while Mr. Sloane embraced the opportunity of " slily thrusting his fangs " into Mr. John Randolph's side. The " very mild, dignified and conciliatory " deportment of the latter, strange to say, was the immediate cause of Mr. T. M. Randolph's anger, who " vociferated " a tirade of abuse, demanded an explanation from his adversary when called on for an apology, and on that explanation being refused, apologized himself in the humblest manner.

The wanton disregard of fact in Mr. Garland's narrative will be best exhibited by an account of the affair deduced from contemporaneous publications in the Va. Argus, the Enquirer and the Intelligencer, of May, June and July, 1806.

From these publications we learn that on the last night of the ninth Congress, Mr. S. R. Williams, while discussing the salt duties, used some warm language, for which he was called to order by Mr. T. M. Randolph. Soon afterwards Mr. John Randolph took the floor and began his remarks by saying, " What has thrown us into this heat?—is it the dinner we have just eaten ? I hope no honorable gentleman who has heretofore kept the noiseless tenor of his way, because we have adjourned for half an hour, has permitted his passions to indulge in an asperity not shown on any former occasion." This "mild," "dignified," and "conciliatory" insinuation that some honorable gentleman was intoxicated, following immediately upon Mr. T. M. Randolph's call to order, was supposed by that gentleman to be pointed at him. On the vote being taken, he requested permission to reply to Mr. John Randolph, a request seconded by the latter in a manner deemed offensive. The permission being given, Mr. T. M. Randolph began his remarks as follows : "It is true, as the gentleman says, that I have not made much noise this session, and it is as true that he has made more than is useful." He then proceeded to animadvert on the course of Mr. John Randolph, in observations at least respectable in manner and style, and wholly different from the miserable tirade ascribed to him by Mr. Garland on the authority of a person writing from memory two weeks after the transaction.[1]

On resuming his seat he was called on by Mr. Garnett, of Va., as the friend of Mr. John Randolph, and asked whether the remarks just made were intended for him ; that if they were, a demand for satisfaction would be made. Mr. T. M. Randolph avowed that his remarks were meant for Mr. John Randolph, and were designed as a retaliation for the offensive expressions of that gentlemen. He professed himself ready to give the satisfaction required, brought his friend, Mr. Coles, and repeated to him in the presence of Mr. Garnett what had passed between that gentleman and himself. In the conversation that ensued, Mr. Garnett stated explicitly that Mr. John Randolph's remarks were not intended for Mr. T. M. Randolph, whereupon the latter expressed his willingness to make "any reparation that a man of honor might make."

Mr. Garnett retired to get a formal disclaimer from his principal, and Mr. T. M. Randolph returned to his seat. Here he was assured by all around him of his mistake, and informed of its being whispered that his retort was in pursuance of a preconcerted plan. Neither Mr. Coles nor Mr. Garnett came ; the session was about to close, the affair seemed to be settled, and there was danger of his losing the only opportunity of repairing the injustice he had done. Accordingly Mr. T. M. Randolph rose, and saying, "I have been told by six or seven gentlemen that the words were meant for another," expressed his regret for what he had said. He unquestionably supposed Mr. Garnett authorized to make the statement that he had made, as is proved by a note appended to the foregoing sentence in the contemporaneous report of the National Intelligencer. It is in these words : "Among them,[2] one whose authority was beyond question."

In the meanwhile Mr. Garnett found Mr. John Randolph, who considered himself so situated that he could make no explanation. Mr. Garnett returned to communicate this fact to Mr. Coles, and to make arrangements for a meeting if Mr. T. M. Randolph should decline to apologize ; but Mr. Coles, who was the private secretary of the President, had been called off on public business. When Mr. Garnett found him, Mr. T. M. Randolph had made his apology to the House, and Messrs. Coles and Garnett determined on consultation to say nothing of Mr. John Randolph's refusal to explain.

And yet, from Mr. Garland's book, it would be supposed that this refusal was communicated to Mr. T. M. Randolph, and even hastened his apology. The fact was not divulged until two or three weeks afterwards, when the anonymous writer, already mentioned, published an account of the scene in the House of Representa-

---

[1] T. M. Randolph's remarks on this occasion will be found in the Annals of Congress, and they more than bear out the assertions of his son.
[2] Id est, T. M. Randolph's informants.

tives so grossly inaccurate that the editor of the Intelligencer, "after correcting his account of the affair by notes taken at the time," published it to refute the misrepresentations of "A Citizen." Mr. John Randolph thereupon published a card in the Enquirer, denouncing the report of the Intelligencer, and especially the note implying that he had authorized Mr. Garnett to make an explanation. Mr. T. M. Randolph followed, in a card stigmatizing Mr. John Randolph's publication as "incorrect," "unjust," "haughty," and "extravagant," declaring that his own pacific conduct was induced by the belief that Mr. Garnett sought "accommodation;" that "a challenge, the thing expected, would have ended discussion," and that "Mr. John Randolph knew he had won no laurel." Neither card was signed by the writer. Messrs. Coles and Garnett confessed that they had suppressed Mr. John Randolph's refusal to explain, and Mr. T. M. Randolph, considering the affair reopened, and doubtless viewing it as if no communications had passed, repaired to Richmond with a second, but no challenge came, and so the matter ended.

For the first part of his narrative, Mr. Garland has adopted the anonymous letter of "A Citizen," without stating that the report of the Intelligencer, "corrected by contemporaneous notes," was published in advance of its regular time for the avowed purpose of refuting such misrepresentations as those made by "A Citizen."

For the latter part of his narrative, he has adopted the statement of Mr. John Randolph, without stating that its correctness was denied by Mr. T. M. Randolph, and that in the all-important fact of the knowledge by the latter of Mr. John Randolph's refusal to explain, it turned out to be erroneous.

Yet the same files of newspapers which furnished one side of the story supplied the other. It is difficult therefore to acquit Mr. Garland of intentional misrepresentation, or at least of great negligence with reference to his facts. If he considered it worthy of recording, it was certainly worth recording correctly. I have endeavored in the above statement to do justice to all concerned.

Very truly, yours,

GEO. W. RANDOLPH.

A letter from President Jefferson to Mr. Duane, editor of the Aurora, March 22d, 1806, contains the following passages:

"That the expedition of Miranda was countenanced by me, is an absolute falsehood, let it have gone from whom it might; and I am satisfied it is equally so as to Mr. Madison. To know as much of it as we could was our duty, but not to encourage it."

This remark was called out by the following circumstances. Miranda having failed in securing the final coöperation of England in his South American projects, and having been expelled from France by Napoleon for alleged political intrigues, came to the United States. By the aid of Samuel J. Ogden and William S. Smith he fitted out a vessel at New York in 1806, with two or three hundred men, and a supply of arms to act against the government of Caraccas. The vessel sailed in

February. The Government ordered Ogden and Smith to be prosecuted for a violation of the neutrality laws. They memorialized Congress to the effect that if they had committed an error they had been led into it " by the conduct of officers of the Executive Government, who now intended to bring upon the memorialists the penalties of the laws, to sacrifice their characters, fortunes, and liberty in expiation of their own errors, or to deprecate the vengeance of foreign governments, by offering the memorialists as a victim to their resentment," and they asked such relief " as the wisdom of Congress might think proper to grant." They also made various imputations against the judges before whom the legal proceedings against them had been instituted. Josiah Quincy, of Massachusetts, presented the memorial containing these allegations to the House, April 21, 1806; and he declared that " the information contained in some of those statements was corroborated by information known to some gentlemen on the floor—that the Executive had been advised of the fitting out of the Leander [Miranda's vessel] time enough to have prevented her sailing."

Alston, of North Carolina, declared that any member of Congress who possessed such information was as criminal as the President or Secretary of State was alleged to be. Jackson, of Virginia, pronounced Quincy's allegations "false " " and a base calumny." Quincy soon attempted to qualify his assertions, and Jackson contradicted the correctness of his explanation. Finally, Quincy utterly retracted, by saying that, " in making the remarks he had offered, he did not mean to criminate the Administration "—that " if his words bore such a meaning, he withdrew them—such was not his intention."

Mr. Early offered a resolution that the charges in the memorial were " unsupported by any evidence which in the least degree criminated the Executive Government of this country "—that the memorial was presented " at a time and under circumstances insidiously calculated " to excite unjust suspicions—that it would be highly improper for Congress to interfere in a matter pending in the courts—and that the memorials be returned by the clerk " to those from whom they came." The previous question was ordered by a vote of seventy-four to fifteen.—The resolution was divided, and the first clause (exonerating the Administration) was carried by a vote of seventy-five against eight;

the second, characterizing the design of the memorial as "insidious," by a vote of seventy to thirteen; the third, declaring it improper for Congress to interfere, by a unanimous vote; the fourth, ordering the memorial to be returned to its makers, by a vote of seventy-one to fourteen. If we consider that about three-fourths of the opposition voted with the majority, or did not vote at all, and that less than half of it voted against any clause of the resolution, a more signal vindication of the Administration could not be conceived.

It might as well here be added, that Miranda's expedition ended in failure. With a little English assistance he took a town or two in Caraccas (or Venezuela) but the inhabitants did not favor him, and he was compelled to reëmbark. He repeated his attempt in 1810, and with more effect, but within a couple of years was defeated, taken a prisoner and sent to Spain, where he died after a four years' incarceration in the dungeons of the Inquisition.

Ogden and Smith were acquitted on their trial for a violation of the neutrality laws; and, as party accusations then ran, by the verdict of a jury packed for that object by the United States marshal, Swartwout, a special friend and adherent of Aaron Burr. Swartwout was turned out of office.

The President, in a letter, April 13th, pressing Wilson C. Nicholas to come into the Senate,[1] in the place of Giles, whose health had again failed, gave the following picture of the political state of that body:

"Giles's absence has been a most serious misfortune. A majority of the Senate means well. But Tracy and Bayard are too dexterous for them, and have very much influenced their proceedings. Tracy has been of nearly every committee during the session, and for the most part the chairman and of course drawer of the reports. Seven Federalists voting always in phalanx, and joined by some discontented Republicans, some oblique ones, some capricious, have so often made a majority as to produce very serious embarrassment to the public operations; and very much do I dread the submitting to them, at the next session, any treaty which can be made with either England or Spain, when I consider that five joining the Federalists can defeat a friendly settlement of our affairs."

[1] He had a short time before (March 24th) pressed Mr. Nicholas to accept a joint commission with Armstrong and Bowdoin (our ministers to France and Spain) to attempt a friendly settlement of all outstanding questions with Spain. Colonel Nicholas's private affairs did not permit his acceptance, and the plan of a third commissioner was soon after dropped.

It was the question of the Presidential succession which produced all these embarrassments—though judging from the records of Congress they are very strongly stated in the preceding extract. We apprehend Mr. Jefferson wrote in a moment of unusual depression.

On the 18th of April the President addressed Mr. Leavitt Harris, American consul at St. Petersburg, inclosing a letter to the Emperor Alexander. It was in answer to one received from that monarch, dated 20th of August preceding. The President's communication was couched in that language of courtesy with which it is the custom to address such potentates, but its pith did not consist of compliments. It made an earnest and, though shrewd, manly appeal to the Czar to exert his powerful interposition in behalf of the rights of neutrals, in the general pacification of Europe, then anticipated in consequence of the death of Pitt and the accession of Fox to the English ministry.

At the same time the President accepted from Harris a bust of Alexander, with many complimentary expressions, and avowing that his respect for the latter induced him to depart from a rule which had hitherto known no exception, not to accept any present beyond "a book or a pamphlet, or some other curiosity of minor value, as well to avoid imputation on his motives of action as to shut out a practice susceptible of such abuse." [1]

Doubtless some diplomacy may be discovered in Mr. Jefferson's conduct on this occasion, but it is certain from his writings and recollected conversations that he felt a sincere regard for that young, virtuous, and able monarch, who, notwithstanding his possession of unlimited authority, entertained many of the liberal views in which he had been educated by La Harpe; and who exhibited them by his inquiries respecting our republican institutions and by a sort of personal overture to the President, which was understood to evince extraordinary respect for his abilities and character. This was the beginning of that friendly understanding between Russia and the United States, which has become traditionary in their policies.

The President's views of the political consequences of the death of Mr. Pitt, and his real feelings towards England, find a

---

[1] This rule was rigidly adhered to until the close of his Administration. We get his ideas of what constitutes " minor value " in the fact that he refused to accept a carved ivory case, directing it to be returned to the donor.

clear exposition in a letter to the American minister to England, Mr. Monroe (May 4th):

"The late change in the ministry I consider as ensuring us a just settlement of our differences, and we ask no more. In Mr. Fox, personally, I have more confidence than in any man in England, and it is founded in what, through unquestionable channels, I have had opportunities of knowing of his honesty and his good sense. While he shall be in the administration, my reliance on that Government will be solid. We had committed ourselves in a line of proceedings adapted to meet Mr. Pitt's policy and hostility, before we heard of his death, which self-respect did not permit us to abandon afterwards; and the late unparalleled outrage on us at New York, excited such sentiments in the public at large, as did not permit us to do less than has been done. It ought not to be viewed by the ministry as looking towards them at all, but merely as the consequences of the measures of their predecessors, which their nation has called on them to correct. I hope, therefore, they will come to just arrangements. No two countries upon earth have so many points of common interest and friendship; and their rulers must be great bunglers indeed, if, with such dispositions, they break them asunder. The only rivalry that can arise is on the ocean. England may, by petty larceny thwartings, check us on that element a little, but nothing she can do will retard us there one year's growth. We shall be supported there by other nations, and thrown into their scale to make a part of the great counterpoise to her navy. If, on the other hand, she is just to us, conciliatory, and encourages the sentiment of family feelings and conduct, it cannot fail to befriend the security of both. We have the seamen and materials for fifty ships of the line, and half that number of frigates; and were France to give us the money, and England the dispositions to equip them, they would give to England serious proofs of the stock from which they are sprung, and the school in which they have been taught; and added to the efforts of the immensity of sea-coast lately united under one power, would leave the state of the ocean no longer problematical. Were, on the other hand, England to give the money, and France the dispositions to place us on the sea in all our force, the whole world, out of the continent of Europe, might be our joint monopoly. We wish for neither of these scenes. We ask for peace and justice from all nations; and we will remain uprightly neutral in fact, though leaning in belief to the opinion that an English ascendency on the ocean is safer for us than that of France."

And he added :

"We begin to broach the idea that we consider the whole Gulf Stream as of our waters, in which hostilities and cruising are to be frowned on for the present, and prohibited so soon as either consent or force will permit us. We shall never permit another privateer to cruise within it, and shall forbid our harbors to national cruisers. This is essential for our tranquillity and commerce."

"The late unparalleled outrage on us at New York," referred to by the President, consisted in the firing a shot by the commander of a British vessel of war (Captain Whitby, of the Leander), into an American coasting vessel, near Sandy Hook, by which a person on board of her was killed. The President immediately (May 3d) issued a proclamation, ordering the Leander and two other ships in her company out of the American waters; calling upon the civil and military officers of the United States to arrest Captain Whitby; and warning all persons against giving aid to those ships, under the penalties of the law.

The President's feelings against the Pitt administration are more strongly expressed in a letter to Mr. Digges, July 1st:

"He [Mr. Jefferson] would be happy to see Mr. Digges and his friends on the fourth of July, and to join in congratulations on the return of the day which divorced us from the follies and crimes of Europe, from a dollar in the pound at least of six hundred millions sterling, and from all the ruin of Mr. Pitt's administration. We, too, shall encounter follies; but if great, they will be short, if long, they will be light; and the vigor of our country will get the better of them. Mr. Pitt's follies have been great, long, and inflicted on a body emaciated with age, and exhausted by excesses beyond its power to bear."

In a letter to Bowdoin, our Spanish minister, July 10th, he declared if the latter could obtain Florida, it would " fill the American mind with joy." He thought that we should cut off the impressment of our seamen by England, and establish the inviolability of our flag. He " sincerely wished to be honestly neutral and truly useful to both belligerents." He warmly invited arrangements with France and Spain which would secure permanent peace and friendship with them.

Thus, to the President's sanguine hopes, the thread of old complications had been cut by the death of Pitt and accession of Fox. The storm which had lowered so darkly from all points of the horizon had suddenly given place to bright sunshine. But its radiance was to be but transient. Fox, striken by incurable disease, was hastening to the grave, and with him were to perish all traces of liberality towards the United States, during the reign of George III.

The year 1806 was also marked by domestic political triumphs. The Republicans carried the Legislature of Massachusetts, and consequently the executive council; and they came within a few votes of electing their Governor. Connecticut and Delaware were now all the Federal States that held out, and it may be doubted whether this, in the former, was not in a great measure owing to the imprudence of some leading Republicans in that State, who, without consulting the President, and greatly to his regret and chagrin, commenced prosecutions in the United States district courts against two or three of their fellow-citizens who had published libels against him.

In August, John Randolph, so signally foiled in Congress in his attempt against the Administration, made a popular appeal against it in the newspapers. He published two articles over the signature of Decius, in which he complained of the conduct of our foreign negotiations in various specified particulars; accused the Cabinet of having one set of opinions for the public and another to secretly influence the action of Congress; insisted that a purchase of the Floridas would be in direct opposition to the President's public message on the subject; and he rung the usual changes in respect to "back-stairs" influence. In proof of his allegations, Mr. Randolph took the liberty of publishing the President's confidential message of December 6th, 1805, from which the injunction of secrecy had not been raised.

The allegations were little besides a repetition of their author's speeches in Congress. But they were answered in the newspapers, by William A. Burwell, a Virginia member of Congress whom we have already had occasion to mention, and of whom Professor Tucker justly remarks, that his "State had seldom had an abler and never an honester representative."[1] Burwell transmitted copies of his replies to the President, and they found him at Monticello, where the Secretary of State and Secretary of War were, at the time, his guests. Both of these officers concurred with the President in recollections which distinctly refuted Randolph at every material point. Those who retain any interest in the controversy, will find these recollections stated in a letter to Burwell published in Mr. Jefferson's correspondence, under date of September 17th.

The autumn of 1805 was made a memorable epoch in American history, by the treasonable projects of Aaron Burr. He left the Vice-Presidency in the spring of that year an utterly ruined man in fame and fortune, and with indictments for murder hanging over him in the States of New York and New Jersey.[2] These circumstances were sufficient to drive a man

---

[1] Life of Jefferson.

[2] Burr had been paying his addresses to a lady in Philadelphia before the duel, and he renewed them immediately afterwards. But he soon found he must fly. At this moment he wrote his daughter: "If any male friend of yours should be dying of *ennui*, recommend him to engage in a duel and a courtship at the same time."

wholly unprincipled and ambitious, into any scheme which
promised to mend his broken fortunes. He proceeded to the
western States with, it would seem, several projects occupying
his mind. One of the nominal ones, at least, was the construction of a canal round the Falls of the Ohio. Jonathan Dayton,
long so conspicuous in New Jersey politics, was concerned in
this speculation, and General Wilkinson, the Commander-in-
Chief of the army, and the newly appointed Governor of the
Louisiana territory, was offered a share in it. Burr reached
Pittsburg on the 30th of April, and early in May stopped at
Blennerhasset's Island, near Marietta, in the Ohio—that scene
painted in such Claude-like glory of coloring by William Wirt.
The "Serpent" entered this "Eden" to forever poison its
peace—to make Blennerhasset and his "angel-like wife" the
dupes and instruments of a desperate and dishonorable adven-
turer.

From thence Burr proceeded to Lexington, and on the 29th
of May reached Nashville, where he met General Andrew Jackson. He continued his Journey to New Orleans, and was received with much attention. Returning to Nashville (August
16th), he spent a week with General Jackson, whom he speaks
of with much admiration in his journal.[1] He retraced his steps
and arrived in Washington in November. This journey develops
nothing of importance, except that Burr threw out hints of some
great enterprise to Wilkinson, which, he carried the idea, was
favored by the Government. But he, at the same time, spoke
with great bitterness of the Administration, and declared that
the people of the West were ripe for a revolt. Wilkinson wrote
to the Secretary of the Navy, apprising him of these facts, and
advising that Burr's movements be closely watched.[2]

Burr spent the winter of 1805–6 in Washington, attempting
to tamper with General Eaton (recently returned from Tripoli),
Commodore Truxton, and others. Every important person of
military ability who was supposed to be at variance with the
Administration, was approached by him, and he made the most
artful efforts to increase their discontents. This was particu-

---

[1] Q. v. in Davis's Life of Burr, vol. ii., p. 372.
[2] Smith did not receive the letter, but Wilkinson's aid-de-camp testified, on Burr's
trial, that the letter was copied by him, and he believed dispatched through the post-
office.

larly the case with Eaton, and having, as he supposed, brought that impetuous man's feelings to the proper point, he advanced, in the explanation of his views, from a talked about expedition against the Mexican provinces (his starting-point with all to whom he broached his projects), to the avowal of a purpose to revolutionize our own western States and to found an empire whose capital was to be New Orleans. He said this must ultimately take place; that an independent government was as much a right of the western people, as it was a right of the Atlantic States to be independent of Great Britain; that if he could gain over the naval commanders, he could turn Congress out of doors, dispose of the President, and establish a government that had "energy." He informed Eaton that Wilkinson took part in his enterprise, and would carry with him all the regular troops in the West; that ten or twelve thousand western volunteers would join his standard; and that many in the Spanish provinces were ready to do the same. He offered Eaton a high command if he would join him.

On receiving these startling disclosures, the latter waited on the President, and proposed to him to send Burr on a foreign mission, alleging that otherwise there would be an insurrection, if not a rebellion, in the western States within eighteen months. The President declined, saying he had entire confidence in the people of those States. At the same time, Eaton communicated the details of his conversation with Burr to two members of Congress from Connecticut.[1]

All these facts were sworn to by Eaton on the subsequent trial of Burr.[2] In explanation of his going to the President with such a proposition, instead of at once disclosing to him all the facts, he said: "On the solitary ground upon which he stood, he was at a loss how to conduct himself, though at no loss as respected his duty—he durst not place his lonely testimony in the balance against the weight of Colonel Burr's character, for by turning the tables on him, which he thought any man capable of such a project, was very capable of doing, he [Eaton] should sink under the weight." He said he perceived "that the sub-

[1] He so testified on Burr's trial, and was not pressed on the point, it being probably understood that the members of Congress (Dana and Smith) would confirm his statements if brought to the witness stand.
[2] Q. v., taken in short hand by David Robinson, vol. i., p. 474 et seq.

ject was disagreeable to the President"—and that " the circumstance of no interrogatories being made to him, he thought imposed silence upon him at that time and place."

The President well knew that General Eaton was " disaffected towards the Government."[1] He had been seen much in the company of Burr—and perhaps, therefore, his motives were suspected.[2] He had a stately way of talking, which sometimes gave an air of extravagance to what he said. The story sounded monstrous—and the President had, as usual, a thorough confidence in the people.

Much doubt has been supposed to rest on the real intentions of Burr; and it has been difficult for impartial men to believe that he meditated a thing which would now seem to have been so purely chimerical as an attempt to dismember the Union without the aid of any great agitating question between its parts —without the prevalence of ostensible disaffection in either part—and without fortune or popularity of his own to bribe or inveigle a large body of men into such an undertaking.[3] There were, however, deep concealed disaffections both in the East and the West. Those in the East will be hereafter more particularly stated, and Burr's contemporaneous knowledge and apparent approbation of them, established on the evidence of an eminent participator in the disaffection, and in the disunion projects to which it gave birth.

It would require a volume to give the mostly unwritten history of the previous intrigues and plots of a set of adventurers sprinkled through the States and territories west of the Alleghanies, which at different periods, or among different persons, tended to various apparent objects, but all of which involved a common idea—a separation of the Western from the Atlantic States. There was another point of agreement between the principal projectors. They all, it is believed, accepted Spanish gold. Spain thus originated the disaffection to prevent the United States from pressing westward on Mexico, forgetting,

---

[1] That is, towards the Administration. The words are quoted from Eaton's testimony.

[2] It will be remembered that it was not far from this time that Burr himself was applying to the President for an office. It would therefore appear that Eaton's conjecture was probably correct as to what would then have been the effect of giving him a foreign mission.

[3] We once, on less examination, scouted (in a published review) the idea that he entertained such a project.

at political blindness which had long cursed her coun-
it success would only give her colonial possessions a
angerous neighbor. It appears probable, indeed, that
the recipients of her bribes in the western States played
her from the first. They had no intention of becoming
ient to Spain. Their grand idea appears to have been
y to dismember the United States, but also Mexico; or
they proposed to unite Mexico with the western Ameri-
:es, and thus build up a vast empire from the Allegha-
the Pacific, which should be equally independent of
nd the United States.

e projects perhaps hardly reached the maturity of defi-
ns—they scarcely rose above hopes—until Burr came to
and combine the elements of conspiracy, and take the
its execution. He was precisely the leader to inspire
.ce among these restless and debauched adventurers, and
is to have habitually relied on such men to effect his

· possessed much cunning and much penetration of a
ar kind; but, like most wholly unprincipled men, he
d the power of evil. He believed every man and
had their easy price. He therefore relied on personal
:es, and petty intrigue and finessing, to attain objects
beyond the reach of such means. He baited mouse-
:pecting to catch elephants in them. His life-long his-
in exemplification of this trait of mind, and it is a life-
l of failures. In every great crisis of his career we find
h intense cunning in his look, and mystery in his rapid
:nts, setting his little traps. But he was always just wise
to be outgeneralled when he came in contact with a
in; he was always just artful enough to beat himself.
: any attempts to be cunning, and by mere force of his
, and a straightforward life, he might have been far
ccessful. He loved intrigue for its own sake. There
ascination in it which blinded his judgment. He was
, embark in it, and was sanguine of success, where a

> not, by any means, intend to say, that Burr had not, at different periods,
particular friends and supporters, some highly honorable men. But our
ply to the *class* who will be found almost invariably foremost in the execution
nes and personal objects.

man of less astuteness, but without his taste for plotting, would have foreseen the certainty of defeat. It takes another trait to complete the character of a rash and ready conspirator. He was proverbially insensible to danger. He was willing to risk his life to carry out the most paltry amour. He was willing to risk it a thousand times in any desperate effort for fortune and power, rather than glide along smoothly in the current of a common success. When we consider his peculiar character, and weigh testimony adduced at his subsequent trial, which was not impeached, or even rendered the subject of a just suspicion,[1] little doubt seems to remain that he contemplated a dismemberment of the Union as a direct result of his enterprise, or rather as a contingent result, which was to follow, if success crowned the first branch of the undertaking.

In August, 1806, Burr again went to the western States. In Kentucky he purchased, or pretended to purchase, of Mr. Charles Lynch, a large tract of land near Nachitoches, which the Spanish Governor of New Orleans had ceded to "Baron P. N. Tut Bastrop," before the sale of Louisiana; and by the conditions of the grant it was to be settled by a certain number of persons within a fixed time nearly expired. Burr agreed to pay $50,000 for the land. It would be remarkable that a bankrupt in fortune, avowedly on the eve of attempting the conquest or revolution of Mexico—an undertaking requiring money, and which, if successful, would bring land enough—should pause to divide means raised on credit in such a "speculation." It is not credible. It seems to have been intended as a pretext to enable him to collect the men he desired without interruption from the civil authorities, and probably to fall back upon for safety in case that interruption should take place, and an attempt be

---

[1] The only fact brought to bear against Eaton's testimony was, that after he had exposed Burr's proposals to him, the Government settled his claims for disbursements, etc., in the Barbary war, allowing him $10,000. Eaton had before been pressing his claims, and we presume that no one at this day is ready to believe that he committed a deliberate perjury which might involve the life of a previous *friend*, for the purpose of obtaining either an earlier or more favorable settlement! And Eaton's testimony was amply confirmed in all its essential substance by that of Colonel Morgan and his two sons, General and Thomas Morgan of Cannonsburg, Ohio. No more respectable men, and few better known men, resided in that State. On Burr's journey west, in 1806, they received him in all honor, as a distinguished friend. His first day's stay at Col. Morgan's was marked by such disclosures that that gentleman conceived it his duty to immediately lay them before the judges of a court sitting in the neighborhood. The judges communicated the facts to the President, advising that Burr be watched. Not the most trivial fact was fished up at the trial which tended to cast a shadow of suspicion on the credibility or perfectly honest intentions of the Morgans.

ade to punish him either for treason or a violation of our
utrality laws.

In the fall of 1806, Blennerhasset and other agents of Burr in
e region of Marietta, Ohio, contracted for the building of boats,
rchased quantities of meal, kiln-dried it for a voyage, enlisted
ch men as they could induce to join them, formed a military
icampment at Blennerhasset's Island, received chests of weapons
ere from some higher point on the Ohio, and were joined by
med and organized parties also from above. They made no
ret of the fact that they were acting in concert with and
der the leadership of Burr. To some, persons they declared
it their object was the conquest of Mexico, of which Burr
s to be king—to others the settlement of the Bastrop grant—
I to others, the formation of a new western empire, which
s to include Mexico, Louisiana, and that portion of the United
tes west of the Alleghanies. It was clearly, nay, indisputably
ved that Blennerhasset avowed the latter project to confiden-
friends whom he attempted to draw into the enterprise.
wrote articles for one of the few newspapers west of the
untains, advocating a separation of the western from the
ern States. He and his associates continually declaimed
inst the connection, complaining how much the West had to
for the support of the Government, without receiving any
efit in return.

General Wilkinson, by order of the President, had collected
or six hundred soldiers at Nachitoches to oppose a threat-
d Spanish irruption. This officer was needy in means,
ensive in his habits, and was supposed not to be averse to
culating adventures. He and Burr were familiar acquaint-
es; and the latter seems to have confidently expected to
ce him an accomplice. They corresponded vaguely on the
ject during the summer, Burr assuming, perhaps to make his
imunications more safe from exposure, that his correspondent
w a good deal more of his plans than was actually disclosed:
Wilkinson, afterwards, alleging that his object was to
w Burr to communicate something which would prove his
designs.

Wilkinson must be won, or he would crush the expedition at
outset; and the time arrived which required a decisive
eriment. In October a younger brother of Colonel John

Swartwout of New York reached Wilkinson's camp at Natchitoches, ostensibly to bear a letter of introduction from Jonathan Dayton to Colonel Cushing, the second in command, but carrying secret dispatches in cipher from both Dayton and Burr to Wilkinson. Burr wrote Wilkinson:

"Yours, postmarked 13th of May, is received. I, Aaron Burr, have obtained funds, and have actually commenced the enterprise. Detachments from different points, and under different pretences, will rendezvous on the Ohio, 1st November —everything internal and external, favors views; protection of England is secured. T—— is going to Jamaica to arrange with the Admiral on that station; it will meet on the Mississippi. ——, England, ——, navy of the United States are ready to join, and final orders are given to my friends and followers: it will be a host of choice spirits. Wilkinson shall be second to Burr only, Wilkinson shall dictate the rank and promotion of his officers. Burr will proceed westward, 1st August, never more to return; with him goes his daughter; the husband will follow in October with a corps of worthies.

"Send forth an intelligent and confidential friend with whom Burr may confer; he shall return immediately with further interesting details; this is essential to concert and harmony of movement. Send a list of all persons known to Wilkinson, west of the mountains, who may be useful, with a note delineating their characters. By your messenger send me four or five commissions of your officers, which you can borrow under any pretence you please; they shall be returned faithfully. Already are orders to the contractors given to forward six months' provisions to points Wilkinson may name: this shall not be used until the last moment, and then under proper injunctions. The project is brought to the point so long desired. Burr guarantees the result with his life and honor, with the honor, and fortunes of hundreds of the best blood of our country.

"Burr's plan of operation is, to move down rapidly from the falls on the 15th of September, with the first 500 or 1,000 men in light boats, now constructing for that purpose, to be at Natchez between the 5th and 15th of December; there to meet Wilkinson; there to determine whether it will be expedient in the first instance to seize on or pass by Baton Rouge. On receipt of this send an answer. Draw on Burr for all expenses, etc. The people of the country to which we are going, are prepared to receive us. Their agents, now with Burr, say, that if we will protect their religion, and will not subject them to a foreign power, that in three weeks all will be settled. The gods invite to glory and fortune; it remains to be seen whether we deserve the boon. The bearer of this goes express to you; he will hand a formal letter of introduction to you from Burr. He is a man of inviolable honor and perfect discretion; formed to execute rather than to project; capable of relating facts with fidelity, and incapable of relating them otherwise. He is thoroughly informed of the plans and intentions of Burr, and will disclose to you as far as you inquire, and no farther. He has imbibed a reverence for your character, and may be embarrassed in your presence. Put him at ease, and he will satisfy you."

Dayton wrote Wilkinson (July 24, 1806):

"It is now ascertained that you are to be displaced in next session. Jefferson will affect to yield reluctantly to the public sentiment, but yield he will. Prepare yourself therefore for it. You know the rest. You are not a man to despair, or even despond, especially when such projects offer in another quarter. Are you ready? Are your numerous associates ready Wealth and glory—Louisiana and Mexico. . . . . Dayton."

Wilkinson, having deciphered Burr's letter, communicated its contents to Colonel Cushing, announcing his determination to march immediately to the Sabine, and make such terms with the Spaniards as would enable him to send the greater part of his force for the defence of New Orleans; and in the meantime to forward the information he had obtained to the President.

Wilkinson inquired of Swartwout what would be the course of Burr's expedition. "He said this territory (Louisiana) would be revolutionized, where the people were ready to join them, and that there would be some seizing he supposed at New Orleans; that they expected to be ready to embark about the 1st of February, and intended to land at Vera Cruz, and to march from thence to Mexico." He also intimated that a forced loan would be made from the bank at New Orleans, for the purpose of equipping the expedition.

Wilkinson made an arrangement with the Spaniards, and reached New Orleans on the 25th of November. Claiborne, Governor of Orleans territory, received the following letter, dated November 12th, from General Andrew Jackson, of Tennessee:

"Put your town [New Orleans] in a state of defence, organize your militia, and defend your city as well against internal enemies as external. My knowledge does not extend so far as to authorize me to go into detail, but I fear you will meet an attack from quarters you do not at present expect. Be upon the alert; keep a watchful eye on our General, and beware of an attack as well from your own country as Spain. I fear there is something rotten in the State of Denmark. You have enemies within your own city that may try to subvert your government, and try to separate it from the Union. You know I never hazard ideas without good grounds, you will keep these hints to yourself. But, I say again, be upon the alert; your government, I fear, is in danger; I fear there are plans on foot inimical to the Union; whether they will be attempted to be carried into effect or not I cannot say, but rest assured they are in operation or I calculate boldly. Beware the month of December. I love my country and government; I hate the Dons; I would delight to see Mexico reduced, but I will die in the last ditch before I would yield a foot to the Dons, or see the Union disunited."

This letter lost none of its force from the fact that it betrayed such strong suspicions of Wilkinson, and that the writer was known to have but recently received and entertained Burr in a friendly manner. Suspicions of the former were common in all of those western States where Burr and his emissaries had moved. Whatever other reasons might have existed, for this, there was a very obvious one in the fact that wherever the conspirators had attempted to extend their plot, their first declaration had been that Wilkinson and other principal men in the army and navy were their active confederates.

The most alarming rumors reached New Orleans. Martial law was proclaimed. A meeting of the citizens was held, at which a voluntary embargo was agreed upon to furnish seamen to man the gunboats in the river. The militia was placed under Wilkinson's command, and numerous volunteers offered their services. Strong bodies of troops were kept under arms, and fortifications rapidly erected.

Dr. Bollman, who had communicated with Wilkinson as an avowed emissary of Burr, Swartwout, who had brought Burr's letters to Wilkinson, and Ogden, another active emissary in the conspiracy, were placed under military arrest. Bollman was immediately brought before a judge of the Superior Court by a writ of *habeas corpus*, and Wilkinson returned to the writ that what he had done had been necessary for the safety of the city, and that he should continue to arrest dangerous persons. He sent Bollman and Swartwout to Washington by sea. Some other arrests took place, and sharp contests arose between the Commander-in-Chief and certain judges—they attempting to discharge his prisoners on *habeas corpus*, and he resisting their interference, and in one instance placing in confinement not only the counsel for the prisoner, but the judge who issued the process. Altogether, the scene was much like one witnessed a few years later in the same city, when the officer placing himself in conflict with the civil laws was General Andrew Jackson.

In the latter part of September the President had received some intimations of Burr's movements, but they were too vague to admit of any action, except maintaining a greater watchfulness. Towards the close of October "the objects of the conspiracy began to be perceived, but still so blended and involved in mystery that nothing distinct could be singled out for pursuit."[1] The President, however, immediately dispatched a special agent to the scene of operations, clothed with powers to call upon the

[1] Special Message, January, 22d, 1807.

civil and military authorities to take such steps as circumstances should require. Learning that boats and stores were collecting on the Ohio, and that an unusual number of suspicious characters were in motion, he also dispatched orders to the Governors of Orleans and Mississippi territories, and to the commanders of the land and naval forces, to be on the alert and prepared to resist all illegal attempts. Special orders were forwarded to Wilkinson.

The first communication of the latter officer was received by the President, November 25th; and on the 27th he issued a proclamation warning all persons to withdraw from unlawful enterprises, and dispatched orders "to every intersecting point on the Ohio and Mississippi from Pittsburg to New Orleans" to put the civil authorities in motion, and to direct the employment of the regulars and militia to seize every man and thing connected with Burr's enterprise. As new facts came to light, orders were issued for still wider preparations.

Daviess, the United States Attorney for the district of Kentucky, had, acting on his own information, offered a motion before the District Court sitting at Frankfort, on the third of November, that Burr be brought before the court, to answer a charge of being engaged in an unlawful enterprise. The judge refused to issue the process, but ordered a grand-jury to be impanelled. Burr appeared in court with his counsel, and declared his readiness to meet an immediate investigation. But Daviess could not procure the attendance of his principal witness, and the jury were discharged. On the 25th, the District Attorney applied for a new grand-jury, and subpoenaed General Adair to attend as a witness. The latter did not appear. Daviess moved to be allowed to attend the grand-jury in their room, to examine the witnesses, which he contended was necessary to bring out and explain the connection of testimony in reference to a plot of which the jury had no knowledge. The motion was denied, and the grand-jury not only threw out the bill, but signed a written declaration expressing their belief that Burr meditated nothing dangerous to the peace and well-being of the United States. A motion was granted that a copy of this paper might be taken for insertion in the newspapers. This triumph of the conspirators was celebrated by a ball at Frankfort; and then Burr and Adair departed together.

This turn of affairs has been thought, in some measure, due to the talents, consummate address, and high popularity of one of Burr's counsel, Henry Clay, who had been, six days before, chosen United States senator, to fill the vacancy occasioned by the resignation of Adair himself—and the star of whose professional and political greatness had just begun to beam splendidly on the western horizon. But if any improper or ill-timed proceedings were in part the result of his efforts, none will doubt that he acted under erroneous impressions of the facts. He undoubtedly at the time wholly discredited the charge against Burr.[1]

The proofs at hand were at best very imperfect—Burr had great tact in glossing over his designs, and stopped at no bold deception—Kentucky, at that time, was rent by bitter party and personal feuds, and Daviess, a warm Federalist, was unjustly suspected of having party and personal objects in view. Wilkinson, as has been already said, was distrusted; and if any information of his later movements had reached Kentucky, it was vague, confused, and contradictory. And an *authorized* attempt on Mexico was one of the most popular things which could be proposed in the West.

Graham, the confidential agent of the Government, proceeded to Marietta, and easily drew from Blennerhasset enough

[1] In Mallory's Life of Mr. Clay (prefixed to an edition of his speeches), is given Burr's letter to Clay, when he solicited his aid. In this he disavowed all criminal or illegal intentions. In justice to Mr. Clay, and as a specimen of Burr's matchless effrontery in falsehood, we subjoin an extract from the letter.

"I have no design, nor have I taken any measure, to promote a dissolution of the Union, or a separation of any one or more States from the residue. I have neither published a line on this subject, nor has any one through my agency or with my knowledge. I have no design to intermeddle with the government or to disturb the tranquillity of the United States, or of its territories, or of any part of them. I have neither given, nor signed, nor promised a commission to any person for any purpose. I do not own a musket, nor bayonet, nor any single article of military stores; nor does any person for me, by my authority, or with my knowledge. My views have been fully explained to, and approved by, several of the principal officers of Government, and I believe are well understood by the Administration, and seen by it with complacency. They are such as every man of honor and every good citizen must approve. Considering the high station you now fill in our national councils. I have thought these explanations proper, as well to counteract the chimerical tales which malevolent persons have so industriously circulated, as to satisfy you that you have not espoused the cause of a man in any way unfriendly to the laws, the Government, or the interests of his country."

Mr. Clay (says Mallory), on reaching Washington as a senator, and seeing the evidence collected against Burr, and particularly the letter in cipher from him to Wilkinson, became apprised of his former client's true character. The same biographer further asserts (vol. i., p. 25) that Clay and Burr next met, after an interval of some years, in the court room of the City Hall in New York. The latter approached the former, " tendering him his hand with the customary salutation." Clay refused to receive his hand. Burr, however, endeavored to engage him in conversation, complimenting him on his conduct at Ghent. Clay "turned a deaf ear, replying very briefly to his inquiries, and giving him no encouragement to proceed." Burr requested an interview. Clay named his lodgings: but the other never came—anticipating, probably, that his cringing pertinacity would meet a still more summary repulse.

to authorize an application (December 2d) to the Governor of Ohio to seize Burr's flotilla in the Muskingum. The Legislature was sitting, and instantly, in secret session, authorized the seizure. The President's proclamation now arrived. Four or five boats coming from Pennsylvania to join Burr (under Major or Colonel Tyler) passed down the river, and Blennerhasset escaped in them, leaving his wife behind. His house and grounds received some very rough usage from a body of militia which next day took possession of them.

Graham hurried on to Frankfort. The Kentucky Legislature was in no mood to reënact the scene which had just been exhibited in the District Court. It immediately ordered the seizure of everything connected with Burr's expedition. Militia were posted on the river to intercept descending boats, but Tyler's escaped in the night. Burr and Adair, after reaching Nashville, had parted, the former descending the Cumberland, and the latter pushing across the country for New Orleans. Burr was joined by Tyler near the close of December. Their united force comprised not far from one hundred men.

About the first of January, Burr reached the Mississippi territory, and, going on shore, saw in a newspaper the measures which had been taken for his reception at New Orleans. He thereupon withdrew to the Louisiana bank of the river, and formed a camp a few miles above Natchez. The President's proclamation soon reached Mississippi. The Governor of that territory called out a detachment of militia, and made preparations to arrest Burr. The latter, after an interview with the Governor (and after his personal safety had been stipulated), surrendered rather than be immediately attacked, and gave recognizances to appear before the Territorial Court. Poindexter, the Attorney-General of Mississippi, believed that Burr was not amenable to the Territorial Court, having committed no offence within its jurisdiction; and he proposed to send the prisoner to Washington. The court overruled the objection, but no evidence against Burr was sent to the grand-jury, and they, of course, found no bill. On the contrary, they presented the Governor for calling out the militia, the mode in which Burr had been compelled to surrender, and the proceedings at New Orleans, which, they declared, "if sanctioned by the Executive of our country, must sap the vitals of our political existence, and crumble this glorious fabric in the dust." Under what influences a grand-jury could have been summoned, who were capable of this indecent action, we are not apprised; but nothing is to be considered marvellous or startling where Burr is found to be an actor in the scene.

The malefactor's respite was short. He learned that Wilkinson had sent military officers to arrest him, and he fled eastward. A reward was offered for his apprehension, and in February he was taken in Alabama, shabbily dressed, and accompanied by one man. He was ultimately carried to Richmond for trial.

During these proceedings, the President's correspondence on the subject was uniformly calm and confident. He wrote General Wilkinson January 3d, 1807, and after stating the seizure of Blennerhasset's flotilla, and that Tyler's could not probably escape, he said: .

"I believe therefore that the enterprise may be considered as crushed, but we are not to relax in our attentions until we hear what has passed at Louisville. If everything from that place upwards be successfully arrested, there is nothing from below that is to be feared. Be assured that Tennessee, and particularly General Jackson, are faithful.

*   *   *   *   *   *   *   *   *

"We had considered Fort Adams as the place to make a stand, because it covered the mouth of the Red river. You have preferred New Orleans on the apprehension of a fleet from the West Indies. Be assured there is not any foundation for such an expectation, but the lying exaggerations of those traitors to impose on others, and swell their pretended means. The very man[1] whom they represented to you as gone to Jamaica, and to bring the fleet, has never been from home, and has regularly communicated to me everything which had passed between Burr and him. No such proposition was ever hazarded to him. France or Spain would not send a fleet to take Vera Cruz; and though one of the expeditions, now near arriving from England, is probably for Vera Cruz, and perhaps already there, yet the state of things between us renders it impossible they should countenance an enterprise unauthorized by us. Still I repeat that these grounds of security must not stop our proceedings or preparations until they are further confirmed. Go on, therefore with your works for the defence of New Orleans, because they will always be useful, only looking to what should be permanent rather than means merely temporary."

He wrote Charles Clay, January 11th:

"Burr's enterprise is the most extraordinary since the days of Don Quixote. It is so extravagant that those who know his understanding would not believe it if the proofs admitted doubt. He has meant to place himself on the throne of Montezuma,

[1] Commodore Truxton.

and extend his empire to the Alleghany, seizing on New Orleans as the instrument of compulsion for our western States.   I think his undertaking effectually crippled by the activity of Ohio.   Whether Kentucky will give him the *coup de grâce* is doubtful; but if he is able to descend the river with any means, we are sufficiently prepared at New Orleans.   I hope, however, Kentucky will do its duty, and finish the matter for the honor of popular government, and the discouragement of all arguments for standing armies."

He wrote Governor Tiffin of Ohio, February 20th, a highly complimentary letter on the zeal manifested by that officer, and by the Legislature of his State, in crushing the conspiracy.   He assigned to Ohio "the most eminent" place in accomplishing this; and he added:

"The hand of the people has given the mortal blow to a conspiracy which, in other countries, would have called for an appeal to armies, and have proved that government to be the strongest of which every man feels himself a part.   It is a happy illustration, too, of the importance of preserving to the State authorities all that vigor which the Constitution foresaw would be necessary, not only for their own safety, but for that of the whole."

He again wrote General Wilkinson, February 3d:

"Although we at no time believed he [Burr] could carry any formidable force out of the Ohio, yet we thought it safest that you should be prepared to receive him with all the force which could be assembled, and with that view our orders were given; and we were pleased to see that without waiting for them, you adopted nearly the same plan yourself, and acted on it with promptitude; the difference between yours and ours proceeding from your expecting an attack by sea, which we knew was impossible, either by England or by a fleet under Truxton, who was at home; or by our own navy, which was under our own eye.   Your belief that Burr would really descend with six or seven thousand men, was no doubt founded on what you knew of the numbers which could be raised in the western country for an expedition to Mexico, under the authority of the Government; but you probably did not calculate that the want of that authority would take from him every honest man, and leave him only the desperadoes of his party, which in no part of the United States can ever be a numerous body.   In approving, therefore, as we do approve, of the defensive operations for New Orleans, we are obliged to estimate them, not according to our own view of the danger, but to place ourselves in your situation, and only with your information.   Your sending here Swartwout and Bollman, and adding to them Burr, Blennerhasset, and Tyler, should they fall into your hands, will be supported by the public opinion.   As to Alexander, who is arrived, and Ogden, expected, the evidence yet received will not be sufficient to commit them.   I hope, however, you will not extend this deportation to persons against whom there is only suspicion, or shades of offence not strongly marked.   In that case, I fear the public sentiment would desert you; because, seeing no danger here, violations of law are felt with strength.   I have thought it just to give you these views of the sentiments and sensations here, as they may enlighten your path.   I am thoroughly sensible of the painful difficulties of your situation, expecting an attack from an overwhelming force, unversed in law, surrounded by suspected persons, and in a nation tender to everything infringing liberty, and especially from the military."

He added:

"You have, doubtless, seen a good deal of malicious insinuation in the papers against you. This, of course, begot suspicion and distrust in those unacquainted[1] with the line of your conduct. We who knew it, have not failed to strengthen the public confidence in you; and I can assure you that your conduct, as now known, has placed you on ground extremely favorable with the public. Burr and his emissaries found it convenient to sow a distrust in your mind of our dispositions toward you; but be assured that you will be cordially supported in the line of your duties."

This letter (which a little careful scrutiny will show to be far more cautiously worded than may at first view appear) was designed to give Wilkinson to understand that the President thus far sustained his conduct to the extent to which it was known—that he would continue to do so, if that conduct should be marked by the proper degree of prudence; but it does not extend to those general and unqualified expressions which we should expect, had he felt entire confidence in the discretion of this officer.[2]

The statement should not be omitted, that pending the measures against Burr, between the time of his expedition becoming publicly known and its final dispersion, numerous military bodies in all parts of the country sent addresses to the President volunteering to march at a moment's notice to put down the conspiracy and all its abettors.

---

[1] Printed "acquainted" in Cong. ed.—an obvious error.

[2] Jefferson's precise feelings toward Wilkinson are expressed more pointedly than elsewhere in a letter to Monroe, January 11th, 1812:

"I have ever and carefully restrained myself from the expression of any opinion respecting General Wilkinson, except in the case of Burr's conspiracy, wherein, after he had got over his first agitations, we believed his decision firm, and his conduct zealous for the defeat of the conspiracy, and although injudicious, yet meriting, from sound intentions. the support of the nation. As to the rest of his life, I have left it to his friends and his enemies, to whom it furnishes matter enough for disputation. I classed myself with neither, and least of all in this time of his distresses, should I be disposed to add to their preasure."

CHAPTER V.

1806—1807.

PENDING the exciting events of Burr's conspiracy, and before
any of the facts were accurately known—and while every current of the atmosphere was surcharged with wild and contradictory reports—the second session of the ninth Congress met at
Washington December 1st, 1806.

189

The President's message announced that the difficulties in our foreign relations were not yet terminated. He declared, however, that the delay in arriving at that result, in the case of the British Government, had not arisen from causes which forbade the expectation of an amicable adjustment during the present session of Congress. He stated that Spain had advanced a force to the Red River—that he had proposed the Sabine as the temporary boundary—that the answer was not yet received—that the official correspondence would develop other particulars. He said the inhabitants of Orleans and Mississippi territories had evinced the utmost promptitude in meeting the requisitions made on them by the Government.

He touched very lightly on Burr's expedition—giving the names of no individuals—only mentioning it as an illegal attempt against Spain : and he said suitable measures had been adopted for its suppression, and for bringing those engaged in it to justice. In concluding this topic, he remarked :

"It was due to that good faith which ought ever to be the rule of action in public as well as in private transactions, it was due to good order and regular government, that while the public force was acting strictly on the defensive and merely to protect our citizens from aggression, the criminal attempts of private individuals to decide for their country the question of peace or war, by commencing active and unauthorized hostilities, should be promptly and efficaciously suppressed."

Whether it would be necessary to increase our regular force, would, he said, depend upon the result of our Spanish negotiations; and this being uncertain, he recommended provisional measures to the consideration of Congress. The approaches to New Orleans ought, he declared, to be effectually guarded, both against outward attacks, and for the " internal support of the country ;" and encouragement to be given to the settlement of the west bank of the Mississippi, " within reach of New Orleans."

A further appropriation was recommended for gunboats, for " repairing fortifications already established, and for the erection of such works as might have real effect in obstructing the approach of an enemy to our seaport towns, or remaining before them."

Again, alluding to Burr's conspiracy, the President said the laws had wisely provided punishment for insurrection, and for enterprises against foreign States. In the latter case, they had given powers of prevention to a certain extent—and he inquired if the same powers would not be reasonable and useful where the enterprise was preparing against the United States. He suggested that if binding over to peace and good behavior could be extended to acts to be done out of the jurisdiction of the United States, it would be effectual in some cases where the offender was now able to keep every indication of his criminal purposes out of sight.

Our Indian relations were pronounced in an amicable and highly favorable condition. Mention was made of the progress of Lewis and Clarke's exploration of the Missouri—of Mr. Freeman's, of the Red River—and of Lieutenant Pike's, of the Mississippi.

The following recommendation was submitted in relation to the slave trade.

"I congratulate you, fellow citizens, on the approach of the period at which you may interpose your authority constitutionally, to withdraw the citizens of the United States from all further participation in those violations of human rights which have been so long continued on the unoffending inhabitants of Africa, and which the morality, the reputation, and the best interests of our country, have long been eager to proscribe. Although no law you may pass can take prohibitory effect till the first day of the year one thousand eight hundred and eight, yet the intervening period is not too long to prevent, by timely notice, expeditions which cannot be completed before that day."

The receipts of the Treasury during the fiscal year, were stated to be near fifteen millions of dollars. From this sum, upwards of three millions of principal, and nearly four millions of interest, had been paid on the public debt—two millions seven hundred thousand on American claims assumed in the purchase of Louisiana—and near two millions in reimbursing the five and a half per cent. stock.

He recommended the suppression of duties on salt, it being "a necessary of life," and the continuance of those composing the Mediterranean fund, "levied chiefly on luxuries," for "a short period," after which they "would become unnecessary for any purpose now within contemplation."

Then came the following passages on the principles on which tariffs should be regulated, and on the duties of the Government in respect to education.

"When both of these branches of revenue shall in this way be relinquished.

there will still ere long be an accumulation of moneys in the treasury beyond the installments of public debt which we are permitted by contract to pay. They cannot, then, without a modification assented to by the public creditors, be applied to the extinguishment of this debt, and the complete liberation of our revenues—the most desirable of all objects, nor, if our peace continues, will they be wanting for any other existing purpose. The question, therefore, now comes forward—to what other objects shall these surpluses be appropriated, and the whole surplus of impost, after the entire discharge of the public debt, and during those intervals when the purposes of war shall not call for them? Shall we suppress the impost and give that advantage to foreign over domestic manufactures? On a few articles of more general and necessary use, the suppression in due season will doubtless be right, but the great mass of the articles on which impost is paid is foreign luxuries, purchased by those only who are rich enough to afford themselves the use of them. Their patriotism would certainly prefer its continuance and application to the great purposes of the public education, roads, rivers, canals, and such other objects of public improvement as it may be thought proper to add to the constitutional enumeration of federal powers. By these operations new channels of communication will be opened between the States; the lines of separation will disappear, their interests will be identified, and their union cemented by new and indissoluble ties. Education is here placed among the articles of public care, not that it would be proposed to take its ordinary branches out of the hands of private enterprise, which manages so much better all the concerns to which it is equal; but a public institution can alone supply those sciences which, though rarely called for, are yet necessary to complete the circle, all the parts of which contribute to the improvement of the country, and some of them to its preservation. The subject is now proposed for the consideration of Congress, because, if approved by the time the State Legislatures shall have deliberated on this extension of the federal trusts, and the laws shall be passed, and other arrangements made for their execution, the necessary funds will be on hand and without employment. I suppose an amendment to the Constitution, by consent of the States, necessary, because the objects now recommended are not among those enumerated in the Constitution, and to which it permits the public moneys to be applied.

"The present consideration of a national establishment for education, particularly, is rendered proper by this circumstance also, that if Congress, approving the proposition, shall yet think it more eligible to found it on a donation of lands, they have it now in their power to endow it with those which will be among the earliest to produce the necessary income. This foundation would have the advantage of being independent on war, which may suspend other improvements by requiring for its own purposes the resources destined for them."

After alluding to the uncertainty of our foreign relations, and their liability to change at any moment, he said:

"Our duty is, therefore, to act upon things as they are, and to make a reasonable provision for whatever they may be. Were armies to be raised whenever a speck of war is visible in our horizon, we never should have been without them. Our resources would have been exhausted on dangers which have never happened, instead of being reserved for what is really to take place. A steady, perhaps a quickened pace in preparations for the defence of our seaport towns and waters; an early settlement of the most exposed and vulnerable parts of our country; a militia so organized that its effective portions can be called to any point in the Union, or volunteers instead of them to serve a sufficient time, are means which may always be ready, yet never preying on our resources until actually called into use. They will maintain the public interests while a more permanent force shall be in course of preparation. But much will depend on the promptitude with which these means can be brought into activity. If war be forced upon us, in spite of our long and vain appeals to the justice of nations, rapid and vigorous movements in its outset will go far towards securing us in its course and issue, and towards throwing its burdens on those who render necessary the resort from reason to force."

The next day he informed Congress, by a special message, that the death of the British minister (Mr. Fox), charged with the duty of negotiating with us, had not interrupted the manifestation of a disposition on the part of that Government for a speedy and amicable termination of those negotiations. Under these circumstances, he recommended a further suspension of the non-importation Act of the preceding session.

Congress almost immediately (December 6th) acted on this recommendation, suspending the execution of that Act to the ensuing first of July, after voting down a proposition supported by the Federalists, Quids, and a few Republicans, that the suspension extend to December 31, 1807. Crowninshield declared, in the debate, that England had never seriously entered into negotiation with us until the passage of this Act—and that but for its passage, it was his opinion she never would have entered into such negotiation. If she found our policy wavering, she would very probably renew her depredations on our commerce, as her whole system of policy was hostile to our growing commercial greatness. This is probably to be taken as the view of the Administration.

But the President was authorized to further suspend the non-importation Act to the second Monday in December following; and on the 3d of February, 1807, the Secretary of State instructed our ministers charged with the negotiation with England, to inform that Government that the President, "trusting to the influence of mutual dispositions and interests in giving an amicable issue to the negotiation, would, if no intervening intelligence forbade, exercise the authority vested in him by the Act of continuing its suspension from the first day of July to the term limited by the Act, and which would afford to Congress, who would then be in session, the opportunity of making due provision for the case."

Burr's conspiracy soon occupied the attention of the House. About the middle of January, 1807, John Randolph introduced a resolution for information on the subject, which passed; and on the 22d, the President replied in a message, giving an outline of the conspiracy so far as it was then known to the Government, and of the civil and military proceedings for its suppression. In regard to surmises that Burr was to receive foreign aid, the President declared they were " without proof or probability "—were " to be imputed to the vauntings of the author of this enterprise, to multiply his partisans by magnifying the belief of his prospects and support." He stated that Burr appeared to have " two distinct objects, which might be carried on either jointly or separately, and either the one or the other first, as circumstances should direct." One was to separate the Union by the Alleghany Mountains—the other to attack Mexico. A third and " merely ostensible " " object was provided," namely, " the settlement of a pretended purchase of a tract of country on the Washita, claimed by a Baron Bastrop." " This was to serve as the pretext for all his preparations, an allurement for such followers as really wished to acquire settlements in that country, and a cover under which to retreat in the event of final discomfiture of both branches of his real design." Finding himself thwarted in his first purpose, by the unshaken " attachment of the western country to the present Union," he had determined to seize on New Orleans, plunder the bank, possess himself of the military and naval stores, and proceed on his expedition to Mexico. The President believed, however, that the expedition " could not threaten serious danger to New Orleans."

Under the circumstances, the President thought Wilkinson had acted properly in sending his prisoners to Washington, " probably on the consideration that an impartial trial could not be expected during the present agitation of New Orleans, and that that city was not as yet a safe place of confinement."

Congress appear to have been more alarmed than the President, and far more alarmed by the documents that accompanied the President's message[1] than by the message itself. The insig-

[1] These were Wilkinson's affidavit of December 14th, 1806 ; Burr's letter to Wilkinson of July 25, 1806 ; Wilkinson's letters to the Government, of December 14th and 18th, 1806—the last covering Bollman's letter to Wilkinson, of September 27, 1806, and its inclosed letter in cipher from Burr.

nificance of Burr's force, when mustered at the mouth of the Cumberland, was not yet known at the capital. The members were fired by an apparent attempt, coming from the judiciary itself, to prevent the confinement of men charged with a dangerous violation of the laws. Giles, J. Q. Adams, and Smith, of Maryland, a Committee of the Senate, almost immediately reported a bill suspending the operation of the writ of *habeas corpus* for three months, in cases of arrest for treason, or for other acts endangering the peace or the neutrality of the United States. The usual three readings were unanimously dispensed with; and the bill unanimously passed the same day, and was sent down as a confidential proceeding to the House.

But the sudden panic subsided before action took place in the latter body, though the interval was but three days. On receiving the Senate's bill, communicated "in confidence," a motion "that the message and bill received from the Senate ought not to be kept secret, and that the doors be now opened," passed— yeas one hundred and twenty-three, nays three. Eppes, the President's son-in-law, immediately moved that the bill be rejected. In his speech on the subject he said:

"Is there a man present who believes, on this statement, that the public safety requires a suspension of the *habeas corpus!* This Government has now been in operation thirty years; during this whole period, our political charter, whatever it may have sustained, has never been suspended. Never, under this Government, has personal liberty been held at the will of a single individual. Shall we, in the full tide of prosperity, possessed of the confidence of the nation, with a revenue of fifteen millions of dollars, and six hundred thousand freemen, able and ready to bear arms in defence of their country, believe its safety endangered by a collection of men which the militia of any one county in our country would be amply sufficient to subdue? Shall we, sir, suspend the chartered rights of the community for the suppression of a few desperadoes—of a small banditti already surrounded by your troops; pressed from above by your militia, met below by your regulars, and without a chance of escape but by abandoning their boats, and seeking safety in the woods? I consider the means at present in operation amply sufficient for the suppression of this combination. If additional means were necessary, I should be willing to vote as many additional bayonets as shall be necessary for every traitor. I cannot, however, bring myself to believe that this country is placed in such a dreadful situation as to authorize me to suspend the personal rights of the citizen, and to give him in lieu of a free Constitution the Executive will for his charter. . . . . Believing that the public safety is not endangered, and that the discussion of this question is calculated to alarm the public mind at a time when no real danger exists, I shall vote for the rejection of the bill in its present stage."

In this last remark we get the reason for the very unusual

proposition to vote down summarily a bill passed by another branch of Congress, without giving it the usual reference. Eppes' motion prevailed—yeas one hundred and thirteen, nays nineteen.   Only two of the leading Republicans voted in the negative, Bidwell and Varnum, both of Massachusetts.   Bidwell opposed the rejection of a bill at that stage; but Varnum went further, and declared that without such a law he apprehended that it would be found impracticable to trace the conspiracy to its source, and bring the offenders to justice.   His fears proved prophetic; but few probably will consider the final escape of a handful of conspirators any counterbalancing evil to that which would have inured from the establishment of such a precedent in legislation.

An incidental circumstance occurred which doubtless aided in producing that strong revulsion of feeling from the Senate's action which was exhibited in the House of Representatives. On the evening of the 22d of January, Bollman and Swartwout, sent by Wilkinson from New Orleans in military custody, reached Washington.   When, on a cooler examination of the President's message of the same day, it appeared that the highest accounts did not place the main division of Burr's flotilla which had descended the Ohio at above fifteen boats, containing three hundred men—or the other branch of it, which had descended the Cumberland, at above two boats—that the Executive did not consider these "fugitives" as threatening serious danger — few made proper allowances for General Wilkinson's high-handed conduct.   Not taking into account the misinformation under which he had acted, many believed he had been influenced by idle terrors.   Others suspected him of exaggerating all the features of the conspiracy for the purpose of acquiring the greater reputation in putting it down.   And there were not wanting those who asserted that whatever there was in the plot, he had been a full accomplice in it, until he judged it safer and more profitable to turn informer.

Bollman's and Swartwout's arrival was communicated to Congress on the 26th of January; and on the 28th, a letter from the commander of Fort Massic giving information that Burr had passed that post on the 31st of the preceding month with only about ten boats manned by six hands each, and "that three boats with ammunition were said to have been arrested by the militia at Louisville."   The President also stated that the militia on the

Ohio would be "able to prevent any further aids passing through that channel." Here was food for further reaction.

Bollman and Swartwout were brought before the Circuit Court in the District of Columbia, and committed for trial on the affidavit of Wilkinson, the testimony of Eaton, and the facts disclosed in the President's message. But the prisoners were brought before Chief Justice Marshall early in February, on a writ of *habeas corpus*, and discharged from custody on the ground that it was not made to appear that they had been connected with the commission of any overt act of treason.

The President's correspondence of the period speaks coolly of this affair. He wrote Nicholson (February 20th), that if the evidence should be found conclusive, these men could be arrested again, "if it should be worth while." He said their "crimes were defeated, and whether they should be punished or not belonged to another department, and was not the subject of even a wish on his part." He did not, however, concur in the Chief Justice's view of the law. He afterwards claimed that if that officer's decision was correct, and if such interference was proper before the executive officers of the Government could possibly gather the testimony concerning the particulars of a distant conspiracy, it was out of the question to attempt to prevent the enlargement of any detected traitor who was disposed either to fly, or to return to the execution of his designs.

On the 7th of February, Broom, the Federal member from Delaware, submitted the following resolution in the House of Representatives:

"*Resolved*, That it is expedient to make further provision, by law, for securing the privilege of the writ of *habeas corpus*, to persons in custody, under, or by color of, the authority of the United States."

The object of this proposition was apparent; and it drew out an animated and protracted debate. The Federalists professed to be deeply alarmed at the dangerous encroachments of executive power, and they painted in glowing colors the danger of military interference in the concerns of civil government. The Republicans ironically congratulated their opponents on their late conversion to these wholesome doctrines. Eppes, now fast rising to leadership in the House, declared that "the greatest monster in human shape was a tyrant in principle, with the rights of man in his mouth—a wretch sunk to the last step in the political ladder, and willing again to mount by principles he never felt." He added:

"Where has this zeal of a certain party for the rights of man so long slumbered? Where was it when the sedition law was passed? Where was it when a member of this House was imprisoned and deprived of his constitutional privilege, for printing a letter from the Secretary of War, acknowledged to be genuine? Where was it when General Hamilton [1] was seized in the western parts of Pennsylvania, without the shadow of authority; driven like a convicted felon before the bayonet to Philadelphia, and there imprisoned for months without the possibility of obtaining a *habeas corpus?* Where was this zeal when the rights of aliens were suspended, that whole class of people placed under the will of the Executive, and a power given by law to seize and ship them? Dead, sir! The rights of man were not much in fashion with the party at that time. Plots, clues to conspiracies, and a gag for the mouth of him who dared to arraign the Federal immaculacy, were then the order of the day. When I shall believe the sympathy which these men affect to feel for a character so recently hunted through the community by them like a wolf, is sincere, I may then credit their attachment to human rights, and not till then.

"The real secret in this business is, that the termination of this affair in the western country does not suit the Federal palate. To reduce an insurrection without an army or navy, is a very anti-Federal thing. They do not understand, and cannot admire that kind of energy in government which derives its force from confidence and attachment on the part of the people."

Broom's resolution was indefinitely postponed, February 19th, by a vote of sixty to fifty-eight. Many Republicans, like T. M. Randolph, W. A. Burwell, and other equally devoted friends of the President, voted in the negative. They were not in favor of the resolution, but preferred a different mode of disposing of it.

On the third day of the session, the portion of the President's message alluding to the prohibition of the African slave-trade had been referred to a select committee of seven. They reported a very stringent bill, prohibiting the importation of slaves. Numerous amendments were offered, and the debate was long and occasionally violent. An amendment which was adopted, placing various restrictions on the coastwise transportation of slaves (from one American State into another) gave offence to many of the friends of the original bill, and caused them to vote against it in the shape in which it finally passed. But on the naked question of preventing the foreign importation, the senti-

---

[1] We take it for granted that this name is misprinted, or rather that something is omitted showing *who* were seized, etc.

ment of the House appears to have been nearly unanimous. The final vote exhibited no distinctly drawn sectional or political lines of division.[1]

On the subject of the recommended naval defences, there were three parties in the House—those in favor of a navy—those in favor of harbor fortifications—and those who wished to combine a system of defence consisting of fortifications and gunboats. The first plan found its advocates from maritime districts; the second from exposed cities on the seaboard; the third from the interior. The two first parties united against the President's plan of gunboats. Early in February, a debate on the latter topic resulted in a call on the President for such information as he possessed, tending to establish the efficacy of this kind of force. He replied on the 10th, in a communication, which presents a clear view of his proposed combined system of land-batteries and gunboats. In regard to the circumstances under which he recommended it, the following will probably be new to many persons. He said:

"On this subject professional men were consulted as far as we had opportunity. General Wilkinson, and the late General Gates, gave their opinions in writing, in favor of the system, as will be seen by their letters now communicated. The higher officers of the navy gave the same opinions in separate conferences, as their presence at the seat of Government offered occasions of consulting them, and no difference of judgment appeared on the subject. Those of Commodore Barron and Captain Tingey, now here, are recently furnished in writing, and transmitted herewith to the legislature."

The House, by a vote of sixty-eight to thirty-six, appropriated $150,000 for building thirty gunboats. The Senate struck out this clause in the bill—leaving the money to be appropriated at the President's discretion in land defences—and returned the bill to the House on the last day of the session. The House probably had the choice of concurring or defeating the entire bill, and it concurred by the following remarkably meagre vote, yeas thirty-nine, nays thirty-six.

[1] Of the select committee who unanimously reported the original stringent non-importation bill, but one voted for the amended bill on its final passage. The final vote took place February 26th, and stood yeas sixty-three, nays forty-nine. The local classification was, so far as our memory serves us, as follows: New Hampshire, yeas two, nays two; Vermont, yeas two, nays two; Connecticut, yeas three, nays one; New York, yeas nine, nays six; Maryland, yeas four, nays four; North Carolina, yeas four, nays five; Kentucky, yeas one, nays two; Virginia, yeas one, the rest nays: South Carolina and Georgia all nays; Pennsylvania, Massachusetts, New Jersey, Tennessee, and Rhode Island, all yeas. Prominent men of both parties voted on each side of the question.

An act was passed authorizing the President to accept the services of thirty thousand volunteers, should they, in his judgment, be needed. The salt tax was repealed; the Mediterranean fund was continued; appropriations were made for the coast survey, and to reward Lewis and Clark for their journey of exploration to the Pacific.

On the 19th of February, the President announced that the terms of a treaty had been agreed on with England, and that our Minister in France had been officially informed that the declaring of the British Islands in a state of blockade (the Berlin decree of November 21, 1806) would not extend to American commerce.

The ninth Congress expired on the 3d of March, 1807.

The President's private letters, during the late session, which demand our notice, are few. In one to Charles Clay, January 11th, we catch a glimpse of Mr. Jefferson's private pecuniary matters:

"Yours of December 19th has been duly received, and I thank you for your friendly attention to the offer of lands adjoining me for sale. It is true that I have always wished to purchase a part of what was Murray's tract, which would straighten the lines of the Poplar Forest, but I really am not able to make a purchase. I had hoped to keep the expenses of my office within the limits of its salary, so as to apply my private income entirely to the improvement and enlargement of my estate; but I have not been able to do it."

On the 13th of January he wrote his "dear and ancient friend," John Dickinson; and the letter contains that groan which breaks sooner or later from the bosoms of all who wield official power and patronage:

"I have tired you, my friend, with a long letter. But your tedium will end in a few lines more. Mine has yet two years to endure. I am tired of an office where I can do no more good than many others, who would be glad to be employed in it. To myself, personally, it brings nothing but unceasing drudgery and daily loss of friends. Every office becoming vacant, every appointment made, *me donne un ingrat, et cent ennemis.* My only consolation is in the belief that my fellow citizens at large give me credit for good intentions. I will certainly endeavor to merit the continuance of that good-will which follows well-intended actions, and their approbation will be the dearest reward I can carry into retirement."

An embarrassment of the Administration in the 9th Congress, had been the want of a recognized and competent leader. There were able young men, and sensible and experienced older ones in the House; but no individual appeared to combine all the qualities requisite for the position. To supply this deficiency, Mr. Jefferson wrote Wilson C. Nicholas (February 28th), desiring him to become the successor of T. M. Randolph, who had determined to retire on account of ill health, and an increasing distaste for Congressional life. Mr. Nicholas consented, was elected, and though not a brilliant or remarkably fluent man, possessed experience, tact, and popular manners, combined with sound ability and sense, and a steady attention to business. He, therefore, well filled the place assigned to him.

The new English treaty negotiated by Messrs. Monroe and Pinkney, was received on the last day of the session of the late Congress, from the British Minister at Washington, Mr. Erskine.[1] It did not, in material particulars, meet the views of the President. The termination of impressments had been one of the main objects of the negotiation. Learning in January (1807), that on some partial and informal promises of the British negotiators, Monroe and Pinkney were on the point of signing a treaty containing no stipulations on this head, the Government forwarded formal instructions to them (February 3d), to make no treaty which did not provide against impressments, informed them that such a one, if already made, could not be ratified, and that they would be expected at once to resume negotiations to supply the omitted article. It unfortunately turned out that a treaty with this omission had actually been signed on the 31st of December preceding. Nor was this all. It was accompanied by a declaration on the part of the British ministers that their Government reserved the power of departing from its stipulations in favor of our rights as a neutral, if the United States submitted to an invasion of those rights from France.[2]

The President wrote Mr. Monroe that the treaty could not be ratified. After mentioning the instructions on the subject of impressment, he added :

"We observed, too, that a written declaration of the British commissioners,

---

[1] He succeeded Mr. Merry on the accession of the Grenville Ministry.
[2] In other words, submitted to the celebrated "Berlin decree" of Bonaparte (Nov. 21st, 1806), declaring the British Islands in a state of blockade, made in retaliation for the British order in council (May 16th, 1806), declaring the coast of France and Germany, from Brest to the Elbe, in a state of blockade.

given in at the time of signature, would of itself, unless withdrawn, prevent the acceptance of any treaty, because its effect was to leave us bound by the treaty and themselves totally unbound. This is the statement we have given out, and nothing more of the contents of the treaty has ever been made known. But depend on it, my dear sir, that it will be considered as a hard treaty when it is known. The British commissioners appear to have screwed every article as far as it would bear, to have taken everything and yielded nothing. Take out the eleventh article, and the evil of all the others so much overweighs the good, that we should be glad to expunge the whole. And even the eleventh article admits only that we may enjoy our right to the indirect colonial trade, *during the present hostilities.* If peace is made this year, and war resumed the next, the benefit of this stipulation is gone, and yet we are bound for ten years, to pass no non-importation or non-intercourse laws, nor take any other measures to restrain the unjust pretensions and practices of the British. But on this you will hear from the Secretary of State. If the treaty cannot be put into acceptable form, then the next best thing is to back out of the negotiation as well as we can, letting that die away insensibly; but, in the meantime, agreeing informally, that both parties shall act on the principles of the treaty, so as to preserve that friendly understanding which we sincerely desire, until the one or the other may be disposed to yield the points which divide us."

In conclusion, he informed Monroe, that the course proposed would leave him to "follow his desire of coming home as soon as he saw that the amendment of the treaty was desperate." In that case, Mr. Pinkney, he remarked, could procrastinate negotiations, "and give us time, the most precious of all things to us." He offered Monroe the governorship of Orleans, which he said he considered, at that period, "the second office in the United States in importance."

That the President allowed Congress to disperse without placing the treaty before the Senate—in other words, that he rejected it without consulting the coördinate branch of the treaty-making power—was the subject of many criticisms among a party which had newly learned to be jealous of Executive encroachments. But if the President had fully made up his mind that he would not assent to the treaty, it is difficult to discover what object there would have been in spending the time of the Senate, and the money of the people, in deliberating over an instrument which could under no circumstances go into effect—which was already practically dead.

The President proved to England that his action was dictated by no hostility towards herself, by continuing by proclamation, the suspension of the Non-Importation Act. It appears from his correspondence of the period, that every member of his

Cabinet concurred in his views in respect to the treaty. He wrote the Secretary of State, April 21st:

"As on a consultation when we were all together, we had made up our minds on every article of the British treaty, and this of not employing their seamen was only mentioned for further inquiry and consideration, we had better let the negotiations go on, on the ground then agreed on, and take time to consider this supplementary proposition. Such an addition as this to a treaty already so bad would fill up the measure of public condemnation. It would, indeed, be making bad worse. I am more and more convinced that our best course is, to let the negotiation take a friendly nap, and endeavor in the meantime to practise on such of its principles as are mutually acceptable. Perhaps we may hereafter barter the stipulation not to employ their seamen for some equivalent to our flag, by way of convention; or, perhaps, the general treaty of peace may do better for us, if we shall not, in the meantime, have done worse for ourselves. At any rate, it will not be the worse for lying three weeks longer."

The following letter to Mr. Bowdoin, then in France, exhibits the tone of the representations which were to be made in other foreign quarters:

" You heard in due time from London, of the signature of a treaty there between Great Britain and the United States. By a letter we received in January, from our ministers at London, we found they were making up their minds to sign a treaty, in which no provision was made against the impressment of our seamen, contenting themselves with a note received in the course of their correspondence, from the British negotiators, assuring them of the discretion with which impressments should be conducted, which could be construed into a covenant only by inferences, against which its omission in the treaty was a strong inference; and in its terms totally unsatisfactory. By a letter of February the 3d, they were immediately informed that no treaty, not containing a satisfactory article on that head, would be ratified, and desiring them to resume the negotiations on that point. The treaty having come to us actually in the inadmissible shape apprehended, we, of course, hold it up until we know the result of the instructions of February 3d. I have but little expectation that the British Government will retire from their habitual wrongs in the impressment of our seamen, and am certain, that without that, we will never tie up our hands by treaty, from the right of passing a non-importation or non-intercourse act, to make it her interest to become just. This may bring on a war of commercial restrictions. To show, however, the sincerity of our desire for conciliation, I have suspended the Non-Importation Act. This state of things should be understood at Paris, and every effort used on your part to accommodate our differences with Spain, under the auspices of France, with whom it is all important that we should stand in terms of the strictest cordiality. In fact, we are to depend on her and Russia for the establishment of neutral rights by the treaty of peace, among which should be that of taking no persons by a belligerent out of a neutral ship, unless they be the *soldiers* of an enemy. Never did a nation act towards another with more perfidy and injustice than Spain has constantly practised against us: and if we have kept our hands off of her till now, it has been purely out of respect to France, and from the value we set on the friendship of France. We expect, therefore, from the friendship of the Emperor, that he will either compel Spain to do us justice, or abandon her to us. We ask but one month to be in possession of the city of Mexico."

The spring elections of 1807 exhibited an increase of Republican strength. That party now elected their Governor in Massachusetts, which gave them all the State executives, as well as legislatures, except in Connecticut and Delaware.

In the letter to Bowdoin, just quoted, the President spoke as follows of Burr's approaching trial:

"Hitherto we have believed our law to be, that suspicion on probable grounds was sufficient cause to commit a person for trial, allowing time to collect witnesses till the trial. But the judges here have decided, that conclusive evidence of guilt must be ready in the moment of arrest, or they will discharge the malefactor. If this is still insisted on, Burr will be discharged; because his crimes having been sown from Maine, through the whole line of the western waters, to New Orleans, we cannot bring the witnesses here under four months. The fact is, that the Federalists make Burr's cause their own, and exert their whole influence to shield him from punishment, as they did the adherents of Miranda. And it is unfortunate that Federalism is still predominant in our judiciary department, which is consequently in opposition to the legislative and executive branches, and is able to baffle their measures often."

Burr arrived at Richmond, in custody, on the 26th of March, and was delivered over to the civil authorities and brought before Judge Marshall for examination. After hearing a three days' argument, the Chief Justice decided not to "insert in the commitment the charge of high treason," but only that of misdemeanor. The prisoner was admitted to bail in the sum of ten thousand dollars for his appearance at the next circuit court of the United States for the Virginia district, to commence at Richmond on the 22d of May.

He had been received by the Federalists in the capital of Virginia as a political martyr. His sureties were highly respectable members of that party. Public and individual demonstrations of sympathy were abundantly and in some instances conspicuously exhibited.

After Burr was held to bail, one of his counsel, Mr. Wickham—a very distinguished lawyer of Richmond—made a dinner party, and among his guests, and sitting at the same table, were seen the Chief Justice of the United States and Aaron Burr, who was soon to be tried before him for a misdemeanor, and who was notoriously soon to be proceeded against for high treason by those representing the Executive of the United States.

Professor Tucker, who was present on the occasion, and who evidently speaks by authority, states that "no one was afterwards more sensible" of the "impropriety" of his conduct than Judge Marshall.' While this will probably mitigate every one's estimate of the original act, none tho less does that act assist in explaining the feelings with which Jefferson, and his friends, looked upon the proceedings of the Chief Justice preliminary to and pending Burr's trials.

The Circuit Court opened at the appointed time, Judges Marshall and Griffin presiding. Burr appeared with an imposing array of counsel—Edmund Randolph, Mr. Wickham, Mr. Botts and Mr. Baker; and Luther Martin, of Maryland, and Charles Lee, formerly Attorney-General of the United States, were associated in the management of the trials at a later stage. For the United States, appeared George Hay (the attorney of the district), William Wirt and Alexander McRae.

The defence claimed the right of challenging the grand jury "for favor," and this being allowed, some eminent Republicans —including W. B. Giles and W. C. Nicholas—were so challenged and "advised" by the Chief Justice to withdraw.

It is not proposed to give here beyond a few characteristic incidents of the various legal proceedings which took place. On the 9th of June, Burr himself moved for a *subpœna duces tecum*, directed to the President, requiring him, or the secretaries having them in charge, to forthwith bring a letter of General Wilkinson to the President, mentioned in a message of the latter to Congress, together with the documents accompanying the letter, a copy of the President's answer to the letter, and the military and naval orders given to the officers of the army and navy at or near New Orleans concerning Burr "or his property."

' After mentioning that the Chief Justice "was a near neighbor and intimate friend of the entertainer," Professor Tucker says: "It is proper to add, this gentleman informed the Chief Justice in the course of the morning, that he expected Colonel Burr to dinner. The Chief Justice considered that, having already accepted the invitation, it might be regarded as undue fastidiousness, and perhaps a censure on his friend, then to decline it. He accordingly went to the dinner, but he had no communication whatever with Burr; sat at the opposite end of the table. and withdrew at an early hour after dinner. . . . . There was an evident impropriety in this association between parties thus related to the public and to each other, and no one was afterwards more sensible of it than the Chief Justice himself, but it was not an act of deliberation, but merely inconsiderate."—*Life of Jefferson.*

Mr. Hay pledged himself, " if possible, to obtain the papers which were wanted, and not only those, but every paper which might be necessary to the elucidation of the case," and " he had no doubt he should obtain them."[1] But he contended that the President could not be compelled to furnish the court with official or other confidential papers in his department, without reference to his own opinion whether the public good would permit their disclosure. He raised other points not important here. The spirit in which the proceedings had been permitted to open will derive some illustration from the following uninterrupted remarks of Mr. Martin :

" I have asserted that Colonel Burr was entitled to a copy of these orders [the official orders of the Navy and War departments]. We intended to show that these orders were contrary to the Constitution and the laws, and that they entitled Colonel Burr to the right of resistance. We intended to show, that by this particular order [that of the Secretary of the Navy to seize or destroy Burr's flotilla] his property and his person were to be destroyed ; yes, by these tyrannical orders, the life and property of an innocent man were to be exposed to destruction. We did not expect these originals themselves. But we did apply for copies, and were refused under Presidential influence. In New York, on the farcical trials of Ogden and Smith,[2] the officers of the Government screened themselves from attending, under the sanction of the President's name. Perhaps the same farce may be repeated here ; and it is for this reason that we apply directly to the President of the United States. . . . . This is a peculiar case, sir. The President has undertaken to prejudge my client by declaring that 'of his guilt there can be no doubt.' He has assumed to himself the knowledge of the Supreme being himself, and pretended to search the heart of my highly respected friend. He has proclaimed him a traitor in the face of that country which has rewarded him. He has let slip the dogs of war, the hell hounds of persecution, to hunt down my friend. And would this President of the United States, who has raised all this absurd clamor, pretend to keep back the papers which were wanted for this trial, where life itself is at stake ?" . . . .

The following is a part of Mr. Wirt's reply :

" I cannot take my seat without expressing my deep and sincere sorrow at the policy which the gentlemen in the defence have thought it necessary to adopt. As to Mr. Martin, I should have been willing to impute this fervid language to the sympathies and resentments of that friendship which he has taken such frequent occasions to express for the prisoner, his *honorable friend.* In the cause of friendship I can pardon zeal even up to the point of intemperance ; but the truth is, sir, that before Mr. Martin came to Richmond, this policy was settled, and on every question incidentally brought before the court, we were stunned with invectives against the Administration. I appeal to your recollection, sir, whether this policy was not

[1] Robertson's Report, vol. i. p. 115.
[2] For their connection with Miranda's expedition from that city.

manifested even so early as in those new and until now unheard of challenges to the grand jury for favor? Whether that policy was not followed up with increased spirit, in the very first speeches which were made in this case; those of Mr. Botts and Mr. Wickham on their previous question pending the attorney's motion to commit! Whether they have not seized with avidity every subsequent occasion, and on every question of mere abstract law before the court, flew off at a tangent to launch into declamations against the Government—exhibiting the prisoner continually as a persecuted patriot—a Russell or a Sydney bleeding under the scourge of a despot.

    •   •   •   •   •   •   •   •

"I beg to know, sir, if the course which gentlemen pursue is not disrespectful to the court itself? Suppose there are any foreigners here accustomed to regular government in their own country, what can they infer from hearing the federal Administration thus reviled to the federal judiciary—hearing the judiciary told that the Administration are 'bloodhounds, hunting this man with a keen and savage thirst for blood—that they now suppose they have hunted him into their toils and have him safe?' Sir, no man, foreigner or citizen, who hears this language addressed to the court, and received with all the complacency at least which silence can imply, can make any inferences from it very honorable to the court. It would only be inferred, while they are thus suffered to roll and luxuriate in these gross invectives against the Administration, that they are furnishing the joys of a Mahometan paradise to the court as well as to their client. I hope that the court, for their own sakes, will compel a decent respect to that Government of which they themselves form a branch!"

The Chief Justice observed, that remarks had been made, on both sides, of which the court did not approve, yet it had hitherto avoided interfering; but it hoped, henceforth, these improprieties would be avoided.

This "hope" appears to have received very little attention. Two days afterwards, Mr. Martin launched out into an attack on the Government, very nearly the same in substance with that already quoted. And he made the following reply to Mr. Wirt:

"The gentleman has told us that respect ought to be paid to the officers of Government. It is granted. I thought so once. I thought that the officers of Government ought to be treated with high respect, however much their conduct ought to be the subject of criticism; and I invariably acted according to that principle. If I have changed my opinion, I owe it to the gentleman himself, and the party he is connected with. They formerly thought differently. That gentleman and his friends so loudly and incessantly clamored against the officers of Government, that they contributed to effect a change in the Administration, and are now, in consequence, basking in the sunshine of office; and therefore they wish to inculcate and receive that respect which they formerly denied to others in the same position," etc.

He was not interrupted, and these invectives were repeated

at intervals without interruption through the subsequent pro-ceedings.

On learning the language that had been tolerated towards himself by the court, the President's patience gave way. Rumor ascribed to Martin a full knowledge of his " honorable friend's" schemes. The President was in possession of a letter which directly implicated him, written by an old Revolutionary captain, named Graybell, then a flour merchant in Baltimore, who was represented to be a man of entire respectability and credibility. The President wrote Hay (June 19th):

"We think you should immediately dispatch a subpœna for Graybell; and while that is on the road, you will have time to consider in what form you will use his his testimony; *e. g.* shall Luther Martin be summoned as a witness against Burr, and Graybell held ready to confront him? It may be doubted whether we could examine a witness to discredit our own witness. Besides, the lawyers say that they are privileged from being forced to breaches of confidence, and that no others are. Shall we move to commit Luther Martin, as *particeps criminis* with Burr? Graybell will fix upon him misprision of treason at least. And at any rate, his evidence will put down this unprincipled and impudent Federal bull-dog, and add another proof that the most clamorous defenders of Burr are all his accomplices. It will explain why Luther Martin flew so hastily to the 'aid of his honorable friend,' abandoning his clients and their property during a session of a principal court in Maryland, now filled, as I am told, with the clamors and ruin of his clients."

Martin was a son-in-law of that Michael Cresap mentioned in the Notes on Virginia as the murderer of Logan's family. Instead of treating this alleged misstatement as a historical error, he acted on the assumption that Mr. Jefferson had substantially invented a tale to disprove a theory ; and after waiting some years (until Mr. Jefferson became the leader of the Republican party) he attacked him in a letter filled with scurrilities.[1] After Mr. Jefferson's accession to the Presidency, Martin was eagerly employed in important cases where the Government was plaintiff or complainant, and he as eagerly availed himself of every such opportunity to attack the President personally with a license and audacity seldom heard at the bar. He is described by his contemporaries as an able, but coarse man—possessed of violent and unrestrained passions—and addicted to deep drinking.[2]

[1] Those who desire to see this specimen of Mr. Martin's style, will find it at p. 211, vol. v. of the London edition of Porcupine's Works.
[2] The fullest personal sketch we have ever seen of Mr. Martin, is from Blennerhasset's diary, kept during Burr's trial. He says:
"As we were chatting after dinner, in *staggered* the whole rear guard of Burr's

Whatever Graybell's testimony against Martin would have amounted to, it is doubtless fortunate that the President's momentary impressions were not acted on. The arrest of one of Burr's counsel during the trial would have afforded room for misconceptions in the public mind, while there was not any danger of serious ones as matters already stood.

On the 13th of June, the Chief-Justice granted the defendant's motion for a *subpœna duces tecum* to the President. Hay, as he declared he would do, had previously written the President for the papers desired by the defence. Mr. Jefferson replied immediately (June 12th), and while reserving to himself " the necessary right of the President of the United States to decide, independently of all other authority, what papers, coming to him as President, the public interests permitted to be communicated, he assured " the Attorney " of his readiness, under that restriction, voluntarily to furnish on all occasions whatever the purposes of justice might require." He stated that the letter of Wilkinson called for by the accused, with every other paper relating to the charges against Burr, had been delivered to the Attorney-General, when the latter went to Richmond in March, and that he (the President) supposed all those papers were delivered by the Attorney-General to Mr. Hay. He promised to write immediately to the former for the desired letter. In regard to orders issued at the War and Navy departments con-

forensic army—I mean the celebrated Luther Martin. who yesterday concluded his fourteen hours' speech. . . . I was too much interested by the little I had seen, and the great things I had heard, of this man's powers and passions, not to improve the present opportunity to survey him in every light the length of his visit would permit. I accordingly recommended our brandy as superior, placing a pint-tumbler before him. No ceremonies retarded the libation. . . . Imagine a man capable, in that space of time, to deliver some account of an entire week's proceedings in the trial, with extracts from memory of several speeches on both sides, including long ones from his; to recite half columns verbatim of a series of papers, of which he said he is the author; to caricature Jefferson ; to give a history of his acquaintance with Burr ; expatiate on his virtues and sufferings, maintain his credit, embellish his fame, and intersperse the whole with sententious reprobations and praises, of several other characters : some estimate, with these preparations, may be formed of this man's powers, which are yet shackled by a preternatural secretion or excretion of saliva which embarrasses his delivery. In this, his manner is rude, and his language ungrammatical ; which is cruelly aggravated upon his hearers by the verbosity and repetition of his style. With the warmest passions which hurry him like a torrent, over those characters or topics that lie most in the way of their course, he has, by practice, acquired the faculty of curbing his feelings, which he never suffers to charge the enemy till broken by the superior numbers of his arguments and authorities, by which he always outflanks him, when he lets loose the reserve upon the centre, with redoubled impetuosity. Yet fancy has been denied to his mind, or grace to his person or habits. These are gross and incapable of restraint, even upon the most solemn public occasions. This is, at all times, awkward and disgusting. Hence his invectives are rather coarse than pointed : his eulogiums more fulsome than pathetic. In short, every trait of his portrait may be given in one word—he is ' *the Thersites of the law.*' "

cerning Burr, he said the request seemed " to cover a correspondence of many months with such a variety of officers, civil
and military, all over the United States, as would amount to
laying open the whole Executive books."   He continued :

"I have desired the Secretary of War [1] to examine his official communications;
and on a view of these, we may be able to judge what can and ought to be done,
towards a compliance with the request. If the defendant alleges that there was
any particular order, which, as a cause, produced any particular act on his part,
then he must know what this order was, can specify it, and a prompt answer can be
given. If the *object* had been specified, we might then have some guide for our
conjectures, as to what part of the Executive records might be useful to him ; but,
with a perfect willingness to do what is right, we are without the indications which
may enable us to do it. If the researches of the Secretary at War should produce
anything proper for communication, and pertinent to any point we can conceive in
the defence before the court, it shall be forwarded to you."

He again wrote to Hay, before receiving the Chief-Justice's
decision in regard to the *subpœna duces tecum,* forwarding the
promised papers from the War department; and he made this
further offer for the benefit of the prisoner :

" To these communications of papers, I will add, that if the defendant supposes
there are any facts within the knowledge of the heads of departments, or of myself,
which can be useful for his defence, from a desire of doing anything our situation
will permit in furtherance of justice, *we shall be ready to give him the benefit of it, by
way of deposition, through any persons whom the court shall authorize to take our
testimony at this place.* I know, indeed, that this cannot be done but by consent
of parties ; and I therefore authorize you to give consent on the part of the United
States. Mr. Burr's consent will be given of course, if he supposes the testimony
useful."

He thus explained his objections to a personal attendance,
and his views in regard to the legal custody of Executive
papers :

" As to our personal attendance at Richmond, I am persuaded the Court is sensible, that paramount duties to the nation at large control the obligation of compliance with their summons in this case ; as they would, should we receive a similar
one, to attend the trials of Blennerhasset and others, in the Mississippi territory,
those instituted at St. Louis and other places on the western waters, or at any place
other than the seat of Government. To comply with such calls would leave the
nation without an executive branch, whose agency, nevertheless, is understood to
be so constantly necessary, that it is the sole branch which the Constitution requires
to be always in function. It could not then mean that it should be withdrawn from
its station by any coördinate authority.

---

[1] The remark was confined to the Secretary of War, because Hay had informed the
President that he (Hay) already had in his possession the order of the Navy department
desired by the defence.

"With respect to papers, there is certainly a public and a private side to our offices. To the former belong grants of land, patents for inventions, certain commissions, proclamations, and other papers patent in their nature. To the other belong mere executive proceedings. All nations have found it necessary, that for the advantageous conduct of their affairs, some of these proceedings, at least, should remain known to their executive functionary only. He, of course, from the nature of the case, must be the sole judge of which of them the public interests will permit publication. Hence, under our Constitution, in requests of papers, from the legislative to the executive branch, an exception is carefully expressed, as to those which he may deem the public welfare may require not to be disclosed; as you will see in the inclosed resolution of the House of Representatives, which produced the message of January 22d, respecting this case. The respect mutually due between constituted authorities in their official intercourse, as well as sincere dispositions to do for every one what is just, will always ensure from the Executive, in exercising the duty of discrimination confided to him, the same candor and integrity to which the nation has in like manner trusted in the disposal of its judiciary authorities. Considering you as the organ for communicating these sentiments to the court, I address them to you for that purpose, and salute you with esteem and respect."

Two days after making these respectful propositions to the court, he saw Judge Marshall's opinion, and the next day (20th) thus wrote to Hay:

"I did not see till last night the opinion of the judge on the *supœna duces tecum* against the President. Considering the question there as *coram non judice*, I did not read his argument with much attention. Yet I saw readily enough, that, as is usual where an opinion is to be supported, right or wrong, he dwells much on smaller objections, and passes over those which are solid. Laying down the position generally, that all persons owe obedience to subpœnas, he admits no exception unless it can be produced in his law books. But if the Constitution enjoins on a particular officer to be always engaged in a particular set of duties imposed on him, does not this supersede the general law, subjecting him to minor duties inconsistent with these? The Constitution enjoins his constant agency in the concerns of six millions of people. Is the law paramount to this, which calls on him on behalf of a single one? Let us apply the judge's own doctrine to the case of himself and his brethren. The sheriff of Henrico summons him from the bench, to quell a riot somewhere in his county. The federal judge is, by the general law, a part of the *posse* of the State sheriff. Would the judge abandon major duties to perform lesser ones? Again; the court of Orleans or Maine commands, by subpœnas, the attendance of all the judges of the Supreme Court. Would they abandon their posts as judges, and the interests of millions committed to them, to serve the purposes of a single individual? The leading principle of our Constitution is the independence of the legislature, executive and judiciary, of each other and none are more jealous of this than the judiciary. But would the executive be independent of the judiciary, if he were subject to the *commands* of the latter, and to imprisonment for disobedience; if the several courts could bandy him from pillar to post, keep him constantly trudging from north to south and east to west, and withdraw him entirely from his Constitutional duties? The intention of the Constitution, that each branch should be independent of the others, is further manifested by the means it has furnished to each, to protect itself from enterprises of force attempted on them by the others, and to none has it given more effectual or diversified means than to the Executive."

The intimation in the last sentence admits of but one interpretation—that the President would, if necessary, protect the constitutional inviolability of his office by force.

As a striking commentary on the practical consequences of the Chief-Justice's position if carried out, just two days after the last quoted letter of the President was written, a great and warlike outrage was inflicted on our national flag. A public vessel (the Chesapeake) was attacked, reduced to submission, and part of her crew forcibly carried off. The insolent victor took soundings before an American city, and threatened an attack on it if certain demands were not complied with. The nation simultaneously shouted to arms. That was the moment when a *subpœna* to bring certain papers to any court, however distant, might have deprived the nation of its Chief Magistrate for one, two, or three months, according to distance and other circumstances! An invader's foot might have pressed our soil, while the Commander-in-Chief was practically deposed by a *subpœna!*

The defendant took no immediate steps to raise the question whether the court would attempt to enforce its process—reserving it probably, if his other chances of escape failed, to be made the occasion of a motion which will presently appear.

Of the manner of treating the Government witnesses, the following is a sample, from the lips of Randolph, usually one of the most moderate of Burr's counsel.

"Of James Wilkinson we are not afraid, in whatever shape he may be produced, in whatever form he may appear before this court. We are only afraid of those effects which desperation may produce in his mind. Desperation, may it please the court, is a word of great fitness in the present case. General Wilkinson we behold first acting as a conspirator to insnare others, afterwards as a patriot to betray others from motives of patriotism. What must be the embarrassment of this man when the awful catastrophe arrives, that he must either substantiate his own innocence by the conviction of another, or be himself regarded as a traitor and conspirator in the event of the acquittal of the accused."

On the 24th of June, the grand-jury came into court, and through their foreman, John Randolph, presented bills of indictment for treason and misdemeanor against Burr and Blennerhasset. Hay moved Burr's commitment, and it was ordered.

He was placed in the city jail. Two days afterwards, three of his counsel made affidavit that they " could not avoid remarking the danger which would most probably result to his health from the situation, inconveniences and circumstances attending the place of his confinement," that they could not " freely and fully perform what they had undertaken for his defence if he remained in the jail aforesaid, deprived as he was of a room to himself." The court thereupon ordered " the front room of the house, now occupied by Luther Martin, Esq.," to be " prepared for the reception and safe keeping of Colonel Aaron Burr," by suitable shutters and door fastenings, and by the employment of a guard of seven men, to be placed at the door and " on the floor of the adjoining unfinished house, and on the same story."

The prisoner being arraigned, plead not guilty, and the court made an order that the marshal summon forty-eight jurors to appear on the 3d day of August following, as a *venire* for the trial.

Hay presented a resolution of the Virginia Council of State, tendering "apartments" in the third story of the penitentiary, " for the use of such persons as should be directed, under the authority of the United States, to be confined therein ;" and he moved Burr's commitment there.   The prisoner's counsel objected to this ; but after a letter was received from Governor Cabell, tendering a selection of the unoccupied rooms of the penitentiary, and stipulating that the prisoner should be under the sole control of the marshal, with authority on the part of that officer to admit any persons he might think proper, to visit " the confined," the court ordered the commitment until the second day of August, when Burr was to be brought back to Martin's house, and to be guarded as before.

Burr wrote his daughter, Mrs. Alston, July 3d :

" I have three rooms in the third story of the penitentiary, making an extent of one hundred feet. My jailer is quite a polite and civil man—altogether unlike the idea one would form of a jailer. You would have laughed to have heard our compliments the first evening."

*   *   *   *   *   *   *

" While I have been writing, different servants have arrived with messages, notes and inquiries, bringing oranges, lemons, pineapples, raspberries, apricots, cream, butter, ice, and some ordinary articles."

" *July* 6, 1807.

" My friends and acquaintances of both sexes are permitted to visit me without interruption, without inquiring their business, and without the presence of a spy. It is well I have an ante-chamber, or I should often be *gêné* with visitors.

"If you come, I can give you a bedroom and parlor on this floor. The bedroom has three large closets, and is a much more commodious one than you ever had in your life."

The trial opened at the appointed time. After the President's letter to Hay of June 20th, already quoted, he again wrote him, June 23d, in regard to the papers wanted by the defence, promising that no pains should be spared to furnish them. His next letter (August 20th) was in answer to Hay, and the only noticeable passages in it are the following:

"Before an impartial jury, Burr's conduct would convict himself, were not one word of testimony to be offered against him. But to what a state will our law be reduced by party feelings in those who administer it? Why do not Blennerhassett, Dayton, etc., demand private and comfortable lodgings? In a country where an equal application of law to every condition of man is fundamental, how could it be denied to them? How can it ever be denied to the most degraded malefactor?"

This was the last letter written by the President to the counsel or to any one connected with the prosecution, during the trial for treason.

Burr's declarations and overtures to Eaton, and other similar ones, some going as far and others not, were proved. It was distinctly proved, by witnesses of the highest respectability, that Burr said or gave it to be understood that he contemplated a division of the Union. Blennerhassett and other agents had avowed this as one of the objects they had in view. Boats and military stores had been provided. Armed men had assembled avowedly as members of a common and concerted expedition. No other head of the expedition had been talked about but Burr. He came and openly assumed its general direction. But he was not personally present at Blennerhassett's Island, at the time the overt act was laid in the indictment. It was thus laid, because then, if at all, had an overt act taken place within the judicial district of Virginia.

The prisoner's counsel finally moved to stop the introduction of evidence in the trial for treason, on the ground—1st, that conformably to the Constitution, no man could be convicted of treason who was not present when the war was levied; 2d, that if this construction was erroneous, no testimony could be received to charge one man with the overt acts of others, until those overt acts, as laid in the indictment, were proved to the satisfaction of the court. The court pronounced its opinion August 31st, sustaining the motion and submitting the case at that stage to the jury. This amounted in effect to a direction to acquit the prisoner on that charge.

The jury retired, and in a few minutes returned with the following verdict: "We of the jury say that Aaron Burr is not proved to be guilty under this indictment by any evidence submitted to us. We therefore find him not guilty." Burr and his counsel objected to the verdict as unusual and irregular, and the former moved that the court "either send back the jury to alter it or correct it itself." Mr. Parker, one of the jury, said: "if he were to be sent back he would find the same verdict; that they all knew that it was not in the usual form; but it was more satisfactory to the jury as they found it; and that he would not agree to alter it." The court decided the verdict should remain as found, and that an entry should be made on the record of "not guilty."

After much discussion, the prisoner was discharged from the indictment for treason and put on trial for a misdemeanor. The *subpœna duces tecum* to the President was issued, and the Attorney of the United States acknowledged its service. He produced the portion of Wilkinson's letter to the President (of November 6th, 1806), which he did not regard as confidential and improper to be disclosed, stating that "the President had devolved on him the exercise of that discretion which constitutionally belonged to himself."

That Mr. Hay exercised the discretion confided to him in no contumacious spirit, and that there was no desire on his part to withhold anything in the letter which could be of benefit to the prisoner, appeared from the fact that he offered, prior to the service of the subpœna, to allow three of Burr's counsel—Wickham, Randolph, and Botts—to examine Wilkinson's letters to the Government. He said, "he would depend on their candor and integrity to make no improper disclosure; and if there should be any difference of opinion as to what were confidential passages, the court should decide."[1] Martin immediately "objected to this as a secret tribunal." He declared "the counsel had a right to hear them publicly without their consent."[2]

[1] Robertson's Report, vol. ii. p. 501.   [2] Ib. p. 502.

Mr. Hay stated more than once that the passages he desired to withhold were those containing the opinions given confidentially by Wilkinson to the Government in respect to individuals in the western country and in New Orleans, which had no connection with the question before the court, and the publication of which would seriously embroil Wilkinson with those persons. He said those opinions may have been changed, and very probably had been changed, since writing the letters.[1] The Chief Justice himself said, "he thought that neither the Government nor court ought to make such use of General Wilkinson's confidential letters as to embroil him with the world."[2]

After the subpœna had been served, Hay again accompanied his refusal to publicly exhibit the entire letter, by an offer to submit it to the inspection of Mr. Wickham, or to submit it to the court and to be controlled by the judgment of the latter. This compromise was pertinaciously refused by the defence; and another storm of vituperation was poured upon the Government for an attempt to set up an odious "State secrecy."

The motive of Burr's counsel was apparent. The court was committed on the legal question; and it must undoubtedly enforce obedience to its process or grant a motion already made by the defence, " that this case should stand continued [postponed] until this [Wilkinson's] letter should be produced and deposited with the clerk."

Judge Marshall said, "that in no case of this kind would a court be required to proceed against the President as against an ordinary individual; the objections to such a course were so strong and obvious that all must acknowledge them;"[3] and he ordered that the letter be publicly produced or that the case be "continued." But he said, if thought proper, the court would order no copy of the letter to be taken for public exhibition—that no use be made of it but what was necessarily attached to the case, and if "necessary to debate it in public, those who took notes might be directed not to insert any part of the arguments on that subject."

How far these restraints would be likely to protect Wilkinson practically from the effects of the disclosure, will be readily estimated. But that officer voluntarily consented to the exhi-

---

[1] Robertson's Rep., vol. ii. pp. 501, 510.   [2] Ib. p. 501.
[3] We have observed no intimation from the Chief Justice in respect to the nature of the "objections."

bition of his letter, and the trial proceeded. We have not space to continue even this imperfect outline. The attorney of the United States considered most of the testimony he had obtained excluded by a subsequent ruling of the Chief Justice, and he moved that the jury be discharged. The court decided this could not be done, except by mutual consent. The jury, therefore, brought in a verdict of " not guilty." The Chief Justice (October 20th) declined to order Burr's commitment elsewhere on the charge of treason, but ordered him committed for trial in Ohio for a misdemeanor. Bail was accepted for his appearance in the sum of three thousand dollars. Burr forfeited his recognizances, and fled to England.

During the progress of the last trial, the President addressed several letters in relation to the case to the United States Attorney. He instructed him (September 4th) to allow none of the witnesses to be paid or permitted to depart, until their testimony had been taken down in writing, either as delivered in court, or in the presence of any of Burr's counsel, who might choose to attend to cross-examine; and he added: " These whole proceedings will be laid before Congress, that they may decide whether the defect has been in the evidence of guilt, or in the law, or in the application of the law, and that they may provide the proper remedy for the past and the future." This letter contains reflections on the motives of the court, but not as pointed as some already given.

It has been claimed that the President interfered improperly in these trials, and that he exhibited an indecorous eagerness for the conviction of the prisoner. An inspection of his correspondence with Hay will show that he had very little to do with the actual management of the cases. His letters principally pertained to testimony which he was asked or required to furnish, and to his own official rights involved in questions entertained by the court. In short, out of, as well as in court, the President appears more in the light of a defendant than an assailant. We have given an instance where the constant and insulting invectives of a lawyer provoked a disposition in him to probe the motives of such malignity; but it appears only as a passing suggestion—nothing came of it. It is true, he reflected severely on the conduct of Judge Marshall. We have uniformly seen that he never spared that gentleman's motives on any occasion where political questions or consequences were to be affected by his judicial or other official action. But this was a private account between themselves. His imputations were not sent to the court or made public. They produced no effect.

While the President was held up in the court-room as a tyrant thirsting for innocent blood, and, by implication, as a wretch instigating perjury to attain his object—while the court was as coolly and authoritatively listening to arguments concerning, and passing upon, the constitutional right of the chief magistrate of the United States to the custody of his own executive papers,[1] and deciding the question whether he should be arrested for contempt, as if he was some subordinate officer of the court—that chief magistrate neither sent nor authorized any commumunication to the court lacking in the decency and respect which was due from the head of one department of the Government to another. He in no way publicly challenged its authority, except to give notice that he should not suffer his department or person to be violated; and we have seen no intimation that this determination was made known to the court in a manner which was considered offensive.

Again, in the capital of a State, four-fifths of whose people and prominent citizens were friends of the Administration, Burr's sympathizers were literally allowed to have their own way, when out of the court-room. At aristocratic " dinner parties," at hotels, on the corners of the streets, in the knots about the court-house, the voices were overwhelmingly in his favor. An intimation that these influences would be likely to bear improperly on the minds of the jury; that the ends of public justice were in danger of being defeated by this " outside pressure," would, in a few hours, have sent twice as many important men into Richmond as that city contained, to roll back this tide of manufactured sympathy. But to the last, Burr was the admired and caressed lion of the town. This does not look much like Government interference.

A lively illustration of the prevailing spirit, and of the President's private feelings, is presented by the following anecdote. Major Gibbons was United States Collector of the port of Rich-

---

[1] Which, by the Constitution, Congress are not authorized to see except at the President's discretion.

mond. He was a man of character, and was seamed with Revolutionary scars; but he was a warm Federalist, and so openly sympathized with Burr that he threw open his house for the constant reception of his friends during the trial. The President was solicited to remove Gibbons. He declined, and was further pressed, until he settled the point by saying jocularly but peremptorily: "Remove the Major! I would sooner divide my last hoe-cake with him."

In discussing Mr. Jefferson's conduct on Burr's trial, it has appeared to be the impression of some candid persons that the Executive cannot properly take any steps whatever in the way of collecting or arranging the testimony for the Government on such an occasion—in a word, take any step directly intended to increase the chances of the prisoner's conviction. This is clearly a mistaken view. It is the constitutional duty of the President to see the laws faithfully executed. It is his business to collect the proofs of conspiracy. The Attorney-General, whose duty it is to prosecute, is his appointee, a part of his Cabinet, his representative. The alleged impropriety of the President's personal interference, rests on the fact that it may bias his mind if called upon to exercise his prerogative of pardoning after conviction. Yet the direct prosecutor, the Attorney-General, gives a vote or voice in the Cabinet whether such pardon shall be granted. In a former administration we have seen a different Cabinet officer marching in person against violators of the law, so that he might be called upon to advise in regard to pardoning men whom he had recently faced in battle; or the chief who had permitted him thus to march, might be called upon to exercise that prerogative in regard to men whose hands were red with the blood of his friend and subordinate, slain in upholding the laws. Even the judge who is to try, may, without either a legal or moral disqualification for the latter duty, believe the prisoner guilty, and may earnestly desire his conviction if guilty. It only needs that he be willing to give him a perfectly fair trial, and to act purely and strictly according to law and evidence.

The President interfered in Burr's trial neither indecorously, nor more than was to be expected in the absence of the Attorney-General;[1] and his letters to Hay and others in

---

[1] This officer was detained at home by the illness of one of his family.

regard to it, may be pointed to with just pride as evidences of his character. The question is not whether he, in private and confidential communications, judged right or wrong of the law, of the motives of Judge Marshall, or of the guilt of the prisoner. That he felt thus strongly—that he was provoked into an obvious exhibition of temper—but throws out in stronger relief, the fact that a spirit of perfect fairness—a willingness to give the prisoner every just and legal advantage—and an avoidance of all trick, or management, to counteract what he believed to be those things on the other side—characterized every line and word he wrote on the subject, however confidential.

Let us now complete what we have to say of Aaron Burr's history. He escaped the punishment of a traitor only to endure a more prolonged punishment. Abroad, according to the rule of his life, he everywhere met with a gleam of success to be rapidly followed by irrevocable overthrow. His brilliant personal parts won admiration, until his insincerity, his want of good faith, and his predisposition to embark in dangerous schemes of any description that remotely promised to better his fortunes, rendered him an object of personal and governmental suspicion. England finally ordered him out of her territories. He went to Sweden and Germany, and reached France in 1810, filled with projects which were to be broached to Napoleon. After spending months in ineffectual attempts to procure an audience, his funds ran low, and he resolved to trust himself again in the United States. But, on application, a passport was denied him, and he found he was under the surveillance of the police. The American diplomatic officers turned their backs on him, and Russel, our chargé d'affaires, in answer to his demand for a passport, replied that he would give him one which would " enable him to surrender himself for trial for the offences with which he stood charged," and " no other." During the latter part of 1810, and until July, 1811, he was begging to be allowed to return home, and was often, if we may credit his journal, literally threatened with starvation. In the last-named year he obtained permission to leave France, and embarked for America; but the vessel was captured and carried into England. He remained there, driven to the most desperate shifts to keep off hunger—subsisting by expedients sometimes akin to beggary—until March, 1812, when he obtained money to pay a passage to Boston.

He arrived in New York in disguise, but finding the Government would not molest him, opened a law-office. The scenes of Richmond, in 1807, were never revived. The aristocratic dinner parties, the press of servants with perfumed billets, the crowding visitors of both sexes had disappeared. He could no longer be used for political purposes. To pay respect to him for the purpose of evincing disrespect to the chief magistrate and government of the country, had ceased to be fashionable; and, in the minds of the great majority of respectable Americans, his familiar association was liable to affix suspicions which were far from agreeable.

In the summer of 1812, his grandson, "who was to have redeemed all his glory, and shed new lustre upon the families" of Burr and Alston, perished, and the mother—the sweet and accomplished Theodosia—soon, it is to be hoped, followed. She left Charleston in November to join her father in New York. The vessel in which she embarked was never again heard of. Whether it went down in a wild gale which soon swept our whole Atlantic sea-board, or whether she was reserved for a fate which it causes a shudder to contemplate, can never be known until that day when the ocean shall give up its secrets and its dead. Horrid rumors occasionally found their way to the ears of Burr. He loved his daughter, but he met the terrors which imagination presented with a bosom of steel—with that stony undauntedness which was one of the most marked traits in his character, and which, with different principles, and under better auspices, might have made him a hero.

His old creditors fell upon him, to use his own words, "with vindictive fury"—especially the holders of his Mexican debts—and he "saw no probability of keeping out of a prison." From that period until 1834, a little shrivelled old man might be occasionally seen in the courts of law engaged in some cause, or flitting silently and alone along the streets of the crowded metropolis. Few seemed to know him, and he addressed himself to but few. He was reserved in speech, and his tread, as of old, was stealthy and cat-like. The age which tames, and the misfortunes which chasten rightly constituted minds, had produced no effect on his. Tottering on the verge of the grave, crushed, forlorn, subsisting on the charity of one who was not of his kindred, it was still his chief ambition to be thought to possess

the manners of Chesterfield and the morals of Rochester. Tl
are no good reasons for supposing that a trace of remorse (
visited his conscience. There is not a shadow of proof that am
all the teeming projects of his brain there was one which had
its object the melioration of man. Finally, paralysis smote l
and for two years he could not move without assistance. {
propped up in bed, he plotted and wrote *billets-doux!* '
curtain dropped on the scene on the 14th of September, 183(

CHAPTER VI.

1807—1808.

BURR's trial attracted comparatively little general notice during its progress, in consequence of the occurrence of more important and exciting events.

On the 22d of June, 1807, the United States frigate Chesapeake, of thirty-eight guns, got under weigh from Hampton Roads for the Mediterranean, carrying Commodore Barron, who, his health being restored, was to resume the command on that station. Lying in Lynnhaven Bay were the British vessels of war Bellona, 74; Leopard, 50 (but carrying, it was said, 56); and the Melampus, 38. The Leopard lifted her anchor, and stood out of the Capes, ahead of the Chesapeake; but this was not a matter to attract any notice, as the British vessels were constantly cruising in the offing. In the afternoon the vessels were near together, and the Leopard hailed, saying she had dispatches for Commodore Barron. She soon sent a boat alongside the Chesapeake, and exhibited an order from Vice-Admiral Berkley to the captains under his command, that in case they fell in with the Chesapeake, out of the American waters, they were to " require to search for deserters " and " proceed and search for the same, and if a similar demand should be made by the American, he was permitted to search for deserters from their service," [1] etc.

Barron replied that he knew of no such deserters as were claimed—that his recruiting officers had been particularly instructed by the Government not to enter British deserters— that his orders did not permit his crew to be mustered by any but their own officers. Observing an appearance of preparation on board the Leopard, he ordered his men to quarters without drum beat, and as quietly as possible. But not suspecting any difficulty, he had put to sea with decks incumbered, with nothing in its proper place, and with a crew that had not once exercised the guns. The rammers, wads, matches, locks, and powder-horns for the latter, were unprepared, so that practically the guns were wholly unserviceable.

As soon as the Leopard's officer returned, that vessel again hailed, now lying on the weather-quarter of the Chesapeake, and within pistol-shot. Commodore Barron answered he did

---

[1] The British minister at Washington had informed our Government that three British deserters were on board the Chesapeake, and he requested that they be delivered up. The Navy department referred the matter to Barron, and he to Captain Gordon, the commander of the vessel. The latter fairly investigated the facts, and found that the men were deserters, but that two of them certainly, and it was supposed the third, were impressed Americans. The facts were reported to the British minister, and he appeared satisfied. Nothing more was heard on the subject until the attack on the Chesapeake. The men taken from the Chesapeake were not those who had been the subjects of the correspondence.

not understand the hail. The Leopard immediately fired a shot ahead, and a few seconds afterwards poured a full broadside into the American vessel. She continued steadily firing from twelve to eighteen minutes, until Barron, after repeatedly desiring that at least one gun be discharged, ordered his colors to be struck, and as they reached the taffrail, a gun was discharged by an officer, who applied with his fingers a coal brought from the galley. Captain Humphreys, of the Leopard, refused to accept the surrender of the ship twice tendered, but he took away four deserters found on board. The Chesapeake returned to Hampton Roads. She was considerably damaged, especially in her spars and rigging. Three of her men were killed, and eighteen wounded. Among the latter were Commodore Barron and his aid, Mr. Broom.[1]

The four men taken from the Chesapeake were tried at Halifax and condemned to be hung. Three who were Americans were subsequently pardoned, on condition of returning to service in the British fleet; but on the British deserter the sentence was executed.

On the return of the Chesapeake, an intense excitement broke out among the American people. The inhabitants of Norfolk and Portsmouth unanimously passed resolutions to hold no further intercourse with the British vessels until the pleasure of the Government should be known. Douglas, the commander of the squadron, wrote the Mayor of Norfolk an insolent letter, July 3d, saying the inhabitants could have war or peace as they desired. Governor Cabell at once ordered out bodies of militia to cover these towns. It would seem that at about the same time, a vessel, on her way to New York, and on board of which were Vice-President Clinton and his daughter, was either endangered or insulted by a British cruiser.[2]

The President immediately dispatched a vessel to England to instruct our ministers to demand reparation for the insult we had received, and on the 2d of July he issued a proclamation forbidding the waters of the United States to all British vessels of war, unless in distress or bearing dispatches. Captain

[1] Courts martial were held on Barron, Captain Gordon, Captain Hall of the marines, and the gunner. The first was entirely acquitted of cowardice, but found guilty of negligence, and was suspended from rank and pay for five years. Gordon and Hall were reprimanded, and the gunner cashiered.

[2] See Jefferson to Clinton, July 6, 1807.

Douglas, however, remained in the neighborhood of Norfolk, and even took soundings of the passage to the town, as if intending an attack on it or on the Chesapeake, Cybele, and some gunboats lying there. These facts flew through the United States, increasing the public indignation; and the nation, as one man, called for instant war. The President wrote General Lafayette soon afterwards:

"I inclose you a proclamation, which will show you the critical footing on which we stand at present with England. Never, since the battle of Lexington, have I seen this country in such a state of exasperation as at present. And even that did not produce such unanimity. The Federalists themselves coalesce with us as to the object, although they will return to their old trade of condemning every step we take towards obtaining it. 'Reparation for the past, and security for the future,' is our motto. Whether these will be yielded freely, or will require resort to non-intercourse, or to war, is yet to be seen. We have actually near two thousand men in the field, covering the exposed parts of the coast, and cutting off supplies from the British vessels."

The following hitherto unpublished letter to Mr. Eppes gives the President's views as to the proper course to be pursued by the Government as well as any of the numerous published ones of the same period; and it alludes to another domestic bereavement—the death of the second child of his deceased daughter, Mrs. Eppes:

To JOHN W. EPPES.

WASHINGTON, *July* 12, '07.

DEAR SIR:

Yours of the 3d is received. At that time, I presume, you had not got mine of June 19th, asking the favor of you to procure me a horse. I have lost three since you left this place; however, I can get along with the three I have remaining, so as to give time for looking up a fourth, suitable in as many points as can be obtained. My happiness at Monticello (if I am able to go there) will be lessened by not having yourself and Francis there; but the circumstance which prevents it is among the most painful that have happened to me in life. Thus comfort after comfort drops off from us, till nothing is left but what is proper food for the grave. I trust, however, we shall have yourself and Francis the ensuing winter, and the one following that, and we must let the aftertime provide for itself. He will ever be to me one of the dearest objects in life.

The affair of the Chesapeake seems to have come in as an interlude during the suspension of Burr's trial. I suspect it will turn out that the order Berkley received from his Government was in equivocal terms, implying force or not as should suit them, to say; and the construction would be governed by Bonaparte's successes or misfortunes. I know that Berkley's order to the ships under him was of that character. However, their orders are to be nothing in our eyes. The fact is what they have to settle with us. Reason and the usage of civilized nations require that we should give them an opportunity of disavowal and reparation. Our own interest, too, the very means of making war, requires that we should give time to our merchants to gather in their vessels and property and our seamen now afloat : and our duty requires that we do no act which shall commit Congress in their choice between war, non-intercourse, and other measures. You will be called as early as the circumstances of health and of an answer from England will recommend, probably some time in October. Should that country have the good sense to do us ample justice, it will be a war saved; but I do not expect it, and every preparation is therefore going on, and will continue, which is within our power. A war need cost us very little, and we can take from them what would be an indemnification for a great deal. For this everything shall be in readiness at the moment it is declared. I have not yet heard how Commodore Douglas has taken the proclamation. That he will obey it, I doubt. Should he not, the moment our 16 gunboats in that quarter are ready they will be able to take off all his small vessels and to oblige his large ones to keep together. I count on their being all ready before the end of this month, and that by that time we shall have 32 in New York, and a good provision of batteries along the shores of the city; for to waste labor in defending the approaches to it would be idle. The only practicable object is to prevent ships coming to before it. We have nothing interesting to us from either London, Paris, or Madrid, except that Yrugo leaves us, and a successor is to come. In the meantime, we have received Foronda as *chargé des affaires*, a most able and amiable man. In consequence of this, Bowdoin will probably go on to Madrid. We shall thus avoid the mischief which the dissensions between him and Armstrong were likely to produce. Present my warm affections to Mr. and Mrs. Eppes and to the family, and accept the same for yourself.

                                                    TH. JEFFERSON.

Steps were immediately taken to put New York, Charleston, and New Orleans in the best practicable state of defence. The Virginia militia effectually cut off all communication between the British fleet in the Chesapeake and the shore, and measures were under discussion to drive it from its present menacing position, when Captain Douglas rendered it unnecessary by returning to the outer bay, and announcing that he contemplated no acts of hostility until the orders of his Government should be received.

Decatur, in command of our naval force at Norfolk, was instructed to leave the British squadron unassailed if it remained quiet in its present situation, but to attack it with all his force should an attempt be made to enter the Elizabeth River. Similar orders were sent to Rodgers at New York, in case British armed vessels attempted to enter the bay. Gallatin and Madison, being both ill with the bilious disease incidental to the climate of Washington in the hot months, and there being no further special reasons for the Cabinet remaining together, they dispersed, after arranging for a constant communication with each other. The President reached Monticello on the 1st of August. Congress was convened for the 26th of October—as early as it was expected an answer would be received from England.

Spain having demanded satisfaction for the pretended participation of the United States in Miranda's expedition, the President wrote to the Secretary of State, August 16th:

"If anything Thrasonic and foolish from Spain could add to my contempt of that Government, it would be the demand of satisfaction now made by Foronda. However, respect to ourselves requires that the answer should be decent, and I think it fortunate that this opportunity is given to make a strong declaration of facts, to wit, how far our knowledge of Miranda's objects went, what measures we took to prevent anything further, the negligence of the Spanish agents to give us earlier notice, the measures we took for punishing those guilty, and our quiet abandonment of those taken by the Spaniards. But I would not say a word in recrimination as to the western intrigues of Spain. I think that is the snare intended by this protest, to make it a set-off for the other. As soon as we have all the proofs of the western intrigues, let us make a remonstrance and demand of satisfaction, and, if Congress approves, we may in the same instant make reprisals on the Floridas, until satisfaction for that and for spoliations, and until a settlement of boundary. I had rather have war against Spain than not, if we go to war against England. Our southern defensive force can take the Floridas, volunteers for a Mexican army will flock to our standard, and rich pabulum will be offered to our privateers in the plunder of their commerce and coasts. Probably Cuba would add itself to our confederation."

Some lively correspondence took place with the British Minister, Mr. Erskine; and on his asking indemnification for water casks, belonging to the British fleet, destroyed by the people of Hampton, after the return of the Chesapeake, the President wrote the Secretary of State:

"It will be very difficult to answer Mr. Erskine's demand respecting the water casks in the tone proper for such a demand. I have heard of one who, having broke his cane over the head of another, demanded payment for his cane. This demand might well enough have made part of an offer to pay the damages done to the Chesapeake, and to deliver up the authors of the murders committed on board her."

And still from another quarter came menaces of hostilities. The Northwestern Indians, who had been tampered with by the Governor of Upper Canada, were in commotion. On the 28th of August, the President proposed to the Secretary of War that the Governors of Michigan, Ohio, and Indiana be at once instructed to enroll bodies of militia, to fall upon such tribes as should take up the war hatchet. He thought, however,

Governors Hull and Harrison should first make an earnest effort to induce the Indians to remain at peace; and he wished the following representations to be made to the latter:

"That we never wished to do them an injury, but on the contrary, to give them all the assistance in our power towards improving their condition, and enabling them to support themselves and their families; that a misunderstanding having arisen between the United States and the English, war may possibly ensue. That in this war it is our wish the Indians should be quiet spectators, not wasting their blood in quarrels which do not concern them; that we are strong enough to fight our own battles, and therefore ask no help; and if the English should ask theirs, it should convince them that it proceeds from a sense of their own weakness, which would not augur success in the end; that at the same time, as we have learnt that some tribes are already expressing intentions hostile to the United States, we think it proper to apprise them of the ground on which they now stand; for which purpose we make to them this solemn declaration of our unalterable determination, that we wish them to live in peace with all nations as well as with us, and we have no intention ever to strike them or to do them an injury of any sort, unless first attacked or threatened; but that learning that some of them meditate war on us, we too are preparing for war against those, and those only who shall seek it; and that if ever we are constrained to lift the hatchet against any tribe, we will never lay it down till that tribe is exterminated, or driven beyond the Mississippi. Adjuring them, therefore, if they wish to remain on the land which covers the bones of their fathers, to keep at peace with a people who ask their friendship without needing it, who wish to avoid war without fearing it. In war, they will kill some of us; we shall destroy all of them. Let them then continue quiet at home, take care of their women and children, and remove from among them the agents of any nation, persuading them to war, and let them declare to us explicitly and categorically that they will do this: in which case, they will have nothing to fear from the preparations we are now unwillingly making to secure our own safety."

How different would have been the character of both of our wars with England, and how different would have been the fate of the red man, if our enemy also had acted on the humane and enlightened policy here shadowed forth![1]

It would appear that the President was less sanguine of a favorable termination of the present negotiation with England than some of his Cabinet. He wrote the Secretary of the Navy, September 3d:

"I do not see the probability of receiving from Great Britain reparation for the wrong committed on the Chesapeake, and future security for our seamen, in the same favorable light with Mr. Gallatin and yourself. If indeed the consequence of the battle of Friedland can be to exclude her from the Baltic, she may temporize with us. But if peace among the *continental* powers of Europe should leave her

[1] The Society of Friends, or "Quakers," at Philadelphia, expressed to the President soon after this, through James Pemberton, their high satisfaction at his uniform course of policy towards the Indians.

free in her intercourse with the powers who will then be *neutral*, the present ministry, perhaps no ministry which can now be formed, will not, in my opinion, give us
the necessary assurance respecting our flag. In that case, it must bring on a war
soon, and if so, it can never be in a better time for us. I look to this, therefore,
as most probably now to take place, although I do most sincerely wish that a just
and sufficient security may be given us, and such an interruption of our property
avoided."

The undaunted and even lively tone of the preceding declarations—when apparently the clouds of war were rising in
every quarter of the heavens against us—the actual preference
expressed, if we must fight England, to make but one job of it
in fighting her and Spain—the readiness, if the unfortunate
Indians could not be induced by a final and solemn warning to
keep at peace, to take the initiative, and carry a prompt war of
invasion into their territories—give a forcible picture of the
President's nerve and moral courage, when his favorite peace
policy was supposed to be no longer available.

We will pass his private correspondence during the summer,
after barely enumerating a portion of his letters and their subjects. We find him complaining to the Count Diodati of the
intolerable weariness of office; acknowledging to M. Silvestre,
the gold medal of the Agricultural Society of Paris, for his
" mould-board of least resistance ;" presenting to John Norvell,
some interesting views on a course of political, and historical
reading, and on the proper manner of conducting a newspaper;
declining, to Governor Sullivan, to make a tour north, during
his Presidency, as a thing which he disrelished, if he did not
consider it actually improper;[1] declining to Mr. Weaver, to be
considered a candidate for reëlection; writing the usual occasional friendly letters to Dupont de Nemours and Lafayette;
thanking Madame de Staël for a work she had sent him, and
assuring her how welcome would be a proposed visit from her

---

[1] His views on this topic have not been, we think, before presented, and they are
worthy of consideration :

" With respect to the tour my friends to the North have proposed that I should make in
that quarter, I have not made up a final opinion. The course of life which General Washington had run, civil and military, the services he had rendered, and the space he therefore occupied in the affections of his fellow citizens, take from his examples the weight
of precedents for others, because no others can arrogate to themselves the claims which
he had on the public homage. To myself, therefore, it comes as a new question, to be
viewed under all the phases it may present. I confess that I am not reconciled to the
idea of a chief magistrate parading himself through the several States, as an object of
public gaze, and in quest of an applause which, to be valuable, should be purely voluntary. I had rather acquire silent good will by a faithful discharge of my duties, than
owe expressions of it to my putting myself in the way of receiving them."

son at Monticello; declaring to his friend, Governor Page, that "he had never removed a man [from office] because he was a Federalist," and "never wished them [the Federalists in office] to give a vote at an election, but according to their own wishes;"[1] and thanking John Nicholas[2] and others, for the offer of volunteers to support the Government.

A letter to his old and beloved friend, Dr. Wistar, of Philadelphia, solicits a little more notice, on account of some incidents which we desire to narrate in connection with it. The President wrote :

"I have a grandson, the son of Mr. Randolph, now about fifteen years of age, in whose education I take a lively interest.   .   .   .   .   .

I am not a friend to placing young men in populous cities, because they acquire there habits and partialities which do not contribute to the happiness of their after life. But there are particular branches of science, which are not so advantageously taught anywhere else in the United States as in Philadelphia. The garden at the Woodlands for Botany, Mr. Peale's Museum for Natural History, your Medical school for Anatomy, and the able professors in all of them, give advantages not to be found elsewhere. We propose, therefore, to send him to Philadelphia to attend the schools of Botany, Natural History, Anatomy, and perhaps Surgery; but not of Medicine."

The grandson here referred to—Colonel Thomas Jefferson Randolph, of Edgehill—informs us that on his way to Philadelphia, on this occasion, he stopped some days with his grandfather at Washington. He says, that not long after his arrival, the latter came into his room and desired him to unpack his trunks and spread out their contents. With the same careful scrutiny that a mother would have given, he examined every article of apparel. He then took out a pencil and paper and commenced making a list of additional things, saying, " you will need this and this, when you get to Philadelphia." After completing the enumeration, he went out with his grandson, and purchased the articles, selecting the best, but constantly consulting the taste of the latter. Pocket and purse underwent the same examination with the same improvement. This, says our informant, was characteristic of his habitual method of treating children. And children always understood him at the first glance. The same was true in a remarkable degree of servants, and, indeed, of all plain and ignorant men. His look, cold to

---

[1] This letter is dated July 17th.   [2] Then of Geneva, New York.

the polished stranger, fell benignantly and lovingly upon the weak, the simple, and the lowly, and they at once felt and returned the sympathy. They never feared him, they never presumed upon him. They were often observed, when they had no idea who he was, to select him out of the most glittering party as the subject of an almost exclusive and obviously admiring attention.

The last remark reminds us of an anecdote which we received from one of the actors in it. Mr. Jefferson and his oldest grandson were riding in a carriage together. A stranger slave in the highway took off his hat and bowed to them. Mr. Jefferson, according to his invariable wont in such cases, touched or raised his hat, and bowed. The grandson, being busy talking, supposed this would do, and made no separate return to the salutation. With gentle but intended reproof in his eye, Mr. Jefferson turned to him, and asked : "Thomas, do you permit a slave to be more of a gentleman than yourself?"

Not far from the year of which we are writing (1807), Mr. Jefferson, while on a visit home, accompanied two of his nephews on horseback to Charlottesville. Here two or three gentlemen were invited to Monticello to dinner. The company did not set off precisely together. Mr. Jefferson, with one or both his nephews and another youngish gentlemen, constituted the advanced guard. A smart shower had fallen during the forenoon, and when they got back to Moore's Creek, the water was running up to the saddle girths of a horse. An ordinary western-appearing man was sitting on the bank with a saddle in his hands. He waited until all the party had entered the stream but Mr. Jefferson, and then asked him for a ride across. To rein up to a stone, suffer him to mount, *en croupe*, and carry him to the opposite bank, was a matter of course. In a few moments the party in the rear, who had witnessed the affair, overtook our besaddled pedestrian, stretching away at a sturdy pace along the foot of Carter's mountain. "I say!" quoth a junior; "what made you let the young men pass and ask that gentleman to carry you over the creek?" "Wall," said Kentucky, in broad patois, "if you want to know, I'll tell you: I reckon a man carries yes or no in his face—the young chaps' faces said no—the old 'un's said yes." "It isn't every man that would have asked the President of the United States for a ride behind him," said the other, expecting, perhaps, to blank the bold visage of Kentucky. If such was his object, however, he was very much mistaken. "You don't say that was Tom Jefferson, do you?" was the reply, and he immediately added: "he's a . . . . . fine old fellow, anyway." "That was the President," was the response. Kentucky looked up and looked round, the locality well known to travellers at once carrying conviction to his mind. He appeared to be in a brown study for a moment; the massive features then relaxed; he burst into a loud laugh, and thus he spoke: "What do you suppose my wife, Polly, will say when I get back to Boone County, and tell her I've rid behind Jefferson? she'll say I voted for the *right man!*"

On another occasion the President was riding along the bank of the Rivanna and saw a very ragged old man waiting at a ford on the opposite shore. He rode across, took him up behind, and brought him over. An intimate friend of Mr. Jefferson told us that he once heard the latter express compunction for not picking up an old soldier, whom he once, during the Revolutionary war, saw sitting, at nightfall, by the roadside, not very near any house. The soldier was very drunk, and Mrs. Jefferson was in the carriage; but he was touched to think that perhaps he had left a man and a "soldier" to lay out through a wet and chilly night.

We have the following anecdote from a gentleman who had it from one of the parties. The President was riding in the environs of Washington, and overtook a man of common but respectable appearance, walking towards "the city." To draw up and salute him was a habitual civility. The stranger asked some political questions, and a conversation on political topics ensued. He exhibited much sense mixed up with much partisan feeling. He strongly censured certain acts of the Administration, and getting warm, finally alluded to some of the indecent personal stories of Callender against the President. Things were getting into an uncomfortable shape for the latter; but instead of obeying his first impulse to ride abruptly away, he asked his companion "if he knew Mr. Jefferson personally?" "No," said the other, "nor do I want to." "But is it fair play to believe and repeat such stories, and then not dare to meet the subject of them face to face and trust to your own senses?'

This man, too, was a Kentuckian—a country merchant of excellent character on his way to the capital, who had stopped a stage out of the city to call on acquaintances. The word "dare" presented the matter in a new phase, and he promptly responded: "I will never shrink from meeting Mr. Jefferson, if he comes in my way." "Will you go to his house to-morrow at —— o'clock, and be introduced to him, if I will meet you there?" "Yes." Promising to be there, and making some excuse for haste, the President then rode rapidly on.

He had hardly gone, before a suspicion darted into the traveller's mind, and he commenced comparing the tall form, the sandy hair, the bold, easy rider, the superb horse, with descriptions he had read of Mr. Jefferson. To think of the question of identity was to settle it at once. At the appointed time next day, the President received the card of Mr. ——, "his yesterday's companion who promised to call at —— o'clock." He was ushered in, now a well dressed man, and he immediately said : "I have called, Mr. Jefferson, to apologize for having said to a stranger " . . . Here the President laughingly interrupted him, by saying—"hard things of an imaginary personage, who is no relation of mine." Mr. —— was not satisfied to have the subject dropped without a more formal *amende ;* but all attempts at explanation were laughingly parried. He soon found himself at his ease in another animated conversation, until, to his utter surprise at such a rapid lapse of time, a servant announced dinner. The President insisted on his staying. Mr. —— firmly declined, until his entertainer archly asked him if he was afraid of meeting Mr. * * * Mr. * * * "Don't mention him," said the other, "and I will stay." The sequel of this strangely struck up acquaintance we need not give, further, than to say that henceforth the ——s, of Kentucky, were fiery Jeffersonians, and that Mr. ——, senior, used often to laughingly caution young people not to be *too* free in talking with strangers.

The foregoing anecdotes do not all, perhaps, illustrate the point we started with, but they illustrate the man.

Here is a glimpse of farming matters in Virginia, in the autumn of 1807, in a letter from the President (November 21st) to Mr. Maury :

"The crops of the present year have been great beyond example. The wheat sown for the ensuing year is in a great measure destroyed by the drought and the fly. A favorable winter and spring sometimes do wonders towards recovering unpromising grain; but nothing can make the next crop of wheat a good one.

"The present aspect of our foreign relations has encouraged here a general spirit of encouragement to domestic manufacture. The Merino breed of sheep is well established with us, and fine samples of cloth are sent on from the North. Considerable manufactures of cotton are also commencing. Philadelphia, particularly, is becoming more manufacturing than commercial."

To gain a clear insight into the relations between the United States and England, growing out of the affair of the Leopard and Chesapeake, it may be well to present the main facts connectedly, instead of mingling them with intervening occurrences. It is to be premised that Mr. Canning, the brilliant *élève* of the late Mr. Pitt, and the uncompromisingness of whose toryism, like that of his archetype, was only equalled by its undauntedness in action, was the British Secretary of State for Foreign Affairs. There was a strong party in England composed of the ship-owners, the navy, the East and West India merchants, and "political characters of great consideration in the state," who were decidedly in favor of plundering, and sweeping away the competition of, American commerce. So strong was this combination, wrote home Monroe, that "it was most certain that nothing could be obtained of the Government on any point but what might be extorted by necessity." Everything, therefore, in the relations of the two countries was in a most uncertain state—the results depending more perhaps on the success of particular interests and political combinations in England than on any other causes.

It has been sometimes assumed that the President's rejection of the treaty formed by Monroe and Pinkney was the origin of all the hostile feeling in England against us, and the foundation of the war of 1812. Canning did afterwards complain that the President had no right to approve what he pleased and condemn what he pleased in the treaty, and instruct the American ministers to attempt to procure amendments in the latter points and consider the former settled. He required that the whole subject be reopened from the beginning, if any part of it was reopened. But in glancing through Monroe's correspondence until he asked his audience of leave, we do not observe an intimation that the rejection of the treaty was complained of or treated as an offensive and much less a hostile act.

The truth was, England had determined to replenish her huge navy through her Bonapartean wars from the preëminent seamen, who were trained in the merchant marine of the United States. If we would submit to this, she was willing to make some concessions in favor of our commerce. But we had received a significant hint, even on this head, at the moment our ministers signed the rejected treaty, in the notice that the provisions in favor of our neutral rights would depend on our degree of submission to France, and that England would practically reserve the sole right of deciding in the latter particular. In short, the complete supremacy which England had obtained on the ocean rendered a war between her and a maritime power as growing and enterprising as the United States absolutely unavoidable, unless the latter were willing to play the part of a very tame jackal to a very hungry lion. We had in reality a second war of independence to fight, as necessary as the first for the preservation of certain essential parts of our independent nationality.

No civilized nation of modern times had claimed the right of forcibly taking deserters from the public vessels of a friend. Consequently, Mr. Canning went through the form of expressing his regrets to the American minister in regard to the affair of the Chesapeake; and he even said that, "if the British officers should prove to have been culpable, the most prompt and effectual reparation should be afforded to the Government of the United States." But he persisted in connecting the question with that of the nationality of the deserters, and with others having as little proper relevancy. His conduct, in short, was obviously evasive, and intended to gain time for political developments at home and warlike ones abroad.

He presently found a new cavil in the circumstance that the President had ordered British armed vessels out of the American waters—assuming that it was an act of retaliation without awaiting explanations. And he next declared that he would not, in diplomatic negotiations with the United States, connect the affair of the Chesapeake with the subject of impressment —that if our ministers' instructions compelled them to connect these topics, further efforts to treat would be useless for the present—that in that event, a minister would be forthwith sent to the United States to arrange the affair of the Chesapeake, but not "empowered to entertain, as connected with this topic, any proposition respecting the search of merchant vessels."

In October, a proclamation was issued by the British king, authorizing and commanding officers of his ships of war "to seize upon, take, and bring away" all his natural-born subjects found serving in merchant vessels of any foreign state. On receiving information that such subjects were serving on board a foreign armed vessel, his officers were to require their delivery, and if it was refused, to so report to the commander-in-chief of the squadron: and the last-named officer was to transmit the fact immediately to the British minister at the "seat of government of that state to which the said foreign ship of war should belong, to demand reparation for the injury," etc.

On it being objected by the American minister that this closed the door to negotiation, Canning replied that it was merely a declaration of the existing law, necessary to be made for the information of his majesty's commanders, since the disavowal of Berkley's conduct in the case of the Chesapeake left them without a guide to their proper action. Towards the close of October, he made a final reply to the proposition of the American ministers, to renew negotiations on the basis of the rejected treaty; and he declined to do so.

Monroe, considering all the objects of his particular mission now at an end, asked his audience of leave, and returned home. Pinkney remained to discharge the duties of a resident minister.

On the 11th of November, 1807, the King of·Great Britain issued orders in council, which showed that the interests which were in favor of plundering our commerce had completely triumphed. These orders declared all ports and places belonging to France and her allies subjected to the same restrictions as if in a state of rigorous blockade, with the exception that neutral vessels might trade in them on clearing from the ports of Great Britain or her allies, "under such regulations as his majesty might think fit to prescribe," and on the condition, also, that on their return voyages they sail directly to the ports of Great Britain or her allies, again submitting to the prescribed "regulations." But if neutrals were found, under any circumstances, carrying French "certificates of origin,"[1] the vessel and

---

[1] "Certificates of origin" were certificates obtained of French agents at the ports of shipment, declaring that the articles of the cargo were not of the produce or manufacture of his Britannic majesty's dominions.

cargo were declared lawful prize. The "regulations" included an onerous "transit duty," and required neutrals to take out a British "license" to trade with the enemies of Great Britain.[1]

Napoleon determined that England should not be benefited by this system, whatever wrongs he might inflict on neutrals, to prevent it, and he issued his "Milan decree" (December 17th, 1807), declaring every vessel denationalized and forfeited which submitted to be searched by British cruisers, or paid duties or license money to that Government, or which was found sailing to or from British ports. These regulations were to be annulled as soon as Great Britain should return to the principles of the laws of nations.

The consequences of all these measures were that American

---

[1] These "regulations" were established by an additional order in council, November 25th, 1807; and by an act of parliament of March 25th, 1808.

The direct war on neutral rights had been commenced by the British orders in council of May 16th, 1806, which declared the whole coast of France and Germany, from Brest to the Elbe—a distance of about eight hundred miles—in a state of blockade! This was retaliated by Napoleon's "Berlin decree," of November 21st, 1806, which declared the British Islands in a state of blockade. The second British order of January, 1807, and the third and crushing one of November, the same year, were avowedly made in retaliation of the Berlin decree. Yet, when that of January was made, it was not pretended that "any injury had accrued to or was apprehended by Great Britain, from an execution of the French decree against the commerce of the United States on the theatre of their neutral rights." (See Madison to Erskine, March 25th, 1808.) In fact, it was notorious that the Berlin decree was not enforced against the United States until about a year after its date and until long after the retaliatory order in council. Alexander Baring (since Lord Ashburton) a distinguished member of the British Parliament, truly said: "No condemnation of an American vessel had ever taken place under it; and so little did the French privateers interfere with the trade of America with this country, that the insurance on it has been but very little higher than in time of profound peace; while that on the American trade with the Continent of Europe has at the same time been doubled and even trebled by the conduct of our cruisers." (*Inquiry into the Causes and Consequences of the Orders in Council*, etc., by Alexander Baring, M.P. London, February, 1808.) There appears, therefore, to be but one explanation of the conduct of England towards the United States. She *began* a species of naval aggression peculiarly injurious to them and profitable to herself. When France retaliated, making an exception in favor of the United States, England made that retaliation a pretext for a new and more serious aggression on the United States! She occupied then the miserable attitude of a power taking advantage of her own wrong to push on a war of commercial regulations in order to plunder an innocent third party.

It was the well settled law of England that there could be no such thing as a paper or mere declaratory blockade, which would authorize confiscation for violating it. In the case of the Betsey, December 18th, 1798, Sir William Scott held: "On the question of blockade, three things must be proved; first, the existence of an *actual blockade*; second, the knowledge of the party; third, some act of violation, either by going in or coming out with a cargo, laden after the commencement of the blockade." (Rob. Adm. Rep. vol. i. p. 93.) This opinion was confirmed in repeated cases extending down to the interpolations in international maritime law, commenced by the earlier orders in council. So scrupulous was England in 1800, that the Maria Schrœder, a neutral vessel, was ordered to be restored for violating the blockade of Havre—it being shown that that blockade was not strictly maintained. (Rob. vol. iii. p. 147.) In 1807, a paper blockade of nearly the whole European continent authorized confiscation, and carrying a "certificate of origin," authorized the condemnation of ship and cargo! Even Reddie, perhaps the most blind apologist of England who has ever written on maritime law, refuses to justify the "regulations" under the British order in council of November, 1807. (Reddie on Maritime International Law, vol. ii. p. 28–31.) Bynkershoek thus, in consonance with reason and justice, lays down the rule which limits the right of retaliation to the aggressor: "Diceres id edictum, jure retorsionis subsistere. Sed retorsio non est, nisi adversus eum, qui ipse damni quid dedit; ac deinde patitur; non vero adversus communem amicum." "Qui injuriam non fecit, non recte patitur."

commerce with any European power (unless we should practically except England) was mostly excluded from the ocean. If it attempted to reach the Continent in violation of British orders, it became the almost certain prey of British cruisers in going or returning. If it stopped and paid the required tribute to England, confiscation awaited it when it reached continental ports.

Congress assembled on the 26th of October. The Federalists were reduced to a still smaller minority than in the preceding Congress. In the Senate, William H. Crawford, of Georgia, soon took the place of Baldwin, deceased;[1] John Pope, of Kentucky, the place of Clay; Jesse Franklin, of North Carolina, the place of Stone; Andrew Gregg, of Pennsylvania, the place of Logan; Jonathan Robinson, of Vermont, the place of Smith; Chauncey Goodrich, of Connecticut, the place of Tracy, deceased; Elisha Matthewson, of Rhode Island, the place of Fenner; and Nahum Parker, of New Hampshire, the place of Plumer. There were but six Federal senators in all: Hillhouse and Goodrich, of Connecticut; Bayard and White, of Delaware; and Pickering and Adams, of Massachusetts. The number was soon to be reduced to five, by Mr. Adams going over to the Republicans.

Among the most prominent Administration members in the House of Representatives were W. C. Nicholas, Eppes and Burwell, of Virginia; Macon and Alston, of North Carolina; Campbell, of Tennessee; Varnum, Crowninshield and Bacon, of Massachusetts; Findley and Smilie, of Pennsylvania; Sloan, of New Jersey; Clinton, Mumford, and Van Cortlandt, of New York; R. M. Johnson and Desha, of Kentucky; and Troup, of Georgia. The most prominent Federalists were Quincy, of Massachusetts; Dana and Davenport, of Connecticut; Key, of Maryland; and Gardenier and Van Rensselaer, of New York. The Quids were represented by three or four members of considerable ability, with John Randolph at their head.

The President's message was calm in its tone. After alluding to the causes which induced the extraordinary mission to Great Britain, he said:

---

[1] To be more particular, he took the place of George Jones, who was appointed by the Governor, on the decease of Baldwin, August 27th, 1807, and who held until November 7th, 1807.

"The instructions given to our ministers were framed in the sincerest spirit of amity and moderation. They accordingly proceeded, in conformity therewith, to propose arrangements which might embrace and settle all the points in difference between us, which might bring us to a mutual understanding on our neutral and national rights, and provide for a commercial intercourse on conditions of some equality. After long and fruitless endeavors to effect the purposes of their mission, and to obtain arrangements within the limits of their instructions, they concluded to sign such as could be obtained, and to send them for consideration, candidly declaring to the other negotiators, at the same time, that they were acting against their instructions, and that their Government, therefore, could not be pledged for ratification. Some of the articles proposed might have been admitted on a principle of compromise, but others were too highly disadvantageous, and no sufficient provision was made against the principal source of the irritations and collisions which were constantly endangering the peace of the two nations. The question, therefore, whether a treaty should be accepted in that form could have admitted but of one decision, even had no declarations of the other party impaired our confidence in it. Still anxious not to close the door against friendly adjustment, new modifications were framed, and further concessions authorized than could before have been supposed necessary; and our ministers were instructed to resume their negotiations on these grounds."

He declared that we were "reposing in confidence" in "this new reference to amicable discussion," when, "by a formal order from the British Admiral," the Chesapeake was attacked. He then stated the steps taken in consequence, but that no answer had yet been received from the British Government.

He complained that the aggressions thus began had been continued by the British commanders remaining in our waters, in defiance of our authority, by habitual violations of our jurisdiction, and by putting to death one of the persons taken from the Chesapeake. He said, these aggravations necessarily led to the policy of admitting no foreign armed vessels into our harbors, or maintaining a force sufficient to control them, and that the expense of the last and its "inconsistence with our principles" would "dispense with those courtesies which would necessarily call for it," and leave us as free to exclude the navy as the army of a foreign power from our limits.

The British order in Council of January 7th, 1807, was thus alluded to:

"To former violations of maritime rights, another is now added of very extensive effect. The government of that nation has issued an order interdicting all trade by neutrals between ports not in amity with them; and being now at war with nearly every nation on the Atlantic and Mediterranean seas, our vessels are required to sacrifice their cargoes at the first port they touch, or to return home without the benefit of going to any other market. Under this new law of the ocean, our trade on the Mediterranean has been swept away by seizures and condemnations, and that in other seas is threatened with the same fate."

"Our differences with Spain," he said, "remained still unsettled." To former grounds of complaint, was now added "a very serious one"—a decree conforming with that of the French Government of November 21st, 1806 (the "Berlin decree"), but whether it "would also be conformed to that in its" favorable "construction and application in relation to the United States," had not been ascertained.

With all other foreign powers, he declared our relations were on their usual footing. A fermentation had been observed among the Northwestern Indians, but had apparently so far subsided as to require no new measures. The appropriations of the last session had been mostly expended on the fortification of New York, Charleston, and New Orleans, as the most exposed points, and, for the same reasons, the gunboats had been chiefly assigned to New York, New Orleans, and the Chesapeake. "Whether our movable force on the water, so material in aid of the defensive works on the land, should be augmented in this or any other form, was left to the wisdom of the Legislature." For manning the gunboats in case of sudden attacks on our harbors, he suggested for consideration, whether our seamen might not justly be formed into a special militia, "to be called on for tours of duty in defence of the harbors where they shall happen to be." When our peace was threatened, the President said he had, without waiting for a law, incurred expenses in laying in stores, and in calling all our gunboats into service, which he trusted would meet the approbation of Congress. "Whether a regular army was to be raised, and to what extent," must depend on the information so shortly expected. In the meantime, he had called on the States for their quotas of militia, and encouraged the acceptance of volunteers; and they were ordered to be organized and ready at a moment's warning.

After alluding to the measures resorted to to break up Burr's enterprise, their complete success, but the defeat of all measures to convict him before the courts, he added:

"You will be enabled to judge whether the defeat was in the testimony, in the law, or in the administration of the law; and wherever it shall be found, the legislature alone can apply or originate the remedy. The framers of our Constitution certainly supposed they had guarded, as well their government against destruction by treason, as their citizens against oppression, under pretence of it; and if these ends are not attained, it is of importance to inquire by what means, more effectual, they may be secured."

The revenue maintained, he said, its flourishing condition. The receipts into the treasury had been nearly sixteen millions of dollars, which, with the five and a half millions in it, in the beginning of the year, had enabled the Government, after meeting current demands and interest, to pay more than four millions of the principal of the funded debt—all of it which was redeemable. A surplus of eight millions and a half was left in the treasury. A part of this might be devoted to commencing an accumulation to meet the installments of the public debts as they should become payable, and a part of it "towards completing the defence of the exposed points of our country, on such a scale as should be adapted to our principles and circumstances."

Bills were before long brought into Congress, appropriating six hundred thousand dollars to cover the expenses incurred by the President—eight hundred and fifty-two thousand dollars to procure additional gunboats—and seven hundred and fifty thousand dollars for fortifications. But decisive action was deferred to await the return of the answer to our demands on England. The vessel dispatched for that purpose did not return until the second week in December.

On the 18th of December, the President sent the following confidential message to Congress:

"The communications now made, showing the great and increasing dangers with which our vessels, our seamen, and merchandise, are threatened on the high seas and elsewhere, from the belligerent powers of Europe, and it being of great importance to keep in safety these essential resources, I deem it my duty to recommend the subject to the consideration of Congress, who will doubtless perceive all the advantages which may be expected from an inhibition of the departure of our vessels from the ports of the United States.

"Their wisdom will also see the necessity of making every preparation for whatever events may grow out of the present crisis."

Accompanying this was a copy of the proclamation of the King of Great Britain ordering the impressment of British seamen in foreign service, and also of a new official declaration of the Emperor of France (made September 18th, 1807), of the construction to be put on the Berlin decree. This authorized the seizure of all English property or merchandise from England or her colonies, whoever the owner, found on board neutral vessels. The question whether the vessels bearing such property or merchandise should be confiscated, was reserved for future decision.

But there was a much more important reason for a recommendation of an immediate embargo. The British orders in council of November 11th, 1807, were known to the Government, though they had not been received in that official shape which made it proper for the President to communicate them formally to Congress.[1]

A bill was passed in the Senate, on the day on which the President's message was received, laying an embargo on the sailing, unless by permission of the President, of any vessel in the ports of the United States for foreign ports, except foreign ships in ballast, or with cargoes taken on board before notification of the act; and coastwise vessels were required to give bonds to land their cargoes in the United States. The vote on

[1] It was long and pertinaciously insisted by the opposition that the President had no information of these orders when he sent in his special message. Mr. Jefferson asserts the contrary in a letter to Madison, July 14th, 1824. Mr. Madison informed Mr. Tucker that the American Government was previously in possession of the information " through an authentic private channel," and that " it was confirmed by a ministerial English newspaper received at the same time. (Tucker's Jefferson, vol. ii. p. 249.) In a published letter to Hon. Harrison Gray Otis, dated March 31, 1808, John Quincy Adams said :

" It is true that these orders were not officially communicated with the President's message recommending the Embargo. They had not been officially received—but they were announced in several paragraphs from London and Liverpool newspapers of the 10th, 11th and 12th of November, which appeared in the National Intelligencer [of Washington City] of 18th December, the day on which the embargo message was sent to Congress. The British Government had taken care that they should not be authentically known before their time—for the very same newspapers which gave this inofficial notice of these orders, announced also the departure of Mr. Rose, upon a special mission to the United States. And we now know that of these all-devouring instruments of rapine, Mr. Rose was not even informed. . . . .

" They were not merely without official authenticity. Rumors had for several weeks been in circulation derived from English prints, and from private correspondences, that such orders were to issue ; and no inconsiderable pains were taken here to discredit the fact. Assurances were given that there was reason to believe no such orders to be contemplated. Suspicion was lulled by declarations equivalent nearly to a positive denial ; and these opiates were continued for weeks after the Embargo was laid, until Mr. Erskine received instructions to make the official communication of the orders themselves, in their proper shape, to our Government."

The following is one of the paragraphs from the Intelligencer, alluded to by Mr. Adams :

" LONDON, November 10.

" A proclamation is now, we understand, in readiness for his majesty's signature, declaring France and the whole of her vassal kingdoms in a state of siege, and prohibiting all intercourse with her or them : and all entrance of vessels into her or their harbors, except of such as have cleared last from a British port, either home or foreign."

The preceding very specific statements of Mr. Adams were published in less than four months after the date of the President's special message, and we have seen no contemporaneous efforts made to specifically meet and disprove them. We have paid the more attention to this point, because we shall presently find Mr. Canning himself tauntingly repeating the ungrounded and foolish assertion of the American opposition.

the final passage stood, yeas twenty-two; nays six.[1] The bill passed the House three days afterwards (Monday, 21st) by a vote of eighty-two to forty-four. It was furiously opposed by the Federalists and Quids; and some firm Republicans voted with them on various grounds, which we have not space to explain.

The President, on the 23d of November, sent to Congress a detailed account of the proceedings and testimony in the trial of Burr. On the 27th, Maclay, of Pennsylvania, moved in the Senate the appointment of a committee to inquire whether John Smith, a senator from Ohio, ought to be expelled "in consequence of the part which he took in the conspiracy of Aaron Burr against the peace and prosperity of the United States." The resolution, after some amendments which gave it a wider scope, passed without a division, and was referred to a committee of seven, of which J. Q. Adams was chairman. That gentleman made a report on the 31st, characterized by his usual vigor of thought and diction; and as the basis on which a majority of the Senate presently acted, it would be omitting a forcible indication of public sentiment in the highest places, not to present glimpses of this able paper. The following are some of its passages:

"It [the Constitution] has not subjected him [Senator Smith] to removal by impeachment; and when the darling of the people's choice has become their deadliest foe, can it enter the imagination of a reasonable man that the sanctuary of their legislation must remain polluted with his presence, until a court of common law, with its pace of snail, can ascertain whether his crime was committed on the right or on the left bank of a river; whether a puncture of difference can be found between the words of the charge and the words of the proof; whether the witnesses of his guilt should or should not be heard by his jury; and whether he was punishable, because present at an overt act, or intangible to public justice, because he only contrived and prepared it? Is it conceivable that a traitor to that country which has loaded him with favors, guilty to the common understanding of all mankind, should be suffered to return unquestioned to that post of honor and confidence, where, in the zenith of his good fame, he had been placed by the esteem of his countrymen, and in defiance of their wishes, in mockery of their fears, surrounded by the public indignation, but inaccessible to its bolt, pursue the purposes of treason in the heart of the national councils? Must the assembled rulers of the land listen with calmness and indifference, session after session, to the voice of notorious infamy, until the sluggard step of municipal justice can overtake his enormities? Must they tamely see the lives and fortunes of millions, the safety of present and

---

[1] The nays were Crawford, Goodrich, Hillhouse. Maclay, Pickering and White. Of the Federal senators, Mr. Adams voted for the bill, and Mr. Bayard was absent.

future ages, depending upon his vote, recorded with theirs, merely because the absurd benignity of general maxims may have remitted to him the forfeiture of his life?

    •   •   •   •   •   •   •   •

"From the volume of printed evidence communicated by the President of the United States to Congress, relating to the trial of Aaron Burr, it appears that a great part of the testimony which was essential to his conviction upon the indictment for treason, was withheld from the jury upon an opinion of the Court, that Aaron Burr, not having been *present* at the overt act of treason alleged in the indictment, no testimony relative to his conduct or declarations elsewhere, and subsequent to the transactions on Blennerhassett's Island could be admitted. And in consequence of this suppression of evidence, the traverse jury found a verdict, 'That Aaron Burr was not proved to be guilty, under that indictment, by any evidence submitted to them.' It was also an opinion of the Court, that none of the transactions, of which evidence was given on the trial of Aaron Burr, did amount to an overt act of levying war, and, of course, that they did not amount to treason. These decisions, forming the basis of the issue upon the trials of Burr, anticipated the event which must have awaited the trials of the bills against Mr. Smith, who, from the circumstances of his case, must have been entitled to the benefit of their application; they were the sole inducements upon which the counsel for the United States abandoned the prosecution against him.

"Your committee are not disposed now to question the correctness of these decisions on a case of treason before a court of criminal jurisdiction. But whether the transactions proved against Aaron Burr did or did not amount, in technical language, to an overt act of levying war, your committee have not a scruple of doubt on their minds, that, but for the vigilance and energy of the Government, and of faithful citizens under its directions, in arresting their progress and in crushing his designs, they would, in a very short lapse of time, have terminated not only in a war, but in a war of the most horrible description, in a war at once foreign and domestic. As little hesitation have your committee in saying, that if the daylight of evidence, combining one vast complicated intention, with overt acts innumerable, be not excluded from the mind by the curtain of artificial rules, the simplest understanding cannot but see what the subtlest understanding cannot disguise, crimes before which ordinary treason whitens into virtue—crimes of which war is the mildest feature. The debauchment of our army, the plunder and devastation of our own and foreign territories, the dissolution of our national Union, and the root of interminable civil war, were but the means of individual aggrandizement, the steps to projected usurpation. If the ingenuity of a demon were tasked to weave, into one composition, all the great moral and political evils which could be inflicted upon the people of these States, it could produce nothing more than a texture of war, dismemberment, and despotism."

The report concluded with a resolution that Smith be expelled for his "participation in the conspiracy of Aaron Burr against the *peace, union, and liberty* [1] of the people of the United States."

Hillhouse moved that Smith be heard by counsel not ex-

---

[1] These words are italicized in the report.

ceeding two. Adams opposed this, and Hillhouse and Bayard replied. The latter, among other things, said:

> "I do not consider the question to be, whether there was a conspiracy of which Burr was the author? That such a conspiracy did exist, I firmly believe; and I further believe that scarcely a man in the United States doubts it. Nor is it the question, whether the course pursued against Burr has been as discreet as it might have been, or whether certain alleged subtleties ought to have been discarded by the courts of law. The only question is, whether John Smith did participate in this conspiracy? If he did, even in the smallest criminal degree, I shall have no hesitation in giving my vote for his expulsion."

Smith was finally heard by counsel, and testimony, oral and written, was submitted. The final question was not reached until April 9th, when the vote stood for expulsion nineteen, against it ten. Two-thirds not voting in the affirmative, the resolution failed. Smith held his seat during the session, and then resigned.

If other Federal senators did not as frankly as Adams and Bayard announce their convictions of Burr's guilt, we think no one avowed an opposite conclusion—or pronounced the President a tyrant for crushing the conspiracy—or intimated that he had consciously sought the conviction of an innocent man. As already remarked, the national feeling had been too seriously and audibly expressed to invite any repetition of the former ambitious demonstrations of sympathy for the accused.

The vote on Smith's expulsion does not appear to have been strictly a party division—though most of the Republicans voted for, and most of the Federalists against it. There were those in each party who believed Smith had been wheedled into Burr's enterprise without understanding its character. Among these was Giles, of Virginia, one of the most decided administration members; and he both spoke and voted against the resolution. His vote, given the other way, would have changed the result.

Further manifestations of deep feeling in Congress in regard to the manner in which Burr's case had been disposed of, were not wanting. Giles introduced a bill in the Senate, February 11th, for the punishment of treason and other offences, in which several new and stringent clauses were introduced, and the aiding or assisting in doing certain traitorous acts by any one, "though not personally present when any such act was done or committed," was made treason, punishable with death. After some amendments, this passed the Senate by a vote of eighteen to ten. Randolph reported a milder bill in the other house, but it provided that any " persons combining, confederating, or conspiring," to do traitorous acts, should " be deemed guilty of a conspiracy to commit treason," punished by fine and imprisonment, and required to give sureties for good behavior at the discretion of the court. No final action appears to have been had on the bill. Congress were so much occupied with the menacing state of our relations with England, that all other topics were comparatively neglected.[1]

Violations of the Embargo Act, by enrolled coasting vessels carrying cargoes to the West Indies, called for a supplementary enactment during the session. Even this did not meet the fraudulent ingenuity brought into exercise to elude its provisions, and still another law became necessary. The debates on the supplementary acts were conducted with unparalleled asperity. Barent Gardenier, one of the Federal members from New York, in discussing the subject (February 10th), declared that the original embargo law had a different object from what it professed—that " it was a sly, cunning measure," and he asked :

" Are the nation prepared for this? If you wish to try whether they are, tell them at once what is your object—tell them what you mean—tell them you mean to take part with the Grand Pacificator ; or else stop your present course. Do not go on forging chains to fasten us to the car of the Imperial Conqueror."

The common accusation of the Federalists at this period, was that the Embargo was designed to favor France in her war with England—that this was the main object of the Government in proposing that measure. On Gardenier's uttering the above

[1] Much stronger public manifestations of feeling in regard to Burr's trial, took place out of Congress, and in a few instances they assumed official forms. The Legislature of Pennsylvania, for example, passed resolutions requesting the members of Congress from that State to use their endeavors to have an amendment of the Constitution submitted to the State legislatures, making Judges of the Supreme Court removable by the President on a joint address of both houses of Congress. These resolutions were presented by Maclay in the Senate, and by Whitehill in the House of Representatives.

Towards the close of December, Randolph moved that the President be requested to institute an inquiry into General Wilkinson's conduct, on the charge that he had received money, in 1796, from the Baron Carondelet, for acting as an agent of the Spanish Government. The resolution finally passed. The President had already, at Wilkinson's request, ordered a Court of Inquiry. Randolph's invective, as usual, had not been restrained within any limits of moderation. Wilkinson sent him a challenge. In his answer, Randolph took the good ground that he was not to be called to an account for words spoken in debate. and the very poor one that he could not descend to the level of a disgraced man. Wilkinson posted him as a coward, and there, we believe, the matter dropped.

remarks, he was called to order by Smilie, Campbell, Montgomery, and several others. The speaker "hoped the gentlemen would keep within the rules of propriety." Mr. Gardenier "hoped the speaker would keep order in the House."[1] As soon as the confusion ceased, he continued :

"If the gentlemen have composed themselves, and are in a condition to hear, I will proceed. I wish first, however, to put them at ease on one point. They are not of sufficient importance to have been the objects at whom I would level anything. I assure the gentlemen I did not mean them."

In the course of his remarks, he said :

"Yes, sir, I do fear that there is an unseen hand which is guiding us to the most dreadful destinies—unseen, because it cannot endure the light. Darkness and mystery overshadow this House and the whole nation. We know nothing—we are permitted to know nothing. We sit here as mere automata ; we legislate without knowing, nay, sir, without wishing to know, why or wherefore. We are told what we are to do, and the Council of Five Hundred do it. We move, but why or wherefore no man knows ; we are put in motion, but how, I for one cannot tell."

Proceeding in this strain, and remarking, "this course will do in this country no longer," the speaker called him to order. Mr. Alston "wished the gentleman might be permitted to proceed." Mr. Gardenier said, "I do not desire permission of that gentleman ; I shall permit myself to proceed," etc.

The next day, Richard M. Johnson, of Kentucky, very severely criticised Gardenier's remarks, and he declared if they were applied to him, that he should consider them "a base, unprincipled calumny." He said if he was called "a tool to others, he pronounced it a slander," and he intimated that he held himself responsible out of the House for his language. G. W. Campbell, of Tennessee, was one of the individuals so discourteously alluded to by Gardenier as beneath his notice. He was one of the most prominent members, a man of grave and pacific demeanor, and, says one of his colleagues, of a "rather Quaker look." Replying to Gardenier on the 22d, he said that when "charges of the most serious nature were made on that floor against a majority of the House—charges that they were acting under and governed by French influence (for this was in substance the allegation)—charges which he believed to be unfounded with respect to every member of the House, of the

----

[1] Three gentlemen were still standing.

majority, and which, so far as regarded himself, he knew to be, and now so declared them, infamous, groundless falsehoods—it might be proper," etc. Gardenier challenged Campbell. The parties met at Bladensburg, and the challenger fell apparently mortally wounded, the ball entering just back of the arm-pit, and coming out near the back-bone.[1] He recovered, however, in about six weeks, and, as if to prove the futility of this kind of arbitrament, returned to his duties neither a sadder, wiser, nor, after a short interval, a more courteous man.

This is not a greatly exaggerated sample of the debates on the Embargo, and of the habitual charges of a considerable number of Federal members of Congress, and of the Federal newspapers, in regard to the objects of that measure.

A bill to raise seven regiments of regulars passed by a vote of ninety-eight to sixteen. Some of the other military measures adopted during the session were as follows: The sum of $852,500 was appropriated to enable the President to construct or purchase one hundred and eighty-eight gunboats. The sum of $1,000,000 was placed at his disposal for fortifications for the defence of our ports and harbors. The sum of $300,000 was appropriated to purchase arms, and $150,000 to purchase salt-petre. The President was authorized to call upon the State Executives to organize, equip, and "hold in readiness to march at a moment's warning," one hundred thousand militia, and to call them into actual service at his discretion. The annual sum of $200,000 was appropriated for providing arms and military equipments for the whole body of the militia of the United States, to be distributed by the States, and the President was authorized to construct arsenals and manufactories of arms at his discretion. The sum of $986,363 was appropriated to defray the first year's expense of the seven regiments of regulars which the President was authorized to enroll.

We will not close our account of the proceedings of this session without recording that the intelligence of the death of the celebrated John Dickinson was received by it with the same manifestations of official respect that had been paid to the memories of Samuel Adams and Edmund Pendleton. Jacob Crowninshield, the distinguished member of the House of Repre-

---

[1] Some particulars of this duel are given in an unpublished letter of Vice-President Clinton, lying before us.

sentatives from Massachusetts, died during this session. Congress adjourned on the 25th day of April.

Mr. Rose, the special minister sent by the British Government to the United States, in pursuance of its intimations to Monroe and Pinkney, had arrived in Washington, January 13th, 1808. He announced that his instructions limited the objects of his mission to a settlement of the affair of the Chesapeake, and that he could not enter even upon this until the President's proclamation, ordering British ships out of the American waters, was withdrawn. The Secretary of State replied (March 5th), that it accorded with reason and the uniform position of England under similar circumstances, that the aggressor should be required to put things into their former condition before entering upon counter demands. But he declared that if the British minister would disclose the terms of a satisfactory reparation, the repeal should be made of the same date with that measure. He stated the reasons why it was proper to couple the subject of impressment with that of reparation for the attack on the Chesapeake—inasmuch as the decision in both cases rested on analogous principles—from an inclination to seize this particular occasion to restore a full harmony—and because the United States intended to offer terms of accommodation which could not but be regarded as satisfactory. Mr. Rose replied (March 17th), declining the proposition, and declaring his mission closed. He soon returned to England.

The President's views of the objects and effects of the Embargo, and of the proper limit of its continuance, appear in a letter to the Attorney-General, March 23d, 1808:

"The Embargo appears to be approved, even by the Federalists of every quarter except yours. The alternative was between that and war, and, in fact, it is the last card we have to play, short of war. But if peace does not take place in Europe, and if France and England will not consent to withdraw the operations of their decrees and orders from us, when Congress shall meet in December, they will have to consider at what point of time the Embargo, continued, becomes a greater evil than war. I am inclined to believe we shall have this summer and autumn to prepare for the defence of our sea-port towns, and hope that in that time the works of defence will be completed, which have been provided for by the legislature."

A letter to Charles Pinckney, a week later, discloses his impressions of the general aspect of national affairs a little before the adjournment of Congress:

"With France we are in no *immediate* danger of war. Her future views it is impossible to estimate. The immediate danger we are in of a rupture with England, is postponed for this year. This is effected by the Embargo, as the question was simply between that and war. That may go on a certain time, perhaps through the year, without the loss of their property to our citizens, but only its remaining unemployed on their hands. A time would come, however, when war would be preferable to a continuance of the Embargo. Of this Congress may have to decide at their next meeting. In the meantime, we have good information that a negotiation for peace between France and England is commencing through the medium of Austria. The way for it has been smoothed by a determination expressed by France (through the Moniteur, which is their Government paper), that herself and her allies will demand from Great Britain no renunciation of her maritime principles, nor will they renounce theirs. Nothing shall be said about them in the treaty, and both sides will be left in the next war to act on their own. No doubt the meaning of this is, that all the *Continental* powers of Europe will form themselves into an armed neutrality, to enforce their own principles. Should peace be made, we shall have safely rode out the storm in peace and prosperity. If we have anything to fear, it will be after that. Nothing should be spared from this moment in putting our militia in the best condition possible, and procuring arms. I hope that this summer we shall get our whole seaports put in that state of defence which Congress has thought proportioned to our circumstances and situation ; that is to say, put *hors d'insulte* from a maritime attack by a moderate squadron. If armies are combined with their fleets, then no resource can be provided but to meet them in the field. We propose to raise seven regiments only for the present year, depending always on our militia for the operations of the first year of war. On any other plan, we should be obliged always to keep a large standing army."[1]

[1] The President's private correspondence during the exciting session of 1807–8, was as diversified in its topics as usual. We find him literally rioting among the fossil remains of mammoths, and other monsters of the extinct world, which the zeal of General William Clarke (the fellow explorer of Lewis, and the brother of the "Hannibal of the West") had exhumed for him at the Big-Bone Licks of the Ohio, and sent on to Washington ; repeatedly urging Dr. Wistar, of Philadelphia, to come and put them in order ; corresponding with Robert R. Livingston, John Taylor of Caroline, and some other friends, on agriculture and cognate topics ; giving his warm approbation to the plan, afterwards successfully carried out, of that great and far-seeing merchant, John Jacob Astor, in relation to establishing a trade with the Northwestern Indians, and promising the latter the countenance and all the reasonable patronage of the Government ; expressing his interest in mineralogical and geographical explorations to Mr. Bettay, who wrote him of silver mines seventeen hundred miles west of St. Louis ; declaring it the duty of our Government to ascertain all the water communications across our continent, etc., etc. On the 1st of January he was reëlected President of the American Philosophical Society.

The explanation of his views on one head, contained in a private letter, will be read with interest by many persons. On the 23d of January he thus replied to a request from the Rev. Mr. Miller, to proclaim a national fast day :

"I consider the Government of the United States as interdicted by the Constitution from intermeddling with religious institutions, their doctrines, discipline, or exercises. This results not only from the provision that no law shall be made respecting the establishment or free exercise of religion, but from that also which reserves to the States the powers not delegated to the United States. Certainly, no power to prescribe any religious exercise, or to assume authority in religious discipline, has been delegated to the General Government. It must, then, rest with the States, as far as it can be in any human authority. But it is only proposed that I should *recommend*, not prescribe, a day of fasting and prayer. That is, that I should *indirectly* assume to the United States an authority over religious exercises, which the Constitution has directly precluded them from. It must be meant, too, that this recommendation is to carry some authority, and to be sanctioned by some penalty on those who disregard it ; not, indeed, of fine and imprisonment, but of some degree of proscription, perhaps in public opinion. And does

Addresses poured upon the President, warmly approving of his measures, and of none more than the Embargo. The Legislatures of Massachusetts, Vermont, Rhode Island, New York, Pennsylvania, Maryland, New Jersey, North Carolina, Orleans Territory, New Hampshire, and South Carolina, addressed him to this effect during the session and the succeeding recess. To these were added similar communications from large popular meetings, or political organizations, in Boston, New York, Philadelphia, Washington, Pittsburg, and other cities—from the Republicans of Connecticut generally, and from those of various counties in other States. He also received a large number of approbatory addresses from religious bodies, principally of the Baptist and Quaker denominations—though the Methodist Churches sent a considerable number. The Baptist Associations very generally addressed him.

The legislatures of Massachusetts, Vermont, Rhode Island, New York, Pennsylvania, Maryland, New Jersey and North Carolina—all, perhaps, that acted, in 1808, before Mr. Jefferson's final refusal to serve a third term had been made public—solicited his continuance in office. The answer to each, on this subject, was as follows:

"That I should lay down my charge at a proper period, is as much a duty as to have borne it faithfully. If some termination to the services of the chief magistrate be not fixed by the Constitution, or supplied by practice, his office, nominally for years, will, in fact, become for life; and history shows how easily that degenerates into an inheritance. Believing that a representative government, responsible at short periods of election, is that which produces the greatest sum of happiness to mankind, I feel it a duty to do no act which shall essentially impair that principle; and I should unwillingly be the person who, disregarding the sound precedent set by an illustrious predecessor, should furnish the first example of prolongation beyond the second term of office.

"Truth, also, requires me to add, that I am sensible of that decline which advancing years bring on; and feeling their physical, I ought not to doubt their mental effect. Happy if I am the first to perceive and to obey this admonition of nature, and to solicit a retreat from cares too great for the wearied faculties of age."

the change in the nature of the penalty make the recommendation the less a *law* of conduct for those to whom it is directed? I do not believe it is for the interest of religion to invite the civil magistrate to direct its exercises, its discipline, or its doctrines; nor of the religious societies, that the General Government should be invested with the power of effecting any uniformity of time or matter among them. Fasting and prayer are religious exercises: the enjoining them an act of discipline. Every religious society has a right to determine for itself the times for these exercises, and the objects proper for them, according to their own particular tenets: and this right can never be safer than in their own hands, where the Constitution has deposited it."

On the 19th of January, Senator Bradley, of Vermont, the chairman of the last Presidential caucus, issued notices calling a meeting of the Republican members of Congress in the Senate chamber on the 23d, for, as it was well understood, the nomination of a President. Eighty-nine (thirty or forty short of the full number) assembled, including John Quincy Adams, and Kirkpatrick, of New York, elected as Federalists. Of the absentees, some were ill, some out of the city, and some kept aloof, because they supported the claims of Mr. Monroe or Vice President Clinton, and it was already well known that Mr. Madison would receive a large majority of the caucus vote. No member attended from New York but Kirkpatrick;[1] but it would be wrong to infer that all the absences were occasioned by the last named cause.[2] For the Presidential nomination, Madison received eighty-three votes, Clinton three, and Monroe three. For the Vice-Presidential nomination, Clinton received seventy-nine votes, John Langdon five, General Dearborn three, and J. Q. Adams one.

The results of the Presidential nomination were embarrassing to the Administration. The defeated candidates and their friends refused to acquiesce in the decision of the caucus, and a protest appeared not long after (March 7th), signed by seventeen Republican members, including Quids.

A large majority of the friends of Clinton and Monroe in Congress, as well as both of those gentlemen, believed that the President and his Cabinet, with perhaps the exception of Gallatin,[3] had exerted their official and personal influence in favor of Madison, and they resented it accordingly in private, though prudence, if no other consideration, prevented them from openly taking an issue which would at once overwhelm all their own hopes.

Between Mr. Clinton and the President, no explanation ever took place; though we may presume one would have taken place had the former lived to settle down in the calm of retirement. Mr. Clinton died in April, 1812.

A letter from Mr. Jefferson to Colonel Monroe (February

---

[1] So we find it stated in a manuscript letter of George Clinton lying before us, and in copy of one written at the time by D. C. Verplank, one of the New York members, to General Bailey, of New York, and forwarded by him to Mr. Clinton.

[2] On the contrary, we learn from his manuscript letters that Mr. Clinton considered some of the absentees his opponents—particularly the senators Mitchell and Smith.

[3] See APPENDIX, No. 21.

18th, 1808), on the subject of the nomination, is too characteristic to be omitted :

> " I see with infinite grief a contest arising between yourself and another, who have been very dear to each other, and equally so to me. I sincerely pray that these dispositions may not be affected between you; with me I confidently trust they will not. For independently of the dictates of public duty, which prescribes neutrality to me, my sincere friendship for you both will ensure its sacred observance. I suffer no one to converse with me on the subject. I already perceive my old friend Clinton, estranging himself from me. No doubt lies are carried to him, as they will be to the other two candidates, under forms which, however false, he can scarcely question. Yet I have been equally careful as to him also, never to say a word on the subject. The object of the contest is a fair and honorable one, equally open to you all; and I have no doubt the personal conduct of all will be so chaste, as to offer no ground of dissatisfaction with each other. But your friends will not be as delicate. I know too well from experience the progress of political controversy, and the exacerbation of spirit into which it degenerates, not to fear for the continuance of your mutual esteem. One piquing thing said draws on another, that a third, and always with increasing acrimony, until all restraint is thrown off, and it becomes difficult for yourselves to keep clear of the toils in which your friends will endeavor to interlace you, and to avoid the participation in their passions which they will endeavor to produce. A candid recollection of what you know of each other will be the true corrective. With respect to myself, I hope they will spare me. My longings for retirement are so strong, that I with difficulty encounter the daily drudgeries of my duty. But my wish for retirement itself is not stronger than that of carrying into it the affections of all my friends. I have ever viewed Mr. Madison and yourself as two principal pillars of my happiness. Were either to be withdrawn, I should consider it as among the greatest calamities which could assail my future peace of mind. I have great confidence that the candor and high understanding of both will guard me against this misfortune, the bare possibility of which has so far weighed on my mind, that I could not be easy without unburdening it."

This did not appease the early *élève* and always dear friend. Monroe had been surrounded by some hot-headed, bitter-spirited advisers and probably informers. He replied to Jefferson warmly, complaining of his conduct in regard to the English mission and treaty. The latter did not lose his temper, but again (March 10th), wrote a long, calm, kind letter of explanations. We presume this healed the breach, for we soon find them again on the footing of their ancient, close and confiding friendship.

In none of his letters to Monroe, while disavowing an interference between him and Madison, does Jefferson disavow a personal choice. There is no doubt his preference was then for Madison. If the latter was not the better, he was at least the older soldier. With ripe experience, and at the very zenith of his splendid intellect, he had been eight years at the President's side. His dispatches and other official papers had displayed a profundity of understanding and knowledge that placed him in the first class of living statesmen.[1]

He never had separated from the President in action, or in an important opinion—was perfectly versed in his policy, and was sure to continue it intelligently and faithfully through another administration. He was a great constitutional jurist, and there were still left unsettled executive questions which needed the decision of such a chief magistrate.

Few persons ever knew Monroe intimately, who did not love him. There was a downrightness—a manliness—a crystal-like integrity in his character, which constantly grew upon associates. Jefferson's frequent remark that he was so perfectly honest, that "if his soul was turned inside out, not a spot would be found on it," has become historic. His countrymen, probably, have not generally—this was a remark of Mr. Madison's[2]—sufficiently appreciated his solid but not showy understanding. Yet if either he or Madison was to be elected President in 1808, there can be but little doubt that seniority in years and deeds better entitled the latter to the preference.[3]

The President had been empowered to partly or wholly

[1] For a specimen, let the reader peruse his examination of the British doctrines in regard to neutral trade, published unofficially in 1806.

[2] The following is from Mr. Trist's Memoranda:

Observations by Mr. Madison, Montpellier, Dec. 8, 1827.

*   *   *   *   *   *

"Mr. Monroe:—his understanding very much underrated—his judgment particularly good. Few men have ever made more of what may be called *sacrifices* in the service of the public. When he considered the interests or the dignity of the country involved, his own interest was never regarded. Besides this cause, his extreme generosity—not only to the numerous members of his family dependent on him—but to friends not united by blood, has greatly contributed to his impoverishment. Perhaps there never was another instance of two men brought so often, and *so directly at points*, who retained their cordiality towards each other unimpaired through the whole. We used to meet in days of considerable excitement, and address the people on our respective sides; but there never was an *atom of ill will* between us. On one occasion we met at a church up here pointing towards the northwest). There was a *nest of Dutchmen* in that quarter, who generally *went together*, and whose vote might very probably turn the scale. We met here at a church. Service was performed, and then they had music with two fiddles. They are remarkably fond of music. When it was all over, we addressed these people, and kept them standing in the snow listening to the discussion of constitutional subjects. They stood it out very patiently—seemed to consider it a sort of fight, of which they were required to be spectators. I then had to ride in the night, twelve miles to quarters; and got my nose frost-bitten, of which I bear the mark now (touching the end of his nose to the left side)."

[3] We have seen how gracefully Jefferson deferred to John Adams's seniority. John Adams was about seven years and a half older than Jefferson. Jefferson was seven years older than Madison. Madison was nine years and a half older than Monroe.

suspend the Embargo during the recess of Congress, should a withdrawal of its edicts by either of the European belligerents call, in his judgment, for that measure. Instructions were immediately addressed by him to the American ministers in France and England, to offer to suspend it, on such conditions, and to hold out the idea to each of those powers that a separate persistence in its edicts by the other would be met by hostilities from the United States.[1]

France returned no definite answer to the proposal. England, flushed by the reverses of her great enemy in the Peninsula, in the summer of 1808, and somewhat relieved by the new theatre thus opened to her commerce, assumed a still more unyielding attitude towards the United States.

Under color of exhibiting sympathy for the patriots of Spain, a strong effort was made, during the summer, to induce the President to suspend the Embargo in relation to that country. He declined, on the grounds that the information in possession of Government in regard to the state of affairs in Spain was yet indefinite, and that Congress was soon to assemble.

The views of our Minister in England on the preceding proposition, and his general views in regard to a repeal of the Embargo, were expressed with great decision to our Government. He characterized the trade which it was proposed to reopen in the Peninsula as a "sordid traffic" with England through an indirect channel, "at a time when it might be said that we were emboldened by French reverses to do what before

---

[1] The opposition subsequently claimed that partiality had been shown to France. On the other hand, Mr. Macon—without having seen the instructions, it is presumed—expressed the opinion in the House of Representatives that partiality had been shown to England. The following sentences from the instructions speak for themselves. The Secretary of State wrote Mr. Pinkney, April 30th, 1808:

"Should the French Government revoke so much of its decrees as violate our neutral rights, or give explanations and assurances having the like effect, and entitling it, therefore, to a removal of the Embargo as it applies to France, it will be impossible to view a perseverance of Great Britain in her retaliating orders, in any other light than that of war, without even the pretext now assumed by her. . . . . Should the British Government take this course, you may authorize an expectation that the President will, within a reasonable time, give effect to the authority vested in him on the subject of the embargo laws."

The same officer wrote General Armstrong, May 2d, 1808:

"Should wiser councils or increasing distresses induce Great Britain to revoke her impolitic orders against neutral commerce, and thereby prepare the way for the removal of the Embargo, as it applies to her, France could not persist in the illegal part of her decrees, if she does not mean to force a contest with the United States. On the other hand, should she set the example of revocation, Great Britain would be obliged, either by following it to restore to France the full benefit of neutral trade, which she needs, or, by persevering in her obnoxious orders after the pretext for them had ceased, to render collisions with the United States inevitable."

we could not resolve upon, or were tempted by the prospect of a scanty profit, exaggerated by our cupidity and impatience, to forget what was due to consistency, to character, to permanent prosperity." Mr. Pinkney continued:

"We sanction, too, the maritime pretensions which insult and injure us. We throw ourselves, bound hand and foot, upon the generosity of a Government that has hitherto refused us justice, and all this when the affair of the Chesapeake, and a host of other wrongs, are unredressed, and when Great Britain has just rejected an overture which she must have accepted with eagerness if her views were not such as it became us to suspect and guard against.

"To repeal the Embargo altogether would be preferable to either of the other courses, but would, notwithstanding, be so fatal to us, in all respects, that we should long feel the wound it would inflict, unless, indeed, some other expedient as strong at least, and as efficacious in all its bearings, can (as I fear it cannot), be substituted in its place.

"War would seem to be the unavoidable result of such a step. If our commerce should not flourish in consequence of this measure, nothing would be gained by it but dishonor; and how it could be carried on to any valuable purpose it would be difficult to show. If our commerce should flourish in spite of French and British edicts, and the miserable state of the world, in spite of war with France, if that should happen, it would, I doubt not, be assailed in some other form. The spirit of monopoly has seized the people and Government of this country. We shall not, under any circumstances, be tolerated as rivals in navigation and trade. It is in vain to hope that Great Britain will voluntarily foster the naval means of the United States. Even as allies we should be subjects of jealousy. It would be endless to enumerate in detail the evils which would cling to us in this new career of vassalage and meanness, and tedious to pursue our backward course to the extinction of that very trade to which we had sacrificed everything else.

"On the other hand, if we persevere, we must gain our purpose at last. By complying with the little policy of the moment, we shall be lost. By a great and systematic adherence to principle, we shall find the end of our difficulties.

"The Embargo, and the loss of our trade, are deeply felt here, and will be felt with more severity every day. The wheat harvest is likely to be alarmingly short, and the state of the Continent will augment the evil. The discontents among their manufacturers are only quieted for the moment by temporary causes. Cotton is rising, and will soon be scarce. Unfavorable events on the Continent will subdue the temper, unfriendly to wisdom and justice, which now prevails here. But, above all, the world will, I trust, be convinced that our firmness is not to be shaken. Our measures have not been without effect. They have not been decisive, because we have not been thought capable of persevering in self-denial, if that can be called self-denial which is no more than prudent abstinence from destruction and dishonor."

England had derived encouragement to persist in her maritime regulations from other and stronger causes than any yet named. These were the refractory language and conduct of a portion of the American press and people in regard to the Embargo. That measure unquestionably bore with severity on the interests of every great class. The farmer lost his markets, and had to pay enormously increased prices for such imported articles as he used. The merchant lost his trade, and the mariner his occupation. Though the outcry came principally from the two last classes, all suffered about equally in proportion to their capital. The farmer had the advantage that he could procure his mere food as easily as before. But its extreme cheapness rendered this an item of little importance to the merchant; and the mariner, if need be, could readily exchange his labor for it. No class lacked for abundant subsistence—but the increase or profits of all were entirely cut off. It was difficult to pay debts contracted when money flowed in its usual channels. It was a period of financial embarrassments—a time for economies—an occasion for those commercial stop-laws which constitutions do not permit, but which the heart of a nation enforces under the penalty of common scorn.

Far different were beginning to be the effects of the Embargo in England. Her annual exports to the United States had already reached about fifty millions of dollars. This money paid for the labor of innumerable artisans, and it kept a multitude of manufacturing establishments in operation. Her exports and the imports received in return, gave employment to an important branch of England's merchant marine. These several interests did not merely depend upon the occupation thus given, for profits or for surplus earnings, but, to a considerable extent, for the actual materials of subsistence. If the artisans of England were thrown out of employment, they did not disappear like a speck among a population overstocked with an unsalable surplus of food. In thirty-six hours after the manufacturing establishment stopped, one half of its hands began to feel the pangs of hunger. A week or a fortnight brought the most provident of them to the same pass. The English operative, bred all his life exclusively to one kind of labor, could not, like an American, turn his hand readily to another. If he could, there was no unfilled place where he might step in, as in America, and acquire a ready subsistence for his family. From the United States the cessation of commerce called forth grumblings on full stomachs—from England, it would soon draw out the shriek of starvation from a class: and the destruction of that class, and of the inter ests dependent upon its labor, when the nation was already suffering under so many commercial and financial disadvantages, would lead to consequences which no sane Government would willingly provoke. It needed but a display of the Revolutionary nerve, at this crisis, for the United States to effectually vindicate their neutral rights without a war—but the nerve was wanting, and the war became necessary.

The expectation, which Mr. Pinkney says existed in England, that we were " not capable of persevering in self-denial," proved painfully true. A large majority of the nation were willing to endure their share of the privation. But sectional and class feelings were only too successfully appealed to among the minority, and they were inflamed to a pitch which was thought to render disunion or civil war the alternative of persistence in the measures of the Government.

This state of things was mainly produced by the efforts of the ultra-Federal leaders in the eastern States—and particularly by those individuals who had desired a dissolution of the Union on the occasion of the accession of Louisiana. They first deluded and then inflamed the public mind in those States, by persuading the inhabitants that they were the victims of partial, and, therefore, tyrannical legislation. They represented the Embargo as a blow aimed intentionally at the prosperity of New England, or at least as a mode of obtaining redress which was more injurious to the United States than to their enemy, and which was chosen by the dominant " Virginia party," because most of the injury would fall on New England.

The disingenuousness of these pretences is made apparent by the most superficial view of the facts. The farmer of the South suffered far more than the farmer of the North. The former was usually much the largest landholder, and his labor was performed by those whom he was required to clothe as well as to feed. He manufactured nothing. His general habits of living were comparatively expensive. He was a consumer of many imported articles. He had been required in ordinary times to annually market a large surplus of products to meet the necessary expenses of his establishment. He had been deriving but very moderate agricultural profits before any commercial restrictions were imposed. Under the Embargo, his markets were destroyed, while his disbursements remained nearly equal —for all the saving he could make by retrenching luxuries was

counterbalanced by the increased cost of his imported nece
ries. It is notorious that these causes led to the bankruptcy
many, and the serious pecuniary embarrassment of multitude
previously opulent Southern planters. Not even the commer
class in New England probably suffered more in proportior
their capital.

The New England agriculturist, on his small farm, hii
little, purchasing little, used to rigid economies, frequei
manufacturing his homespuns and some other necessaries, r
the best markets which remained, and favored indirectly t
smuggling trade of considerable extent,[1] suffered much less.
the aggregate, there can be but little doubt that the landholo
of Virginia lost twice as much from the effects of the Emba
as the landholders of Massachusetts.

The right by which the Federal leaders claimed that 1
England enjoyed such a preponderance in commercial and n
gation interests that an injury to those interests constitute
special and " sectional " attack on her, is exemplified by
statistics contained in the following table of exports:

	Foreign and domestic productions and manufactures exported from 1791 to 1802 inclusive.	Foreign productions and manufactures exported from 1803 to 1813 inclusive.	Domestic productions and manufactures exported from 1803 to 1813 inclusive.	TOTAL.
New Hampshire, ...	$3,829,000	$1,386,000	$3,147,000	$8,362,(
Massachusetts,.......	98,770,000	81,324,000	54,985,000	235,079,(
Rhode Island,........	14,113,000	6,953,000	7,789,000	28,855,(
Connecticut,.........	12,328,000	501,000	11,614,000	24,443,(
Vermont,...........	165,000	1,075,000	1,217,000	2,457,(
New York,..........	129,941,000	78,052,000	85,283,000	293,276,(
New Jersey,.........	491,000	107,000	815,000	1,313,(
Pennsylvania, ...	124,744,000	65,118,000	44,796,000	234,658,(
Delaware, ...	3,009,000	1,713,000	1,097,000	5,819,(
Maryland,..........	101,026,000	50,214,000	36,630,000	187,870,(
Virginia,...........	53,125,000	2,355,000	42,833,000	98,313,(
North Carolina	6,764,000	61,000	7,055,000	13,880,(
South Carolina, ...	83,631,000	14,420,000	50,523,000	148,574,(
Georgia, ...	12,162,000	190,000	18,584,000	30,900,(
Orleans Territory,....			16,408,000	16,408,(
Dist. of Columbia,....			13,144,000	13,144,(

Total of five Eastern States,..................... $299,192,000
Total of four Middle States,................ 534,766,000
Total of six Southern States and Dist. of Columbia,.. 509,089,000

[1] This remark will find an explanation in facts to be subsequently stated.

The following exhibits the tonnage of some of the principal ports of the Union during the year in which the Embargo was repealed, and the succeeding one:[1]

Tonnage of	In 1809.	In 1810.
Boston,	133,257	149,121
Newburyport,	36,574	39,100
Portland,	33,007	32,599
Salem,	43,537	41,462
Bath,	23,033	20,344
New York,	243,533	268,548
Philadelphia,	121,443	125,258
Baltimore,	102,434	103,444
Norfolk,	40,940	47,643
Charleston,	40,819	52,888
Portsmouth,	27,719	28,820

The President thus alluded to the conduct of the Federalists in a letter to Dr. Leib, June 23d, 1808:

"They are now playing a game of the most mischievous tendency, without perhaps being themselves aware of it. They are endeavoring to convince England that we suffer more by the Embargo than they do, and if they will but hold out awhile, we must abandon it. It is true, the time will come when we must abandon it. But if this is before the repeal of the orders of council, we must abandon it only for a state of war. The day is not distant, when that will be preferable to a longer continuance of the Embargo. But we can never remove that, and let our vessels go out and be taken under these orders, without making reprisal. Yet this is the very state of things which these Federal monarchists are endeavoring to bring about; and in this it is but too possible they may succeed. But the fact is, that if we have war with England, it will be solely produced by their manœuvres. I think that in two or three months we shall know what will be the issue."

In August he wrote the Secretary of War that "the infractions in the Embargo in Maine and Massachusetts were open." Smuggling into and from Canada, especially through Lake Champlain, was common, and was so openly carried on that parties went armed to resist the government officers. The President wrote Dearborn, August 9th, that insurrection was threatened in Boston if the importation of flour was stopped, and that the "next post would stop it"—that he feared the governor "was not up to the tone of the parricides"—and he

---

[1] The table of exports is arranged from sums and statements purporting to be derived from official sources, which we find already collected in Matthew Carey's Olive Branch, and the general accuracy of that statistician is presumed to be a sufficient guaranty of their correctness. Sums of less than a thousand dollars, it will be observed, are not taken into account. The tonnage statistics are from the same source.

desired his correspondent, on the first symptom of a forcible opposition to the law, to "fly to the scene and aid in suppressing any commotion." He advised Governor Tompkins, of New York, August 15th, to call out a body of militia to put down combinations of armed men who had resisted the execution of the embargo laws on the Canada frontier, fired upon the public guards, and wounded at least one of them dangerously. He ordered General Wilkinson, August 30th, to send all the recruits for the army in the State of New York to Sackett's Harbor, Oswegatchie, and Plattsburgh. Military force became necessary to support the authority of the revenue officers in several of the Eastern ports, and gunboats were sent into those ports for that purpose.

West of Lake Champlain, the refractory manifestations were prevented from spreading, and they were ultimately quelled by the energy of the Executive of New York—the patriotic and gallant Daniel D. Tompkins. Most of the New England Executives, on the other hand, entered reluctantly and tardily on measures of suppression, and some of them fostered the popular discontents, by personally acting with, and even taking the lead of the most violent denouncers of the measures of the Government. The collectors, in various instances, evinced "worse than negligence" in the execution of their duties, and it became necessary for the President to remove them.[1]

The Cabinet passed the summer amidst constant harassments—and much of·the President's time was taken up in deciding on individual applications for exemptions from the provisions of the Embargo. Whoever will take the pains to glance into his decisions on these, will be astonished at the extent of investigation they display, if not at the rigorous impartiality they manifest.[2]

---

[1] See President to Secretary of War, August 9th.

[2] For example, William Gray, of Salem, the first ship-owner of the United States—who had come out almost alone from among the great Federal merchants of New England, to support the Embargo—who had recently succeeded in defeating the Salem resolutions against that measure—was refused the privilege of sending a vessel to carry some important testimony to a distant country. Here is the clear, brief and decisive response:

Mr. Gray's case.

"His late rational and patriotic conduct would merit any indulgence consistent with our duty; but the reason and the rule against permitting long voyages at present, are insurmountable obstacles. It is to be hoped some circuitous means of sending his proofs can be found. A vessel may go from England as well as from here."

But at about the same time, a Chinese Mandarin, who had been staying at New York,

General Armstrong wrote home from France, advising an immediate occupation of the Floridas. The President thus commented on the recommendation in a letter to the Secretary of State, of September 13th (1808):

"This letter of June 15th, is written after the cession by Carlos to Bonaparte of all his dominions, when he supposed England would at once pounce on the Floridas as a prey, or Bonaparte occupy it as a neighbor. His next will be written after the people of Spain will have annihilated the cession, England become the protector of Florida, and Bonaparte without title or means to plant himself there as our neighbor."

He wrote the Governor of Louisiana, October 29th:

"The patriots of Spain have no warmer friends than the Administration of the United States, but it is our duty to say nothing and to do nothing for or against either. If they succeed, we shall be well satisfied to see Cuba and Mexico remain in their present dependence; but very unwilling to see them in that of either France or England, politically or commercially. We consider their interests and ours as the same, and that the object of both must be to exclude all European influence from this hemisphere. We wish to avoid the necessity of going to war, till our revenue shall be entirely liberated from debt. Then it will suffice for war, without creating new debt or taxes."

Here is the germ of what has been termed the "Monroe doctrine." We shall find it taking its definite and ultimate form among the political maxims of Mr. Jefferson—and that it was proposed by him to Monroe before the latter (some years from the date of which we write) officially proclaimed it a policy of his administration.

The whole tenor of the President's correspondence, during the summer, shows that he was sincerely anxious for a friendly adjustment with England—that "to nobody would a repeal" of the orders in council "be so welcome as to himself."[1] Mr. Pinkney wrote from London, June 5th, that he was to have a free conference with Mr. Canning in a few days. On the 29th of June, he informed the Government that he had had a long interview with Mr. Canning that day, which had given him hopes of a repeal of the orders in council, if he would authorize an expectation of the repeal of the Embargo; and he also

was permitted to hire a vessel to take him and his property home, the President basing his permission on the ground of national comity, and that the case came fairly within the view of the first section of the embargo law!

[1] Letter to Lieper, May 25th.

thought satisfaction would be made for the attack on the Chesapeake. The results of these expected negotiations will be hereafter given.

On receiving this intelligence, the President directed a suspension of orders which he had authorized for calling out a hundred thousand militia, and he wrote the Secretary of State, "if they repeal their orders, we must repeal our Embargo. If they make satisfaction for the Chesapeake, we must revoke our proclamation, and generalize its operation by a law. If they keep up impressments, we must adhere to nonintercourse, manufacturers' and a navigation act."

But the President's anticipations of a speedy adjustment, if he entertained any, were very transient. It is not, indeed, probable that he expected anything more favorable than another period of temporizing. His views of the real nature of our relations with both England and France, are disclosed in the following hitherto unpublished letter:

To John W. Eppes.

Monticello, *Sept.* 20th, '08.

Dear Sir:

Your letter of the 5th, mentioning that you should be at Eppington till the 14th and then proceed to Cumberland, did not get here till the 15th; it had either been put into the post-office at Richmond after the mail hour, or loitered there a week. I thank you for your attention to the purchase of a horse. I now send for him, and the bearer goes first to Cumberland, and if yourself or the horse should not be there, he will go on as shall be necessary. I will thank you to inform me by him of what blood he is by the dam, if you know it. I shall leave this for Washington on the 28th. We had a marriage in our family on the 17th, between Anne and Mr. Bankhead. All are well here.

A letter from Mr. Pinkney expresses a hope that the British Government will repeal their orders on his engagement that we will repeal our embargo. He infers this from a conversation with Canning; but I have little faith in diplomatic inferences, and less in Canning's good faith. Bonaparte being absent from Paris, we can get nothing important from thence. His beginning now for the first time to condemn our vessels augurs nothing friendly. I hope Spain will give him serious employment; for although nothing in the newspapers, except the public documents, is at all to be believed as to details, yet the information from our consuls shows a determined resistance. I am happy to hear of your own confirmed health as well as Francis's, and shall hope to see you both at Washington as usual. I salute you with affection and respect.

Th. Jefferson.

The following letters in regard to Indian affairs explain themselves and the occasions under which they were written;

and they are worthy of the notice of all just and humane persons. The President wrote to Merriwether Lewis, Governor of Louisiana Territory,[1] August 21st (1808):

"I regret that it has been found necessary to come to open rupture with the Osages, but, being so, I approve of the course you have pursued—that of drawing off the friendly part of the nation—withdrawing from the rest the protection of the United States, and permitting the other nations to take their own satisfaction for the wrongs they complain of. I have stated to General Dearborn that I think we may go further, and as the principal obstacle to the Indians acting in large bodies is the want of provisions, we might supply that want, and ammunition also, if they need it. With the Sacs and Foxes I hope you will be able to settle amicably, as nothing ought more to be avoided than the embarking ourselves in a system of military coercion on the Indians. If we do this, we shall have general and perpetual war. When a murder has been committed on one of our stragglers, the murderer should be demanded. If not delivered, give time, and still press the demand. We find it difficult, with our regular government, to take and punish a murderer of an Indian. Indeed, I believe we have never been able to do it in a single instance. They have their difficulties also, and require time. In fact, it is a case where indulgence on both sides is just and necessary, to prevent the two nations from being perpetually committed in war, by the acts of the most vagabond and ungovernable of their members. When the refusal to deliver the murderer is permanent, and proceeds from the want of will, and not of ability, we should then interdict all trade and intercourse with them till they give us complete satisfaction. Commerce is the great engine by which we are to coerce them, and not war. I know this will be less effectual on this side the Mississippi, where they can have recourse to the British; but this will not be a long-lived evil. By this forbearing conduct towards the Mississippian Indians for seven years past, they are become satisfied of our justice and moderation towards them, that we have no desire of injuring them, but, on the contrary, of doing them all the good offices we can, and they are become sincerely attached to us; and this disposition, beginning with the nearest, has spread and is spreading itself to the more remote, as fast as they have opportunities of understanding our conduct. The Sacs and Foxes, being distant, have not yet come over to us. But they are on the balance. Those on this side the Mississippi, will soon be entirely with us, if we pursue our course steadily. The Osages, Kanzas, the Republican, Great and Wolf Panis, Matas, Poncaras, etc., who are inclined to the Spaniards, have not yet had time to know our dispositions. But if we use forbearance, and open commerce with them, they will come to, and give us time to attach them to us."

And he again wrote to Governor Lewis, three days later:

"Isham Lewis arrived here last night and tells me he was with you at St. Louis about the second week in July, and consequently, after your letter of the 1st of that month, that four Iowas had been delivered up to you as guilty of the murder which had been charged to the Sacs and Foxes, and that you supposed three of them would be hung. It is this latter matter which induces me to write again.

---

[1] Appointed Governor by the President in 1807.

"As there was but one white murdered by them, I should be averse to the execution of more than one of them, selecting the most guilty and worst character. Nothing but extreme criminality should induce the execution of a second, and nothing beyond that. Besides their idea that justice allows only man for man, that all beyond that is new aggression, which must be expiated by a new sacrifice of an equivalent number of our people, it is our great object to impress them with a firm persuasion that all our dispositions towards them are fatherly; that if we take man for man, it is not from a thirst for blood or revenge, but as the smallest measure necessary to correct the evil, and that though all concerned are guilty, and have forfeited their lives by our usages, we do not wish to spill their blood as long as there can be a hope of their future good conduct. We may make a merit of restoring the others to their friends and their nation, and furnish a motive for obtaining a sincere attachment. There is the more reason for this moderation, as we know we cannot punish any murder which shall be committed by us on them. Even if the murderer can be taken, our juries have never yet convicted the murderer of an Indian. Should these Indians be convicted, I would wish you to deliver up to their friends at once, those whom you select for pardon, and not to detain them in confinement until a pardon can be actually sent you. That shall be forwarded to you as soon as you shall send me a copy of the judgment on which it shall be founded."

The circumstances which led to the celebrated "Batture Case" between the President and Edward Livingston, arose, or rather came to a head, during the summer of 1808.[1]

---

[1] The Batture was "a shoal or elevation of the bottom of the river [Mississippi] adjacent to the bank of the suburb St. Mary [in the city of New Orleans], produced by the successive depositions of mud during the annual inundations of the river, and covered with water only during those inundations. At all other times it had been used by the city, immemorially, to furnish earth for raising the streets and courtyards, for mortar, and other necessary purposes, and as a landing or quay for unloading firewood, lumber, and other articles brought by water." It extended "from one hundred and twenty-two to two hundred and forty-seven yards from the water's edge into the river." While covered with water (from February to July inclusive), it was the port for all the small craft and boats from the upper country, which, in high water, "could land or lie nowhere else in the neighborhood of the city." It was estimated, even then, to be worth half a million of dollars, could it be used for private purposes. But it had been considered the public property time out of mind, and had been treated as such during the French and Spanish governments in the island. (It will be understood that we follow the general historical version of the facts as they are given by Mr. Jefferson in his paper on the Batture case.) The owner of the adjacent property (J. Gravier) suddenly, in 1805, claimed, and commenced a suit against the city to recover, the whole Batture. On the 14th of December, 1806, he executed a deed of two-thirds of the property to one Peter de la Bigarre, on condition that the latter should pay the expenses of the suit and $50,000 additional, if the land was recovered—the land to remain meanwhile unsold and hypothecated for the purchase-money till paid; and Bigarre was to receive nothing if the suit failed.

The President, when this matter was brought before him, came to the conclusion that this "was a mere speculation on the chance of a lawsuit in which" the parties "were to divide the spoils if successful and to lose nothing if they failed"—"a criminal purchase of a pretence title." He believed also that Bigarre was the mere instrument, in this matter, of Edward Livingston, who had originated and contrived all the steps in the affair; and this appears to have been the impression of the inhabitants of New Orleans generally. The deed to Bigarre was not executed before witnesses or notaries, nor recorded until the day before the court decided on the title, and when the nature of their decision was known to the parties.

The court, two against one, adjudged the title of the whole Batture to be in Gravier. This produced much popular excitement, and it was freely charged that the court had been bribed. When Mr. Livingston appeared as the owner, and commenced certain excavations on the land (August, 1807), his workmen were driven away by the people. This happened several times, until Governor Claiborne restored order by promising to immediately dispatch an agent to place the subject before the General Government, in which, he claimed, lay the title of the disputed land.

A grand-jury, composed of the most respectable characters in the territory, made a presentment, in November, against Livingston's structures on the Batture, in which they said: "Whether it be private or public property, is immaterial, so long as the laws do not permit such use of it as to injure and obstruct the navigation: and we present it as our opinion, that all such measures should be taken as are consistent with law to arrest these operations which are injurious for the present, and, in changing the course of the river, are hazardous in the extreme."

To show the kind and degree of hazard these structures produced, it was brought in proof before the President, that in consequence of them, the Batture was by one single particular tide extended seventy-five or eighty feet further into the river, and raised from two feet to five feet and ten inches generally. The tide already, it was in proof, generally brought the water within eight or ten inches of the top of the levee, or artificial banks of the river, and sometimes within two or three inches of the top, so that "it splashed over with the wind." None need to be told that the plain on which New Orleans stands is lower than the surface of the river, and that a breach in the levee might therefore cause that city and the adjacent country to be submerged almost instantly under the descending torrents of the largest river in North America.

Governor Claiborne repeatedly called the attention of the General Government to the subject, invoking its interposition, and declaring that otherwise he could not be responsible for the peace, or even the safety, of New Orleans. The President submitted the facts to the Attorney-General, and that officer (October 28th, 1807) gave it as his opinion that the title to the disputed land was in the United States. Gravier's title was considered wholly defective on various grounds. The United States had been no party to the suit of Gravier against the city, the court had not undertaken to decide on the right of the United States, and if it had so undertaken, the question was wholly out of its competence or jurisdiction.

By the act of Congress of 1807, chap. 91, it had been enacted, "If any person should take possession of any lands ceded to the United States by treaty, he should forfeit all right to them, if any he had; and it should be lawful for the President of the United States to direct the marshal, or the military, to remove him from the lands; providing, however, that this removal should not affect his claim until the Commissioners[*] should have made their reports, and Congress decided thereon." This law was expressly designed to prevent the seizure and possession ("nine points of the law") of the most valuable tracts in the newly-acquired territory of French Louisiana, by greedy speculators, under all sorts of fictitious and fraudulent claims. And, inasmuch as the new territory (where the title had not been legally vested in individuals) belonged equally to the people of all the States, Congress reserved the ultimate decision of these claims to itself, and did not delegate it to local courts, or any other local tribunals.

The President called a Cabinet consultation on this subject, November 27th, 1807, at which the Attorney-General and heads of departments were present. After a long and equally careful scrutiny into the facts, and an investigation into not only the Spanish, French, and United States laws, in regard to riparian possessions, but the analogous statutes and customs of other nations, running back to the most remote antiquity, the Cabinet came unanimously to the conclusion, that the Executive was "authorized and in duty bound, without delay to arrest the aggressions of Mr. Livingston on the public rights, and on the peace and safety of the city of New Orleans, and that orders should be immediately dispatched for that purpose."[†] The Secretary of State, accordingly, wrote Governor Claiborne, November 30th, inclosing instructions for the marshal "to remove immediately, by the civil power, any persons from the Batture Ste. Marie, who had taken possession since the 3d of March, and authorizing the governor, if necessary, to use military force; for which purpose a letter of the same date was written by the Secretary at War to the commanding officer at New Orleans." The instructions were delivered to the marshal, January 25th, 1808. At the order of this officer, Livingston's workmen peaceably retired. They soon returned, however, by direction of their principal, and informed the marshal that they were commanded not to give up the Batture until they should be compelled to do so by an adequate armed force.

In the meantime, Livingston "obtained from a single judge of the Superior Court of the Territory, an order, purporting to be an injunction, forbidding the marshal to disturb Edward Livingston in his possession of the Batture, under pain of a contempt of court." This was not the first nor last instance of a single New Orleans judge (invested by the acts Congress, from which he solely derived authority, with merely common law and no chancery jurisdiction) attempting, on a mere *ex parte* hearing, to arrest by his fiat both the laws of Congress and the officers acting under the direct authority of the Executive of the United States for their execution.

The marshal of Orleans disobeyed the judicial injunction, and dispossessed Mr. Livingston. The latter made no further attempts to resume his work. Three weeks after his dispossession, the Territorial Legislature passed an act prescribing the terms on which riparian proprietors should proceed, and this gave Mr. Livingston an opportunity to resume his enterprise under its conditions; but he had elected to seek his remedy from Congress and courts of law. The Orleans Legislature also passed a vote of thanks to the President for his interposition.

On the 7th of March, 1808, the President, by message, informed Congress of the general facts in this case, mentioning his own measures " to prevent any change in the state of things, and to keep the grounds clear of intruders," "until this question could be decided under legislative authority." He nowhere attempted to pass upon the real title, regarding the possession as " the only charge of the Executive," and he committed the question of title to Congress, "the only authority competent to its decision."* He admitted that if that title was ultimately found to rest in Mr. Livingston, the latter would be entitled to damages from the parties, which, without right, had received the intermediate profits.

Mr. Livingston appealed to the public in a pamphlet, and applied to Congress for relief. He also commenced suits for damages against Mr. Jefferson and the marshal who dispossessed him. From Congress he derived no satisfaction, though the matter was pressed for several terms. The Attorney-General, after two years more of consideration (and after Mr. Jefferson had retired from office), reaffirmed his former opinion. The Legislature of Orleans Territory also renewed their vote of thanks in February, 1810, pending the suit of Livingston against Jefferson. The latter was decided adversely to the plaintiff (1811), on a technical point, we think, without reaching the merits of the case. The suit was not renewed by Mr. Livingston, and here the matter dropped, so far as Mr. Jefferson was concerned. Livingston afterwards, however, recovered possession of a portion of the Batture, on Gravier's title—and even this had risen so enormously in value, that it enabled him to pay all the expenses which he had been at, to most honorably discharge all his earlier liabilities, and still to realize a large fortune.

On the legal questions involved in the Batture case, we do not, of course, assume to decide, though acting on the proofs before the President and Cabinet, it would be difficult for us to see on what possible sound rule, in regard to riparian possessions, an adjacent owner could be entitled to embank round and exclude the river at high water from any mud deposit or shoal, over which it was necessary for the river at such times to flow, in order not to be so dammed up or obstructed as to lead to inundation, or to a change in the bed of the stream, or to other practical injurious consequences, always liable to ensue in such cases. (For example, the filling up of the stream above or below the obstruction, to the entire destruction of existing docks, or rendering it necessary to extend them much further to reach deep water—thus constantly changing the frontage, and more and more obstructing the stream.) If the adjacent owners of shoals, uncovered in low water, are entitled, as a matter of course, to inclose them against high water, the Hudson, and many other of the finest navigable streams of our country, might thus be rendered wholly unnavigable in ten years. The owner of a far projecting shoal on one side of a river, might thus drive the descending waters of the next "fresh" on the lands of the opposite owner, and lead, in some instances, to their complete abrasion, so that henceforth the bed of the stream would pass where they had stood. And let us imagine an adjacent owner " docking out," beyond high water mark, from "one hundred and twenty-two to two hundred and forty-seven yards " into the North or East Rivers at the city of New York, or into the Delaware at Philadelphia ! It is unnecessary to further demonstrate the complete and self-evident absurdity of such a doctrine.

We repeat, we speak of facts as they were on proof before the President, and consequently as they appeared to his mind and to the minds of his Cabinet. How differently they were made to appear on the trial, we are not apprised, as we have not looked up the record of the case, considering the accuracy of the testimony in regard to the character of the Batture of no consequence in estimating the President's motives or even the degree of prudence which he exercised. He acted on abundant testimony; and, in reality, it was only the question of possession, and not the question of title, which the President interfered with. Here he had the direct authority of an act of Congress. And he had not then, or afterwards, the slightest direct or indirect personal interest in the matter.

As we have several times cited Mr. Jefferson's paper in this celebrated case, we should, in justice to Mr. Livingston, make an explanation. That paper does not conceal the idea that the latter acted throughout the whole transaction the part of a trickish, unprincipled, greedy speculator and adventurer. Mr. Jefferson unquestionably enter-

* See his Paper on the Batture case, Works, Cong. Ed., vol. viii. p. 601.

is view of Livingston's character, and he considered him doubly dangerous by
[his great talents and perfect knowledge of all the turnings and windings of
etice. It is proper also to say, that this was the prevailing impression, at the
the most prominent and best men in Orleans Territory. The Creole population,
y, regarded and feared him as a great incarnation of wickedness and subtlety.
is little doubt that gross exaggerations had crept into these popular concep-
his character. We are ready to believe that the President, influenced by the
tations of the Government officers and prominent inhabitants of the territory,
tle injustice to his motives and his actions. Mr. Jefferson was proverbially scant
arity towards great speculations and great speculators. There might have been
king prejudices. It is not to be denied that the prevailing impressions of Living-
litical career were far from favorable. He was spontaneously selected by both
s that Republican in Congress, in the election of 1801, who would be the first to
to Burr, if any one did so. Jefferson, at that period, had no suspicions of him.
him an office. Livingston became a defaulter in that office. He went South
rnished name. He was accused of favoring Burr's schemes in 1806. He appeared
nnsel at New Orleans. All these circumstances, with his attempted specula-
l the public sentiment at New Orleans, conspired to beget unfavorable and exag-
prejudices.
uld be difficult to believe, that at all periods of his life, Edward Livingston was
dy scrupulous man. Yet there is just as little doubt that, at the meridian of a
hich became splendid, and from thence to its close, he possessed the full confi-
the most just and intelligent of his compatriots. He became a lawgiver and
n, who received and was entitled to the common confidence of his country.
of the surest indications that could be adduced that he was really a right-hearted
o be found in the fact that, subsequently to the bitter contests we have recorded,
y voluntarily made an overture towards the restoration of friendly relations with
rson. This overture was made not when the great orb of the latter was blaz-
zenith, and when the ambitious were eager to bask in its beams, but when it was
the horizon; and Livingston's own star now needed no reflected brightness.
it and tone of Jefferson's answer showed that he had completely changed his opi-
his earlier Batture antagonist.

CHAPTER VII.

1808—1809.

THE President made his usual two visits to Monticello in the summer of 1808. His unpublished letters of this period to Mr. Eppes give some traces of his private life, but they disclose nothing of particular interest.[1]

---

[1] Mr. F. W. Eppes was again married, but he maintained as much as before towards Mr. Jefferson, the attitude of an affectionate and affectionately cherished son-in-law.

To Thomas Jefferson Randolph.

Washington, *October 24th*, 1808.

Dear Jefferson :

I inclose you a letter from Ellen, which, I presume, will inform you that all are well at Edgehill. I received yours without date of either time or place, but written, I presume, on your arrival at Philadelphia. As the commencement of your lectures is now approaching, and you will hear two lectures a day, I would recommend to you to set out from the beginning with the rule to commit to writing every evening the substance of the lectures of the day. It will be attended with many advantages. It will oblige you to attend closely to what is delivered to recall it to your memory, to understand, and to digest it in the evening ; it will fix it in your memory, and enable you to refresh it at any future time. It will be much better to you than even a better digest by another hand, because it will better recall to your mind the ideas which you originally entertained and meant to abridge. Then, if once a week, you will, in a letter to me, state a synopsis or summary view of the heads of the lectures of the preceding week, it will give me great satisfaction to attend to your progress, and it will further aid you by obliging you still more to generalize and to see analytically the fields of science over which you are travelling. I wish to hear of the commissions I gave you for Rigden, Voight, and Ronaldson, of the delivery of the letters I gave you to my friends there, and how you like your situation. This will give you matter for a long letter, which will give you as useful an exercise in writing as a pleasing one to me in reading.

God bless you and prosper your pursuits.

TH. JEFFERSON.

A month later, was written to the same grandson, that beautiful letter of advice, given in both editions of Mr. Jefferson's Works, from which we have already extracted the author's recital of his own experiences and triumphs over temptation in early life.[1]

The Presidential election of 1808 was conducted with extreme heat, particularly in the eastern States. The Federal gains were important. The great chief whom the Republicans had so long centered upon—the leader who never had a rival in his own party—was no longer before the people for their suffrages. Three Republican candidates were in nomination, and though two of them, in the final result, ostensibly withdrew but a very few electoral votes from Mr. Madison, the division had weakened the moral as well as the numerical strength of the party.[2] The sectional feelings and class interests, roused into action by the Embargo, swept back into the opposition, all

---

[1] See vol. I., p. 22.

[2] Monroe received no electoral votes, but he had a strong party in Virginia, and the genuine Quids were generally violently opposed to Madison.

the New England States but one, in which the Republicans had recently triumphed.

The following was the result of the electoral vote:

	For President.			For Vice-President.				
	James Madison.	George Clinton.	Charles C. Pinckney.	George Clinton.	James Madison.	James Monroe.	John Langdon.	Rufus King.
New Hampshire...	—	—	7	—	—	—	—	7
Massachusetts	—	—	19	—	—	—	—	19
Rhode Island	—	—	4	—	—	—	—	4
Connecticut	—	—	9	—	—	—	—	9
Vermont	6	—	—	—	—	—	6	—
New York	13	6	—	13	3	3	—	—
New Jersey.......	8	—	—	8	—	—	—	—
Pennsylvania	20	—	—	20	—	—	—	—
Delaware.........	—	—	3	—	—	—	—	3
Maryland	9	—	2	9	—	—	—	2
Virginia	24	—	—	24	—	—	—	—
North Carolina....	11	—	3	11	—	—	—	3
South Carolina....	10	—	—	10	—	—	—	—
Georgia	6	—	—	6	—	—	—	—
Kentucky	7	—	—	7	—	—	—	—
Tennessee	5	—	—	5	—	—	—	—
Ohio	3	—	—	—	—	—	3	—
	122	6	47	113	3	3	9	47

To get a clear view of the attitude of parties in Congress and throughout the country during the eventful winter of 1808–9, it is necessary that we understand the history of our diplomatic negotiations with England down to that period. We have seen what was the effect of Mr. Canning's personal deportment and official communications on the mind of Mr. Pinkney early in the summer of 1808—that the latter believed reparation for the affair of the Chesapeake was about to be made to the United States, and that the other principal questions in dispute between the two countries were on the point of being amicably adjusted.

Mr. Canning's seeming friendly dispositions appear to have been assumed, not only to gain time, but to draw out our minister who was opening himself with the frankness of a confidence carried to the utmost limits of proper official reserve. The British minister had been all smiles and smoothness. What must have cost him far more, he had kept under that habitual tendency to light stinging persiflage, deepening occasionally into impertinent sarcasm, which he carried into official intercourse and even into official papers, where he felt dislike or encountered opposition. Mr. Canning could do a gracious thing graciously, and so can anybody else. He could render himself a most agreeable and apparently friendly personal or business associate. Sidney Smith aptly characterized him as a "diner-out of the first lustre." But where he acted the agreeable to carry out a design, it was exceedingly difficult for him to keep up appearances long, not because he hated insincerity, but because he preferred his jest to his interest. Every shake of the mask gave a glimpse of a face behind it leering with impudence and derision.

His toryism was not ranker than that of his great master, Mr. Pitt. On the contrary, the growth of public opinion rendered it visibly milder—especially towards the close of his career. The one always sacrificed everything that stood in the way of his views. The other often provoked by his trifling where nothing was to be gained. Pitt appears to have been an earnest man. When he sunk broken-hearted into his grave, all men knew that a mighty pillar of a nation's greatness had fallen. His party felt they had suffered an irreparable loss. Canning lived to be cast off by the Tories, and to have such upright and truthful men as the Duke of Wellington utterly refuse to act with him politically—more, they asserted, from his insincerity and unsteadiness than from any important differences of opinion. His great talents have never been disputed. His real character has been the subject of most conflicting opinions. We have given that version of it which seems most consistent with facts. and which was certainly exhibited in his entire course towards our country. Pinkney considered his conduct, in 1808, tainted by the most gratuitous artifice—and there even rose direct questions of veracity between them.

No well-informed American of any party will doubt the perfect sincerity of character of William Pinkney, of Maryland. He was one of those rare men who engage in nothing with friend or foe, to which they cannot carry a loyal and stainless good faith. His education, knowledge of the world, and talents placed him above simple credulity or subsequent jealousy. Indeed on the score of talent, an American can have no unwillingness to have his side of the correspondence measured against Mr. Canning's; and if the future attorney-general of the United States, and the future first American forensic orator of his day, lacked Mr. Canning's ability in any department (but that of a mere wit), it was, probably, only from the want of equal experience in that department.[1]

After Mr. Pinkney wrote home his favorable dispatches already mentioned of June 29th, 1808, he continued to have apparently the most friendly intercommunications with Canning. Two of these took place on the 22d and 29th of July, in which the latter encouraged the greatest freedom, and appeared anxious to draw out the American Minister as far as possible. But before the close of the last interview Canning apprised Pinkney that their discussions must henceforth be in writing—and that without an explicit proposal in writing, on which the British Government could deliberate and act, nothing further could be effected.

The American minister had no objection to place his proposition in writing—a demand for the revocation of the orders in council, and a stipulation, when this should take place, that the Embargo should be immediately suspended as far as it regarded Great Britain—provided he could be given to understand what would be the answer before preparing his note. Canning did not press the preparation of the note, but he declared that if it was written, his Government must be left free to act upon it, without an intimation in advance. Pinkney, fearing a written correspondence might lead to unnecessary discussion, attempted to change his determination, but in vain. He was compelled, therefore, to submit a written proposition, or in effect, to drop the negotiation—and he had been led to suppose that the most favorable dispositions were felt towards an immediate accommodation. He accordingly prepared a note, and delivered it on the 26th of August. (It is dated 23d in

---

[1] Colonel Benton's Thirty Years' View has few more warmly written pages than those devoted to the character of Mr. Pinkney (q. v. vol. i., pp. 19, 20). John Randolph's annunciation of Pinkney's death in the House of Representatives, in 1828, has become historic:

"I rise" [said Mr. Randolph] "to announce to the House the not unlooked-for death of a man who filled the first place in the public estimation in this or in any other country. We have been talking of General Jackson, and a greater than him, is, not here, but gone for ever. I allude, sir, to the boast of Maryland, and the pride of the United States—the pride of all of us, but more particularly the pride and ornament of the profession of which you, Mr. Speaker (Mr. Phillip P. Barbour), are a member and an eminent one."

the correspondence.)   It embraced the proposal already mentioned.

A month afterwards (September 23d), Canning replied in two separate communications.   In the first, he gave as the reason for his requiring written instead of verbal communications, " a recollection of the misrepresentation which took place in America of former conferences between them "—though he acquitted Pinkney of having originated it.   He mentioned that his share " in the preceding verbal communications had been null, and intimated that he had always discouraged them and engaged in them with reluctance.   On one point, indeed, he confessed he had been " particularly anxious to receive precise information, and upon which, from Mr. Pinkney's candor and frankness, he was fortunate enough to obtain it."   As the latter had connected in his overtures the suspension of the Embargo with the repeal of the order in council of 11th November, as well as the preceding one of the 7th of January, he had been desirous to ascertain whether that of November had been known to the Government of the United States " previously to the passage of the President proposing the Embargo, so as to be a moving consideration to that Message," and " had the satisfaction to learn that such was not the fact "—that rumors of it might have reached America, but that there was no certain knowledge of it in the possession of the American Government.

The second letter announced the determination of the British Government to adhere to the orders in council as a necessary act of retaliation against France; that his majesty regarded the American Embargo as " manifestly unjust " towards England, as according to every principle of justice," " redress ought have been first sought from the party originating the wrong;" that " by some unfortunate concurrence of circumstances, without any hostile intention, the American Embargo did come in aid of the ' blockade of the European continent' precisely at the very moment when, if that blockade could have succeeded at all, this interposition of the American Government would most effectually have contributed to its success."   The tone of both the letters is well exemplified in the following Canning-re paragraph:

" His majesty would not hesitate to contribute, in any manner in his power, to restore to the commerce of the United States its wonted activity; and if it were possible to make any sacrifice for the repeal of the Embargo, without appearing to deprecate it as a measure of hostility, he would gladly have facilitated its removal, *as a measure of inconvenient restriction upon the American people.*"

The broad insinuation, or rather charge against the veracity of the American Government, in the first letter, is palpable. The paragraph last quoted was an impertinence worthy of a pettifogger in the theatre of a police court, or of the smartness of an actor in low comedy. Pinkney himself was placed by a false declaration in the mortifying posture of a minister who had not waited to have his official secrets wormed from him, but who had hastened, with more than rustic simplicity, to voluntarily expose them. All this (if his word can be taken) came without the shifting of a circumstance, or a particle of premonition, on the heel of a continuous train of those friendly and cordial assurances which had led him to feel confident of a ready and favorable adjustment. This was purely Canning-like.

But, to borrow a forensic phrase, he "took nothing by his motion." Pinkney replied in the language of a gentleman, for he knew no other. But he followed up his antagonist keenly and nervously, and exposed him at every point. The letter (dated October 10th) is too long to quote, and we will take space to mention but two of its allegations. He declared that all their oral communications had been directly invited and encouraged by Canning; and he explicitly denied having given the information attributed to him in regard to a knowledge of the last orders in council by the American Government when the Embargo was recommended. And he said all that he did utter on that subject was conjectural, and that he "professed" at the time "to speak, and did in fact speak from general information only."

Canning's next official communication to him was dated November 22d, after the meeting of the American Congress; and there is nothing in it, or in their subsequent correspondence, that demands our particular attention.

Congress convened on the 7th of November. The President's Message began by mentioning the propositions which had been made to England and France in regard to the Embargo, and their rejection. This experiment having failed, that law, he said, had necessarily remained in full force. It had been borne, in general, with patriotism; it had saved our mariners and our property; it had given us time to prepare defensive and provisional measures; it had demonstrated our moderation and firmness to other nations, and the necessity of uniting in support of the laws and the rights of our country, to ourselves; and it "had thus long frustrated those usurpations and spoliations which, if resisted, involved war—if submitted to, sacrificed a vital principle of our national independence." The proper course to be pursued henceforth was referred to the wisdom of Congress.

The instructions which had been given to our ministers at London and Paris were laid before Congress. It appeared from their correspondence, that in addition to the rejection of our recent offers, England had taken no steps to make redress for the attack on the Chesepeake, still adhering to her inadmissible preliminary, and "now bringing it into connection with the distinct and irrelative case of the orders in council."

With the other nations of Europe, and with the Barbary powers, the President said, no material changes had occurred in our relations since the last session. Negotiations with Spain had been alternately suspended and resumed, and now "necessarily experienced a pause under the extraordinary and interesting crisis which distinguished her internal situation."

"With our Indian neighbors," the President stated, " the public peace had been steadily maintained," notwithstanding some instances of individual wrong, the perpetrators of which had been given up. He continued:

"And, generally, from a conviction that we consider them as part of ourselves, and cherish with sincerity their rights and interests, the attachment of the Indian tribes is gaining strength daily—is extending from the nearer to the more remote, and will amply requite us for the justice and friendship practised towards them. Husbandry and household manufacture are advancing among them, more rapidly with the southern than the northern tribes, from circumstances of soil and climate; and one of the two great divisions of the Cherokee nation have now under consideration to solicit the citizenship of the United States, and to be identified with us in laws and government, in such progressive manner as we shall think best."

The appropriations of the last session for harbor fortifications, he said, had been expended, and most of the works would be completed during the season, except at New York and New

Orleans. Further appropriations would be necessary to render the former entirely secure against naval enterprise. A view of what had been done at the several places, and what it was proposed further to do, would be communicated as soon as the several reports were received.

Of the gun-boats authorized to be constructed, it had been thought necessary to build but one hundred and three during the present year. A sufficient number of officers had been appointed to carry on the business of recruiting in the new regiments of regulars, and their success was believed to have been satisfactory. No general detachments of militia and volunteers had been called into service as authorized by the act of the preceding session; but some small and special ones had been found necessary to prevent evasions of the Embargo on our northern frontier. These, and the armed vessels employed, had, in a good measure, repressed those evasions.

The power to call out a large force ought, he thought, to be continued for the ensuing season. The uniform reorganization of the militia—the "best security" of "a people who are free"—was earnestly urged. The public factories for the making of arms had been enlarged, and additional machinery erected, "in proportion as artificers could be found or formed." Their effect was already more than doubled; and contracts had been entered into with private manufactories to supply the arms directed to be procured for the militia.

The following paragraph touched on the subject of the new manufactories springing up in consequence of the suspension of our foreign commerce:

"The suspension of our foreign commerce, produced by the injustice of the belligerent powers, and the consequent losses and sacrifices of our citizens, are subjects of just concern. The situation into which we have thus been forced, has impelled us to apply a portion of our industry and capital to internal manufactures and improvements. The extent of this conversion is daily increasing, and little doubt remains that the establishments formed and forming will—under the auspices of cheaper materials and subsistence, the freedom of labor from taxation with us, and of protecting duties and prohibitions—become permanent."

He stated that the receipts in the treasury during the past year amounted to about eighteen millions of dollars, which, with the eight and a half millions in the treasury at the close of the preceding year, had enabled the Government, after meet-

ng current demands, to pay two millions three hundred thou-
and dollars of the principal of our funded debt, leaving a
urplus of near fourteen millions. Of this, five millions three
undred and fifty thousand dollars would be necessary to pay
rhat would be due on the 1st of January, 1809, which would com-
lete the entire redemption of the eight per cent. stock. These
ayments, with those made in the six and a half years preceding,
rould extinguish thirty-three millions five hundred and eighty
housand dollars of the principal of the funded debt, being
he whole which could be paid or purchased according to law.
his would liberate the revenue from about two million dollars
f interest. The accumulation of our surplus revenue, beyond
rhat could be applied to the payment of the public debt, when
'the freedom and safety of our commerce should be restored,"
nerited, he said, the consideration of Congress. He asked
rhether it should lie unproductive in the public vaults—whether
he revenue should be reduced—or whether it should "rather
e appropriated to the improvement of roads, canals, rivers,
ducation, and other great foundations of prosperity and union,"
nder powers already possessed by Congress, or such an amend-
nent of the Constitution as might be approved by the States.
ind he asked, whether while we remained "uncertain of the
ourse of things," the time might not be advantageously
mployed in obtaining such an amendment.

The Message closed as follows:

"Availing myself of this the last occasion which will occur of addressing the
ro houses of the legislature at their meeting, I cannot omit the expression of
y sincere gratitude for the repeated proofs of confidence manifested to me by
emselves and their predecessors since my call to the Administration, and the many
dulgences experienced at their hands. The same grateful acknowledgments are
e to my fellow-citizens generally, whose support has been my great encouragement
der all embarrassments. In the transaction of their business I cannot have
aped error. It is incident to our imperfect nature. But I may say with truth,
y errors have been of the understanding, not of intention; and that the advance-
ent of their rights and interests has been the constant motive for every measure.
n these considerations I solicit their indulgence. Looking forward with anxiety
their future destinies, I trust that, in their steady character unshaken by diffi-
lties, in their love of liberty, obedience to law, and support of the public autho-
ties, I see a sure guaranty of the permanence of our republic; and retiring from
e charge of their affairs, I carry with me the consolation of a firm persuasion that
aven has in store for our beloved country long ages to come of prosperity and
appiness."

Congress opened with various propositions in regard to the Embargo, all of which were referred to a committee, which reported November 22d, that the United States could not, without a total sacrifice of their honor and independence, submit to the decrees of England and France—that it was expedient to exclude the ships and merchandise of both those powers from the United States—that the country ought to be placed at once in a state of defence. The report repudiated the idea of a permanent suspension of commerce, and took the ground that the continuance of that suspension was only a preferable alternative to a war with both powers at once, which it was assumed would be necessary if we sought then to forcibly vindicate our rights, inasmuch as both were willful aggressors, and that to open hostilities with one, singly, would be tantamount to a submission to the pretensions of the other. Resolutions carrying out these views were presented. The debate on them was most vehement, and a final vote was retarded by all the expedients of parliamentary warfare. The resolution that the United States could not, "without a sacrifice of their rights, honor, and independence," submit to the edicts of England and France against their commerce, passed with but two dissenting votes, and that for putting the country in a state of defence, unanimously. The resolution that it was expedient to prohibit, by law, the admission of British public or private ships into American ports passed, yeas ninety-two, nays twenty-nine. The resolution was extended to the ships of France, by a vote of ninety-seven to twenty-four; and then to all belligerents, "having in force orders or decrees violating the lawful commerce and neutral rights of the United States," by a vote of ninety-six to twenty-six.

Thus, after a year's experiment, and after all the outcry and even resistance which had been raised against the Embargo, the vote in the House of Representatives for sustaining it was sixteen greater than that by which the law was originally passed.

The same question, substantially, had been earlier debated and disposed of in the Senate. Mr. Hillhouse had offered a resolution, November 11th, for the repeal of the Embargo. This was voted down December 2d, yeas six, nays twenty-five. On the 8th of December, Giles introduced a stringent bill, making further provision for enforcing that law. In the debate,

Pickering distinctly took the ground that this and all the other measures of the Government towards France and England were especially intended for the benefit of the former, and were in accordance with the wishes, if they had not been actually entered into "in obedience to a requisition of the French Emperor!" The bill passed December 21st, yeas twenty, nays seven, the nays being the same number which had originally been given against the Embargo.[1]

The President had seen no reason to change his earlier views in respect to the merely temporary and provisional character of this law. He wrote Dr. Eustis (January 14th, 1809), on receiving the resolutions of confidence passed by the Republicans of Boston:[2]

"The moment for exerting these united [governmental] powers, to repel the injuries of the belligerents of Europe, seems likely to be pressed upon us. They have interdicted our commerce with nearly the whole world. They have declared it shall be carried on with such places, in such articles, and in such measure only, as they shall dictate; thus prostrating all the principles of right which have hitherto protected it. After exhausting the cup of forbearance and conciliation to its dregs, we found it necessary, on behalf of that commerce, to take time to call it home into a state of safety, to put the towns and harbors which carry it on into a condition of defence, and to make further preparation for enforcing the redress of its wrongs, and restoring it to its rightful freedom. This required a certain measure of time, which, although not admitting specific limitation, must, from its avowed objects, have been obvious to all; and the progress actually made towards the accomplishment of these objects, proves it now to be near its term. While thus endeavoring to secure, and preparing to vindicate that commerce, the absurd opinion has been propagated, that this temporary and necessary arrangement was to be a permanent system, and was intended for its destruction."

His communications had always conveyed the same general idea, yet one of the principal grounds of local agitation was that the Embargo was intended as a permanent measure. There was a deeper reason for this pretence than appeared on the surface. Men who had themselves voted for or sustained an embargo during a former administration—who had empow-

---

[1] The political character of the division had changed but to the extent of one vote. James Lloyd, Jr., a Federalist and opponent of the Embargo, had taken the place of J. Q. Adams, from Massachusetts, at the opening of the session—the latter having resigned his seat in consequence of being superseded, and of his constituents disapproving his support of the Embargo. Crawford of Georgia, and Maclay of Pennsylvania, Republicans, had originally voted against the measure. Crawford now voted for it, and Maclay was absent.—Gilman of New Hampshire, originally voted for it, and now against it. The change against the Embargo among the New England senators was two votes.

[2] Passed on the 19th of December, 1808.

ered a president to impose one at his discretion,[1] could not very
well claim that it was not authorized under the constitutional
powers of Congress to "regulate commerce." But it was
difficult to incite the law abiding people of New England to
oppose factiously the execution of what they believed to be a
constitutional law, and impossible to rouse among them, in
opposition to such a law, that storm of excitement which
would gradually lead on to sedition and disunion. Accordingly,
the Federal leaders made a subtle distinction. Because the
present Embargo was not limited in its duration to a specified
time, they assumed, contrary to the open disclaimers of the
President and his political "organs," that it was intended to be
permanent, and that it therefore involved the *destruction* of
commerce by an authority which could only legally "regulate"
it. This narrow quibble was the fulcrum on which the lever of
resistance and all its train of consequences rested.

When the news of the "Enforcing Law" (as the bill introduced into Congress by Giles was generally designated) reached
Massachusetts, a violent excitement burst forth. Several collectors resigned rather than encounter the consequences of the
public fermentation. Newspapers appeared in mourning. The
contest between the people and the General Government, it was
asserted, rested on the same principles as in 1776. Governor
Lincoln (the Lieutenant-Governor who had succeeded to the
executive chair on the death of Sullivan) was another Hutchinson; President Jefferson was another George III. If possible,
the present oppressors were governed by more flagitious motives
than those of 1776. George III. and his government were
seeking the good of some portion of the realm. If they
oppressed America, it was for the benefit of England. But it
was declared that the tyrant Jefferson was only gratifying his
fell and inextinguishable sectional hate against the prosperity
of New England, while he benefited no other portion of the
country; and that he was meanly cringing, as usual, at the feet
of the French Emperor, who repaid his subserviency only by
contumely and injury. Resistance and disunion were called
for in the newspapers and by the votes of numerous town
meetings.[2]

[1] As in Act of June 4th, 1794.
[2] Hillhouse, a U. S. Senator from Connecticut, declared in Congress in the debate on

Gore, as chairman of a committee in the Massachusetts Legislature, reported (January 28th, 1809), that if our Government had met the Berlin decree as it did that issued by the Directory in 1798, the English orders in council would not have been made. "Let Congress," declared the report, "repeal the Embargo, annul the convention with France, forbid all commercial intercourse with the French dominions, arm our public and private ships, and unfurl the republican banner against the imperial standard." "This done, the English orders would cease to operate." Our trade, except with France and her dependencies, "would again recover and flourish." Agriculture and all other avocations would thrive. These propositions might have been expected, perhaps, to find favor with a few ruined and desperate ship-owners, and a very small class always found among merchants, hardened into insensibility to every appeal but that of avarice; but the American historian will

the Enforcing Law, that the people were not bound to submit; and he did not believe they would submit. The Boston Centinel said "every man would presume" he was not bound to obey the Embargo—that "if the petitions did not produce a relaxation or removal of the Embargo, the people ought immediately to assume a higher tone." The Boston Repertory said, if it was not repealed, it would be soon set "at defiance"— that "it behoved" the people of Massachusetts "to speak, for strike they must, if speaking did not answer." The Boston Gazette exclaimed: "It is better to suffer the amputation of a limb, than to lose the whole body. We must prepare for the operation." . . . "Wherefore, then, is New England asleep: wherefore does she submit to the oppression of enemies in the South? Have we no Moses who is inspired by the God of our fathers, and will lead us out of Egypt." A handbill, circulated at Newburyport, contained the following : "You have reposed confidence in a coward" (Jefferson). . . . "Nerve your arms with vengeance against the despot who would wrest the inestimable germ of your independence from you, and you shall be conquerors. Give ear no longer to the siren voice of democracy and Jeffersonian liberty. It is a cursed delusion, adopted by traitors, and recommended by sycophants."

Resolutions were passed in town meeting at Augusta, Maine (January 16th 1809), which, after denouncing the preceding "criminal apathy" of the people on the subject, declared, that henceforth "silence would be crime, and resistance would become a virtue of the first magnitude." A town meeting at Boston, Massachusetts, adopted a memorial to the Legislature (January 25th, 1809), requesting its "interposition to procure for them relief from the grievances they now suffered. . . . Relief against the unconstitutional measures of the General Government"—and declaring that its power "was adequate to this object was evident from the organization of the confederacy." A town meeting at Bath passed resolutions (December 27th, 1808), requesting the Legislature to take such "immediate steps for relieving the people, either by themselves alone, or in concert with other commercial States, as the extraordinary circumstances of their situation might require." A town meeting at Topsfield (January 15th, 1809) resolved that a war with Great Britain "would be unjust, unnecessary, and extremely to be deplored;" that war was not a necessary alternative of the repeal of the Embargo ; "but should this be the alternative, it ought to be a war with France, and not with Great Britain"—that our people "might find many sources of profitable employment without interfering in any degree with those principles of maritime law which Great Britain deemed essential to her existence, and which, in an eventful moment like the present, she would never yield"—that "neither the honor nor the permanent interests of the United States required that they should drive Great Britain, if it were in their power, to the surrender of those claims so essential to her in the mighty conflict in which she was at present engaged : a conflict interesting to humanity, to morals, to religion, and to the last struggle of liberty." A full collection of the newspapers of the period would probably enable us to multiply to thousands these examples of expressions directly in favor of, or leading to, resistance and disunion.

always blush to record that they received the sanction of an American Legislature. The Massachusetts General Court accepted Gore's report (February 3d) by a vote of one hundred and ninety-five to one hundred and twenty-seven! It also declared the Enforcing Law "unjust, oppressive, and unconstitutional, and not legally binding "—but advised a resort to the State courts, rather than to open resistance to prevent its execution.[1]

We shall not stop to give an analysis of the Enforcing Law. It is accessible to all in the statutes of the United States. There is no ground for hesitation in declaring that, in conferring powers on the Executive, it fell short of rather than exceeded a considerable list of Acts passed on similar occasions during the

[1] This report placed a large portion of the Federal leaders of Massachusetts in a singular predicament. The "Boston Memorial," of January 20th, 1806, after touching on the aggressions of France and Spain, proceeded to declare that it was the object of the memorialists "to confine their animadversions to the more alarming, because more numerous and extensive, detentions and condemnations of American vessels by Great Britain, and to advert to the principles recently avowed and adopted by her courts relative to neutral trade in articles of colonial produce—principles which, if admitted or practised upon in all the latitude which might be fairly inferred to be intended, would be destruction to the navigation, and radically impair the most lucrative commerce of our country." After much additional and stronger denunciation of the conduct of England, the memorialists proceeded, in conclusion, to declare : "In all events, fully relying that the subject of our differences with Great Britain will receive the due consideration of Government; and that such measures will, in consequence, be promptly adopted as will tend to disembarrass our commerce—assert our rights—and support the dignity of the United States, your memorialists have the honor to remain," etc. This paper was signed by James Lloyd, jr., David Green, Arnold Welles, David Sears, John Coffin Jones, George Cabot, and Thomas H. Perkins, a committee chosen by and acting in behalf of the merchants of Boston generally.

Even Mr. Pickering, who declared in a published letter to Governor Sullivan (February 16th, 1808), that Great Britain had "really done" our commerce "no essential injury," voted for a resolution in the United States Senate, February 10th, 1806, which declared the captures and condemnations which had already taken place under British orders, "an unprovoked aggression upon the property of the citizens of the United States —a violation of their neutral rights—and an encroachment upon their national independence."

Mr. Gore, himself, had not been perfectly uniform in his British subserviency. At a meeting held in Faneuil Hall, on the 16th of July, 1807, John Quincy Adams, Harrison Gray Otis, William Eustis, Christopher Gore, Charles Jones, John C. Jones, Thomas H. Perkins, Jonathan Mason, and John Warren, were appointed a committee to prepare a report, which contained the following resolutions :

"*Resolved*. That we consider the unprovoked attack made on the United States armed ship Chesapeake, by the British ship of war Leopard, a wanton outrage on the lives of our fellow-citizens, a direct violation of our national honor, and an infringement of our national rights and sovereignty.

"*Resolved*, That we most sincerely approve the Proclamation, and the firm and dispassionate course of policy pursued by the President of the United States, and we will cordially unite with our fellow-citizens in affording effectual support to such measures as our Government may further adopt in the present crisis of our affairs."

The Boston town meeting, held six days earlier, unanimously passed still stronger resolutions in commendation of the course of the Government, and closed with the following :

"*Resolved*, unanimously, That though we unite with our Government in wishing most ardently for peace on just and honorable terms, yet we are ready cheerfully to coöperate in any measures, however serious, which they may judge necessary for the safety and honor of our country, and will support them with our lives and fortunes."

administrations of the first and second Presidents, and which had received the general support and approval of the Federal party. As a prominent example among these, it is only necessary to cite the Act of June 4th, 1794.

When the President's opening message to Congress was sent in (November 8th, 1808), the Government had recently received Pinkney's and Canning's correspondence down only to the letter of the British minister, which was dated September 23d. As this was criminatory in its character towards the American Government and its minister, it would " have accorded neither with propriety, nor with the wishes of Mr. Pinkney," to make it public, until his answer was received to make public at the same time. " When that answer afterwards arrived " (we quote the President's message of January 11th, 1809), " it was considered as what had passed in conversation had been superseded by the written and formal correspondence on the subject, the variance in the statements of what had verbally passed, was not of sufficient importance to be made the matter of a distinct and special communication."

Our Government was driven from its silence by a remarkable circumstance. Canning's last named communication to Pinkney, suddenly appeared in the New England Palladium, published in Boston, and the official paper for printing the Acts of the Massachusetts Legislature. This called for the transmission of the whole correspondence to Congress by the President.

Canning's misstatements and sarcasms were received with an ecstasy of delight by a class of partisans in the United States. But the tone of his paper, the place of its appearance, his obvious motive in thus carrying his controversy with the American minister into the American newspapers,[1] and finally, the free communication and good understanding between himself and certain politicians in Massachusetts which the circumstances seemed to betray, produced disgust among the high-minded men of all parties. In Congress, this feeling was too strong to be prudently encountered. Quincy sat silent. Even

---

[1] It has never, that we are aware, been shown how the publishers of the Palladium came in possession of this paper. They certainly did not receive it from Mr. Pinkney or our Government. Nobody else could have been in possession of it but the British Minister or Cabinet, or some person who received it from them. It is, therefore, not only fair but necessary to assume that Mr. Canning directly or indirectly caused or permitted this publication.

Gardenier did not go beyond a feeble effort to turn the thing into ridicule, by asking if it was " necessary to array the representatives of the nation against the humble editors of a newspaper ?"   Key, the distinguished Federal member from Maryland, said :

"I consider the late publication as the most direct and insidious attempt of a foreign government to take advantage of and influence the parties in this country, and that, too, by dishonorable means.   The paper alluded to could only have been in possession of our own Administration or of the British Government.   It came not from us ; it must have proceeded from the other—and from what view ?   Had fair information been the object, the letter of Mr. Pinkney in reply would also have been made public, that one might have been confronted with the other.   If it proceeded from that quarter, the separation of the reply from the letter, is evincive of the attempt to impose on the people.   I consider it an attempt to set the people at variance with their Government, and an insolent attempt of a foreign nation to interfere in our affairs in three points of view.   First.   Mr. Pinkney is expressly exonerated from the charge of misrepresentation ; but no man can understand it otherwise than as having allusion to the Executive of the country—an insinuation which there is no proof to support, and in support of which none can be adduced. Whatever difference of political opinion may exist between us on some points, I respect the Administration on the whole, and every honest man of every political opinion must side with me.   Secondly.   There is an insinuation that the President of the United States had only permitted our minister at London individually, not formally, to make a proposition on the subject of the Embargo.   This is unfounded in fact, because the documents before the House prove to the contrary.   Thirdly. A question is raised whether actual knowledge of the orders in council of November, was in possession of our Government at the time of laying the Embargo, which Mr. Pinkney has fully explained, that the American papers showed that it was well known before the passage of the Embargo, that such would probably be the measures adopted by the British Government.   It is upon these three great questions that this letter is insidiously calculated to deceive the American people."

A bill passed the House January 20th, by a vote of eighty to twenty-six, for an extra session of Congress on the fourth Monday of May then next.   It passed the Senate on the 26th without a division.   This was a test question on sustaining the policy of the Administration, sketched in the following letter, written the next day by the President to Monroe.

"The idea of sending a special mission to France or England is not entertained at all here.   After so little attention to us from the former, and so insulting an answer from Canning, such a mark of respect as an extraordinary mission, would be a degradation against which all minds revolt here.   The idea was hazarded in the House of Representatives a few days ago, by a member, and an approbation expressed by another, but rejected indignantly by every other person who spoke, and very generally in conversation by all others : and I am satisfied such a propo-

sition would get no vote in the Senate. The course the legislature means to pursue, may be inferred from the Act now passed for a meeting in May, and a proposition before them for repealing the Embargo in June, and then resuming and
maintaining by force our right of navigation. There will be considerable opposition
to this last proposition, not only from the Federalists, old and new, who oppose
everything, but from sound members of the majority. Yet it is believed it will
obtain a good majority, and that it is the only proposition which can be devised
that could obtain a majority of any kind. Final propositions will, therefore, be
soon dispatched to both the belligerents through the resident ministers, so that
their answers will be recived before the meeting in May, and will decide what is to
be done. This last trial for peace is not thought desperate. If, as is expected,
Bonaparte should be successful in Spain, however every virtuous and liberal sentiment revolts at it, it may induce both powers to be more accommodating with us.
England will see here the only asylum for her commerce and manufactures, worth
more to her than her orders of council. And Bonaparte, having Spain at his feet,
will look immediately to the Spanish colonies, and think our neutrality cheaply
purchased by a repeal of the illegal parts of his decrees, with, perhaps, the Floridas
thrown into the bargain. Should a change in the aspect of affairs in Europe produce this disposition in both powers, our peace and prosperity may be revived and
long continue. Otherwise, we must again take the tented field, as we did in 1776,
under more inauspicious circumstances.

"There never has been a situation of the world before, in which such endeavors
as we have made would not have secured our peace. It is probable there never
will be such another. If we go to war now, I fear we may renounce forever the
hope of seeing an end of our national debt. If we can keep at peace eight years
longer, our income, liberated from debt, will be adequate to any war, without new
taxes or loans, and our position and increasing strength will put us *hors d'insulte*
from any nation. I am now so near the moment of retiring, that I take no part in
affairs beyond the expression of an opinion. I think it fair, that my successor
should now originate those measures of which he will be charged with the execution and responsibility, and that it is my duty to clothe them with the forms of
authority. Five weeks more will relieve me from a drudgery to which I am no longer
equal, and restore me to a scene of tranquillity, amidst my family and friends, more
congenial to my age and natural inclinations. In that situation, it will always be
a pleasure to me to see you, and to repeat to you the assurances of my constant
friendship and respect."

The vote on engrossing for a third reading, a bill for raising
an army of fifty thousand volunteers, was taken January 23d,
and it stood, yeas seventy-two, nays forty-five. In the affirmative, voted the Administration supporters proper; in the negative, the two extremes—the anti-maritime party, who favored
the continuance of the Embargo long enough to bring England
to terms, though it should exterminate our own commerce—
and the maritime Federalists, who were as much opposed to a
war with England as to the Embargo; who, in reality, had
but one policy toward that power, namely, submission.

Before the bill for an extra session had passed the Senate (January 25th), Mr. Nicholas, of Virginia, the administration leader in the House, and understood to represent the personal views of the President, after declaring that we ought now to look for war and prepare for war if the Embargo did not within a reasonable time effect its purpose—that if redress was our object, defence was not sufficient, and that therefore " extensive preparation " was now called for—introduced the following resolution :

" *Resolved*, As the opinion of this House, that the United States ought not to delay beyond the ——— day of ——— to repeal the Embargo laws, and to resume, maintain and defend the navigation of the high seas against any nation or nations having in force edicts, orders, or decrees, violating the lawful commerce and neutral rights of the United States."

On the 30th, after some debate on this resolution, Mr. Nicholas so modified it, that it declared that if the obnoxious orders or decrees were not repealed by the day to be inserted in the blank, letters of marque and reprisal should be issued against the offending powers ; and he moved to fill the blank with the 1st day of June.

This proposition, taken in conjunction with the President's letter to Monroe, and with another to his son-in-law, Randolph, presently to be quoted, make the fact certain that he was in favor of suspending the Embargo at the specified time, and then resorting to hostilities, if necessary.

John Randolph moved as an amendment, a repeal of the Embargo "forthwith." This being voted down by a considerable majority, the question recurred on filling the blank with the first day of June. The "war party in peace and the peace party in war" (as they were subsequently well designated in Congress by Robert Y. Hayne, of South Carolina), strongly opposed Nicholas's resolution. Dana, of Connecticut, ridiculed this "contingent declaration of war." But he claimed that the Embargo should be given up, because it could not be enforced.[1]

Gardenier amused the House by earnestly advocating the

---

[1] He said : " Do gentlemen recollect how much danger menaces the sentiment of attachment to their country when foreign indulgences (as the liberty of trading derived from the contiguity of the British provinces) are given to the citizens of any portion of a country which refuses to allow them those privileges ? . . . . I deem it useless to rely on the patriotism of the people, when the Government forgets the cement of patriotism. What is country ? That portion of the globe where we have friends, freedom and protection."

President's peace policy, not only in the substance but in the identical line of argument in which its friends were accustomed to support it. We do not find Quincy's name in the debate. He was, perhaps, brooding over the conduct of his political friends on a recent occasion, when, after he had made an imposing demonstration, looking toward an impeachment of the President, not one of those friends was found ready to countenance his attempt.[1]

Pending the debate on Nicholas's resolution, a new party, or rather a new party wing, developed itself. The Republicans of New England became alarmed by the insurrectionary manifestations at home, and anxious for some middle course. After various desultory propositions,[2] they settled down in favor of the plan of an earlier repeal of the Embargo, and a permission thenceforth to our merchant vessels to arm in their own defence. On the 3d of February a motion to make the date of the repeal the 4th of March instead of the 1st of the succeeding June, pre-

[1] On the 26th of January, Mr. Quincy had risen "to perform a great duty!" It was a "painful" duty, but the "occasion called for it!" Every member "who had reason to believe a high crime or misdemeanor had been committed, was bound to state that opinion to the House, and move such an inquiry as the nature of the supposed offence demanded." He then stated that "Benjamin Lincoln, Esq.," Collector of the Port of Boston, offered his resignation to the President at the end of 1806, and again in September, 1807; assigning at both times his utter inability from age and infirmity to perform the duties of the office; that on the first occasion the President promised to appoint a successor, and on the second made no answer; that consequently the incumbent held the place a year longer; that the office had been "thus kept in effect vacant for more than two years," to reserve it for "a favorite of the Executive, Henry Dearborn, Secretary of War." As a preliminary to impeachment, he offered two resolutions, asking the President to lay his correspondence with Mr. Lincoln before the House, and to appoint a committee to inquire into the facts. The House, by a vote of ninety-three to twenty-four, agreed to consider the resolutions. Mr. Quincy made a speech. He thought it a high offence that the United States had been kept paying an individual $5000 a year for inadequate services, and against his own wishes.

This "Benjamin Lincoln, Esq.," was one of the oldest, if not the oldest, surviving major-general of the Revolutionary army. He had been appointed to the command of the Southern Department in 1778; had commanded at the fall of Charleston; had led the central division at Yorktown; had served as Secretary of War; and had subsequently held several high civic and diplomatic appointments. He had always been a decided Federalist; and had been made Collector of Boston in 1789, after being defeated for a reëlection as Lieutenant Governor by Samuel Adams. He never had actually sent in his resignation, until after the passage of the Enforcing Law.

The cruelty and criminality of retaining him two years longer in a lucrative office which he could perform the duties of by deputy—and doing this for such a purpose, when any number of young and well qualified Republicans could have been found willing to take the place though but for that short period—gave great diversion to many of the members. Others possessing less humor, treated Mr. Quincy and his proposed impeachment with anything but sportiveness. At length the important vote drew on. The yeas and nays were called on the resolutions. The yeas stood one (Mr. Quincy)—the nays one hundred and seventeen!

[2] For example, Story, who had at an earlier date, stoutly defended the Embargo, moved to fit out "fifty fast sailing frigates"—and this, we believe, is usually cited to show that the party who opposed the Embargo, were for immediate and adequate preparations for war!

vailed, yeas seventy; and the repealing clause then passed, yeas seventy-six.[1]

The President thus wrote his son-in-law:

To Thomas Mann Randolph.

Washington, *February* 7, 1809.

Dear Sir:

    I thought Congress had taken their ground firmly for continuing their Embargo till June, and then war. But a sudden and unaccountable revolution of opinion took place the last week, chiefly among the New England and New York members, and in a kind of panic they voted the 4th of March for removing the Embargo, and by such a majority as gave all reason to believe they would not agree either to war or non-intercourse. This, too, was after we had become satisfied that the Essex Junto had found their expectation desperate, of inducing the people there to either separation or forcible opposition. The majority of Congress, however, has now rallied to the removing the Embargo on the 4th of March, non-intercourse with *France* and *Great Britain*, trade everywhere else, and continuing war preparations. The further details are not yet settled, but I believe it is perfectly certain that the Embargo will be taken off the 4th of March.

The proposition to allow merchant vessels to arm, was next brought forward (or rather revived) by Randolph, and was supported by the Federalists, Quids, and the eastern and northern Republicans, who shrunk from direct war measures. The supporters of the Administration fell back on a non-intercourse law introduced earlier in the session. They were in favor of commercial restrictions of some kind, which would operate as a retaliation on England, or of open war. They had no partiality for a hybrid system, which offered the strongest inducements to illicit trade, and, among abandoned characters, the most dangerous temptations to piracy.

They now vigorously rallied, and on the 9th of February the Non-intercourse bill was referred back to the committee which reported it, yeas sixty-one, nays forty-one. On the motion of Alston, of North Carolina, and after a struggle carried through the night, the House, at 5 o'clock A.M. discharged the committee of the whole from the further consideration of the resolution for permitting the arming of merchant vessels, yeas sixty-five, nays fifty-five. On motion of the same gentleman, and after a debate protracted by the minority till the House became thinned out by physical exhaustion, all the resolutions offered by the oppo-

---

[1] We find these votes thus stated at pp. 1334, 1350 of Annals of Congress, 1808-9, second session, and the nays, if any, not mentioned.

sition were referred to the committee having in charge the Non-intercourse bill, yeas fifty-five, nays thirty-six.

On the 11th of February, Nicholas reported from that committee an Act which, as finally passed, interdicted the entrance of English or French public vessels into the ports and harbors of the United States, and all intercourse with them after the 1st of March ensuing; declared private vessels of those nations forfeited which entered the limits of the United States after the 20th of May; entirely cut off importations from those nations and their dependencies after the 20th of May; and connected with these provisions, ample means of enforcement so far as the power of the United States was adequate to that object.

The debate on the bill continued until the 27th of February, often exhibiting great vehemence.[1] Innumerable substitutes and amendments were offered without any important ones being carried. The bill passed, yeas eighty-one, nays forty. The bill to raise fifty thousand volunteers was lost in the Senate. The President was authorized to equip as many of the public vessels as he should deem necessary. Some other acts passed, looking to an extension of our defences, but none of them require notice. Illinois was erected into a territory this session. The tenth Congress closed on the 3d of March, and with it Mr. Jefferson's Presidential term.

The *coup d'œil* given of his Administration would be very incomplete without some explanation of that sudden vacillation in the Republican ranks, on Nicholas's resolution, which led to the only defeat of the Government on any leading national question during Mr. Jefferson's Presidency

We have recently presented his letter to his son-in-law on this subject. The following to a former Cabinet colleague, was written while all the facts, it must be presumed, were fresh in his memory:

TO GENERAL DEARBORN.

MONTICELLO, *July* 16, 1810.

DEAR GENERAL AND FRIEND:

Your favor of May the 31st was duly received, and I join in congratulations with you on the resurrection of republican principles in Massachusetts and New

---

[1] As a specimen of the avowals of some of the extreme and outspoken Federalists, it may be stated that Gardenier (February 18th) attempted to show that Great Britain had a right to issue her orders in council—that we could not, pending the Berlin decree, have honorably traded with France, independently of those orders—that the proposition that we were " paying tribute for going to a place where we could not go, was merely ideal "—and he repeated the customary insinuation, that the measure before the House was intended to meet the wishes of the French Emperor.

Hampshire, and the hope that the professors of these principles will not again easily be driven off their ground. The Federalists, during their short-lived ascendency, have, nevertheless, by forcing us from the Embargo, inflicted a wound on our interests which can never be cured, and on our affections which will require time to cicatrize. I ascribe all this to one pseudo-Republican, Story.[1] He came on (in place of Crowninshield, I believe) and staid only a few days; long enough, however, to get complete hold of Bacon, who giving in to his representations became panic struck, and communicated his panic to his colleagues, and they to a majority of the sound members of Congress. They believed in the alternative of repeal or civil war, and produced the fatal measure of repeal. This is the immediate parent of all our present evils, and has reduced us to a low standing in the eyes of the world. I should think that even the Federalists themselves must now be made, by their feelings, sensible of their error. The wealth which the Embargo brought home safely, has now been thrown back into the laps of our enemies; and our navigation completely crushed, and by the unwise and unpatriotic conduct of those engaged in it. Should the orders prove genuine, which are said to have been given against our fisheries, they too, are gone: and if not true as yet, they will be true on the first breeze of success which England shall feel: for it has now been some years that I am perfectly satisfied her intentions have been to claim the ocean as her conquest, and prohibit any vessel from navigating it, but on such a tribute as may enable her to keep up such a standing navy as will maintain her dominion over it. She has hauled in, or let herself out, been bold or hesitating, according to occurrences, but has in no situation done anything which might amount to an acknowledged relinquishment of her intentions. I have ever been anxious to avoid a war with England, unless forced by a situation more losing than war itself. But I did believe we could coerce her to justice by peaceable means, and the Embargo, evaded as it was, proved it would have coerced her had it been honestly executed. The proof she exhibited on that occasion, that she can exercise such an influence in this country as to control the will of its Government and three-fourths of its people, and oblige the three-fourths to submit to one-fourth, is to me the most mortifying circumstance which has occurred since the establishment of our government. The only prospect I see of lessening that influence, is in her own conduct, and not from anything in our power. Radically hostile to our navigation and commerce, and fearing its rivalry, she will completely crush it, and force us to resort to agriculture, not aware that we shall resort to manufactures also, and render her conquests over our navigation and commerce useless, at least, if not injurious to herself in the end, and perhaps salutary to us, as removing out of our way the chief causes and provocations to war."

After the exposure and publication of the fact that the Governor of Canada dispatched an agent named John Henry, to Massachusetts, in the beginning of 1809, to correspond with the disaffected, and produce an understanding between them and England, Mr. Jefferson wrote John Adams, April 20th, 1812:

"Of this mission of Henry, your son had got wind in the time of the Embargo, and communicated it to me. But he had learned nothing of the particular agent,

[1] Joseph Story, afterwards a justice of the U. S. Supreme Court.

although, of his workings, the information he had obtained appears now to have been correct. He stated a particular which Henry has not distinctly brought forward, which was, that the eastern States were not to be required to make a formal act of separation from the Union, and to take a part in the war against it; a measure deemed much too strong for their people: but to declare themselves in a state of neutrality, in consideration of which they were to have peace and free commerce, the lure most likely to insure popular acquiescence. Having no indications of Henry as the intermediate in this negotiation of the Essex Junto, suspicions fell on Pickering, and his nephew Williams, in London. If he was wronged in this, the ground of his suspicion is to be found in his known practices and avowed opinions, as that of his accomplices in the sameness of sentiment and of language with Henry, and subsequently by the fluttering of the wounded pigeons."

On the 25th of December, 1825, Mr. Jefferson gave another account of the transaction in answer to inquiries addressed to him by William B. Giles, then Governor of Virginia. In this he stated that J. Q. Adams called on him during the Embargo, and declared to him that "he had information of the most unquestionable certainty," that persons in the eastern States, and Massachusetts particularly, were in negotiation with agents of the British Government, "the object of which was an agreement that the New England States should take no further part in the war then going on"—that "without formally declaring their separation from the Union," "they should withdraw from all aid and obedience to them"—that in consideration of this, their commerce and navigation were to be free from interruption by England, and they were to be treated in all particulars as neutrals. He said that Mr. Adams declared "there was imminent danger that the convention would take place "— that to enable the friends of the Union to make head against these plans, "the repeal of the Embargo was absolutely necessary." And he finally declared that "from that moment, and influenced by that information, he saw the necessity of abandoning it, and instead of effecting our purpose by this peaceful weapon, we must fight it out, or break the Union "—that "he then recommended to his friends to yield to the necessity of a repeal of the Embargo, and to endeavor to supply its place by the best substitute, in which they could procure a general concurrence."

This is manifestly a contradictory explanation of the repeal of the Embargo, and of the writer's feelings at the time, from that given in the earlier letters which have been quoted. The cou-

temporary solution would naturally be the best one, and particular circumstances leave no reasonable doubt on that point. The letter to Giles was written at a period of great debility, during the author's eighty-third year, and within less than six months of his death. In the opening of the letter he deplored being called upon for recollections of transactions so far back, saying that his memory had " become almost a blank." [1]

We have stated more than once, that Mr. Jefferson's memory was never specially retentive of particular incidents; and that he preserved his remarkable general accuracy in writing of them by references to his own or to published records. In the present case, he spoke of a matter which was the subject of no record, and he was probably misled by impressions directly drawn from, or raised by some chord of association touched by, Giles's communications.[2] And his errors are so great and manifest, that we cannot help conjecturing that he wrote during some unusual access of disease, which either peculiarly affected his memory, or prevented him from giving his usual attention to his statements. Thus, where he mentions the war " then going on," he obviously confounds the period just preceding the repeal of the Embargo—that is, the opening of the year 1809— with the period of the second war with Great Britain, which was not declared until 1812.[3] Again, Mr. Adams subsequently asserted, and we have no doubt correctly, that the direct personal interview between them, alluded to by Mr. Jefferson, took place in March, 1808, a year earlier than mentioned by the latter. It is easy to see what a train of secondary errors of memory must have been involved in these two important primary ones.

There can be no doubt that Mr. Jefferson, by these mistakes, did great injustice to his own action in 1809, and to his declara-

---

[1] He erroneously thought, however, that the substance of Mr. Adams's communications " was of a character too awful, too deeply engraved in his mind, and influencing too materially the course he had to pursue, ever to be forgotten."

[2] This is but conjecture, as we have not Giles's letter before us. Mr. Jefferson was evidently, also, making a particular effort to do justice, at a critical moment, to the past conduct of a gentleman (John Quincy Adams) whose measures, at the time of writing, he was severely censuring to the same correspondent. This desire may have unconsciously affected his statements. Giles published the censures, and omitted the tribute to Mr. Adams's early services; and it was to repair this injustice that the legatee of Mr. Jefferson's papers published the latter. Portions of a warm correspondence between that legatee and Governor Giles, growing out of this publication, are before us.

[3] Mr. Adams embarked for Russia in August, 1809, and did not return until August, 1817.

ions then and at approximate periods. But, fortunately, he
lid none, in the substance, to anybody else. His letter to Giles
ras made public (after his death) in 1828. Mr. Adams, then a
andidate for reëlection to the Presidency, "authorized" the
National Intelligencer to publish a paper of corrections and ex-
ilanations. In this, having mentioned the errors which we have
lready stated, he took some pains to show that his communica-
ions in 1809, instead of being made to the President, were
rritten to Giles, Nicholas, and others, "as the solicited advice
if friend to friend, both ardent friends to the Administration
and to their country." For all practical purposes, then, this
ras as much a communication to the President as if the letters
iad been directed to him.

But in regard to his actual warnings and accusations against
he Federalists, Mr. Adams put the case in a much stronger
ight than did Mr. Jefferson. He said:

> "He [Adams] urged that a continuance of the Embargo much longer would
> certainly be met by forcible resistance, supported by the Legislature, and probably
> y the judiciary of the State [Massachusetts]. That to quell that resistance, if
> force should be resorted to by the Government, it would produce a civil war; and
> hat in that event, he had no doubt the leaders of the party would secure the
> coöperation with them of Great Britain. That their object was, and had been for
> several years, a dissolution of the Union, and the establishment of a separate con-
> sideration, he knew from unequivocal evidence, although not provable in a court of
> aw; and that in case of a civil war, the aid of Great Britain to effect that purpose,
> would be as surely resorted to, as it would be indispensably necessary to the
> design."

Here we have a charge against the leaders of the Massachusetts Federalists of a wish and design, entertained in 1809, and
for years previously, to permanently divide the Union. And
this accusation is deliberately reiterated twenty years after the
events, by the President of the United States, and declared to
be supportable by "unequivocal evidence." It is due to Mr.
Adams to say that he made and published substantially similar
allegations in 1809.[1]

His communication, published in the Intelligencer in 1828,

---

[1] For example, in his third article, in the Boston Patriot, reviewing the writings of
Mr. Ames, he said: "They [Ames's principles] are the principles of a faction, which,
has succeeded in obtaining the management of this commonwealth, and which aspired to
the government of the Union. Defeated in this last object of their ambition, and sensible that the engines by which they have attained the mastery of the State are not sufficiently comprehensive, nor enough within their control to wield the machinery of the
nation, their next resort was to dismember what they could not sway, and to form a new
confederacy, to be under the glorious shelter of British protection."

drew out a reply from some of the parties supposed to be implicated by its charges. Mr. Adams retorted, making his allegations more specific, and was again answered. We shall
hereafter call attention to this correspondence, and to some
interesting resulting disclosures.

To return to Mr. Jefferson's connection with the public
measures of 1809. It admits of no question that he did not
abandon the attitude assumed in Nicholas's resolution voluntarily, as he supposed when he wrote to Giles in 1825. He was
driven to that abandonment—in other words, beaten on the
question by the defection of the eastern and northern Republicans. And he firmly believed to the end of his life (and we
understand that Madison and Gallatin fully acquiesced in that
belief) that had this resolution passed and been firmly acted
on, we should have attained our objects with both England and
France, without the subsequent degradations we endured, or
war with either of those powers.

It has been a common and continued assertion among those
whose illegal resistance and threats of dividing the Union, first
neutralized to a material extent the proper results of the
Embargo, and then led to its premature repeal, that it wholly
failed in its intended effect on other nations, and consequently
brought unnecessary injury on our own. Pertinacity and zeal
would be expected in a line of argument necessary to excuse
the writers for conduct which the nation regarded as "moral
treason."[1] Descendants and successors are excusable for the
same pertinacity.

An English and French view of this subject may not be
uninteresting. The disquisitions of the Edinburgh Review, the
great organ of the English Whigs, on maritime international
law, and on the effects of the commercial regulations of different nations, display at this period a knowledge of facts and
cogency of argument that has caused them to be repeatedly
quoted as conspicuous authority by writers on maritime law.[2]
The number of this Review for November, 1812, says:

"It was long the anxious business of the American minister, as appears from

---

[1] This was the clinging epithet applied to their conduct by the celebrated Felix
Grundy.

[2] E. g. See Reddie on International Maritime Law, *passim*. He generally quotes
them as, and therefore admits them to be, *adverse* authority.

the document before us, to procure by persuasion an abandonment of the measures hostile to the American trade. He urged his case on views of justice and of general policy—he calmly combated the pretexts by which he was met—he boldly and pointedly asserted that the claims of this country must, sooner or later, be abandoned; and he added, what ought never to be forgotten, that they were unjust, and that time, therefore, could do nothing for them. His representations were met by declarations of 'what his Majesty owed to the honor, dignity, and essential rights of his crown,' and by all the other sounding commonplaces usual on such occasions. These sentiments were afterwards explained at greater length, and promulgated to the world in the deliberate record of a state paper. But in spite of the honor of majesty thus pledged to these obnoxious measures, they were repealed. A laborious investigation into their merits ended in their unqualified reprobation and abandonment—their authors were unable to look in the face *the scenes of beggary, disorder, and wretchedness which their policy had brought on the country; they were borne down by the cries of suffering millions—and they yielded at length to necessity, what they had formerly refused to justice.* This was clearly, therefore, an act of unwilling submission. It bore not the stamp of conciliation; and the only inference to be drawn from it was, that the plotters of mischief, being fairly caught in their own snare, were glad to escape, on any terms, from the effects of their ill-considered measures."

*   *   *   *   *   *   *   *

"There is not a man in the kingdom who can doubt, that if the orders in council had been rescinded six months sooner, the war might have been entirely avoided, and all other points of difference between the countries adjusted upon an amicable footing. Nor is there an individual who has attended at all to the progress of the dispute, who does not see that it was embittered from the first, and wantonly urged to its present fatal issue by the insolent, petulant, and preposterous tone of those very individuals who insisted on that miserable experiment, and plunged their own country in wretchedness, only to bring down upon it the reluctant hostility of its best customers and allies. If those mischievous and despicable councils were once cordially renounced—if this paltry and irritating tone were forever interdicted at our public offices—if the negotiation were committed to a man acceptable to Americans, and free from the suspicion of insincerity, which the character of our late diplomatic communications with her have so naturally excited; we are fully persuaded that a speedy and honorable termination might yet be put to this unnatural contest, which, if it be purely ruinous and disreputable to us, promises to be so much more detrimental than beneficial to our opponent."

These views, it is believed, were substantially concurred in by the leading Whig statesmen of Great Britain.

The Emperor of the French was generally conceded to be a good judge of the effects of measures designed to annoy or injure a national antagonist. He declared to R. L. Livingston (a kinsman of Chancellor Livingston, then in France) that the Embargo was a " wise measure," and that " he did not wish us to go to war with England, knowing we had no ships to carry on that war." [1] Mr. Pickering, and other Federalists in Congress,

---

[1] Mr. Livingston communicated these statements to the President in a letter dated

specifically imputed similar views to the Emperor, and we may therefore conclude that they were repeated on various occasions. That these opinions were based on purely selfish considerations, no one will doubt; and it is this which gives them their highest value as testimony. It certainly was for the interest of France that the United States adopt the mode of redress which would be most damaging to England. If the United States chose the alternative of war with the latter, France had but to repeal her decrees against their commerce, and the Embargo would cease as regarded herself. She would then in effect have the United States for her allies in the war. Yet Napoleon preferred the continuance of non-intercourse with us, if it was at the same time continued against England, to the possession of both our intercourse and alliance!

The argument of mere authority is not conclusive—and here is not the place for an extended array of facts or reasoning on the subject. But it may be safely asserted on statistics already presented, that to have permitted our commerce to go abroad on the ocean, would have been to expose it to certain destruction. If we had cringed to the power which was the first and by far the greatest practical aggressor on our rights—which had impressed several thousands of our citizens during her present war,[1] while her opponent had not impressed one—which had recently attacked and outraged our national flag within sight of our own shores and refused reparation, while her antagonist had offered no insult to that flag—if, under these circumstances, we had adopted the proposition of Mr. Gore and the Massachusetts Legislature to repeal our commercial restrictions as to England and make war on France, what commercial reward could we have expected for our voluntary degradation? We could have traded with England and her colonies—and with a few other countries not embraced in the iron bands of Napoleon's conti-

September 22d, 1808, and the latter replied October 15th, 1808. The *words* we quote are from the reply.

[1] John Quincy Adams, in his published letter to Otis, already referred to (dated March, 1808), said:

"Examine the official returns from the department of State. They give the names of between four and five thousand men impressed since the commencement of the present war, of which number not one-fifth part were British subjects. The number of naturalized Americans could not amount to one-tenth—I hazard little in saying that more than three fourths were native Americans. If it be said that some of these men, though appearing on the face of the returns American citizens, were really British subjects, and had fraudulently procured their protections; I reply, that this number must be far exceeded by the cases of citizens impressed which never reach the department of State. The American Consul in London estimates the number of impressments during the war, at nearly three times the amount of the names returned."

nental system. But we should have still remained shut out from the principal portion of the important and profitable trade of the world ; and even where our trade could have thus crawled by British permission, it would have been compelled to encounter British competition. Our ministers in England believed that it was more to destroy our rivalry in commerce and navigation, than to directly affect France, that the orders in council had been issued. What we had to expect from abject submission may therefore be estimated.

On the other hand, could the objects sought by the Embargo have been attained by submitting to the maritime regulations of France, and making war on England? This would have equally placed us in the attitude of a volunteer and cringing auxiliary to our national aggressor. The practical commercial advantage gained would be trifling, because, if Napoleon could throw open to us the ports of the European continent and of dependent countries, England could prevent us from entering them. And, moreover, a spirit was abroad in a section of our own country, which would have rendered the hazard of a civil war imminent, if the English sympathies and prejudices of its people had been furnished with so strong a provocation to exhibit themselves.

Was any feasible and honorable substitute for the Embargo ever offered by those who heaped mountains of invective and ridicule on that measure? It seems to be supposed by many that they at least proposed the heroic alternative of war. The maritime class from interest, and the Federalists from principle, were habitually the advocates of a great navy—and desultory and impracticable propositions in this direction were made by them, during the continuance of the Embargo. Their Congressional orators, too, like Mr. Quincy, declared the Government could not be "kicked into a war."[1] But when a serious move was made towards war, they were always foremost in the opposition. And they united with a few panic-struck Republicans and all the other fragments of opposition, to vote down a distinct proposition submitted by the Administration party, to terminate the Embargo in about four months, and follow it by issuing letters of marque and reprisal.

---

[1] Speech in House of Representatives, January 19th, 1809.

The commercial interests had been the first to denounce the English maritime regulations. The seizures which took place under the orders in council of November 6th, 1793, produced a tempest of excitement among them. Nothing but the organization of an imposing embassy (Mr. Jay's) arrested the current of the public mind in favor of war. The same interests were the first to call for redress or war, when in 1805 England enforced the rule of 1756 towards neutrals [1]—a rule which fell with great severity on our expanded commerce.[2] These interests becomingly resented the British orders in council of 1806-7. The outrage on the Chesapeake had called out a lively burst of feeling from the maritime Federalists in the very emporium of New England.[3] Yet when the Embargo was resisted by the same class to the verge of insurrection, they proposed no practical alternative but a submission to the maritime regulations of England! This, probably, shows that there was no feasible and honorable substi-

---

[1] The Boston Memorial, January 20th, 1806 (signed in behalf of themselves and their constituents, the merchants of Boston generally, by James Lloyd, jr., David Green, Arnold Welles, David Sears, John Coffin Jones, George Cabot, and Thomas H. Perkins), declared these orders "would annihilate or greatly diminish the commerce of neutral nations"—that they "only served to invite depredation, to bankrupt ourselves and enrich others, until such commerce be swept from the ocean," etc.—that they were "unsound in point of principle, offensive in practice"—that the memorialists trusted "that such measures would, in consequence, be promptly adopted as would tend to disembarrass our commerce, assert our rights, and support. the dignity of the United States."

The merchants and chamber of commerce of New Haven, in a memorial signed by Henry Dagget, president of the chamber of commerce (February 7th, 1806), more vehemently declared that "all nations should combine against such innovations on their rights"—should firmly resist every encroachment upon the rights of neutral commerce"—and they pledged themselves "to give aid and support to every measure of Government calculated to accomplish this important object."

The merchants of Newburyport used equally decisive language as to the evil and the remedy, in a memorial dated December, 1805, and signed by a committee of merchants, consisting of Ebenezer Stocker, Stephen Howard, Edward Tappan, John Pearson, William Bartlet, Moses Howard, and William Earls.

The inhabitants of Salem, generally, in a strong memorial, dated January 20, 1806, pronounced the orders "a mere pretext for predatory seizures," and declared that if "conciliation could not effect the purpose of justice, and an appeal to arms was the last and necessary protection of honor, they felt no disposition to decline the common danger"—that "they felt no hesitation to pledge their lives and properties in support of the measures which might be adopted to vindicate the public rights, and redress the public wrongs." The committee signing this paper, were John Hathorne, Joseph Sprague, Jonathan Mason, Benj. Crowninshield, jr., Joseph White, jr., and Joseph Story.

The New York Memorial was as strong as that of Boston, and was signed in behalf of the merchants generally, by John Broome, Oliver Wolcott, and forty-seven others, including the principal Federal merchants of the city.

The Philadelphia Memorial held the same tone, and was signed by a committee of twenty, including Thomas Fitzsimmons, and the principal Federalists.

[2] The value of exports from the United States, foreign and domestic, during the first four years of General Washington's Presidency, was less than $100,000,000. During the first four years of Mr. Jefferson's Presidency, it exceeded $330,000,000, and about half of it ($163,287,000) was foreign—chiefly the production of the colonies of enemies of Great Britain, so that it was exposed to capture under the English regulations of 1805.

[3] See note 1, p. 284.

tute for commercial restrictions but war. That fact was distinctly asserted in a memorial presented to the Government just before the final declaration of war, by some of the principal commercial characters of New York. The memorialists were headed by the profoundly sagacious John Jacob Astor, and three-quarters of them were Federalists.[1]

It must always be conceded that the Embargo was only a choice of evils. It was a hard and painful alternative, but for a time was probably the best one. As one of its most eloquent defenders, John Quincy Adams, remarked, "the orders in council, if submitted to, would have degraded us to the condition of colonies—if resisted, would have fattened the wolves of plunder with our spoils. The Embargo was the only shelter from the tempest—the last refuge of our violated peace." [2]

And, finally, the policy on which it was based, has the convincing argument of ultimate success in its favor. The effect of the Non-intercourse law on France and England was the same in kind with that of the Embargo, and its extent was less. Those nations, finally, repealed their obnoxious maritime regulations against us, on condition that we would repeal that law. It weighs nothing against the evidence furnished by this fact, that the English repeal did not take place until five days after our declaration of war against her. She acted without any knowledge of that declaration.

One of the characteristics of Mr. Jefferson's Presidency which stands forth most prominently, is its perfect consistency with the principles he avowed before his accession to that office. Indeed, the remark extends to all parts of his public life. He underwent one great ostensible change of political principle—that which took place in the minds of Franklin, the Adamses, Patrick Henry, and Washington, in 1775 or 1776—the change from acquiescence in a constitutional mixed government to the warm support of a purely representative one. In Mr. Jefferson's case, it came so rapidly and was so complete, that we cannot help suspecting the earlier feeling was the result of habit, and that the latter accorded with the natural biases of his mind.

[1] See APPENDIX, No. 22.
[2] These words occur in Mr. Adams's letter to Harrison Gray Otis, published in 1808, to justify his own vote for the Embargo, and to answer Pickering's letter to Governor Sullivan against that measure. Yet Mr. Adams lived to sneer, seemingly, at this and other measures of the Administration, which he also contemporaneously voted for, and violently supported in the partisan publications of the day!

Most of the great leaders of the Revolution became conscientious Republicans; but they stopped short of democracy—and those who reached it, reached it gradually. Mr. Jefferson's mind appears to have had no subsequent growth in this direction. His republicanism and his democracy were not like rills gradually swelled into rivers by new accessions; they were like those outlets of seas, which are as deep and broad at their sources as at their mouths. More than most statesmen, he passed through all those political vicissitudes which make both victory and retaliation sweet—which wed the heart to the possession of power—which foster the disposition to wield power arbitrarily. He retired from public life without having done an act, or expressed a sentiment which any candid and intelligent friend or opponent will adjudge to imply an intentional deviation from the principles he professed.

He passed through public life, too, unchanged, unchilled, unhardened, in his private feelings. His faith in humanity had only increased, his hopes of the world's future had only grown brighter.

His relations with his Cabinet and with the other officers of the executive departments had been uniformly of the most agreeable character. Not a transient or trifling misunderstanding—not a cold word had ever occurred between him and one of them. Separated from each other by irreconcilable estrangements, after his firm and gentle influence ceased to form the bond of union between them, all of them agreed through life in remaining the devoted political admirers and personal friends of their former chief. It would be doing injustice to Mr. Jefferson's Federal opponents in Congress, to omit to say, that it is believed that those of them who became familiarly acquainted with him, thenceforth, without a single exception, laid aside their personal prejudices, and ceased to attack him in public or private. Among his staunchest friends were the wives and daughters of some very eminent Federalists. His servants at Washington were so attached to him that several of them wept on taking leave of him.

We shall offer no extended review of his Administration. It originated or reaffirmed nearly all the State maxims that still continue to control our government; and these and their daily workings are open to all. It may at least be said, that henceforth our policies were our own. We were an independent nation in spirit as well as form. We had a system which was supposed to be adapted to our particular wants and situation as a people, and which was our free choice. We were no longer copyists or colonists in spirit—we were Americans.

Mr. Jefferson's feelings in bidding a final farewell to office, after holding it with but a few brief intervals for nearly half a century, were thus described by him in a letter to his old friend Dupont de Nemours, written two days before the expiration of his Presidency:

"Within a few days I retire to my family, my books and farms; and having gained the harbor myself, I shall look on my friends still buffeting the storm with anxiety indeed, but not with envy. Never did a prisoner, released from his chains, feel such relief as I shall on shaking off the shackles of power. Nature intended me for the tranquil pursuits of science, by rendering them my supreme delight. But the enormities of the times in which I have lived, have forced me to take a part in resisting them, and to commit myself on the boisterous ocean of political passions. I thank God for the opportunity of retiring from them without censure, and carrying with me the most consoling proofs of public approbation. I leave everything in the hands of men so able to take care of them, that if we are destined to meet misfortunes, it will be because no human wisdom could avert them. Should you return to the United States, perhaps your curiosity may lead you to visit the hermit of Monticello. He will receive you with affection and delight; hailing you in the meantime with his affectionate salutations and assurances of constant esteem and respect."

Addresses poured in upon him, on his approaching retirement, from every part of the Union. They came from legislatures, and popular bodies—from State, city, county, and town, conventions and meetings—from political, ecclesiastical, military, industrial, and almost all other associations. We will quote one of them as presenting the spirit of the whole. The following address (written by William Wirt) was moved in the Virginia Legislature, and passed, February 6th, by a vote of about five to one:

SIR:

The General Assembly of your native State cannot close their session without acknowledging your services in the office which you are just about to lay down, and bidding you a respectful and affectionate farewell.

We have to thank you for the model of an administration conducted on the purest principles of republicanism; for pomp and state laid aside; patronage discarded; internal taxes abolished; a host of superfluous officers disbanded; the monarchic maxim that a national debt is a national blessing, renounced, and more than thirty-three millions of our debt discharged; the native right to near one hun

dred millions of acres of our national domain extinguished; and without the guil
or calamities of conquest, a vast and fertile region added to our country, far mor
extensive than her original possessions, bringing along with it the Mississippi an
the port of Orleans, the trade of the West to the Pacific ocean, and in the intrinsi
value of the land itself, a source of permanent and almost inexhaustible revenu
These are points in your Administration which the historian will not fail to seize, t
expand, and to teach posterity to dwell upon with delight. Nor will he forget oc
peace with the civilized world, preserved through a season of uncommon difficul
and trial; the good will cultivated with the unfortunate aborigines of our countr
and the civilization humanely extended among them; the lesson taught the inhab
tants of the coast of Barbary, that we have the means of chastising their piratic
encroachments, and awing them into justice; and that theme, which, above a
others, the historic genius will hang upon with rapture, the liberty of speech an
the press preserved inviolate, without which genius and science are given to man i
vain.

In the principles on which you have administered the government, we see onl
the continuation and maturity of the same virtues and abilities which drew upo
you in your youth the resentment of Dunmore. From the first brilliant and happ
moment of your resistance to foreign tyranny until the present day, we mark wit
pleasure and with gratitude the same uniform and consistent character—the sam
warm and devoted attachment to liberty and the Republic, the same Roman lov
of your country, her rights, her peace, her honor, her prosperity.

How blessed will be the retirement into which you are about to go! Ho
deservedly blessed will it be! For you carry with you the richest of all reward
the recollection of a life well spent in the service of your country, and proofs th
most decisive of the love, the gratitude, the veneration of your countrymen.

That your retirement may be as happy as your life has been virtuous an
useful; that our youth may see in the blissful close of your days, an addition
inducement to form themselves on your model, is the devout and earnest prayer o
your fellow-citizens who compose the General Assembly of Virginia.

To this address, transmitted by his friend Governor Joh
Tyler (father of ex-President Tyler), Mr. Jefferson returned th
following reply:

February 16th, 1809.

I receive with peculiar sensibility the affectionate address of the Gener
Assembly of my native State, on my approaching retirement from the office wit
which I have been honored by the nation at large. Having been one of those wh
entered into public life at the commencement of an era the most extraordinar
which the history of man has ever yet presented to his contemplation, I clai
nothing more, for the part I have acted in it, than a common merit of having, wit
others, faithfully endeavored to do my duty in the several stations allotted me. I
the measures which you are pleased particularly to approve, I have been aided b
the wisdom and patriotism of the national legislature, and the talents and virtues o
the able coadjutors with whom it has been my happiness to be associated, and t
whose valuable and faithful services I with pleasure and gratitude bear witness.

From the moment that to preserve our rights a change of government becam
necessary, no doubt could be entertained that a republican form was most con
sonant with reason, with right, with the freedom of man, and with the charactu

and situation of our fellow citizens. To the sincere spirit of republicanism are naturally associated the love of country, devotion to its liberty, its rights, and its honor. Our preference to that form of government has been so far justified by its success, and the prosperity with which it has blessed us. In no portion of the earth were life, liberty and property ever so securely held; and it is with infinite satisfaction that withdrawing from the active scenes of life, I see the sacred design of these blessings committed to those who are sensible of their value and determined to defend them.

It would have been a great consolation to have left the nation under the assurance of continued peace. Nothing has been spared to effect it; and at no other period of history would such efforts have failed to ensure it. For neither belligerent pretends to have been injured by us, or can say that we have in any instance departed from the most faithful neutrality; and certainly none will charge us with a want of forbearance.

In the desire of peace, but in full confidence of safety from our unity, our position, and our resources, I shall retire into the bosom of my native State, endeared to me by every tie which can attach the human heart. The assurances of your approbation, and that my conduct has given satisfaction to my fellow citizens generally, will be an important ingredient in my future happiness; and that the supreme Ruler of the universe may have our country under his special care, will be among the latest of my prayers.

Mr. Jefferson was present at the inauguration of his successor, and soon afterwards set out for home. The inhabitants of the county of his birth and residence (Albemarle) had proposed to meet and escort him to Monticello, with imposing ceremonies. He quietly put aside the request by declaring that he could not decide on the day of his return, and he added:

"But it is a sufficient happiness to me to know that my fellow-citizens of the country generally entertain for me the kind sentiments which have prompted this proposition, without giving to so many the trouble of leaving their homes to meet a single individual. I shall have opportunities of taking them individually by the hand at our court-house and other public places, and of exchanging assurances of mutual esteem. Certainly it is the greatest consolation to me to know, that in returning to the bosom of my native county, I shall be again in the midst of their kind affections: and I can say with truth that my return to them will make me happier than I have been since I left them."

The proposed ovation gave way to an address, and it was thus answered:

To the Inhabitants of Albemarle County, in Virginia.

April 3, 1809.

Returning to the scenes of my birth and early life, to the society of those with whom I was raised, and who have been ever dear to me, I receive, fellow-citizens and neighbors, with inexpressible pleasure, the cordial welcome you are so good as to give me. Long absent on duties which the history of a wonderful era made incumbent on those called to them, the pomp, the turmoil, the bustle and splendor of office, have drawn but deeper sighs for the tranquil and irresponsible occupations of private life, for the enjoyment of an affectionate intercourse with you, my neighbors and friends, and the endearments of family love, which nature has given us all, as the sweetener of every hour. For these I gladly lay down the distressing burden of power, and seek, with my fellow-citizens, repose and safety under the watchful cares, and labors and perplexities of younger and abler minds. The anxieties you express to administer to my happiness, do, of themselves, confer that happiness; and the measure will be complete, if my endeavors to fulfill my duties in the several public stations to which I have been called, have obtained for me the approbation of my country. The part which I have acted on the theatre of public life, has been before them, and to their sentence I submit it; but the testimony of my native county, of the individuals who have known me in private life, to my conduct in its various duties and relations, is the more grateful, as proceeding from eye-witnesses and observers, from triers of the vicinage. Of you, then, my neighbors, I may ask, in the face of the world, " whose ox have I taken, or whom have I defrauded? Whom have I oppressed, or of whose hand have I received a bribe to blind mine eyes therewith?" On your verdict I rest with conscious security. Your wishes for my happiness are received with just sensibility, and I offer sincere prayers for your own welfare and prosperity.

CHAPTER VIII.

1809.

THE ex-President reached Monticello in the middle of March; he thus wrote to his successor on the 17th:

'I had a very fatiguing journey, having found the roads excessively bad, though I have seen them worse. The last three days I found it better to be on horseback, and travelled eight hours through as disagreeable a snow storm as I was ever in. Feeling no inconvenience from the expedition but fatigue, I have more confidence in my *vis vitæ* than I had before entertained. The spring is remarkably backward. No oats sown, not much tobacco seed, and little done in the gardens. Wheat has suffered considerably. No vegetation visible yet but the red maple, weeping willow and lilac. Flour is said to be at eight dollars at Richmond, and all produce is hurrying down."

He expressed, in the same letter, much solicitude in respect to the events of the next four or five months. He predicted a smooth administration to his successor, if peace could be preserved, and he declared that in " the present maniac state of Europe," he would not " estimate the point of honor by the ordinary scale." Still, he thought war " might become a less losing business than unrestricted depredation." The whole spirit of this communication clearly shows, if any proofs were needed of that fact, that he had not regarded Nicholas's resolution of the preceding session as a measure likely to lead to war—though he had been willing to risk war, to compel a recognition of our neutral rights.

A correspondence of a free and closely confidential character in regard to measures of Government, continued to be maintained between the late and the acting President—the only example of the kind, it is believed, in our history. The relations which existed between Jefferson and Madison, were not those merely of kindred politicians, who had acted long and harmoniously together, or of every-day social friends. They were the strongest ties which can knit those of the same sex together—similar principles, similar intellectual capacities, similar degrees of knowledge, similar tastes and views, and finally similar personal interests—for with so general a concurrence on political questions, the public fortunes of the men had become necessarily embarked in the same bottom. They were just far enough removed from each other by the difference of age and experience for one to naturally lead and the other to gracefully follow; and yet they were not sufficiently apart to bring the dissimilar feelings of widely separated epochs of life into inharmonious contact. Madison was still in the full meridian of manhood; Jefferson had not passed the mellow autumn of old age.[1]

There were enough minor contrasts in their minds and manners to give an agreeable piquancy to their intercourse. Madison was purely a reasoner; he was an unrivalled logician. Jefferson could reason if the occasion demanded; but it was rather his taste and his habit to reflect silently, and only

---

[1] Madison was fifty-eight and Jefferson sixty-six years of age.

announce naked and sententious conclusions. He was averse to personal argumentation, and he abhorred it when it approached the precincts of controversy. It has often been said that Madison was a shade the most conservative. He was naturally, probably, several shades more conservative, and he had far more caution. He struck not out on so bold a wing into theory—conformed not practice to theory so fearlessly—and had not the same daring decision to defy the world on the strength of an intellectual, a moral, or a political conviction. He had less enthusiasm, less nerve, less of that force of will which sweeps along everything in its course, less marked and salient points of every description. He also had less genius. But Mr. Madison had equal talent, a sufficiency of passive firmness, more circumspection, and if he did not naturally and resistlessly control the portion of society inclined towards his views, he did not rouse a war *ad internecionem* with the other portion by the boldness and vehemency of his antagonism.

Jefferson, one of the kindest-hearted and most philanthropic men of his times, stands caricatured in the minds of many candid persons into a personification of intolerance, nay, ferocious bigotry, because he always spoke out and wrote out all he thought at the moment. His language never withheld from view a fiery tinge of the feeling that dictated it; he never smothered either the spark or the flame. There was a special excuse for him. He was engaged in a contest with a party who had without provocation transcended all the decencies of civilized life in their assaults on him, and to whose false, coarse, malignant, insulting and persistent accusations his own replies were only the milk of retaliation. John Adams was a well abused man, but the depraved ingenuity of his tormentors never invaded the domestic circle, to strike at him through the feelings of his children—to charge him with practices within that circle, and under the knowledge of his daughters, which, of all others, would have been most revolting to the pride of womanhood, the most lacerating to the respect and tenderness of filial love.

The persecution and calumny which dogged Jefferson to the grave, and did not even then surcease, fell lightly on Madison. There were, perhaps, two or three reasons for this. Perhaps Mr. Jefferson's adversaries had at length discovered, that this was not the most successful way of keeping the public favorites from the Presidency. Certainly no similar tactics were resorted to by any party for many subsequent years. Then, as heretofore remarked, it was Jefferson who was the founder of the obnoxious system, the apostle of the hated creed; and on such the rage of opponents, and particularly of conquered opponents, falls with tenfold more violence than on the lieutenant or successor, however closely he may follow in the footsteps of his predecessor.

But in truth, Madison owed much of his immunity to a kind of prudence which Jefferson never possessed. He so far concurred in all of the practical political views of the former, that it would be difficult, we apprehend, to point out an important difference. Nay, he had separated from the great first President, who had so loved and trusted him, to follow the standard of Jefferson. He sat eight years in the Cabinet of the latter without a recorded non-concurrence of views. But in expressing an opinion for the public ear, he carefully abstained from all but the pure logic of argument. He went not a word beyond the necessary point. He questioned no one's motives—he retaliated no hostile personal assault. He never suffered an extraneous sentiment calculated to provoke prejudice to creep into his writings, or even his conversation. Where such expressions became necessary, he guarded, so far as circumstances would allow, against their publicity, and he took especial pains to recall and destroy his private political correspondence.

Jefferson, on the other hand, was a perfectly fearless talker and writer. We find him making some efforts, in his earlier career, to prevent the publication of letters which might compromise him as the leader of a party, and always dreading to get into the newspapers; but an inspection of his entire correspondence will show, that no man was ever more gratuitously open on the most dangerous topics. It was next to impossible for him to suppress an abstract conclusion, growing out of or suggested by his topic, however much his keen knowledge of men might admonish him of the danger thus incurred. In his conversation he was still more communicative. His political lieutenants often stood aghast at his freedom.[1] And he added

---

[1] General Smith's statement, that his friends often thought him too free in conversation, has already been seen, in a letter to R. H. and J. A. Bayard. Professor Tucker, who knew Mr. Jefferson personally, makes a similar statement. Dr. Dunglison, his family physician, will hereafter be found mentioning the same characteristic in these

greatly to the effect of his disclosures by the energy of his expressions. The thought that, uttered by another, would have attracted little notice, often hissed like a fiery missile, in his nervous and burning diction. And it also often happened that the pith of his comparison, or the epigrammatic point of his expression, kept the Congreve rocket flying, which otherwise would have speedily dropped to the ground. The effect of his startling abstractions has already been well illustrated in the case of conservative and excellent Charles Carroll. Mr. Jefferson, in the animation of writing and speaking, generally forgot to put in the limitations—the "ifs" and "buts," which not only take off the sharp edge of the thought, but leave such convenient holes for prudent men to creep out at!

But after all, it is these daring, eagle-pinioned men who alone win the goal of transcendent and overmastering popularity. People admire and trust, but rarely love those colder-blooded champions, who go to the feast as well as to the battle armed in full panoply, on whose bosoms the Gorgon shield repels sympathy as well as danger. Such never win the mystic pass-words to the human heart, which, like the cries of the brute creation to one another, at once excite the feeling that calls them forth—which at once muster the squadrons of the air and the plain for battle, or scatter them in flight. The mighty leader of mankind must be something more than a sage; something more than a skillful executive tactician—he must be, at heart, a hero. He must be ready on great occasions, to spurn all middle prudences. He must be as ready to raise the song of martyrdom as the shout of victory. He must rejoice in danger, when danger must be met. His sword must flame as fiercely in the van of battle, and his foot be as eager to scale the rampart, or tread the fatal breach as the least considerable and the bravest under his command. He who would rely on men to the death, must show that he holds his life as cheap as theirs.

Far be it from us to intimate, that any little cunning, much less a shade of duplicity, marked the character of Madison. Nature had constituted him a different man, in some particulars, from his predecessor; and it was as appropriate and right

---

pages: and he personally related to us some amusing incidents which grew out it. We never have met an individual who knew Mr. Jefferson personally, who had not almost habitually noticed this peculiarity, and who did not speak of it as a matter of common notoriety and remark among Mr. Jefferson's associates.

that the one should follow out his own peculiarities as the othe
Men may not only differ, without blame, in their modes of actio
but each will play his part most efficiently who plays his natur
one. If, when extraneous moot-questions came up, Madis
relapsed into grave silence, it was like Washington; if he pa
ried unnecessary curiosity by a neat turn, it was like Frankli
His caution was purely defensive. He never employed it
assail, or surprise, or take an advantage of an opponent. It wa
the result of temperament and not of cowardice. He was pa
sionless, because reason and logic guided the steady movemen
of all his faculties.

It has been perhaps already remarked, that Jefferson an
Madison were peculiarly calculated to be useful to each othe
One prompted—the other restrained. One determined—tl
other followed up and supplied the chain of argument, or lil
the cable-trier, cautiously smote each link, to make sure that
had no flaw.

They also had that difference in personal peculiarities whic
seasons intercourse, and draws closer the bands of friendship.

Jefferson was six feet two and a half inches in height; Mac
son five feet and between six and six and a half inches.[1] Je
ferson's movements were unrestrained, swinging, and bol
Madison's though graceful, were precise. Calm authority a
in Jefferson's eye, and lurked in the firm intonations of h
voice. In a stage coach, in a crowd, in any situation, he
once attracted notice—at once was recognized by high and lo
as a leader of men. The impression which his looks conveye
was that of great firmness and gentleness combined—of powerf
energy in perfect repose. Madison, in public, appeared to
stranger like a polished and contemplative professional man
student, who was taking a look out on the busy world.

A characteristic of Mr. Jefferson's conversation has bee
given—its boldness. It did not, as he became advanced in lit
often evince enthusiasm; he made no effort at sustained br
liancy; and he utterly lacked wit. His discourse abounde
with information and thought, and was garnished with ol
fashioned courtesy and compliment, as old architecture exhibi

---

[1] We mention the last fact with this precision, not recollecting to have seen it el
where published, and having it on the personal authority of Mr. Madison's Private
cretary, Hon. Edward Coles.

rich and quaint carving. This was in the style of the pre-Revolutionary court of Virginia, or of that of Louis XVI., partly rubbed off by later associations.[1] His conversation, however, was always pleasing to the listeners, and occasionally, with the young, deepened into that earlier strain, when his thoughts spontaneously arranged themselves into the striking and stately diction of his early writings. It then fell with indescribable force on the ears of his hearers.

Mr. Madison too had the old-school elegance, and superabounded with information. His discourse, without being didactic and frigid, was weighty. He, perhaps, was never impassioned; and was rather taciturn in public. But among private friends he was a delightful and humorous talker; and in very small and very confidential circles, blazed out into unrestrained facetiousness, and occasional brilliant flashes of wit. He told a story admirably; and had a long list of pet anecdotes against Jefferson, at which their victim always laughed until his eyes ran over. Many of these have been repeated to us by those who " were there to see." We wish we could give specimens; but the aroma would all exhale in the recital. Some, perhaps most of them, indeed, require the living narrator, as their humor depends more upon the manner than the matter. Mr. Madison's fund of geniality and liveliness was inexhaustible, and it defied age or pain. A gentleman who was intimate at Montpellier, long after its owner's retirement, mentioned to us visiting him on one occasion, when he was severely indisposed and confined to his bed. When the family and guests sat down to dinner, the invalid desired the door of his apartment to be left open " so that he could hear what was going on." Every few moments he was heard to cry out in a feeble but most humorous voice, " Doctor, are you pushing about the bottles?— do your duty, Doctor, or I must cashier you."

He had the power of completely interesting and amusing Jefferson in any of the moods of his mind, and this is no small bond of amity between even grave statesmen. A companion to unbend with—before whom care and blue-devils always fly— is a very serious luxury to a king or a beggar; is one that

---

[1] Curiously enough, Mr. Jefferson's complimentary language in his letters has been regarded as an evidence of insincerity and hollowness, by some persons of this abrupt generation, who have not chanced to learn that there ever existed any different model of manners from their own.

monarchs cannot always command. And when this player on David's harp, is, additionally, the steady friend and trusted counsellor, the luxury becomes as complete as it is unusual.

Jefferson and Madison delighted to manifest their confidence in each other. When Madison was asked his opinion by a common friend, he very often replied by putting another question: "what says Mr. Jefferson?" Ask Jefferson for information and he would not unfrequently answer, "go to Mr. Madison—that was his measure—he knows a good deal more about it than I do." On being told this, Madison would smilingly say—"it was his measure, not mine—I only helped carry it into execution." They always spoke of each other with warm expressions of respect and attachment. We mention these facts on the authority of those who were intimately familiar with them, and that of members of their respective families.

The late President, as has been said, freely corresponded with his successor on public affairs. But he did not fall into the senile mistake of putting on Mentor-like airs to the full-grown disciple—or of descending to details of advice after the manner of those conceited and uneasy persons, who, having once acted an important part, are impressed with a lively conviction that nobody will ever again entirely fill it—that after nature created themselves she broke the mould of excellence. Jefferson rarely gave an unasked opinion; and he gradually retrenched and finally almost discontinued writing to the President on public measures, owing to the foolish and scandalous insinuations of the press, that the latter acted under his influence.

During the last session of the tenth Congress, and pending the action of that body on the Embargo and Non-intercourse Acts, some private correspondence had taken place between Madison and Gallatin, on one side, and Erskine, the resident British minister, on the other, with a view to adjust the difficulties between the two countries. The conduct of Erskine was frank and amicable. He obviously was sincerely desirous of an arrangement honorable to both sides. He wrote home communicating the propositions he had received, and what he believed to be the fair intentions of the new Cabinet towards his country, and in return received instructions from Mr. Canning, which he supposed authorized him to form a liberal treaty. One was accordingly made, and it was promulgated April 19th, 1809, with proclamation of the President, suspending the Non-intercourse laws, after the 10th of June, in reference to Great Britain and her dependencies.

Mr. Jefferson evinced high gratification at the prospect of his honorable termination of disputes; and when it was apparently effected, he "sincerely congratulated" the President April 27th), declaring that from whatever motives on the part of England it originated, "he rejoiced in it as the triumph of our forbearing, yet persevering, system." He wrote to his correspondent: "It will lighten your anxieties, take from the cabal its most fertile ground of war, will give us peace during our time, and by the complete extinguishment of the public debt, open upon us the noblest application of revenue that has ever been exhibited by any nation." He regretted that Great Britain proposed to send a minister to form a commercial treaty. He said she never had made such a treaty on equal terms with any nation, "and we had no right to expect to be the first." He continued:

"It will confirm the English, too, in their practice of whipping us into a treaty. They did it in Jay's case, were near it in Monroe's, and on the failure of that, have applied the scourge with tenfold vigor, and now come on to try its effect. But it is the moment when we should prove our consistence, by recurring to the principles we dictated to Monroe, the departure from which occasioned our rejection of his treaty, and by protesting against Jay's treaty being ever quoted, or looked at, or even mentioned. That form will forever be a millstone round our necks unless we now rid ourselves of it once for all. The occasion is highly favorable, as we never can have them more in our power."

He remarked, in reference to our other great European opponent, and in reference to the extension of our own national limits southwardly:

"As to Bonaparte, I should not doubt the revocation of his edicts, were he governed by reason. But his policy is so crooked that it eludes conjecture. I fear his first object now is to dry up the sources of British prosperity by excluding her manufactures from the continent. He may fear that opening the ports of Europe to our vessels will open them to an inundation of British wares. He ought to be satisfied with having forced her to revoke the orders on which he pretended to retaliate, and to be particularly satisfied with us, by whose unyielding adherence to principle she has been forced into the revocation. He ought the more to conciliate our good will, as we can be such an obstacle to the new career opening on him in the Spanish colonies. That he would give us the Floridas to withhold intercourse with the residue of those colonies, cannot be doubted. But that is no price; because they are ours in the first moment of the first war; and until a war they are of no particular necessity to us. But, although with difficulty, he will consent to our receiving Cuba into our Union, to prevent our aid to Mexico and the other provinces. That would be a price, and I would immediately erect a column on the southernmost limit of Cuba, and inscribe on it a *ne plus ultra* as to us in that direction. We should then have only to include the North in our confederacy, which would be of course in the first war, and we should have such an empire for liberty as she has never surveyed since the creation; and I am persuaded no constitution was ever before so well calculated as ours for extensive empire and self-government."

Mr. Erskine's treaty did not receive the approbation of his Government, and its ratification was refused. One of the grounds of its condemnation was that it obtained no adequate security for the good faith of the United States. The latter had already practically exhibited more confidence in Great Britain —and the President was driven to acknowledge his error by revoking his proclamation of April 19th. As if more unmistakably to mark the temper of the British cabinet, Mr. Erskine was recalled, and his place filled by "Copenhagen Jackson," as he was commonly termed in the United States, from his having conducted those negotiations with Denmark which terminated in the battle of Copenhagen and the capture of the Danish navy by England. Jackson's connection with this outrage on a neutral power, was sufficient to render him suspected and odious in the United States; and, in addition to this, he was well known to be, personally, a cold, hard, illiberal tool of the party in England which was most hostile to the United States. Thus, if England had, in sending Mr. Erskine, accidentally relaxed for a moment in the policy towards us, attributed to her by Governeur Morris—the policy of "attempting to catch flies with vinegar"—she now promptly repaired the mistake.

It is curious to look back upon the list of British ministers in this country, from the organization of the government down to the war of 1812—if not somewhat later—the Hammonds, the Merrys, the Jacksons, the Fosters, etc. We except the gentlemanly Erskine from all remark, because, though he was grievously misled in some particulars by that faction in our country who always took the British ministers into their keeping, he was undoubtedly a high-souled and liberally disposed man. The others were petty, petulant, third-rate diplomatists, who were not really fit to fill the secretaryships of legation in respectable missions. They came into our land to tease, to scold, to squab-

le about straws; to carry the narrow bitter spirit of pettifog-
ers into diplomatic negotiation; and most impoliticly, not to
ıy insultingly, of all, to throw themselves body and soul into
ıe arms of a political faction violently hostile to the Adminis-
ation, and representing scarcely a tithe of the American
eople—to take all the coloring of their views of American
ffairs from that faction—to adopt and send home its statements
-to countenance it directly and almost avowedly by their
ıfluence, and by having their governments countenance it to
ıe greatest practicable extent in all the propositions, and even
nputations (as in Canning's answer to Pinkney) engrafted into
ı official communications. The discourtesy, impropriety, and
ıexpediency of this treatment are made apparent by the
ıisunderstandings which so often existed between the govern-
ıents on comparatively insignificant points, and which, in con-
unction with Mr. Canning's "paltry and irritating tone,"[1]
radually wore out the patience of the American people and
roduced a desire for the war of 1812 among as large a proportion
f them as had originally desired the war of the Revolution.

The treaty with Erskine had gratified the moderate men of
ll parties. Even the Federal disunion leaders were compelled
ı affect satisfaction, or to remain silent, so wide-spread and
nanimous was this feeling among the popular masses in their
wn party. Madison was claimed as a Federalist and invited to
'ederal banquets in some quarters, while in others it was exult-
ıgly insisted that the threats of New England had frightened
im into a sound policy. The Federal newspapers loudly
laimed that this amicable and easy solution of long-standing
ifficulties proved that England had always been well disposed
ıwards us and ready to make a similar arrangement, if Mr.
efferson had been found willing to accept it. Some went so
ır as to assert that "she had requested Mr. Jefferson to do the
ıme thing," but that he had refused, it being his policy "to
eep alive in the minds of our people a perpetual irritation
gainst the Government of Great Britain."

When the news of the rejection came, the same party made
more striking display of its colonial spirit. Some of the
ıewspapers which contained the avowals quoted in the preceding
ıaragraph, now asserted that "Mr. Erskine surrendered every-

[1] See Edinburgh Review, quoted in last chapter.

thing and got nothing in return "—that he " acted contrary to
his instructions "—that our Government having cajoled him into
an arrangement which it was aware he was unauthorized to
make, had proceeded to carry it into execution on its own part,
merely to obtain a pretext for raising a clamor against the
Government of Great Britain—that the whole arrangement, on
our side, " so far from being a proof of a disposition to make
peace and settle our differences, was the strongest evidence
of a hostile temper, because Mr. Madison knew that the revulsion and disappointment occasioned by it among our own citizens
would excite new clamors." [1]

---

[1] When the treaty was promulgated, the Boston Gazette said: " We shall not stop
to inquire whether the spirited and vigorous measures of New England—their determined
public declarations that they would not submit to an unnecessary and destructive war,
have induced the Administration to listen to the same terms which Great Britain has
always been ready to offer, and to which we have uniformly contended she was sincerely
disposed." The Philadelphia United States Gazette declared "she [England] had
requested Mr. Jefferson to do the same thing." The Federal Republican (of Baltimore-
Hanson's paper, afterwards destroyed by a mob) said: " Peace with England—The war
party and French partisans are thrown into complete confusion. The perseverance of
the eastern States, aided by the returning sense of a formidable body of the people of
the southward, have driven Administration from its ground. Since Mr. Jefferson has
retired in disgrace into private life, his successor has been compelled to abandon the
ruinous policy under which the country has so long suffered. With the magnanimity
and frankness characteristic of a great and enlightened nation, England made a second
attempt to renew the terms of amity and peace between the two nations." " As to the
revocation of the orders in council, it is merely necessary to observe, that the terms
which our government has now accepted might have been obtained at any time past.
They were always in our power." " It was the policy of Mr. Jefferson to keep alive in
the minds of our people a perpetual irritation against the Government of Great Britain;
we are happy to find that Mr. Madison has more liberal views." We have purposely
scattered the three last preceding extracts from Hanson's paper over a surface of three
months (they were respectively of April 21st, May 3d, and June 10th), to show that
these were not the momentary expressions of the Federalists, drawn out by surprise,
but their continuous ones, until they learned that England had rejected the treaty. Such
quotations might be swelled to a volume.

Now per contra. On receiving news of the rejection, the Federal Republican at once
declared: " Mr. Erskine surrendered everything and got nothing in return." " For our
part we have had but one opinion from the commencement of this mysterio is affair—and
we have made bold to express it. It is that Mr. Erskine acted contrary to his instructions
—and Secretary Smith knew what these instructions were." " That adjustment, so far
from being a proof of a disposition to make peace and settle our differences, is the
strongest evidence of a hostile temper, because Mr. Madison knew that the revulsion and
disappointment occasioned by it among our citizens, would excite new clamors" etc.
(December 9th). " Our Administration, if they understood their business, must have
been aware that they were negotiating with an unauthorized individual" (December
11th). " It is proved, beyond a doubt, that the Government might, with just as much
propriety, have cajoled with General Smith, or any other individual, concluded a convention, proceeded to carry it into execution on their part, and then raised a clamor against
the Government of Great Britain and accused them of perfidy and breach of faith for not
recognizing and fulfilling the stipulations" (December 28th). The Boston Palladium
said: " By letters from well-informed men in England, we are assured that the conduct
of Mr. Erskine is condemned by all parties in that country; that the temper of the public is far beyond that of the ministry. A very general opinion prevails there, that it will
be very difficult to keep any terms with this country; that we are governed by men
devoted to the interests of France, who are determined to insist on terms from England
which never can be obtained." The "well-informed" English correspondents of the
Boston Federalists did not probably read both sides. Bell's Weekly (London) Messenger
said: " The disavowal of Mr. Erskine's act is of a piece with the general conduct of
England towards America. Whenever circumstances have in any way admitted it, our
tone towards America has always been insulting, and our conduct everything but

But the rejection was very differently received by the mass
' the American people. It was not generally believed that
'r. Erskine had exceeded his instructions; but most persons in
ality cared nothing for that nice question, feeling that the treaty
as a fair one for England and no more than a fair one for the
nited States, and that its rejection, with the accompanying
rcumstances, evinced a disposition on the part of the former
)wer so unjust and contemptuous towards us, that we could not
rther expect or honorably seek redress by negotiation.

The popular feeling in respect to the new English minister
d his offers to our Government, is represented in the following
therto unpublished letter :

To Hon. John W. Eppes, Washington.

Monticello, Dec. 8, '09.

ar Sir:

I should sooner have informed you of Francis's safe arrival here, but that the
) you meditated to North Carolina rendered it entirely uncertain where a letter
ald find you. Nor had I any expectation you could have been at the first meet-
of Congress, till I saw your name in the papers brought by our last post. Dis-
ointed in sending this by the return of the post, I avail myself of General
rke's journey to Washington for its conveyance. Francis has enjoyed constant
l perfect health, and is as happy as the day is long. He has had little success as
with either his traps, or bow and arrows. He is now engaged in a literary con-
; with his cousin, Virginia, both having begun to write together. As soon as he
) to s (being now only at h), he promises you a letter.

You will expect no political news here. You are at the source from whence it
) flow. I find here but one general sentiment of indignation against Mr. Jack-
, both as to the matter and manner of his offers. I am not disappointed as to
matter, but as to his manner I am. I expected he would be oily, wily and able.
ed him rude, malignant, and muddy-headed. As to the question what is to be
e, I do not puzzle myself with it. Satisfied that that will be done which is
st and best, I am predetermined to concur in it, well knowing that if we all pull
ther, we shall be safe, in whatever direction we move. Knowing the drudgery
etter-writing which oppresses the members, I shall ask nothing from you but to
rm us at times of your health, and be assured of my constant affection and
ect.

Th. Jefferson.

Mr. Jefferson, as we have seen, had been very deeply grati-

dly. . . . In our prosperity we have bullied America, and when things are not
l with us, we have vented our strife in injurious language and unworthy conduct.
ards her. Whilst there were any hopes in Spain, America could get nothing direct
l us. But disappointment brought us to our senses, and the negotiation was
rwed. The coalition war on the continent has since broke out, and we begin to.
at our condescension. In this manner has the American negotiation been on and
turing some years—our demands rising with our hopes and prosperity, and our ·
eration coexistent with our disappointment."

fied at the prospect of a solid peace with England,[1] and he was
proportionably disappointed. The effect of the rejection was still
more serious on a class of young, ardent and splendid men, like
Clay, Calhoun and Grundy, who were soon to be the leaders of
the Republican party. It converted them into determined advocates of war. In this they got a year or two ahead of the
seniors; but England took good care to leave no chance for a
chasm between front and rear, for she swelled her aggressions
until the coldest were ready to draw the sword.

The following extract from a letter from Mr. Jefferson to
Governor Jay (April 7th, 1809), embodies views several times
expressed at about the same period:

> "An equilibrium of agriculture, manufactures and commerce, is certainly
> become essential to our independence. Manufactures sufficient for our consumption,
> of what we raise the raw material (and no more). Commerce sufficient to carry the
> surplus produce of agriculture beyond our own consumption, to a market for
> exchanging it for articles we cannot raise (and no more). These are the true limits
> of manufactures and commerce. To go beyond them is to increase our dependence
> on foreign nations and our liability to war."

Dissensions in Mr. Madison's Cabinet called out several
letters from Mr. Jefferson during the year. The President had
retained the same gentlemen who served with himself in his
predecessor's Cabinet, except Dearborn, Secretary of War, who
had determined to retire some time before the close of Mr. Jefferson's term, and who only deferred his resignation for the
latter event. The State Department, which had been held by
Madison, was filled by Robert Smith, the Secretary of the
Navy; and Paul Hamilton, of South Carolina, was appointed to
the Navy department. General Dearborn's place at the War
bureau, was filled by Dr. William Eustis, the former member
of Congress from Boston. Gallatin, Granger, and Rodney
retained their places. Feuds presently sprung up among these
previously harmonious associates, and particularly between Smith
and Gallatin. These extended to their friends in Congress, and
became so serious, that Gallatin thought of retiring. Jefferson
implored him not to do so in a letter dated October 11th (1809)
from which we take the following:

[1] In a letter of the period to his bosom confidant, General Dearborn, he spoke
England as a power " with which mutual interests would urge a mutual and affectionate
intercourse."

" I consider the fortunes of our republic as depending, in an eminent degree, on
he extinguishment of the public debt before we engage in any war: because, that
one, we shall have revenue enough to improve our country in peace and defend it
1 war, without recurring either to new taxes or loans. But if the debt should once
more be swelled to a formidable size, its entire discharge will be despaired of, and
re shall be committed to the English career of debt, corruption and rottenness,
losing with revolution. The discharge of the debt, therefore, is vital to the des-
inies of our government, and it hangs on Mr. Madison and yourself alone. We
hall never see another President and Secretary of the Treasury making all other
bjects subordinate to this. Were either of you to be lost to the public, that great
ope is lost. I had always cherished the idea that you would fix on that object the
measure of your fame, and of the gratitude which our country will owe you."

These entreaties prevailed.

One of Mr. Jefferson's occasional occupations, during 1809,
ras the careful perusal of Marshall's Life of Washington, and
he correction of what, in his opinion, "was wrong" in that
roduction. He commenced committing to paper (so he wrote
Barlow, Oct. 8th) "such facts and annotations as the reading of
hat work brought into his recollection." He promised to send
hese to his correspondent, to be used in a history of the United
States, which the latter then contemplated writing. Barlow did
not proceed with the work, and whether the memoranda were
ent to him does not appear. No such paper is in possession of
Mr. Jefferson's family; and if it is among his papers in the
State department at Washington, its publication in Professor
Washington's (Congress) edition of his Works would have been
xpected. We are inclined to think, from several circumstances,
hat the design ultimately resolved itself into the revision of his
Ana, and prefixing an introduction to them in 1818.

Mr. Jefferson communicated to Dr. Barton, in September, a
very disagreeable loss. In removing his effects from Washing-
on, a large trunk, sent round by water, was broken open by
hieves on the James River, and its contents cast into the stream.
These consisted of fifty Indian vocabularies, which he had spent
hirty years in collecting, and probably with better opportunities
han ever had been, or ever could again be, possessed by any
ther individual. Some of these dialects were already nearly or
quite extinct, and others had become commingled by the crowd-
ng together and mixture of the different clans, as they receded.
before the whites. But a few muddy and defaced leaves of this
great collection were ever recovered. It is difficult to conceive

a more annoying loss to the owner, or to the student in our aboriginal philology and history.

Among his casual opinions worth mention, we find a recommendation of county circulating libraries—his determination (no new one with him) to confine his contributions for literary, charitable and other useful institutions to those in some degree under his supervision, instead of making his gratuities inconsiderable by scattering them over a vast surface—and his severe denunciation of the growing custom of making speeches two or three days long in Congress.

The spring of 1809 had been unusually cold and backward in Virginia. Mr. Jefferson did not succeed in getting in a large breadth of crops, and the season turned out a very unpropitious one. To add to injuries occasioned by weather, his lands, during his residence in Washington, had been, in spite of all his efforts, deteriorating in fertility. Under the evils of absenteeism and overseers, important directions had been neglected, or obeyed in a half-way and slovenly manner. Everything was out of repair. There had been one standing excuse for every short-coming: "The force had been worked as hard as it could be, without disobeying his orders." His directions had always been imperative to overtask his servants under no circumstances—that whatever else suffered, they must not suffer—that where there was a doubt on this subject, they must have the benefit of it. The consequences were, that not much hard work was done at Monticello; and the "sick-list" was reached with a facility which possibly sometimes encouraged deception. In these respects, matters were not materially mended by his return home. He made good economical arrangements on paper, but he could not endure to see sweat flow to secure their performance. His "force" did not perform the amount of labor ordinarily required by good farmers of the most humane dispositions, nor nearly so much as is commonly performed by white hired laborers. He generally went to bed the most tired, if not the only tired man, on his farm. He thus described his habits of life in a letter to Kosciusko (February 26th, 1810):

"My mornings are devoted to correspondence. From breakfast to dinner, I am in my shops, my garden, or on horseback among my farms; from dinner to dark, I give to society and recreation with my neighbors and friends; and from candle light to early bed-time, I read. My health is perfect; and my strength considerably reinforced by the activity of the course I pursue; perhaps it is as great as usually falls to the lot of near sixty-seven years of age. I talk of ploughs and harrows, of seeding and harvesting, with my neighbors, and of politics too, if they choose, with as little reserve as the rest of my fellow-citizens, and feel, at length, the blessing of being free to say and do what I please, without being responsible for it to any mortal. A part of my occupation, and by no means the least pleasing, is the direction of the studies of such young men as ask it. They place themselves in the neighboring village, and have the use of my library and counsel, and make a part of my society. In advising the course of their reading, I endeavor to keep their attention fixed on the main objects of all science, the freedom and happiness of man. So that coming to bear a share in the councils and government of their country, they will keep ever in view the sole objects of all legitimate government.

    *   *   *   *   *   *   *   *

" Instead of the unalloyed happiness of retiring unembarrassed and independent, to the enjoyment of my estate, which is ample for my limited views, I have to pass such a length of time in a thraldom of mind never before known to me. Except for this, my happiness would have been perfect. That yours may never know disturbance, and that you may enjoy as many years of life, health and ease as yourself shall wish, is the sincere prayer of your constant and affectionate friend."

In the last paragraph, we have the writer's first particular allusion, in his correspondence, to his pecuniary difficulties, and it is one of the very few he ever uttered. The disastrous sequel of those difficulties is well known, but the causes which led to them have been misunderstood and grossly misrepresented. It is due to him that the public should know whether he was a weak visionary, squandering his property in absurd undertakings, or whether his fortunes sunk as any other man's whose forte was not acquisition would be likely to sink, under similar circumstances. And it is now time to enter upon this inquiry.

His property, patrimonial and acquired, his income in earlier life, and his business habits, have already been stated.[1] He has been quoted as saying, that the estate inherited by his wife, "after the debts should be paid," about equalled his own "patrimony," by which latter word it was conjectured he meant property. But these debts had to be paid more than once, and they proved a canker to his fortune. It has been seen that his wife's share of the British debt on her father's estate, was £3,749 12s., that he made sales of property at three different periods to meet it, and that it ultimately " swept nearly half of his estate."[2]

---

[1] See vol. L, 65, et seq.   [2] See Col. Randolph's letter to us. ib.

The first of these sales took place in 1776. He disposed of lands to the amount of £4,200, and not receiving his pay in hand, offered the bonds to Mr. Evans, the agent of the creditors. They were declined. The creditors, of course, fairly had their option in this, but the result, without proving beneficial to them, was particularly injurious to their debtor. The bonds, by the conditions of the subsequent treaty of peace, would have been payable in gold and silver to British holders, and the makers of them were amply responsible. But, although Mr. Jefferson had sold before the emission of paper money, and at hard money prices, he was compelled to receive his pay in the former when it was worth but about two and a half per cent. of its nominal value.

The State of Virginia, crushed under the calamities of the war, was then calling on her citizens who owed money to British subjects, to bring it into the treasury to be applied to the support of the war—stipulating to become answerable for the British debts. Mr. Jefferson deposited in the treasury the paper money he had received in payment of his bonds. English remittances were generally suspended during the war, owing to the great risk of capture. Subsequently to the war, and before Virginia had determined what action to take in regard to the discharge of her engagements, Mr. Jefferson wrote to his English creditors, from Paris (January 5th, 1787), a letter, from which we take a few extracts:

"I am desirous of arranging with you such just and practicable conditions as will ascertain to you the terms at which you will receive my part of your debt, and give me the satisfaction of knowing that you are contented. What the laws of Virginia are, or may be, will in no wise influence my conduct. Substantial justice is my object, as decided by reason, and not by authority or compulsion."

After mentioning his deposit in the Virginia treasury to the credit of his correspondents, he added:

"Subsequent events have been such, that the State cannot, and ought not, to pay the same nominal sum in gold or silver, which they received in paper; nor is it certain what they will do: my intention being, and having always been, that, whatever the State decides, you shall receive my part of your debt fully. I am ready to remove all difficulty arising from this deposit, to take back to myself the demand against the State, and to consider the deposit as originally made for myself, and not for you." [1]

[1] He however stated a variety of considerations, not necessary here to be repeated, which ought, he thought, to exempt him from the payment of interest during the war

Mr. Jefferson ultimately derived so much from his deposit 1 the State Treasury, that he was wont, in after years, as he de past the goodly farm which had been thus sacrificed, to ay, smilingly, to some accompanying grandchild : "I owned hat once, and sold it for a great-coat !" He was wont, also, to ay, that he had a second time paid his British debts to Lord ornwallis. When that officer plundered and ravaged his state of Elk Island,' he inflicted direct and necessarily resulting amages, which, according to Mr. Jefferson's estimate, more han equalled the amount of his British debt and its interest uring the war. The second and third sales made by Mr. Jef- erson to make his "third payment" of that debt, took place at nfavorable periods, and the final effect on his estate has been een.

His remaining property consisted of about ten thousand cres of land, the contents of his house, etc., and about one hun- red and fifty slaves. Most of the land was fertile and favora- ly situated. Well managed, and increased in value by the ubsequent rise in property as the country became more thickly ettled, it should have made him an independent, and, in ur country, and among the rural class, a rich man. There ere periods before his death when considerable portions of his state would have sold for fifty dollars an acre.'

As a member of the Virginia Assembly, as a member of ongress, and as Governor of Virginia, Mr. Jefferson's official alaries had not more than met the extra expenses which the ffices occasioned. His salary in France did not meet expenses.' s Secretary of State, he had generally lived rather retiredly and lainly, and his salary nearly equalled his expenditures. As ice-President, he for the first and last time derived some pecu- iary advantage from an office. During his Presidency his isbursements exceeded his income—but a portion of them went o the completion of his house, and to the improvement and mbellishment of his estate. In none of these offices was his tyle of living noticed either for parsimony or extravagance ; hough, as a general thing, he had much of a particular kind of ompany, in addition to the usual throngs who flutter about

---

1 See vol. i., p. 340. et seq.
2 See his letter to Madison, February 17th, 1826.
3 But some of these were incurred for valuable articles which continued in his posses- ion, such as books and pictures.

official mansions. Travellers, learned men, investigators in every department of mind and matter, were drawn to his board as if by a natural affinity.

It is probable that the surplus income of his farms about met the excess of his expenses over his official salaries, in all his public positions except the Presidency—and it would have done so in that office but for the Embargo. When that measure fell with such crushing effect on all who purchased luxuries, Mr. Jefferson made no change in his manner of living, and he consequently left office owing $20,000.

We have given his land-roll for 1794, showing that he then owned 10,647 acres of land, and some city lots. In 1809, he owned 10,004 acres, with the same smaller parcels. The farms were generally the same, except that he had given fifteen hundred acres of his Bedford estate to one of his daughters—and on the other hand, had acquired about eight hundred acres on Buffalo Creek, and one hundred adjoining his Albemarle possessions. He had now a valuable mansion, containing many costly articles, including an expensive library. The number of his servants in Albemarle was one hundred and fourteen, and in Bedford, eighty-six.[1] His farms had the ordinary complement of "stock,"[2] and there was a flouring-mill at Monticello of considerable cost, and several small manufacturing shops.[3] Altogether, the value of his property was probably not far from $200,000.

---

[1] We do not find that Mr. Jefferson had sold any slaves for the sixteen preceding years. Sixty-six had been included in the marriage settlements of his daughters, and some liberated. Some idea of the mortality among this class of people, may be derived from the following facts. From 1801 to 1810 inclusive, there died in Mr. Jefferson's family—none in 1801, 1802, 1803, or 1804; one in 1805; three in 1807; one in 1808; three in 1809; three in 1810. The deaths were mostly among aged persons and very young children.

[2] Some agricultural reader in a different region of the country, may be curious to know what and how much this implies. In the winter of 1809–10, the census of the "store stock"—that is, the stock wintered over after annual sales, putting down provisions, etc.—included (says the farm-book), in Albemarle, 13 work horses, 10 mules, 15 cows, 21 other cattle, 49 sheep, and 118 swine; in Bedford, 11 work horses, 30 cows, 55 other cattle, 46 sheep, and 194 swine.

[3] The mill, including its canal or race, ultimately cost $30,000. Its profits were reduced by the damage occasionally suffered from the floods of the Rivanna. Mr. Jefferson's memoranda mention that on the 22d of April, 1804, a "fresh" carried the water above the hoppers in the toll-mill—and this wanted six feet of the height of water in a fresh in 1795, and nine feet of that of the "great fresh" on the 26th of May, 1771! In February, 1810, three inches of rain fell in an hour, creating a flood which did incredible damage in the abrasion of the sloping plowed lands—but the rise in the stream is not stated. On the 9th and 10th of November, 1810, there fell four and three-quarter inches of rain in forty-eight hours: the water entered the mill four feet deep, and swept away so much of the dam that it required a considerable outlay and some months of labor to repair it. On the 29th of July, 1814, twelve and one-eighth inches of rain fell in twenty hours. The Rivanna rose fifteen feet, and "Hardware [creek] was said to have risen thirty-feet perpendicular."

Among the shops we have referred to, was a nailery, where six tons of nails were

It would seem that with so much apparently productive capital the debt we have mentioned should have constituted but a slight burden on Mr. Jefferson's estate. There were drawbacks on the availability of that capital which persons unfamiliar with Southern life might readily overlook. The lands were immediately profitable no further than they could be worked; and the whole number of slaves on a plantation gives no definite idea of the effective farm labor. By Mr. Jefferson's roll of slaves in 1810, it appears that out of the two hundred composing the whole number, ninety-five were under fourteen years of age, and twenty over fifty years of age. From those in the prime of life must be deducted the sick, nurses, cooks, etc. The planter must have his mechanics, " door yard " and menial servants—and though these save expenditure in one direction, they are withdrawn from the class which produce the main salable staples of the farm. And those too young or too old for work must be supported from the products of the land, and in part from the proceeds of its marketed staples.

Mr. Jefferson's family was not large nor particularly expensive. It came to consist of the family of his son-in-law, Mr. Randolph,[1] and generally of some other relatives. To the

made by hand in 1810. There was a weaving shop, containing five looms, but its product was as yet trifling.

[1] Mr. Jefferson could not endure separation from his only remaining daughter. His son-in-law's affairs gradually became hopelessly embarrassed. Mr. Randolph was a generous man and lavished liberal sums on kinsmen deprived of what he considered their just patrimony, by the consequences of a second marriage. The Embargo and the succeeding Non-intercourse seriously affected his property. He engaged in the manufacture of flour during the war, and was unfortunate in it—mostly losing by the consequences of one accident an amount of flour worth about thirty thousand dollars. His affairs were additionally broken up by absence from home. He was appointed colonel of the 20th U. S. regiment in 1813, and marched to Canada. He resigned in 1814, in consequence of a misunderstanding with General Armstrong, the Secretary of War. He was elected Governor of Virginia in 1819, and held the office three years, the full continuous period permitted by the constitution. But the main sources of his misfortunes, and many of his traits of character are thus described in a letter to us from one who knew him intimately, and loved him tenderly :

" It was in the service of persons having very small claims on him, that he wasted his patrimony and even his wife's fortune. . . He could not say No to importunate pleaders, to distressed kinsmen or neighbors, distressed oftentimes by the result of their own folly. He stood security again and again for men, to whose selfish entreaties and false statements he sacrificed his fortune and his peace of mind; and was always crippled by debts not of his own contracting. . . He was for a long time persuaded that his embarrassments were only temporary, and that all he wanted was time and economy to work through his difficulties. . . . He might have retrieved his fortunes, but the same fatality of character pursued him. Again and again he yielded to the solicitations of his friends; again and again he believed their solemn assurances—' Your name, only your name, we pledge our sacred honor that you shall never be called on to pay a. farthing.' But he always was called on to pay not ' one farthing,' but generally the whole amount of the debt. From this it might be supposed that Colonel Randolph was. what is called an easy tempered man, gentle, and easily entreated. Not so: his temper was irritable and violent. It was firmness that he needed, not fire.

" He had other weaknesses which neutralized the effects of many high qualities, and

latter and to family friends his hospitality was profuse; they came and went singly and in families—staying three months, six months, or longer according to inclination. Accomplished young kinswomen habitually passed two or three of the summer months there, as they would now at a fashionable watering-place. They married the sons of Mr. Jefferson's friends, and then came with their families; first one child, then two, three, four, five, six—babies, small children, school-boys, little girls, young ladies, nurses and tutors! As a specimen of Virginia life, we will mention that a friend from abroad came to Monticello with a family of six persons, and remained ten months. A second visit brought the same train six months—and so on.

This was according to the recognized usages of hospitality in the Ancient Dominion. All this was to be expected in the abode of the head of a family connection, supposed to be entirely independent in his circumstances, always receiving his relatives and friends with out-stretched arms, always retarding their departure and urging their return. Nor would this, under ordinary circumstances, have proved the source of pecuniary embarrassment to him.

We come now to the real causes of his misfortunes, and to avoid a frequent recurrence to them, shall extend the view over some years not yet reached in this narrative. In the first

gifts of nature and education. He had fine talents, a superior education, an active mind, a strong and active body, great courage, but it was as if some bad fairy, presiding at his birth, had, by a fatal curse, paralyzed the power to profit by these advantages. He could make great efforts, but just at the moment he was to receive their reward, some strange relaxation, some sudden intermission would render all his previous labors abortive. He would stand like one in a dream, lose all apparent interest in the completion of his work, and see the fruit of his toils perish before his eyes for want of energy to continue and carry out his own plans. For example, his income, like that of other gentlemen farmers in Virginia, was derived from his crops. He was himself a scientific agriculturist, and at the same time, an excellent practical farmer. He was indefatigably industrious, superintending all the details of the farming operations. He loved the life of the fields, and delighted in the occupation it afforded him. He was one of the best botanists in the State; . . was an excellent classical scholar, and might often be seen under the shade of a tree with a favorite Greek or Latin author in his hand. These refined tastes interfered not in the least degree with the business of the plantation; and he generally succeeded in raising the best crops, without in any way abusing or harassing his slaves, towards whom he was eminently humane. I have seldom known a kinder master.

"After months of anxious attention and intelligent supervision the object would be attained—large and beautiful harvests would reward his care. They were gathered into his barns, and nothing remained but to get them conveyed to market, in Richmond, seventy miles distant, and there sold. Here would come in the torpor of which I spoke. All the excitement of pleasant occupation was over; what remained to be done was irksome. His whole nature and tastes were repugnant to commerce of any kind. He could neither buy nor sell, nor bargain. His harvests remained in his barns, or if taken to Richmond, in the warehouses there, till the golden moment for disposing of them was over; so that a common saying among his neighbors, was, that no man made better crops than Colonel Randolph, and no man sold his crops for worse prices."

place, a long and scarcely interrupted series of unfavorable seasons followed Mr. Jefferson's retirement. Thus the summer of 1810 in his region was cold and backward, the breadth of crops small, and the produce limited. This was followed by an unfavorable winter, and the crops of 1811 did not exceed two-thirds the usual product. The Hessian fly increased its ravages. These specifications might be continued, but it would be to no purpose. The agricultural staples of Virginia were kept at ruinous prices by Embargo and Non-intercourse laws from 1807 until war was declared in 1812. The crops of the last-named year chanced to be fine ones, but those of the interior were caught unsold by the "Ninety-day Embargo." The rigorous blockade of the Chesapeake from an early period in 1813 left no chance for exportation, and consequently no considerable market for products during the remainder of the war. The Virginia farmers often fed their wheat to their horses.

To these causes must be added monetary revulsions, both during and after the war, by which credit was prostrated, the currents of trade stopped, markets destroyed, and landed property reduced almost to its original wilderness prices. The war left the nation in debt and with a disordered currency. The merchants were ruined by the sudden fall in the price of their imported goods. The Southern farmer was relieved in this quarter, and he found his former markets for certain products; but the general disarrangement of trade and currency neutralized these benefits. The Bank of the United States was chartered in 1816; and then followed a period of paper money plethora almost as disastrous to the agricultural interests as the preceding depression. The rage for speculation was maddening. Lands sold at high prices, but the pay was "rags." And times of high prices bring no relief to those whose consumption (as in Mr. Jefferson's case) exceeds their production. The bubble was soon blown to bursting. What followed is vividly portrayed by Colonel Benton in his Thirty Years' View:

"The years of 1819 and 1820 were a period of gloom and agony. No money, either gold or silver: no paper convertible into specie: no measure or standard of value left remaining. The local banks (all but those of New England), after a brief resumption of specie payments, again sank into a state of suspension. The bank of the United States, created as a remedy for all those evils, now at the head of the evil, prostrate and helpless, with no power left but that of suing its debtors, and selling their property, and purchasing for itself at its own nominal price. No price for property or produce. No sales but those of the sheriff and the marshal. No purchasers at execution sales but the creditor, or some hoarder of money. No employment for industry—no demand for labor—no sale for the product of the farm—no sound of the hammer, but that of the auctioneer, knocking down property. Stop laws—property laws—replevin laws—stay laws—loan-office laws—the intervention of the legislator between the creditor and the debtor; this was the business of legislation, in three-fourths of the States of the Union—of all south and west of New England. No medium of exchange but depreciated paper; no change even, but little bits of foul paper, marked so many cents, and signed by some tradesman, barber, or innkeeper: exchanges deranged to the extent of fifty or one hundred per cent. Distress the universal cry of the people; relief the universal demand thundered at the doors of all legislatures, State and federal."

The period from Mr. Jefferson's retirement from public life to his death, was one that called for pecuniary prudence in all classes of men—a husbanding of means, and an avoidance of expenditure—an extinguishment, so far as practicable, of outstanding debts, and the contraction of no new ones. The principal causes which rendered these ends unattainable in his case, are thus described by an eye-witness:

MY DEAR MR. RANDALL: ——, 1856.

*   *   *   *   *   *   *   *   *

Mr. Jefferson was not an improvident man. He had habits of order and economy, was regular in keeping his accounts, knew the value of money, and was in no way disposed to waste it. He was simple in his tastes, careful, and spent very little on himself. 'Tis not true that he threw away his money in fantastic projects and theoretical experiments. He was eminently a practical man. He was, during all the years that I knew him, very liberal, but never extravagant.

*   *   *   *   *   *   *   *   *

To return to his visitors: they came of all nations, at all times, and paid longer or shorter visits. I have known a New England judge bring a letter of introduction to my grandfather, and stay three weeks. The learned Abbé Correa, always a welcome guest, passed some weeks of each year with us during the whole time of his stay in the country. We had persons from abroad, from all the States of the Union, from every part of the State, men, women, and children. In short, almost every day for at least eight months of the year, brought its contingent of guests. People of wealth, fashion, men in office, professional men military and civil, lawyers, doctors, Protestant clergymen, Catholic priests, members of Congress, foreign ministers, missionaries, Indian agents, tourists, travellers, artists, strangers, friends. Some came from affection and respect, some from curiosity, some to give or receive advice or instruction, some from idleness, some because others set the example, and very varied, amusing and agreeable was the society afforded by this influx of guests. I have listened to very remarkable conversations carried on round the table, the fireside, or in the summer drawing-room.

*   *   *   *   *   *   *   *   *

There were few eminent men of our country, except perhaps some political adversaries, who did not visit him in his retirement, to say nothing of distinguished foreigners. Life at Monticello was on an easy and informal footing. Mr. Jefferson always made his appearance at an early breakfast, but his mornings were most commonly devoted to his own occupations, and it was at dinner, after dinner, and in the evening that he gave himself up to the society of his family and his guests. Visitors were left free to employ themselves as they liked during the morning hours, to walk, read, or seek companionship with the ladies of the family, and each other. M. Correa passed his time in the fields and the woods; some gentlemen preferred the library; others the drawing-room; others the quiet of their own chambers; or they strolled down the mountain side and under the shade of the trees. The ladies in like manner, consulted their ease and inclinations, and whiled away the time as best they might.

All the visitors at Monticello were not of so agreeable a stamp. We have it from an equally authoritative source, that with this constant influx of well-bred guests, came also swarms of impertinent gazers who, without introduction, permission or any ceremony whatever, thrust themselves into the most private of Mr. Jefferson's out-of-door resorts, and even into his house, and stared about as if they were at a public show. This nuisance increased as years advanced. There are a number of persons now living who have seen groups of utter strangers, of both sexes, planted in the passage between his study and dining-room, consulting their watches, and waiting for him to pass from one to the other to his dinner, so that they could momentarily stare at him. A female once punched through a window-pane of the house, with her parasol, to get a better view of him. He was waylaid in his rides and walks. When sitting in the shade of his porticoes to enjoy the coolness of the approaching evening, parties of men and women would sometimes approach within a dozen yards, and gaze at him point-blank until they had looked their fill, as they would have gazed on a lion in a menagerie. And he was compelled to submit to such things, shut himself up in a room, or evince a resentment as foreign from his manners as it was really from his feelings. These intrusions annoyed him, but they excited sensations of regret and pity rather than of anger.

It is painful to record such facts. In nineteen cases out of twenty they were undoubtedly the sins of ignorance instead of intentional impertinence, and at heart were often really the highest compliments which uncultivated men could pay to the great setting political luminary. They wanted to tell their children, and have it told to their grandchildren, that they had seen Thomas Jefferson.

We have already introduced to the reader old Wormley, a grey-haired servant of Mr. Jefferson. We once stood with him before the dilapidated pile of Monticello. The carriage-houses, three in number, were at the moment under our eye. Each would hold a four-horse coach. We inquired—"Wormley, how often were these filled, in Mr. Jefferson's time?" "Every night, sir, in summer, and we commonly had two or three carriages under that tree," said he, pointing to a large tree. "It took all hands to take care of your visitors?" we suggested. "Yes, sir, and the whole farm to feed them," was the concise and significant reply. The last was a literal truth, and expressed less than the fact. We find in a list of Mr. Jefferson's allotments of his servants, between farming, mechanical and menial occupations, as early as 1810, that the house servants (including children) numbered thirty-seven. The whole Monticello estate, so far as he had laborers to work it, did not in some years furnish a surplus of food sufficient for his guests, and their horses and servants! The general mode of travelling then in Virginia was on horseback, or by carriages drawn by at least two horses; and strangers who came from a distance, very generally took carriages from some Virginia town. Male and female servants much more commonly accompanied travellers than now. Mrs. Randolph, who presided over the domestic establishment at Monticello, being once asked, what was the greatest number of guests she had ever been called upon to provide beds for over night, replied, "she believed fifty!" Not only was everything which was raised at Monticello thus consumed, or exchanged for articles of consumption, but heavy drafts were often made on the Bedford estate.

And such a horde of fashionable company consume something besides common farm products. When Mr. Jefferson first reached what he fancied was to be retirement, he was asked by his daughter on what scale he desired to live—how he would have the appointments of his table. "I will live like a plain country gentleman," was the answer. But this standard could not be easily followed, under the actual circumstances. A delicious Virginia ham on its bed of greens, engirdled by its rim of eggs (à la Old Dominion), and a slice of chicken or turkey might do very well for a "plain country gentleman's" dinner two or three times a week, and these could be had for the asking on every Virginia farm. But people of fashion, to say nothing of "New England judges," might not expect to be kept "three weeks" on ham and turkey! Claret might suffice for a "plain country gentleman," particularly if, as in Mr. Jefferson's case, he preferred it to all other summer wines. His visitors might choose something else; and it is not for the hospitable and supposed wealthy entertainer to impose his tastes on his guests.¹ No person need be told that "entertaining handsomely" is an expensive amusement.

Mr. Jefferson could not know, when he left public life, either the general or special pecuniary disadvantages which awaited him. His temper, as in youth, was sunny and hopeful. After an unfavorable season, or unpropitious event, he always looked forward with confidence for a better next one—and if that did not come, he reasoned there was a double chance for good "fortune" the third time! In a word, nothing discouraged him. But because he owed a debt of some magnitude, he thought it a duty to cut off every expense which he regarded as superfluous, and he attempted to do so from the moment of his

---

¹ This reminds us of an illustrative anecdote. Mr. C——, a Virginia gentleman of the old noblesse, and an excellent, kind-hearted man, was visiting Mr. Madison. He had been long estranged from Mr. Jefferson; but the topic of difference coming up between him and Madison, the representations of the latter greatly mollified his feelings. Just at that point, a young friend of Madison (our informant) was on the point of leaving Montpellier in a carriage for Monticello, expecting to return immediately. Madison suddenly proposed to C—— to jump in and go along. The latter was taken all aback at the idea of making a visit to Jefferson—and yet he was not half so reluctant to go as he fancied he would have been! Madison observing his hesitation, good-humoredly insisted on his proceeding. He had no time to reflect, and in ten minutes was on the way. Before reaching Monticello, and especially while climbing the mountain, he drew some long breaths and looked very sober. Our informant thought that for "about a second" he discovered a look of surprise on Jefferson's face as they entered the house, but he advanced instantly and saluted his guest with as prompt cordiality as if he had been looking for him. C—— did not get at his ease quite as readily. When they sat down to the dinner-table, he was placed by the side of Mr. Jefferson. The ice soon broke, and C—— began to talk with great animation. Jefferson reminding him that he remembered his tastes, had some old and particularly fine Madeira placed before him. But no; C—— declared he would stick to claret with his host. They sat a couple of hours, the guest growing more and more delighted. When they rose from the table Jefferson retired for a few moments. C—— took our informant aside, and very seriously asked, "Do you suppose I could get a glass of good brandy here? I have been so amused by Jefferson that here I have been sipping his . . . . acid, cold French wine, until I am sure I shall die in the night (he had already stipulated to stay over night!) unless I take an antidote." His travelling companion knew all the ways at Monticello. He directed the faithful Burwell (Mr. Jefferson's favorite servant) to take a bottle of brandy to a private room, as C—— was willing to throw no imputations on his host's tastes, and so the movement must be concealed from him! Next day he returned to Montpellier, lauding Jefferson to the skies, but sorely puzzled to understand "why a man of so much taste should drink cold, sour French wine!" He insisted to Mr. Madison that it would injure Jefferson's health. He talked himself warm on the topic. He declared it would kill him—that some night he would be carried off by it! Finally, he insisted that Madison write and urge him to change his wine. His altered tone towards Jefferson, and his warm solicitude in the particular just named, afforded great amusement to Madison and Jefferson. The trio thenceforth remained fast friends.

retirement. No more expensive pictures, books, or other articles of luxury were purchased. It is true, he built a neat house on his Bedford property, but the labor was mostly performed by his servants, and the interior was finished at convenient intervals. He did not feel the pressure of pecuniary embarrassment at the time, and his convenience, his spirits, if not his health demanded that he have a roof to which he could occasionally fly for relief and rest from the traveller-thronged caravansera of Monticello. Besides this, we know no considerable expense he could have avoided, unless he chose to repulse the visits of his countrymen, and shut his doors on the ancient rites of hospitality customary among men of his rank.

It has been conceded that his farming operations, though conducted on sound and customary agricultural principles, were carried out with too great a fear of overtasking his dependents —that he was indulgent to a fault. He was sometimes cheated by overseers, for he was unsuspecting among common men. But these slight drawbacks were temporary, and had little to do with ultimate results. His oldest grandson began to take the management of his estate in 1814, and, not long afterwards, he assumed its entire control, and continued it to the period of Mr. Jefferson's death. The grandson was a vigorous and successful farmer.

Occasional gleams of good fortune came, but the general course of diminution and loss was inevitable, unless as already said, Mr. Jefferson chose to change the social customs of his life. If he did not adopt the latter alternative, who has the right to complain or condemn! "Whose ox did he" thereby "take—or whom did he defraud?" His debts were all paid before or after his death, even to his subscription of two hundred dollars to build a Presbyterian church in Charlottesville. His contributions to religious, educational, and charitable objects through his life, would have made his old age opulent! There is not a circumstance connected with the causes, progress, or sequel of his pecuniary misfortunes over which manhood should blush, or friendship desire to draw a veil.

Without prodigality, without idleness or improvidence, without embarking a dollar in speculation, he was reduced to comparative poverty. The bulk of his property was literally eaten up by his countrymen. But so stoutly did he and the

brave hearts around him struggle—so cheerfully and self-deny-
ingly did his entire family retrench where retrenchment was prac-
icable—that he still would have had more than enough to carry
him comfortably to the end, had he not (as we shall by and by
relate more in detail) lost a large sum of money by indorsing
for a friend. Indorsing was entirely contrary to his habits, but
on this occasion there was not the slightest apparent prospect
of danger, and the circumstances were such that it would have
been very difficult to refuse. It was thus reserved for one of the
dearest of his friends to give that *coup de grâce* which shrouded
Monticello in gloom, consigned it to stranger hands and early
decay, exposed its aged and tottering owner to the jeers of
brutal partisans, and broke the noble heart that dealt the
unwilling blow.

It is now time that we attempt to give some description of
Monticello and its surroundings—the gathering point of so
much intellect, learning, wit, beauty, and fashion, until the
festal song was succeeded by the funeral dirge.

The general topography of the surrounding country has been
noted. The public road from Charlottesville, by which Monticello was oftenest approached, after leading to the foot of
" Carter's Mountain," winds along its lower slopes, until it commences ascending the edge of the wooded ravine which separates that hill from Monticello. In the notch between their
summits the road crosses over to the latter, and thence descends
its southwestern declivity towards Milton. Opposite the crossing, a gate opens on a private carriage road to Mr. Jefferson's former mansion, about half a mile distant. The slight
further ascent is mostly through the natural growth of forest
trees, among which, and coming to the carriage road, is the
family burial-place. On emerging from the forest, the visitor
finds himself on a slightly crowning area of a few acres, the
summit of the mountain, cleared of the original trees except
here and there clumps or single ones occasionally grouped with
fine transplanted native or exotic species. On a small levelled
space on the very apex, stands the house formerly surrounded
by ornamented grounds, and nearly embowered in trees.

It is a long brick structure of a lofty balustraded single
story, the central portion surmounted by a fine dome. There
are spacious porticoes in front and rear, and the sides termi-

nate in piazzas resting on brick arches. The former appearance of the house will be better understood from the vignette in our first volume, than from any description we can give.[1] The piazzas open on "terraces," which extend a few yards from the sides, and then turn back at right angles, and are continued to the "pavilions." Their roofs are flat, and on a level with the underpinning of the house, so that they furnished a favorite promenade in the evening and in damp weather.[2] This arrangement was rendered practicable by the slope of the hill, and one of its principal objects was to prevent the view from the house being obstructed by outbuildings. The pavilions rose a story higher. The east (or to be more particular, the southeast) one was the house and home at which Mr. Jefferson arrived with his bride at midnight, in the "great snow" of 1772. It is probable that such recollections caused it to be preserved in the subsequent building plan, and that the west pavilion ("Colonel Randolph's study") was built to match it.

Entering the mansion by the northeast portico, the former visitor found himself in a lofty, nearly square hall, the main central room of the building. On the right, were disposed horns of the moose, elk, and different varieties of American deer—and hanging from their antlers or tastefully grouped about, were Indian and Mexican antiquities, articles of costume, war clubs, shields, spears, bows, quivers of arrows, and almost every conceivable specimen of aboriginal art. On the left, were arranged bones of the mastodon and other fossil monsters, disentombed on the Ohio; and massive specimens of minerals, and other natural curiosities, were appropriately interspersed. After gazing a moment at these objects, the eye settled with a deeper interest on busts of Jefferson and Hamilton, by Ceracchi, placed on massive pedestals on each side of the main entrance—"opposed in death as in life," as the surviving original sometimes remarked, with a pensive smile, as he observed the notice they attracted.

The hall opened by folding glass doors on a semi-octagonal drawing-room immediately in its rear, and which extended

---

[1] The vignette presents but the central portion of the house, and one side or wing. The other wing corresponded with the one seen.
[2] But a small portion of one terrace appears in the vignette, and this is surmounted by a temporary sloping roof.

rough the remaining depth of the building to the southwest
rtico. This apartment was neatly furnished, and had a floor
'parquetry.' A harpsichord stood in one corner; and the walls
ere hung with fine portraits in oil of Columbus, Americus
espucius, Andrea Doria, Castrucio Castracani, Raleigh, Cor-
r—Mr. Jefferson's "trinity," Bacon, Newton, and Locke—
'ashington, John Adams, Madison, and Monroe. On either
le of the door opening on the portico, were busts of the Empe-
rs Alexander and Napoleon.

To the right (that is, west) of the drawing-room was a dining-
om, and still further on, a semi-octagonal tea-room. On
ackets in these, were busts of Washington, Franklin, Vol-
ire, Lafayette, and Paul Jones. Washington's (by Houdon)
ore a wreath of *immortelles*. Some admirer in France sen·
ese to Mr. Jefferson's family, to crown his bust on his birth
iy. He ordered them, instead, to be wreathed around the
ow of Washington, and there they thenceforth remained
itil Mr. Jefferson's death.

In the front of this part of the house, were two commo-
ous apartments for guests, containing beds in alcoves.

To the left or east of the hall was Mrs. Randolph's
om, and in the rear, Mr. Jefferson's; and beyond these, was
e library, extending through the depth of the house. The
ched piazza beyond, was ultimately sashed with glass, and
nverted into a flower conservatory, so that the windows and
ass doors of the library opened upon both its beauty and its
agrance. The "work-shop," so often spoken of by describers
 Mr. Jefferson's habits, was originally the eastern extremity
the library.

The alcove for the bed in Mr. Jefferson's private room,
ened, also, on that apartment—an arrangement which wooed
ery passing breath of air, and the odors of the conservatory
summer. In the winter, the library side was closed by cloth
ngings.'

---

¹ This, like much other equally elaborate workmanship, was the handiwork of Mr.
ferson's own servants—John Hemings and his sable apprentices.
² The upper story was cut up into numerous bedrooms (brought into all conceivable·
ipes by the irregular form of the house), except the dome, which was finished into a
gle, fine apartment, known as "the ladies' drawing-room." Several of the upper·
oms were lit by sky-lights, and light was also carried down from these to some of the
rer rooms through ornamented funnels.
Most, if not all, the lower doors were of glass; though some of them had wooden or-
re coverings, to be closed when necessary. The furniture was neat and just sufficient.

The view from Monticello is superb. On the west, the already described valley between the Northwest Range and the Blue Ridge, lies stretched out like a map under the feet. On the east, the eye sweeps to the limits of its vision over that great plain which constitutes the sea-margin of the United States from New England to Mexico. From this vast and sombre sea of verdure,[1] there rises but one eminence high enough to break the level of half of the entire horizon seen from Monticello. This is Willis's Mountain, forty miles distant from the latter, and directly south of it.

Though no larger than the greater Egyptian pyramid,[2] this hill makes a unique addition to the scenery, by exhibiting the phenomenon of looming to a remarkable degree. This occurs only in the morning, but no other persistent conditions are known to be required for its appearance. Sometimes the conical summit seems to shoot in an immense column to the clouds. At others, it assumes the forms of a hemisphere, a square, a pine tree, a parachute, an inverted cone, and others as fantastic and as variant from the reality. The Blue Ridge, also, though not to an equal degree, exhibits this phenomenon where it is seen from Monticello at about forty or fifty miles' distance and still further off. One of its appearances is very striking. The lofty chain seems cloven

Marble and brescia tables, French mirrors, and handsome sofas, abounded. The beds were generally in alcoves. There were many indications of elaborate contrivance to secure convenience in the minor arrangements. The cookery was French, and admirable—the table elegant—and the plate just sufficient neither to attract notice by its profusion or meagreness. The last remark will apply to all the equipments of Monticello. Taste and elegance were everywhere visible—and the mean between sumptuousness and the opposite extreme, was always exactly hit.

The portions of the terraces at right angles with the front and rear wall of the house, contained the offices ; and the other portions were covered ways, connecting the offices with the cellars of the house, and also furnishing the servants entrance. Articles for the table were carried from the kitchens through the covered ways, and raised to the dining-room by a dumb-waiter. Thus, the discomfort (in a warm climate) of a kitchen in the house was avoided—and also the ludicrous spectacle which sometimes meets the eye of the guest in houses with detached kitchens, who chances to look out of the *wrong* window when dinner is coming to the table.

Along the southeastern terrace ran a road, and along the lower side of it were the mechanic shops we have so often mentioned. Behind and below these, commenced the terraced gardens, of different breadths, according to the desired size, dropping down the southeastern slopes. The first was for culinary vegetables, the second for grapes, the third for figs, and so on ; and orchards for different kinds of tree fruits extended below. The flowers were mostly cultivated in plats and borders on the lawns. On the rear lawn, an elliptical gravel walk, " the round-about walk," commenced at the portico and extended some distance outside of the space hemmed in by the buildings. Spiral roads twisted around the mountain, in various directions, for rides and walks—and it might thus be conveniently ascended or descended, without resort to the highway.

[1] We speak of these objects as they appeared in 1851.

[2] Mr. Jefferson was wont to call the attention of visitors to it, as presenting a pretty correct idea of the appearance of the pyramid of Cheops at the same distance. The latter is stated by Stevens, we believe, to be eight hundred feet square at its base, and four hundred and sixty-one feet high. Older writers make it much larger.

to its base, by a wooded or bare and rocky gorge. Perhaps a green valley stretches through, and other ranges of mountains are seen rising beyond. To one unacquainted with these optical illusions, they bring unutterable amazement. It is as if he had stepped into a land of enchantment, where, according to the superstitions of past ages, necromancers or genii were sporting with the forms and consistency of the solid globe. And what must have been the emotions of the former Indian inhabitant—the wild and roving Tuscarora, whose hunting-grounds embraced this region—as he paused, startled in the morning chase, to witness these tremendous transfigurations of the most massive and immobile objects in nature !

Mr. Jefferson used to say if the county of Fluvanna (lying directly east of Albemarle) was a lake, and Willis's Mountain a volcano, his scenery would be perfect. There is, indeed, a lack of water in the landscape, but we should be loth to exchange the masquerading mountain for the burning one. As a whole, there are doubtless more extensive, and even more beautiful prospects than this, but they are rare, and are scarcely ever commanded from points having the climate, soil, and easiness of access which render them desirable sites for human dwellings. In all these respects combined, and in healthiness, Monticello possesses advantages over most other situations which can be found in our country.

The fineness and salubrity of the climate are indeed remarkable. An English traveller who early visited this region, found an evident change of complexion in the inhabitants from that of residents of the lower country, and among females of the most ordinary class, "many a one that would be a fit subject to be painted for a Lavinia." "It is truly delightful," exclaims this gentleman, " to behold the groups of females assembled here at times to gather the cherries and other fruits which grow in the greatest abundance in the neighborhood of almost every habitation. Their shapes and complexions are charming; and the carelessness of their dresses, which consists of little more, in common, than a simple bodice and petticoat, makes them appear still more engaging." "The common people in this neighborhood appeared to me to be of a more frank and open disposition, more inclined to hospitality, and to live more contentedly on what they possessed, than the people of the same class in any other part of the United States I passed through." [1]

[1] Travels through the United States in 1795, 1796 and 1797, by Isaac Weld, jr. London, 1799.

It is some years since we looked into Mr. Weld's book, and common-placed a few pages; and we have long since forgotten "what manner of man he was of." But there is a fragrant smack of good taste and close observation, certainly, in the passage above quoted, and a glow of coloring that would have delighted old Beverly. Mr. Weld's carelessly-dressed women, in "simple bodice and petticoat," have disappeared from the Old Dominion—at least from the regions of it we have visited; but there is, to this day, if we mistake not, less frigid precision in dress, less over-dressing, in the families of the wealthy planters in the interior of that State, than among Northern females, in a corresponding position. When among the former, Ben Jonson's lines from the "Silent Woman," have often occurred to us:

> " Give me a look, give me a face,
> That makes simplicity a grace;
> Robes loosely flowing, hair as free,
> Such sweet neglect more taketh me
> Than all the adulteries of art:
> They strike mine eyes, but not my heart."

Or Herrick's " Delight in Disorder:"

> " A sweet disorder in the dress,
> (A happy kind of carelessness):
> A lawn about the shoulders thrown
> Into a fine distraction;
> An erring lace, which here and there
> Enthralls the crimson stomacher;
> A cuff neglectful, and thereby
> Ribands that flow confusedly;
> A winning wave, deserving note
> In the tempestuous petticoat;
> A careless shoe-string, in whose tie
> I see a wild civility:
> Do more bewitch me, than when art
> Is too precise in every part."

A Virginia woman is too free, too lithe in her movements to keep up the unvarying precision of a lay-figure. She walks abroad as if the earth was made to walk upon, though saucy breezes throw ribbons and ringlets and "erring laces" into never so "fine" a "distraction." She rides anything else than a dumb-jockey, or a city miss fresh from the riding academy; nay, if the road be shady, or the green-sward looks temptingly elastic and says (as everybody knows it does sometimes say): "Come take a run over me," the Virginia woman does not always find it in her heart to refuse the challenge: but down goes the riding-whip, and the next moment her blood mare, with straight thin neck, broad red nostril, and eye lit to flame, is skimming like a low flying bird over the ground.

It is difficult for one whose eye is accustomed only to females brought up at the feet of the fashionable Fadladeens, to conceive the graceful and free movements of a high-bred Virginia woman, when roused into full action, not in the ball room at Saratoga or Newport, but at home, with the turf of the Old Dominion under her feet, and the skies of the Old Dominion over her head. We once approached an old Virginia farm-house, with its owner, who had been for some days absent. A few hundreds yards off, we suddenly stopped to gaze, for, at that moment, dashing round from the rear of the mansion, and darting like mad through the trees, came a troop of riders at full speed, all of them females but one. Sweeping round the house, they disappeared; but a circuit of a few moments again brought them in front, when, discovering us, they reined up for an instant; and then, affecting vast dismay, made a rush at a high carriage gate, on one side of the lawn, to escape. The foremost rider galloping past it almost without drawing rein, bent to one side, raised and dashed it open, and then, wheeling his horse, darted through with another rider, and went clattering down a rocky path, as the gate, made to swing shut, closed with a bang. Two more performed the same feat, and the last of the train made an effort to shoot through at the same time. This was a girl of perhaps a dozen years old, and she was mounted on by far the largest horse in the party. "There goes my horse whom I bade nobody ride!" exclaimed our companion, mock gravity very scantily hiding his expression of good-natured amusement. But the last rider was too late. The gate was shutting on her, and it appeared that it must inevitably catch her powerful horse between its head and the shutting-post. We held our breath. But a

It was towards the close of his Presidency that Mr. Jefferson began to think seriously of building a house at Poplar Forest. But the first idea was conceived much sooner, and he used to say from his having been confined there for three days, in one of the two rooms of an overseer's house, during a great rain storm. Finding nothing but an almanack to read, he finally, in despair, fell to computing how long it would take to pay the national debt. The usual pocket-book of logarithms chanced to be absent, and he had slowly to run over interminable masses of figures. But he persisted and finally ascertained to his satisfaction that the internal taxes could be abolished, and the debt still be paid in eighteen years by the increase of revenue and a proper retrenchment in expenditures. This occurred in 1801, and it led him to introduce the original of the passage in his first message, commencing with the words, "Other circumstances, combined with the increase of numbers," etc. The original was more definite and precise in its statements; but Gallatin did not agree with its conclusions, and the other members of the Cabinet held back from expressing an opinion. Nicholas and most of the chiefs of the Virginia delegation were open-mouthed against it, fearing it would only end in disappointing popular expectation. But Gallatin, on a careful reëxamination of the President's data and estimates, changed his mind, and the passage, with some modifications, was inserted. The three days among the overseer's dogs and children, were therefore not unfruitful ones. And they suggested a more convenient resort from long rain storms, and an uninterrupted retreat for the solitary study of high problems.

The house at Poplar Forest was not completed until a number of years after the close of Mr. Jefferson's Presidency. It was situated in that part of Bedford, on the confines of Campbell

---

sharp, prompt, fearless pull on the reins of the heavy curb-bit suddenly arrested the horse, and it was done with such vigor and such a will, that the great animal threw his forefeet high in the air, and the gate *seemed* to swing under the uplifted hoofs, as it closed. In another moment, it was seized by the little rider, thrown open, and away she went with whip flying, to overtake her companions. We thought of the wild, fearless, graceful riders of the western plains, and wondered whether the blood of Pocahontas, which flowed in the veins of the merry party, had anything to do with the matter!

A day or two afterwards, we were walking with our friend in the neighboring highway. He picked up a horse-shoe, gazed at it a moment curiously, and ejaculated with a smile: "I thought as much;" and then, turning to us, remarked: "That's ——'s " (naming a son): "I know his mark. Whenever the roads are passable, he tucks up his coat-tails, and then de'll take the hindmost until he throws at least two shoes! I believe," he continued, "there must be something in our climate to make hard riders — our boys and girls can never rest with trotting a horse for a mile!"

county, which is near the city of Lynchburg. The following is an agreeable picture of it, and of its scenes and accessories:

——————— ———, 1856.

MY DEAR MR. RANDALL:

   •   •   •   •   •   •   •   •

     The house at Poplar Forest was very pretty and pleasant. It was of brick, one story in front, and, owing to the falling of the ground, two in the rear. It was an exact octagon, with a centre-hall twenty feet square, lighted from above. This was a beautiful room, and served as a dining-room. Round it were grouped a bright drawing-room looking south, my grandfather's own chamber, three other bedrooms, and a pantry. A terrace extended from one side of the house; there was a portico in front connected by a vestibule with the centre room, and in the rear a verandah, on which the drawing-room opened, with its windows to the floor.

   •   •   •   •   •   •   •   •

     Mr. Jefferson, from the time of his return home in 1809, was in the habit of visiting this Bedford plantation, but it was some years before the house was ready for the reception of his family. It was furnished in the simplest manner, but had a very tasty air; there was nothing common or second-rate about any part of the establishment, although there was no appearance of expense. As soon as the house was habitable, my grandfather began to take the ladies of his family, generally two at a time, with him, whenever he went. His first visit of a fortnight or three weeks was in the spring—the second, of about six weeks, in early or late autumn. We have staid as much as two months at a time. My mother went occasionally—not very often—for she had too much to do at home. I . . . . generally accompanied him with one of my younger sisters. Mr. Jefferson greatly enjoyed these visits. The crowd at Monticello of friends and strangers, of stationary or ever-varying guests, the coming and going, the incessant calls upon his own time and attention, the want of leisure that such a state of things entailed as a necessary consequence, the bustle and hurry of an almost perpetual round of company, wearied and harassed him in the end, whatever pleasure he may have taken, and it was sometimes great, in the society and conversation of his guests. At Poplar Forest he found in a pleasant home, rest, leisure, power to carry on his favorite pursuits—to think, to study, to read—whilst the presence of part of his family took away all character of solitude from his retreat. His young grand-daughters were there to enliven it for him, to make his tea, preside over his dinner table, accompany him in his walks, in his occasional drives, and be with him at the time he most enjoyed society, from tea till bed time. The weather was generally fine (the autumn climate of this part of Virginia is delightful, and even the spring is pleasant), the neighbors, who were to a man exceedingly attached to him, were very friendly, without being oppressive in their attentions. There were some excellent people among those Bedford neighbors of ours, and something touching in their affection for their old friend, whose arrival they watched for with pleasant anticipation, and hailed with a sort of loyal satisfaction. It was no sooner known in the neighborhood that Mr. Jefferson had arrived, than our neighbors hastened to help our housekeeping with all kinds of fruit, vegetables, poultry, game (I remember once a quarter of a bear's cub), the product of rich farms and an abundant country.

     By and by the gentlemen came dropping in—the ladies soon followed—we were invited out to dine, and the neighbors came to dine with us—but not often enough to consume much time, or interrupt our home occupations. I remember among these neighbors a certain "Parson" Clay, as he was called, who must have been an Episcopal clergyman before the Revolution, to whose four sons my grandfather used to lend books, and who astonished me with their names of Cyrus, Odin, Julius and Paul.

My grandfather was very happy during these sojourns in a comparatively simple and secluded district—far from noise and news—of both of which he got too much at Monticello; and we, his grand-daughters, were very happy too. It was a pleasant change for us, a variety in life and manners. We saw, too, more of our dear grandfather at those times than at any other. He was most desirous that we should find congenial occupations, and we had books, drawing materials, embroidery, and never felt time heavy on our hands. He interested himself in all we did, thought, or read. He would talk to us about his own youth and early friends, and tell us stories of former days. He seemed really to take as much pleasure in these conversations with us, as if we had been older and wiser people. Such was the influence of his affectionate, cheerful temper, that his grandchildren were as much at their ease with him, as if they had not loved and honored and revered him more than any other earthly being. I . . . . not only listened with intense interest to all he said, but answered with perfect freedom, told my own opinions and impressions, gave him my own views of things, asked questions, made remarks, and, in short, felt as free and as happy as if I had been with companions of my own age. My grandfather missed my mother of course. Her company had become very necessary to him, but her absence seemed the only drawback on his unalloyed satisfaction during these short and highly prized intervals of rest and leisure.

Our days at Poplar Forest were cheerful and uneventful. We met in the morning for an early breakfast, which, like all his other meals, he took leisurely. Whilst sipping his coffee or tea he talked with us, and if there was anything unusual to be done, arranged our plans for the day. The forenoon, whilst we followed our own desires, he passed in the drawing room with his books. With the exception of an occasional visitor, he was seldom interrupted until the hour of his ride. We dined about three, and as he liked to sit over his wine (he never took more than three glasses, and these after, and not during dinner), I always remained at table till he rose. His conversation was at this time particularly pleasant—easy, flowing, and full of anecdote. After dinner he again retired for some hours, and later in the afternoon walked with us on the terrace, conversing in the same delightful manner, being sometimes animated, and sometimes earnest. We did not leave him again till bed-time, but gave him his tea, and brought out our books or work. He would take his book from which he would occasionally look up to make a remark, to question us about what we were reading, or perhaps to read aloud to us from his own book, some passage which had struck him, and of which he wished to give us the benefit. About ten o'clock he rose to go, when we kissed him with warm, loving, grateful hearts, and went to our rest blessing God for such a friend.

Mr. Jefferson had decidedly one of the evenest and most cheerful tempers I ever knew. He enjoyed a jest, provided it were to give pain to no one, and we were always glad to have any pleasant little anecdote for him—when he would laugh as cheerily as we could do ourselves, and enter into the spirit of the thing with as much gaiety.

It was pleasant to see him in company with the country gentlemen of the neighborhood, they treated him with so much affectionate and respectful frankness—were so much at their ease with him, whilst they held him in such high honor. Their wives too were as happy as queens to receive him, and when he called or dined with them, were brimful of satisfaction and hospitable devotion. This frank and free homage, paid by independent people, who had nothing to gain, to one whose public character had merited their approbation, and whose private virtues they loved and revered, was equally honorable to those who rendered and him who received it.

Our journeys to and from Bedford, were almost always pleasant. The weather at the season of our visit was good of course, though we were once or twice caught by an early winter. The roads were not bad for country roads. My grandfather travelled in his own carriage, with his own horses, his faithful Burwell on horse-back by his side. It took us nearly three days to make the hundred miles.[1] We always stopped at the same simple country inns, where the country-people were as much pleased to see the "Squire," as they always called Mr. Jefferson, as they could have been to meet their own best friends. They set out for him the best they had, gave him the nicest room, and seemed to hail his passage as an event most interesting to themselves. These were pleasant times, but I have dwelt on them long enough. . . . . .

> With great regard, my dear Mr. Randall,
>
> Very truly yours.

A younger grand-daughter of Mr. Jefferson's wrote her husband many years ago:

"In his journeys to Bedford, he always took two of us along with him. I often now think of those journeys, generally made in good weather, and with every attention to our comfort. Early in the morning, he was sure to have some additional wrapping to put over the shoulders of each of us, generally a large cape off from one of his cloaks, and if the weather was cold we were wrapped in his furs. His cheerful conversation, so agreeable and instructive, his singing as we journeyed along, made the time pass pleasantly, even travelling through the solitudes of Buckingham and Campbell counties over indifferent roads. Our cold dinner was always put up by his own hands; a pleasant spot by the road-side chosen to eat it, and he was the carver and helped us to our cold fowl and ham, and mixed the wine and water to drink with it. During those visits to Poplar Forest, he took us to see all his neighbors, and to Lynchburgh sometimes to see the place, and to make some purchase to please us in the shops."

In the above pictures of Poplar Forest there is one omission. In the drawing-room there was what Mr. Jefferson called his petit-format library, contained in four cases, each of which was perhaps between three and four feet in width and height. The books, to economize space, were generally of the smallest sized editions published. He had first made this collection for his convenience at Washington. It contained upwards of one hundred volumes of British, a considerable collection of Italian and French, and a few favorite Greek and Latin poets, and a larger

---

[1] Poplar Forest could be reached from Monticello by travelling about eighty miles, but the roads were far rougher.

number of prose writers of the same languages—all, it is unnecessary to say, in the original. These, with the last three or four new books and reviews, brought from Monticello, were the delights which, with the society of his grand-daughters, and the occasional visits of neighbors who mixed the courtesy and simplicity of the old Virginia planter with the culture and self-respect of gentlemen, filled up that round of quiet enjoyments which contrasted, a portion of the time, so pleasingly with the hotel-like bustle and want of privacy at Monticello.

It was at Ford's tavern, one of the stopping-places between Monticello and Poplar Forest, that the following incident occurred on one of Mr. Jefferson's trips from one to the other. He was alone, and on alighting was shown into the best room where a very respectable looking stranger was sitting. The latter, who was a clergyman, soon opened a conversation without having the least idea to whom he was talking. He incidentally introduced the subject of certain mechanical operations which he had recently witnessed. Mr. Jefferson's inquiries and remarks, as he afterwards declared, soon satisfied him that he was conversing with some eminent engineer. Agriculture next came up, and then he made up his mind that Mr. Jefferson was a large farmer. Finally, the topic of religion was broached, and the clergyman became strongly suspicious that his companion was another clergyman, but he confessed that he could not discover to what particular persuasion he leaned! There was something in Mr. Jefferson's presence that did not invite the indulgence of personal curiosity, and no "leading questions," were put to him. At ten o'clock he retired to bed. The clergyman immediately sought the landlord and asked who had been his companion. "What, don't you know the Squire?—that was Mr. Jefferson," was the reply. "Not President Jefferson?" "Yes, President Jefferson!" "Why," exclaimed the clergyman, "I tell you that was neither an atheist nor irreligious man—one of juster sentiments I never met with." [1]

We have seen Mr. Jefferson in several personal phases, and it is now time to look in upon him in the interior of his family in purely domestic life, for, sooth to say, some periods of the year brought a comparative cessation of company.

[1] We have this from one who had more than once heard it from the lips of the good "parson" himself.

MY DEAR MR. RANDALL—

You seem possessed of so many facts and such minute details of Mr. Jefferson's family life, that I know not how I can add to the amount. . . . . When he returned from Washington, in 1809, I was a child, and of that period I have childish recollections. He seemed to return to private life with great satisfaction. At last he was his own master and could, he hoped, dispose of his time as he pleased, and indulge his love of country life. You know how greatly he preferred it to town life. You recollect as far back as his 'Notes on Virginia,' he says: 'Those who labor in the earth are the chosen people of God.' With regard to the tastes and wishes which he carried with him into the country, his love of reading alone would have made leisure and retirement delightful to him. Books were at all times his chosen companions, and his acquaintance with many languages gave him great power of selection. He read Homer, Virgil, Dante, Corneille, Cervantes, as he read Shakspeare and Milton. In his youth he had loved poetry, but by the time I was old enough to observe, he had lost his taste for it, except for Homer and the great Athenian tragics, which he continued to the last to enjoy. He went over the works of Eschylus, Sophocles and Euripides, not very long before I left him.[1] Of history he was very fond, and this he studied in all languages, though always, I think, preferring the ancients. In fact, he derived more pleasure from his acquaintance with Greek and Latin than from any other resource of literature, and I have often heard him express his gratitude to his father for causing him to receive a classical education. I saw him more frequently with a volume of the classics in his hand than with any other book. Still he read new publications as they came out, never missed the new number of a review, especially of the Edinburgh, and kept himself acquainted with what was being done, said, or thought in the world from which he had retired.

He loved farming and gardening, the fields, the orchards, and his asparagus beds. Every day he rode through his plantation and walked in his garden. In the cultivation of the last he took great pleasure. Of flowers, too, he was very fond. One of my early recollections is of the attention which he paid to his flower-beds. He kept up a correspondence with persons in the large cities, particularly, I think, in Philadelphia, for the purpose of receiving supplies of roots and seeds both for his kitchen and flower garden. I remember well when he first returned to Monticello, how immediately he began to prepare new beds for his flowers. He had these beds laid off on the lawn, under the windows, and many a time I have run after him when he went out to direct the work, accompanied by one of his gardeners, generally Wormley, armed with spade and hoe, whilst he himself carried the measuring-line. I was too young to aid him, except in a small way, but my sister, Mrs. Bankhead, then a young and beautiful woman, ... was his active and useful assistant. I remember the planting of the first hyacinths and tulips, and their subsequent growth. The roots arrived, labelled each one with a fancy name. There was Marcus Aurelius, and the King of the Gold Mine, the Roman Empress, and the Queen of the Amazons, Psyche, the God of Love, etc., etc., etc. Eagerly, and with childish delight, I studied this brilliant nomenclature, and wondered what strange and surprisingly beautiful creations I should see rising from the ground when spring returned, and these precious roots were committed to the earth under my grandfather's own eye, with his beautiful grand-daughter Anne standing by his side, and a crowd of

---

[1] The writer left Monticello the year before Mr. Jefferson's death.

happy young faces, of younger grandchildren, clustering round to see the progress, and inquire anxiously the name of each separate deposit.   Then, when spring returned, how eagerly we watched the first appearance of the shoots above ground. Each root was marked with its own name written on a bit of stick by its side, and what joy it was for one of us to discover the tender green breaking through the mould, and run to grandpapa to announce, that we really believed Marcus Aurelius was coming up, or the Queen of the Amazons was above ground!   With how much pleasure compounded of our pleasure and his own, on the new birth, he would immediately go out to verify the fact, and praise us for our diligent watchfulness. Then, when the flowers were in bloom, and we were in ecstasies over the rich purple and crimson, or pure white, or delicate lilac, or pale yellow of the blossoms, how he would sympathize in our admiration, or discuss with my mother and elder sister new groupings and combinations and contrasts.   Oh, these were happy moments for us and for him !

It was in the morning, immediately after our early breakfast, that he used to visit his flower-beds and his garden.   As the day, in summer, grew warmer, he re- tired to his own apartments, which consisted of a bed-chamber and library opening into each other.   Here he remained until about one o'clock, occupied in reading, writing, looking over papers, etc.   My mother would sometimes send me with a message to him.   A gentle knock, a call of "come in," and I would enter, with a mixed feeling of love and reverence, and some pride in being the bearer of a com- munication to one whom I approached with all the affection of a child, and some- thing of the loyalty of a subject.   Our mother educated all her children to look up to her father, as she looked up to him herself—literally looked up, as to one stand- ing on an eminence of greatness and goodness.   And it is no small proof of his real elevation, that as we grew older and better able to judge for ourselves, we were more and more confirmed in the opinions we had formed of it.

About one o'clock my grandfather rode out, and was absent perhaps two hours; when he returned to prepare for his dinner, which was about half-past three o'clock. He sat some time at table, and after dinner, returned for a while to his room, from which he emerged before sunset to walk on the terrace or the lawn, to see his grand- children run races, or to converse with his family and friends.   The evenings, after candle-light, he passed with us, till about ten o'clock.   He had his own chair and his own candle a little apart from the rest, where he sat reading, if there were no guests to require his attention, but often laying his book on his little round table or his knee, whilst he talked with my mother, the elder members of the family, or any child old enough to make one of the family-party.   I always did, for I was . . . . the most active, and the most lively of the young folks, and most wont to thrust myself forward into notice.

————————

————, 185-.

My dear Mr. Randall:

    *   *   *   *   *

With regard to Mr. Jefferson's conduct and manners in his family, after I was old enough to form any judgment of it—I can only repeat what I have said before —and I say it calmly and advisedly, with no spirit of false enthusiasm or exaggera- tion—I have never known anywhere, under any circumstances, so good a domestic character as my grandfather Jefferson's.   I have the testimony of his sisters and of his daughter, that he was in all the relations of private life, at all times, just what he was when I knew him. My mother was ten years old when her mother died. Her impression was, that her father's conduct as a husband had been admirable in its ensemble, charming in its details. She distinctly recalled her mother's passionate attachment to him, and her exalted opinion of him. On one occasion she heard her blaming him for some generous acts which had met with an ungrateful return —"but," she exclaimed, "it is always so with him—he is so good himself that he cannot understand how bad other people may be." . . . On one occasion my mother had been punished for some fault, not harshly nor unjustly, but in a way to make an impression. Some little time after, her mother being displeased with her for some trifle, reminded her in a slightly taunting way of this painful past. She was deeply mortified, her heart swelled, her eyes filled with tears, she turned away, but she heard her father say in a kind tone to her mother, "My dear, a fault in so young a child once punished should be forgotten." My mother told me she could never forget the warm gush of gratitude that filled her childish heart at these words, probably not intended for her ear. These are trifling details, but they show character. . . . .

My grandfather's manners to us, his grandchildren, were delightful. I can characterize them by no other word. He talked with us freely, affectionately, never lost an opportunity of giving a pleasure or a good lesson. He reproved without wounding us, and commended without making us vain. He took pains to correct our errors and false ideas, checked the bold, encouraged the timid, and tried to teach us to reason soundly and feel rightly. Our smaller follies he treated with good-humored raillery, our graver ones with kind and serious admonition. He was watchful over our manners, and called our attention to every violation of propriety. He did not interfere with our education, technically so called, except by advising us what studies to pursue, what books to read, and by questioning us on the books which we did read. I was . . . . . . thrown most into companionship with him. I loved him very devotedly, and sought every opportunity of being with him. As a child I used to follow him about, and draw as near to him as I could. I remember when I was small enough to sit on his knee and play with his watch chain. As a girl I would join him in his walks on the terrace, sit with him over the fire during the winter twilight, or by the open windows in summer. As child, girl and woman, I loved and honored him above all earthly beings. And well I might. From him seemed to flow all the pleasures of my life. To him I owed all the small blessings and joyful surprises of my childish and girlish years. His nature was so eminently sympathetic, that with those he loved, he could enter into their feelings, anticipate their wishes, gratify their tastes, and surround them with an atmosphere of affection. I was fond of riding, and was rising above that childish simplicity when, provided I was mounted on a horse, I cared nothing for my equipments, and when an old saddle or broken bridle were matters of no moment. I was beginning to be fastidious, but I had never told my wishes. I was standing one bright day in the portico, when a man rode up to the door with a beautiful lady's saddle and bridle before him. My heart bounded. These coveted articles were deposited at my feet. My grandfather came out of his room to tell me they were mine.

When about fifteen years old, I began to think of a watch, but knew the state of my father's finances promised no such indulgence. One afternoon the letter-bag was brought in. Among the letters was a small packet addressed to my grandfather. It had the Philadelphia mark upon it. I looked at it with indifferent, incurious eye. Three hours after, an elegant lady's watch with chain and seals was in my hand, which trembled for very joy. My Bible came from him, my Shakspeare, my first writing-table, my first handsome writing-desk, my first Leghorn hat, my first silk dress. What, in short, of all my small treasures did not come from him ? . . My sisters, according to their wants and tastes, were equally thought of, equally provided for. Our grandfather seemed to read our hearts, to see our invisible wishes, to be our good genius, to wave the fairy wand, to brighten our young lives by his goodness and his gifts. But I have written enough for this time—and indeed what can I say hereafter, but to repeat the same tale of love and kindness. . .

I remain, my dear Mr. Randall,

Very truly yours,

A younger grand-daughter of Mr. Jefferson wrote to her husband:

St. Servan,[1] May 26th, 1839.

Faithful to my promise, dearest ———, I shall spend an hour every Sunday in writing all my childish recollections of my dear grandfather, which are sufficiently distinct to relate to you. My memory seems crowded with them, and they have the vividness of realities; but all are trifles in themselves, such as I might talk to you by the hour, but when I have taken up my pen, they seem almost too childish to write down. But these remembrances are precious to me, because they are of him, and because they restore him to me as he then was, when his cheerfulness and affection were the warm sun in which his family all basked and were invigorated. Cheerfulness, love, benevolence, wisdom, seemed to animate his whole form. His face beamed with them. You remember how active was his step, how lively and even playful were his manners.

I cannot describe the feelings of veneration, admiration and love that existed in my heart towards him. I looked on him as a being too great and good for my comprehension; and yet I felt no fear to approach him, and be taught by him some of the childish sports that I delighted in. When he walked in the garden and would call the children to go with him, we raced after and before him, and we were made perfectly happy by this permission to accompany him. Not one of us in our wildest moods ever placed a foot on one of the garden beds, for that would violate one of his rules, and yet I never heard him utter a harsh word to one of us, or speak in a raised tone of voice, or use a threat. He simply said, "do," or "do not." He would gather fruit for us, seek out the ripest figs, or bring down the cherries from on high above our heads with a long stick, at the end of which there was a hook and a little net bag. . . . One of our earliest amusements was in running races on the terrace, or around the lawn. He placed us according to our ages, giving the youngest and smallest the start of all the others by some yards, and so on, and then he raised his arm high with his white handkerchief in his hand, on which our eager eyes were fixed, and slowly counted three, at which number he dropt the handkerchief and we started off to finish the race by returning to the starting-place and receiving our reward of dried fruit—three figs, prunes or dates to the victor, two to the second, and one to the lagger who came in last. These were our summer sports with him.

I was born the year he was elected President, and except one winter that we spent with him in Washington, I never was with him during that season until after

[1] In France.

he had retired from office. During his absences, all the children who could write corresponded with him. Their letters were duly answered,[1] and it was a sad mortification to me that I had not learned to write before his return to live at home, and of course had no letter from him. Whenever an opportunity occurred, he sent us books, and he never saw a little story or piece of poetry in a newspaper suited to our ages and tastes, that he did not preserve it and send it to us; and from him we learnt the habit of making these miscellaneous collections by pasting in a little paper book made for the purpose, anything of the sort that we received from him or got otherwise.[2]

On winter evenings, when it grew too dark to read, in the half hour that passed before candles came in, as we all sat round the fire, he taught us several childish games, and would play them with us. I remember that "cross questions," and "I love my love with an A," were two I learned from him; and we would teach some of ours to him. When the candles were brought, all was quiet immediately, for he took up his book to read, and we would not speak out of a whisper lest we should disturb him, and generally we followed his example and took a book—and I have seen him raise his eyes from his own book and look round on the little circle of readers, and smile and make some remark to mamma about it. When the snow fell we would go out as soon as it stopped to clear it off the terraces with shovels, that he might have his usual walk on them without treading in snow.[3]

He often made us little presents. I remember his giving us "Parents' Assistant,"[4] and that we drew lots, and that she who drew the longest straw had the first reading of the book—the next longest straw entitled the drawer to the second reading—the shortest, to the last reading and the ownership of the book. Often he discovered, we knew not how, some cherished object of our desires, and the first intimation we had of his knowing the wish was its unexpected gratification. Sister Anne gave a silk dress to sister Ellen. Cornelia [then eight or ten years old] going up stairs, involuntarily expressed aloud some feelings which possessed her bosom on the occasion, by saying, "I never had a silk dress in my life." The next day a silk dress came from Charlottesville for Cornelia—and (to make the rest of us equally happy) also a pair of pretty dresses for Mary and myself. One day I was passing hastily through the glass door from the hall to the portico; there was a broken pane which caught my muslin dress and tore it sadly. Grandpapa was standing by and saw the disaster. A few days after he came into mamma's sitting-room with a bundle in his hand, and said to me, "I have been mending your dress for you." He had himself selected for me another beautiful dress. I had for a

---

[1] Of the letters addressed to Mrs. Bankhead, we know nothing. She died early, and they are probably lost. Those addressed to the next grand-daughter were numerous, No copies were kept of them, and they were all lost at sea—while following their owner to a Northern city. The younger grand-daughters were too young to receive more than one or two apiece from him. For specimens of these, addressed to children five or six years old, see APPENDIX, No. 23.

[2] Some of these harmless scrap-books were mistaken by a visitor (or writer in the newspapers, who claimed to derive his information from a visitor) for collections by Mr. Jefferson of all the attacks made on him in the public journals! There was not a trace of truth in the statement. Mr. Jefferson very rarely read, and never took pains to preserve an attack on himself.

[3] The writer of the above, assured us personally, that the task here described was too eagerly coveted to be permitted to a domestic—and that it would have been a gratification to the little shovellers, to sweep the long terraces with their hair, to express their love for him for whose feet they were preparing them.

[4] Miss Edgworth's works were collected as they appeared, and given to the children. Mr. Jefferson was a hearty admirer of Miss Edgworth—notwithstanding the very few novels he ever read.

long time a great desire to have a guitar. A lady of our neighborhood was going to the West and wished to part with her guitar, but she asked so high a price that I never in my dreams aspired to its possession. One morning on going down to breakfast, I saw the guitar. It had been sent up by Mrs. ——— for us to look at, and grandpapa told me that if I would promise to learn to play on it I should have it. I never shall forget my ecstasies. I was but fourteen years old and the first wish of my heart was unexpectedly gratified. . . . .

Pages more might be filled with written and oral recollections of the same tenor. The flight of years has not dimmed the love with which all those of his household regarded him; and the impression which he left on their memories, is far too deeply stamped for anything but death to efface. But, as one of the narrators has asked, " what can be said hereafter but to repeat the same tale of love and kindness?"

CHAPTER IX.

1810—1813.

WE again recur to Mr. Jefferson's correspondence during 1810. His indignation at the conduct of both Great Britain and

'rance remained unabated. He wrote Dr. Jones, a Virginia
lember of Congress, March 5th:

"Our difficulties are indeed great, if we consider ourselves alone. But when
ewed in comparison with those of Europe, they are the joys of Paradise. In the
ernal revolution of ages, the destinies have placed our portion of existence amidst
ch scenes of tumult and outrage, as no other period, withing our knowledge, had
esented. Every government but one on the continent of Europe, demolished, a
nqueror roaming over the earth with havoc and destruction, a pirate spreading
isery and ruin over the face of the ocean. Indeed, my friend, ours is a bed of
ses. And the system of government which shall keep us afloat amidst this wreck
' the world, will be immortalized in history. We have, to be sure, our petty
quabbles and heart burnings, and we have something of the blue devils at times, as
 these raw-heads and bloody-bones who are eating up other nations. But happily
r us, the Mammoth cannot swim, nor the Leviathan move on dry land: and if we
ill keep out of their way, they cannot get at us."

Commenting in a letter to Mr. Law on "the miserable policy"
ursued by England " of teasing and embarrassing us by ally-
ng itself with a faction here, not a tenth of the people, noisy
nd unprincipled," he thus met the charge of having been
nfluenced by enmity in his own official conduct towards that
ountry:

" With respect to myself, I saw great reason to believe their ministers were
eak enough to credit the newspaper trash about a supposed personal enmity in
yself towards England. This wretched party imputation was beneath the notice
f wise men. England never did me a personal injury, other than in open war;
nd for numerous individuals there, I have great esteem and friendship. And I
ust have had a mind far below the duties of my station, to have felt either national
artialities or antipathies in conducting the affairs confided to me. My affections
ere first for my own country, and then, generally, for all mankind; and nothing
ut minds placing themselves above the passions, in the functionaries of this
ountry, could have preserved us from the war to which their provocations have
een constantly urging us."

In two or three letters during the year, he expressed antici-
ations of "a crush" in the "internal structure" of England,
wing to the remarkable state of her monetary affairs. These
iews were not confined to him or his party; and in looking
ack over the circumstances of the times, it only appears won-
erful that they were not realized.[1]

1 The Bank of England had suspended specie payments in February, 1797, and they
ere not resumed until 1823, a period of twenty-six years. The bank had, we think,
out a million and a quarter of specie in its vaults at the time of suspension. Its circu-
tion prior to that event, was eleven or twelve millions of pounds. In 1810, when
r. Jefferson wrote, its circulation had reached eighteen millions: and before 1820, it
d reached thirty millions, or one hundred and fifty millions of dollars. The notes of

A Russian Ambassador [Count Pahlen] reached the United States in the summer of 1810, and one of his first steps was to convey to Mr. Jefferson by the orders of the Emperor Alexander assurances of that monarch's continued friendly regard. The reply did not fail to urge the customary views in relation to the union of maritime policies between Russia and the United States.

We find Mr. Jefferson proposing to William Duane (August 12th) to publish Baxter's abridgment and continuation of Hume's history of England—although he admitted that the work lacked equally in style and profundity. The avowed object was to supplant a book which had "undermined the free principles of the English government," and the style of which had rendered it "the manual of every student." He also proposed the publication of De Tracy's Commentary on Montesquieu, the manuscript of which had been confided to him by the author for that purpose, should he consider it advisable. Duane translated and published it, the proof-sheets being seen by Mr. Jefferson. Duane proposed a revision of the Notes on Virginia, and Jefferson replied that "he did contemplate some day the making additions and corrections to them; but he was inclined to take the benefit of his whole life to make collections and observations, and let the editing them be posthumous." He never found time, if he did inclination, to make the effort; and on the whole, it perhaps may be considered fortunate.[1]

We shall close these brief extracts from his correspondence

the bank were as irredeemable, at the time, as our own old continental currency: the debts of England were rolling up with frightful velocity; and reasoning from all the analogies the world had ever presented, nearly all foreigners throughout Christendom looked daily for a giving way of commercial confidence, and some tremendous consequent convulsion. That this did not occur, is not only a better proof of England's enormous resources than even her iron struggle with Napoleon, but perhaps the best proof her history contains of the inflexible, all-defying and all-sacrificing national spirit of her people.

[1] On some of the topics treated in the original work, especially the political ones, his later views would have been valuable. But the attempt to carry them all out on a scale befitting his reputation elsewhere, would have involved a vast range of inquiry—and the preparation of almost an encyclopædia of the sciences. Was he prepared for this? The original when written was a wonderful compilation in some departments. It also had strong original features to commend it—was a most felicitous application of the philosophy of science to the business and interests of society. But while Mr. Jefferson had been "governing men and guiding States," the chariot wheels of science had not tarried. Men just as able as himself to press forward its investigations, had separately taken up its branches, and unfolded vast new reaches of fact and theory. Could an old man, sixty-seven years old, though perfectly at his leisure, go back and overtake them—and then add something worthy of the time and pen of an eminent statesman? There can be but one rational answer to this question. There can be no doubt the first deliberate reflection Mr. Jefferson gave to the subject, suggested the inevitable conclusion.

rith the following from a letter to David Howel, 15th :

e or two newspapers a week, but with reluctance give even that time nd Horace, and so much other more agreeable reading ; indeed, I ɔ to exercise of the body than of the mind, believing it wholesome to ·, in recollection, my ancient friendships, and suffer no new circum- alloy with them. I do not take the trouble of forming opinions on ɡ among them, because I have such entire confidence in their integ- m as to be satisfied all is going right, and that every one is doing his tion confided to him. Under these impressions, accept sincere assu- continued esteem and respect for yourself personally, and my best r health and happiness."

.nited space will be devoted to the correspondence of as the usual literary and political variety, but perhaps w essentially new views, or statements which connect n an interesting light with important passing events. ter to Mr. Eppes, not heretofore published, Mr. Jeffer- ɔferred to the boundary of Louisiana, and certain pertaining to that question :

To John W. Eppes.   Monticello, *Jan.* 5, 1811.

ro letters of Dec. 14th reached this place just after I had left it for s has occasioned the delay of the answer. I now inclose you the ,uested on the boundaries of Louisiana. It is a bad polygraph copy ; egible. There is nothing secret in the paper, and therefore it may be you please, except that I would not have it printed, but with the President. With his sanction, if it be thought material to satisfy the on the solidity of a right, the assertion of which may lead to war, it L But the paper I send you wants a very material appendix. This ɔgical table of all the facts relating to the discovery and history of :h I compiled from all the authors I possess or could obtain who have iisiana, with a reference to the authority of every fact. This is not ɾ papers, and I have no conception what has become of it, unless it office of State. I sent both papers to that office, and perhaps only the principal paper may have been returned to me. I write by this ·raham, to examine, and if he has not the original of the chrono- o lend me his copy, from which I will send you one. With respect ·ies, they are as well ascertained as those of any unsettled country ell as the boundaries of several of these States, about which disputes as the boundaries of many of the unsettled northern countries of

.   .   .   .   .   .

on considered the main branch of the Rio Bravo the western boundary ı far as that river extended. See his letter to Mellish, December 31, 1816.

I proposed to Francis, as you desired, his staying here. He asked me if I had written to you to ask permission for his stay. I told him I had, and that you left it to himself. He said at once he would stay. I have put him into his Latin grammar, rather to learn him to exercise his memory in getting by heart, than from an expectation that he may otherwise profit from it as yet. I observe he gets very readily and perfectly. I inclose you a letter from him. Accept assurances of my constant affection.

TH. JEFFERSON.

He expressed the following opinions in regard to the colonization of American people of color in Africa, and in regard to the duties of our Government in the premises:

TO MR. JOHN LYNCH.

MONTICELLO, *January* 21, 1811.

SIR:

You have asked my opinion on the proposition of Mrs. Mifflin, to take measures for procuring, on the coast of Africa, an establishment to which the people of color of these States might, from time to time, be colonized under the auspices of different governments. Having long ago made up my mind on this subject, I have no hesitation in saying that I have ever thought it the most desirable measure which could be adopted for gradually drawing off this part of our population, most advantageously for themselves as well as for us. Going from a country possessing all the useful arts, they might be the means of transplanting them among the inhabitants of Africa, and would thus carry back to the country of their origin, the seeds of civilization which might render their sojournment and sufferings here a blessing in the end to that country."

After mentioning his own correspondence when President, with other governments, undertaken at the instance of the Virginia Executive, to procure an "asylum to which these people might be occasionally sent," and after giving some particulars of the Sierra Leone establishment, he added:

"You inquire further, whether I would use my endeavors to procure for such an establishment security against violence from other powers, and particularly from France? Certainly, I shall be willing to do anything I can to give it effect and safety. But I am but a private individual, and could only use endeavors with private individuals; whereas, the National Government can address themselves at once to those of Europe to obtain the desired security, and will unquestionably be ready to exert its influence with those nations for an object so benevolent in itself and so important to a great portion of its constituents. Indeed, nothing is more to be wished than that the United States would themselves undertake to make such an establishment on the coast of Africa. Exclusive of motives of humanity, the commercial advantages to be derived from it might repay all its expenses. But for this, the national mind is not yet prepared. It may perhaps be doubted whether many of these people would voluntarily consent to such an exchange of situation, and very certain that few of those advanced to a certain age in habits of slavery, would be capable of self-government. This should not, however, discourage the experiment, nor the early trial of it; and the proposition should be made with all the prudent cautions and attentions requisite to reconcile it to the interests, the safety, and the prejudices of all parties."

The misunderstandings in Mr. Madison's Cabinet, already adverted to, had continued to increase, and they found incitements in the differing opinions of its members in regard to the proper policy to be pursued towards England and France. Gallatin's and Smith's opposition to each other's views became more personal and extreme, and the President was accused by the friends of the latter, of leaning too strongly towards the Secretary of the Treasury. It is certain that the President had very great confidence in the ability and experience of Gallatin. He had originally intended to make him Secretary of State, but had been compelled to forego his purpose reluctantly, and at the last moment, owing to the anticipated opposition of a party in the Senate, who were friends of the individual designated to that office.[1]

[1] We are enabled to state the following facts from an unquestionable source. The President made up his mind to offer the State department to Gallatin. The latter was consulted, and was highly gratified at the proposal, because it would afford him a relief from the long drudgery he had undergone in the Treasury department, and because having personally favored George Clinton's nomination to the Presidency rather than Mr. Madison's, it came as an acceptable token of unbroken regard from the latter. But as a warm opposition was anticipated, it was considered best to keep the matter a secret until the nomination was sent to the Senate. Giles was very hostile to Gallatin; and both Robert Smith and his brother General Samuel Smith (then in the Senate) were opposed to his transfer to the State department; the main objection of the latter being (we are informed by one of his family) that it was unbecoming that a foreign born citizen should be selected to conduct our correspondences with *foreign* nations.

The contemplated appointment of Gallatin to the State department began to be suspected because no other individual was mentioned for the place; and it became fully disclosed by a ruse on the part of a lady. She cordially congratulated Mrs. Gallatin on her husband's promotion, and the latter, taken by surprise, admitted that it was an agreeable lightening of his official labors, etc. It was not long before Giles, with his customary rapidity of action, placed *seventeen* written objections to Gallatin's appointment in the President's hands, requesting that they might also be communicated to Gallatin. The President very quietly suggested that if they were intended for Gallatin, Giles had better himself deliver them! There was an immediate mustering of heads among the hostile senators. Gallatin became alarmed, and asked the President to leave him in his present situation. But Madison's passive determination of character now shone forth, and he peremptorily refused. He said, if the Senate intended to dictate his nominations, or otherwise reject unexceptionable men, there would never be a better time than then for him to find out whether he was President or not; and the American people must decide whether he had done wrong in making, or the Senate in rejecting, the nomination. Finally, Gallatin frankly admitted, that, after his long services, he could not endure the idea of a rejection. "That," said Mr. Madison, "puts a different face on the matter; though he greatly regretted that Mr. Gallatin had not thought of this earlier, and before he [the President] had completed all his arrangements." (It is not probable that we use the exact words of Mr. Madison, but we have felt authorized to place them in quotation marks, as we received them substantially as his from one who often heard the matter talked of by him.) Gallatin was permitted to remain in the Treasury department, and in recasting the Cabinet, Robert Smith was designated to the State department.

We are not aware of any facts that go to show that the opposition of Smith's friends

The differences in the Cabinet corresponded with those between two Republican wings or factions in the Senate, and finally the feud began to exhibit itself in the newspapers. Duane, of the Aurora, passed some public strictures on Gallatin. Thereupon Lieper (Jefferson's old friend, and correspondent in Philadelphia) and some other eminent Republicans withdrew necessary pecuniary accommodations which they had been in the habit of extending to Duane. The latter appealed to Jefferson for aid. The answer (March 28th, 1811) paid a noble tribute to Gallatin, and avowed the writer's continued confidence in him, but he informed the editor of the Aurora that his own services in the cause of Republicanism "constituted too strong a claim on the good wishes of every friend of elective government, to be effaced by a solitary case of difference of opinion." Mr. Jefferson promised to write to a friend at Richmond to organize a plan of extensive assistance, and he closed with an earnest exhortation to a firm support of the Administration, and against "schismatizing on either men or measures." He declared "principles alone could justify that."

Duane was not controlled by this advice. He continued his censures on the Secretary of the Treasury, and finally extended them to the President. When the Aurora containing these was received in Richmond, William Wirt, who had been charged with the execution of the plan for Duane's aid by Jefferson, immediately wrote to the latter that nothing further could be done in that direction. Jefferson apprised Duane of this, not concealing the opinion that his conduct had rendered such a result inevitable. This letter (dated April 30th) contains an avowal of the writer's opinions in respect to the duty of sacrificing individual views to party unity, which present an important feature in his political code. He said:

"I have thought it well that you should know exactly the feelings here, because if you get similar information from other respectable portions of the Union, it will naturally beget some suspicion in your own mind, that, finding such a mass of opinion variant from your own, you may be under erroneous impressions, meriting reëxamination and consideration. I think an editor should be independent, that is, of personal influence, and not be moved from his opinions on the mere authority of any individual. But with respect to the general opinion of the political section

to Gallatin was made with any reference to the appointment of the former. And at all events, no one acquainted with the character of the Smiths, will suspect either of them of dishonorable conduct or motives.

with which he habitually accords, his duty seems very like that of a member of Congress. Some of these indeed think that independence requires them to follow always their own opinion, without respect for that of others. This has never been my opinion, nor my practice, when I have been of that or any other body. Differing on a particular question from those whom I knew to be of the same political principles with myself, and with whom I generally thought and acted, a consciousness of the fallibility of the human mind, and of my own in particular, with a respect for the accumulated judgment of my friends, has induced me to suspect erroneous impressions in myself, to suppose my own opinion wrong, and to act with them on theirs. The want of this spirit of compromise, or of self-distrust, proudly, but falsely, called independence, is what gives the Federalists victories which they could never obtain, if these brethren could learn to respect the opinions of their friends more than of their enemies, and prevents many able and honest men from doing all the good they otherwise might do. I state these considerations, because they have often quieted my own conscience in voting and acting on the judgment of others against my own; and because they may suggest doubts to yourself in the present case. Our Executive and legislative authorities are the choice of the nation and possess the nation's confidence. They are chosen because they possess it, and the recent elections prove it has not been abated by the attacks which have for some time been kept up against them. If the measures which have been pursued are approved by the majority, it is the duty of the minority to acquiesce and conform. It is true indeed that dissentients have a right to go over to the minority, and to act with them. But I do not believe your mind has contemplated that course, that it has deliberately viewed the strange company into which it may be led, step by step, unintended and unperceived by itself. The example of John Randolph is a caution to all honest and prudent men, to sacrifice a little of self-confidence, and to go with their friends, although they may sometimes think they are going wrong. After so long a course of steady adherence to the general sentiments of the Republicans, it would afflict me sincerely to see you separate from the body, become auxiliary to the enemies of our government, who have to you been the bitterest enemies, who are now chuckling at the prospect of division among us, and, as I am told, are subscribing for your paper. The best indications of error which my experience has tested, is the approbation of the Federalists. Their conclusions necessarily follow the false bias of their principles. I claim, however, no right of guiding the conduct of others; but have indulged myself in these observations from the sincere feelings of my heart. Retired from all political interferences, I have been induced into this one by a desire, first of being useful to you personally, and next of maintaining the Republican ascendency. Be its effect what it may, I am done with it, and shall look on as an inactive, though not an unfeeling, spectator of what is to ensue. As far as my good will may go, for I can no longer act, I shall adhere to my government, executive and legislative, and as long as they are Republican, I shall go with their measures, whether I think them right or wrong; because I know they are honest, and are wiser and better informed than I am. In doing this, however, I shall not give up the friendship of those who differ from me, and who have equal right with myself to shape their own course. In this disposition be assured of my continued esteem and respect."

The criticism on Duane's course implied in these remarks, wounded his feelings. Jefferson disavowed such an intention, but adhered to his position. The temper of the celebrated editor of the Aurora was naturally vehement, and it had been rendered intolerant towards opponents by the bitter persecutions he had endured. But he was a sincere Republican, and he exhibited his native good sense on the present occasion by not only dropping all resentment, but by going much oftener than before for advice to the friend whose "wounds" had proved so "faithful."

A statement of the various complaints made at this period against Gallatin by the opposing branch of the Republicans will be found in a letter from Jefferson to Wirt, dated May 3d, 1811. The following passages from it further exhibit the writer's breadth of toleration in differences of opinion with honest and able members of his own party, and they also show that he found something to call for his toleration in the leaders of both wings:

> "Mr. Gallatin's support of the bank has, I believe, been disapproved by many. He was not in Congress when that was established, and therefore had never committed himself, publicly, on the constitutionality of that institution, nor do I recollect ever to have heard him declare himself on it. I know he derived immense convenience from it, because they gave the effect of ubiquity to his money wherever deposited. Money in New Orleans or Maine was at his command, and by their agency transformed in an instant into money in London, in Paris, Amsterdam, or Canton. He was, therefore, cordial to the bank. I often pressed him to divide the public deposits among all the respectable banks, being indignant myself at the open hostility of that institution to a government on whose treasuries they were fattening. But his repugnance to it prevented my persisting. And if he was in favor of the bank, what is the amount of that crime or error in which he had a majority save one in each House of Congress as participators? yet on these facts, endeavors are made to drive from the Administration the ablest man except the President, who ever was in it, and to beat down the President himself, because he is unwilling to part with so able a counsellor."

Mr. Wirt was authorized to show the letter to Mr. Ritchie, editor of the Richmond Enquirer, who was a decided friend of the President, but was understood not to be as cordial to Gallatin. In fact, there is little doubt that this letter was written specially for the eye of an editor, who, for a union of ability and discretion with statesmanlike views, had never been equalled in his party, and who consequently wielded a most important influence. Mr. Jefferson often pronounced Thomas Ritchie "the first editor of the United States."

Among the early letters of this year we find interesting ones on various topics to Dr. Rush, De Tracy, Humboldt, Paganel, Dupont de Nemours, Kosciusko, etc. To the latter he thus spoke of the Spanish-American revolution:

"Spanish America is all in revolt. The insurgents are triumphant in many of the States, and will be so in all. But then the danger is that the cruel arts of their oppressors have enchained their minds, have kept them in the ignorance of children and as incapable of self-government as children. If the obstacles of bigotry and priestcraft can be surmounted, we may hope that common sense will suffice to do everything else. God send them a safe deliverance."

His hopes and fears on the same subject are more fully expressed in other letters of the period. His wishes for peace, and indignation at the conduct of the European belligerents, find their customary expressions. Some advice (July 22d) to Barlow who was about departing as American minister to France, in respect to the proper deportment to be observed towards Napoleon, is worth perusal:

"He has understanding enough, but it is confined to particular lines. Of the principles and advantages of commerce he appears to be ignorant, and his domineering temper deafens him moreover to the dictates of interest, of honor, and of morality. A nation like ours, recognizing no arrogance of language or conduct, can never enjoy the favor of such a character. The impression, too, which our public has been made to receive from the different styles of correspondence used by two of our foreign agents, has increased the difficulties of steering between the bristling pride of the two parties. It seems to point out the Quaker style of plain reason, void of offence: the suppression of all passion, and chaste language of good sense. Heaven prosper your endeavors for our good, and preserve you in health and happiness."

When it was understood that Foster, the British minister who had succeeded Jackson, had formally declared to our Government that the orders in council would be persisted in, Mr. Jefferson at once arrived at the conclusion that war was our only alternative. He wrote to a gentleman in England, September 16th, 1811:

"We have hitherto been able to avoid professed war, and to continue to our industry a more salutary direction. But the determination to take all our vessels bound to any other than her ports, amounting to all the war she can make (for we fear no invasion), it would be folly in us to let that war be all on one side only, and to make no effort towards indemnification and retaliation by reprisal. That a contest thus forced on us by a nation a thousand leagues from us both, should place your country and mine in relations of hostility, who have not a single motive or interest but of mutual friendship and interchange of comforts, shows the monstrous character of the system under which we live."

But hearing an unfounded rumor of the death of George III, he thus wrote Mr. Eppes on the 29th of the same month:

"In this event [the revocation of the orders in council] we may still remain at peace, and that probably concluded between the other powers. I am so far, in that case, from believing that our reputation will be tarnished by our not having mixed in the mad contests of the rest of the world, that, setting aside the ravings of pepper-pot politicians, of whom there are enough in every age and country, I believe it will place us high in the scale of wisdom, to have preserved our country tranquil and prosperous during a contest which prostrated the honor, power, independence, laws, and property of every country on the other side of the Atlantic. Which of them have better preserved their honor? Has Spain, has Portugal, Italy, Switzerland, Holland, Prussia, Austria, the other German powers, Sweden, Denmark, or even Russia? And would we accept of the infamy of France or England in exchange for our honest reputation, or of the result of their enormities, despotism to the one, and bankruptcy and prostration to the other, in exchange for the prosperity, the freedom, and independence which we have preserved safely through the wreck?"

Mr. Jefferson wrote to General Dearborn, August 14th, that should England force on a war with us, "he foresaw a possibility of a separate treaty between her and the Essex men on the principles of neutrality and commerce"—that "Pickering here and his nephew Williams there, could easily negotiate this." He also said:

"Tell my old friend, Governor Gerry, that I gave him glory for the rasping with which he rubbed down his herd of traitors. Let them have justice and protection against personal violence, but no favor. Powers and preëminences conferred on them are daggers put into the hands of assassins, to be plunged into our own bosoms in the moment the thrust can go home to the heart. Moderation can never reclaim them. They deem it timidity, and despise without fearing the tameness from which it flows. Backed by England, they never lose the hope that their day is to come, when the terrorism of their earlier power is to be merged in the more gratifying system of deportation and the guillotine. Being now *hors de combat* myself, I resign to others these cares. A long attack of rheumatism has greatly enfeebled me, and warns me that they will not be very long within my ken."

The severe expressions of this letter were called out by a course of conduct on the part of the Federalists, a full account of which would carry us too far from the objects of this work. Mr. Jefferson had pretty good proofs that a strong disunion feeling had continued to manifest itself among influential individuals in New England from the year 1803, if not indeed from 1796.[1] He had the most specific assurances from J. Q. Adams and others, that such feelings existed, and even took the form of definite designs in the years 1808 and 1809. On the 14th of January, 1811, Josiah Quincy of Massachusetts declared in Congress, in the debate on the bill to enable the people of the territory of Orleans to form a constitution and State government, that the passage of the bill " would justify a revolution in this country," and he subsequently added :

> " I am compelled to declare it as my deliberate opinion that if this bill passes, the bonds of this Union are virtually dissolved; that the States which compose it are free from their moral obligations, and that, as it will be right of all, so it will be the duty of some, to prepare definitely for a separation—amicably if they can, violently if they must." [2]

Being called to order, Quincy, " to save all misapprehension," reduced his declarations to writing in the above form. He was, at the time, the leading Federal member of the House.

At the Federal caucus held in Boston on the Sunday evening preceding the State elections of 1811, resolutions were passed denouncing the Non-intercourse law, and in favor of " the election of such men to the various offices of the State government, as would oppose by peaceable but firm measures, the execution of laws which, if persisted in, must and would be resisted." Gerry, the Republican candidate, was chosen governor, and in his opening message, in June, denounced such doctrines as " seditious." The Legislature went further, and declared the holders of them " inceptive traitors " and " domestic partisans of a foreign power." Gerry removed them from office wherever they held by the tenure of the Executive will; and it was for this Jefferson had " given him glory " in the preceding letter to Dearborn.[3]

---

[1] A brief summary of these proofs will be found in APPENDIX No. 24.
[2] See Annals of Congress, by Gales and Seaton.
[3] The real spirit of Jefferson's remarks will be better understood after perusing a letter written by him not long afterwards (June 11th, 1812) to Gerry himself:
" What, then, does this English faction with you mean? Their newspapers say rebellion. and that they will not remain united with us unless we will permit them to govern the majority. If this be their purpose, their anti-republican spirit, it ought to be met at once. But a Government like ours should be slow in believing this, should put forth its whole might when necessary to suppress it, and promptly return to the paths of reconciliation. The extent of our country secures it, I hope, from the vindictive passions of the petty incorporations of Greece. . . . .
But I trust that such perverseness will not be that of the honest and well-meaning mass of the Federalists of Massachusetts; and that when the questions of separation and rebellion shall be nakedly proposed to them, the Gores and the Pickerings will find their

Mr. Jefferson had an attack of illness during the summer, and he thus described it and its effects in a letter to Dr. Rush, August 17th:

"I have had a long attack of rheumatism, without fever and without pain, while I keep myself still. A total prostration of the muscles of the back, hips and thighs, deprived me of the power of walking, and leaves it still in a very impaired state. A pain when I walk, seems to have fixed itself in the hip, and to threaten permanence. I take moderate rides, without much fatigue; but my journey to this place, in a hard-going gig, gave me great sufferings, which I expect will be renewed on my return as soon as I am able. The loss of the power of taking exercise would be a sore affliction to me. It has been the delight of my retirement to be in constant bodily activity, looking after my affairs. It was never damped as the pleasures of reading are, by the question of *cui bono!* for what object? I hope your health of body continues firm. Your works show that of your mind. The habits of exercise which your calling has given to both, will tend long to preserve them. The sedentary character of my public occupations sapped a constitution naturally sound and vigorous, and draws it to an earlier close. But it will still last quite as long as I wish it. There is a fullness of time when men should go, and not occupy too long the ground to which others have a right to advance. We must continue while here to exchange occasionally our mutual good wishes. I find friendship to be like wine, raw when new, ripened with age, the true old man's milk and restorative cordial. God bless you and preserve you through a long and healthy old age."

Like most other vigorous and healthy men, he was much inclined to consider his "constitution sapped" whenever he suffered temporarily under the effects of severe disease. His rheumatic malady had commenced about a month before writing the above. After a continuance of three weeks, it was so far abated, that he rode to Poplar Forest, from which the preceding letter was written. He went there for two objects—to escape the company at Monticello, and because he thought this period of forced inaction would afford an excellent opportunity to review his early mathematical studies. For the last, he had now, as he supposed, a special object, being determined to take upon himself the mathematical education of his oldest grandson. This scheme did not proceed far.

levees crowded with silk-stocking gentry, but no yeomanry; an army of officers without soldiers. I hope, then, all will still end well; the Anglomen will consent to make peace with their bread and butter, and you and I shall sink to rest, without having been actors or spectators in another civil war. . . . .
We have not timed these things well together, or we might have begun a re-alliance between Massachusetts and the Old Dominion, faithful companions in the war of Independence, peculiarly tallied in interests, by each wanting exactly what the other has to spare; and estranged to each other, in latter times, only by the practices of a third nation, the common enemy of both. Let us live only to see this re-union, and I will say with old Simeon, 'Lord, now lettest thou thy servant depart in peace, for mine eyes have seen thy salvation.' In that peace may you long remain, my friend, and depart only in the fullness of years, all passed in health and prosperity. God bless you."

He wrote to Rush that he had "forgotten much" of his mathematical knowledge—that he "recovered it with more difficulty than when in the vigor of his mind he originally acquired it"—that it was strange "that old men should not be sensible that their minds keep pace with their bodies in the progress of decay"—and he declared that had no other considerations impelled him to retire from the Presidency, "the fear of becoming a dotard, and of being insensible of it, would of itself have resisted all solicitations to remain."

These expressions sound like the vagaries of a sick man. Their tone was undoubtedly deepened by illness, but Mr. Jefferson was inclined, in certain moods of the mind, to this habit of self-depreciation. The impression that age was telling on his faculties, seems to have been persistent with him after his retirement from public life. But he had no such dread of its effects on others. Very little did he reason in that strain in his reply to the remonstrance against Judge Bishop's appointment as collector of New Haven. Very little did he act on that hypothesis in the deference he paid to the wisdom of the Wythes, the Pendletons, the Samuel Adamses, and the Dickinsons, when they were advanced a score of years beyond his own present age. His respect for the counsel of the aged was proverbial among his acquaintances.

The correspondence of 1812 opens with a most agreeable circumstance—a complete reconciliation between John Adams and Jefferson. Their common friend and old fellow-laborer in the Revolution, Dr. Rush, had written to Mr. Jefferson early in 1811, deploring the alienation. The latter, in reply, spoke most kindly of Mr. Adams and his public services, and declared that the present state of things had not continued "from the want of sincere desire and of effort" on his part to restore their ancient relations. He inclosed the correspondence between himself and Mrs. Adams in 1804, which he said had not before been communicated to any one, leaving his friend to decide whether the circumstances "admitted of a revival of friendly intercourse," and declaring that "he should certainly not be wanting in anything on his part which might second his [Rush's] efforts." The latter probably judged that Mr. Jefferson had made sufficient overtures, for here the subject appears to have dropped.

On the 5th of December, 1811, Mr. Jefferson again wrote to

Dr. Rush on the same subject. He said that "two of the Mr. Coles, his neighbors and friends, brothers of the one who lived with him as Secretary at Washington, took a tour to the northward during the last summer"[1]—that by the invitation of Mr. Adams, they passed a day with him at Braintree—that in a conversation with them on political subjects, he "adverted to the unprincipled licentiousness of the press against himself [Jefferson], adding, 'I always loved Jefferson, and still love him.'" "This," continued the latter, "is enough for me;" and he declared to Rush that he should only wait for an "apposite occasion to express to Mr. Adams his unchanged affections for him." He said that "from this fusion of mutual affections, Mrs. Adams was of course separated—it would only be necessary that he never name her."

One of the Messrs. Coles[2] has furnished us with recollections of his conversations with Mr. Adams on this occasion, and they will be found in Appendix.[3]

The interview appears to have led Mr. Adams also to determine to seek a reconciliation with his estranged friend, and he has the honor—no small one—of having made the first overture. A letter addressed to him by Jefferson, January 21st, 1812, thanks him "beforehand" for "the specimens of homespun" he had forwarded by post, and which were not yet arrived. This of course, implies that Mr. Adams had communicated the transmission of the articles in advance. Thenceforth their correspondence was free, at times frequent, and it was always marked on both sides by singular unreserve. There are more of Jefferson's subsequent letters to Adams in print than to any other one correspondent, and Adams not unfrequently overflowed with two or three letters to Jefferson's one. We shall have frequent occasion to refer to this correspondence—and, happily, to record another reconciliation which grew out of it.

A letter from Jefferson to Nelson, April 2d, 1812, shows that the former considered a speedy war with Great Britain

---

[1] The sentence here quoted (copied from the original by a member of Dr. Rush's family), is given in Randolph's and the Congress edition, with the omission of the name Coles, and also of the words "brothers of the one who lived with me as Secretary at Washington,"—which, without a name, would have designated the individuals.

[2] Hon. Edward Coles, now of Philadelphia, and several times before mentioned in this work.

[3] SEE APPENDIX, No. 25.

table, and he wrote to Mr. Maury in England on the same
ct on the 25th of the same month :

ur two countries are to be at war, but not you and I. And why should our
antries be at war, when by peace we can be so much more useful to one
r ? Surely the world will acquit our Government from having sought it.
before has there been an instance of a nation's bearing so much as we have
   Two items alone in our catalogue of wrongs will forever acquit us of being
gressors ; the impressment of our seamen, and the excluding us from the
   The first foundations of the social compact would be broken up, were we
ively to refuse to its members the protection of their persons and property,
n their lawful pursuits. I think the war will not be short, because the object
land, long obvious, is to claim the ocean as her domain, and to exact transit
from every vessel traversing it. This is the sum of her orders of council,
were only a step in this bold experiment, never meant to be retracted if it
be permanently maintained. And this object must continue her in war with
world. To this I see no termination, until her exaggerated efforts, so much
l her natural strength and resources, shall have exhausted her to bank-
."

n the 1st of June the President recommended a declaration
r against Great Britain, and it was declared on the 18th of
nonth. Jefferson wrote to Kosciusko on the 28th that "our
nt enemy would have the sea to herself, while we should
ually predominant at land, and should strip her of all her
ssions on this continent." His view of the kind of war
h it would be expedient for the United States to wage,
rs in the same letter :

he partisans of England here have endeavored much to goad us into the
f choosing the ocean instead of the land, for the theatre of war. That would
neet their strength with our own weakness, instead or their weakness with
ength. I hope we shall confine ourselves to the conquest of their posses-
nd defence of our harbors, leaving the war on the ocean to our privateers.
will immediately swarm in every sea, and do more injury to British com-
than the regular fleets of all Europe would do. The government of France
scontinue their license trade. Our privateers will furnish them much more
ntly with colonial produce, and whatever the license trade has given them.
lave apprehended we should be overwhelmed by the new improvements of
hich have not yet reached us. But the British possess them very imper-
and what are these improvements ? Chiefly in the management of artillery,
h our country admits little use. We have nothing to fear from their armies,
ill put nothing in prize to their fleets. Upon the whole, I have known no
tered into under more favorable auspices."

e wrote the President the next day, that " to continue the
opular, two things were necessary," to stop Indian barba-

rities, and to furnish markets for our produce. The first was to be obtained by the conquest of Canada, the other by protecting our coasting trade by " lining our coast with vessels of pilot-boat construction, filled with men, armed with carronades, and only so much larger as to assure the mastery of the pilot-boats," taken from us by the British, and kept as tenders to their larger vessels. It was these last, he contended, which had done the principal damage to our trade in the Revolution, and would do so again unless prevented by the same swift-sailing class of vessels, the construction of which he thought was unknown to the English. He wrote to Duane (now Colonel Duane), that "the acquisition of Canada this year as far as the neighborhood of Quebec, would be a mere matter of marching, and would give us experience for the attack of Halifax the next, and the final expulsion of England from the American Continent."

These anticipations may appear to have been without reasonable foundation, in view of the result. It may be asked what means we had to achieve the conquest of Canada? We at least had as good troops as that province then contained, and we had the overwhelming superiority of numbers. Mr. Jefferson's first letter (to Duane, October 1st), after General Hull's surrender, vigorously sketched the causes of our miscarriage, and pointed to those which would prevent us from again having equal chances of success:

"Whether the head of the War department[1] is equal to his charge, I am not qualified to decide. I knew him only as a pleasant, gentlemanly man in society; and the indecision of his character rather added to the amenity of his conversation. But when translated from the colloquial circle to the great stage of national concerns, and the direction of the extensive operations of war, whether he has been able to seize at one glance the long line of defenceless border presented by our enemy, the masses of strength which we hold on different points of it, the facility this gave us of attacking him, on the same day, on all his points, from the extremity of the lakes to the neighborhood of Quebec, and the perfect indifference with which this last place, impregnable as it is, might be left in the hands of the enemy to fall of itself; whether, I say, he could see and prepare vigorously for all this, or merely wrapped himself in the cloak of cold defence, I am uninformed.

*   *   *   *

"I fear that Hull's surrender has been more than the mere loss of a year to us. Besides bringing on us the whole mass of savage nations, whom fear and not affection had kept in quiet, there is danger that in giving time to an enemy who can send rein-

[1] William Eustis of Massachusetts, who resigned and was succeeded by General John Armstrong of New York, January 13th, 1813.

forcements of regulars faster than we can raise them, they may strengthen Canada and Halifax beyond the assailment of our lax and divided powers. Perhaps, however, the patriotic efforts from Kentucky and Ohio, by recalling the British force to its upper posts, may yet give time to Dearborn to strike a blow below. Effectual possession of the river from Montreal to the Chaudiere, which is practicable, would give us the upper country at our leisure, and close forever the scenes of the tomahawk and scalping-knife."

Mr. Jefferson this year increased his household manufactures of linens, cottons, and woollens, to the extent of supplying his own establishment with coarse articles; and he to some degree engaged in, and encouraged others to engage in, the breeding of sheep for wool growing purposes. The Batture case occupied a portion of his attention. His health was much better than in the preceding summer. The following hitherto unpublished letter gives a glimpse of his pecuniary affairs.

To John W. Eppes.

MONTICELLO, *June 5th*, 1812.

DEAR SIR :

I learnt accidentally, a day or two ago, that you were proposing to sell Pantops, and had offered it to some persons in this neighborhood. This is done, I have no doubt, after mature consideration, and under the view that it will be most beneficial to Francis, of whose interests no one can be a more faithful depository than yourself. Candor obliges me to say that an estate so closely and constantly under my eye could not pass out of the family without sentiments of regret, which would be renewed as often as the object should meet the eye. This induces me to request that I may have the refusal of it on the same terms on which you might be willing to sell it to others. These I understand to be on payments of considerable length, and this circumstance may bring it within my means. You know of the debt brought on me by my Washington residence. I have got through more than half of it, and confide that two years more will clear me of the residue. I could then, without inconvenience, begin to set apart annually, a portion of the price, so as to make sure of the whole in time. At ten dollars the acre, the price at which I am told it is offered, it would be a very safe purchase, if brought within the term in which I could accomplish it. Except indeed, that there is an event which we should all deprecate, but which may happen in opposition to all our prayers, and would transfer the reversionary inheritance without regard to any contract you or I could make. This should be contemplated beforehand to guard against the too heavy effects of an evicted title.

Peter Carr is enlarging the plan of his school, in which he expects the aid of Wood, whose superior qualifications in different branches of science are well known. It will unquestionably be the best situation in the State should you propose to place.Francis at any distance from you. Whatever my cares and attentions could add would be ensured by my tender affections for him, as well as my friendship for you. With my friendly respects to Mrs. Eppes, be assured of my constant attachment and respect to yourself.

TH. JEFFERSON.

When this letter was written, war prices were anticipated for the finest crops which had been harvested for a series of years; the blockade of the Chesapeake was an event which no one was looking for; the stream of company to Monticello had not reached flood tide; and altogether the aspect of things was calculated to foster impressions which were to prove most delusive. We are inclined to think that when Mr. Jefferson speaks of having extinguished half his Washington debt, he did not keep sufficiently in view smaller ones incurred for current expenditures which he had reason to expect would be met, from time to time, by current receipts.

He was importuned from several quarters to become a candidate for the Presidency in 1812. Some thought he would conduct the war with more energy than Madison; others were apprehensive that the latter might be defeated in his reëlection by a combination of his Republican opponents and the Federalists. A written specimen of Jefferson's way of answering such overtures will be found in a letter from him to Thomas C. Flournoy, dated October 1st, 1812.[1] We quote a few sentences:

"You probably do not know Mr. Madison personally, or at least intimately, as I do. I have known him from 1779, when he first came into the public councils, and, from three and thirty years trial, I can say conscientiously that I do not know in the world a man of purer integrity, more dispassionate, disinterested, and devoted to genuine Republicanism; nor could I in the whole scope of America and Europe point out an abler head. He may be illy seconded by others, betrayed by the Hulls and Arnolds of our country, for such there are in every country, and with sorrow and suffering we know it. But what man can do will be done by Mr. Madison. I hope, therefore, there will be no difference among Republicans as to his reëlection, and we shall know his value when we have to give him up, and to look at large for his successor."

We have to record a more singular proposition to the ex-President, made after the warlike disasters of 1812. This was, that he become Secretary of State in Mr. Madison's Cabinet instead of Monroe, the latter taking the place of Eustis in the War department. This would have formed a Cabinet which would indeed have commanded the confidence of the nation, and demolished all the chances of success which Mr. Madison's competitor could have possessed. It is hardly probable, however, that the latter consideration entered seriously into the

[1] Congress edition, vol. vi. p. 82. It is not given in Randolph's edition.

objects of this proposal, for Madison's election could not reasonably-have been considered doubtful. Jefferson's reply will be found in a letter to Colonel Duane, dated, October 1st. He declared, "he possessed so much of the Roman principle, as to deem it honorable for the general of yesterday to act as corporal to-day, if his services could be useful to his country ; holding that to be false pride which postponed the public good to any private or personal considerations." But he said, "the hand of age was upon him, that the decay of bodily faculties apprised him that those of the mind could not be unimpaired, had he not still better proofs." He added much more in the same strain.

The most remarkable part of the affair remains to be told. Mr. Madison actually proposed this arrangement to Mr. Jefferson.[1] Whether he did so, merely to meet the wishes of friends, or in the expectation of a possible acceptance of the offer, we have no means of knowing, but there is probably little doubt that the former was his motive.

The second session of the twelfth Congress opened, November 2d, 1812, under rather gloomy auspices. The American navy had already covered itself with imperishable glory by a series of such exploits as the masterly escape of the Constitution from the fleet of Commodore Broke, the capture of the Guerriere by the former vessel, of the Alert by the Essex, of the Frolic by the Wasp, of the Macedonian by the United States; and before the close of the year, though not until after the meeting of Congress, of the Java by the United States. On the other hand, a series of abortive attempts and disasters, alleviated only by occasional gleams of success, had been the result of our efforts on land.

Party excitement in and out of Congress was intense. Some of the Federal leaders and newspapers, particularly in New England, had encouraged Great Britain to persist in her orders in council, by tauntingly declaring that our government had no idea of war; that it kept up irritations merely for party purposes; that it did not dare in reality to open hostilities. When war was declared, the same partisans denounced it as unnecessary, unjust, and undertaken from the most criminal motives. To complaints were soon added open threats of disunion. None

[1] We have this on the authority of an intimate friend of Mr. Madison, now living, who heard the fact from his own lips.

earlier or more eagerly urged the latter alternative than a portion of the "pulpit politicians" of Massachusetts.[1]

We have seen the declaration of Quincy, the New England
Federal leader in Congress, that the Government could not be
" kicked into a war." In a debate in the same body, January
5th, 1813, on a bill to add twenty thousand men to the existing
army establishment, Mr. Quincy said:

"I desire, therefore, that it may be distinctly understood, both by this House and

[1] E. g. The Boston Repertory, in an article (January 9th, 1810) under the caption
"Smoke! Smoke!" exclaimed: "Will our Administration never be understood? Shall
we forever be the dupes of a contemptible farce, which has been exhibiting for years to
make people wonder and stare? My life on it, our Executive have no more idea of
declaring war than my grandmother." The Repertory declared (April 18th, 1810):
"Our Government will not make war on Great Britain, but will keep up a constant irritation on some pretence or other, for the sake of maintaining influence as a party."
The same paper said (Dec. 24th, 1811): "We are firmly persuaded that the majority
in Congress do not mean to declare war at present, that they dare not; and that all their
threats are but contemptible vaporing," etc. The Philadelphia Gazette (January 10th,
1812), in speaking of the proposed war, and of the Republicans in Congress, said:
"They shrink from it." . . . "They are frightened as the aspect becomes a
little serious, and wish to go home and think about it." The Baltimore Federal
Gazette said: "If you think a vote to raise 25,000 men looks like a war, quiet your
apprehensions. You do not understand what is here called management. There will,
as I believe, be no war. The war-whoop, the orders in council, the non-importation, the
Presidential caucusing, will vanish before summer." Such extracts might be indefinitely multiplied, and we will turn now to the pulpit.
Rev. David Osgood, D.D., pastor of the church at Medford, Massachusetts, in a discourse delivered April 10th, 1810, and subsequently printed, said: "The strong prepossessions of so great a portion of my fellow citizens, in favor of a race of demons, and
against a nation of more religion, virtue, good faith, generosity, and beneficence, than
any that now is, or ever has been upon the face of the earth, wring my soul with
anguish, and fill my heart with apprehensions and terror of the judgments of heaven
upon this sinful people." . . . In a printed discourse of the same gentleman, delivered June 27th, 1812, occur the following, among other equally virulent declarations:
"If, at the command of weak or wicked rulers, they undertake an unjust war; each man
who volunteers his services in such a cause, or loans his money for its support, or by his
conversation, his writings, or any other mode of influence encourages its prosecution,
that man is an accomplice in the wickedness, loads his conscience with the blackest
crimes, brings the guilt of blood upon his soul, and in the sight of God and His law is a
murderer." "My mind has been in a constant agony, not so much at the inevitable loss
of our temporal prosperity and happiness, and the complicated miseries of war, as at its
guilt, its outrages against heaven, against all truth, honesty justice, goodness—against
all the principles of social happiness." "Were not the authors of this war in character
nearly akin to the deists and atheists of France; were they not men of hardened hearts,
seared consciences, reprobate minds, and desperate wickedness, it seems utterly incon-
ceivable that they should have made the declaration." "One hope only remains, that
this last stroke of perfidy may open the eyes of a besotted people; that they may awake
like a giant from his slumbers, and wreak their vengeance on their betrayers, by driving
them from their stations, and placing at the helm more skillful and faithful hands." "If,
at the present moment, no symptoms of civil war appear, they certainly will soon, unless
the courage of the war-party should fail them." "A civil war becomes as certain as
the events that happen according to the known laws and established course of nature."
In a published discourse of the Rev. J. S. J. Gardiner, A.M., rector of Trinity Church,
Boston, delivered April 9th, 1812, occur, among many similar ones, the following
expressions: "It is a war unexampled in the history of the world: wantonly proclaimed
on the most frivolous and groundless pretences, against a nation from whose friendship we might derive the most signal advantages, and from whose hostility we have
reason to dread the most tremendous losses." "Every provocation has been offered to
Great Britain on our part, and our resentment has risen in proportion as she has shewn
a conciliating spirit." "What consequence is it to you if they be repealed, if you are
sold to Napoleon, as you have reason to believe, by the slaves who have abused your
confidence." "Let no considerations whatever, my brethren, deter you at all times, and

this nation, that it is my unequivocal belief that the invasion of Canada, which is avowed by the Cabinet to be its purpose, is intended by it, that continuance of the war and not peace is its object. . . . . I say, then, sir, that I consider the invasion of Canada, as a means of carrying on this war, as cruel, wanton, senseless, and wicked. . . . . Never was there an invasion of any country worse than this, in point of moral principle, since the invasion of the West Indies by the Buccaneers, or that of the United States by Captain Kidd. Indeed both Kidd and the Buccaneers had more apology for their deed than the American Cabinet. . . . . When in the usual course of Divine Providence, who punishes nations as well as individuals, His destroying angel shall on this account pass over this country—and sooner or later, pass it will—I may be permitted to hope that over New England his hand will be stayed. Our souls are not steeped in the blood which has been shed in this war. The spirits of the unhappy men who have been sent to an untimely audit, have borne to the bar of divine justice no accusations against us. . . . . I say, then, sir, without hesitation, that in my judgment the embarrassments of our relations with Great Britain, and keeping alive between this country and that a root of bitterness has been, is, and will continue to be, a main principle of the policy of this American Cabinet. They want not a solid settlement of our differences. . . . . The men who now, and who for these twelve years past, have, to the misfortune of this country, guided its councils and directed its destinies, came into power on a tide which was raised and supported by elements constituted of British prejudices and British antipathies. . . . . The transfer of power was effected undeniably, principally on the very ground of those prejudices and antipathies which existed in the nation against Great Britain, and which had been artfully fomented by the men now in power and their adherents, and directed against their predecessors. These prejudices and passions constitute the main pillar of the power of these men. In my opinion, they will never permit it to be wholly taken away from them."

He said he knew " that while he uttered these things, a thousand tongues and a thousand pens were preparing without doors to overwhelm him, if possible, in their pestiferous gall." But he added :

" It is not for such a man [as himself] to hesitate or swerve a hair's breadth from his country's purpose and true interests, because of the yelpings, the howlings, and snarlings of that hungry pack which corrupt men keep directly or indirectly in pay, with the view of hunting down every man who dare develop their purposes ; a pack composed, it is true, of some native curs, but for the most part of hounds and spaniels of very recent importation, whose backs are seared by the lash, and whose necks are sore with the collars of their former masters." [1]

in all places, from execrating the present war." "As Mr. Madison has declared war, let Mr. Madison carry it on." "The Union has been long since virtually dissolved, and it is full time that this part of the disunited States should take care of itself." In a discourse delivered July 23d, the same year, Mr. Gardiner said: "The alternative then is, that if you do not wish to become the slaves of those who own slaves, and who are themselves the slaves of French slaves, you must either, in the language of the day, cut the connexion, or so far alter the national compact as to insure yourselves a due share in the government." These extracts, in the substance, might be increased without limit: though such violences of mere language were not perhaps common.

[1] Much more was added in the same strain and with equal violence of temper. He broadly intimated that Monroe was to be appointed to command the army for the

Tallmadge of Connecticut was convinced from the "prophesies" that God was pouring the full vials of his wrath upon the nations—that "the people of Great Britain had been exerting themselves to spread the knowledge and influence of that religion which alone could remove the malady and heal the nations"—and he wished to know if "these fair and happy prospects should be checked and perhaps blasted forever by this unhappy war?"—if it was "unworthy the legislators of a Christian people to reflect that they were now waging an offensive war, and one which in its consequences might be found to be directed against Him who was the God of armies?" He said, "when he reflected on these awful and solemn events, he could not but weep for his infatuated country, and if he had an angel's voice, he would call on every rational creature in these United States and entreat them to pause and consider before our country's doom should be forever sealed." Wheaton of Massachusetts closed a speech with the declaration that "his soul sickened at the thought of progressing in this war."

Mr. Clay, then speaker, rose to reply to these various assaults, January 8th, 1813. He was so feeble from recent illness that he was compelled to sit down before closing his remarks, and to defer their conclusion until the next day. We have space only for those in which he depicted the conduct of the opposition, and in which he replied to Quincy's attack on Mr. Jefferson and his Administration. Mr. Clay said:

"If gentlemen would only reserve for their own Government, half the sensibility which is indulged for that of Great Britain, they would find much less to condemn. Restriction after restriction has been tried; negotiation has been resorted to, until further negotiation would have been disgraceful. Whilst these peaceful experiments are undergoing a trial, what is the conduct of the opposition? They are the champions of war—the proud, the spirited, the sole repository of the nation's honor—the men of exclusive vigor and energy. The Administration, on the contrary, is weak, feeble, and pusillanimous—'incapable of being kicked into a war.'

conquest of Canada, and that after three or four years he was to return at the head of his forces, a candidate for the Presidency. He added: "And whoever is candidate for the Presidency, with an army of thirty thousand veterans at his heels, will not be likely to be troubled with rivals, or to concern himself about votes. A president elected under such auspices, may be nominally a president for years; but really, if he pleases, a president for life."

Mr. Quincy again and again, during his speech, spoke of the "wise, moral, reflecting people," "the wise and thoughtful people of" New England, etc., etc. He spoke of the Federalists as comprising "almost all the moral sense and nine-tenths of the intelligence" of New England. He characterized the New England Republicans "as toads and reptiles which spread their slime in the drawing-room." In the corrected report of his speech he, however, struck out this last sentence. (See Annals of Congress, 12th Congress, 2d session, p. 600.)

The maxim, 'not a cent for tribute, millions for defence,' is loudly proclaimed. Is the Administration for negotiation? The opposition is tired, sick, disgusted with negotiation. They want to draw the sword and avenge the nation's wrongs. When, however, foreign nations, perhaps emboldened by the very opposition here made, refuse to listen to the amicable appeals which have been repeated and reiterated by the Administration, to their justice and to their interest—when, in fact, war with one of them has become identified with our independence and our sovereignty, and to abstain from it was no longer possible, behold the opposition veering round and becoming the friends of peace and commerce. They tell you of the calamities of war, its tragical events, the squandering away of your resources, the waste of the public treasure, and the spilling of innocent blood. 'Gorgons, hydras, and chimeras dire.' They tell you that honor is an illusion! Now, we see them exhibiting the terrific forms of the roaring king of the forest. Now, the meekness and humility of the lamb! They are for war and no restrictions, when the Administration is for peace. They are for peace and restrictions, when the Administration is for war. You find them, sir, tacking with every gale, displaying the colors of every party, and of all nations, steady only in one unalterable purpose—to steer, if possible, into the haven of power.

"During all this time, the parasites of opposition do not fail, by cunning sarcasm, or sly innuendo, to throw out the idea of French influence, which is known to be false, which ought to be met in one manner only, and that by the lie direct.

* * * * * *

"Yet, preposterous and ridiculous as the insinuation is, it is propagated with so much industry, that there are persons found foolish and credulous enough to believe it. You will, no doubt, think it incredible (but I have, nevertheless, been told it is a fact), that an honorable member of this House, now in my eye, recently lost his election by the circulation of a silly story in his district, that he was the first cousin of the Emperor Napoleon. The proof of the charge rested on the statement of facts, which was undoubtedly true. The gentleman in question, it was alleged, had married a connection of the lady of the President of the United States, who was the intimate friend of Thomas Jefferson, late President of the United States, who some years ago, was in the habit of wearing red French breeches. Now, taking these premises as established, you, Mr. Chairman, are too good a logician not to see that the conclusion necessarily follows!

* * * * * *

"Next to the notice which the opposition has found itself called upon to bestow upon the French Emperor, a distinguished citizen of Virginia, formerly President of the United States, has never for a moment failed to receive their kindest and most respectful attention. An honorable member from Massachusetts (Mr. Quincy), of whom I am sorry to say it becomes necessary for me, in the course of my remarks, to take some notice, has alluded to him in a remarkable manner. Neither his retirement from public office, his eminent services, nor his advanced age, can exempt this patriot from the coarse assaults of party malevolence. No, sir! in 1801, he snatched from the rude hand of usurpation the violated constitution of his country, and that is his crime. He preserved that instrument in form, and substance, and spirit, a precious inheritance for generations to come, and for this he can never be forgiven. How vain and impotent is party rage, directed against such a man! He is not more elevated by his lofty residence, upon the summit of his own favorite mountain, than he is lifted by the serenity of his mind and the consciousness of a well-spent life, above the malignant passions and bitter feelings of the day. No! his own beloved Monticello is not more moved by the storms that beat against its sides, than is this illustrious man by the howlings of the whole British pack, set loose from the Essex kennel! When the gentleman to whom I have been compelled to allude, shall have mingled his dust with that of his abused ancestors; when he shall have been consigned to oblivion, or if he lives at all, shall live only in the treasonable annals of a certain junto, the name of Jefferson will be hailed with gratitude, his memory honored and cherished as the second founder of the liberties of the people, and the period of his Administration will be looked back to as one of the happiest and brightest epochs of American history—an oasis in the midst of a sandy desert. But I beg the gentleman's pardon; he has indeed secured to himself a more imperishable fame than I had supposed; I think it was about four years ago that he submitted to the House of Representatives, an initiative proposition for an impeachment of Mr. Jefferson. The House condescended to consider it. The gentleman debated it with his usual *temper, moderation,* and *urbanity.* The House decided upon it in the most solemn manner, and although the gentleman had somehow obtained a second, the final vote stood, one for, and one hundred and seventeen against the proposition!"

It was in the same speech that Mr. Clay, after quoting Quincy's former sentiment uttered on the floor of the House in favor of disunion, " peaceably if we can, forcibly if we must," and after declaring his conviction that " no man, who had paid any attention to the tone of certain prints, and to transactions in a particular quarter of the Union [New England] for several years past, could doubt the existence of such a plot " (" the dismemberment of the Union "), closed his retort in this strain: " But I will quit this unpleasant subject; I will turn from one whom no sense of decency or propriety could restrain from soiling the carpet on which he treads, to gentlemen who have not forgotten what is due to themselves, to the place in which we are assembled, or to those by whom they are opposed."

Having given some illustration of the spirit of parties, continuous details must be left to professed history.

Mr. Madison was rechosen to the Presidency in 1812, receiving one hundred and twenty-eight electoral votes to eighty-nine cast for DeWitt Clinton. Elbridge Gerry received one hundred and thirty-one electoral votes for the Vice-Presidency to eighty-six cast for Jared Ingersoll.

The war on land, during 1813, without being as unfortunate as that of the preceding year, was far from being successful in its results. At sea we lost no credit for good conduct—but it required the crowning victory of Lake Erie to give us a decided preponderance of success in naval actions. And all had been made aware, if the fact needed any demonstration, that our navy

ould give no adequate protection to our sea-board. The Dela-
rare and Chesapeake bays were closely blockaded early in the
·ear, at once paralyzing the commerce which had flowed
hrough those great avenues of trade. If the principal ports of
Vew England were left open, it was to repay and foster the
upposed English partialities of a disaffected faction of its
·eople, and not from the want of naval strength in our enemy.

Mr Jefferson's views in regard to the progress of the war
ippear in various letters during the year. The following,
uddressed to General Bailey, February 6th, presents a sufficient
:xample of them:

"Our first entrance on them [the events of the war] has been peculiarly inaus-
·icious. Our men are good, but force without conduct is easily baffled. The
Creator has not thought proper to mark those in the forehead who are of stuff to
make good generals. We are first, therefore, to seek them, blindfold, and then let
them learn the trade at the expense of great losses. But our turn of success will
:ome by and by, and we must submit to the previous misfortunes which are to be
the price of it. I think with you on the subject of privateers. Our ships of force
·ill undoubtedly be blockaded by the enemy, and we shall have no means of annoy-
ng them at sea but by small, swift-sailing vessels; these will be better managed
und more multiplied in the hands of individuals than of the government. In short,
:hey are our true and only weapon in a war against Great Britain, when once Canada
und Nova Scotia shall have been rescued from them. The opposition to them in
:ongress is merely partial. It is a part of the navy fever, and proceeds from the
lesire of securing men for the public ships, by suppressing all other employments
·rom them. But I do not apprehend that this ill-judged principle is that of a
najority of Congress. I hope, on the contrary, they will spare no encouragement
o that kind of enterprise. Our public ships, to be sure, have done wonders. They
nave saved our military reputation sacrificed on the shores of Canada; but in point
·f real injury and depredation on the enemy, our privateers without question have
·een most effectual. Both species of force have their peculiar value." [1]

We find him making several practical suggestions to the
President and Secretary of State. He proposed forming a
classified and better armed and disciplined militia from the

[1] There was a good reason why our navy so much excelled the conduct of our land
troops for at least the two first years of the war. The latter were, at the opening of the
struggle, a rural militia, and most of their officers knew no more of the art of war, than
was to be learned at semi-annual militia musters and picked out of military treatises—
ibout as good a preparation for actual war as would be wading in water knee deep, and
reading treatises on swimming, to prepare a novice in that art to keep afloat in a rough sea.
England herself has recently learned in the Crimea that even the best drilled soldiers not
reasoned by actual service, cut but a sorry figure beside such troops as the French
Zouaves fresh from the fields of Algeria.
Our navy labored under no such disadvantages. It had but recently gone through
the school and the glorious experiences of the Barbary war. Our officers had been
weeded by trial, and those fitted for great commanders were legibly "marked in the
forehead." And never had more been "marked" within so limited a space and scale
of operations!

young men of the country. He recommended employing gun-boats in the Chesapeake, and cutting a canal from Lynhaven river to the east branch of the Elizabeth for their retreat. He suggested keeping our navy together in fleets in fortified harbors, for the purpose of compelling the enemy to also keep together in large fleets, and thus lose the ability to block up every harbor and river, and cut off our entire coasting trade by scattered cruisers. This was the maritime policy of the Revolution—but on reading Monroe's answer to his suggestions, Mr. Jefferson became satisfied that it was not adapted to existing circumstances.

The public movements and avowals in New England pointing towards insurrection or disunion, drew out an expression from him, in a letter to James Martin, September 20th, in which he seemed to favor the idea that it would be well to " solemnly put the question " to those States, whether they would remain in the Union, in obedience to the laws, or leave it? He had no doubt that a majority of their people would decide to remain.

The anti-war excitement in New England had gone on rapidly increasing since the demonstrations already recorded. On the 15th of June (1813), Josiah Quincy, who was now out of Congress, and a member of the Massachusetts Senate, reported a preamble and resolution in the latter body adverse to passing a vote of thanks to Captain Lawrence for the capture of the Peacock. The preamble set forth that former resolutions of this kind had " given great discontent to many of the good people of the commonwealth, it being considered by them as an encouragement and excitement to the continuance of the present unjust, unnecessary and iniquitous war;" that the Senate had a high sense of the " naval skill and military and civil virtues of Capt. James Lawrence," and were "withheld from acting on said proposition solely from considerations relative to the nature and principles of the present war;" and " to the end that all misapprehension on this subject might be obviated," the following resolution was offered :

" *Resolved*, as the sense of the Senate of Massachusetts, that, in a war like the present, waged without justifiable cause, and prosecuted in a manner which indicates that conquest and ambition are its real motives, it is not becoming a moral and religious people to express any approbation of military or naval exploits which are not immediately connected with the defence of our seacoast and soil."

The preamble and resolution were adopted, and remained on the journals of the Massachusetts Senate nearly eleven years, when they were expunged by the order of that body.   Fifteen days before their adoption, Lawrence had sailed from Boston roads in the unlucky frigate Chesapeake, to meet the Shannon. The Chesapeake was captured. The naval historian, Cooper, says, that at the close of the action, "both ships were charnel-houses."   Lawrence fell mortally wounded, using an exclamation which has become a household word among Americans— "Don't give up the ship."

The Massachusetts Senate was doubtless unapprised of this catastrophe, at the time of its action just mentioned. But neither it, nor the governor, nor council, nor the prominent Federalists of Boston, were unapprised of the time when the mangled corpses of Lawrence and his first-lieutenant, Ludlow, were borne back from Halifax for funeral rites and interment. They did not attend his funeral, and a Federal newspaper of Boston, to deter its partisans from being present, threw out the innuendo that the ceremonies to be observed on the occasion were political in their object.[1]

On the 26th of June, Quincy, from a joint committee of both houses of the Massachusetts Legislature, presented a report and resolutions, declaring that the admission of States "not comprehended within the original limits of the United States," was unauthorized by the letter "or the spirit" of the Constitution, and that "it was the interest and duty of the people of Massachusetts to oppose the admission of such States into the Union, as a measure tending to the dissolution of the confederacy." The report and resolutions were adopted.

On the 15th of July a remonstrance was agreed to by the same Legislature, denouncing the continuance of the war after the repeal of the British orders in council, as improper and impolitic, because it exhibited distrust of the good faith of England, and countenanced the imputation of coöperation with France—which would tend to stir up the entire British people against us. It denounced the war as unjust, because we had not removed proper causes of complaint by providing against

---

[1] The Boston Advertiser asked: "What honor can be paid where a Crowninshield is chief mourner and a Story chief priest?" Capt. G. Crowninshield had gone at his own expense in a cartel to Halifax. and brought back the bodies. Joseph Story. Associate Justice of the U. S. Supreme Court, was to deliver the funeral oration at Salem.

employing British seamen—and because we had not exhausted negotiation on the subject of impressment. "Under such circumstances," said this remarkable paper, "silence towards the Government would be treachery to the people." The Legislature concluded with an appeal to "the Searcher of all hearts," to attest "the purity of their motives!"

If this document meant to assert that we had not offered to make any reasonable arrangements to prevent the employment of British seamen, provided England would cease to impress ours, it asserted a palpable and gross untruth. And what terms are fit to characterize a declaration, coming from men of common information, that we had not fairly exhausted negotiation?[1]

The eastern ultra-Federalists were in the habit of asserting at this period that the number of impressments had been very small. A committee of the Massachusetts Legislature actually reported to that body that the number of impressed citizens of that State on board of British public vessels, at the opening of the war, was only eleven. General credit was ostensibly given to the declaration made by Pickering in his letter to Governor Sullivan in 1808, that Great Britain only "desired to obtain her own subjects," that "the evil we complained of arose from the impossibility of always distinguishing the persons of the two nations." The best information which could be obtained placed the number of impressments of American citizens prior to the declaration of war, as high at least as six thousand; and the accuracy of the report of the Massachusetts Legislative Committee can therefore be readily estimated. Mr. Pickering's assertions corresponded as little with known facts as they did with his own official declarations when he was Secretary of State.[2]

---

[1] Not a President, not a Secretary of State, not an American minister in England since the formation of our government, had omitted to earnestly remonstrate against impressment, and urge a fair and pacific settlement of the question. Our appeals were utterly disregarded. When the practice had recently led to an outrage on one of our national vessels which England herself did not pretend to justify, she haughtily refused to allow any negotiations for the removal of the cause of the offence to be connected with the subject of reparation. She defiantly chose this period to legalize and extend the practice, by a royal proclamation. And finally, after more than twenty years of attempted negotiation on our part, she formally refused to treat with us further on the topic, and at the same time continued impressments on the broadest and most fraudulent scale. See next note.

[2] In Pickering's instructions to Rufus King, Minister at the Court of London, June 8th, 1796, he said: "The long but fruitless attempts that have been made to protect American seamen from British impresses, prove that the subject is in its nature difficult. . . . But there is another cogent reason for an exemption from impresses in the British colonies —that the practice will be, as it has always been, subject to monstrous abuses; and the supreme power is so remote that the evils become irremediable before redress can even be sought for." He officially wrote Mr. King, September 10th, 1796: "For the

It is not here asserted that the better class of New England
Federalists either engaged in, or directly advocated the propriety

British Government, then, to make professions of respect to the rights of our citizens and
willingness to release them, and yet deny the only means of ascertaining those rights, is an
insulting tantalism." He officially reported to Congress, December 9th, 1799 : " Admiral
Parker paid no attention to the agent's application on behalf of our impressed seamen ;
the admiral having determined, and informed the agent of the determination, that no
proofs would be regarded by him, unless specially presented by the American Government through the British minister ; nor then but in the single case of native Americans.
Under this determination there will be detained, not only the subjects of his Britannic
Majesty, naturalized since the peace of 1783, but all who, born elsewhere, were then resi-
dent in, and had become citizens of the United States ; also, all foreigners, as Germans,
Swedes, Danes, Portuguese, and Italians, who voluntarily serve in the vessels of the
United States. And it is a fact that such foreigners have frequently been impressed ;
although their languages and other circumstances demonstrate that they were not
British subjects."
   We could readily select many other equivalent declarations from the official dispatches and reports of Pickering.
   Rufus King, our minister to England, is accused in no quarter of having entertained
unreasonable prejudices against that government. He officially wrote Pickering, April
13th, 1797, that since the preceding July he had applied for the discharge of two hundred and seventy-one impressed seamen who, as Americans, had claimed his interference—that the admiralty had ordered eighty-six of them to be discharged, had
detained thirty-seven as British subjects or as " American volunteers," and in regard
to the remaining one hundred and forty-eight, made no answer, " the ships on board of
which these seamen were detained having in many instances sailed before an examination was made, in consequence of his application." And King further declared : " It is
certain that some of those who have applied to me are not American citizens, but the
exceptions are in my opinion few ; and the evidence, exclusive of certificates, has been
such, as in most cases to satisfy me that the applicants were real Americans, who had
been forced into the British service ; and who, with singular constancy have generally
persevered in refusing pay and bounty, though in many instances they have been in the
service more than two years." King wrote home to the Secretary of State, March 15th,
1799, " that not only seamen who spoke the English language, and who were evidently
English or American subjects, but also all Danish, Swedish. and other foreign seamen,
who could not receive American protections, were indiscriminately taken from their
voluntary service in our neutral employ and forced into the war, in the naval service
of Great Britain." Silas Talbot, American agent in the West Indies, for the relief of
impressed seamen, wrote Pickering, July 4th, 1797, that Captain Otway, of the British
frigate Ceres, ordered American seamen to be brought to the gangway and whipped for
writing to their agent to get them discharged."
   Marshall's complaints when Secretary of State were as pointed and as criminatory
towards the British Government as Pickering's—and we need not say that the same was
true of all the Republican Secretaries of State.
   We could present the resolutions passed by the merchants of nearly all the principal
American cities, at different periods, specially denouncing the gross and abusive
impressment of our seamen by England. A Federal meeting held in the city of New
York, April 26th, 1806, appointed a committee, two of whom were Rufus King and
Oliver Wolcott, to report resolutions on the subject. The resolutions declare among
other things, " that the suffering foreign armed ships to station themselves off our
harbor, and there to stop, search, and capture our vessels—to impress, wound, and murder our citizens, is a gross and criminal neglect of the highest duties of Government, and
that an Administration which patiently permits the same is not entitled to the confidence
of a brave and free people." The resolutions passed unanimously.
   Commodore Rogers forwarded to the Secretary of the Navy (January 14th, 1813),
the muster books of the Moselle and Sappho captured by him, by which it appeared that
about an eighth of their seamen—that is to say, between thirty and forty—were
impressed Americans ; and Rogers remarked : " It will appear . . . if there is only
a quarter part of that proportion on board their other vessels, that they have an infinitely
greater number of Americans in their service than any American has yet had an idea
of." Ten Americans were found on board of the Guerriere—and Captain Dacre declared
to the court martial which afterwards tried him, that " what considerably weakened his
quarters, was permitting the Americans belonging to the ship to quit their quarters "
when the Constitution hoisted her colors ; and he manfully added, " that though it
deprived him of the men, he thought it was his duty."
   Impressments were often, in all cases where resistance was attempted, conducted
with unsparing severity. But even where nothing but bold remonstrance was interposed, the cutlass and club were freely resorted to. Those who refused to go on duty

of smuggling or furnishing supplies to the enemy. But some of them publicly held a line of argument which was well calculated to teach baser men that such offences were venial under existing circumstances; and it is certain that those practices were

were scourged, placed in irons, brought up again and scourged on the raw wounds of past whippings, until they succumbed. Their American protections in many instances were torn up before their eyes. At their pretended examinations, when taken on board British ships, commanders often treated their statements with brutal levity, affecting not to hear a portion of what they said, or turning it off with a joke, that showed that they made no pretensions to justice. Sometimes wretches whom everybody on board knew had never seen the prisoner before, would emerge from the press-gang and say: "Sir, I know this fellow. He was a schoolmate of mine. Tom, you know well enough, so don't sham Yankee any more." We cannot encumber these pages with the special proofs of the preceding statements, but every one of them rests on the affidavits of American seamen of known and unquestionable character—and some of them were sworn to in different instances by a number of such witnesses. The tearing up of protections and the whippings were pretty uniform circumstances among the petty British commanders. The scene of the captain affecting not to hear, the press-gang witness, etc., took place on board the Ceres.

To show that the most positive testimony of American citizenship was treated with contempt, not only by petty military officials, but that it (as we have understood, Mr. King already to intimate), met with intentional neglect and evasion from the highest British tribunals having cognizance of the subject, we are induced to give the particulars of a case—not because it presents more striking features than others, but because we chance to know near relatives of the impressed man, and therefore have a moral personal certainty on the question of his nativity; and because we possess a sad and illustrative sequel of the affair, not, so far as we know, hitherto made public. Hiram Thayer was born in the town of Greenwich, Connecticut. A letter from Commodore Decatur to the Secretary of the Navy, dated New London, March 18th, 1814, stated the following facts: That Thayer was impressed in 1803, and when the British ship Statira was put in commission, about 1808, he was transferred to her. Gen. Lyman, the American consul at London, had applied to the Lords Commissioners for his discharge in vain. A certificate of his nativity from the selectmen, town clerk, and minister of Greenwich were forwarded to Mitchell, the resident agent for American prisoners at Halifax; but still he was not released. He wrote to his father that on representing his case to Captain Stackpole of the Statira the latter told him if he refused to fight his countrymen "he should be tied to the mast and shot at like a dog." The Statira was one of the blockading squadron off New London in 1814, and on the 14th of March, Decatur sent off John Thayer, the father, with a flag, to ask the release of his son, and carrying a note to Captain Capel from Decatur, saying "that he felt persuaded that the application of the father, furnished as he was, with conclusive evidence of the nativity and identity of his son, would induce an immediate order for his discharge." "The son," says Decatur, "descried his father at a distance in the boat, and told the lieutenant of the Statira, it was his father," and he adds: "I understand the feelings manifested by the old man on receiving the hand of his son, proved beyond all other evidence the property he had in him. There was not a doubt left on the mind of a single British officer of Hiram Thayer's being an American citizen. And yet he is detained, not a prisoner of war, but compelled under the most cruel threats, to serve the enemies of his country." Thayer "had so recommended himself by his sobriety, industry, and seamanship," as to be appointed a boatswain's mate: two hundred and fifty pounds sterling were then due him—but he refused to receive any bounty, or advance, lest it might afford some pretext for denying him his discharge when a proper application should be made for it. Captain Capel "regretted it was not in his power to comply with" Decatur's "request;" but he said he would "forward his application to the commander-in-chief by the earliest opportunity, and he had do doubt he would order his immediate discharge."

Here, we believe published accounts drop the story of Hiram Thayer. We knew an uncle of his, who was a member of the New York Legislature in 1845, and also other members of his family. The uncle wrote a letter for our inspection in which he states that Hiram Thayer was not discharged until some time after the close of the war—that he then wrote to his father that he should be home at a specified time—that the father proceeded to the port to which he was to return—that when the ship arrived in which he was expected, the unfortunate father was informed that his son had fallen overboard and perished—that a trunk and some clothing bearing the name of his son were delivered to him, etc.

carried to an enormous extent by persons who had property and commercial connections sufficient to render it practicable. Lowel, in his contemporaneously published "Road to Ruin," said:

"*Encouraged and protected from infamy by the just odium against the war,* they engage in lawless speculations, sneer at the restraints of conscience, laugh at perjury, mock at legal restraints, and acquire an ill-gotten wealth at the expense of public morals, and of the more sober, conscientious parts of the community. . . .

"Administration hirelings may revile the northern States, and the merchants generally, for this monstrous depravation of morals, this execrable course of smuggling and fraud. But there is a just God, who knows how to trace the causes of human events, and He will assuredly visit upon the authors of this war all the iniquities of which it has been the occasion. If the guilty deserve our scorn or our pity, the tempters and seducers deserve our execration."

A sheriff's officer in New Hampshire, recovered a letter (dated August 16th, 1813) signed by five respectable citizens of that State, in which they made the following assurances to a British official, in regard to one Curtis Coe, an American, imprisoned as a spy at Three Rivers:

"From our acquaintance with Mr. Coe, his character and politics, we are confident that his object is far from being unfriendly to the motives which induced your government in repelling the attacks made on you by our Executive. His politics have uniformly been what we style staunch Federalism, and his object, we believe, no other than trafficking with your citizens in defiance of some of our laws. His language and conduct with us have uniformly belied even the semblance of an enemy to your government, or any of your usages in repelling the measures which our Executive has tried to enforce."

The revenue laws were constantly interrupted, and oftentimes defeated in their execution by vexatious processes and proceedings in the State courts. A member of Congress declared that he knew of fifty-six writs having been served upon a United States collector within one week. American vessels were, in a number of instances, captured, carrying British permits or licenses, and Croke, the British vice-admiralty judge at Halifax, declared in an official decision, that the object of these licenses was to directly benefit the military service of Great Britain—to give subsistence to her armies in Spain.[1] Individ-

---

[1] This decision was delivered August 2d, 1813, in the case of the Orion. This vessel sailed from New York for Lisbon, May 15th, 1813. It should be remarked that this infamous traffic does not appear to have been confined to Eastern ports. The British consul at Boston, Andrew Allen, was arrested and brought before Judge Davis, of the District Court, for countersigning one of these licenses. He was ordered to enter into recognizances for his appearance and trial at the next Circuit Court. He forfeited his recognizance, and fled to Canada. His counsel were Harrison Gray Otis and William Sullivan --the latter the author of "Familiar Letters on the Public Men of the Revolution," etc.

uals were repeatedly detected in selling provisions and stores to the enemy. On the 2d of December, 1813, formal notice was given that the British blockade previously confined to the ports and harbors of the Chesapeake, Delaware, New York, Charleston, Port Royal, Savannah, and the Mississippi, was extended to all the ports, rivers, etc., on both sides of Long Island Sound. The ports east and north of this remained unblockaded, and vessels departed from, and returned to them with so little interruption, that the fact was commented on with censure in the British House of Commons.[1]

The Executives of Massachusetts and Connecticut had refused to submit the militia of those States to orders issued by the President. In November, 1813, Chittenden, Governor of Vermont, by proclamation, ordered home the militia of his State from Canada. The officers, through their Commander, Lieutenant-Colonel Dixon, replied that they regarded the governor's proclamation "with mingled emotions of pity and contempt for its author." The bearer of it was held to bail for trial at Albany. A resolution was subsequently offered in Congress to instruct the Attorney-General to prosecute Chittenden for attempting to induce desertion. Though it was promptly withdrawn at the request of the Republican representatives from Vermont, Otis took occasion to offer resolutions in the Legislature of Massachusetts, pledging that State to the support of Vermont, or any other State, whose constitutional rights were invaded; and the resolutions passed.[2]

Commodore Decatur, in command of the frigate United States 44, the Macedonian 38, and the Hornet 18, was chased into New London by a greatly superior force, June 1st, 1813. Here these ships remained closely blockaded during the remainder of the war, and the blockading squadron had the advantage of commanding at the same time the best point on the entire sea-board of the United States for destroying their coasting trade. Decatur would

---

[1] It was finally extended to the whole coast in April, 1814.

[2] The Pennsylvania Legislature, as soon as apprised of these proceedings, passed resolutions pronouncing Chittenden's conduct worthy of punishment, and denouncing Otis's resolutions as an effort to arrest, by intimidation, an execution of the laws. And Pennsylvania avowed its determination under all circumstances to uphold the General Government in lawful measures to punish persons, whatever their station, for directly or indirectly aiding and comforting the enemy.

The New Jersey Legislature went further, avowing its "contempt and abhorrence of the ravings of an infuriated faction, whether issuing from a legislative body, a maniac governor, or discontented and ambitious demagogues;" and declaring that the people of New Jersey were prepared "to resist internal insurrection with the same readiness" that they would the invasion of a foe.

all probability have escaped but for intelligence communi-
ted from the town to the enemy. He officially informed
a Secretary of the Navy (December 20th, 1813) that he
tempted to get to sea on a dark and tempestuous night—that
soon as his movements to that end became apparent, signals
the enemy were made, by burning blue lights on both points
the harbor's mouth, and he declared : "There is not a doubt
at they [the enemy] have, by signals or otherwise, instan-
neous information of our movements. Notwithstanding these
nals have been repeated, and seen by twenty persons at least
this squadron, there are men in New London who have the
rdihood to affect to disbelieve it, and the effrontery to avow
sir disbelief." During a severe storm of wind and rain, in
arch, 1814, Decatur issued orders for the instant embarkation
his officers. In a very short time blue lights were thrown
like rockets from Long Point, and were immediately an-
ered by three guns from the British fleet. These signals were
tnessed by all the officers and men in the American look-
t boats, and also by some of the officers at Fort Trumbull.
iey were known to be signals by those who were perfectly
niliar with that species of marine communication. It is pro-
r to say these treasonable practices were admitted and
verely reprobated by a portion of the Federalists.

The newspapers representing the extreme Federalists, of
urse, reflected the spirit which prompted these actions. The
ston Daily Advertiser published a series of articles openly
commending the New England States to form a separate peace,
ging that it was lawful and proper to do so, and if Congress
ould refuse its assent, it would be for wise and prudent men to
cide what ought to be done. In not a few papers the American
oops were openly ridiculed, and their successes deplored.[1]

[1] "Ingersoll, in his " Historical Sketch of the Second War between the United States
America and Great Britain," etc., says :
"Harrison's victory over Proctor was publicly deplored. The Salem Gazette of the
l October, 1813, announced : ' At length the handful of British troops, which, for
re than a year have baffled the numerous armies of the United States in the invasion
Canada, deprived of the genius of the immortal Brock, have been obliged to
ld to superior power and numbers.' The Boston Daily Advertiser of the next day,
l of October, 1813, added : 'We shall surrender all our conquests at a peace. It is,
eed a hopeful exploit for Harrison, with five thousand troops, who have been assem-
ng and preparing ever since July, 1812, to fight and conquer four hundred and fifty
rn out, exhausted British regulars, whom the Indians had previously deserted.' In
ode Island, infected by contagion with Massachusetts, a journal pronounced Har-
on's victory the triumph of a crowd of Kentucky savages over a handful of brave men
o more than a march and their capture without fighting.''

Jefferson's letters during 1813, express anything but appro-bation of the conduct of France.[1] To Baron Humboldt (December 6th), he declared views in regard to the American Indians which sound like the dirge of that unfortunate race :

> "You know, my friend, the benevolent plan we were pursuing here for the happiness of the aboriginal inhabitants in our vicinities. We spared nothing to keep them at peace with one another. To teach them agriculture and the rudiments of the most necessary arts, and to encourage industry by establishing among them separate property. In this way they would have been enabled to subsist and multiply on a moderate scale of landed possession. They would have mixed their blood with ours, and been amalgamated and identified with us within no distant period of time. On the commencement of our present war, we pressed on them the observance of peace and neutrality, but the interested and unprincipled policy of England has defeated all our labors for the salvation of these unfortunate people. They have seduced the greater part of the tribes within our neighborhood, to take up the hatchet against us, and the cruel massacres they have committed on the women and children on our frontiers taken by surprise, will oblige us now to pursue them to extermination, or drive them to new seats beyond our reach. Already we have driven their patrons and seducers into Montreal, and the opening season will force them to their last refuge, the walls of Quebec. We have cut off all possibility of intercourse and of mutual aid, and may pursue at our leisure whatever plan we find necessary to secure ourselves against the future effects of their savage and ruthless warfare. The confirmed brutalization, if not the extermination of this race in our America, is, therefore, to form an additional chapter in the English history of the same colored man in Asia, and of the brethren of their own color in Ireland, and wherever else Anglo-mercantile cupidity can find a two-penny interest in deluging the earth with human blood. But let us turn from the loathsome contemplation of the degrading effects of commercial avarice."

In three letters to Mr. Eppes, then chairman of the Finance Committee in Congress, he gave his opinions at length on the subject of the banks and currency. The United States Bank had expired by the limitation of its charter in 1811, and it was now earnestly urged in Congress that the want of it mainly led to the distressing derangement prevailing in monetary affairs, and that its recharter was the only means of curing the evil, and providing the sound circulating medium necessary for the efficient prosecution of the war. Some of the earlier Republican opponents of the Bank had already begun to yield to these views. Mr. Jefferson maintained his uncompromising hostility. We can enter upon no analysis of his reasoning, and must refer the reader to the letters. Their general purport was to propose as a substitute for the bank, to issue Treasury bills

---

[1] Particularly see one to Madame de Staël, dated May 24th.

emitted on a specific tax appropriated for their redemption. And he even went so far as to pronounce the whole system of State banks, as then organized, unsubstantial and fraudulent—productive of evil at best, and always ready to explode and carry ruin throughout the community. He considered State banks necessary for the accommodation of business men—but thought they should offer nothing but cash in exchange for discounted bills.

If we may credit the statements of an intelligent statistician, who was not a partisan of the Administration, the currency found disturbing agents not necessarily arising from the prosecution of the war, or from other legitimate causes. Matthew Carey records in his Olive Branch, that in the winter of 1813–14, the Boston banks being in a condition to do so, entered vigorously upon an attempt " to stop the wheels of government by draining the banks in the Middle and Southern States of their specie, and thus producing an utter disability to fill the loans " which the Government was attempting to effect. Mr. Carey at first placed the amount of specie which they withdrew in eight months from the Middle and Southern banks at four millions of dollars, but subsequent inquiries satisfied him that it was between seven and eight millions. He said " the banks from New York to Norfolk inclusively, as well as most of those to the westward, were literally drained of their specie, and nearly reduced to bankruptcy." " A fearful alarm spread through the community. The issue was looked for with terror. . . . The banks throughout the middle and southern States were obliged to curtail their discounts. Bankruptcies took place to a considerable extent. Even wealthy men, who were wholly unprepared for such a crisis, suffered great inconvenience. Some who had subscribed to the loans were unable to comply with their engagements ; and others were withheld from subscribing by the general pressure for money. In consequence, the loan, then pending, partially failed, to the very great embarrassment of the Government, and distress of the public. This was the nefarious object in view."

To show that there could be no pretext on the part of the Boston banks of a want of specie, our author gives an abstract of the statements of six Boston banks, officially published by the Secretary of the commonwealth, in January, 1814, by which it appeared that the specie then in their vaults was $4,945,444, while their notes in circulation were but $2,000,601.

But the Boston bankers did not allow their hoard of specie to lie idle. Between July 1st, 1814, and January 1st, 1815, it was reduced from $5,468,604 to $1,999,368. It did not flow back into the collapsed arteries of American circulation. Mr. Carey declares, on what he claims to be specific proof, that it was drawn into the British provinces to pay for Government bills and for smuggled goods; that an arrangement was made "with agents of the Government of Lower Canada, whereby an immense amount of British Government bills, drawn in Quebec, were transmitted for sale to New York, Philadelphia, and Baltimore, and disposed of to moneyed men on such advantageous terms as induced them to make large purchases. . . . These bills were forwarded through trusty persons in Boston, and the proceeds being placed to their credit, added immensely to the command the Boston banks had acquired, by the extent of the smuggling trade, over those in the middle and southern States." This commercial intercourse with the enemy was so ostentatiously managed that Mr. Carey copies an advertisement of British Government bills for sale, taken from the Boston Daily Advertiser in 1814.[1]

Meanwhile, the Federal press and pulpit of Massachusetts so violently denounced the citizens of that State who should take any part of the Government loans, that the agents of the Government were compelled to advertise that the names of subscribers should not be made known.[2]

---

[1] See Olive Branch, seventh edition, pp. 315–319. Lowell, the author of the "Road to Ruin," made a contemporaneous denial of such arrangements. Thereupon Carey said: "That these bills to an immoderate amount, were transmitted from Quebec; that they were drawn for the support of the armies employed in hostilities against this country; that they were paid for in specie, devoted to the support of those armies, are facts too stubborn to be set aside. I hereby publicly dare him [Mr. Lowell], or any other person in the Union, to disprove any of them. They are abundantly sufficient to establish the iniquity of the case." We are not aware that any explanations were ever made which tended to relieve the reputation of the parties charged with these transactions.

[2] See advertisement of Gilbert and Dean, brokers, in Boston Chronicle, and of Jesse Putnam in Boston Gazette, April 14th, 1814.

The Boston Gazette, April, 1814, said: "Some will say, will you let the country become bankrupt? no, the country will never become bankrupt. But, pray, do not prevent the abusers of their trust becoming bankrupt. Do not prevent them from becoming odious to the public and replaced by better men. Any Federalist who lends money to Government, must go and shake hands with James Madison, and claim fellowship with Felix Grundy. Let him no more call himself a Federalist and friend to his country. He will be called by others infamous. . . . It is very grateful to find that the universal sentiment is that any man who lends his money to the Government at the present time, will forfeit all claim to common honesty and common courtesy among all true friends of the country. God forbid that any Federalist should ever hold up his hand to pay Federalists for money lent to the present rulers; and Federalists can judge

The restored amity of Jefferson and Adams had stood a near chance of being again wrecked at the outset. · After Priestley's death, a letter to him in 1801 by Jefferson, was published by Belsham, which reflected with severity on the idea that "we were to look backwards, not forwards, for improvement," and which remarked that "the President himself" (Mr. Adams) had countenanced the latter idea "in one of his answers to addresses." Mr. Adams, on receiving Belsham's publication, in 1813, called Jefferson's attention to this statement. In reply (June 15th, 1813) the latter exhibited the mingled tact and dignity—consideration for the feelings of another, and respect for himself—which always characterized him in this perplexing class of explanations. He pointed out to Mr. Adams the particular answer to an address which he had referred to '— retracted nothing—reaffirmed his abstract idea—and even ventured to tell Mr. Adams that he considered his expressions on that occasion "lent to the prejudices of his friends." This last was treading on delicate ground, but the mixture of frankness and courtesy prevailed. Mr. Adams was never implacable when kindly approached.

A new and strong tie was beginning indeed to bind the stately old men together. They were speedily becoming the last of the signers of the Declaration of Independence—the last of the great actors and leaders of 1776. Their common and dearly loved friend, Rush, had died in April, 1813, after a brief illness, and when the ink on Jefferson's last letter to him was yet fresh." [2] In his first letter to Adams after that event (May 27th), Jefferson said:

whether Democrats will tax their constituents to pay interest to Federalists." The Boston Centinel proclaimed similar views. In Number 5 of the Road to Ruin, Lowell said: "Money is such a drug (the surest sign of the former prosperity and present insecurity of trade) that men, against their consciences, their honor, their duty, their *professions and promises*, are willing to lend it secretly, to support the very measures which are both intended and calculated for their ruin." The words which we have italicized in the preceding sentence were contemporaneously construed to imply that a voluntary or extorted agreement had been made by the Federal moneyed men of Boston, not to take any shares in the Government loans.

Rev. Elijah Parish, D.D., thus "held forth" at Byfield, April 7th, 1814: "No peace will ever be made, till the people say there shall be no war. If the rich men continue to furnish money, the war will continue till the mountains are melted with blood—till every field in America is white with the bones of the people."

[1] Jefferson designated that to the young men of Philadelphia. This will be found in Mr. Adams's Works, dated May 7th, 1798, and it contains the following sentences: "Without wishing to damp the ardor of curiosity, or influence the freedom of inquiry, I will hazard a prediction that after the most industrious and impartial researches, the longest liver of you all will find no principles, institutions, or systems of education more fit in general, to be transmitted to your posterity, than those you received from your ancestors." (Adams's Works, vol. ix., p. 188.

[2] The letter is dated March 6th, 1813.

"Another of our friends of seventy-six is gone, my dear sir, another of the co-signers of the independence of our country. And a better man than Rush could not have left us, more benevolent, more learned, of finer genius, or more honest. We, too, must go; and that ere long. I believe we are under half a dozen at present; I mean the signers of the Declaration. Yourself, Gerry, Carroll, and myself, are all I know to be living. I am the only one south of the Potomac. Is Robert Treat Payne, or Floyd living?[1] It is long since I have heard of them, and yet I do not recollect to have heard of their deaths."

Appended to a letter from Adams to Jefferson, dated July 15th, 1813, we find the following :

I have been looking for some time for a space in my good husband's letters to add the regards of an old friend, which are still cherished and preserved through all the changes and vicissitudes which have taken place since we first became acquainted, and will, I trust, remain as long as

"A. ADAMS."

Here was voluntary and frank retraction on the part of Mrs. Adams, from the position in which she had placed herself in her correspondence with Jefferson in 1804. Henceforth a succession of friendly messages passed between her and her early friend. She wrote to him and he replied. We regret that the letters have escaped publication.[2] Mrs. Adams, like her husband, never again met Mr. Jefferson, but she had the opportunity, and eagerly availed herself of it, to bestow kindly and assiduous attentions on some of his family. They gratefully appreciated those attentions then, and most warmly remember them now.

Mrs. Adams lost none of the imposing features of her character in the decline of life. An observing and intelligent gentleman who was a guest at Quincy within a year or two of her death, has given us a description of his visit. Mr. Adams shook as if palsied; but the mind and the heart were evidently sound. His spirits seemed as elastic as a boy's. He joked, laughed heartily, and talked about everybody and everything, past and present, with the most complete *abandon*. He seemed to our highly educated informant to be a vast encyclopedia of written and unwritten knowledge. It gushed out on every possible topic, but was mingled with lively anecdotes and sallies, and he exhi-

---

[1] Judge Payne died at his residence in Boston, May 11th, 1814, aged eighty-four. General William Floyd died on his farm, on the Mohawk river, New York, August 4th, 1821, aged eighty-six years.

[2] One from Jefferson to Mrs. Adams is given in his Works, under date of January 11th, 1817. It was in answer to one from her, dated December 15th, 1816.

bited a carelessness in his language which suggested anything but pedantry or an attempt at "fine talking." In short, the brave old man was as delightful as he was commanding in conversation. While the guest was deeply enjoying this interview, an aged and stately female entered the apartment, and he was introduced to Mrs. Adams. A cap of exquisite lace surrounded features still exhibiting intellect and energy, though they did not wear the appearance of ever having been beautiful. Her dress was snowy white, and there was that immaculate neatness in her appearance which gives to age almost the sweetness of youth. With less warmth of manner and sociableness than Mr. Adams, she was sufficiently gracious, and her occasional remarks betrayed intellectual vigor and strong sense. The guest went away, feeling that he never again should behold such living specimens of the "great of old."

Mr. Jefferson's style as a writer has attracted so much notice, that his account of the manner in which it was formed, and his opinions on one or two important questions in respect to our language, will be matters of curiosity to a class of readers. On receiving from John Waldo a copy of his "Rudiments of English Grammar," Mr. Jefferson wrote to him, August 16th, 1813:

"I am entirely unqualified to give that critical opinion of it which you do me the favor to ask. Mine has been a life of business, of that kind which appeals to a man's conscience, as well as his industry, not to let it suffer, and the few moments allowed me from labor have been devoted to more attractive studies, that of grammar having never been a favorite with me. The scanty foundation, laid in at school, has carried me through a life of much hasty writing, more indebted for style to reading and memory, than to rules of grammar. I have been pleased to see that in all cases you appeal to usage, as the arbiter of language; and justly consider that as giving law to grammar, and not grammar to usage. I concur entirely with you in opposition to Purists, who would destroy all strength and beauty of style, by subjecting it to a rigorous compliance with their rules. Fill up all the ellipses and syllepses of Tacitus, Sallust, Livy, etc., and the elegance and force of their sententious brevity are extinguished."

After citing several illustrations in the Latin, he says:

"Wire-draw these expressions by filling up the whole syntax and sense, and they become dull paraphrases on rich sentiments. . . . . . I am no friend, therefore, to what is called *Purism*, but a zealous one to the *Neology* which has introduced these two words without the authority of any dictionary. I consider the one as destroying the nerve and beauty of language, while the other improves both, and adds to its copiousness. I have been not a little disappointed, and made suspicious of my own judgment, on seeing the Edinburgh Reviews, the ablest critics of the age, set their faces against the introduction of new words into the English language; they are particularly apprehensive that the writers of the United States will adulterate it. Certainly so great a growing population, spread over such an extent of country, with such a variety of climates, of productions, of arts, must enlarge their language to make it answer its purpose of expressing all ideas, the new as well as the old. The new circumstances under which we are placed, call for new words, new phrases, and for the transfer of old words to new objects. An American dialect will therefore be formed; so will a West-Indian and Asiatic, as a Scotch and an Irish are already formed. But whether will these adulterate or enrich the English language? Has the beautiful poetry of Burns, or his Scottish dialect, disfigured it? Did the Athenians consider the Doric, the Ionian, the Æolic, and other dialects, as disfiguring or as beautifying their language? Did they fastidiously disavow Herodotus, Pindar, Theocritus, Sappho, Alcæus, or Grecian writers? On the contrary, they were sensible that the variety of dialects, still infinitely varied by poetical license, constituted the riches of their language, and made the Grecian Homer the first of poets, as he must ever remain, until a language equally ductile and copious shall again be spoken.

"Every language has a set of terminations, which make a part of its peculiar idiom. Every root among the Greeks was permitted to vary its termination, so as to express its radical idea in the form of any one of the parts of speech; to wit, as a noun, an adjective, a verb, participle, or adverb; and each of these parts of speech again, by still varying the termination, could vary the shade of idea existing in the mind."

Having exhibited the convenience that would result from adopting the last-named system in the English language, Mr. Jefferson presents and illustrates by numerous examples two other available sources of copiousness: first, the joining in one word the root and every other member of its family with prepositions and other words; and, second, the joining in one word one family of roots with another. He then adds:

"If we wish to be assured from experiment of the effect of a judicious spirit of Neology, look at the French language. Even before the revolution, it was deemed much more copious than the English; at a time, too, when they had an academy which endeavored to arrest the progress of their language, by fixing it to a Dictionary, out of which no word was ever to be sought, used, or tolerated. The institution of parliamentary assemblies in 1789, for which their language had no apposite terms or phrases, as having never before needed them, first obliged them to adopt the Parliamentary vocabulary of England; and other new circumstances called for corresponding new words; until by the number of these adopted, and by the analogies for adoption which they have legitimated, I think we may say with truth, that a Dictionnaire Néologique of these would be half as large as the dictionary of the academy; and that at this time it is the language in which every shade of idea, distinctly perceived by the mind, may be more exactly expressed, than in any language at this day spoken by man. Yet I have no hesitation in saying that the English

, is founded on a broader base, native and adopted, and capable, with the
dom of employing its materials, of becoming superior to that in copiousness
hony. Not indeed by holding fast to Johnson's Dictionary ; not by raising
od cry against every word he has not licensed ; but by encouraging and
ag new compositions of its elements. Learn from Lye and Benson what
uage would now have been if restrained to their vocabularies. Its enlarge-
ıst be the consequence, to a certain degree, of its transplantation from the
of London into every climate of the globe ; and the greater the degree the
»cious will it become as the organ of the development of the human mind."

e same views are several times expressed in other parts of
»fferson's correspondence, and he often urged them in con-
ion. A familiar illustration employed by him to exhibit
nefit of sacrificing strict accuracy to attain force, was the
on one of his seals, written, "Rebellion *to* tyrants is
nce to God," instead of "Rebellion *against* tyrants is
nce to God."

e critical examiner of Mr. Jefferson's writings will observe
is practice corresponded with his theory in the latter par-
:, not only in familiar writing, but in some of his most
ate productions. His ideas of style will be perfectly
stood after reading the following extracts from a letter ho
to his grandson, Francis Eppes (January 19th, 1821).
ing of Thomas Paine and Lord Bolingbroke, he said :

ese two persons differed remarkably in the style of their writing, each
a model of what is most perfect in both extremes of the simple and the
    No writer has exceeded Paine in ease and familiarity of style, in perspi-
? expression, happiness of elucidation, and in simple and unassuming
a. In this he may be compared with Dr. Franklin ; and indeed his Common
as, for awhile, believed to have been written by Dr. Franklin, and published
»e borrowed name of Paine, who had come over with him from England.
)lingbroke's, on the other hand, is a style of the highest order. The lofty,
cal, full-flowing eloquence of Cicero. Periods of just measure, their
s proportioned, their close full and round. His conceptions, too, are bold
ong, his diction copious, polished and commanding as his subject. His
i are certainly the finest samples in the English language, of the eloquence
for the Senate."

ıe copiousness and splendor of Lord Bolingbroke's diction,
.bitual vigor and frequent felicity of expression, the liveli-
ınd ease with which his sonorous sentences are thrown
ıer, the boldness and ardor of his manner, are conceded by
. But his construction of sentences is often defective,
d by nice rules of rhetoric. Sometimes his defects rise to

positive errors. He goes sweeping on like a large and rapid stream which cannot wait, so to speak, to find a smooth way round all the impediments it encounters, but occasionally rushes over them broken into roughness and foam. No stickler for frigid accuracy would, without any reservations, have assigned him the literary rank Mr. Jefferson does; and certainly no such person would have introduced the above unqualified comparison between him and Cicero. Jefferson was as familiar with the writings of Lord Shaftesbury as those of Bolingbroke. His description of the style of the latter will be generally thought to apply even better to that of the former. Shaftesbury has more sustained grandeur, and is vastly more *accurate*. But in attaining accuracy, he often sacrifices nerve, and always lacks nature and spontaneity. The careful word-artist is always before us —never the freely-moving, warm-blooded man. Jefferson always, therefore, expressed a decided preference for the style of Bolingbroke.[1]

[1] He agreed with Quinctilian in the following particulars: "In universum, si sit necesse, duram potiùs atque asperam compositionem malim esse, quam effeminatam ac enervem, qualis apud multos. Ideòque, vincta quædam de industria sunt solvenda, ne laborata videantur; neque ullum idoneum aut aptum verbum prætermittamus, gratia lenitatis."

CHAPTER X.

1814—1816.

aval campaign of 1814, resulted less successfully than
ding ones, though several large vessels were put into
· during the year. Our navy lost nothing in honor

but the preponderance of strength against it was overwhelming, and opportunities did not occur for those even-handed encounters in which it had previously won so much reputation. On Lake Champlain, however, came a bright flash of former success. The victory of McDonough at Plattsburgh, achieved just a year and a day after that of Perry on Lake Erie, approached the latter in brilliancy, and preserved for our navy its darling place in the national pride and affections.

On land, where our real strength lay, the campaign was checkered with successes and reverses. Our National Capital, then an unfortified village, suffered the humiliation which nearly every European capital had suffered within a few years, of being captured by an enemy. But it encountered a barbarity which neither Cossack nor Jacobin had inflicted on any capital of the Old World, in having its public, and a portion of its private, edifices, first rifled and then burnt to the ground—altogether "an enterprise," as Sir James Mackintosh well remarked in the British House of Commons, "which most exasperated a people, and least weakened a government of any recorded in the annals of war."

But the generals had now been found who, to recur to Jefferson's phrase, were "marked in the forehead." The battle of Chippewa, where a superior body of veteran English troops was nearly routed; Bridgewater or Lundy's Lane where midnight darkness did not arrest the hand to hand strife, or hush the roar of battle rising high over the eternal thunder of Niagara; the splendid sortie of Fort Erie; the victory of Plattsburgh—the adjunct of McDonough's victory in the bay; Jackson's train of unexampled successes in the South, ending with the crowning triumph of New Orleans—demonstrated what American troops could do when properly commanded. No pretence could now be set up by enemies without or British idolaters within, that we overwhelmed our enemy by numerical superiority—or by possessing the advantage in point of discipline. In these encounters, the British had the larger force. Nor is this all. British official statements will show that their regular troops employed in Canada during 1814, outnumbered all the regulars of the United States.[1]

_____

[1] Their newspapers and their officers talked of making a serious "invasion" of the

Lieutenant General Drummond was acting on the offensive hen the actions in the Canadian peninsula, which have been entioned, were fought. He was attempting to drive before m a comparative handful of American troops, under General rown, preparatory to an anticipated descent upon the State of ew York. He consequently had his choice of time for fighting, d in making all the important dispositions of the campaign.

On the score of time of service, and seasoning in practical war, e British troops also possessed a decided advantage. Napoon was a prisoner. England was pouring the veterans of the eninsular war into Canada—and had her existence as a nation en staked on the result, she could not have sent choicer or ore honorably distinguished troops. The very men who had shed to the assault at Ciudad Rodrigo, and quelled the murous defence of Badajos; the very horses that had charged, e sabres that had flashed, and the cannon that had thundered Corunna, Talavera, Salamanca and Vittoria—rushed to the sault, charged, flashed and thundered at Chippewa, Bridgeater, and New Orleans. When at Chippewa, Major Jessup, aping from his second horse, ordered the 25th United States giment of infantry to cease firing and to try the bayonet, his mpletely successful charge was directed against the far fuller 00th British regiment of infantry, commanded by the Marquis f Tweedale, who had been an aid-de-camp of Wellington in pain, and learned his lessons of war under that great comander.[1] Brown, Scott, Ripley, Porter, Miller, Brady, Nichos, Jessup, Leavenworth, McNeil, McRee, McFarland, Wood, lindman, Arrowswith, Austin, Jones, Smith—not to mention ch subordinates as Worth, Towson, Ritchie, Harris, Bliss, iddle, and that young and gallant inheritor of a great name, ho here found his last field, Ambrose Spencer—all these[2] and he men they commanded at Bridgewater, where bayonet contantly crossed bayonet; where, in the language of General

---

nited States—and some of the former, apparently in earnest, ventured amusing specuions on the probability of the United States being wholly, or in part, reconquered.
[1] The present Duke of Wellington married a daughter of the Marquis of Tweedale.
[2] We name the most conspicuous American officers engaged in the action, except iose below the rank of captain—without intending to make any distinction between iose of the same rank, by the order in which we have placed their names. All may be ld to have distinguished themselves equally according to rank. And as we have not arched for the names of our commanders beyond two or three historical accounts of e battle lying at hand, it is altogether probable we have omitted names as well entitled be in the list, as those placed there.

Drummond's official report, "in so determined a manner were the American attacks directed against his guns, that his artillery-men were bayoneted by them in the very act of loading, and the muzzles of the American guns were advanced within a few yards of his own;" when in the thick darkness regiments fired and charged by the light of each others volleys; when but one out of four of the whole American force escaped death or wounds; and when the Americans drove their enemy entirely from the field, and then retired at their own time, and in perfect order, to their camp—they were opposed to a superior number of the same officers and men who had aided to tame the pride of Victor, Massena, Marmont and Soult.[1]

The war of 1812 closed in a blaze of American triumph. The incidents of the negotiation and the particular terms of the treaty do not belong here. The latter was concluded in December, 1814, and proclaimed in the United States in February, 1815. It left the boundaries and relations of the two nations as before the war. As it contained no stipulations against British impressments, it has been often asserted by the detractors of Mr. Madison's Administration and of the Republican party, that it failed in securing the first and principal object for which the war had been undertaken. Those who take this view, look at the form, and disregard the substance. The orders in council had been repealed. Impressments ceased. It is true, that with the peace then reigning in Europe, England had no further immediate occasion for impressment; but if she renewed it, we could also renew the war with the return of the occasion—strengthened by our intermediate growth, and by the assistance of her enemy, whose hostilities should again force her to resort to this method of filling her navy. Our resistance and retaliation would thus be at least co-existent with the practical aggression. Jefferson, so peculiarly decided on the subject of impressment, approved of the peace on the terms in which it was made, and by one of those felicitous characterizations habitual to him

[1] And in illustration of the material of the American soldier, the statement ought not to be omitted that six or seven hundred of those who won the field of Bridgewater, were volunteers. They took full part in the action, and the commander-in-chief himself bore witness that "Porter's volunteers" "were not excelled by the regulars in meeting the charge" that "precipitated by the incitement of their gallant commander," they fell upon the enemy's line hand to hand, broke it, and compelled many to surrender. The literal massacre of New Orleans, inflicted in part by irregular troops, also fell upon the English veterans from Spain, three to one more numerous than the victors.

politics, he defined its character, and established a national
icy for the future.   He wrote to the President, before learning
t the treaty was ratified : " I presume that, having spared to
pride of England her formal acknowledgment of the atrocity
mpressment in an article of the treaty, she will concur in a
vention for relinquishing it. Without this, she must under-
id that the present is but a *truce*, determinable on the first
of impressment of an American citizen, committed by any
er of hers."   He wrote to a former member of his Cabinet,
ieral Dearborn, March 17th, 1815 :

Peace was indeed desirable; yet it would not have been as welcome without
uccesses of New Orleans. These last have established truths too important not
e valued; that the people of Louisiana are sincerely attached to the Union;
their city can be defended; that the Western States make its defence their
liar concern; that the militia are brave; that their deadly aim countervails the
wuvering skill of their enemy; that we have officers of natural genius now
ing forward from the mass; and that, putting together all our conflicts, we can
the British by sea and by land, with equal numbers. All this being now
ed, I am glad of the pacification of Ghent, and shall still be more so, if, by a
mable arrangement against impressment, they will make it truly a treaty of
e, and not a mere *truce*, as we must all consider it, until the principle of the war
tiled."

And the following to another Cabinet associate, Rodney, dis-
ies his secret feelings towards England at this period.   After
idemning in burning language the conduct of the rulers of
h France and England, and the deep "hatred" of the latter
'ards the United States, he continued :

'What nourishment and support would not England receive from an hundred
ons of industrious descendants, whom some of her people now born will live to
here. What their energies are, she has lately tried. And what has she not to
from an hundred millions of such men, if she continues her maniac course
atred and hostility to them. I hope in God she will change. There is not a
on on the globe with whom I have more earnestly wished a friendly intercourse
qual conditions. On no other would I hold out the hand of friendship to any.
ow that their creatures represent me as personally an enemy to England. But
i only can believe this, or those who think me a fool. I am an enemy to her
lts and injuries. I am an enemy to the flagitious principles of her administra-
, and to those which govern her conduct towards other nations. But would she
i to morality some place in her political code, and especially would she exercise
mcy, and at least neutral passions towards us, there is not, I repeat it, a people
arth with whom I would sacrifice so much to be in friendship."

The "truce," or "armistice," as Mr. Jefferson termed it in

other letters, was never broken. Having learned that the United States had finally and firmly resolved to fight rather than endure the impressment of their citizens, England forever relinquished the practice. There were good reasons enough, without treaty stipulations, for her discontinuing a method of recruiting her navy which cost her the lives of more men than she thus obtained, and also ten times the price of obtaining an equal number of men by subsidy.[1]

An "armistice" on purely equal terms was not very discreditable when made with a power which, after twelve years of such war as the world never before witnessed, had finally sent Napoleon a captive to St. Helena, and now had her thousand cruisers, her unemployed armies, and those resources which had subsidized Europe to devote exclusively to the struggle with us. Nor was it very discreditable for the United States to make peace, when the practical causes of the war were removed, though we failed to extort that formal relinquishment from our antagonist which the Armed Neutrality (consisting of Russia, France, Spain, Portugal, Austria, Prussia, Denmark, Sweden, Holland and Naples) had thirty years earlier failed to extort from the same power. We had achieved our great object—for henceforth we were in fact, as well as in name, an independent nation.

Mr. Jefferson's correspondence during 1814 is unusually large and interesting. A letter to Thomas Leiper, January 1st, discloses the fruitful sources of so many contemporaneous and more especially posthumous attacks on himself:

"Thus am I situated. I receive letters from all quarters, some from known friends, some from those who write like friends, on various subjects. What am I to do? Am I to button myself up in Jesuitical reserve, rudely declining any answer, or answering in terms so unmeaning, as only to prove my distrust? Must

---

[1] Jefferson wrote to the Rev. Mr. Worcester, January 29th, 1816:

"It is alleged that Great Britain took from us before the late war near one thousand vessels, and that during the war we took from her fourteen hundred. That before the war she seized and made slaves of six thousand of our citizens, and that in the war we killed more than six thousand of her subjects, and caused her to expend such a sum as amounted to four or five thousand guineas a head for every slave she made. She might have purchased the vessels she took for less than the value of those she lost, and have used the six thousand of her men killed for the purposes to which she applied ours, have saved the four or five thousand guineas a head, and obtained a character of justice which is valuable to a nation as to an individual. These considerations, therefore, leave her without inducement to plunder property and take men in future on such dear terms. I neither affirm nor deny the truth of these allegations."

Where he speaks of "making slaves," he alludes of course to impressments into the British navy.

hdraw myself from all interchange of sentiment with the world. I cannot do
It is at war with my habits and temper. I cannot act as if all men were
thful, because some are so ; nor believe that all will betray me, because some
I had rather be the victim of occasional infidelities, than relinquish my general
dence in the honesty of man."

In a letter to Dr. Walter Jones, January 2d, we get the
st connected delineation of General Washington which ever
:eeded from Mr. Jefferson's pen. Its date shows that it was
matured, his final conception of the subject—that undoubt-
· on which he chose to go before the bar of posterity. In
point of view, it possesses an interest independent of its
nsic value. Considering it too long for insertion here, and
willing to present it except in its entire form, we shall trans-
t to the Appendix of these volumes.[1]

n answer to a letter from Mr. Samuel Greenhow, who
ied to him for aid to a Bible society, and who stated to him
there were families in Virginia destitute of the Bible, Mr.
:rson (January 31st) expressed his surprise at the latter
rtion, but presuming that the society " had evidence of the
" he inclosed a draft of fifty dollars to his correspondent,
icerely agreeing with him that there never was a more pure
sublime system of morality delivered to man than is to be
d in the four Evangelists."

He wrote his friend Joseph C. Cabell, January 31st, in
rer to the question, " whether the States could add any
.ifications to those which the Constitution had prescribed for
r members of Congress," that he had never reflected on the
ect, but had "taken up an off-hand opinion " that they
d not. Further consideration suggested doubts, the grounds
rhich are stated ; but he virtually recommended that no
ent legislative action be taken on the subject. His opinion
mes somewhat illustrative of his political character, from
fact that it really applied to an attempt then making by the
ublicans, in the Virginia Legislature, to prohibit Congres-
al districts from electing non-residents as their members of
gress—aimed, it was said, against the expected election of
a Randolph by a district beyond the Blue Ridge, provided he
ild be beaten, as was then anticipated, in his own. Mr. Jeffer-
expressed the wish that his opinions be permitted to go no

[1] See Appendix No. 26.

further. He said " he wanted to be quiet," and " in general, to
let it be understood that he meddled little or not at all with
public affairs;" but he added : " There are two subjects, indeed,
which I shall claim a right to further as long as I breathe, the
public education, and the subdivision of counties into wards; I
consider the continuance of republican government as absolutely
hanging on these two hooks." [1]

A letter to Gideon Granger, of March 9th, gives the testimony of the writer on various questions of fact in the political
history of his own administration, which were much mooted in
their day, and in regard to which controversy has hardly yet
died away.[2] He wrote Horatio G. Spafford, March 17th:

" Blackstone and Hume have made tories of all England, and are making tories
of those young Americans whose native feelings of independence do not place
them above the wily sophistries of a Hume or a Blackstone. These two books, but
especially the former, have done more towards the suppression of the liberties of
man, than all the million of men in arms of Bonaparte and the millions of human
lives with the sacrifice of which he will stand loaded before the judgment seat of
his Maker. I fear nothing for our liberty from the assaults of force; but I have
seen and felt much, and fear more from English books, English prejudices, English
manners, and the apes, the dupes, and designs among our professional crafts."

He wrote Thomas Cooper, September 10th, on the suspension of specie payments by the banks:

" The crisis, then, of the abuses of banking is arrived. The banks have pronounced their own sentence of death. Between two and three hundred millions
of dollars of their promissory notes are in the hands of the people, for solid pro-

[1] To the second of these "hooks" Mr. Jefferson was thought, by many of his neighbors, to attach a very disproportionate importance. The investigations of later writers,
and particularly of De Tocqueville, have diffused much additional information on the subject among those who, unfamiliar with the practical effects of town or ward governments,
were disposed to regard them as unimportant. Mr. Jefferson's political system would have
lacked its apex, or rather its foundation, had he not thus distinctly recognized the principle
that the more nearly government is brought home to the people, the more purely, efficiently
and cheaply will it be administered; and that every community is the best judge of its own
individual concerns. On any other theory, it would be difficult to say why we need our
county and State organizations, each independent of all others in a certain sphere. On
any other theory, pure consolidation would present the standard of utility.
[2] It appears from this letter that Granger sent an agent to Virginia in 1800, to give
information " of the danger resulting " from Burr's " intrigues;" that in 1803-4, Jefferson, on Granger's advice, " procured Erastus Granger to inform De Witt Clinton of the
plan to elevate Burr in New York;" that in 1803-4, Jefferson believed Burr to be at the
bottom of the intrigues to form a coalition of the five eastern States with New York and
New Jersey, "either to overawe the Union by the combination of their power and their
will, or by threats of separating themselves from it;" that Jefferson employed
G. Granger to procure the dismission of the prosecutions for libels on himself, commenced in Connecticut during his presidency. The letter also points out all the earliest
sources of his information in regard to the conspiracy of Burr in 1805-6.
The opinion expressed that Burr was at the bottom of the eastern disunion intrigues
of 1803-4 will recall Plumer's account of a conversation between Burr and some of the
Federal leaders on that subject, given in an earlier cited number of the Appendix.

duce and property sold, and they formally declare they will not pay them. This is an act of bankruptcy of course, and will be so pronounced by any court before which it shall be brought. But *cui bono?* The law can only uncover their insolvency, by opening to its suitors their empty vaults. Thus by the dupery of our citizens, and tame acquiescence of our legislators, the nation is plundered of two or three hundred millions of dollars, treble the amount of debt contracted in the Revolutionary war, and which, instead of redeeming our liberty, has been expended on sumptuous houses, carriages and dinners. A fearful tax! if equalized on all; but overwhelming and convulsive by its partial fall. The crush will be tremendous; very different from that brought on by our paper money. That rose and fell so gradually that it kept all on their guard, and affected severely only early or long-winded contracts. Here the contract of yesterday crushes in an instant the one or the other party. The banks stopping payments suddenly, all their mercantile and city debtors do the same; and all, in short, except those in the country, who, possessing property, will be good in the end. But this resource will not enable them to pay a cent on the dollar. From the establishment of the United States Bank, to this day, I have preached against this system, but have been sensible no cure could be hoped but in the catastrophe now happening. The remedy was to let banks drop gradually at the expiration of their charters, and for the State governments to relinquish the power of establishing others. This would not, as it should not, have given the power of establishing them to Congress. But Congress could then have issued treasury notes payable within a fixed period, and founded on a specific tax, the proceeds of which, as they came in, should be exchangeable for the notes of that particular emission only. This depended, it is true, on the will of the State legislatures, and would have brought on us the phalanx of paper interest. But that interest is now defunct. Their gossamer castles are dissolved, and they can no longer impede and overawe the salutary measures of the Government. Their paper was received on a belief that it was cash on demand. Themselves have declared it was nothing, and such scenes are now to take place as will open the eyes of credulity and of insanity itself, to the dangers of a paper medium abandoned to the discretion of avarice and of swindlers. It is impossible not to deplore our past follies, and their present consequences, but let them at least be warnings against like follies in future. The banks have discontinued themselves. We are now without any medium; and necessity, as well as patriotism and confidence, will make us all eager to receive treasury notes, if founded on specific taxes. Congress may now borrow of the public, and without interest, all the money they may want, to the amount of a competent circulation, by merely issuing their own promissory notes, of proper denominations, for the larger purposes of circulation, but not for the small. Leave that door open for the entrance of metallic money. And, to give readier credit to their bills, without obliging themselves to give cash for them on demand, let their collectors be instructed to do so, when they have cash; thus, in some measure, performing the functions of a bank, as to their own notes. Providence seems, indeed, by a special dispensation, to have put down for us, without a struggle, that very paper enemy which the interest of our citizens long since required ourselves to put down, at whatever risk. The work is done. The moment is pregnant with futurity, and if not seized at once by Congress, I know not on what shoal our bark is next to be stranded. The State legislatures should be immediately urged to relinquish the right of establishing banks of discount. Most of them will comply on patriotic principles, under the convictions of the moment; and the non-complying may be crowded into concurrence by legitimate devices."

Several letters on scientific topics are scattered through the correspondence of the year. In one, he gives a long series of reasons for adhering to the Linnæan classification in natural history, instead of changing to that of Blumenbach and Cuvier;[1] in another, a formula and explanation of Lord Napier's theorem for the solution of right-angled spherical triangles, etc., etc. Among his literary opinions we find him declaring the Edinburgh Review " unrivalled in merit," and that if it should be " continued by the same talents, information, and principles," it " would become a real Encyclopedia, justly taking its station in our libraries with the most valuable depositories of human knowledge." Its antagonist, the Quarterly, " appeared to him a pigmy against a giant." In a letter to the compiler of the " American Speaker," he declared that he thought Eugene Aram's defence of himself " the finest thing" " which the English language had produced." He considered the speeches of Aram, of Carnot in 1803 on the proposition to declare Bonaparte consul for life, and of Logan to Lord Dunmore, " as worthily standing in a line with those of Scipio and Hannibal in Livy, and of Cato and Cæsar in Sallust." He spoke in his usual contemptuous vein of Plato, in a letter to Mr. Adams, and the latter expressed his hearty concurrence.

Receiving from the Chevalier De Onis a copy of the new Constitution of Spain, he complained of its establishing a state religion, but said there was one provision in it " which would immortalize its inventors "—that which " after a certain epoch, disfranchised every citizen who could not read and write." This was proportioning the remedy to the disease. Mr. Jefferson never proposed or considered such a qualification for voting desirable in his own country.

Before dropping this summary of the miscellaneous letters of the year, we will quote one addressed to an individual of that class of good persons who every now and then feel that they have a special " call " to attempt the religious conversion of some very eminent man—especially an eminent man suspected of heterodox views. Mr. Jefferson was both suspected and accused in that direction; and being a favorite with the

---

[1] Because the Linnæan had obtained general consent, which another might find it impossible to do; and because it furnished a sufficient groundwork for supplementary insertions as new productions were discovered.

body of his countrymen, he received a double share of this kind of attention. The following letter carries its own explanation of circumstances;

TO MR. MILES KING.

MONTICELLO, *September* 26, 1814.

SIR:

I duly received your letter of August 20th, and I thank you for it, because I believe it was written with kind intentions, and a personal concern for my future happiness. Whether the particular revelation which you suppose to have been made to yourself were real or imaginary, your reason alone is the competent judge. For dispute as long as we will on religious tenets, our reason at last must ultimately decide, as it is the only oracle which God has given us to determine between what really comes from him and the phantasms of a disordered or deluded imagination. When he means to make a personal revelation, he carries conviction of its authenticity to the reason he has bestowed as the umpire of truth. You believe you have been favored with such a special communication. Your reason, not mine, is to judge of this; and if it shall be his pleasure to favor me with a like admonition, I shall obey it with the same fidelity with which I would obey his known will in all cases. Hitherto I have been under the guidance of that portion of reason which he has thought proper to deal out to me. I have followed it faithfully in all important cases, to such a degree at least as leaves me without uneasiness; and if on minor occasions I have erred from its dictates, I have trust in him who made us what we are, and know it was not his plan to make us always unerring. He has formed us moral agents. Not that, in the perfection of his state, he can feel pain or pleasure in anything we may do; he is far above our power; but that we may promote the happiness of those with whom he has placed us in society, by acting honestly towards all, benevolently to those who fall within our way, respecting sacredly their rights, bodily and mental, and cherishing especially their freedom of conscience, as we value our own. I must ever believe that religion substantially good which produces an honest life, and we have been authorized by one whom you and I equally respect, to judge of the tree by its fruit. Our particular principles of religion are a subject of accountability to our God alone. I inquire after no man's, and trouble none with mine; nor is it given to us in this life to know whether yours or mine, our friends or our foes, are exactly the right. Nay, we have heard it said that there is not a Quaker or a Baptist, a Presbyterian or an Episcopalian, a Catholic or a Protestant in heaven; that, on entering that gate, we leave those badges of schism behind, and find ourselves united in those principles only in which God has united us all. Let us not be uneasy then, about the different roads we may pursue, as believing them the shortest, to that our last abode; but, following the guidance of a good conscience, let us be happy in the hope that by these different paths we shall all meet in the end. And that you and I may there meet and embrace, is my earnest prayer. And with this assurance I salute you with brotherly esteem and respect.

These appeals were oftener made, or rather meditated to be made, in person. The former residents of Monticello have recollections of several visits from fervent neophytes and zealous brethren bent on this errand—and occasionally came a tough old polemic, to do battle like Christian with Apollyon, yet not choosing, like Christian, the Valley of Humiliation as the theatre of the combat. Whatever the species, they all found courteous welcome at Monticello—and were never prohibited from attempting to perform their self-assigned task. But they invariably encountered something for which they were not prepared. Brought face to face with an aged and dignified statesman, whose every word bespoke knowledge, reflection, and moral elevation, these well-meaning people discovered that it was not so easy to deliver an uninvited homily to such a man in his own house. They generally contented themselves with a modest hint—stayed to dinner, and perhaps over night, well pleased guests—and when they departed warmly shook the hand of their entertainer, and ever afterwards spoke kindly of him.

Mr. Jefferson's continued views on the subject of negro slavery, are made very fully to appear, in a letter addressed this year to Edward Coles. It presents no change of opinions—nothing new on the subject—but as it exhibits many of his views in connection—as it has not been published in either edition of Mr. Jefferson's Works, and as we know it to be authentic, (having seen the original), we give it a place at full length in the Appendix.[1]

It is rather entertaining to observe in the customary correspondence between Jefferson and John Adams, in 1814, the old head of the " French Party," in the United States, denouncing the imperial captive of St. Helena, in the most burning language of aversion and scorn,[2] and the old head of the " English Party" putting in extenuations for Napoleon generally, and particularly as compared with " John Bull," whom Mr. Adams declared to be a " greater tyrant and miser[3] usurper"—" quite as unfeeling,

_____

[1] See APPENDIX, No. 27.

[2] Mr. Jefferson is habitually unsparing and sometimes unquestionably unjust to Napoleon, particularly in this letter. Napoleon not only embodied the political ideas for which Jefferson had no toleration, but he had been the direct means of overthrowing that form of a constitution in his country which Jefferson had fondly hoped would ripen into substance and reality. The Republican chief had charity for those hereditary monarchs, whom he believed to be honest and well-meaning men, but none whatever for those who overthrew freer governments and climbed to a throne. And at this period Napoleon's civic ability (most scornfully characterized by Jefferson), was comparatively little known—remained completely obfuscated by the glare of his military achievements. Lastly, Jefferson could not forgive one whom he thought only less guilty than the rulers of England in aggressions on the United States, and in unnecessarily keeping in operation that train of causes which produced the existing war between England and the latter.

[3] We find this so printed in the Cong. Ed. of Mr. Jefferson's works—but the word " miser " is probably a typographical error.

as unprincipled, more powerful"—and " who had shed more blood than Bonaparte."

Mr. Jefferson made the following allusion to the situation of the agriculturists of Virginia, and to his own pecuniary affairs, in a letter to Mr. Short, November 28th.

" These are my views of the war. They embrace a great deal of sufferance, trying privations, and no benefit but that of teaching our enemy that he is never to gain by wanton injuries on us. To me this state of things brings a sacrifice of all tranquillity and comfort through the residue of life. For although the debility of age disables me from the services and sufferings of the field, yet, by the total annihilation in value of the produce which was to give me subsistence and independence, I shall be like Tantalus, up to the shoulders in water, yet dying with thirst. We can make indeed enough to eat, drink and clothe ourselves; but nothing for our salt, iron, groceries and taxes, which must be paid in money. For what can we raise for the market? Wheat? we can only give it to our horses, as we have been doing ever since harvest. Tobacco? it is not worth the pipe it is smoked in. Some say Whisky; but all mankind must become drunkards to consume it. But although we feel, we shall not flinch. We must consider now, as in the Revolutionary war, that although the evils of resistance are great, those of submission would be greater. We must meet, therefore, the former as the casualties of tempests and earthquakes, and like them necessarily resulting from the constitution of the world."

We have omitted for a long period to chronicle his elections to honorary memberships in foreign and domestic societies. In 1814, he was elected a member of the New York Historical Society, of the American Antiquarian Society, and of the Agronomic Society of Bavaria.[1] His favorite American Philosophical Society had continued to reëlect him its president, in spite of his desire to retire. In November 1814, he kindly but peremptorily signified that he could no longer " consent to hold honors without requital which justly belonged to others." His resignation was accepted, and he was succeeded by his cherished friend, Dr. Wistar.

On learning the destruction of the Congressional library by the British at Washington, he wrote to Samuel H. Smith.

MONTICELLO, *September* 21, 1814.

DEAR SIR: •   •   •   •   •

I presume it will be among the early objects of Congress to re-commence their collection. This will be difficult while the war continues, and intercourse with,

[1] We have seen a large collection of diplomas, in almost every language of Europe, conferring degrees, honorary memberships, etc., on him—also numerous medals awarded to him on various occasions.

Europe is attended with so much risk. You know my collection, its condition and extent. I have been fifty years making it, and have spared no pains, opportunity or expense, to make it what it is. While residing in Paris, I devoted every afternoon I was disengaged, for a summer or two, in examining all the principal bookstores, turning over every book with my own hand, and putting by everything which related to America, and indeed whatever was rare and valuable in every science. Besides this, I had standing orders during the whole time I was in Europe, on its principal book-marts, particularly Amsterdam, Frankfort, Madrid and London, for such works relating to America as could not be found in Paris. So that, in that department particularly, such a collection was made as probably can never again be effected, because it is hardly probable that the same opportunities, the same time, industry, perseverance and expense, with some knowledge of the bibliography of the subject, would again happen to be in concurrence. During the same period, and after my return to America, I was led to procure, also, whatever related to the duties of those in the high concerns of the nation. So that the collection, which I suppose is of between nine and ten thousand volumes, while it includes what is chiefly valuable in science and literature generally, extends more particularly to whatever belongs to the American statesman. In the diplomatic and parliamentary branches, it is particularly full. It is long since I have been sensible it ought not to continue private property, and had provided that at my death, Congress should have the refusal of it at their own price. But the loss they have now incurred, makes the present the proper moment for their accommodation, without regard to the small remnant of time and the barren use of my enjoying it. I ask of your friendship, therefore, to make for me the tender of it to the library committee of Congress, not knowing myself of whom the committee consists. I inclose you the catalogue, which will enable them to judge of its contents. Nearly the whole are well bound, abundance of them elegantly, and of the choicest editions existing. They may be valued by persons named by themselves, and the payment made convenient to the public. It may be, for instance, in such annual installments as the law of Congress has left at their disposal, or in stock of any of their late loans, or of any loan they may institute at this session, so as to spare the present calls of our country and await its days of peace and prosperity. They may enter, nevertheless, into immediate use of it, as eighteen or twenty wagons would place it in Washington in a single trip of a fortnight.

He stated, that he would like to retain a few books "chiefly classical and mathematical," and one of his five Encyclopædias, until his death, and then have them go to Congress and be paid for—it being his object to place the library entire in their hands, or preserve it so at home.

He had, in a letter to Dr. Cooper, written before the destruction of the library of Congress, stated his own to be " the best chosen collection of its size probably in America, and containing a great mass of what was most rare and valuable, and especially of what related to America."

On the 7th of October, the Joint Library Committee of Congress, reported (by Mr. Goldsborough) as follows:

"That they have received from Mr. Samuel H. Smith an offer from Mr. Jefferson, late President of the United States, of the whole of his library for Congress, on such terms as they consider highly advantageous to the nation, and worthy the distinguished gentleman who tenders it. But the means placed at the disposal of the Committee being very limited, and totally inadequate to the purchase of such a library as that now offered, the committee must have recourse to Congress either to extend their powers, or adopt such other as they may think most proper.

"Should it be the sense of Congress to confide this matter to the Committee, they respectfully submit the following resolution:

"*Resolved*—By the Senate and House of Representatives of the United States of America in Congress assembled, that the Joint Library Committee of the two Houses of Congress be, and they are hereby authorized and empowered to contract, on their part, for the purchase of the library of Mr. Jefferson, late President of the United States, for the use of both Houses of Congress."

When the Senate next met, October 10th, Mr. Jefferson's letter to Smith was communicated, and the above resolution read a third time and unanimously passed. On its being taken up in the House, T. J. Oakley, of New York, moved an amendment, which would change the specific authority of the Committee to purchase Mr. Jefferson's library into a general one to purchase *a* library. This was negatived, by a vote of fifty-three yeas to eighty-seven nays.

Mr. Cyrus King, of Massachusetts, moved an amendment, limiting the Committee to the purchase of such parts of the library as they should deem suitable for the purpose. Several speakers contended that the extent and cost of the purchase was too large—that the selection embraced too many works in foreign languages—that some were too "philosophical" in their character, and others objectionable on other grounds. Voltaire's writings, and Callender's "Prospect Before Us," were specially named among the objectionable productions. King's amendment failed —yeas forty-seven, nays ninety-one. Mr. J. Reed, of Massachusetts, moved to limit the price to be paid to $25,000. This failed, yeas thirty-seven, nays one hundred and three. Timothy Pickering, of Massachusetts, moved an amendment, providing for a selection of the books, and it failed, yeas fifty-two, nays ninety-six. Finally, Oakley moved an amendment, which was generally accepted, requiring the sanction of Congress before the purchase should be completed.

The Senate proceeded to consider the amended resolution, October 20th. Mr. Mason, of New Hampshire, moved that its further consideration be postponed to the first Monday in April.

The vote stood yeas seven, nays twenty-one. The resolution then passed without a division.

A bill, providing that the sum of $23,950 be paid to Mr. Jefferson for his library (in Treasury notes of the issue ordered by the law of March 4th, 1814), passed the Senate December 3d, without a division. This bill came up in the House for its final reading on the 26th of January, 1815. A motion to postpone indefinitely failed—yeas sixty-nine, nays seventy-three. Mr. Cyrus King, of Massachusetts, moved to recommit the bill, with instructions to the committee to report a new section authorizing the selection of such of the books as might be "necessary or useful to Congress in their deliberations," and the disposal of the remainder at public sale. This proposition received fifty-six affirmative votes. Mr. King subsequently moved to recommit the bill, with instructions to report a section "authorizing the Library Committee, as soon as said library should be received at Washington, to select therefrom all books of an atheistical, irreligious and immoral tendency, if any such there were, and send the same back to Mr. Jefferson, without any expense to him." Mr. King afterwards thought proper to withdraw this motion. On the final passage of the bill, the vote stood, yeas eighty-one, nays, seventy-one. Among those who voted in the negative were a number of political and personal friends of Mr. Jefferson, who, while they scorned the grounds of objection avowed by some of their Federal associates, believed that the existing situation of the finances of the country rendered it inexpedient to devote so large a sum to the purchase of a Congressional library.

It has been seen that the valuation of the books was referred by Mr. Jefferson to such persons as Congress should designate. The joint Library Committee made all the arrangements on the part of that body, but it is due to them to say that the placing of the price below a sum at which more than three to one of Congress, including nearly half of the Federal members, had refused to limit it, is understood to have been in pursuance of the wishes and suggestions of Mr. Jefferson. The price did not probably much exceed half the original cost of the books, and they had been purchased under the most favorable circumstances. They were generally uninjured, and the margins of many of them were covered with valuable citations, and annotations, in Mr. Jefferson's own hand.

The Hartford Convention met near the close of 1814—a sort of comet in our political sky, appearing differently to different spectators, but to most clad with dire menaces of present, or dire portents of future disaster. We cannot carry out our preceding sketches of political history in any proportion, nor understand clearly a mooted point in Mr. Jefferson's political views and assertions, without some account of the meeting of this body and of its results.

The proceedings of the Massachusetts Legislature in 1814 were, on various occasions, highly factious and disorganizing; and the elections which took place in that State retained the leaders of faction in power, with scarcely diminished majorities. It was evident that the latter were determined to compel the National Government to submit to the dictation of the New England Federalists—in some important particulars, or to establish a separate Eastern Confederacy. These designs were substantially avowed on legislative floors, by the press, and from the pulpit. Some of the measures alluded to will be described in another place.[1] Prospects of peace with Great Britain, caused a delay in ultimate steps; but when the insolent terms demanded by that power of the American Commissioners sent to treat for peace, roused anew the war spirit of the Middle and Southern States, and rendered it probable that the struggle would be continued to a decisive result, the Massachusetts malcontents adopted a bolder line of action.

On the 8th of October, a joint committee of the Legislature reported, by their chairman, Harrison Gray Otis, that the United States Constitution had failed in securing the objects of its establishment—that the provisions that it contained for amendment were inadequate to the existing emergency—that the people were consequently authorized to resort to such means to secure that result as their safety demanded—that " no reason precluded the right to obviate those dissensions which unfitted our government for peace or war"—and consequently, that a Convention of the States concurring in these views was expedient. It was also recommended to raise and officer a state army of ten thousand men, and provide a million of dollars for its support. The report was adopted by a vote of three to one, and

[1] See APPENDIX, No. 28.

George Cabot, Harrison Gray Otis, Nathan Dane, Joseph Lyman, and eight other less conspicuous individuals were appointed delegates to the Hartford Convention.[1]

Equally violent proceedings took place in the Connecticut Legislature. That body denounced the proposed system of filling the regular army by compulsory drafts from the militia, as unconstitutional and oppressive, and, by a very strong vote, it authorized the Governor, in case such a law should pass Congress, to call a special session of the Legislature to provide for the protection of the people. It denounced the war as criminal in its object, and as, under the circumstances, a violation of the political compact between Government and the people. It appointed Goodrich, Hillhouse, and five other persons delegates to the Hartford Convention.

The Rhode Island Assembly, by a vote of nearly two to one, adopted a report in the same general tone, and appointed four delegates.

The statement should not be omitted, that in a part, if not in all of these States, some portion of the legislative declarations having reference to the Convention contained words or phrases which, separately taken, conveyed the idea that nothing was contemplated repugnant to the obligations of those States as members of the Union. This probably served as an excuse for such hesitating persons as could persuade themselves that an isolated and ambiguous declaration of this kind meant more than the context—more than the general tenor and spirit of the entire legislative proceedings of the period—more than the open avowals of the chief actors—more than the exhortations of the press and the pulpit in favor of revolution or disunion.[2]

[1] A protest was drawn up by Levi Lincoln (son of that Levi Lincoln who had been a member of Mr. Jefferson's Cabinet), and signed by seventy-six members of the House. Thirteen members of the Senate also made a protest, headed by the celebrated John Holmes, who had himself been a Federalist until that party engaged in its present schemes, and who thenceforth denounced it in a series of speeches, which for directness and pith, are almost unrivalled in the annals of partisan contests.

[2] The Boston Gazette asked, "Is there a patriot in America who conceives it his duty to shed his blood for Bonaparte, for Madison, for Jefferson, and that host of ruffians in Congress, who have set their face against us for years, and spirited up the brutal part of the populace to destroy us? Not one. Shall we then be any longer held in slavery, and driven to desperate poverty by such a graceless faction? Heaven forbid!"

Another Boston Journal said:

"To the cry of disunion, the plain and obvious answer is that the States are already separated; the bond of union is broken by President Madison. As we are now going on, we shall certainly be brought to irretrievable ruin. The Convention cannot do a more popular act, not only in New England, but throughout the Atlantic States, than to make a peace for the good of the whole. The Convention must report to their constituents on the subject of peace and war. If they find that it is to continue, it is to be

s which thus formally appointed dele-
Convention, that project did not receive
or Gilman, of New Hampshire, declined
islature of his State. In Vermont, Gover-
mself foremost in hostility to the National
not choose to trust the majority of Federalists
re to act on the question. The recent victories
and Macomb on the borders of the State, had
ord in the popular bosom, which did not vibrate
y with projects of this description.

ederalists of the middle and southern States were
opposed to the war, and individuals, and even a few
acted in the same spirit with the Massachusetts leaders.[1]

that they will recommend, and that the States will adopt the recommendation, uo men or money shall be permitted to go out of New England, until the militia enses already incurred are reimbursed, nor until the most ample provision is made the defence of the New England States, during the continuance of the war."

The Baltimore Federal Republican said, (November 17th, 1814): "On or before the 4th of July, if James Madison is not out of office, a new form of government will be in operation in the Eastern section of the Union. Instantly after, the contest in many States will be, whether to adhere to the old or join the New Government. . . Mr. Madison cannot complete his term of service if the war continues."

The New York Commercial Advertiser said: "Old Massachusetts is as terrible to the American, now, as she was to the British Cabinet in 1775; for America too, has her Butes and her Norths. Let then, the commercial States breast themselves to the shock, and know that to themselves they must look for safety. All party bickerings must be sacrificed on the altar of patriotism. Then, and not till then, shall they humble the pride and ambition of Virginia, whose strength lies in their weakness; and chastise the insolence of those madmen of Kentucky and Tennessee, who aspire to the Government of these States, and threaten to involve the country in all the horrors of war."

The Rev. Elijah Parish, D.D., in a published discourse delivered at Byfield, April 7th, 1814, among a multitude of similar things, said: "The Israelites became weary of yielding the fruit of their labors to pamper their splendid tyrants. They left their political woes. They separated. Where is our Moses? Where is the rod of his miracles? Where is our Aaron? Alas! no voice from the burning bush has directed them here. . . . Such is the temper of the American Republicans, so called. A new language must be invented before we attempt to express the baseness of their conduct, or describe the rottenness of their hearts? . . . New England if invaded, would be obliged to defend herself. Do you not then owe it to your children, and owe it to your God, to make peace for yourselves. . . . The full vials of despotism are poured on your heads, and yet you may challenge the plodding Israelite, the stupid African, the feeble Chinese, the drowsy Turk, or the frozen exile of Siberia to equal you in tame submission to the powers that be. . . . Here we must trample on the mandates of despotism, or here we must remain slaves forever. . . . God will bring good from every evil. The furnaces of Egypt lighted Israel to the land of Canaan. . . . How will the supporters of this anti-christian warfare endure their sentence—endure their own reflections—endure the fire that forever burns—the worm which never dies—the hosannas of heaven—while the smoke of their torments ascends for ever and ever."

The number of similar extracts might be doubled, from the Rev. Doctor's discourse. It will be remembered that in the Introduction of his Ana, Mr. Jefferson speaks of the "pulpit-lyings and slanderings and maniacal ravings of their Gardiners, their Osgoods, and their Parishes." We have in a preceding chapter given specimens of the two first of these worthies, and a slight one of the third. The trio is now complete.

[1] An amusing instance of this, coupled with a characteristic denunciation of Republicanism, occurs in a charge to a grand jury, by Judge Martin of Maryland—our previous acquaintance, Luther Martin. He said: "The horrid atrocities of France are proofs that fallen man, for whose restraint governments were created, is a more deformed and debased monster than the beasts of the earth. Wriggling themselves into place, Republicans become demagogues; and republicanism is by no means inseparably united with

But the majority took the position of Dexter, that it is the duty of the citizen to sustain his country in a war lawfully declared; and not a few bore arms, or furnished money to the Government by aiding to take up its loans. The young and rising men of the party supported the Government almost in a body; and that support soon extended to the general measures of the Republicans and became permanent. Thus an educated and able class, bred in conservative views, who under different circumstances would have continued the Federal party through another generation, and rendered it perhaps permanent as a reasonable and healthful opposition—being forced to choose between a reactionary conservatism, coupled with strong English partialities on one side, and democracy and their country on the other, patriotically chose the latter, and thus cut off forever the line of Federal succession.

The Hartford Convention met on the 15th of December, 1814, consisting of the delegates whose appointments have been mentioned, two irregular volunteer delegates from New Hampshire and one from Vermont—in all, twenty-six persons. It sat with locked doors in an upper room of a stone house, and remained in mysterious gestation for about three weeks.

The only part of its proceedings which the Convention allowed to become public was a report of the delegates to their legislatures (January 4th, 1815), which, after a good deal of preface, advised them to await the decision of Congress on certain pending measures, and then, if necessary, to protect their State sovereignties—or in other words, to prevent those

virtue. False philosophy, conceived in hell, and nursed by the devil, propagated in Europe all their wretchedness, too extensively introduced into the United States. The American Revolution was completed by men of virtue, morality, and religion: but the sun does not shine on a people who have, since then, so deteriorated in virtue, morality, and religion: their depreciation began with that of paper money, and for twenty years Europe has been spewing on this devoted country an almost unremitting torrent of her filthiest feculency, tainting a mass, become still more rotten. Vainly do we attribute our evils to a violation of sailors' rights, or to a weak government. Providence punishes us for our sins with war, the worst of curses, worse than famine or pestilence. No guilt can be more inexpiable than that of him who, without just cause, plunges a nation into war. In the sight of Heaven, such a man will be viewed as the willful, deliberate murderer of every individual who loses his life in its prosecution, and his soul is stained by every drop of blood thereby. They who add sin to sin with greediness in prosecuting the war with which we are afflicted by an avenging God, are those truly guilty of moral treason. I hold it, gentlemen, as a sound and incontrovertible truth, a truth of which I cannot doubt, that no citizen can more righteously divest himself of his allegiance to his government without its consent, than his government can, without his consent, deprive him of its protection. This truth is formed in the very nature of civil society. The contrary doctrine is the spawn of folly and knavery, whatever wiseacres of modern growth may tell us."

The grand jury, not to be outdone in this extra official courtesy and frankness, prepared a written reply in which they expressed their contempt for "the absurd and unconstitutional ground of the court's remarks in defence of perpetual allegiance." etc.

measures from being executed. They proposed the following amendments to the Constitution : to make free population the exclusive basis of representation—to make the President elective but for one term—to render persons of foreign birth ineligible to sit in Congress or hold any civil office under the general government—to prevent an embargo from being imposed for a period exceeding sixty days—to prevent Congress from interdicting commercial intercourse, admitting new States, declaring war, or authorizing hostilities except in case of invasion, without the concurrence of two-thirds of both houses of Congress. They recommended that in case the United States "should refuse their consent to arrangements whereby the New England States, separately or in concert, might be empowered to assume upon themselves the defence of their territory against the enemy, and appropriate therefor such part of the revenue raised in those States as might be necessary," that a new convention meet in Boston in June; and in case of emergency, the officers of the present Convention were authorized to again call it together.

Here were the proposed sweeping constitutional changes—the proposed separate action, or rather inaction, of New England in respect to the war ; but when it came to the new and more rapid mode of constitution changing, which it had been recently declared was demanded by the "public safety," the Convention shrunk back. Revolution was postponed to try the effect of another menace.

The legislatures of Massachusetts and Connecticut accepted the report of their delegates in January, 1815, and appointed "commissioners" to proceed to Washington to make the proposed demand on the National Government. The commissioners of Massachusetts were H. G. Otis, William Sullivan,[1] and Thomas II. Perkins ; those of Connecticut, Calvin Godard and Nathaniel Terry. Pending the session of the Hartford Convention, and subsequently, various steps were resorted to by the legislatures of Connecticut and Massachusetts to annoy the United States authorities and thwart their measures, especially those for raising troops for the army.[2]

---

[1] Author of "Familiar Letters on Public Men of the Revolution," etc., which contain such peculiarly violent assaults on Mr. Jefferson.

[2] The City Corporation of Hartford passed an ordinance, preventing United States troops from parading, or recruiting stations being opened within the limits of the most opulous parts of the city; but it was suspended when Jessup, the commander of the United States troops, informed the Mayor of the city (Goodrich, one of the members

To prevent a recurrence to this topic, a page of history will be anticipated. The commissioners, or envoys, of Massachusetts and Connecticut set out for the national capital under what, to their partizans, appeared imposing circumstances. It was indeed an apparently propitious time to impose terms on the general government. If our troops had learned to fight, money, the sinew of war, was wholly wanting, and the public finances were seemingly embarrassed beyond the power of speedy extrication. Our navy was driven from the ocean. England, relieved by the peace in Europe, could precipitate her whole strength upon us. The demands of the Federalists began to rise. A New York journalist of that party declared that "the greatest curse which could befall the nation would be a peace with Great Britain under the present Administration." Dark hints that Mr. Madison must "resign," or that an "explosion was at hand," began to be heard.[1]

The commissioners, or envoys, were proceeding, when suddenly the news of the victory of New Orleans and the peace of

---

of the Hartford Convention) that he should submit to no local regulations which conflicted with the laws of the United States. Jessup wrote to the War department, January 20th, 1815 : "No regard is paid to the claim or authority of the United States. A soldier was recently arrested for debt, and is now confined in jail. Another was fined, and being without funds, was thrown into prison, where he must remain until the fine is paid. In some parts of the country suits have been commenced against the officers for debts of soldiers: and we are threatened daily with prosecutions in consequence of the enlistment of minors. The legislature will commence in this city early in the next week : the ostensible object for which it is called is, ' to take into consideration *the alarming state of public affairs*,' but, if I mistake not, its real object will be found to be resistance to the laws of the Union."

The legislature of Connecticut passed an act February 3d, requiring the State judges to discharge on *habeas corpus* all minors enlisted without consent of their parents, guardians, and masters. The following scale of penalties was prescribed : for inducing a minor to leave the State to enlist into the army of the United States a fine not exceeding $500, and imprisonment not exceeding a year ; for thus enlisting a minor a fine of $500 ; for advertising or suffering to be posted on his house an advertisement for the enlistment of minors, a fine of $100 and three months' imprisonment. The attorneys of the State were ordered to prosecute by information all breaches of this law. Massachusetts soon passed a similar act. The mails were stopped on Sunday in Connecticut, and various other annoyances resorted to.

A collision would have most likely ensued between the State and National authorities in Connecticut but for the mingled exhibition of decision, good temper, and admirable management of Lieutenant-Colonel Jessup, the splendid young soldier of Chippewa and Bridgewater, who yet bore the unhealed wounds of those encounters on his person. His conduct, under the trying circumstances in which he was placed, forms a delightful page of American history—but here is not the place for it.

[1] The Boston Gazette asked : "Do the Democrats think that a Madison, whose highest ambition is to balance a sentence and round a period—that the rhetorician who once glimmered in harmless debate in times of peace, can now balance the conflicting parties of our country, or direct the energies of a powerful nation?" The Baltimore Federal Gazette published a letter from Washington, dated January 5th, 1815, the day on which the Hartford Convention adjourned, intimating that an "explosion was at hand"—"that the President would be called on to resign." The Federal Republican declared : "We believe, and have for some time believed, that there is no hope of preserving this Union six months, if six weeks, unless Mr. Madison resigns or is removed from office."

Ghent successively sped over the land.   Here was a sudden turn of affairs !   The bubble was punctured, and it instantly burst.   The "Northern Confederacy," or "Confederacy of Commercial States," supposed to be so menacing while England could be called in as an ally, suddenly dwindled into a handful of malcontents, who could easily be put down by the people of their own States.   Derision succeeded indignation in the public mind.   The afterwards celebrated Henry Wheaton advertised a reward in his paper (the New York National Advocate) for the discovery of some unfortunate gentlemen who had started for Washington in the service of the Hartford Convention, but who had missed their way, and it was feared had drowned themselves.   This sally was received with universal merriment, and was followed by others.   It was perhaps fortunate for the envoys that they were considered only fit subjects for ridicule.   At Washington, they exhibited themselves but little to the public eye; neither displayed their credentials to the President nor delivered their ultimatum to the Government—and they took an early opportunity to very quietly return home.

Much controversy and speculation have arisen on the nature of the secret proceedings of the Hartford Convention.   Its journal, after a number of years, was dragged to light; but as would perhaps be expected whatever the proceedings, nothing important was disclosed by it.   Several of its members, and others who claimed to be to a greater or less extent in its secrets, published long explanations of its origin, object, and official acts.   It is somewhat remarkable that none of these explanations agree, and still more so that those made at different periods by the same member—the reputed parent of the project—exhibit a like discrepancy.[1]

[1] We allude of course to Mr. H. G. Otis. This versatile gentleman, itching with national ambition, strove in agony, if not abasement, to remove the brand of national odium which was burnt as if into the flesh of every member of the Convention.   He made his first essay as a member of the United States Senate—but resigned before the close of his term.   He offered at least three public explanations at different periods, of the views and objects of the Hartford Convention.   We shall not enter upon any examination of them in detail, or into comparisons, except to generally illustrate the remark in the text.   In the "Appeal to the citizens of the United States," January 28th, 1820, signed by Otis and eleven other persons, and more especially in Otis's elaborate defence of the Convention in twelve published letters, he claimed that its originators and members had great and affirmative public objects in view, and that the latter assembled to seriously discuss and decide upon measures for their practical attainment.   He expressly declared in the Appeal that the power of raising State troops "to be employed in the State raising the same, or in any adjoining State, and providing for their pay and subsistence," was "the most important object aimed at by *the institution* of the Convention and by the report of that body."   And he said of its deliberations: "There calm and collected, like

The origin and objects of the Convention need no explanations. They are sufficiently spread on official records by its originators, and it is difficult to perceive why particular importance should attach to its secret proceedings, so long as they are not needed to furnish criteria of party motives, and so long as they concededly produced no practical results. In fact, we fully credit the statement in which all the explainers are fortunately enabled to substantially concur, that nothing important was officially done or determined beyond what has become public.[1]

the Pilgrims from whom they descended, and not unmindful of those who had achieved the independence of their country, they deliberated on the most effectual means of preserving for their fellow citizens and their descendants, the civil and political liberty which had been won and bequeathed to them."

Would anybody, after reading claims as lofty as these, and especially after reading Otis's legislative report of October 8th, 1814, expect to find this gentleman afterwards intimating that, after all, the members of the Hartford Convention were only, as children say, "playing pretend"—only suffering themselves to be made the "safety-valve" for the escape of the "steam" of a popular "fermentation;" and that in the legislative measures which *instituted* the Convention, they but acted the part of "unwilling agents?" In Mrs. Willard's History of the United States, published in 1843, is given (at p. 351) an "extract" from a letter, which she says was written to her by Otis in answer to her request to him "to give a brief view of the motives of those engaged in promoting the measure." It is to be presumed that Otis was informed that his statements were desired for historical purposes, and consequently that they purport to give the spirit or substance of a *complete* explanation. The following is the extract entire :

"The Hartford Convention, far from being the original contrivance of a cabal, for any purpose of faction or disunion, was a result growing by natural consequences out of existing circumstances. More than a year previous to its institution, a convention was simultaneously called for by the people, in their town meetings, in all parts of Massachusetts. Petitions to that effect were accumulated on the tables of the Legislative chamber. They were postponed for twelve months, by the influence of those who now sustain the odium of the measure. The adoption of it was the consequence, not the source of a popular sentiment ; and it was intended by those who voted for it, as a *safety-valve* by which the steam arising from the fermentation of the times might escape, not as a boiler in which it should be generated. Whether good or ill, it was a measure of the people, of States, of Legislatures. How unjust to brand the *unwilling agents*, the mere committee of legislative bodies, with the stigma of facts which were first authorized, and then sanctioned by their constituted assemblies."

[1] The character of the members favors this conclusion. They were rich men, indignant at the stoppage of their gains by commercial restrictions and war—colonists in spirit, who, like Tallmadge, thought a war against England was a war against religion and order—aristocrats dreaming of the restoration of those palmy days when political wisdom and rights sprung from hair-powder and shoe-buckles—sectional fanatics, unwilling to have the "moral and religious" people of New England form part of any political compact which they could not control—politicians who were keen consolidationists when they were the Ins at Washington, but who regarded their own banishment from the theatre of national politics as a procedure which demanded the formation of a "confederacy" which would better appreciate their capacities for government. But even among the latter class, by far the most dangerous one, ran the conservatism of personal character, of caste, and of the cautious New England mind. There was not among the members one hopeless enough to be desperate, depraved enough to delight in blood and disorder, or warm enough in temperament to become a dangerous enthusiast.

The contemporaneous views on this subject of the best informed New England Republicans, and of those who personally and well knew the prime actors in the Hartford Convention, are shown in the stirring speeches of John Holmes in the Massachusetts Senate. We quote from two of them :

"You boast of forbearance : but you forbore only because afraid to go further. You complain of Southern aggrandizement, with ten members in the Senate, an undue proportion, according to your population. Massachusetts has become contemptible, a

[r. Jefferson regarded the preliminary measures by which
]onvention was introduced, and that assembly itself, with
1e indignation which was generally felt for them by the
iblicans, and by a great majority of the Federalists out of
hree States represented in the Convention. But he never
·tained a particle of alarm for the result, or a particle of
1st in the fidelity of the mass of the people, even in the
·sented States. He wrote to Mr. Short, November 28th,
, a little more than a fortnight before the meeting of the
·ention :

ome apprehend danger from the defection of Massachusetts. It is a dis-
ble circumstance, but not a dangerous one. If they become neutral, we are
:nt for one enemy without them, and in fact we get no aid from them now.
·r administration determines to join the enemy, their force will be annihilated
1ality of division among themselves. Their Federalists will then call in the
h army, the Republicans ours, and it will only be a transfer of the scene of
om Canada to Massachusetts; and we can get ten men to go to Massachu-
'or one who will go to Canada. Every one, too, must know that we can at
oment make peace with England at the expense of the navigation and fisheries
sachusetts. But it will not come to this. Their own people will put down
factionists as soon as they see the real object of their opposition; and of this
int, New Hampshire, and even Connecticut itself, furnish proofs."

.ese views are substantially repeated in a letter to Mr.

·d of reproach. Your conduct has disgusted the people everywhere. In the
State of New York they have risen against your cabal and hurled defiance in
·eth. There is amongst us a reckless, daring and ambitious faction, who, I do not
e to proclaim, prefer the British Government, *monarchy and all.*

fraid to overthrow the Constitution, you try to undermine it by pretence of
·ment. You called it perfect while you were in pay. The friends of peace,
ng that the country could not be kicked into war, forced it on; and failing to
ss themselves of the administration, tried to destroy the government. An
orized and unconstitutional assemblage at Hartford are to change a Constitution
·d unfit for either war or peace, but which you dare not attack openly. The
; paper of your party, whose editor, as a member of this legislature, voted for the
ies, has openly and uniformly declared that there must be redress, even by
·e and resistance. But violence is dangerous, and therefore you undermine by
ions. Opposition provoked the war and protracts it. The enemy takes pos-
; of a large extent of your country. Instead of expelling him from it, you appoint
ention to divide the States, unless you are permitted to rule them. The Hartford
1tion exploded in a mission to Washington. If Great Britain has not lost confi-
in Massachusetts scolding, threatening, vaporing, evaporating, she prolongs the
·ut that is all. She makes the war disastrous, and calls it disgraceful, which dis-
the enemy she courts. Amid all its atrocious Vandalism, which of you has ever
·d that England is in the right? If there is such a one, I am ready to ask his
1. You accuse the late President Jefferson of causing the war and defending it.
1y excuse his predecessor, President Adams, who still more vigorously defends
·r, and whom you consider ten times worse than Jefferson. You object to de-
; Louisiana, which all your party wanted to take by force from Spain, to rush
vasion and war, but which, peaceably acquired by purchase, you will not defend.
luping England into the war, you continue to deceive her: you dupe her again by
on of our common enemy and reproach of our General Government. The war
en as useful and glorious as that of the Revolution, and eventually will be so
ized. But Massachusetts must join it, or all the disgrace will be hers."

Mellish, of December 10th. On the 27th of the same month, and during the sitting of the Hartford Convention, he wrote the Abbé Correa, that the British Negotiators at Ghent were only insisting on the cession of a part of Maine, as " a thread to hold by until they could hear the result, not of the Congress of Vienna, but of Hartford," but " when they should know, as they would know, that nothing would be done there, they would let go their hold and complete the peace of the world by agreeing to the *status ante bellum*." He wrote Governor Plumer of New Hampshire, January 31st, 1815, very warmly stigmatizing the " agitators and traitors," declaring them to be stipendaries of England and employed to destroy our Government; but he excepted a portion of the actors from these remarks, and expressed the usual contempt of the ability of the Convention to produce any important results.[1]

News of the treaty of Peace reached Washington, February 11th, and Monticello on the 13th. Mr. Jefferson wrote to Lafayette on the 14th:

"The Marats, the Dantons, and Robespierres of Massachusetts are in the same pay, under the same orders, and making the same efforts to anarchize us, that their prototypes in France did there. I do not say that all who met at Hartford were under the same motives of money, nor were those of France. Some of them are Outs, and wish to be Ins; some the mere dupes of the agitators, or of their own party passions, while the Maratists alone are in the real secret; but they have very different materials to work on. The yeomanry of the United States are not the *canaille* of Paris. We might safely give them leave to go through the United States recruiting their ranks, and I am satisfied they could not raise one single regiment (gambling merchants and silk-stocking clerks excepted) who would support them in any effort to separate from the Union. The cement of this Union is in the heart-blood of every American. I do not believe there is on earth a government established on so immovable a basis. Let them, in any State, even in Massachusetts itself, raise the standard of separation, and its citizens will rise in mass, and do justice themselves on their own incendiaries. If they could have induced the Government to some effort of suppression, or even to enter into discussion with them, it would have given them some importance, have brought them into some notice. But they have not been able to make themselves even a subject of conversation, either of public or private societies. A silent contempt has been the sole notice they excite; consoled, indeed, some of them, by the *palpable* favors of Philip. Have then, no fears for us, my friend. The grounds of these exist only in English newspapers, edited or endowed by the Castlereaghs or the Cannings, or some other such models of pure and uncorrupted virtue. Their military heroes by land and

[1] In a letter to Monroe, then Secretary of War, January 1st, while specially mentioning the existing " causes of uneasiness," Jefferson does not even allude to the Convention.

sea, may sink our oyster boats, rob our hen roosts, burn our negro huts, and run off. But a campaign or two more will relieve them from further trouble or expense in defending their American possessions."

And to General Dearborn, March 17th :

"Oh, Massachusetts! how have I lamented the degradation of your apostasy! Massachusetts, with whom I went with pride in 1776, whose vote was my vote on every public question, and whose principles were then the standard of whatever was free or fearless. But then she was under the counsels of the two Adamses ; while Strong, her present leader, was promoting petitions for submission to British power and British usurpation. While under her present counsels, she must be contented to be nothing ; as having a vote, indeed, to be counted, but not respected. But should the State once more buckle on her republican harness, we shall receive her again as a sister, and recollect her wanderings among the crimes only of the parricide party, which would have basely sold what their fathers so bravely won from the same enemy. Let us look forward, then, to the act of repentance, which, by dismissing her venal traitors, shall be the signal of return to the bosom and to the principles of her brethren ; and if her late humiliation can just give her modesty enough to suppose that her southern brethren are somewhat on a par with her in wisdom, in information, in patriotism, in bravery, and even in honesty, although not in psalm singing, she will more justly estimate her own relative momentum in the Union. With her ancient principles, she would really be great, if she did not think herself the whole."

Some of these are doubtless to be regarded as the exaggerated expressions of a man indignant at disloyal conduct, and not, in private letters, chary of epithets towards those who were daily and publicly, on one theatre or another, heaping purely gratuitous insults on his own head. He employed the common party language and imputations of the day. But it is hardly probable that any member of the Hartford Convention, however obsequious his veneration for England, was literally in the pay of its Government. There certainly was no Marat or Danton in the number. A large proportion of the delegates were men of irreproachable private character,[1] and we believe they acted far more wisely and temperately than it was intended they should, by the real authors of the measure.[2]

[1] Cabot, the President, though believed to be one of the most decided of that reactionary party who preferred a mixed government on the English model, to a purely representative one, was a virtuous and benevolent man in private life, and unquestionably *honest* in his political views. Thomas H. Perkins, one of the Commissioners to the General Government, appointed by Massachusetts, is reputed to have been an admirable man in his personal and business relations. Many other less conspicuous actors were equally estimable in private life.

[2] It is not probable that they would have remained in session three weeks, if agreed at the outset. And as they made another appeal to Congress, a step which a report adopted by the Massachusetts Legislature in 1814 had expressly condemned, we are

So deep an odium fell upon the Hartford Convention, that a distinguished New England Federalist is said to have prosecuted a person for slander, for charging him with some connection with that assemblage.[1] There can be little doubt that the public condemnation fell less on its imputed object, unpopular as it was, than on the manner in which that object was sought to be attained. Had the real disunionists boldly avowed their purpose—had they candidly explained the causes and presented fair instead of false issues—had they not taken advantage of a dangerous war to dictate conditions to their country—had they not shown more sympathy for a foreign enemy than for portions of the American people—had they not throughout practised, or countenanced baser men in practising, a petty, trickish, mercenary, and annoying system of measures towards the Government, and an injurious one towards the nation—the mass of their countrymen might have condemned their aims, but they never would have heaped upon the members of the Convention that mountain weight of political scorn and detestation which was not, in a single instance, afterwards removed, or sensibly lightened, until the victim sunk into the grave. Who were the real designers, and who were the instruments or dupes in this apparent attempt to juggle a people into revolution, is still very imperfectly known. No satisfactory history has ever appeared of the rise and fall of the "Eastern Confederacy" scheme, which made some external demonstrations at three different periods, and which finally exploded in the Hartford Convention.

The Boston Convention which was to have been the sequel of that of Hartford, was not held, or in the language of President J. Q. Adams, it was "turned over to the receptacle of things lost upon earth." The constitutional amendments proposed by the Hartford Convention were passed by no States which were not formally represented in that body—and they were rejected by some[2] with strong expressions of contempt.

Turning to Mr. Jefferson's private affairs, and to his farm-book in 1815, it appears that the roll of negroes at Monticello,

strongly inclined to believe that the majority of *business men* in the Convention, voted down the *political wire pullers* who were expected to control them.

[1] Daniel Webster is said thus to have prosecuted Theodore Lyman—the last a son of one of the members of the Hartford Convention.

[2] For example, Pennsylvania.

included one hundred and thirty-five; the number at Poplar Forest is not given. His sowing of wheat extended to four hundred and twenty bushels. We find no record of the products of the year, and infer from the omission, that they were neither so large nor so small as to occasion particular remark. The farm-book contains the usual particulars and annual estimates in respect to the domestic manufacture of wool, cotton, and hemp. Mr. Jefferson had not yet learned how utterly inadequate this kind of manufacturing would prove to withstand the reflux of importation after the close of the war.

In a letter, of March 2d, 1815, to Jean Baptiste Say, the celebrated French writer on political economy, appear some interesting, because definite and reliable, agricultural, economical, and other statistics of Virginia. Say was contemplating emigrating to America, to engage in cotton manufacturing, and was inclined to select his residence in the immediate neighborhood of Mr. Jefferson. His inquiries drew from the latter the statements from which the following are selected. After giving a scale of the rise in lands from 1793 to 1811, illustrated by particular examples, showing that they ascended, during that period, from four to sixteen dollars, and from seven to twenty dollars per acre, Mr. Jefferson declared that, owing to the "dropsical state of our medium," this did not give a true idea of their actual value, which he supposed to be from twelve to fifteen dollars an acre. The "best farmers, such as Mr. Randolph, his son-in-law," he said, "got from ten to twenty bushels of wheat to the acre; the worst, such as himself, from six to eighteen." The labor of an able-bodied man cost sixty dollars a year, and he was clothed and fed by his employer—a woman half that sum. A good plow-horse was worth fifty or sixty dollars; a draught-ox, from twenty to twenty-five; a milch cow from fifteen to eighteen; a sheep two dollars; beef five cents, mutton and pork seven cents, and butter from twenty to twenty-five cents a pound; a turkey or goose fifty cents; a chicken, eight and one-third cents; and a dozen of eggs the same. We will close the extracts with a word descriptive of his Albemarle neighbors:

"The Society is much better than is common in country situations; perhaps there is not a better *country* society in the United States. But do not imagine this a Parisian or an academical society. It consists of plain, honest, and rational neighbors, some of them well informed and men of reading, all superintending their farms, hospitable and friendly, and speaking nothing but English. The manners of every nation are the standard of orthodoxy within itself. But these standards being arbitrary, reasonable people in all allow free toleration for the manners, as for the religion of others."

He wrote to Mr. Wendover, March 13th,[1] some views in respect to the right of the clergy to discuss political questions in the pulpit, which do not appear elsewhere in his writings. He said that human concerns, moral and physical, were so vast, that no person could qualify himself to instruct others in all of them, and that consequently they were divided into departments, each of which might occupy the time and attention of a single individual who purposed to teach them. Thus there were separate teachers of mathematics, medicine, law and religion. Congregations associated together, and employed a religious teacher of their particular sect, and contributed to pay him a salary "for the trouble of delivering them at such periods as they agree on, lessons in the religion they profess." Mr. Jefferson continued:

"If they want instruction in other sciences or arts, they apply to other instructors; and this is generally the business of early life. But I suppose there is not an instance of a single congregation which has employed their preacher for the mixed purposes of lecturing them *from the pulpit* in Chemistry, in Medicine, in Law, in the science and principles of Government, or in anything but religion exclusively. Whenever, therefore, preachers, instead of a lesson in religion, put them off with a discourse on the Copernican system, on chemical affinities, on the construction of government, or the characters or conduct of those administering it, it is a breach of contract, depriving their audience of the kind of service for which they are salaried, and giving them, instead of it, what they did not want, or, if wanted, would rather seek from better sources in that particular art or science. In choosing our pastor we look to his religious qualifications, without inquiring into his physical or political dogmas, with which we mean to have nothing to do. I am aware that arguments may be found, which may twist a thread of politics into the cord of religious duties. So may they for every other branch of human art or science. Thus, for example, it is a religious duty to obey the laws of our country; the teacher of religion, therefore, must instruct us in those laws, that we may know how to obey them. It is a religious duty to assist our sick neighbors; the preacher must, therefore, teach us medicine, that we may do it understandingly. It is a religious duty to preserve our own health; our religious teacher, then, must tell us what dishes are wholesome, and give us recipes in cookery, that we may learn how to prepare them. And so, ingenuity, by generalizing more and more, may amalgamate all the branches of science into any one of them, and the physician who is paid to visit the sick, may give a sermon instead of medicine, and the merchant to whom money is sent for a hat, may send a handkerchief instead of it?"[2]

[1] The letter is indorsed "not sent."
[2] He did not deny that a congregation might, if they chose, agree with their preacher

Mr. Jefferson confined this view to abstract or legal rights. There is another one of expediency, in regard to which the opinion of Mr. Burke may be perused with some interest in this connection. He said:

"Politics and the pulpit are terms that have little agreement. No sound ought to be heard in the church but the voice of healing charity. The cause of civil liberty and civil government gains as little as that of religion by this confusion of duties. Those who quit their proper character to assume what does not belong to them, are for the greater part both ignorant of the character they leave, and of the character they assume. Wholly unacquainted with the world, in which they are so fond of meddling, and inexperienced in all its affairs, on which they pronounce with so much confidence, they know nothing of politics but the passions they excite. Surely the church is a place where one day's truce ought to be allowed to the dissensions and animosities of mankind."

Several letters are addressed to Professor' Girardin, in the early part of 1815, in reference to events to be described in the continuation of Burk's History of Virginia. Girardin was then preparing that work at Milton, two or three miles from Monticello. In one of his letters Mr. Jefferson mentioned how he wished to be treated, during his life, by writers of history:

"As to what is to be said of myself, I of course am not the judge. But my sincere wish is that the faithful historian, like the able surgeon, would consider me in his hands, while living, as a dead subject, that the same judgment may now be expressed which will be rendered hereafter, so far as my small agency in human affairs may attract future notice; and I would of choice now stand as at the bar of posterity. ' Cum semel occidaris, et de te ultima Minos fecerit arbitria.' The only exact testimony of a man is his actions, leaving the reader to pronounce on them his own judgment. In anticipating this, too little is safer than too much; and I sincerely assure you that you will please me most by a rigorous suppression of all friendly partialities. This candid expression of sentiments once delivered, passive silence becomes the future duty.

He also contributed some materials to Wirt's Life of Patrick Henry, during the year. His family remember that he was particularly active during the summer in both indoor and outdoor improvements, inventions, scientific investigations, etc. He

to instruct them in law. or medicine. or politics—but in that case he said, it must be by the consent of every individual member, " because the association being voluntary, the mere majority had no right to apply the contributions of the minority to purposes unspecified in the agreement of the congregation." Out of the pulpit, he thought "the preacher had the right, equally with every other citizen, to write or express his sentiments," on politics or other subjects, " his leisure time being his own, and his congregation not obliged to listen to his conversation, or to read his writings."

' He was a Professor for a time in William and Mary College—in what department we are not informed.

contrived a leather top for a carriage, which could be readily arranged to exclude rain, or leave the vehicle entirely un-covered—and which worked essentially on the plan of the modern extension-top carriage. He invented a machine for breaking hemp, which he first had moved by the gate of his saw-mill, and afterwards by a horse. It answered its purpose completely, and produced a material saving in expense. His fertile ingenuity also gave birth to many minor contrivances. He measured the heights of Monticello and various contiguous hills—and of the peaks of Otter when he made his autumn visit to Poplar Forest. Altogether he spent an active and agreeable year.

In one of his earliest letters in 1816, addressed to his Revolu-tionary compatriot, the venerable Charles Thomson, he thus described his bodily condition and habits:

"I retain good health, am rather feeble to walk much, but ride with ease, passing two or three hours a day on horseback,[1] and every three or four months taking in a carriage a journey of ninety miles to a distant possession, where I pass a good deal of my time. My eyes need the aid of glasses by night, and with small print, in the day also; my hearing is not quite so sensible as it used to be; no tooth shaking yet; but shivering and shrinking in body from the cold are now experienced, my thermometer having been as low as 12° this morning. My great-est oppression is a correspondence afflictingly laborious, the extent of which I have long been endeavoring to curtail. This keeps me at the drudgery of the writing-table all the prime hours of the day, leaving for the gratification of my appetite for reading, only what I can steal from the hours of sleep. Could I reduce this episto-lary corvée within the limits of my friends and affairs, and give the time redeemed from it to reading and reflection, to history, ethics, mathematics, my life would be as happy as the infirmities of age would admit, and I should look on its consummation with the composure of one ' *qui summum nec metuit diem nec optat.*' "

In a letter written to John Adams, about three months afterwards, he shows how well he preserved the elasticity of his early feelings and his characteristic view of human life:

"You ask, if I would agree to live my seventy or rather seventy-three years over again? To which I say, yea. I think with you, that it is a good world on

---

[1] He alluded to a bodily habit, not mentioned here, in a letter to Mr. Maury, June 16th, 1815:

" Your practice of the cold bath thrice a week during the winter, and at the age of seventy, is a bold one, which I should not, *à priori*, have pronounced salutary. But all theory must yield to experience, and every constitution has its own laws. I have for fifty years bathed my feet in cold water every morning (as you mention), and having been remarkably exempted from colds (not having had one in every seven years of my life on an average). I have supposed it might be ascribed to that practice. When we see two facts accompanying one another for a long time, we are apt to suppose them re-lated as cause and effect."

the whole; that it has been framed on a principle of benevolence, and more pleasure than pain dealt out to us. There are, indeed (who might say nay), gloomy and hypochondriac minds, inhabitants of diseased bodies, disgusted with the present, and despairing of the future; always counting that the worst will happen, because it may happen. To these I say, how much pain have cost us the evils which have never happened! My temperament is sanguine. I steer my bark with Hope in the head, leaving Fear astern. My hopes, indeed, sometimes fail; but not oftener than the forebodings of the gloomy. There are, I acknowledge, even in the happiest life, some terrible convulsions, heavy set-offs against the opposite page of the account. I have often wondered for what good end the sensations of grief could be intended. All our other passions, within proper bounds, have a useful object. And the perfection of the moral character is, not in a stoical apathy, so hypocritically vaunted, and so untruly too, because impossible, but in a just equilibrium of all the passions. I wish the pathologists then would tell us what is the use of grief in the economy, and of what good it is the cause, proximate or remote."

     •   •   •   •   •   •   •   •

"There is a ripeness of time for death, regarding others as well as ourselves, when it is reasonable we should drop off, and make room for another growth. When we have lived our generation out, we should not wish to encroach on another. I enjoy good health; I am happy in what is around me, yet I assure you I am ripe for leaving all, this year, this day, this hour."

Should we suppose that every word in this off-hand correspondence implied settled opinions or ideas—that he wrote nothing in it merely as speculation, to embody the passing doubt of the moment, or to draw out another's opinions and experiences—that his language never partook of the exaggeration of expression customary in epistolary writing—we should much wonder to hear Mr. Jefferson, in the above extract, asking what were the uses of grief in the moral economy. But that wonder ceases when we remember that in the same paragraph he declared his belief that the world was framed on a principle of benevolence, and when we know that none more uniformly than he felt or expressed complete resignation to the Divine will, under the infliction of the most agonizing griefs which he ever encountered.[1]

Some of Mr. Jefferson's earliest letters in 1816, were directed against the prevailing bank-mania. He wrote Colonel Yancey, January 6th:

"Like a dropsical man calling out for water, water, our deluded citizens are clamoring for more banks, more banks. The American mind is now in that state

---

[1] Let the reader turn back for an example to his letter to Governor Page, on the death of Mrs. Eppes. After receiving Mr. Adams's answer to his question above, he wrote back, August 1st, 1816: "To the question, indeed, on the utility of grief, no answer remains to be given. You have exhausted the subject. I see that with the other evils of life, it is destined to temper the cup we are to drink."

of fever which the world has so often seen in the history of other nations. We are under the bank bubble, as England was under the South Sea bubble, France under the Mississippi bubble, and as every nation is liable to be, under whatever bubble, design, or delusion may puff up in moments when off their guard. We are now taught to believe that ledgerdemain tricks upon paper can produce as solid wealth as hard labor in the earth. It is vain for common sense to urge that *nothing* can produce but *nothing*; that it is an idle dream to believe in a philosopher's stone which is to turn everything into gold, and to redeem man from the original sentence of his Maker, 'in the sweat of his brow shall he eat his bread.'"

The whole of this letter will be read with interest in his published Works. Taught, as they imagined, by the events of the war, many of the ablest and most conscientious Republican opponents of a National Bank, yielded at this period to the supposed necessity of such an institution. A bill passed Congress chartering the bank of the United States, with a capital of $35,000,000;[1] and it was approved by President Madison, April 10th, 1816. Mr. Jefferson, as usual, uttered no complaints at the proceedings of his friends—but his own opinions remained unchanged, as clearly appears by several letters of the period.[2]

In a letter to Benjamin Austin, January 9th, he avowed that he had changed the opinions expressed in the Notes on Virginia against home manufactures. Having explained the circumstances that existed when that work was written, and the completely changed ones produced by the subsequent maritime and commercial regulations of the European powers, he said that he who continued against domestic manufactures, must be for reducing us to dependence on foreign nations—that manufactures, to the extent of our own supply, were as necessary to our independence as to our comfort. It has been inferred from this and one or two other letters, and from a passage in one of his Presidential Messages, that Mr. Jefferson favored a protective tariff sufficient to build up domestic manufactures—and this by a second inference has been assumed to be a high protective tariff. At a later period, he declared himself in favor of a revenue tariff, with such incidental protection as could be properly afforded within its limits,[3]—and this, it is believed, is as far as he ever advocated *protection*.

[1] The capital of the first bank had been but $10,000.000.
[2] See a letter to John Taylor of Caroline, May 28th: to William H. Crawford, June 20th, 1816, etc.
[3] See his letter to Mr. Pinckney, September 30th, 1820.

Mr. Jefferson's attention was drawn, in 1816, by the Governor of Virginia (his friend Wilson C. Nicholas, then in the third year of his office), to a general system of improvements for the defence, education, and development of the material resources of the State. His replies, dated April 2d, and 19th, will be found to contain many broad and valuable views, but they cannot be given here. Passing over several political letters of interest, we come to one which demands notice.

The first Constitution of Virginia, established in 1776, had, from the period of the publication of Jefferson's Notes on Virginia, constantly encountered the objections against it raised in that work; and these, instead of diminishing by the lapse of time, had acquired force in the public mind. Several attempts had been made to procure a revision of the instrument, but it had been prevented by the eastern counties. The western counties, smarting under a recent defeat of this kind, in 1816, invited a meeting of delegates to promote the object. Samuel Kercheval, a western gentleman, published some letters in favor of a revision, and inclosed them to Jefferson, soliciting his views. The reply was long, and exhibits all the power and daring of its author's earlier political disquisitions. He "besought" Kercheval, however, in a second letter, not "to admit of the possibility" of that reply being published, saying that "many good people would revolt from its doctrines," and that he wished "to leave to those who were to live under it, the settlement of their own Constitution, and to pass in peace the remainder of his time"—that if his "opinions were sound, they would occur to others, and would prevail by their own weight without the aid of names." The letters will be given in the Appendix.[1]

Professor Tucker, generally correct, and always candid authority, mentions the following facts in regard to Jefferson's first communication to Kercheval:

"As his letter had an extensive circulation notwithstanding his caution, and eventually found its way into the newspapers, the fear that some of them [his views] deemed most exceptionable, would be adopted, under the known influence of his name, and his presumed efforts in their favor, induced many who would otherwise have desired a revision of the Constitution to postpone it during his life."[2]

Another able and candid Virginia writer, critically versed

[1] See APPENDIX, No. 29.   [2] Tucker's Life of Jefferson, vol. ii., p. 390.

in both the written and unwritten history of his State, Dr. Grigsby, says in his discourse on the Virginia Convention of 1776:

> The first Constitution of Virginia withstood, for near fifty years, his [Jefferson's] attacks in the Notes; but when he threw his thoughts into the shape of a letter to Kercheval, the fate of that instrument was sealed. The phrases of that letter were at once stereotyped in the public voice; and it was amusing to observe on the court green, and in debate, how those phrases passed current with men who had never seen or heard of the letter, and who believed that they were clothing their own thoughts in their own words."

Professor Tucker further says, that " when the revision did take place in 1829, several of " Mr. Jefferson's " principles were deliberately rejected in the Convention—one or two by large majorities." He might, had he written late enough, have added, that at a succeeding Convention, in 1851, some of the rejected "principles" were adopted. But irrespective of the fate of his propositions, or of their intrinsic soundness, few more striking tributes have ever been paid to the influence of an aged and retired statesman than are to be found in the fact, that many friends of a revision dared not have it take place during his life, for fear that his bare opinions—for nobody expected his appearance there—would bear down all opposition in the Constitutional Convention of a State which swarmed with able public men.

Mr. Jefferson wrote a letter to Sir John Sinclair, July 31st, in which, after reciprocating the congratulations of the latter on the termination of the war between their respective nations, and saying that amicable dispositions towards England had been strong on the part of every American Administration, " from the first to the present one," he made the following important declaration:

> "During the first year of my own administration, I thought I discovered in the conduct of Mr. Addington some marks of comity towards us, and a willingness to extend to us the decencies and duties observed towards other nations. My desire to catch at this, and to improve it for the benefit of my own country, induced me, in addition to the official declarations from the Secretary of State, to write with my own hand to Mr. King, then our Minister Plenipotentiary at London, in the following words: [here follows the extract from a letter to Mr. King, of July 13th, 1802, given at page 15 of this volume, except that the first sentence is slightly altered to leave out the irrelevant matter in respect to the *occasion* of writing.[1] And then Mr. Jefferson proceeds to say.] " My expectation was that Mr. King would show

---

[1] And there are two wholly unimportant verbal deviations produced, probably by the copier or printer.

this letter to Mr. Addington, and that it would be received by him as an overture towards a cordial understanding between the two countries. He left the ministry, however, and I never heard more of it, and certainly never perceived any good effect from it."

In a letter to James Maury, four years earlier (April 25th, 1812). Mr. Jefferson alluded to the same facts.[1] In Mr. Trist's Memoranda occurs the following record of some remarks made by Mr. Jefferson, January 7th, 1826—about six months before his death:

"When I came into office, I wrote to Mr. King, pressing him to retain his office. A short time after, I wrote him a letter with my own hand,[2] which it was my intention he should show to the Ministry, declaring that it then was (as it always has been), my wish that we keep on good terms with that nation. People have taken up an erroneous notion I was hostile to them. *This letter was never shown.* Some time after, however, I wrote one to Sir John Sinclair, containing an expression of similar sentiments, which *was* shown, and which produced an immediate change in *the conduct* of the British Ministry."

The letter to Sinclair here referred to was dated June 30th, 1803, and has been given at page 67 of this volume. And Mr. Jefferson might have added that ten days later he addressed a letter of similar import to the Earl of Buchan, which was also undoubtedly shown.[3]

---

[1] The following is an extract from the letter:

"The English newspapers suppose me the personal enemy of their nation. I am not so. I am an enemy to its injuries, as I am to those of France. If I could permit myself to have national partialities, and if the conduct of England would have permitted them to be directed towards her, they would have been so. I thought that in the administration of Mr. Addington, I discovered some dispositions toward justice, and even friendship and respect for us, and began to pave the way for cherishing these dispositions, and improving them into ties of mutual good will. But we had then a Federal minister there, whose dispositions to believe himself, and to inspire others with a belief in our sincerity, his subsequent conduct has brought into doubt; and poor Merry, the English minister here, had learned nothing of diplomacy but its suspicions, without head enough to distinguish when they were misplaced. Mr. Addington and Mr. Fox passed away too soon to avail the two countries of their dispositions."

[2] Mr. Trist supposed he meant to be understood that the first named letter was written by the Secretary of State.

[3] His feelings towards England in 1816, are strongly illustrated by a letter he wrote to Monroe. Various courses having been proposed in Congress to perpetuate the memory of the British outrage in destroying the Capitol, and an inscription on the new building being the one generally preferred, the Secretary of State consulted Mr. Jefferson as to its tenor. The latter replied October 16th, proposing that if there was any inscription it should be as follows: "Founded 1791—Burnt by a British army 1814—Restored by Congress 1817." But he questioned the utility of any inscription. He said the "barbarism of the conflagration would immortalize that of the nation." But he thought that in future England had vastly more to dread from us than we from her—that she was "falling from her transcendent sphere"—and he added:

"It is for the interest of all that she should be maintained, *nearly* on a par with other members of the republic of nations. Her power, absorbed into that of any other, would be an object of dread to all, and to us more than all, because we are accessible to her alone, and through her alone. The armies of Bonaparte with the fleets of Britain, would change the aspect of our destinies. Under these prospects should we perpetuate hatred against her? Should we not, on the contrary, begin to open ourselves to other and more rational dispositions? It is not improbable that the circumstances of the war and her own circumstances may have brought her wise men to begin to view

He informed a member of his family, in conversation, that no circumstance ever gave him more pain than the conduct of Mr. King on this occasion, that it was with difficulty he could bring himself to believe it, and that he shuddered to learn that the Federal leaders were willing to inflict serious injury on their country for the sake of injuring his Administration.

The precise proofs which he had that his letter was not shown, are not within our knowledge. We would fain hope that there may have been some mistake or misapprehension in the matter—either that Mr. King did communicate the letter —that he did not receive it—or that he mistook its intended destination. The last would be a most flimsy excuse, and the second is entirely improbable. Mr. King's unpublished correspondence may fortunately establish the first fact. He was an ultra-Federalist, and one of the fondest of the admirers of England—but his conduct during the war of 1812, would seem to show that he had no foreign or partisan partialities strong enough to interfere with the calls of honor and patriotism.

A number of Mr. Jefferson's unpublished family letters in 1816 are before us. They abound in the usual expressions of strong affection, and they show that he was deeply interesting himself in the education of his grandchildren.

Mr. Eppes, since his second marriage, had been much sepa-

us with other and even with kindred eyes. Should not our wise men, then, lifted above the passions of the ordinary citizen, begin to contemplate what *will* be the interests of our country on so important a change among the elements which influence it? I think it would be better to give her time to show her present temper, and to prepare the minds of our citizens for a corresponding change of disposition, by acts of comity towards England, rather than by commemoration of hatred. These views might be greatly extended. Perhaps, however, they are premature, and that I may see the ruin of England nearer than it really is."

In a letter to John Adams, November 25th, Mr. Jefferson expressed equivalent views; and he said that were England "under a government which could treat us with justice and equity, he should himself feel with great strength the ties which bound us together, of origin, language, laws and manners; and he was persuaded the two people would become in future, as it was with the ancient Greeks, among whom it was reproachful for Greek to be found fighting against Greek in a foreign army."

Mr. Adams was in a less placable mood. He saw no prospect of a change in the Government of England, and less of any relenting on its part towards the United States. He replied:

"Instead of ' turning their eyes to us,' their innate feelings will turn them from us. They have been taught from their cradles to despise, scorn, insult, and abuse us. They hate us more vigorously than they do the French. They would sooner adopt the simple monarchy of France than our republican institutions.   *   *   *   *

" Britain will never be our friend till we are her master.

" This will happen in less time than you and I have been struggling with her power; provided we remain united. Aye! there's the rub! I fear there will be greater difficulties to preserve our Union, than you and I, our fathers, brothers, friends, disciples, and sons have had to form it. Towards Great Britain, I would adopt their own maxim. An English jockey says, ' if I have a wild horse to break, I begin by convincing him I am his master; and then I will convince him that I am his friend.' I am well assured that nothing will restrain Great Britain from injuring us but fear."

iated from Mr. Jefferson, by distance of residence, and by the pressure of his private business, between sessions of Congress. But the fond grandfather had generally contrived to keep Francis Eppes with himself, or in schools near his residence. Mr. Eppes senior, had prepared to relieve him of this care in 1816, by sending his son to a school in North Carolina. Mr. Jefferson, with customary delicacy, but with evident solicitude, attempted to prevent this arrangement from being carried into effect. Here is a characteristic passage from one of his letters:

"I am almost afraid to propose to you to yield to me the expense and direction of his education. Yet I think I could have it conducted to his advantage. Certainly no expense which could be useful to him, and no attention on my part would be spared; and he could visit you at such times as you should wish. If you say yea to this proposition, he might come on to me at Poplar Forest, for which place I shall set out about the 6th of April, and shall be there to about the 21st; and could I hear from you soon after my arrival there, I could be taking preparatory steps for his reception and the course to be pursued. All this is submitted to your good pleasure. Patsy, supposing Mrs. Eppes to have an attachment to flowers, sends her a collection of seeds."

Mr. Eppes, of course, consented that his son remain. Mr. Jefferson, after minutely describing the school he had selected, added:

"I am sensible, my dear sir, of the delicacy of your sentiments on the subject of expense. I am indeed an unskillful manager of my farms, and sensible of this from its effects, I have now committed them to better hands, of whose care and skill I have satisfactory knowledge, and to whom I have ceded the entire direction.[1] This is all that is necessary to make them adequate to all my wants, and to place me at entire ease. And for whom should I spare in preference to Francis, on sentiments either of duty or affection? I consider all my grandchildren as if they were my children, and want nothing but for them. It is impossible that I could reconcile it to my feelings, that he alone of them should be a stranger to my cares and contributions. You must then, permit me to come in for my share, and to do something which may give me somewhat of the parental character with him; not to the diminution of what he feels and owes to you, or of your authority; but yet to be something affectionate in his eyes. We will both, then, do what falls in our way. I have accordingly advanced to Mr. Mitchell, for the ensuing session, for so they divide the year. And it is all but nothing; being no more than I paid to Mr. Maury for my own education, fifty-five years ago."

In the last paragraph the reader obtains a hint of Mr. Jefferson's pecuniary expectations at this period. The rose color of hope, as usual, predominated. It was strange that with the accu-

---

[1] The individual here referred to was his grandson, Thomas Jefferson Randolph.

mulating facts constantly under his eyes—with an army of guests constantly devouring his substance—amidst money fluctuations which rendered every business arrangement and expectation wholly unreliable—he should have seemed to imagine that unskillful farming had been the leak in the vessel, or that any skill in farming would stop it. In this private letter to a favorite son-in-law, he does not allude to the real cause of his straitening circumstances. He never alluded to it but once or twice, it is believed, and then only to his daughter and oldest grandson.

The bark was not yet in the rapids—but one less hopeful and more familiar with the progress of pecuniary misfortune, would have already heard the roar of the nearing whirlpool.

We select the following from his letters of this period to the grandson mentioned in the preceding extracts:

To Francis Eppes, Millbrook.

Monticello, May 21, 1814.

I send you, my dear Francis, a Greek grammar, the best I know for the use of schools. It is the one now the most generally used in the United States. I expect you will begin it soon after your arrival at the New London Academy. You might, while at home, amuse yourself with learning the letters, and spelling and reading the Greek words, so that you may not be stopped by that when Mr. Mitchell puts you into the grammar. I think you will like him, and old Mr. and Mrs. Deshavens, from the character I have of them. I am sure Mr. Mitchell will do everything for you he can, and I have no fear that you will not do full justice to his instruction. But, while you endeavor, by a good store of learning, to prepare yourself to become a useful and distinguished member of your country, you must remember that this can never be, without uniting merit with your learning. Honesty, disinterestedness, and good nature are indispensable to procure the esteem and confidence of those with whom we live, and on whose esteem our happiness depends. Never suffer a thought to be harbored in your mind which you would not avow openly. When tempted to do anything in secret, ask yourself if you would do it in public; if you would not, be sure it is wrong. In little disputes with your companions, give way rather than insist on trifles, for their love and the approbation of others will be worth more to you than the trifle in dispute. Above all things, and at all times, practise yourself in good humor; this of all human qualities is the most amiable and endearing to society. Whenever you feel a warmth of temper rising, check it at once, and suppress it, recollecting it would make you unhappy within yourself, and disliked by others. Nothing gives one person so great an advantage over another, under all circumstances. Think of these things, practise them, and you will be rewarded by the love and confidence of the world. I have some expectation of being at Poplar Forest the third week of June, when I hope I shall see you going on cleverly, and already beloved by your tutors, curators, and companions, as you are by yours affectionately,

Th. Jefferson.

CHAPTER XI.

1817—1822.

An intelligent traveller, Lieutenant Hall, of the British army, made a visit to Monticello at this period, and he has left the following account of it.[1]

[1] Travels in Canada and the United States in 1816 and 1817, by Lieut. Francis Hall.

"Having an introduction to Mr. Jefferson [said Mr. Hall] I ascended his little mountain, on a fine morning, which gave the situation its due effect. The whole of the sides and base are covered with forest, through which roads have been cut circularly so that the winding may be shortened at pleasure: the summit is an open lawn, near to the south side of which the house is built, with its garden just descending the brow: the saloon, or central hall, is ornamented with several pieces of antique sculpture, Indian arms, mammoth bones, and other curiosities collected from various parts of the Union. I found Mr. Jefferson tall in person, but stooping and lean with old age, thus exhibiting the fortunate mode of bodily decay which strips the frame of its most cumbersome parts, leaving it still strength of muscle and activity of limb. His deportment was exactly such as the Marquis de Chastellux describes it above thirty years ago. 'At first serious, nay, even cold,' but in a very short time relaxing into a most agreeable amenity, with an unabated flow of conversation on the most interesting topics discussed in the most gentlemanly and philosophic manner. I walked with him round his grounds, to visit his pet trees and improvements of various kinds; during the walk he pointed out to my observation a conical mountain, rising singly at the edge of the southern horizon of the landscape: its distance, he said, was forty miles, and its dimensions those of the greater Egyptian pyramid; so that it accurately represents the appearance of the pyramid at the same distance; there is a small cleft visible on its summit, through which the true meridian of Monticello exactly passes; its most singular property, however, is, that on different occasions it looms, or alters its appearance, becoming sometimes cylindrical, sometimes square, and sometimes assuming the form of an inverted cone. Mr. Jefferson had not been able to connect this phenomenon with any particular season or state of the atmosphere, except that it most commonly occurred in the forenoon. He observed that it was not only wholly unaccounted for by the laws of vision. but that it had not as yet engaged the attention of philosophers so far as to acquire a name; that of looming, being in fact, a term applied by sailors to appearances of a similar kind at sea. The Blue Mountains are also observed to loom, though not in so remarkable a degree.

"It must be remarkable to recall and preserve the political sentiments of a man who has held so distinguished a station in public life as Mr. Jefferson. He seemed to consider much of the freedom and happiness of America to arise from local circumstances. 'Our population,' he observed, 'has an elasticity by which it would fly off from oppressive taxation.' He instanced the beneficial effects of a free government, in the case of New Orleans, where many proprietors who were in a state of indigence under the dominion of Spain, have risen to sudden wealth, solely by the rise in the value of land, which followed a change of government. Their ingenuity in mechanical inventions, agricultural improvements, and that mass of general information to be found among Americans of all ranks and conditions, he ascribed to that ease of circumstances which afforded them leisure to cultivate their minds, after the cultivation of their lands was completed. In fact I have frequently been surprised to find mathematical and other useful works, in houses which seemed to have little pretensions to the luxury of learning. 'Another cause,' Mr. Jefferson observed, 'might be discovered in the many court and county meetings which brought men frequently together on public business, and thus gave them habits, both of thinking, and expressing their thoughts on subjects, which in other countries are confined to the privileged few.' Mr. Jefferson has not the reputation of

14th Light Dragoons, H. P. London, printed for Longman, Hurst, Rees, and Orme & Brown, Paternoster Row, 1819.

being very friendly to England; we should, however, be aware that a partiality in this respect, is not absolutely the duty of an American citizen; neither is it to be expected that the policy of our government should be regarded in foreign countries with the complacency with which it is looked upon by ourselves; but whatever may be his sentiments in this respect, politeness naturally repressed any offensive expression of them; he talked of our affairs with candor, and apparent good will, though leaning perhaps to the gloomier side of the picture. He did not perceive by what means we could be extricated from our present financial embarrassments, without some kind of revolution in our government. On my replying that our habits were remarkably steady, and that great sacrifices would be made to prevent a violent catastrophe, he acceded to the observation, but demanded if those who made the sacrifices would not require some political reformation in return. His repugnance was strongly marked to the despotic principles of Bonaparte, and he seemed to consider France, under Louis XVI. as scarcely capable of a republican form of government; but added that the present generation of Frenchmen had grown up with sounder notions which would probably lead to their emancipation. Relative to the light in which he views the conduct of the allied sovereigns, I cannot do better than insert a letter of his to Dr. Logan, dated 18th October, 1813, and published in the American newspapers:

"'DEAR SIR: I thank you for the extract in yours of August 16th, respecting the Emperor Alexander. It arrived here a day or two after I had left this place, from which I have been absent about seven or eight weeks. I had, from other information, formed the most favorable opinion of the virtues of the Emperor Alexander, and considered his partiality to this country as a prominent proof of them. The magnanimity of his conduct on the first capture of Paris, still magnified everything we had believed of him, but how he will come out of his present trial remains to be seen: that the sufferings which France had inflicted on other countries, justified some reprisals cannot be questioned, but I have not yet learned what crimes Poland, Saxony, Belgium, Venice, Lombardy, and Genoa, had merited for them not merely a temporary punishment, but that of permanent subjugation, and a destitution of independence and self-government. The fable of Æsop and the Lion dividing the spoils, is, I fear, becoming true history, and the moral code of Napoleon and the English government, a substitute for that of Grotius of Puffendorf, and even of the pure doctrines of the great Author of our own religion. We were safe ourselves from Bonaparte, because he had not the British fleets at his command. We were safe from the British fleets because they had Bonaparte at their back; but the British fleets and the conquerors of Bonaparte being now combined, and the Hartford nation drawn off to them, we have uncommon reason to look to our own affairs. This, however, I leave to others, offering prayers to Heaven, the only contribution of old age, for the safety of our country. Be so good as to present me affectionately to Mrs. Logan, and to accept yourself the assurance of my esteem and respect.

"'TH. JEFFERSON.

"The same anxiety for his country's independence seems to have led him to a change of opinion on the relative importance of manufactories in America. He thus expresses himself in answer to an address from the American Society for the Encouragement of Manufactures: 'I have read with great satisfaction the eloquent pamphlet you were so kind as to send me, and sympathize with every line of it. I was once a doubter whether the labor of the cultivator, aided by the creative powers of the earth itself, would not produce more value than that of the manufacturer alone, and unassisted by the dead subject on which he acted ; in other words, whether the more we could bring into action of the energies of our boundless territory, in addition to the labor of our citizens, the more would not be our gain. But the inventions of the latter times by labor-saving machines, do as much now for the manufacturer as the earth for the cultivator. Experience too, has proved that mine was but half the question ; the other half is, whether dollars and cents are to be weighed in the scale against real independence. The question is then solved, at least so far as respects our own wants. I much fear the effect on our infant establishment of the policy avowed by Mr. Brougham, and quoted in the pamphlet. Individual British merchants may lose by the late immense importations, but British commerce and manufactories in the mass will gain by beating down the competition of ours in our own markets, etc.'

"The conversation turning on American history, Mr. Jefferson related an anecdote of the Abbé Raynal, which serves to show how history, even when it calls itself philosophical, is written. The Abbé was in company with Dr. Franklin, and several Americans at Paris, when mention chanced to be made of his anecdote of Polly Baker, related in his sixth volume, upon which one of the company observed that no such law as that alluded to in the story existed in New England: the Abbé stoutly maintained the authenticity of his tale, when Dr. Franklin, who had hitherto remained silent, said, ' I can account for all this ; you took the anecdote from a newspaper, of which I was at that time editor, and happening to be very short of news, I composed and inserted the whole story.' ' Ah! Doctor,' said the Abbé, making a true French retreat, ' I had rather have your stories, than other men's truths.'

"Mr. Jefferson preferred Botta's Italian History of the American Revolution to any that had yet appeared, remarking, however, the inaccuracy of the speeches.—Indeed, the true history of that period seems to be generally considered as lost. A remarkable letter on this point lately appeared in print, from the venerable Mr. John Adams, to a Mr. Niles, who had solicited his aid to collect and publish a body of revolutionary speeches. He says, ' of all the speeches made in Congress from 1774 to 1777, inclusive of both years, not one sentence remains, except a few periods of Dr. Witherspoon, printed in his works.' His concluding sentence is very strong. ' In plain English, and in a few words, Mr. Niles, I consider the true history of the American Revolution, and the establishment of our present constitutions, as lost forever ; and nothing but misrepresentations, or partial accounts of it, will ever be recovered.'

"I slept a night at Monticello, and left it in the morning, with such a feeling as the traveller quits the mouldering remains of a Grecian temple, or the pilgrim a fountain in the desert. It would indeed argue a great torpor, both of understanding and heart, to have looked without veneration and interest on the man who drew up the Declaration of American Independence, who shared in the councils by which her freedom was established ; whom the unbought voice of his fellow-citizens called to the exercise of a dignity, from which his own moderation impelled him, when such an example was most salutary, to withdraw ; and who, while he dedicates the evening of his glorious days to the pursuits of science and literature, shuns none of the humbler duties of private life ; but, having filled a seat higher than that of kings, succeeds with graceful dignity to that of the good neighbor, and becomes the friendly adviser, lawyer, physician, and even gardener of his vicinity. This is the still small voice of philosophy, deeper and holier than the lightnings and earthquakes which have preceded it. What monarch would venture thus to exhibit himself in the nakedness of his humanity? On what royal brow would the laurel replace the diadem? But they who are born and educated to be kings, are not expected to be philosophers. This is a just answer, though no great compliment, either to the governors or the governed."—Chap. xxxv., 374 to 385.

Lieutenant Hall, it appears from his Work, came near finding a "watery grave" in fording the Rivanna, on his return. His horse and wagon were swept down the stream, but he and his servant escaped, and his equipage was finally saved by the efforts of Mr. Jefferson's domestics. Our traveller then arrived at Richmond without further adventures. He often quotes Mr. Jefferson's opinions, evidently profoundly impressed with the greatness and benignity of his character.

Mr. Jefferson's first published letter in 1817, was addressed to Mrs. Adams.

TO MRS. ADAMS.

MONTICELLO, Jan. 11, 1817.

I owe you, dear Madam, a thousand thanks for the letters communicated in your favor of December 15th, and now returned. They give me more information than I possessed before, of the family of Mr. Tracy.[1] But what is infinitely interesting, is the scene of the exchange of Louis XVIII. for Bonaparte. What lessons of wisdom Mr. Adams must have read in that short space of time! More than fall to the lot of others in the course of a long life. Man, and the man of Paris, under those circumstances, must have been a subject of profound speculation! It would be a singular addition to that spectacle, to see the same beast in the cage of St. Helena, like a lion in the tower. That is probably the closing verse of the chapter of his crimes. But not so with Louis. He has other vicissitudes to go through.

I communicated the letters, according to your permission, to my grand-daughter, Ellen Randolph,[2] who read them with pleasure and edification. She is justly sensible of, and flattered by your kind notice of her; and additionally so, by the favorable recollections of our northern visiting friends. If Monticello has anything which has merited their remembrance, it gives it a value the more in our estimation; and could I, in the spirit of your wish, count backwards a score of years, it would not be long before Ellen and myself would pay our homage personally to Quincy. But those twenty years! Alas! where are they? With those beyond the flood. Our next meeting must then be in the country to which they have flown—a country for us not now very distant. For this journey we shall need neither gold nor silver in our purse, nor scrip, nor coats, nor staves. Nor is the provision for it more easy than the preparation has been kind. Nothing proves more than this, that the Being who presides over the world is essentially benevolent. Stealing from us, one by one the faculties of enjoyment, searing our sensibilities, leading us, like the horse in his mill, round and round the same beaten circle,

——To see what we have seen,
To taste the tasted, and at each return
Less tasteful; o'er our palates to decant
Another vintage—

[1] The Count de Tracy.   [2] Now Mrs. Joseph Coolidge, of Boston.

until satiated and fatigued with this leaden iteration, we ask our own *congé.* I heard once a very old friend, who had troubled himself with neither poets, nor philosophers, say the same thing in plain prose, that he was tired of pulling off his shoes and stockings at night, and putting them on again in the morning. The wish to stay here is thus gradually extinguished; but not so easily that of returning once in awhile, to see how things have gone on. Perhaps, however, one of the elements of future felicity is to be a constant and unimpassioned view of what is passing here. If so, this may well supply the wish of occasional visits. Mercier has given us a vision of the year 2,440; but prophecy is one thing, and history another. On the whole, however, perhaps it is wise and well to be contented with the good things which the master of the feast places before us, and to be thankful for what we have, rather than thoughtful about what we have not. You and I, dear Madam, have already had more than an ordinary portion of life, and more, too, of health than the general measure. On this score I owe boundless thankfulness. Your health was, some time ago, not so good as it has been; and I perceive in the letters communicated, some complaints still. I hope it is restored; and that life and health may be continued to you as many years as yourself shall wish, is the sincere prayer of your affectionate and respectful friend.

He wrote Mr. Adams the same day, and closed his letter thus:

"One of our fan-coloring biographers, who paints small men as very great, inquired of me lately, with real affection too, whether he might consider as authentic, the change in my religion much spoken of in some circles. Now this supposed that they knew what had been my religion before, taking for it the word of their priests, whom I certainly never made the confidants of my creed. My answer was—'say nothing of my religion. It is known to my God and myself alone. Its evidence before the world is to be sought in my life; if that has been honest and dutiful to society, the religion which has regulated it cannot be a bad one.'—Affectionately adieu."

The subject of religion occupies considerable space in the correspondence of Jefferson and Adams. The latter was evidently extremely fond of speculating on this topic, and of drawing out his friend. He who reads their letters, and then suffers his memory to revert to the vehement appeals made to the American people in 1800 to vote for Adams and against Jefferson, on the ground of a difference in their religious beliefs, will obtain an instructive commentary on the propriety of political partisans assuming to sit in judgment on the hearts and private religious opinions of candidates for office.

Mr. Monroe succeeded Mr. Madison in the Presidency, in 1817. It was an event in which Mr. Jefferson experienced great satisfaction, as he had perfect confidence in Monroe personally, and he believed an "Administration in republican forms and principles" for twenty-four consecutive years, "would so consecrate them in the eyes of the people as to secure them against the danger of a change." The President appointed John Quincy Adams Secretary of State, and Jefferson thus wrote to the senior Adams on that subject: "I congratulate Mrs. Adams and yourself on the return of your excellent and distinguished son, and our country still more, on such a minister of their foreign affairs; and I renew to both the assurance of my high and friendly respect and esteem."

Mr. John Q. Adams wrote to Mr. Jefferson, October 4th, propounding several inquiries. These were answered November 1st, and the letter closed thus: "I have barely left myself room to express my satisfaction at your call to the important office you hold, and to tender you the assurance of my great esteem and respect." Jefferson's feelings towards the younger Adams were purely amicable, as this letter implies. He had a high opinion of his integrity and ability—particularly of his ability as a writer. He always, however, to some extent distrusted his temper and judgment. He said, in 1816 or 1817, to one from whose lips we have it: "Monroe showed his usual good sense in appointing Adams. They were made for each other. Adams has a pointed pen: Monroe has sound judgment enough for both, and firmness enough to have *his* judgment control." He said to another gentleman, also our personal informant: "Monroe always saw his point, but could not always *express* very well how he got there. Give Adams a conclusion, and he could always assign the best reasons for it."

Mr. Jefferson took an active part in measures set on foot in 1817, to establish the "Central College" of Virginia, which afterwards ripened into the University. Two of the "Visitors," besides himself, were ex-President Madison, and President Monroe. They met to deliberate on the subject, in the opening of May, at Monticello.

We have the customary range of correspondence during the year. To Dr. Humphreys he expressed his warm approbation of colonizing the American negroes in Africa. To Mr. Adams, he declared that Botta had given the History of the American Revolution "with more detail, precision, and candor, than any writer he had yet met with," but he wholly objected to "putting speeches into mouths that never made them, and fancying motives of action which we [the actors] never felt." He wrote

Dr. Stuart that he hoped " the policy of our country would settle down with as much navigation and commerce only as our own exchanges would require." To the same he said:

> " You say I must go to writing history. While in public life I had not time, and now that I am retired, I am past the time. To write history requires a whole life of observation, of inquiry, of labor and correction. Its materials are not to be found among the ruins of a decayed memory. At this day I should begin where I ought to have left off."

He repeated his early views on expatriation to Dr. Manners. He said it was a right which " we do not claim under the charters of kings or legislators, but under the King of kings." He wrote to Humboldt in respect to the " gigantic undertaking " in New York, " for drawing the waters of Lake Erie into the Hudson," saying the expense would be great, but the beneficial effects incalculable.[1] He predicted to De Marbois, that the United States would proceed successfully for ages; and that " contrary to the principle of Montesquieu, it would be seen that the larger the extent of country the more firm its Republican structure, if founded not on conquest, but in principles of compact and equality." In a letter to Gallatin (June 16th), he applauded the " proof of the innate good sense, the vigilance and the determination of the people to act for themselves," evinced by their spontaneously dropping or defeating the members of Congress who voted for the Compensation Law, when " the newspapers were almost entirely silent" on the subject, and the leaders the other way.[2]

He highly approved, in this same letter, of the President's veto of the Internal Improvement bill, which he considered an unconstitutional enactment; but he thought that the States would be ready to amend the Constitution so as to confer the power of making

---

[1] Joshua Forman, of New York, one of the prominent originators of its great canal, visited Washington in 1809, to converse with President Jefferson on that subject, and to attempt to obtain the coöperation of the General Government. He represented Mr. Jefferson as saying, that " it was a very fine project, and might be executed a century hence." etc., but not now. In a letter to Governor Clinton in 1822, Mr. Jefferson seemed to put a different version on his views—namely, that he thought "New York had *anticipated* by a full century, the ordinary progress of improvement."—See *North American Review*, No. 65, p. 507.

[2] The Fourteenth Congress, at its first session, passed an act (March 19, 1816), abolishing the per diem allowance of members of Congress, and prescribing that they should receive an annual salary of $1.500. At their next session the act was repealed (Feb 6th, 1817), "*after the close of the present Session of Congress.*" Mr. Jefferson said : "the unpopularity of the Compensation Law was completed, by the manner of repealing it as to all the world except themselves."

l improvements on the General Government. It will be
:ted that he more than once advanced the same idea in
sidential messages, and even suggested the commencement
tical steps towards effecting the change. It is understood
: took this view, because he labored under the impression,
at it would be a necessary concession to some of the States
ilarly the western ones), to preserve the Union; and second-
: internal improvements between States, apart from their
 and apart from the wishes of the people, would of them-
form indissoluble links of union. It was not then foreseen
ivate enterprise would soon create these public works. In
ht of analogy, probably no doubt can be entertained that
on would have entirely preferred their construction by
ter means, or that had he lived at this day, he would be
t to oppose the constitutional amendment which we have
in suggesting.

also wrote to Gallatin :

ee of our papers have presented us the copy of an act of the Legislature of
k, which, if it has really passed, will carry us back to the times of the dark-
-y and barbarism, to find a parallel. Its purport is, that all those who shall
 join in communion with the religious sect of Shaking Quakers, shall be
:ivilly dead, their marriages dissolved, and all their children and property
: of their hands. This act being published nakedly in the papers, without
signatures, or any history of the circumstances of its passage, I am not
i hope it may have been a mere abortive attempt."

ne interesting particulars in regard to the journals of
and Clarke, in their western expedition, will be found in
to Mr. Duponceau of Philadelphia; and various details of
on's educational plans for Virginia, in letters to his
l and highly valued friend M. Correa.
i general indoor occupations of the year are thus mourn-
escribed to Mr. Adams :

::
irty-three volumes read in one year, and twelve of them quarto! Dear
[envy you! Half a dozen of octavos in that space of time are as much
llowed. I can read by candle-light only, and stealing long hours from my
· would that time be indulged to me, could I by that light see to write.
irise to one or two o'clock, and often from dinner to dark, I am drudging
iting table. And all this to answer letters in which neither interest nor
n on my part enters; and often from persons whose names I have never
:ard. Yet, writing civilly, it is hard to refuse them civil answers. This is

the burden of my life, a very grievous one indeed, and one which I must get rid of. Delaplaine lately requested me to give him a line on the subject of his book, meaning, as I well knew, to publish it. This I constantly refuse; but in this instance yielded, that in saying a word for him, I might say two for myself. I expressed in it freely my sufferings from this source; hoping it would have the effect of an indirect appeal to the discretion of those strangers, and others, who, in the most friendly dispositions, oppress me with their concerns, their pursuits, their projects, inventions and speculations, political, moral, religious, mechanical, mathematical, historical, etc., etc., etc. I hope the appeal will bring me relief, and that I shall be left to exercise and enjoy correspondence with the friends I love, and on subjects which they, or my own inclinations present. In that case your letters shall not be so long on my files unanswered, as sometimes they have been, to my great mortification."

The remark has been perhaps too long deferred, that Mr. Jefferson, after his retirement, kept copies of only a very small portion of his letters; and consequently that neither his published works, nor his manuscripts in the possession of the Government, furnish any just idea of the extent of his correspondence. We shall, hereafter, see that his published writings for a particular year include considerably less than *one-fiftieth* part of the letters which he wrote.

Another fact should have been earlier noticed. While the Congress edition of Jefferson's writings is much fuller than Randolph's, it omits many important letters published in the latter. The tenor of the omitted letters will show at once that they belong to no particular class which it could have been thought desirable by the editor of the Congress edition to exclude; and some of them are more important than those given by him, in many instances. The omission therefore has no obvious explanation.[1]

[1] The readiest one would be that Professor Washington made his publication exclusively from the *manuscripts* purchased by the Government from the legatee of Mr. Jefferson's papers, and that the omitted letters had been lost from the collection before it was sold to the Government. But Professor Washington clearly was not confined to the *manuscripts*, for he gives Jefferson's youthful letters to John Page, which were not included among them, and for which he was indebted to Professor Tucker's life of Jefferson. (Tucker obtained the letters from Page himself, and first published them to the world.) Nor does Professor Washington make this departure from the *manuscripts* an exceptional one, by mentioning it as such, or by specifying the source from which he derived the letters. Again, a careful comparison of the chasms, blanks, asterisks, etc., in the letters which Randolph and Washington both publish—many of which did not exist in the originals—will show a coincidence between editors acting at different times, and under different circumstances, which has but one probable solution. That probable solution is, that Professor Washington was willing to make the same omissions that Randolph had made, and therefore used Randolph's printed copies of the letters, (so far as they went) instead of making written ones from the original manuscripts. This would be the most delicate course which could be pursued towards a family editor, and would save a vast amount of unnecessary copying. If this hypothesis is correct, an immense mass of mixed written and printed matter, which required arranging with con-

Mr. Jefferson suffered from an attack of illness early in
118, which if not really dangerous, was supposed sufficiently
to attract much public attention; and his family were over-
helmed with letters from every part of the United States,
aking inquiries, and expressing the solicitude and sympathy
the writers. He apparently fully recovered his health, but
e wear of the machine, the advancing debility of old age,
id the predisposition to disease, had doubtless been consider-
)ly increased. His correspondence during the year is much
ss than usual.

A letter to Mr. Wirt congratulates the latter on his accession
the Attorney-Generalship of the United States; and asks his
lvice as to the proper court in which to prove the will of
eneral Kosciusko, which he had left in the hands of Mr.
ifferson as his executor. The great Pole died at Soleure, in
witzerland, in consequence of a fall from his horse, October
ith, 1817, in the sixty-first year of his age. Mr. Jefferson deeply
iplored the loss of " his most intimate, and much beloved
iend." [1]

erable care went into the hands of the printers. Carelessness in any of the parties
ring the arrangement, or even the handling of this matter, might have led to the
:idental and unnoticed loss of some of the printed letters. Whether the loss extended
manuscript papers, we cannot say, having no catalogue of those of Mr. Jefferson,
ich are in the possession of the Government.

A fact which might escape the notice of cursory readers, and seem to render some
the citations in this biography inaccurate, should here be named. The *index of*
ters in the Congress edition of Mr. Jefferson's writings, is *incomplete.*

Our citations have been generally made merely by giving dates of the letters, without
)cifying in which edition they are to be found. A reference to the edition in every
tance would have been inconvenient, and would have required much space.

[1] Jefferson and Kosciusko were bosom friends, and kept up a correspondence for a
ig number of years, and until the death of the latter. After " Warsaw's last Cham-
in "—who has been felicitously described as possessing, in his capacity of a com-
nder, the " integrity of Washington and the activity of Cæsar,"—fell on the fatal field
Macziewice; and after he refused the estates and other presents offered him by the
iperor Paul, he set out for the United States, intending probably to make them his
ure residence. He reached America in 1797. Like all the other continental foreigners
io visited our shores, he became attached to Jefferson: and he earnestly sympathized
Jefferson's political views. He had gallantly served the United States in their Revo-
ionary struggle, and had been warmly applauded and esteemed by Washington: but
s did not prevent him from being insultingly attacked by anti-Republican partisans,
rticularly by the foul-mouthed Cobbet. It was even thought that he was one of the
itemplated objects of the Alien-law. He returned to France in 1798. He had refused
receive back his sword from the Emperor Paul, saying: " I will no longer wear
ord, for I have no longer a country ;" and accordingly Napoleon never found it prac-
able to make him a tool, by delusive promises in favor of his country, as he did some
ler brave and noble Poles. On Kosciusko's death, the women of Poland went into
narning. The Senate solicited his body, and it was carried back at the expense of the
iperor Alexander, and deposited with becoming honors in the tomb of the ancient
igs of Poland.

He is understood to have been supported towards the close of his life by the interest
money received from our Government as a compensation for his military services. He
ested this in government funds, and left it under the charge of Jefferson. Some
ticulars of his will are to be found in letters from Jefferson to Wirt, January 5th, and
K. Jullien, July 23d, 1818.

Death took another of Jefferson's cherished friends, in 1818. Mrs. Adams died near the close of October, and as soon as the sad intelligence reached Monticello, the following letter was written :

To John Adams.

Monticello, *November* 18, 1518.

The public papers, my dear friend, announce the fatal event of which your letter of October the 20th had given me ominous foreboding. Tried myself in the school of affliction, by the loss of every form of connection which can rive the human heart, I know well, and feel what you have lost, what you have suffered, are suffering, and have yet to endure. The same trials have taught me that for ills so immeasurable, time and silence are the only medicine. I will not, therefore, by useless condolences, open afresh the sluices of your grief, nor, although mingling sincerely my tears with yours, will I say a word more where words are vain, but that it is of some comfort to us both that the term is not very distant, at which we are to deposit in the same cerement, our sorrows and suffering bodies, and to ascend in essence to an ecstatic meeting with the friends we have loved and lost, and whom we shall still love and never lose again. God bless you and support you under your heavy affliction.

Th. Jefferson.

The publication of Wirt's glowing life of Henry, produced some reclamations in other quarters. Jefferson's assertion, quoted in the work, that " Mr. Henry certainly gave the first impulse to the ball of revolution," drew a letter from Dr. Waterhouse of Massachusetts, questioning the accuracy of this statement. Jefferson replied (March 3d):

" I well recollect to have used some such expression in a letter to him, and am tolerably certain that our own State being the subject under contemplation, I must have used it with respect to that only.

*   *   *   *   *   *   *   *

The fact is, that one new idea leads to another, that to a third, and so on through a course of time, until some one, with whom no one of these ideas was original, combines all together, and produces what is justly called a new invention, I suppose it would be as difficult to trace our revolution to its first embryo. We do not know how long it was hatching in the British cabinet before they ventured to make the first of the experiments which were to develop it in the end and to produce complete parliamentary supremacy. Those you mention in Massachusetts as preceding the stamp act, might be the first visible symptoms of that design. The proposition of that act in 1764, was the first here. Your opposition. therefore, preceded ours, as occasion was sooner given there than here, and the truth, I suppose, is, that the opposition in every colony began whenever the encroachment was presented to it. This question of priority is as the inquiry would be who first of the three hundred Spartans, offered his name to Leonidas?"

Several letters have been quoted in this work, giving

Mr. Jefferson's views on a proper course of education for young men. The following answer (March 14th, 1818) to inquiries from N. Burwell, contains, it is believed, his fullest expression on a proper course of education for females:

" A plan of female education has never been a subject of systematic contemplation with me. It has occupied my attention so far only as the education of my own daughters occasionally required. Considering that they would be placed in a country situation where little aid could be obtained from abroad, I thought it essential to give them a solid education, which might enable them, when become mothers, to educate their own daughters, and even to direct the course for sons, should their fathers be lost, or incapable, or inattentive. My surviving daughter accordingly, the mother of many daughters as well as sons, has made their education the object of her life, and being a better judge of the practical part than myself, it is with her aid and that of one of her élèves, that I shall subjoin a catalogue of the books for such a course of reading as we have practised.

A great obstacle to good education is the inordinate passion prevalent for novels, and the time lost in that reading which should be instructively employed. When this poison infects the mind, it destroys its tone and revolts it against wholesome reading. Reason and fact, plain and unadorned, are rejected. Nothing can engage attention unless dressed in all the figments of fancy, and nothing so bedecked comes amiss. The result is a bloated imagination, sickly judgment, and disgust towards all the real businesses of life. This mass of trash, however, is not without some distinction; some few modeling their narratives, although fictitious, on the incidents of real life, have been able to make them interesting and useful vehicles of a sound morality. Such, I think, are Marmontel's new moral tales, but not his old ones, which are really immoral. Such are the writings of Miss Edgeworth, and some of those of Madame Genlis. For a like reason, too, much poetry should not be indulged. Some is useful for forming style and taste. Pope, Dryden, Thomson, Shakspeare, and of the French, Molière, Racine, the Corneilles, may be read with pleasure and improvement.

The French language, become that of the general intercourse of nations, and from their extraordinary advances, now the depository of all science, is an indispensable part of education for both sexes. In the subjoined catalogue, therefore, I have placed the books of both languages indifferently, according as the one or the other offers what is best.

The ornaments, too, and the amusements of life, are entitled to their portion of attention. These, for a female, are dancing, drawing, and music. The first is a healthy exercise, elegant, and very attractive for young people. Every affectionate parent would be pleased to see his daughter qualified to participate with her companions and without awkwardness at least, in the circles of festivity, of which she occasionally becomes a part. It is a necessary accomplishment, therefore, although of short use; for the French rule is wise, that no lady dances after marriage. This is founded in solid physical reasons, gestation and nursing leaving little time to a married lady when this exercise can be either safe or innocent. Drawing is thought less of in this country than in Europe. It is an innocent and engaging amusement, often useful, and a qualification not to be neglected in one who is to become a mother and an instructor. Music is invaluable where a person has an ear. Where they have not, it should not be attempted. It furnishes a delightful recreation for the hours of respite from the cares of the day, and lasts us through life. The taste of this country, too, calls for this accomplishment more strongly than for either of the others.

I need say nothing of household economy, in which the mothers of our country are generally skilled, and generally careful to instruct their daughters. We all know its value, and that diligence and dexterity in all its processes are inestimable treasures. The order and economy of a house are as honorable to the mistress as those of the farm to the master, and if either be neglected, ruin follows, and children destitute of the means of living.

This, sir, is offered as a summary sketch on a subject on which I have not thought much. It probably contains nothing but what has already occurred to yourself, and claims your acceptance on no other ground than as a testimony of my respect for your wishes, and of my great esteem and respect."

When the above list of approved novels for young ladies' perusal is examined, the modern reader will not be likely to forget that Waverley, Guy Mannering, the Antiquary, and Old Mortality were then before the world. Rob Roy and the Heart of Mid Lothian appeared in 1818. It is easy to see why such writers as Radcliffe and Godwin—to say nothing of an earlier English school of able, but immoral, or at least indelicate authors—were excluded from the catalogue. But Scott's works are generally thought to exhibit vastly more perfection as novels, than any Mr. Jefferson named; and surely he did not sigh for higher standards of character, more beautiful delineations of every virtue, more certain visitations of the avenging Nemesis to the bosom of guilt, more terrible retributions for crime, than are uniformly interwoven into the plot and moral of the "Waverley Novels."

This relegation of Scott must have been intentional. Mr. Jefferson had read none of his fictions, because he would not read them. But, at the entreaties of grand-daughters, he had listened to occasional passages or pages from several of them. They were not to his taste. In prose as in poetry, he did not relish the romantic school. He detested the political civilization of the middle ages, and especially the feudal system, as cordially as Scott admired them. He as warmly sympathized with common humanity as Scott did with kings and nobles. In short, he was as thorough a radical in heart and grain as the great novelist was a tory. He thought, therefore, that the pictures of social and political civilization drawn by the latter had an untruthful, if not dangerous coloring. But the issue taken with the delineator was rather ludicrous than serious. His taste in regard to the romantic was similar to that of Cervantes—per-ips had been fashioned on it. The Bois-Guilberts and the ront de Bœufs, to him were all cousin-germans of Don Quix- :e. It is recollected by members of his family, that he could ot endure the character of the stately and chivalrous Norman ice of men—always speaking of them as "tyrants and robbers." lis partiality for the Saxon element in English character, laws ad manners, was strong and often avowed.

Jefferson expressed the following views in regard to the eople of the western American States, in a letter to Mr. .dams (May 17th, 1818):

"They are freer from prejudices than we are, and bolder in grasping at truth. he time is not distant, though neither you nor I shall see it, when we shall be but secondary people to them. Our greediness for wealth, and fantastical expense ive degraded, and will degrade, the minds of our maritime citizens. These are le peculiar vices of commerce."

In a letter to Robert Walsh (Dec. 4th), he paid a beautiful ribute to the character of Franklin, and inclosed that paper of necdotes concerning him which is now familiar to the reading ublic.[1]

Here are the reform theories of a temperate man on the ubject of temperance, forty years ago, in a letter to M. de Neu- ille:

"I rejoice, as a moralist, at the prospect of a reduction of the duties on wine, by ur National Legislature. It is an error to view a tax on that liquor as merely a tax n the rich. It is a prohibition of its use to the middling class of our citizens, nd a condemnation of them to the poison of whisky, which is desolating their omes. No nation is drunken where wine is cheap; and none sober, where the earness of wine substitutes ardent spirits as the common beverage. It is, in truth, he only antidote to the bane of whisky. Fix but the duty at the rate of other ierchandise, and we can drink wine here as cheap as we do grog; and who will not refer it? Its extended use will carry health and comfort to a much enlarged circle. very one in easy circumstances (as the bulk of our citizens are) will prefer it to tho oison to which they are now driven by their government. And the treasury itself ill find that a penny apiece from a dozen, is more than a groat from a single one. his reformation, however, will require time. Our merchants know nothing of the

---

[1] While he distinctly admitted that it was "to Mr. Adams's perseverance alone" he ad always understood that our country was indebted for the reservation of the fisheries, the first treaty of peace with England, he said he had "never heard on any au- hority worthy of notice," that Franklin would have waived the formal recognition of ur Independence; and he declared on his own knowledge, that the charge against him f subserviency to France "had not a shadow of foundation." He said, Franklin pos- sed the confidence of the French Government to such a degree "that it might be truly id, that they were more under his influence than he under theirs." He attributed the isrepresentations of Franklin's conduct principally to Dr. Arthur Lee.—(See vol. i . 156.)

infinite variety of cheap and good wines to be had in Europe; and particularly in France, in Italy, and the Grœcian Islands."

He wrote to his old friend, Mr. Macon, Jan. 12th, 1819:

"I read no newspaper now but Ritchie's, and in that chiefly the advertisements, for they contain the only truths to be relied on in a newspaper. I feel a much greater interest in knowing what has passed two or three thousand years ago, than in what is now passing. I read nothing, therefore, but of the heroes of Troy, of the wars of Lacedæmon and Athens, of Pompey and Cæsar, and of Augustus too, the Bonaparte and parricide scoundrel of that day. I have had, and still have, such entire confidence in the late and present Presidents, that I willingly put both soul and body into their pockets."

The following letter gives too minute an account of Mr. Jefferson's physical habits and condition, and of his habits in some other particulars, not to be quoted entire.

To Doctor Vine Utley.

MONTICELLO, *March 21, 1819.*

Sir,—Your letter of February the 18th came to hand on the 1st instant: and the request of the history of my physical habits would have puzzled me not a little, had it not been for the model with which you accompanied it, of Dr. Rush's answer to a similar inquiry. I live so much like other people, that I might refer to ordinary life as the history of my own. Like my friend the Doctor, I have lived temperately, eating little animal food, and that not as an aliment, so much as a condiment for the vegetables, which constitute my principal diet. I double, however, the Doctor's glass and a half of wine, and even treble it with a friend; but halve its effects by drinking the weak wines only. The ardent wines I cannot drink, nor do I use ardent spirits in any form. Malt liquors and cider are my table drinks, and my breakfast, like that also of my friend, is of tea and coffee. I have been blest with organs of digestion which accept and concoct, without ever murmuring, whatever the palate chooses to consign to them, and I have not yet lost a tooth by age. I was a hard student until I entered on the business of life, the duties of which leave no idle time to those disposed to fulfill them; and now, retired, and at the age of seventy-six, I am again a hard student. Indeed, my fondness for reading and study revolts me from the drudgery of letter writing. And a stiff wrist, the consequence of an early dislocation, makes writing both slow and painful. I am not so regular in my sleep as the Doctor says he was, devoting to it from five to eight hours, according as my company or the book I am reading interests me; *and I never go to bed without an hour, or half an hour's previous reading of something moral, whereon to ruminate in the intervals of sleep.* But whether I retire to bed early or late, I rise with the sun. I use spectacles at night, but not necessarily in the day, unless in reading small print. My hearing is distinct in particular conversation, but confused when several voices cross each other, which unfits me for the society of the table. I have been more fortunate than my friend in the article of health. So free from catarrhs that I have not had one (in the breast, I mean) on an average of eight or ten years through life. I ascribe this exemption partly to the habit of bathing my feet in cold water every morning, for sixty years past. A fever of more than twenty-four hours I have not had above two or three times in my life. A periodical headache has afflicted me occasionally, once, perhaps, in six or eight years, for two or three weeks at a time, which seems now to have left me ; and, except on a late occasion of indisposition, I enjoy good health ; too feeble, indeed, to walk much, but riding without fatigue six or eight miles a day, and sometimes thirty or forty. I may end these egotisms, therefore, as I began, by saying that my life has been so much like that of other people, that I might say with Horace, to every one " *nomine mutato, narratur fabula de te.*" I must not end, however, without due thanks for the kind sentiments of regard you are so good as to express towards myself ; and with my acknowledgments for these, be pleased to accept the assurances of my respect and esteem.

The book oftenest chosen for reading for an *hour or half an hour* before going to bed was a collection of extracts from the Bible. During the year 1803, while Mr. Jefferson was in Washington, " overwhelmed with other business," he spent two or three nights " after getting through the evening task of reading the letters and papers of the day,"[1] in cutting such passages from the evangelists as he believed emanated directly from the lips of the Saviour, and he arranged them in an octavo volume of forty-six pages. This selection is thus described by him to his Revolutionary friend, Charles Thompson, January 9th, 1816 :

" I, too, have made a wee-little book from the same materials,[2] which I call the Philosophy of Jesus ; it is a paradigma of his doctrines, made by cutting the texts out of the book, and arranging them on the pages of a blank book, in a certain order of time or subject. A more beautiful or precious morsel of ethics I have never seen ; it is a document in proof that *I am a real Christian*, that is to say, a disciple of the doctrines of Jesus, very different from the Platonists, who call *me* infidel and *themselves*[3] Christians and preachers of the Gospel, while they draw all their characteristic dogmas from what its author never said nor saw. They have compounded from the heathen mysteries a system beyond the comprehension of man, of which the great reformer of the vicious ethics and deism of the Jews, were he to return on earth, would not recognize one feature. If I had time I would add to my little book the Greek, Latin, and French texts, in columns side by side."

It was in the winter of 1816–17, it is believed, that Mr. Jefferson carried out the design last expressed. In a handsome morocco-bound volume, labelled on the back, "Morals of Jesus," he placed the parallel texts in four languages. The first collec-

---

[1] See letter to Mr. Short, October 31st, 1819 ; and to Mr. Vanderkemp, April 25th, 1816.

[2] The letter was in acknowledgment of a presentation by Mr. Thompson of his Harmony of the Four Gospels.

[3] The italics in this letter were underscored in the original.

tion of English texts, mentioned in the letter to Thompson, is not preserved in Mr. Jefferson's family, but his grandson, Mr. George Wythe Randolph, has obtained for us a list of its contents.[1] That, in different languages, is in the possession of his oldest grandson, Colonel Thomas Jefferson Randolph. A full citation of the passages in both volumes will be given in the Appendix.[2] It is remarkable that neither of these collections were known to Mr. Jefferson's grandchildren until after his death. They then learned from a letter addressed to a friend that he was in the habit of reading nightly from them before going to bed.[3]

In a reply to Mr. Spafford, who had requested materials for writing his life, Mr. Jefferson stated (May 11th, 1819), that he had kept no narrative of the public transactions in which he had borne a part with a view to history—that a life of constant action had left him no time for recording—that he had always been thinking of what was next to be done—and that what was done was then dismissed and obliterated from memory. He added : ·

"Numerous and able coadjutors have participated in these efforts, and merit equal notice. My life, in fact, has been so much like that of others, that their history is my history, with a mere difference of feature."

After mentioning a few authorities, he continued :

"These publications furnish all the details of facts and dates which can interest anybody, and more than I could now furnish myself from a decayed memory, or any notes I retain. While, therefore, I feel just acknowledgments for the partial selection of a subject for your employment, I am persuaded you will perceive there is too little new and worthy of public notice to devote to it a time which may be so much more usefully employed."

On the 9th of July he made the memorable answer to John Adams in regard to the "Mecklenburg Declaration of Independence," which has drawn out so much discussion, and which has already been noticed in this work.[4]

---

[1] This is sometimes mentioned as Mr. Jefferson's "Collection for the Indians," it being understood that he conferred with friends on the expediency of having it published in the different Indian dialects as the most appropriate book for the Indians to be instructed to read in.

[2] See APPENDIX No. 30.

[3] This is stated in a letter to us from Colonel Randolph, which will appear in this volume.

[4] See APPENDIX No. 2.

Judge Marshall, presiding in the United States Circuit Court Richmond, this year, held that in suits brought by a foreigner ainst the citizen of a State, the federal courts possessed a ntrolling power over the State courts. The opinion was ly controverted by Judge Roane in a series of articles blished in the Richmond Enquirer over the signature of ampden. Roane forwarded these to Mr. Jefferson, who re- ed (September 6th) fully concurring in his views on the ques- n decided by the court and advancing beyond them in others. nderstanding Roane to admit that the judiciary was the last ort for explaining the Constitution " in relation to the other partments of the Government," he earnestly reasserted what d been a standing doctrine of his own Administration, that ach department was truly independent of the others, and had equal right to decide for itself what is the meaning of the nstitution in the cases submitted to its action." His letter ntains several interesting arguments and citations on this portant question.

Mr. Jefferson had two brief but serious attacks of disease in 19. The first terminated near the beginning of autumn. e second, a spasmodic stricture of the ilium, came upon him the 7th of October, and threatened his life. The crisis was vorably passed on the fourth day, but a dose of calomel pro- ced salivation, and he suffered much from its disagreeable nsequences. He was on horseback again, however, before e close of the month.

Several literary and critical letters during the year, show at his mental activity was unimpaired, and that it was kept constant exercise.

We find Mr. Jefferson's first allusion to the " Missouri iestion " in a letter to Mr. Adams of December 10th. Mis- uri had applied for the usual permission to form a State nstitution, at the preceding session of Congress. A motion a northern member to insert a clause in the act, prohibiting e further introduction of slaves into the new State, and anting freedom to the children of slaves already there, on aching the age of twenty-five, had prevailed in the House, it had been struck out in the Senate. The House refused to ncur, and the Senate to recede; and so the bill was lost. enaces of disunion were freely thrown out in the debate. The next Congress was to assemble on the 6th of December (1819), and in the meantime, this agitating question spread to the State legislatures and popular masses, producing that excitement which would be expected where political and social feelings so deep, and interests so important were brought into collision.[1]

Four days after the meeting of Congress, Jefferson wrote to Adams:

"The banks, bankrupt law, manufactures, Spanish treaty, are nothing. These are occurrences which, like waves in a storm, will pass under the ship. But the Missouri question is a breaker on which we lose the Missouri country by revolt,[1] and what more, God only knows. From the Battle of Bunker's Hill to the treaty of Paris we never had so ominous a question. It even damps the joy with which I hear of your high health, and welcomes to me the consequences of my want of it. I thank God that I shall not live to witness its issue. *Sed hæc hactenus.*"[2]

It is not necessary to record here the various propositions

---

[1] The interests which the southern States had involved in the settlement of the question, are too obvious to require mention. Those in the northern States are thus described by an anti-slavery writer:

"The late discussions on the extension of slavery beyond the Mississippi, had roused up, as if from a long sleep, the anti-slavery sentiment of the North. The American convention for promoting the abolition of slavery, in abeyance since the abolition of the slave trade, revived, and reassembled once more at Philadelphia. But these speculative philanthropists, few and weak, would have been able to accomplish little had not the politicians come to their aid. Jealousy of southern domination had, as we have seen, made the northern Federalists dissatisfied with the purchase of Louisiana; it had led them to protest against the erection of the territory of Orleans into a State, and had moved the Hartford Convention to propose the abolition of the slave representation—a proposal quite as much, perhaps, as any suspected plots against the Union, the unpardonable sin of that body. This feeling had been shared, and, on more than one occasion, exhibited by the northern Democrats also, especially those of New York, who had reflected, not without some bitterness, on the political insignificance in which they had so long been held. The keeping out of new States, or the alteration of the Constitution as to the basis of representation—to which proposal of Massachusetts, reëchoed from Hartford, the other northern States had returned no answers at all, or unfavorable ones—were projects too hopeless, as well as too unpopular in their origin, to be renewed. The extension to the new territory, west of the Mississippi of the ordinance of 1787 against slavery, seemed to present a much more feasible method of accomplishing substantially the same object. This idea spreading with rapidity, still further obliterated old party lines, tending to produce at the North, a political union, for which the Federalists had so often sighed, similar to that which, prevailing throughout the South for the last twenty years, had given to that section so entire a control over the policy of the General Government, both foreign and domestic."—(Hildreth's Hist. of U. S. 2d Ser., vol. iii. p. 682.)

*   *   *   *   *

"Otis of Massachusetts, who, at the last session, as well as on several occasions before, had exhibited his strong sympathy for the slaveholders, of which, indeed, he lived to give still further proofs, now on behalf of a northern ascendency and with the prospect of a new political party on that basis, exerted all his eloquence against them."—(Ib., p. 688.)

[2] The delegate of Missouri had intimated this solution at the preceding session.

[3] Mr. Adams's answer to this, was as follows:

"The Missouri question, I hope, will follow the other waves under the ship, and do no harm. I know it is high treason to express a doubt of the perpetual duration of our vast American Empire, and our free institutions; and I say as devotedly as Father Paul, *esto perpetua*, but I am sometimes Cassandra enough to dream that another Hamilton and another Burr, might rend this mighty fabric in twain, or perhaps into a leash; and a few more choice spirits of the same stamp, might produce as many nations in North America as there are in Europe."

and counter propositions, which preceded the final action of Congress on the Act to authorize the people of the Missouri territory to form a constitution and State government.

A clause which prohibited Slavery in the new State, was struck out in the House of Representatives and the following proviso carried:

"Sec. 8. And be it further enacted, that in all the territory ceded by France to the United States, under the name of Louisiana, which lies north of thirty-six degrees and thirty minutes north latitude, not included within the limits of the State contemplated by this act, slavery and involuntary servitude, otherwise than in the punishment of crimes, whereof the parties shall have been duly convicted, shall be, and is hereby, forever prohibited: Provided always, That any person escaping into the same, from whom labor or service is lawfully claimed, in any State or territory of the United States, such fugitive may be lawfully reclaimed and conveyed to the person claiming his or her labor or service, as aforesaid."

The bill passed the Senate and was approved on the 6th of March, 1820:

Mr. Jefferson was originally opposed to the slavery-restriction clause of the bill—and equally so to the establishment of the "Missouri Compromise line," as it was called. We present his expressions on the subject together. He wrote to J. C. Cabell, January 22d, 1820:

"If our Legislature does not heartily push our University, we must send our children for education to Kentucky or Cambridge. If, however, we are to go a begging anywhere for our education, I would rather it should be to Kentucky than to any other State, because she has more of the flavor of the old cask than any other. All the States but our own are sensible that knowledge is power. The Missouri question is for power." [1]

To H. Nelson, March 12th:

"I thank you, dear sir, for the information in your favor of the 4th instant, of the settlement, *for the present*, of the Missouri question. I am so completely withdrawn from all attention to public matters, that nothing less could arouse me than the definition of a geographical line, which on an abstract principle is to become the line of separation of these States, and to render desperate the hope that man can ever enjoy the two blessings of peace and self-government. The question sleeps for the present, but is not dead."

To Mark Langdon Hill, April 5th:

"I congratulate you on the sleep of the Missouri question. I wish I could say·

---

[1] The letter containing this is in neither edition of Mr. Jefferson's works. We find it in the History of the University of Virginia, soon to be more particularly noticed.

on its death, but of this I despair. The idea of a geographical line once suggested will brood in the minds of all those who prefer the gratification of their ungovernable passions to the peace and union of their country. If I do not contemplate this subject with pleasure, I do sincerely that of the independence of Maine and the wise choice they have made of General King in the agency of their affairs."

To William Short, April 13th :

"Although I had laid down as a law to myself, never to write, talk, or even think of politics, to know nothing of public affairs, and therefore had ceased to read newspapers, yet the Missouri question aroused and filled me with alarm. The old schism of Federal and Republican threatened nothing, because it existed in every State, and united them together by the fraternism of party. But the coincidence of a marked principle, moral and political, with a geographical line, once conceived, I feared would never more be obliterated from the mind; that it would be recurring on every occasion and renewing irritations, until it would kindle such mutual and mortal hatred, as to render separation preferable to eternal discord. I have been among the most sanguine in believing that our Union would be of long duration. I now doubt it much, and see the event at no great distance, and the direct consequence of this question; not by the line which has been so confidently counted on; the laws of nature control this; but by the Potomac, Ohio, Missouri, or more probably, the Mississippi upwards to our northern boundary. My only comfort and confidence is, that I shall not live to see this; and I envy not the present generation the glory of throwing away the fruits of their fathers' sacrifices of life and fortune, and of rendering desperate the experiment which was to decide ultimately whether man is capable of self-government. This treason against human hope, will signalize their epoch in future history, as the counterpart of the medal of their predecessors."

To John Holmes, April 22d :

"I thank you, dear sir, for the copy you have been so kind as to send me of the letter to your constituents on the Missouri question. It is a perfect justification to them. I had for a long time ceased to read newspapers, or pay any attention to public affairs, confident they were in good hands, and content to be a passenger in our bark to the shore from which I am not distant. But this momentous question, like a fire-bell in the night, awakened and filled me with terror. I considered it at once as the knell of the Union. It is hushed, indeed, for the moment. But this is a reprieve only, not a final sentence. A geographical line, coinciding with a marked principle, moral and political, once conceived and held up to the angry passions of men, will never be obliterated; and every new irritation will mark it deeper and deeper. I can say, with conscious truth, that there is not a man on earth who would sacrifice more than I would to relieve us from this heavy reproach, in any *practicable* way. The cession of that kind of property, for so it is misnamed, is a bagatelle which would not cost me a second thought, if, in that way, a general emancipation and *expatriation* could be effected: and, gradually, and with due sacrifices, I think it might be. But as it is, we have the wolf by the ears, and we can neither hold him, nor safely let him go. Justice is in one scale, and self-preservation in the other. Of one thing I am certain, that as the passage of slaves from one state to another, would not make a slave of a single human being who would not be so without it, so their diffusion over a greater surface would make them individually happier, and proportionally facilitate the accomplishment of their emancipation, by dividing the burden on a greater number of coadjutors. An abstinence too, from this act of power, would remove the jealousy excited by the undertaking of Congress to regulate the condition of the different descriptions of men composing a State. This certainly is the exclusive right of every State, which nothing in the Constitution has taken from them and given to the General Government. Could Congress, for example, say, that the non-freemen of Connecticut shall be freemen, or that they shall not emigrate into any other State?

" I regret that I am now to die in the belief, that the useless sacrifice of themselves by the generation of 1776, to acquire self-government and happiness to their country, is to be thrown away by the unwise and unworthy passions of their sons, and that my only consolation is to be, that I live not to weep over it. If they would but dispassionately weigh the blessings they will throw away, against an abstract principle more likely to be effected by union than by scission, they would pause before they would perpetrate this act of suicide on themselves, and of treason against the hopes of the world. To yourself, as the faithful advocate of the Union, I tender the offering of my high esteem and respect."

To William Pinkney, September 30th :

" The Missouri question is a mere party trick. The leaders of Federalism, defeated in their schemes of obtaining power by rallying partisans to the principle of monarchism, a principle of personal not of local division, have changed their tack, and thrown out another barrel to the whale. They are taking advantage of the virtuous feelings of the people to effect a division of parties by a geographical line; they expect that this will insure them, on local principles, the majority they could never obtain on principles of Federalism; but they are still putting their shoulder to the wrong wheel; they are wasting Jeremiads on the miseries of slavery, as if we were advocates for it. Sincerity in their declamations should direct their efforts to the true point of difficulty, and unite their councils with ours in devising some reasonable and practicable plan of getting rid of it. Some of these leaders, if they could attain the power, their ambition would rather use it to keep the Union together, but others have ever had in view its separation. If they push it to that, they will find the line of separation very different from their 36° of latitude, and as manufacturing and navigating States, they will have quarrelled with their bread and butter, and I fear not that after a little trial they will think better of it, and return to the embraces of their natural and best friends. But this scheme of party I leave to those who are to live under its consequences. We who have gone before have performed an honest duty, by putting in the power of our successors a state of happiness which no nation ever before had within their choice. If that choice is to throw it away, the dead will have neither the power nor the right to control them. I must hope, nevertheless, that the mass of our honest and well-meaning brethren of the other States, will discover the use which designing leaders are making of their best feelings, and will see the precipice to which they are led, before they take the fatal leap. God grant it, and to you health and happiness."

To Richard Rush, October 20th :

" A hideous evil, the magnitude of which is seen, and at a distance only, by the one party, and more sorely.felt and sincerely deplored by the other, from the difficulty of the cure, divides us at this moment too angrily. The attempt by one party to prohibit willing States from sharing the evil, is thought by the other to render desperate, by accumulation, the hope of its final eradication. If a little time, however, is given to both parties to cool, and to dispel their visionary fears, they will see that concurring in sentiment as to the evil, moral and political, the duty and interest of both is to concur also in divining a practicable process of cure. Should time not be given, and the schism be pushed to separation, it will be for a short term only; two or three years' trial will bring them back, like quarrelling lovers, to renewed embraces and increased affections. The experiment of separation would soon prove to both that they had mutually miscalculated their best interests. And even were the parties in Congress to secede in a passion, the soberer people would call a convention and cement again the severance attempted by the insanity of their functionaries. With this consoling view, my greatest grief would be for the fatal effect of such an event on the hopes and happiness of the world. We exist, and are quoted as standing proofs that a government, so modelled as to rest continually on the will of the whole society, is a practicable government. Were we to break to pieces, it would damp the hopes and the efforts of the good, and give triumph to those of the bad through the whole enslaved world. As members, therefore, of the universal society of mankind, and standing in high and responsible relation with them, it is our sacred duty to suppress passion among ourselves, and not to blast the confidence we have inspired of proof that a government of reason is better than one of force."

To Lafayette, December 26th:

"With us things are going on well. The boisterous sea of liberty indeed, is never without a wave, and that from Missouri is now rolling towards us, but we shall ride over it as we have over all others. It is not a moral question, but one merely of power. Its object is to raise a geographical principle for the choice of a president, and the noise will be kept up till that is effected. All know that permitting the slaves of the south to spread into the west will not add one being to that unfortunate condition, that it will increase the happiness of those existing, and by spreading them over a larger surface, will dilute the evil everywhere, and facilitate the means of getting finally rid of it, an event more anxiously wished by those on whom it presses than by the noisy pretenders to exclusive humanity. In the meantime, it is a ladder for rivals climbing to power."

We shall continue here, in connection, Mr. Jefferson's expressions on this topic through another phase of the question. The sixteenth Congress again convened November 13th, 1820. The constitution framed by Missouri, and its application for admission as a State were presented by its delegate. The constitution forbade the State legislature to abolish slavery,[1] and it autho-

---

[1] Colonel Benton in his Thirty Years' View says:

"This prohibition, not usual in State constitutions, was the effect of the Missouri controversy and of foreign interference, and was adopted for the sake of peace—for the sake of internal tranquillity—and to prevent the agitation of the slave question. which could only be accomplished by excluding it wholly from the forums of election and legis-

rized that body to pass laws to prohibit the emigration of free
people of color into the State. A resolution to admit Missouri
under this constitution was voted down,[1] and a vehement contest
was continued in Congress until March, 1821, when a resolution
finally passed (by a vote of eighty-six to eighty-two in the
House, and twenty-eight to fourteen in the Senate) to admit the
State into the Union "on an equal footing with the original
States, in all respects whatever," on condition that the clause in
its constitution, in regard to the emigration of free negroes into
the State, should never be construed to authorize the passage of
any law by which "any citizen of either of the States in this
Union should be excluded from the enjoyment of any of the
privileges and immunities to which such citizen is entitled under
the Constitution of the United States." If the legislature of the
State should signify its assent to this "fundamental condition"
by the fourth Monday in the succeeding November, the President was to make proclamation of the fact, and the admission
of the State was to be thus completed.

Jefferson wrote to John Adams, January 22d, 1821:

" Our anxieties in this quarter are all concentrated in the question, what does
the Holy Alliance in and out of Congress mean to do with us on the Missouri question? And this, by the by, is but the name of the case, it is only the John Doe
or Richard Roe of the ejectment. The real question, as seen in the States afflicted
with this unfortunate population, is, are our slaves to be presented with freedom and
a dagger? For if Congress has the power to regulate the conditions of the inhabitants of the States, within the States, it will be but another exercise of that power,
to declare that all shall be free. Are we then to see again Athenian and Lacede-
monian confederacies? To wage another Peloponnesian war to settle the ascendency between them? Or is this the tocsin of merely a servile war? That remains
to be seen: but not, I hope, by you or me. Surely, they will parley awhile, and
give us time to get out of the way. What a Bedlamite is man? But let us turn
from our own uneasiness to the miseries of our southern [South American]
friends."

lation. I was myself the instigator of that prohibition, and the cause of its being put
into the constitution—though not a member of the convention—being equally opposed
to slavery agitation and to slavery extension."—(Vol. i., p. 8.)
    [1] The principal stand taken against it was on the clause authorizing a prohibition
of the emigration of free colored persons. But Colonel Benton says : "The real point of
objection was the slavery clause, and the existence of slavery in the State, which it
sanctioned and seemed to perpetuate. (Thirty Years' View, vol. i. p. 9.) Mr. Hildreth
says : " Maine being already fairly in the Union, that obstacle was out of the way; to
admit Missouri, a joint resolution would be necessary : and the intention was freely
avowed not to admit her, unless this obnoxious clause [that in regard to the emigration
of free colored persons] was first withdrawn or modified. Indeed. there were those who
wished to improve the opportunity to reconsider the action of the last session, and to
keep Missouri out altogether, except on condition of the exclusion of slavery."—(History of U. S., second series, vol. iii. p. 703.)

To J. C. Cabell, January 31st:

"Harvard will still prime it over us with her twenty professors. How many of our youths she now has, learning the lessons of anti-Missourianism, I know not; but a gentleman lately from Princeton, told me he saw there the list of the students at that place, and that more than half were Virginians. These will return home, no doubt, deeply impressed with the sacred principles of our Holy Alliance of restrictionists."

To General Breckenridge, February 15th :

.   .   .   "All, I fear, do not see the speck in our horizon which is to burst on us as a tornado, sooner or later. The line of division lately marked out between different portions of our confederacy, is such as will never, I fear, be obliterated, and we are now trusting to those who are against us in position and principle, to fashion to their own form the minds and affections of our youth. If, as has been estimated, we send three hundred thousand dollars a year to the northern seminaries, for the instruction of our own sons, then we must have there five hundred of our sons, imbibing opinions and principles in discord with those of their own country. This canker is eating on the vitals of our existence, and if not arrested at once, will be beyond remedy. We are now certainly furnishing recruits to their school."

To Judge Roane, March 9th :

"Last, and most portentous of all, is the Missouri question. It is smeared over for the present; but its geographical demarcation is indelible. What it is to become, I see not; and leave to those who will live to see it. The University will give employment to my remaining years, and quite enough for my senile faculties."

To General Dearborn, August 17th :

"I rejoice with you that the State of Missouri is at length a member of our Union. Whether the question it excited is dead, or only sleepeth, I do not know. I see only that it has given resurrection to the Hartford Convention men. They have had the address, by playing on the honest feelings of our former friends, to seduce them from their kindred spirits, and to borrow their weight into the Federal scale. Desperate of regaining power under political distinctions, they have adroitly wriggled into its seat under the auspices of morality, and are again in the ascendency from which their sins had hurled them. It is, indeed, of little consequence who governs us, if they sincerely and zealously cherish the principles of union and republicanism."

Notwithstanding Mr. Jefferson's several illnesses in 1819, he took an active part in personally superintending the erection of the buildings of the University of Virginia. Some account must now be given of this darling child of his old age, though the appearance of a history of the institution, under the authority of the gentleman to whom, next to Mr. Jefferson, it owes its existence and present foundation, renders anything more than a rapid outline of the facts unnecessary here.[1]

The following letter contains a sufficient sketch of those facts :

To Henry S. Randall.

University of Virginia, *August 9th*, 1851.

Dear Sir :

I have been requested by my friend, Mr. George W. Randolph, of Richmond, to acquaint you with the origination of this University, with a view to the biography of its great founder, on which you are engaged.

*   *   *   *   *   *

A seminary called the "Albemarle Academy," had, since 1803, subsisted in Charlottesville, but had fallen into a declining condition, when in 1814 a motive of private speculation led to an effort to revive it. Mr. Jefferson's coöperation being requested, he proposed an enlargement of the plan into a college. The idea was received with great favor, and sixty thousand dollars was soon subscribed in the central counties of Virginia,[2] and the buildings were commenced under the direction of Mr. Jefferson, Mr. Madison, Mr. Monroe, and several other gentlemen of distinction as a Board of Visitors. It was at this period that Mr. Jefferson developed the views of education stated above [in the passages we have omitted where the line of asterisks appears], which I derive from a letter of his of 7th September, 1814, to Mr. Peter Carr, one of the most intelligent of his co-laborers in the work of establishing the college. The institution was incorporated in February, 1816, by the name of "The Central College," and under the illustrious auspices of its *President Visitors* it attracted such attention and favor, as to enable Mr. Jefferson to renew the suggestion of a comprehensive plan of public education. Within a few days from the date of the act of incorporation, the president and directors of the literary fund were directed by joint resolution of both houses to report to the next General Assembly a system comprehending an university, and such additional colleges, academies, and schools, as would diffuse the benefits of education throughout the commonwealth. A report was accordingly made, recommending a plan,[3] not dissimilar to that proposed by Mr. Jefferson in 1779, and a bill to carry it into effect was passed by the House of Delegates, but lost in the Senate.[4] At the

---

[1] "Early History of the University of Virginia, as contained in the letters of Thomas Jefferson and Joseph C. Cabell, hitherto unpublished, with an appendix consisting of Mr. Jefferson's bill for a complete system of education, and other illustrative documents; and an introduction comprising a brief historical sketch of the University, and a biographical notice of Joseph C. Cabell." J. W. Randolph, Richmond, Va., 1856. 8vo. pp. 528.

The name of the able and impartial editor of the work is not given. The correspondence between Jefferson and Cabell is a highly interesting one apart from the subject of the University, and it fills three hundred and seventy-seven pages. But a small number of Jefferson's letters here given appear in either edition of his works.

[2] We may add to Professor Minor's statement that Mr. Jefferson subscribed $1,000. It was chiefly to his influence that the ready filling up of the subscription was owing. Nine other gentlemen subscribed $1,000 each, namely, George Divers, John Harris, Reuben Lindsay, sen., James Monroe, Wilson C. Nicholas, and John Patterson, of Albemarle ; John H. Cocke, of Fluvanna ; Joseph C. Cabell, of Nelson ; and James Madison, of Orange. We think Professor Minor has accidentally somewhat overstated the total sum subscribed.

[3] Drawn up by Mr. Jefferson at the request of some of the committee.

[4] It was not passed by the Senate avowedly that the sense of the public might be

ensuing session, in February, 1818, an act was passed appropriating from the revenues of the literary fund forty-five thousand dollars *per annum* for the primary
education of the poor, and fifteen thousand dollars *per annum* for the support of a
university, which in the course of the next year was located on the site of the
Central College, and the college, of course, merged in it. In January, 1819, the
law organizing the University was enacted, but the institution did not commence
operations until 1825, the interval having been employed in the erection of buildings, which Mr. Jefferson resolved should be models of architectural taste. The
cost of the structure, about three hundred thousand dollars, very far exceeding
public expectation, occasioned so much dissatisfaction as repeatedly to threaten the
abandonment of the enterprise. The effect, however, has been very apparent in
improving the architecture of the country, whilst it tends to beget, perhaps, in
those who from time to time visit it, some feeling of State pride which it is not
unwise to cherish.   .   .   .   .

I am, with great respect,

Your obedient servant,

JOHN B. MINOR.[1]

The site of the University had not been fixed by the law
creating it, but it was enacted that twenty-four Commissioners
be appointed by the Executive, one taken from each Senate district, to report to the next legislature, first, a proper site ; second,
a plan of building ; third, the branches of learning to be taught;
fourth, the number and description of professorships ; fifth, such
general provisions as might properly be enacted by the Legislature for the better organizing and governing the institution.
The Commissioners were to assemble at Rockfish Gap, on the
Blue Ridge, August 1st, 1818, to discharge these duties. Professor Tucker, in his life of Mr. Jefferson, states the following
interesting facts:

"The meeting, though assembled for the sole purpose of ascertaining a single
statistical fact, was by the weight of character of those who composed it, an impressive one, as it numbered among its members the President of the United States,
Mr. Monroe, and the two ex-Presidents Jefferson and Madison, besides several
judges, and leading members of the State Legislature. Yet it was remarked by the
lookers on, that Mr. Jefferson was the principal object of regard, both to the members and spectators; that he seemed to be the chief mover of the body—the soul
that animated it; and some who were present, struck by these manifestations of

taken on the bill or plan; and to effectuate this, it was ordered by a joint resolution of
both Houses, that the report which preceded the bill, the bill itself and proposed amendments, Mr. Jefferson's original bill of 1779, and his late letter to the president of the
Albemarle Academy (Peter Carr), should be printed and distributed throughout the
State.

[1] John T. Lomax was the first professor of Law in the University. Being appointed
a judge about five years afterwards, he resigned, and was succeeded by John A. G.
Davis. On his death, in 1840, he was succeeded by Henry St. George Tucker. On his
vacation of the office, two chairs of law were formed, and John B. Minor, LL.D., and
J. P. Holcombe, appointed to them.

:ference, conceived a more exalted idea of him, on this simple and unpretending
:casion, than they had ever previously entertained."

Mr. Tucker is in error in saying, that the sole object
f the meeting was to ascertain a single statistical fact. The
ommissioners sat four days, and adopted a long report, drawn
p by Mr. Jefferson, in regard to the several specified objects of
1eir appointment.'

In February, 1819, the first Board of Visitors of the Univer-
ty was chosen, and it consisted of Thomas Jefferson, James
[adison, Chapman Johnson, James Breckenridge, Robert B.
aylor, John H. Cocke, and Joseph C. Cabell. On the 29th day
f March, 1819, the Visitors held their first meeting, and unani-
1ously appointed Mr. Jefferson rector.

The buildings were erected on three sides of a square or
1wn, fronting inwards. One side is occupied by the rotunda
nd some other structures for the common use of the students,
1d two sides by professors' houses (called "pavilions"), and
1tervening rows of students' apartments but one story in height,
ced with colonnades. The pavilions, ten in number, display
veral different architectural orders. Their columns, capitals,
:c., and those of the rotunda, were executed in Italy. This
1ixture of orders destroys unity of effect, but the result is gene-
lly regarded as agreeable. Students' rooms thus constructed
re greatly more conducive to comfort and health, and to escape
case of fire, than those arranged in the ordinary way in large
nd lofty buildings; but they are also greatly more expensive in
roportion to the number of persons to be accommodated. Some
eculiarities and inconveniences about the buildings will here-
fter be mentioned in descriptions which we shall quote. Mr.
afferson had substantially the entire control of the plan and
1anner of completing the edifices, and for reasons which are
ery exactly expressed by Professor Tucker:

"Though every essential part of the establishment required the sanction of the
1ard of Visitors, yet on almost all occasions they yielded to his views, partly from

And it would appear from the report "signed and certified by the Members pre-
1t," that President Monroe did not attend. The names appended to the report are,
L Jefferson, Creed Taylor, Peter Randolph, Wm. Brockenbrough, Arch'd Ruther-
rd, Arch'd Stuart, James Breckenridge, Henry E. Watkins, James Madison, A. T.
1son, Hugh Holmes, Phil. C. Pendleton, Spencer Roane, John M. C. Taylor, J. G. Jack-
1, Phil. Slaughter, Wm. H. Cabell, Nat. H. Claiborne, Wm. A. C. Dade, William Jones,
d Thomas Wilson.

the unaffected deference which most of the Board had for his judgment and experience, and partly for the reason often urged by Mr. Madison, that as the scheme was originally Mr. Jefferson's, and the chief responsibility for its success or failure would fall on him, it was but fair to let him execute it in his own way." [1]

It is a rule adopted by some practical men to estimate carefully and minutely the cost of the labor and materials for an edifice, and then double the sum to ascertain the actual eventual cost. If the owner or builder has an architectural mania, the first estimate should be tripled. Mr. Jefferson had this mania pretty well developed, and the expense of the University structures swelled far beyond his expectations, or those of the public. Two or three times the embryo institution came near being wrecked by this cause—the Legislature hesitating, and sometimes refusing to make new appropriations. There was a strong party in that body deeply opposed to the institution, for reasons which will hereafter appear, and even cautious friends occasionally got out of patience. When driven to the wall, Mr. Jefferson always proposed some plan, or made some appeal which proved irresistible.

During his struggles to make the University, in all particulars, what he conceived it ought to be, he had many able and zealous coadjutors; but there was one whom it would be unjust to pass over without special notice, Joseph Carrington Cabell. Of an ancient and opulent family, abounding with honored names —the son of Colonel Nicholas Cabell, of Liberty Hall, distinguished in the Revolution—the nephew of the still more distinguished William Cabell, of Union Hill[2]—his mother of the talented and patriotic family of Carrington—himself cultivated by a finished education, and foreign travel, and uniting in an eminent degree, ability, discretion, and earnestness of character—a zealous lover of education—a warm friend of Jefferson, but independent in his own views—he was most wisely selected as the confidant and legislative mover in the University undertaking. Never was a trust better fulfilled; and in the language of General Dade, in the Virginia Senate, in 1828, "in promoting that monument of wisdom and taste [he] was second only to the im-

---

[1] Life of Jefferson. vol. ii., p. 431.
[2] Dr. Grigsby, in his Discourse on the Virginia Convention of 1776, says of William Cabell, of Union Hill: "What Washington was on the banks of the Potomac, Cabell was on the banks of the Upper James." He owned 25,000 acres of the best lands in Nelson and Amherst counties, and his hospitality was similar in its scale and character to that of Mount Vernon and Monticello.

-nortal Jefferson."[1]   Cabell succeeded Mr. Madison in the Rectorship, and died in that office in 1856.[2]

An exciting episode in the history of the University occurred in 1820. The Board of Visitors of Central College had, it is presumed at Mr. Jefferson's instance, agreed with the celebrated Dr. Cooper (celebrated as Priestley's friend, as a victim of the Sedition Law, and as a man of profound education and capacity), to take a professorship, as soon as the institution should open. The appointment was continued when the college was converted into the University. Cooper was reputed to be a Unitarian.

The appointment transpiring, the clergy of Virginia at once, to use Mr. Jefferson's words, raised a " hue and cry ;" and he complained that they directed it as much against the institution as against Cooper's appointment. Perhaps jealousies had previously existed as to what religious direction a school under the auspices of the overthrower of hierarchy would be likely to take; and Cooper's appointment confirmed, or furnished a good pretext for those jealousies. The censures of the clergy found a decided and dangerous echo in the Legislature. Mr. Jefferson was annoyed and provoked by the storm about his ears, and his private letters exhibit keen resentment. He warmly lashed the clergy, as desiring to restore a " Holy Inquisition," and especially the Presbyterians, whom he accused of taking the lead in the matter. But he exhibited his usual good sense in *action*, by causing the engagement with Cooper to be cancelled on terms equitable and satisfactory to the latter.

Some blame ought, doubtless, to attach to both the parties to this controversy. It cannot be claimed that Mr. Jefferson acted discreetly in employing first, and therefore conspicuously, a Professor in a *State* University, whose religious opinions were obnoxious to nearly the entire body of the religious people of that State. It could not have been necessary, in order to obtain pro-

---

[1] The historian of the University, in speaking of the founders of that Institution, says: " If in this connection, the thanks of posterity are principally due to Mr. Jefferson and Mr. Cabell, it should not be forgotten that they had most efficient coadjutors; as Messrs. Watson, Boadnax, Samuel Taylor, R. Morris (of Hanover), Gordon. Stevenson, and many others from the East ; and Johnson, Baldwin, Blackburn, and above all, a Breckenridge from the West." (Introduction, p. xxxvi.) We shall add one name to this list, that of Colonel Thomas Mann Randolph, who, after retiring from the office of Governor, reëntered the Legislature from Albemarle ; and we find repeated allusions to his efficient aid, in Cabell's letters.

[2] He succeeded Mr. Madison in 1834, but resigned two years later, and Chapman Johnson was appointed. Mr. Johnson resigned in 1845, and Cabell was reappointed, and continued in the office until his death.

per literary and other qualifications. If the appointment was made with special reference to Cooper's theological creed, and an expected propagation of it through him, no candid man could deny that, under the circumstances, it exhibited a reprehensible motive, and involved a violation of the spirit of all Mr. Jefferson's professions in regard to the proper and constitutional mode of treating the different religious sects in the foundation of the University.

But the clergy had no right, without waiting for further developments, to go beyond the obnoxious appointment, and preach a crusade against the *institution*.[1] And no liberal member of that profession would have assumed, that the mere appointment showed that Mr. Jefferson had the propagation of Cooper's religious opinions in view, had they understood what was his uniform conduct in regard to the religious creeds of others. The man who never communicated his inner religious beliefs to more than half a dozen persons—who never communicated them to his own family, except so far as he conceived it necessary to show he was not an infidel [2]—who declined communicating them to his family on the express ground that it would be improper, inasmuch as it might *influence their views*—would not be likely to turn proselyter on so public and comprehensive a scale as that of a State University. Mr. Jefferson well knew that suspicious and watchful eyes were upon him—that an attempt to propagate tenets obnoxious to the Virginia churches, by means of the University, could not be concealed for a day, and that such an attempt, if clearly made to appear, would at once prove fatal to the institution.

There was a magnanimous class of clergymen and gentlemen in Virginia who had objected to Cooper's appointment, but who were completely satisfied by his withdrawal, and by the subsequent appointments. The more distant echoes of the misunderstanding did not so rapidly die away, or rather, new charges were brought against Mr. Jefferson's religious "designs" in founding the University. Long after Cooper's appointment

---

[1] We do not apply this remark to *all* who denounced the selection of Cooper. We apprehend it does not apply to the *leading* Presbyterian assailant, the Rev. Dr. John Rice, who preached, and edited a religious paper at Richmond. We have not seen his articles, but the apparently candid editor of the History of the University describes him as a courteous and liberal man, a non-combatant in politics, a zealous advocate of education, and a known friend of the University.

[2] See his letter to his daughter Martha, ante, p. 45.

eased to be talked about, and the professorships had been
therwise filled (filled under Mr. Jefferson's immediate auspices,
nd according to his wishes), long after the "Father of the Uni-
ersity" slept in his grave on Monticello, a Review, of high
terary character, and known to be supplied with matter by able
lerical pens, assumed that Mr. Jefferson intended the Univer-
ity as "a machine" "for the work of proselyting;" that
ardent, generous, gifted, and unsuspecting youth was here made
he victim of a deliberate, cold-blooded, calculating design for
ts corruption."[1] In view of these statements and various oral
raditions of analogous tenor, as old as the great political struggle
f 1800, we took pains to ascertain from the two surviving original
»rofessors, who remain in the United States, what were the reli-
;ious opinions of themselves and colleagues, and how far they
ınd reason to believe those opinions influenced their selection.
[he following replies were received:

To Henry S. Randall.

Philadelphia, May 28, 1856.

)ear Sir,
          I am not able to give you all the information you require relative to the
łrst Visitors and Professors of the University. The Visitors, I believe were Messrs.
Iefferson, Madison, Monroe, Chapman Johnson, Joseph C. Cabell, Gen. John II.
Jocke, and George Loyall. But I am not able to say whether they were Unitarians
ォ Trinitarians. I believe that all the first Professors belonged to the Episcopal
Jhurch, except Dr. Blaetterman, who, I believe, was a German Lutheran; but I
hink there was no one except Mr. Lomax, the Professor of Law, and now a judge,
rho was a communicant. I don't remember that I ever heard the religious creeds
f either Professors or Visitors discussed or inquired into by Mr. Jefferson, or any
ıne else.   *   *   *   *   *   *   *
          I am, very respectfully yours.

George Tucker.

To Henry S. Randall.

Philadelphia, June 1, 1856.

Ĭy dear Sir:
     *   •   * I have not the slightest reason for believing that Mr.
Iefferson was, in any respect, guided in his selection of Professors of the University
)f Virginia by religious considerations. The question was certainly never asked me
by Mr. Gilmer, who chose some of the Professors in England, myself among the rest;
ınd in all my conversations with Mr. Jefferson, no reference was made to the subject. I was an Episcopalian a> was Mr. Tucker, Mr. Long, Mr. Key, Mr. Bonnycastle,
ınd Dr. Emmet. Dr. Blaetterman, I think, was a Lutheran; but I do not know

---

[1] See the New York Review and Quarterly Church Journal, March, 1837, p. 19.

so much about his religion as I do about that of the rest. There certainly was not a Unitarian among us.[1]

*   *   *   *   *   *   *   *

I am, my dear Sir,

Faithfully yours,

ROBLEY DUNGLISON.

The Review last quoted[2] also declared, " The University was opened, and, as is well known, all religious instruction was excluded." Long before the institution "opened," namely on the 7th of October 1822, Mr. Jefferson in his annual report, as Rector, to the President and Directors of the Literary Fund, said :

"In the same report of the Commissioners of 1818,[3] it was stated by them that in conformity with the principles of our constitution, which places all sects of religion on an equal footing, with the jealousies of the different sects in guarding that equality from encroachment or surprise, and with the sentiments of the Legislature in favor of freedom of religion, manifested on former occasions, they had not proposed that any professorship of divinity should be established in the University; that provision, however, was made for giving instruction in the Hebrew, Greek, and Latin languages, the depositories of the originals and of the earliest and most respected authorities of the faith of every sect; and for courses of ethical lectures, developing those moral obligations in which all sects agree; that proceeding thus far without offence to the constitution, they had left at this point to every sect to take into their own hands the office of further instruction in the peculiar tenets of each.

"It was not, however, to be understood that instruction in religious opinions and duties was meant to be precluded by the public authorities, as indifferent to the interests of society. On the contrary, the relations which exist between man and his Maker, and the duties resulting from those relations, are the most interesting and important to every human being, and the most incumbent on his study and investigation. The want of instruction in the various creeds of religious faith existing among our citizens, presents therefore a chasm in a general institution of the useful sciences. But it was thought that this want, and the intrustment to each society of instruction in its own doctrines, were evils of less danger than a permission to the public authorities to dictate modes or principles of religious instruction—or than opportunities furnished them of giving countenance or ascendency to any one sect over another. A remedy, however, has been suggested

---

[1] Messrs. Long and Key were subsequently appointed to professorships in the London University. Professor Bonnycastle continued in the Virginia University until his death, in 1841, and Professor Emmet (son of Thomas Addis Emmet), until his death in 1842. There was not an obscure man among the professors appointed during Mr. Jefferson's life—not one whose private character and general religious principles do not readily admit of sufficient showing to satisfy all whether he was likely to prove, or was probably selected with reference to being made, an instrument for the religious *corruption* of youth, under anybody's definition of that word.

[2] We simply quote the New York Review and Quarterly Church Journal as containing the only tangible public examples, within our convenient reach, of assertions in regard to the University, which in their general import have not been uncommon among the enemies of Jefferson.

[3] Drawn up by Mr. Jefferson.

romising aspect, which, while it excludes the public authorities from the domi-
. of religious freedom, would give to the sectarian schools of divinity the full
:fit of the public provisions made for instruction in the other branches of
10e. These branches are equally necessary to the divine as to the other pro-
onal or civil characters, to enable them to fulfill the duties of their calling with
:rstanding and usefulness. It has, therefore, been in contemplation, and sug-
ed by some pious individuals who perceive the advantages of associating other
ies with those of religion, to establish their religious schools on the confines of
University, so as to give to their students ready and convenient access and
ndance on the scientific lectures of the University, and to maintain by that
ns those destined for the religious professions on as high a standing of science
of personal weight and respectability, as may be obtained by others from the
:fits of the University. Such establishments would offer the further and great
intage of enabling the students of the University to attend religious exercises
the professor of their particular sect, either in the rooms of the building,
destined to that purpose under impartial regulations, as proposed in the same
rt of the Commissioners, or in the lecturing room of such professor. To such
iositions the Visitors are disposed to lend a willing ear, and would think it their
' to give every encouragement by assuring those who might choose such a
tion for their schools, that the regulations of the University should be so
ified and accommodated as to give every facility of access and attendance to
r students with such regulated use also, as may be permitted to the other stu-
s, of the library, which may hereafter be acquired, either by public or private
iBcence ; but always understanding that these schools shall be independent of
University and of each other. Such an arrangement would complete the circle
he useful sciences embraced by this institution, and would fill the chasm now
ting, on principles which would leave inviolate the constitutional freedom of
;ion, the most inalienable and sacred of all human rights over which the people
authorities of this State, individually and publicly, have ever manifested the most
:hful jealousy ; and could their jealousy be now alarmed, in the opinion of the
islature, by what is here suggested, the idea will be relinquished on any surmises
isapprobation which they may think proper to express."

If the proposition here made to the different sects, on terms
liberal, had been accepted by them, the University of Vir-
ia would now comprise the most extensive school of Theology
:he world.' It was not accepted.

The omission in the plan of the University, to make provision for religious instruc-
, has been misconstrued by many candid persons because they have not understood
rue nature of that institution. They look round on the American colleges, and see
:a provision generally made in them. But these schools have mostly been founded by
icular sects, and if they have received State aid, it has been in consideration that
rs, founded by other sects, have received a proportionate degree of aid. By such an
agement, each college may employ religious teachers of the denomination of its
ders, without requiring the State, when extending its aid, to give preference to a
icular sect, and without unfairness in practice—because every pupil can choose his
school, and because it is presumable that the number of both colleges and scholars
ich sect, will be proportioned to the number of that sect, and consequently to its
ributions to and claims on the public treasury. But none of our State governments
, at least of late years, assessed their population, or taken their public money to
i up a general and *exclusive* system of schools placed under the religious supervision
ie sect; nor have they invited a struggle between sects by allowing a majority of

Mr. Jefferson's offer was no empty flourish. Among the enactments the University were engrafted the following:

CHAPTER II. SEC. I.

27. Should the religious sects of this State, or any of them, according to the invitation held out to them, establish within, or adjacent to, the precincts of the University, schools of instruction in the religion of their sect, the students of the University will be free, and expected to attend religious worship at the establishment of their respective sects, in the morning, and in time to meet their School in the University at its stated hour.

28. The students of such religious schools, if they attend any School of the Uni-

patrons or pupils to say what sect shall exercise such supervision, either generally or in each particular school. No sect is now allowed to preach or otherwise inculcate its tenets in the common schools of any State. In most of the States there is no provision for religious instruction in the common schools; and in some it is directly prohibited, unless as a purely voluntary affair outside of school hours. And we believe it is now generally held that no pupil shall be compelled to join in any religious *services* contrary to the faith or expressed wishes of his parents. Yet it is not customary to speak of this as an intended "*exclusion*" of religion from the schools—as proof of a design to *corrupt* unsuspecting youth.

The Virginia University was intended to be as exclusive in its benefits, so far as the appropriation of the public funds went, as is the system of common schools in any State. Its free pupils were to be selected from a secondary class of schools, and the free pupils of this secondary class, from the primary schools—all forming parts of a State system of education, of which the primary schools were to be the base, and the Virginia University was to be the apex—all mainly supported by public funds taken from the treasury, or raised by taxation on the people, without reference to their religious beliefs. It was a part of the avowed plan and intention of the founders of the University, that it, and it alone, should *complete* the education of the free pupils supported by the public funds. It follows, then, that if that institution was placed under the religious supervision or influence of any particular sect, the public money of all sects would be used for the benefit of one. Nor could this difficulty be obviated, as has been sometimes partially done, by employing (literary) professors of different sects to take turns in leading in religious services and preaching, because, in an institution belonging to the whole State, and purely exclusive in its benefits, it would be necessary to give *every* sect contributing to the public funds, its turn in leading in religious services and preaching, and consequently, officers of the institution to discharge these duties. But there are, doubtless, three times as many sects in Virginia as there are professors of the University; and probably nobody would consent to employ the public funds in maintaining an army of mere chaplains. And again, how could the religious services be *proportioned* among the sects? Should the Unitarian occupy the pulpit as often as the Episcopalian, one representing ten or twenty as many tax-payers as the other? Or should separate chapels be built for all the sects?

There were but two *practicable* alternatives. Mr. Jefferson presented one. The other was to leave religious instruction in the University on the same footing in which it is left in the common schools of the different States. The rejection of Mr. Jefferson's proposal, rendered the second alternative inevitable.

While there can be no good ground for treating the attitude of the Virginia University and of the common schools of the States as an antagonistic one to religion, it appears to us that no reflecting man can fail to deplore the unnatural divorce between religious and intellectual culture, which circumstances compel in the public schools of our country, unless we choose to establish State religions, or unless we throw back popular education on that voluntary basis which never has succeeded in supplying even rudimentary education to the general mass of any numerous people. Never was there a more false, or a more dangerous dogma—quite too prevalent in our country—that "our common schools," of themselves, insure society and the State; that a knowledge of reading, writing, and one or two other elementary branches, is a sufficient pledge in general of good citizenship. Home and church influences may supply the religious "chasm," as Mr. Jefferson termed it, in public education—but these influences are sometimes wanting—and in all cases they would be vastly strengthened and benefited by a systematic daily religious culture in the schools. The want of the latter element is the great defect of American public education.

versity, shall be considered as students of the University, subject to the same regu-
ations, and entitled to the same rights and privileges.

And these continue to be laws of the University to the present time. A letter from Jefferson to Dr. Cooper, of November 2d, 1822, shows that he then was under the expectation that the religious sects would accept the offer thus made to them, and that he considered it highly desirable that they should do so.

We go back to Mr Jefferson's miscellaneous correspondence in 1820. The appalling sacrifice of private property which took place that year in Virginia, was thus described to H. Nelson, March 12th, fully verifying Colonel Benton's already quoted statements:

"This State is in a condition of unparalleled distress. The sudden reduction of the circulating medium from a plethory to all but annihilation is producing an entire revolution of fortune. In other places I have known lands sold by the sheriff for one year's rent; beyond the mountain we hear of good slaves selling for one hundred dollars, good horses for five dollars, and the sheriffs generally the purchasers. Our produce is now selling at market for one-third of its price, before this commercial catastrophe, say flour at three and a quarter and three and a half dollars the barrel. We should have less right to expect relief from our legislators if they had been the establishers of the unwise system of banks. A remedy to a certain degree was practicable, that of reducing the quantum of circulation gradually to a level with that of the countries with which we have commerce, and an eternal abjuration of paper. But they have adjourned without doing anything. I fear local insurrections against these horrible sacrifices of property."

On hearing that Spain had declined to ratify the treaty of the previous year, for the cession of the Floridas, by which the United States had surrendered Texas to Spain, Jefferson wrote to the President (May 14th):

"I confess to you I am not sorry for the non-ratification of the Spanish treaty. Our assent to it has proved our desire to be on friendly terms with Spain: their dissent, the imbecility and malignity of their government towards us, have placed them in the wrong in the eyes of the world, and that is well; but to us the province of Techas will be the richest State of our Union, without any exception. Its southern part will make more sugar than we can consume, and the Red river, on its north, is the most luxuriant country on earth. Florida, moreover, is ours. Every nation in Europe considers it such a right. We need not care for its occupation in time of peace, and, in war, the first cannon makes it ours without offence to anybody. The friendly advisements, too, of Russia and France, as well as the change of government in Spain, now ensured, require a further and respectful forbearance. While their request will rebut the plea of proscriptive possession, it will give us a right to their approbation when taken in the maturity of circumstances. I really think, too, that neither the state of our finances, the condition of our country, nor the public opinion, urges us to precipitation into war. The treaty has had the valuable effect of strengthening our title to the Techas, because the cession of the Floridas in exchange for Techas imports an acknowledgment of our right to it. This province, moreover, the Floridas and possibly Cuba, will join us on the acknowledgment of their independence, a measure to which their new government will probably accede voluntarily."

In a letter to Short, August 4th, we have the "Monroe Doctrine" full blown:

"From many conversations with him, [M. Correa, appointed minister to Brazil, by the Government of Portugal], I hope he sees, and will promote in his new situation, the advantages of a cordial fraternization among all the American nations, and the importance of their coalescing in an American system of policy, totally independent of and unconnected with that of Europe. The day is not distant, when we may formally require a meridian of partition through the ocean which separates the two hemispheres, on the hither side of which no European gun shall ever be heard, nor an American on the other; and when, during the rage of the eternal wars of Europe, the lion and the lamb, within our regions, shall lie down together in peace.   *   *   *   *

"The principles of society there and here, then, are radically different, and I hope no American patriot will ever lose sight of the essential policy of interdicting in the seas and territories of both Americas, the ferocious and sanguinary contests of Europe. I wish to see this coalition begun."

Mr. Jefferson did not approve of all the measures adopted by the Republican party in Congress, under Mr. Monroe's Administration. He lost, however, none of his personal confidence in the President's principles. In a letter to Mr. Ritchie, December 25th, he thus hinted at the measures he disliked:

"As to the two Presidents, late and now in office, I know them both to be of principles as truly republican as any men living. If there be anything amiss, therefore, in the present state of our affairs, as the formidable deficit lately unfolded to us indicates, I ascribe it to the inattention of Congress to their duties, to their unwise dissipation, and waste of the public contributions. They seemed, some little while ago, to be at a loss for objects whereon to throw away the supposed fathomless funds of the treasury. I had feared the result, because I saw among them some of my old fellow-laborers, of tried and known principles, yet often in their minorities. I am aware that in one of their most ruinous vagaries, the people were themselves betrayed into the same phrensy with their representatives. The deficit produced, and a heavy tax to supply it, will, I trust, bring both to their sober senses."

All the Republicans were not so tolerant towards Monroe's course, but he was reëlected President, in 1820, without any opposition. Only one vote in the electoral college was cast against him, that of Governor William Plumer of New Hampshire, who was elected on the Republican ticket.

Various expressions of familiar opinions, made during this year, do not require repetition. To several correspondents Mr. Jefferson complained that the wrist fractured or dislocated in France in 1786, and which had never entirely recovered, was now becoming so stiff from the effects of age, that writing was a slow and painful operation to him. His general health was not good. As early as November of the preceding year (1819) he had been nearly rendered unable to walk, by a swelling of his limbs, occasioned by debility; but he continued to ride daily to the University, a distance, going and returning, of eight miles, to superintend the erection of the buildings. He placed a tele-scope on one of the terraces of his house, which enabled him to see from thence how the workmen were employed at all hours of the day. He was earnestly urged by his physician in the opening of 1820, to suspend this unremitting care and activity, by making a long visit to Poplar Forest; but he could not then tear himself from his favorite employment, and the journey was deferred until November. It was consequently made with much less benefit, and at the close of the year he felt himself only in a state of " slow and uncertain convalescence."

His constitution, however, rallied in the spring of 1821, and this was a year to him of health and activity. His appearance at this time of life may be judged by Sully's portrait at West Point, which the painter made a journey to Monticello to execute.

Timothy Pickering wrote to Mr. Jefferson in February, 1821, inclosing to him a discourse of the Rev. Dr. Channing, and making what was regarded as some kind of personal overture, as appears in the following paragraph of the reply, dated February 27th:

" I have received, sir, your favor of the 12th, and I assure you I received it with pleasure. It is true, as you say, that we have differed in political opinions; but I can say with equal truth, that I never suffered a political to become a personal difference. I have been left on this ground by some friends whom I dearly loved, but I was never the first to separate. With some others, of politics different from mine, I have continued in the warmest friendship to this day, and to all, and to yourself particularly, I have ever done moral justice."

This is as purely characteristic as was the fact that Picker ing, three years later, without a particle of new personal aggression from Mr. Jefferson, made that most offensive and malignant attack on him which has already been noticed in connection with the Mazzei letter.

Jefferson wrote to General Dearborn, August 17th :

"I am happy to hear of his [John Adams's] good health. I think he will outlive us all, I mean the Declaration-men, although our senior since the death of Colonel Floyd. It is a race in which I have no ambition to win. Man, like the fruit he eats, has his period of ripeness. Like that, too, if he continues longer hanging to the stem, it is but a useless and unsightly appendage."

Adams wrote to Jefferson, September 24th :

"As Brother Floyd has gone, I am now the oldest of the little Congressional group that remain. I may, therefore, rationally hope to be the first to depart; and as you are the youngest and most energetic in mind and body, you may therefore rationally hope to be the last to take your flight, and to rake up the fire, as Father Sherman, who always staid to the last, and commonly two days afterwards, used to say, 'that it was his office to sit up and rake the ashes over the coals.' And much satisfaction may you have in your office."

Mr. Jefferson's customary views in regard to the independence of the different branches of the General Government of each other, and of the attempts of the judiciary to encroach on the executive and legislative departments, are frequently repeated in 1821. Col. Taylor of Caroline, Judge Roane, and Jefferson's son-in-law Governor Randolph (elected Governor in 1819), desired him to permit some of his letters on this topic to be published. He declined on the ground that they were not " exactly proper " for publication—that they " contained matter which might give offence to the judges without adding strength to the opinion." He therefore prepared a draft which he allowed to be printed in which all offensive expressions were omitted.

He wrote Mr. Macon, November 23d, the same year:

"My confidence, as you kindly observed, has been often abused by the publication of my letters for the purposes of interest or vanity, and it has been to me the source of much pain to be exhibited before the public *in forms not meant for them.* I receive letters expressed in the most friendly and even affectionate terms, sometimes, perhaps, asking my opinion on some subject. I cannot refuse to answer such letters, nor can I do it drily and suspiciously. Among a score or two of such correspondents, one perhaps betrays me. I feel it mortifyingly, but conclude I had better incur one treachery than offend a score or two of good people. I sometimes expressly desire that my letter may not be published; but this is so like requesting a man not to steal or cheat, that I am ashamed of it after I have done it."

There are other interesting letters of 1821, but the correspondence of the year was lighter than usual, owing to the activity of Mr. Jefferson's occupations.

He wrote, March 6th, 1822, to Jedediah Morse, who proposed to him to become a member of a Society for the civilization and improvement of the Indian tribes. It was to consist of ex-Presidents, heads of Departments, the United States Judiciary, Governors of States, Members of Congress, General Officers of the Army, Presidents of Colleges and Theological Seminaries, the Clergy, etc., etc., *ex officio*, and of such private individuals as would pay a certain price for membership. Mr. Jefferson declared that the expressed object of the association was " one which he had ever had much at heart," but he declined to become a member of it, stating his objections at length to its nature and magnitude. These were in part similar to those urged at an earlier day by himself and Franklin against the Cincinnati.

Party animosity continued to burn against Jefferson. He was accused in the newspapers by a writer signing himself " A Native Virginian," of having overdrawn his account as Minister to France, to the amount of one thousand one hundred and forty-eight dollars! Jefferson replied, May 13th, in a public letter to Messrs. Ritchie & Gooch, of the Richmond Enquirer. The assailant returned to the charge, sustaining himself by quoting pretended entries from the public accounts—aware, doubtless, that their forged character could not be proved from the original documents, which were destroyed in the Register's office when the public buildings were burned by the British in 1814. Unfortunately, however, for this ingenious knave, Mr. Jefferson had preserved a press copy of his public account with the Government. In his answer, he also cited numerous entries in his private account books. We have been at the pains to examine the originals, and those feeling any further curiosity in the matter will find it explained in Appendix.[1]

Nothing can be given more strictly (and it may be added, interestingly) biographical, at this period, than the following:

[1] See APPENDIX, No. 31.

TO JOHN ADAMS.

MONTICELLO, *June* 1, 1822.

It is very long, my dear sir, since I have written to you. My dislocated wrist is now become so stiff that I write slow and with pain, and therefore write as little as I can. Yet it is due to mutual friendship to ask once in a while how we do. The papers tell us that General Stark is off at the age of 93. Charles Thompson still lives at about the same age, cheerful, slender as a grasshopper, and so much without memory that he scarcely recognizes the members of his household. An intimate friend of his called on him not long since; it was difficult to make him recollect who he was, and, sitting one hour, he told him the same story four times over. Is this life?

> " With lab'ring step
> To tread our former footsteps? pace the round
> Eternal?—to beat and beat
> The beaten track? to see what we have seen,
> To taste the tasted? o'er our palates to decant
> Another vintage?"

It is at most but the life of a cabbage; surely not worth a wish. When all our faculties have left, or are leaving us, one by one—sight, hearing, memory—every avenue of pleasing sensation is closed, and athumy, debility, and malaise left in their places—when friends of our youth are all gone, and a generation is risen around us whom we know not, is death an evil?

> " When one by one our ties are torn,
> And friend from friend is snatched forlorn,
> When man is left alone to mourn,
> Oh! then how sweet it is to die!
> When trembling limbs refuse their weight,
> And films slow gathering dim the sight,
> When clouds obscure the mental light
> 'Tis nature's kindest boon to die!"

I really think so. I have ever dreaded a doting old age; and my health has been generally so good, and is now so good, that I dread it still. The rapid decline of my strength during the last winter has made me hope sometimes that I see land. During summer I enjoy its temperature, but I shudder at the approach of winter, and wish I could sleep through it with the dormouse, and only wake with him in spring, if ever. They say that Stark could walk about his room. I am told you walk well and firmly. I can only reach my garden, and that with sensible fatigue. I ride, however, daily. But reading is my delight. I should wish never to put pen to paper; and the more because of the treacherous practice some people have of publishing one's letters without leave. Lord Mansfield declared it a breach of trust, and punishable at law. I think it should be a penitentiary felony; yet you will have seen that they have drawn me out into the arena of the newspapers;[1] although I know it is too late for me to buckle on the armor of youth, yet my indignation would not permit me passively to receive the kick of an ass.

To turn to the news of the day, it seems that the Cannibals of Europe are going to eating one another again. A war between Russia and Turkey is like the battle of the kite and snake. Whichever destroys the other, leaves a destroyer the less

---

[1] Alluding to his letters to Ritchie & Gooch, in reply to a "Native Virginian."

for the world. This pugnacious humor of mankind seems to be the law of his nature, one of the obstacles to too great multiplication provided in the mechanism of the universe. The cocks of the henyard kill one another. Bears, bulls, rams, do the same. And the horse, in his wild state, kills all the young males, until worn down with age and war, some vigorous youth kills him, and takes to himself the harem of females. I hope we shall prove how much happier for man the Quaker policy is, and that the life of the feeder is better than that of the fighter; and it is some consolation that the desolation by these maniacs of one part of the earth is the means of improving it in other parts. Let the latter be our office, and let us milk the cow, while the Russian holds her by the horns, and the Turk by the tail. God bless you, and give you health, strength, and good spirits, and as much of life as you think worth having.

Mr. Adams suggested the publication of this letter, to protect the writer of it, in future, from the annoyances of which he complained. Jefferson so far assented as to leave the matter to the discretion of his friend. The following mournfully sounding extract from his reply, contains some astonishing statements:

"I do not know how far you may suffer, as I do, under the persecution of letters, of which every mail brings a fresh load. They are letters of inquiry, for the most part, always of good will, sometimes from friends whom I esteem, but much oftener from persons whose names are unknown to me, but written kindly and civilly, and to which, therefore, civility requires answers. Perhaps the better known failure of your hand in its function of writing may shield you in greater degree from this distress, and so far qualify the misfortune of its disability. I happened to turn to my letter-list some time ago, and a curiosity was excited to count those received in a single year. It was the year before the last. I found the number to be one thousand two hundred and sixty-seven, many of them requiring answers of elaborate research, and all to be answered with due attention and consideration. Take an average of this number for a week or a day, and I will repeat the question suggested by other considerations in mine of the 1st. Is this life? At best it is but the life of a mill-horse, who sees no end to his circle but in death. To such a life, that of a cabbage is paradise. It occurs then, that my condition of existence, truly stated in that letter, if better known, might check the kind indiscretions which are so heavily oppressing the departing hours of life. Such a relief would, to me, be an ineffable blessing. But yours of the 11th, equally interesting and affecting, should accompany that to which it is an answer. The two, taken together, would excite a joint interest, and place before our fellow-citizens the present condition of two ancient servants, who having faithfully performed their forty or fifty campaigns, *stipendiis omnibus expletis*, have a reasonable claim to repose from all disturbance in the sanctuary of invalids and superannuates."

What a lesson this to the herd of epistolary lion-hunters, and to a smaller and less ambitious class of persecutors, who only forget that some thousands of other persons are as likely as themselves to desire the opinions or the autograph of such a man as

Jefferson ! The latter here carries the idea, that he expected to answer all these letters. We have already stated that it was his uniform custom to answer every one the matter and language of which gave it the appearance of having come from a respectable person. The number of letters for the year here referred to (1820), published in the larger or Congress edition of his works, is twenty —less than a sixty-third of those presumably written. He left, at his death, copies of about sixteen thousand letters written by himself[1]—and this was a trifling number compared with those which he had written without retaining copies.

In a letter to William T. Barry, July 2d, Jefferson said:

" Whether the surrender of our opponents, their reception into our camp, their assumption of our name, and apparent accession to our objects, may strengthen or weaken the genuine principles of republicanism, may be a good or an evil, is yet to be seen. I consider the party division of whig and tory the most wholesome which can exist in any government, and well worthy being nourished, to keep out those of a more dangerous character."

The first part of this remark applies to the support of Monroe by the Federalists, at his second election, and the obliteration of ancient party lines during the " era of good feeling," as it was called. Mr. Jefferson was a compromiser in action among political friends, a conciliator in practice towards opponents, but never a syncretist in principle. He lived to believe that the fears above expressed were vindicated by the results.

Mr. Adams wrote to Mr. Jefferson, October 15th, saying that he had always imputed to the latter the measure of constructing vessels of war to protect our Mediterranean commerce, in Washington's Administration—that he believed "the navy was" Jefferson's " child." He assigned several reasons for this opinion, and said that he had " personal evidence " that " Hamilton was averse to the measure," and " that Washington was averse to a navy, he had full proof from his own lips, in many different conversations, some of them at length, in which he [Washington] always insisted that it was only building and arming ships for the English." He supposed Knox to have " assisted in ushering " the child " into the world," and that if the Attorney-

---

[1] And he had preserved about twenty-six thousand letters, addressed to him. We state both of these numbers on the authority of the legatee of his manuscript papers, Colonel T. J. Randolph.

General (whom he erroneously supposes to have been Bradford instead of Randolph) was on the same side, "the majority was clear."

Jefferson replied November 1st, that he had himself favored the construction of the vessels—that he "thought General Washington approved of building vessels of war to that extent" —that he knew General Knox did—that Hamilton and Randolph's opinions on the occasion were entirely forgotten by him —that his correspondent, Mr. Adams, "was well known to have ever been an advocate of the wooden walls of Themistocles," etc.

To a grandson, absent from Monticello, Mr. Jefferson wrote the following letters :

TO FRANCIS EPPES, MILLBROOK.

MONTICELLO, *Jan.* 1, 1819.

DEAR FRANCIS,

   Leschot has repaired Mrs. Eppes's watch, and changed the pipe of the key, but the watch was so short a time in his hands that she could not be well regulated ; she will therefore probably need further regulation to make her keep good time. I am sorry you are disappointed in your teacher, but it depends on yourself whether this is of any consequence. A master is necessary only to those who require compulsion to get their lessons. As to instruction, a translation supplies the place of a teacher. Get the lessons first by dictionary, and then instead of saying it to a master, go over it with the translation, and that will tell you whether you have got it truly. Dacier's Horace is admirable for this. As to parsing, you can do that by yourself, both as to parts of speech and syntax. You can perfect yourself too in your Greek grammar, as well alone as with a teacher. Your Spanish, too, should be kept up. All depends on your own resolution to stick as closely to your book as if a master was looking over you. If Dr. Cooper comes to us he will open our Grammar School the 1st of April. We shall be decided in a few days, and I will let you know. . . . . Present my respects to Mrs. Eppes, and be assured of my constant affection.

              TH. JEFFERSON.

TO FRANCIS EPPES, MILLBROOK.

POPLAR FOREST, *Sept.* 21, 1820.

DEAR FRANCIS,

   I leave at Flood's, with this letter, a packet containing three small volumes, from my petit format library, containing several tragedies of Euripides, some of Sophocles, and one of Æschylus. The first you will find easy, the second tolerably so ; the last, incomprehensible in his flights among the clouds. His text has come to us so mutilated and defective, and has been so much plastered with amendments by his commentators, that it can scarcely be called his. I inclose you our measured distances expressed in miles and cents. We leave this to-morrow morning, and shall be at Monticello the next night. From there you shall hear from me about the end of the first week of October. By that time I shall either see Dr. Cooper, or know that I shall not see him. I was deceived in the weather the day we left Millbrook. We passed through two hours of very heavy rain, and got to Flood's at 11 o'clock, where we staid the day. We didn't suffer ourselves, but the servants got very wet. Present our cordial love to the family. Ever and affectionately yours,

TH. JEFFERSON.

To FRANCIS EPPES, COLUMBIA, SOUTH CAROLINA.

MONTICELLO, Oct. 6, 1820.

DEAR FRANCIS,

Your letter of the 28th came to hand yesterday, and as I suppose you are now about leaving Richmond for Columbia, this letter will be addressed to the latter place. I consider you as having made such proficiency in Latin and Greek that, on your arrival at Columbia, you may at once commence the study of the sciences, and as you may well attend two professors at once, I advise you to enter immediately with those of Mathematics and Chemistry; after these go on to Astronomy, Natural Philosophy, Natural History, and Botany. I say nothing of Mineralogy or Geology, because, I presume, they will be comprehended in the Chemical course. Nor shall I say anything of other branches of science, but that you should lose no time on them until the accomplishment of those above-named, before which time we shall have opportunities of further advising together. I hope you will be permitted to enter at once into *a course* of *mathematics*, which will itself take up all that is useful in Euclid, and that you will not be required to go formally through the usual books of Geometry. That would be a waste of time which you have not to spare, and if you cannot enter the Mathematical school without it, do not enter it at all, but engage in the other sciences above mentioned. Your Latin and Greek should be kept up assiduously, by reading at spare hours; and discontinuing the desultory reading of the schools, I would advise you to undertake a regular course of History and Poetry, in both languages. In Greek go first through the Cyropædia, and then read Herodotus, Thucydides, Xenophon's Hellenics and Anabasis, ——'s Alexander, and Plutarch's Lives, for prose reading—Homer's Iliad and Odyssey, Euripides, Sophocles, in poetry, and Demosthenes in oratory, alternating prose and verse as most agreeable to yourself. In Latin, read Livy, Cæsar, Sallust, Tacitus, Cicero's Philosophies, and some of his orations in prose—and Virgil, Ovid's Metamorphoses, Horace, Terence and Juvenal for poetry; after all these, you will find still many of secondary grade to employ future years, and especially those of old age and retirement. Let me hear from you as soon as you shall have taken your stand in college, and give me a general view of the courses pursued there, and from time to time afterwards advise me of your progress. I will certainly write to you occasionally; but you will not expect it very frequently, as you know how slowly and painfully my stiffened wrist now permits me to write, and how much I am oppressed by a general and revolting correspondence, wearing me down with incessant labor, instead of leaving me to the tranquil happiness with which reading and lighter occupations would fill pleasantly what remains to me of life. I had written to Dr. Cooper that I should leave Monticello for Poplar Forest, about the 11th of this month. He informs me he cannot be here so soon as that, but will call on me a'

Poplar Forest in the third week of the month. Adieu, my dear Francis. Consider how little time is left you, and how much you have to attain in it, and that every moment you lose of it is lost for ever. Be assured that no one living is more anxious than myself to see you become a virtuous and useful citizen, worthy of the trusts of your country, and wise enough to conduct them advantageously, nor any one more affectionately yours.

TH. JEFFERSON.

To FRANCIS EPPES, COLUMBIA, SOUTH CAROLINA.

POPLAR FOREST, Dec. 13, 1820.

DEAR FRANCIS:

Yours of Oct. 31st, came to me here Nov. 28th, having first gone to Monticello. I observe the course of reading at Columbia which you note. It either is, or ought to be, the rule of every collegiate institution to teach to every particular student the branches of science which those who direct him think will be useful in the pursuits proposed for him, and to waste his time on nothing which they think will not be useful to him. This will certainly be the fundamental law of our University, to leave every one free to attend whatever branches of instruction he wants, and to decline what he doesn't want. If this be not generally allowed at Columbia, I hope they may be induced to indulgence in your case, in consideration of the little time you have left, and which you cannot afford to waste on what will be useless to you, or can be acquired by reading hereafter without the aid of a teacher. As I do not know any professors at Columbia but Dr. Cooper, request in my name his interest and influence to be permitted to adapt your studies to your wants. Reviewing what you say are the courses of the four classes, I pass over the 1st and 2d, which you are done with, and should select for you from the 3d, Algebra, Geometry, Trigonometry, and Natural Philosophy; and from the 4th, Logarithms and Chemistry, to which I should add Astronomy, Botany, and Natural History, which you do not mention in any of the classes. I omit Blair's Rhetoric, Watt's Logic, Kaimes, Paley, Butler, etc., which you can read in your closet after leaving college, as well as at it. And in Mathematics I do not think you have time to undertake either Conic Sections or Fluxions. Unless you can be indulged in this selection I shall lament very much indeed, the having advised your going to Columbia, because time is now the most pressing and precious thing in the world to you, and the greatest injury which can possibly be done you is to waste what remains on what you can acquire hereafter yourself, and prevent your learning those useful branches which cannot well be acquired without the aids of the college. Whether our University will open this time twelvemonth or be shut up seven years, will depend on the present Legislature's liberating our funds by appropriating $100,000 more from the Literary Fund. If you watch the newspapers you will see what they do, and be able to judge what may be expected. Ellen and Virginia are here with me. We leave this the day after to-morrow for Monticello, where we hope to meet your aunt, who will be returning at the same time from Richmond. We learn by your letter to Virginia, that Wayles is with you. To him and to yourself I tender my affectionate attachment. To Dr. Cooper also, give my friendly souvenirs; the difficulty with which I write puts that much out of my power.

TH. JEFFERSON

To Francis Eppes, Columbia, South Carolina.

Monticello, *Apr.* 8, 1821.

DEAR FRANCIS:

Yours of March 27th has been duly received. The effect of what our Legislature did for us at their last session is not exactly what you suppose. They authorized us to borrow another $60,000, pledging, however, our own funds for repayment. This loan enables us to finish all our buildings of accommodation this year, and to begin the library, which will take three years to be completed. Without waiting for that, it is believed that when the buildings of accommodation are finished, the Legislature will cancel the debt of $120,000, and leave our funds free to open the institution. We shall then require a year to get our professors into place. Whether the Legislature will relinquish the debt the next session, or at some future one, is not certain. In the meantime you cannot do better than to stay where you are until the end of 1822, confining your studies to Mathematics, Natural Philosophy, Natural History, and Rhetoric; all other branches you can pursue by yourself, should we not open here by that date.

I note what you say of the late disturbances in your college. These dissentions are a great affliction on the American schools, and a principal impediment to education in this country. The source of discontent arising from dieting the students, we shall avoid here by having nothing to do with it, and by leaving every one to board where he pleases. Nor do I see why this remedy might not have been resorted to in your late case, rather than that of making it a ground of difference with the professors. There may have been reasons, however, of which I am uninformed. The family here is all well, always remember you with affection, and receive your letters with gratification. To theirs I add the assurance of my affectionate love.

TH. JEFFERSON.

To Francis Eppes, Columbia, South Carolina.

Monticello, *June* 27th, 1831.

DEAR FRANCIS:

Your letter of May 7th was received in due time, and in it you ask my opinion as to the utility of pursuing metaphysical studies. No well educated person should be entirely ignorant of the operations of the human mind, to which the name of metaphysics has been given. There are three books on this subject, Locke's Essay on the Human Understanding, Tracy's Elements of Idiology, and Stewart's Philosophy of the Human Mind; any one of which will communicate as much on the subject as is worth attention. I consider Tracy as the most correct metaphysician living; and I inclose you a small tract of his worth reading, because it is short, profound, and treats an interesting question, to wit, that on the certainty of human knowledge. He prostrates the visions of Malebranche, Berkeley, and other skeptics, by resting the question on the single basis of "We Feel." With him who denies this basis there can be no ground of reasoning at all. To pursue the science further is following a will-of-the-wisp, and a very useless waste of time, much better given to sciences more palpable, and more useful in the business of life. Tracy's Review, or Commentaries on Montesquieu is the best elementary book on government which has ever been published. Being afraid to publish it in France, he sent his manuscript to me, 1809, and I got it translated and published in Philadelphia, in 1811. It will be the text-book of the political lectures of the University. The buildings of the University (except the library) will all be finished the ensuing winter. Towards this object the Legislature permitted an advance of $120,000 from the Literary Fund, but under the name of a loan, taking in pledge our annuity of $15,000. If it is to be really redeemed by this, many years will be necessary to clear that fund, but it is hoped they will consider it as an appropriation, and discharge the annuity. Within one year after that discharge, we may open the institution, as it will require that time to bring our professors into place. Mr. Watts[1] when here asked me for a copy of the report containing the plan of that institution; I did not know then that I had a spare copy; I have since found one which I inclose for his acceptance, with the tender of my great respect. Our family is all well, remember you always with affection, and join me in hope you will be able to visit us during your next vacation, as they do in assuring you of our constant attachment.

TH. JEFFERSON.

TO FRANCIS EPPES, COLUMBIA, SOUTH CAROLINA.

POPLAR FOREST, Nov. 17, 1821.

DEAR FRANCIS:

On my return to this place on the 6th inst., I found here your letter of Oct. 22d. I learnt from that with real affliction that it was doubtful whether you would be permitted at Columbia to pursue those studies only which will be analogous to the views and pursuits of your future life. It is a deplorable consideration that, although neither your father nor myself have spared any effort in our power to press on your education, yet so miserable are the means of education in our State that it has been retarded and baffled to a most unfortunate degree; and now that you have only a single year left, you cannot be permitted to employ that solely in what will be useful to you. Every institution, however, has a right to lay down its own laws, and we are bound to acquiescence. There seems, from your letter, to be still a possibility that you may be permitted to remain as an irregular student; that is the most desirable event; if not, then to obtain from Dr. Cooper and Mr. Wallace the favor of attending them as a private student, unconnected with the college. From them you can receive every instruction necessary for you, to wit, in Mathematics, Astronomy, Natural Philosophy, and Chemistry. If that cannot be permitted, there will remain nothing but the disastrous alternative of again shifting your situation. I know nothing of the plan or degree of instruction at Chapel Hill; perhaps you might be excluded there also, by similar rules. If so, William and Mary is your last resource. There students are permitted to attend the schools of their choice and those branches of science only which will be useful to them in the line of life they propose. The objection to that place is its autumnal unhealthiness. The thankfulness you express for my cares of you bespeaks a feeling and good heart; but the tender recollections which bind my affections to you are such as will forever call for everything I can do for you, and the comfort of my life is the belief that you will deserve it. To my prayers that your life may be distinguished by its worth, I add the assurance of my constant and affectionate love.

TH. JEFFERSON.

[1] Beaufort T. Watts, Secretary of State, S. C.

TO FRANCIS EPPES, MILLBROOK.

MONTICELLO, *April* 9, 1822.

DEAR FRANCIS:

Your letter of March 22d did not reach me till a few days ago; that of Feb. 6th had been received in that month. Being chiefly a statement of facts it did not seem to require an answer, and my burden of letter-writing is so excessive as to restrain me to answers absolutely necessary. I think with you that you had now better turn in to the study of the law. As no one can read a whole day closely on any one subject to advantage, you will have time enough in the other portions of the day to go on with those essential studies which you have not as yet completed. If you read law from breakfast four or five hours, enough will remain before dinner for exercise. The morning may be given to Natural Philosophy and Astronomy, the afternoon to Rhetoric and Belles Lettres, and the night to history and ethics. The first object will be to procure the necessary law-books for reading. They will come twenty-five per cent. cheaper from England than bought here, and some indeed can only be had there. I will subjoin a catalogue of what should be obtained as soon as practicable, and their cost there. About as much the next year will be a sufficient library for reference in practice. The course of reading I should advise, would be Coke's Littleton, and his other Institutes, Bacon's Abridgment, Blackstone's Commentaries, Woodson's Lectures, and Reeves in Common Law; and in Chancery, the abridgment of cases in equity, Bridgman's Digested Index, and Fonblanque, interspersing some select case from the reporters both in law and equity. The course will employ two years to be superficial, and three to be profound. This may be done at Millbrook or Monticello as well as in the lawyer's office. You know, of course, that you are as much at home at Monticello as at Millbrook, so that you can choose freely, or divide your time between them to your own wish. You would have perhaps less interruption by company at Millbrook, but access here to books which may not be there. I have fortunately just received from England, Thomas's Coke's Littleton, a most valuable work. He has arranged Coke's matter in the method of Blackstone, adding the notes of Lords Hale and Nottingham and Hairgraves, adding also his own which are excellent. It is now, beyond question, the first elementary book to be read—as agreeable as Blackstone, and more profound. This will employ you fully till the other books can be received from England. They will cost there about $200, to which is to be added duties, about thirty dollars freight and charges. If I can be useful in procuring them, I shall be so with pleasure. The sum I have to pay your father, is about sufficient to accomplish it, and shall be so applied if it is his pleasure. I shall be in Bedford during the last week of this month and the first of the next; you will of course visit us there or here, when we can make more particular arrangements. I have here the two best works on Natural Philosophy, and Astronomy, Hauy and Biot, which I have imported for you from Paris, knowing they were not to be had here. Present me affectionately to Mr. and Mrs. Eppes, and be assured of my warmest attachment to yourself.

TH. JEFFERSON.

———

Bracton, English; Brooke's Abridgment, 4to. edition; Thomas's Coke's Littleton, 3 vols. 8vo.; Coke's 2d, 3d, and 4th Institutes, 3 vols. 8vo.; Bacon's Abridgment, by Gwyllim, 7 vols. 8vo., the last edition; Comyn's Digest, by Manning, a new edition; Blackstone's Commentaries, by Christian, 15th edition, 4 vols. 8vo.; Woodson's Lectures, 3 vols. 8vo.; Reeves' History of the English Law, 4 vols. 8vo.; Jacob's Law Dictionary, by Ruffhead, fol.; Abridgment of Cases in Equity; Bridgman's Digested Index of Cases in Chancery, 3 vols. 8vo.; Fonblanque's Treatise of Equity, 5th edition, 1819, 2 vols., 8vo.

To Francis Eppes, Millbrook.

Monticello, June 12, 1822.

Dear Francis :

I received while at Poplar Forest yours of May 13th, and am glad to learn that you find Coke's Littleton not as difficult as you expected. The methodical arrangement of his work, and the new notes and cases, have certainly been a great improvement. According to your information I have retained in my hands enough to import for you this edition of Coke's Littleton and Bacon's Abridgment. The present high exchange, our enormous duties, and other charges bring them very high. Still I observe the Bacon will come at $15 89, which is $4 less than the American price. The Coke's Littleton being a new publication, comes to $10 a volume, of which more than $1 a volume is our own duty. At the close of your reading of the first volume we shall hope to see you. I suppose you have heard that the Trists have lost their mother.

Ever affectionately yours,
Th. Jefferson.

CHAPTER XII.

1823—1825.

A LITTLE before the close of 1822 Mr. Jefferson met with an accident, which caused him a good deal of inconvenience. Descending from one of his terraces, a decayed step gave way under his feet, and he was precipitated at full length to the

486

round, breaking his left arm. The bone became well knitted gain in course of a couple of months, but the hand and fingers emained useless for a long period, in consequence of an edema-ous swelling. Indeed, the use and strength of the arm and hand rere never entirely recovered. His right wrist, as before stated, ontinued to grow stiffer and feebler as the debility of age in-reased—and therefore he was henceforth partially crippled in oth hands. This added intolerably to the weariness and irk-omeness of writing.

His correspondence in 1823 opens with a letter to Mr. Edward Everett (February 24th), which contains several histo-ical facts already cited, and some not uninteresting literary riticisms. Here are his comments on style to a celebrated aaster of style:

> " By analyzing too minutely we often reduce our subject to atoms, of which the mind loses its hold. Nor am I a friend to a scrupulous purism of style. I readily sacrifice the niceties of syntax to euphony and strength. It is by boldly neglecting the rigorisms of grammar, that Tacitus has made himself the strongest writer in the world. The hypercritics call him barbarous; but I should be sorry to exchange his barbarisms for their wire-drawn purisms. Some of his sentences are as strong as language can make them. Had he scrupulously filled up the whole of their syn-ax, they would have been merely common. To explain my meaning by an English xample, I will quote the motto of one, I believe, of the regicides of Charles I., 'Rebellion *to* tyrants is obedience to God." [1] Correct its syntax, " Rebellion *against* yrants is obedience to God," it has lost all the strength and beauty of the anti-besis.

The publication of O'Meara's Voice from St. Helena, mate-ially changed Mr. Jefferson's estimate of Napoleon's civic qua-ities, and moved him to commiseration for his personal suffer-ngs:

> " I have just finished [he wrote Mr. Adams, February 25th] reading O'Meara's Bonaparte. It places him in a higher scale of understanding than I had allotted him. I had thought him the greatest of all military captains, but an indifferent statesman, and misled by unworthy passions. The flashes, however, which escaped from him in these conversations with O'Meara, prove a mind of great expansion, although not of distinct development and reasoning. He seizes results with rapidity and penetration, but never explains logically the process of reasoning by which he

[1] He here quotes from the Epitaph on John Bradshaw, already mentioned as having been found among his papers, with a note attached by him. conjecturing that it was only a supposititious epitaph, and in reality an *inspiration* of Dr. Franklin. (See vol. i. pp. 231, 232.) If the last conjecture was correct (and Dr. Franklin was certainly fond, on occasion, of playing the part of a literary Puck), still, for aught we know, the motto may have belonged to Bradshaw.

arrives at them. This book, too, makes us forget his atrocities for a moment, in commiseration of his sufferings. I will not say that the authorities of the world, charged with the care of their country and people, had not a right to confine him for life, as a lion or tiger, on the principle of self-preservation. There was no safety to nations while he was permitted to roam at large. But the putting him to death in cold blood, by lingering tortures of mind, by vexations, insults and deprivations, was a degree of inhumanity to which the poisonings and assassinations of the school of Borgia, and the den of Marat never attained. The book proves, also, that nature had denied him the moral sense, the first excellence of well-organized man. If he could seriously and repeatedly affirm that he had raised himself to power without ever having committed a crime, it proves that he wanted totally the sense of right and wrong. If he could consider the millions of human lives which he had destroyed, or caused to be destroyed, the desolations of countries by plunderings, burnings, and famine, the destitutions[1] of lawful rulers of the world without the consent of their constituents, to place his brothers and sisters on their thrones, the cutting up of established societies of men and jumbling them discordantly together again at his caprice, the demolition of the fairest hopes of mankind for the recovery of their rights and amelioration of their condition, and all the numberless train of his other enormities; the man, I say, who could consider all these as no crimes, must have been a moral monster, against whom every hand should have been lifted to slay him."

In two letters to Judge Johnson of South Carolina (March 4th, and June 12th), Mr. Jefferson complains that the Republican side of American history has not yet been written :

"We have been too careless of our future reputation, while our tories will omit nothing to place us in the wrong. Besides the five-volumed libel[2] which represents us as struggling for office, and not at all to prevent our government from being administered into a monarchy, the life of Hamilton is in the hands of a man who, to the bitterness of the priest, adds the rancor of the fiercest Federalism. *Mr. Adams' papers too, and his biography, will descend of course to his son, whose pen, you know, is pointed, and his prejudices not in our favor.* And doubtless other things are in preparation, unknown to us. On our part we are depending on truth to make itself known, while history is taking a contrary set which may become too inveterate for correction."

He proceeds to say that Mr. Madison will probably leave something historical, but that it will be principally confined to the period " between the dissolution of the old and commencement of the new government." He says that he has not had time to prepare anything himself, but that his letters, " all preserved,"[3] will give daily occurrences and views from 1790 till

---

[1] This word is thus printed in both editions of Mr. Jefferson's Works—but it was probably an error in the first copying, which was followed in the later edition without a reference to the original MSS., or it may have been a slip of Mr. Jefferson's pen. The sense would point to the substitution of the word dethronements.

[2] Judge Marshall's Life of Washington is here referred to.

[3] This means of course, all possessing political importance.

: public life; and that, being written "in the warmth and
ess of fact and feeling, they will carry internal evidence
hat they breathe is genuine," and will "command more
:tion than anything he could have written after his retire-
' He adds:

lections from these, after my death, may come out successively as the
· of circumstances may render their appearance seasonable. But multiplied
ly, multiplied views will be necessary to give solid establishment to truth.
known to one which is not known to another, and no one knows everything.
sum of individual knowledge which is to make up the whole truth, and to
correct current through future time."

ıd in the second letter:

story may distort truth, and will distort it for a time, by the superior efforts
tation of those who are conscious of needing it most. *Nor will the opening
' our present government be seen in their true aspect, until the letters of the
v held in private hoards, shall be broken up and laid open to public view.*
treasure will be found in General Washington's Cabinet, when it shall pass
hands of as candid a friend to truth as he was himself? when no longer,
ar's notes and memorandums in the hands of Anthony, it shall be open to
ı priests of Federalism only, and garbled to say so much and no more, as
ir views!" [1]

e remark in regard to the light to be shed on our political
7, on the views of men and the objects of parties, by the
ng up of *private hoards of letters*, has been most signally
d. The published correspondences of Adams, Hamilton,
Jefferson, etc., leave no materials wanting for a genuine
r of the general course and aims of the two great Ame-
parties.
ıe of the preceding extracts implies that Jefferson did not
er John Q. Adams personally friendly to himself. A
re example of the proof on which he based this conclusion
here be given, but it does not appear to be called for.
the same letter to Johnson will be found the customary
in regard to the tenor of a class of decisions in the
ne Court of the United States. It also contains some
ony on the subject of the authorship of Washington's
ell Address, which distinctly confutes a modern theory
his paper was wholly, or principally, the production of
ton.

one will forget that this was written before the publication of General Wash
Writings, by Mr. Sparks.

President Monroe failing to meet Mr. Jefferson as usual on his spring visit home (the latter being at Poplar Forest), consulted him by letter in regard to the attitude which our country ought to assume on the interference of the Allied Powers in the concerns of Spain. Mr. Jefferson replied (June 11th):

"On the question you propose, whether we can, in any form, take a bolder attitude than formerly in favor of liberty, I can give you but commonplace ideas. They will be but the widow's mite, and offered only because requested. The matter which now embroils Europe, the presumption of dictating to an independent nation the form of its government, is so arrogant, so atrocious, that indignation, as well as moral sentiment, enlists all our partialities and prayers in favor of one, and our equal execrations against the other. I do not know, indeed, whether all nations do not owe to one another a bold and open declaration of their sympathies with the one party, and their detestation of the conduct of the other. But farther than this we are not bound to go; and indeed, for the sake of the world, we ought not to increase the jealousies, or draw on ourselves the power, of this formidable confederacy. I have ever deemed it fundamental for the United States, never to take active part in the quarrels of Europe."

The reasons for this policy were further and most cogently urged; and he thought all we could do for Spain was to make our "neutrality as partial" to her, "as would be justifiable without giving cause of war to her adversary." He added:

. . . . . . "The foothold which the nations of Europe had in either America, is slipping from under them, so that we shall soon be rid of their neighborhood. Cuba alone seems at present to hold up a speck of war to us. Its possession by Great Britain would indeed be a great calamity to us. Could we induce her to join us in guaranteeing its independence against all the world *except Spain*, it would be nearly as valuable to us as if it were our own But should she take it, I would not immediately go to war for it; because the first war on other accounts will give it to us; or the island will give itself to us, when able to do so."

He believed, from the indications of circumstances, that the English Government was playing false with Spain—enacting "a theatrical farce in which the five powers were the actors, England the Tartuffe, and her people the dupes."

The views above expressed in regard to Cuba were soon retracted. An intelligent inhabitant of that island visited Mr. Jefferson at Monticello, and informed him that the Cubans would be satisfied to remain as they were, but were sensible that could not be; that their next choice would be independence, if they could see a prospect of being supported in it; but failing in this, that they would prefer incorporation either with the United States or Mexico; that there was not a man in the island who was in favor of its becoming a subordinated colony, for it could be no more, to England. Thereupon, Mr. Jefferson again wrote the President, June 3d:

"I had supposed an English interest there quite as strong as that of the United States, and therefore, that to avoid war, and keep the island open to our own commerce, it would be best to join that power in mutually guaranteeing its independence. But if there is no danger of its falling into the possession of England, I must retract an opinion founded on an error of fact. We are surely under no obligation to give her, gratis, an interest which she has not; and the whole inhabitants being averse to her, and the climate mortal to strangers, its continued military occupation by her would be impracticable. It is better, then, to lie still in readiness to receive that interesting incorporation when solicited by herself. For, certainly, her addition to our confederacy is exactly what is wanting to round our power as a nation to the point of its utmost interest."

In October, the South American question acquired a new and momentous interest. It was rumored and believed, both in England and the United States, that the Holy Alliance, not content with meddling with the affairs of Spain, now proposed to interfere between her and her revolted colonies, and to impose conditions on the latter. Whatever might have been the secret policy of England earlier, this giant stride towards universal domination alarmed her, and Mr. Canning, formerly so fond of showing disrespect to the United States, now invoked their interposition, promising the full support of England. President Monroe at once placed the question before Mr. Jefferson. The reply rings like a battle-shout:

To the President.

Monticello, October 24, 1823.

Dear Sir,—The question presented by the letters you have sent me, is the most momentous which has ever been offered to my contemplation since that of Independence. That made us a nation, this sets our compass and points the course which we are to steer through the ocean of time opening on us. And never could we embark on it under circumstances more auspicious. Our first and fundamental maxim should be, never to entangle ourselves in the broils of Europe. Our second— never to suffer Europe to intermeddle with cis-Atlantic affairs. America, North and South, has a set of interests distinct from those of Europe, and peculiarly her own. She should therefore have a system of her own, separate and apart from that of Europe. While the last is laboring to become the domicile of despotism, our endeavor should surely be, to make our hemisphere that of freedom. One nation, most of all, could disturb us in this pursuit; she now offers to lead, aid, and accompany us in it. By acceding to her proposition, we detach her from the band of despots, bring her mighty weight into the scale of free government, and emancipate, a continent at one stroke, which might otherwise linger long in doubt and difficulty. Great Britain is the nation which can do us the most harm of any one, or all on earth; and with her on our side, we need not fear the whole world. With her, then, we should most sedulously cherish a cordial friendship; and nothing would tend more to knit our affections than to be fighting once more, side by side, in the same cause. Not that I would purchase even her amity at the price of taking part in her wars. But the war in which the present proposition might engage us, should that be its consequence, is not her war, but ours. Its object is to introduce and establish the American system, of keeping out of our land all foreign powers, of never permitting those of Europe to intermeddle with the affairs of our nations. It is to maintain our own principle, not to depart from it. And if, to facilitate this, we can effect a division in the body of the European powers, and draw over to our side its most powerful member, surely we should do it. But I am clearly of Mr. Canning's opinion, that it will prevent instead of provoking war. With Great Britain withdrawn from their scale and shifted into that of our two continents, all Europe combined would not undertake such a war. For how would they propose to get at either enemy without superior fleets? Nor is the occasion to be slighted which this proposition offers, of declaring our protest against the atrocious violations of the rights of nations, by the interference of any one in the internal affairs of another, so flagitiously begun by Bonaparte, and now continued by the equally lawless Alliance, calling itself Holy.

But we have first to ask ourselves a question. Do we wish to acquire to our own confederacy any one or more of the Spanish provinces? I candidly confess, that I have ever looked on Cuba as the most interesting addition which could ever be made to our system of States. The control which, with Florida Point, this island would give us over the Gulf of Mexico, and the countries and isthmus bordering on it, as well as all those whose waters flow into it, would fill up the measure of our political well-being. Yet, as I am sensible that this can never be obtained, even with her own consent, but by war; and its independence, which is our second interest (and especially its independence of England), can be secured without it, I have no hesitation in abandoning my first wish to future chances, and accepting its independence, with peace and the friendship of England, rather than its association, at the expense of war and her enmity.

I could honestly, therefore, join in the declaration proposed, that we aim not at the acquisition of any of those possessions, that we will not stand in the way of any amicable arrangement between them and the mother country; but that we will oppose, with all our means, the forcible interposition of any other power, as auxiliary, stipendiary, or under any other form or pretext, and most especially, their transfer to any power by conquest, cession, or acquisition in any other way. I should think it, therefore, advisable, that the Executive should encourage the British government to a continuance in the dispositions expressed in these letters, by an assurance of his concurrence with them as far as his authority goes; and that as it may lead to war, the declaration of which requires an act of Congress, the case shall be laid before them for consideration at their first meeting, and under the reasonable aspect in which it is seen by himself.

I have been so long weaned from political subjects, and have so long ceased to take any interest in them, that I am sensible I am not qualified to offer opinions on them worthy of any attention. But the question now proposed involves consequences so lasting, and effects so decisive of our future destinies, as to re-kindle all the interest I have heretofore felt on such occasions, and to induce me to the

rd of opinions, which will prove only my wish to contribute still my mite towards
ıng which may be useful to our country. And praying you to accept it at
what it is worth, I add the assurance of my constant and affectionate friend-
and respect.   TH. JEFFERSON.

Thus the " Monroe doctrine " was proposed to President
nroe between five and six weeks before he gave it that offi-
  promulgation in a message to Congress, which stamped it
h his name. The message was dated December 2d, 1823.
nnounced that " we owed it to candor to declare . . . that
  should consider any attempt " on the part of European
:ons " to extend their system to any portion of this hemis-
re as dangerous to our peace and safety," etc. The tenor of
reasoning coincides with that of Mr. Jefferson's letter.[1]
A circumstance occurred this year in the intercourse of
'erson and the elder Adams, which requires some preli-
ary explanation. When Mr. Jefferson was generally talked
n 1803, as a candidate for a second Presidential term, Wil-
ı Cunningham applied to Mr. Adams for information to be
d in publications, the object of which was to defeat Jeffer-
's reëlection. Mr. Adams wrote some letters to him, which
e more or less free in their tone ; and he continued these
ond the immediate occasion, and for a number of succeeding
rs. All these communications were transmitted to Cunning-
ı under his promise that they should not be made public dur-
Mr. Adams's life. The former died in 1823, and his son, dis-
arding his father's promise, published the letters that year.
öre anything but a few extracts from the " Cunningham Let-
," had met Jefferson's eye, he wrote to Mr. Adams (October
h), and after alluding to his own health, to the University,
  in the tone of an ordinary friendly letter, he closed in a
in which is well worth attentive examination :

[1] Putting aside these things, however, for the present, I write this letter as due to
ındship coëval with our government, and now attempted to be poisoned, when
ate in life to be replaced by new affections. I had for some time observed in the
ic papers, dark hints and mysterious innuendoes of a correspondence of yours with
ınd, to whom you had opened your bosom without reserve, and which was to be
ı public by that friend or his representative. And now it is said to be actually

It need scarcely be added, that this maxim of State policy has not been traced
ı to Mr. Jefferson from any other motive than to truly record a historical fact. No
dent ever did, or ever can, originate all the important policies or maxims of his
inistration. It is the real glory of a ruler to choose wisely from all the plans which
ı before him, whether they originate in his own mind, or in the minds of others.

published. It has not yet reached us, but extracts have been given, and such as seemed most likely to draw a curtain of separation between you and myself. Were there no other motive than that of indignation against the author of this outrage on private confidence, whose shaft seems to have been aimed at yourself more particularly, this would make it the duty of every honorable mind to disappoint that aim, by opposing to its impression a seven-fold shield of apathy and insensibility. With me, however, no such armor is needed. The circumstances of the times in which we have happened to live, and the partiality of our friends at a particular period, placed us in a state of apparent opposition, which some might suppose to be personal also ; and there might not be wanting those who wished to make it so, by filling our ears with malignant falsehoods, by dressing up hideous phantoms of their own creation, presenting them to you under my name, to me under yours, and endeavoring to instill into our minds things concerning each other the most destitute of truth. And if there had been, at any time, a moment when we were off our guard, and in a temper to let the whispers of these people make us forget what we had known of each other for so many years, and years of so much trial, yet all men who have attended to the workings of the human mind, who have seen the false colors under which passion sometimes dresses the actions and motives of others, have seen also those passions subsiding with time and reflection, dissipating like mists before the rising sun, and restoring to us the sight of all things in their true shape and colors. It would be strange indeed, if, at our years, we were to go back an age to hunt up imaginary or forgotten facts, to disturb the repose of affections so sweetening to the evening of our lives. Be assured, my dear sir, that I am incapable of receiving the slightest impression from the effort now made to plant thorns on the pillow of age, worth, and wisdom, and to sow tares between friends who have been such for near half a century. Beseeching you then, not to suffer your mind to be disquieted by this wicked attempt to poison its peace, and praying you to throw it by among the things which have never happened, I add sincere assurances of my unabated and constant attachment, friendship, and respect."

Unfortunately here the curtain drops on this affair. We cannot but believe Mr. Adams answered in a way befitting his character—and if so, the letter may have contained remarks or concessions which Jefferson's delicacy chose to put beyond the reach of perpetuation. Or, Mr. Adams (in his eighty-ninth year) may have been ill, and their correspondence thus have become interrupted, until the topic could be as appropriately passed over as revived, between friends who understood each other. Only three subsequent letters between them are published in either edition of Mr. Jefferson's works—one from Jefferson to Adams, January 8th, 1825 ; one from Adams to Jefferson, January 23d, 1825 (entirely taken up with denouncing the laws of different nations against heresy) ; one from Jefferson to Adams, March 25th, 1826, introducing his grandson, Thomas Jefferson Randolph. We have seen no other letters of the period between them, in any collection of Mr. Adams's correspondence

John Quincy Adams was named as a candidate for the Presidency in 1823. His competitors were General Andrew Jackson, William H. Crawford, Henry Clay, and John C. Calhoun. Jefferson wrote to his intimate friend, General Samuel Smith, May 3d:

"On the question of the next Presidential election, I am a mere looker on. I never permit myself to express an opinion, or to feel a wish on the subject. I indulge a single hope only, that the choice may fall on one who will be a friend of peace, of economy, of the Republican principles of our Constitution, and of the salutary distribution of powers made by that between the general and the local governments."

He wrote to another intimate friend, Mr. Short, September 8th, inviting him to Monticello, and adding:

.   .   .   .   .   "You must be contented with the plain and sober family, and neighborly society, with the assurance that you shall hear no wrangling about the next President, although the excitement on that subject will then be at its acme. Numerous have been the attempts to entangle me in that imbroglio. But at the age of eighty, I seek quiet and abjure contention. I read but a single newspaper, Ritchie's Enquirer, the best that is published or ever has been published in America.   .

He wrote to Lafayette, November 4th:

"We are all, for example, in agitation, even in our peaceful country. For in peace as well as in war, the mind must be kept in motion. Who is to be next President, is the topic here of every conversation. My opinion on that subject is what I expressed to you in my last letter. The question will be ultimately reduced to the northernmost and southernmost candidate. The former will get every Federal vote in the Union, and many Republicans; the latter, all of those denominated *of the old school*; for you are not to believe that these two parties are amalgamated, that the lion and the lamb are lying down together. The Hartford Convention, the victory of Orleans, the peace of Ghent, prostrated the name of Federalism. Its votaries abandoned it through shame and mortification; and now call themselves Republicans. But the name alone is changed, the principles are the same."

The "Northernmost" candidate was Mr. Adams, and the "Southernmost," Mr. Crawford. Jefferson came to "feel a wish" between the candidates. His preference was decidedly for Mr. Crawford, though he abstained from any interference even in conversation, except among the members of his own family.

In a letter to George Ticknor of Boston (the elegant author of the History of Spanish Literature, etc.), Mr. Jefferson defended the system of allowing students in a university the uncontrolled choice of their studies, after reaching a certain age and grade of elementary qualification. He declared the " rock he most dreaded was the discipline of the institution," because " the insubordination of our youth was now the greatest obstacle to their education." He informed Ticknor that the last of the University buildings would be nearly finished by the autumn of 1824, and he invited him to then make a visit to Monticello and contribute his knowledge of the regulations and discipline of the European institutions of learning to aid in shaping those of the United States.

Some preceding letters from Jefferson to Ticknor have been passed without notice, as their topics were principally literary. The latter had visited Monticello in 1814, carrying flattering letters of introduction from Mr. Adams and others. He remained there some days, attracting an unusual share of the attention and regard of Mr. Jefferson and his family, by the pleasingness of his manners, and his uncommonly ripe scholarship. Until he became satisfied that it would be better to draw the body of the professors of the University from abroad, Jefferson had been anxious that Ticknor should fill one of the chairs. The latter visited Europe in 1815, with warm letters of introduction from Jefferson to the American Minister, Lafayette, Dupont de Nemours, Say, and others. He was also commissioned to purchase such books as Mr. Jefferson wished from abroad, to furnish a new, but, compared to his former one, very limited library. Ticknor accepted the invitation to visit Monticello in 1824, and we shall have, hereafter, some incidents of the visit.

Mr. Jefferson's absorbing topic throughout 1824 was the University. The buildings were nearly prepared for use; but the professors, the library, etc., were yet to be procured, and the general machinery was to be put in motion. The pecuniary rubs were not over, nor was the opposition in the Legislature quieted. Adverse schemes were set on foot by local and denominational feelings and interests. But the faithful Cabell worked day and night—Jefferson's great hold on the public heart was unbroken— and things in the main continued to go on successfully. He wrote Cabell[1] in February, in regard to the selection of professors:

[1] We regret that we have not room for Cabell's letter to which this is a reply. See History of University, p. 288.

"You know we have all, from the beginning, considered the high qualifications of our professors, as the only means by which we could give to our institution splendor and preëminence over all its sister seminaries. The only question, therefore, we can ever ask ourselves, as to any candidate, will be, is he the most highly qualified?

.   .   .   .   .

"We are next to observe, that a man is not qualified for a professor, knowing nothing but merely his own profession. He should be otherwise well educated as to the sciences generally; able to converse understandingly with the scientific men with whom he is associated, and to assist in the councils of the faculty on any subject of science on which they may have occasion to deliberate. Without this, he will incur their contempt, and bring disreputation on the institution.   .   .   .   .

"In the course of the trusts I have exercised through life with powers of appointment, I can say with truth, and with unspeakable comfort, that I never did appoint a relation to office, and that merely because I never saw the case in which some one did not offer, or occur, better qualified;[1] and I have the most unlimited confidence that in the appointment of professors to our nursling institution, every individual of my associates will look with a single eye to the sublimation of its character, and adopt, as our sacred motto, "*detur digniori.*" In this way it will honor us, and bless our country."

It was determined to send to England for all the professors except those of Moral Philosophy and Law—and for reasons given by Mr. Jefferson to our Minister to that country, Mr. Rush, in a letter of introduction which was borne by the special agent sent to engage the professors. In this (dated April 26th) he said:

.   .   .   .   .   "We have determined to receive no one who is not of the first order of science in his line; and as such in every branch cannot be obtained with us, we propose to seek some of them at least, in the countries ahead of us in science, and preferably in Great Britain, the land of our own language, habits, and manners. But how to find out those who are of the first grade of science, of sober correct habits and morals, harmonizing tempers, talents for communication, is the difficulty. Our first step is to send a special agent to the Universities of Oxford, Cambridge, and Edinburgh, to make the selection for us; and the person appointed for this office is the gentleman who will hand you this letter—Mr. Francis Walker Gilmer—the best educated subject we have raised since the Revolution, highly qualified in all the important branches of science, professing particularly that of the Law, which he has practised some years at our Supreme Court with good success and flattering prospects. His morals, his amiable temper and discretion, will do justice to any confidence you may be willing to place in him, for I commit him to you as his mentor and guide in the business he goes on. We do not certainly expect to obtain such known characters as were the Cullens, the Robertsons, and Porsons of Great Britain, men of the first eminence established there in reputation and office, and with emoluments not to be bettered anywhere. But we know that there is

_____

[1] Mr. Jefferson had forgotten. He unquestionably did, in one or two instances, refuse to appoint relatives, *purely* on the ground that they were relatives, and he avowed that ground, and defended it as necessary under the circumstances.

another race treading on their heels, preparing to take their places, and as well and sometimes better qualified to fill them. These while unsettled, surrounded by a crowd of competitors, of equal claims and perhaps superior credit and interest, may prefer a comfortable certainty here for an uncertain hope there, and a lingering delay even of that. From this description we expect we may draw professors equal to those of the highest name. The difficulty is to distinguish them.

*   *   *   *   *

"On this head our hope and trust is in you. Your knowledge of the state of things, your means of finding out a character or two at each place, truly trustworthy, and into whose hands you can commit our agent with entire safety, for information, caution and coöperation, induces me to request your patronage and aid in our endeavors to obtain such men, and such only, as will fulfill our views. An unlucky selection in the outset would forever blast our prospects. From our information of the character of the different Universities, we expect we should go to Oxford for our classical professor, to Cambridge for those of Mathematics, Natural Philosophy and Natural History, and to Edinburgh for a professor of Anatomy, and the elements or outlines only of Medicine."

Mr. Jefferson was much censured, or "squibbed," as he termed it, for sending abroad for professors; and even the latter, on their arrival in our country, did not escape some unfriendly criticisms from offended professional brethren. Whether as good a selection could have been made in our own country, from those who were unengaged—and such were certainly all Mr. Jefferson had in view when he expressed his fears to Rush, that men of the first order of science, in "every branch," could not be obtained at home—we shall not take it upon ourselves to say. The Visitors of the University thought not, and that was a very sufficient reason for *their* action. It at least can be safely asserted, that the selection which was made, was an eminently good one.

In a letter (February 4th) to Mr. Sparks, who had forwarded him a copy of the North American Review,[1] containing an article on African emancipation and colonization, Mr. Jefferson gave his views at considerable length on those subjects. There is nothing in the general principles expressed, different from those in the Notes on Virginia, but some of the practical propositions in regard to *means* vary. He said:

"I shall speak in round numbers, not absolutely accurate, yet not so wide from truth as to vary the result materially. There are in the United States a million and a half of people of color in slavery. To send off the whole of these at once, nobody conceives to be practicable for us, or expedient for them. Let us take twenty-five years for its accomplishment, within which time they will be doubled. Their estimated value as property, in the first place (for actual property has been lawfully

---

[1] Which was then edited by Mr. Sparks.

sted in that form, and who can lawfully take it from the possessors?) at an aver-
ge of two hundred dollars each, young and old, would amount to six hundred mil-
lns of dollars, which must be paid or lost by somebody. To this add the cost of
eir transportation by land and sea to Mesurado, a year's provision of food and
othing, implements of husbandry and of their trades, which will amount to three
ndred millions more, making thirty-six millions of dollars a year, for twenty-five
ars, with insurance of peace all that time, and it is impossible to look at the ques-
n a second time. I am aware that at the end of about sixteen years, a gradual
traction from this sum will commence, from the gradual diminution of breeders,
d go on during the remaining nine years. Calculate this deduction, and it is still
possible to look at the enterprise a second time. I do not say this to induce an
ference that the getting rid of them is forever impossible. For that is neither my
inion nor my hope. But only that it cannot be done in this way. There is, I
ink, a way in which it can be done; that is, by emancipating the after-born, leav-
g them, on due compensation, with their mothers, until their services are worth
eir maintenance, and then putting them to industrious occupations, until a proper
e for deportation. This was the result of my reflections on the subject five and
rty years ago, and I have never yet been able to conceive any other practicable
an. It was sketched in the Notes on Virginia, under the fourteenth query. The
timated value of the new-born infant is so low (say twelve dollars and fifty cents),
at it would probably be yielded by the owner gratis, and would thus reduce the
x hundred millions of dollars, the first head of expense, to thirty-seven millions
d a half; leaving only the expenses of nourishment while with the mother, and
transportation. And from what fund are these expenses to be furnished? Why
x from that of the lands which have been ceded by the very States now needing
is relief? and ceded on no consideration, for the most part, but that of the ge-
ral good of the whole. These cessions already constitute one fourth of the States
f the Union. It may be said that these lands have been sold; are now the pro-
rty of the citizens composing those States; and the money long ago received and
pended. But an equivalent of lands in the territories since acquired, may be ap-
opriated to that object, or so much, at least, as may be sufficient; and the object,
though more important to the slave States, is highly so to the others also, if they
ere serious in their arguments on the Missouri question. The slave States, too,
more interested, would also contribute more by their gratuitous liberation, thus
king on themselves alone the first and heaviest item of expense.

After assigning several reasons in favor of attempting this
eneral colonization in St. Domingo, instead of Africa, he added
 reference to his proposed means of defraying the expense:

"I am aware that this subject involves some constitutional scruples. But a libe-
l construction, justified by the object, may go far, and an amendment of the con-
itution, the whole length necessary. The separation of infants from their mothers,
o, would produce some scruples of humanity. But this would be straining at a
at and swallowing a camel."

A letter to Robert J. Garnett, February 14th, shows that
[r. Jefferson was very ill satisfied with the tendency of a
lass of measures which received the approbation of Congress,

towards the close of Mr. Monroe's Administration—particularly those for internal improvements. He thought the Federalists, with nothing changed but their names, were now in possession of one branch of the government, were strong in another, and were " openly marching by the road of construction " to " that consolidation which had always been their real object." To check this, he proposed the following constitutional amendments: first, " the limitation of the term of the Presidential service;" second, " the placing the choice of President effectually in the hands of the people ;" third, " the giving to Congress the power of internal improvement, on condition that each State's federal proportion of the moneys so expended, should be employed within the State." [1]

To Mr. Isaac Englebrecht, who requested something from Mr. Jefferson's pen, the latter declared (February 25th), that he knew " nothing more moral, more sublime, more worthy of preservation than David's description of the good man in his 15th Psalm," and he transcribed it for his correspondent, from Brady and Tate's version, commencing :

> " Lord, who's the happy man that may to thy blest courts repair,
> Not stranger-like to visit them, but to inhabit there," etc.

On the 4th of April, he addressed a letter to Edward Livingston, who had inclosed to him his speech in Congress in favor of internal improvements. While courteously dissenting from its positions, Mr. Jefferson pays a tribute to "those powers of reasoning and persuasion of which he had formerly seen . . so many proofs." The whole tone of the letter was kind, and indicated a cordial reconciliation between the writer and one of the ablest of his contemporaries.

To John II. Pleasants (April 19th), Mr. Jefferson expressed, in substance, the same general views in regard to the existing Constitution of Virginia, which were given to Mr. Kercheval eight years earlier.

On the 5th of June, he replied to a letter from Major John Cartwright, of England. The latter had also forwarded to him " his volume on the English Constitution." (The Constitution Produced and Illustrated, published in 1823.) This toughest and

---

[1] See ante, p. 443.

rdiest of English reformers—this Whig Cobbet, with the prin-
les and tastes of a gentleman—this " old radical," this " heart
sedition," " the old heart in London from which the veins of
lition in the country were supplied," as Canning styled him,
the House of Commons—this man who counted among his
rsonal friends Fox, and Sheridan, and Wilberforce, and Whit-
ead, and Price, was, of course, an admirer of Jefferson.' The
mmunication of the latter to him is too long for even analysis
re. He agreed with Cartwright, in deriving the English Consti-
tion from the Saxons, and said that this was set at naught by the
orman conquerors, etc. Jefferson proceeded to cite a multi-
de of authorities to prove the judicial dictum untrue that
hristianity was a part of the common law, and to show when
d how it was interpolated into English decisions. The body
'these citations constitute but an abridgment from an article
Jefferson's common-place book, when he was a law student.'

Cartwright received this letter on the 13th of July, and ob-
rved with high satisfaction, that the signature was as firm as
at to the Declaration of Independence. He published it; and
a biography states that he again wrote to Jefferson, on the
3th of the same month. This letter was long in reaching its
estination, and a knowledge of the publication of the former
e preceded it. Jefferson wrote Edward Everett (October
5th) :

" Your letter of September the 10th gave me the first information that mine to
jor Cartwright had got into the newspapers; and the first notice, indeed, that he
d received it. I was a stranger to his person, but not to his respectable and pa-
iotic character. I received from him a long and interesting letter, and answered
with frankness, going without reserve into several subjects, to which his letter
d led, but on which I did not suppose I was writing for the newspapers. The
iblication of a letter in such a case, without the consent of the writer, is not a fair
actice.

" The part which you quote, may draw on me the host of judges and
vines."

He then proceeds to elaborate and fortify portions of his ar-
ument.

Cartwright was already in his grave. On the 23d of Septem-
er, 1824, a philanthropist as true, and a reformer as brave as

---

1 In 1774 Cartwright published a series of letters favoring American Independence.
ee his Life and Correspondence, edited by his niece, F. D. Cartwright, 2 vols. 8vo.
ndon, 1826.)
2 See vol. i. p. 52.

history mentions, died with rapturous exclamations on his tongue, on learning that Iturbide's schemes had failed, and that the liberties of Mexico were considered out of danger. As he died under the displeasure of Mr. Jefferson (though unapprised of it) it is with with real satisfaction we transcribe the following passage from Mr. Trist's memoranda:

Sunday, October, 1824, Mr. Jefferson said: 'I have got a letter from Cartwright, and he has explained the reason of my letter getting into the papers. The very day (I believe) on which he received it, a man was condemned to three years imprisonment, on the ground that the Scriptures are a part of the common law.'"

The writer of the above informs us, that this was spoken in a tone which indicated that Cartwright's explanation was received as an amply sufficient one.

On the 29th of June, Mr. Jefferson wrote the communication to Martin Van Buren, in regard to the Mazzei letter, and to the fresh charges of Pickering on that subject, which has already been cited, and sufficiently noticed.[1]

In July he received a letter from Henry Lee, the son of Gen. Henry or Harry Lee, of the Revolution, which proved the opening of an unfortunate acquaintance.[2] Lee's letter inclosed the prospectus of a newspaper he was about to start. Mr. Jefferson replied with great courtesy, and subscribed for the paper. His letter closed thus:

"A paper which shall be governed by the spirit of Mr. Madison's celebrated report, of which you express in your prospectus so just and high an approbation, cannot be false to the rights of all classes. The grandfathers of the present generation of your family I knew well. They were friends and fellow-laborers with me in the same cause and principle. Their descendants cannot follow better guides. Accept the assurance of my best wishes and respectful consideration."

General Lafayette made his triumphal visit to the United States in 1824. He landed at New York, in August, and his progress through the country was one entire ovation. On the first of October he wrote to Mr. Jefferson, from Philadelphia, informing him that he proposed to visit his neighborhood; and the latter immediately sent him a warm invitation to come to Monticello.

Jefferson wrote to Richard Rush, four days afterwards, that

[1] See vol. ii. p. 365 et seq.   [2] See APPENDIX, No. 32.

the people of the United States were thrown into a "delirium," of joy by the visit of Lafayette ; and he added:

"He is making a triumphant progress through the States, from town to town, with acclamations of welcome, such as no crowned head ever received. It will have a good effect in favor of the General with the people in Europe, but probably a different one with their sovereigns. Its effect here, too, will be salutary as to ourselves, by rallying us together, and strengthening the habit of considering our country as one and indivisible, and I hope we shall close it with something more solid for him than dinners and balls."

The last hint was subsequently improved upon by its author's proposing that Congress testify its gratitude to the nation's guest, and former benefactor, by making a handsome pecuniary provision for him. The losses which Lafayette had incurred, and his liberal style of living, it was supposed would render this form of testimonial the most convenient one to him in his declining years. The proposition was fortunately timed, and there was but one voice in regard to it. Congress responded to the popular sentiment by voting Lafayette $200,000 and a township of land, "in consideration of his important services and expenditures during the American Revolution."

Finally, Lafayette, surrounded by a gallant escort of mounted Virginia gentlemen, with Revolutionary banners displayed, and amidst peals of martial music, approached Monticello. Jefferson would have gone forth to some distance to meet him, but this was prohibited. The cavalcade wound up the mountain, and entered the lawn in front of the house; the fanfare of trumpets ceased ; every head was uncovered. Lafayette stepped down from his carriage, and Jefferson advanced rapidly from his door to meet him. Though time had dealt its blows on the former, his person was as erect as when, almost fifty years before, he had traversed the plains in sight of which he now stood, a fugitive or a pursuer of British invaders. But the taller and more powerful frame of Jefferson was bent and emaciated. As the old men threw themselves into each other's arms, overcome by emotion, tears streamed from nearly every eye. Lafayette's visit to Monticello proved a delightful one, both to himself and to Jefferson. Of the subjects of their discourse we have already had a sample.'

' See vol. ii. pp. 374, 375, note.

A banquet was given to Lafayette, by the citizens of Charlottesville. Jefferson, Madison, Monroe, and many other distinguished Virginians were present. Everything passed off pleasantly and splendidly. Mr. Madison was peculiarly felicitous in some comments uttered by him, in reply to a toast on the career and public services of the "Nation's Guest." One of the toasts drank was as follows: "Thomas Jefferson and the Declaration of Independence—alike identified with the cause of liberty." Mr. Jefferson thereupon handed Mr. Southall some written remarks, which that gentleman read in reply.[1]

Lafayette's second visit to Monticello and Charlottesville will be found sufficiently mentioned in the memoranda of Dr. Dunglison, hereafter to be given.

Mr. George Ticknor made his expected visit to Monticello in December, 1824, accompanied by his wife, and by Daniel Webster. They remained some days, and it appears that Mr. Webster soon afterwards[2] reduced to writing a series of pretty minute recollections of what he saw and heard there. These are published in the recent edition of his correspondence, edited

---

[1] These contain nothing remarkable, but as they are not found in either edition of Mr. Jefferson's Works, we will transcribe them:

"I will avail myself of this occasion, my beloved neighbors and friends, to thank you for the kindness which now, and at all times, I have received at your hands. Born and bred among your fathers, led by their partiality into the line of public life, I labored in fellowship with them through that arduous struggle which, freeing us from foreign bondage, established us in the rights of self-government: rights which have blessed ourselves, and will bless, in their sequence, all the nations of the earth. In this contest, all did our utmost, and, as none could do more, none had pretensions to superior merit.

"I joy, my friends, in your joy, inspired by the visit of this our ancient and distinguished leader and benefactor. His deeds in the war of independence you have heard and read. They are known to you and embalmed in your memories, and in the pages of faithful history. His deeds, in the peace which followed that war, are perhaps not known to you; but I can attest them. When I was stationed in his country, for the purpose of cementing its friendship with ours, and of advancing our mutual interests, this friend of both, was my most powerful auxiliary and advocate. He made our cause his own, as in truth it was that of his native country also. His influence and connections there were great. All doors of all departments were open to him at all times; to me, only formally and at appointed times. In truth, I only held the nail, he drove it. Honor him then, as your benefactor in peace, as well as in war.

"My friends, I am old, long in the disuse of making speeches, and without voice to utter them. In this feeble state, the exhausted powers of life leave little within my competence for your service. If, with the aid of my younger and abler coadjutors, I can still contribute anything to advance the Institution, within whose walls we are now mingling manifestations to this our guest, it will be, as it ever has been, cheerfully and zealously bestowed. And could I live to see it once enjoy the patronage and cherishment of our public authorities with undivided voice, I should die without a doubt of the future fortunes of my native State, and in the consoling contemplation of the happy influence of this institution on its character, its virtue, its prosperity, and safety.

"To these effusions for the cradle and land of my birth, I add, for our nation at large, the aspirations of a heart warm with the love of country: whose invocations to heaven for its indissoluble union, will be fervent and unremitting while the pulse of life continues to beat, and, when that ceases, it will expire in prayers for the eternal duration of its freedom and prosperity."

[2] The volume is not now before us. We believe that it is stated or intimated that Mr. Webster's recollections were recorded *after* the termination of his visit.

by his son, and we present a few extracts. Mr. Webster thus describes Mr. Jefferson's personal appearance:

"Mr. Jefferson is now between eighty-one and eighty-two, above six feet high, of an ample, long frame, rather thin and spare. His head, which is not peculiar in its shape, is set rather forward on his shoulders; and his neck being long, there is, when he is walking or conversing, a habitual protrusion of it. It is still well covered with hair, which, having been once red, and now turning gray, is of an indistinct sandy color.

"His eyes are small, very light, and now neither brilliant nor striking. His chin is rather long, but not pointed. His nose small, regular in its outline, and the nostrils a little elevated. His mouth is well-formed, and still filled with teeth; it is strongly compressed, bearing an expression of contentment and benevolence. His complexion, formerly light and freckled, now bears the marks of age and cutaneous affection. His limbs are uncommonly long; his hands and feet very large, and his wrists of an extraordinary size. His walk is not precise and military, but easy and swinging. He stoops a little, not so much from age as from natural formation. When sitting, he appears short, partly from a rather lounging habit of sitting, and partly from the disproportionate length of his limbs.

"His dress, when in the house, is a grey surtout coat, kerseymere stuff waistcoat, with an under one faced with some material of a dingy red. His pantaloons are very long and loose, and of the same color as his coat. His stockings are woollen, either white or gray; and his shoes of the kind that bear his name. His whole dress is very much neglected, but not slovenly.[1] He wears a common round hat. His dress, when on horseback, is a grey straight-bodied coat, and a spencer of the same material, both fastened with large pearl buttons. When we first saw him he was riding; and, in addition to the above articles of apparel, wore round his throat a knit white woollen tippet, in the place of a cravat, and black velvet gaiters under his pantaloons. His general appearance indicates an extraordinary degree of health, vivacity, and spirit. His sight is still good, for he needs glasses only in the evening. His hearing is generally good, but a number of voices in animated conversation confuse it.

"Mr. Jefferson rises in the morning as soon as he can see the hands of his clock, which is directly opposite his bed, and examines his thermometer immediately, as he keeps a regular meteorological diary. He employs himself chiefly in writing till breakfast, which is at nine. From that time till dinner he is in his library, excepting that in fair weather he rides on horseback from seven to fourteen miles. Dines at four, returns to the drawing-room at six, when coffee is brought in, and passes the evening till nine in conversation. His habit of retiring at that hour is so strong, that it has become essential to his health and comfort. His diet is simple, but he seems restrained only by his taste. His breakfast is tea and coffee, bread always fresh from the oven, of which he does not seem afraid, with sometimes a slight accompaniment of cold meat. He enjoys his dinner well, taking with his meat a large proportion of vegetables. He has a strong preference for the wines of the Continent, of which he has many sorts of excellent quality, having been more than

[1] Several, indeed most, of these minutiæ convey the impression that Mr. Webster was not closely observant of physical peculiarities. We will give two or three examples. Mr. Jefferson's eyes were not small. He was a large-boned, strong man, but it is odd that Mr. Webster should not have observed that his "wrists" were swollen out of their natural size and even shape, from causes which have been mentioned. His dress, though certainly conformed to no fashion, was not "much neglected" in any signification which we are able to attach to those words, etc. etc.

commonly successful in his mode of importing and preserving them. Among others we found the following, which are very rare in this country, and apparently not at all injured by transportation: L'Ednau, Muscat, Samian, and Blanchette de Limoux. Dinner is served in half Virginian, half French style, in good taste and abundance. No wine is put on the table till the cloth is removed.

"In conversation, Mr. Jefferson is easy and natural, and apparently not ambitious; it is not loud, as challenging general attention, but usually addressed to the person next him. The topics, when not selected to suit the character and feelings of his auditor, are those subjects with which his mind seems particularly occupied; and these, at present, may be said to be science and letters, and especially the University of Virginia, which is coming into existence almost entirely from his exertions, and will rise, it is to be hoped, to usefulness and credit under his continued care. When we were with him, his favorite subjects were Greek and Anglo-Saxon, historical recollections of the times and events of the Revolution, and of his residence in France from 1783-4 to 1789."

Mr. Webster represents Mr. Jefferson as describing Patrick Henry somewhat as we have seen him described in Mr. Trist's Memoranda.[1] He thus gives Mr. Jefferson's observations on Wirt's Life of Henry:

"His biographer sent the sheets of his work to me as they were printed, and at the end asked for my opinion. I told him it would be a question hereafter, whether his work should be placed on the shelf of history or of panegyric. It is a poor book, written in bad taste, and gives so imperfect an idea of Patrick Henry, that it seems intended to show off the writer more than the subject of the work."

And thus on the character of General Jackson:

"I feel much alarmed at the prospect of seeing General Jackson President. He is one of the most unfit men I know of for such a place. He has had very little respect for laws or constitutions, and is, in fact, an able military chief. His passions are terrible. When I was President of the Senate he was a senator; and he could never speak on account of the rashness of his feelings. I have seen him attempt it repeatedly, and as often choke with rage. His passions are, no doubt, cooler now; he has been much tried since I knew him, but he is a dangerous man."

These descriptions appearing to us to lack some of those gradations and qualifications in expression which are essential to convey accurate impressions, we sought an opinion on them from one as familiar with Mr. Jefferson, with his views and modes of expression, as any person ever was, and received the following reply:

——, 1857.

MY DEAR MR. RANDALL:

. . . . . . First, on the subject of Mr. Jefferson's personal appearance. Mr. Webster's description of it did not please me, because, though I will not stop to

[1] See vol. i. p. 40.

quarrel with any of the details, the general impression it was calculated to produce seemed to me an unfavorable one ; that is, a person who had never seen my grandfather, would, from Mr. Webster's description, have thought him rather an ill-looking man, which he certainly never was.

    *   *   *   *   *   *   *   *

"It would be, however, very difficult for me to give an accurate description of the appearance of one whom I so tenderly loved and deeply venerated. His person and countenance were to me, associated with so many of my best affections, so much of my highest reverence, that I could not expect other persons to see them as I did. One thing I will say, that never in my life did I see his countenance distorted by a single bad passion or unworthy feeling. I have seen the expression of suffering, bodily and mental, of grief, pain, sadness, just indignation, disappointment, disagreeable surprise, and displeasure, but never of anger, impatience, peevishness, discontent, to say nothing of worse or more ignoble emotions. To the contrary, it was impossible to look on his face without being struck with its benevolent, intelligent, cheerful, and placid expression. It was at once intellectual, good, kind, and pleasant, whilst his tall, spare figure, spoke of health, activity, and that *helpfulness*, that power and will, 'never to trouble another for what he could do himself,' which marked his character.

"His dress was simple, and adapted to his ideas of neatness and comfort. He paid little attention to fashion, wearing whatever he liked best, and sometimes blending the fashions of several different periods. He wore long waistcoats when the mode was for very short, white cambric stocks fastened behind with a buckle, when cravats were universal. He adopted the pantaloon very late in life, because he found it more comfortable and convenient, and cut off his queue for the same reason. He made no change except from motives of the same kind, and did nothing to be in conformity with the fashion of the day. He considered such independence as the privilege of his age.

"You ask me if Mr. Webster had not 'too strongly colored the Jackson portrait.' I cannot pretend to know what my grandfather said to Mr. Webster, nor can I believe Mr. Webster capable of misstatement. Still I think the copy of the portrait incorrect, as throwing out all the lights and giving only the shadows. I have heard my grandfather speak with great admiration of General Jackson's military talent. If he called him a 'dangerous man,' 'unfit for the place' to which the nation eventually called him, I think it must have been entirely with reference to his general idea that a military chieftain was no proper head for a peaceful republic as ours was in those days. I do not myself remember to have heard him say anything about General Jackson in connection with this subject, except that he thought his nomination a bad precedent for the future, and that a successful soldier was not the sort of candidate for the Presidential chair. He did not like to see the people run away with ideas of military glory.

"In like manner, I never heard him speak of Wirt's Life of Patrick Henry with the amount of severity recorded by Mr. Webster. My impression is that here too, Mr. Webster, from a very natural impulse, and without the least intention of misrepresentation, has put down only those parts of Mr. Jefferson's remarks which accorded with his own views, and left out all the extenuations—the '*circonstances attendantes*,' as the French say. This, of course, would lead to an erroneous impression. Of Mr. Wirt's book, my grandfather did not think very highly, but the unkind remark, as far as Mr. Wirt was personally concerned, unaccompanied by anything to soften its severity, is, to say the least, very little like Mr. Jefferson.

"Mr. Webster's account of his visit to Monticello, seems to me written in no unfair or unfriendly spirit, but was rather hasty, superficial, and never intended for the public eye."

No member of Mr. Jefferson's family ever heard him mention Wirt's Life of Henry in the *tone* attributed to him by Mr. Webster. His family often heard him speak of that work, and of Mr. Henry himself, with playful freedom—laugh at what he conceived the artificial "dressing up" the latter had received at the hands of Wirt. But they always understood him to admire both of the men far too much to feel any inclination to allude to them, or to anything which had emanated from them, with intentional disrespect. Wirt was notoriously a marked favorite with him, through life. His whole correspondence, and his Memoir written at the age of seventy-seven, exhibit his unbounded admiration of Henry in certain particulars, and his dislike or severe animadversion in none. Henry and he came to differ very widely in politics, and the former literally died leading a gallant political sortie against the conquering Republicans. On one occasion at least, his keen native humor was directed personally against Jefferson. With his inimitable look and tone, he with great effect declared, that he did not approve of gentlemen's "abjuring their native victuals."[1] This gave great diversion to Jefferson. He loved to talk about Henry, to narrate anecdotes of their early intimacy; to paint his taste for unrestrained nature in everything; to describe his bonhomie, his humor, his unquestionable integrity, mixed with a certain waywardness and freakishness; to give illustrations of his shrewdness, and of his overwhelming power as an orator. But he never closed an amusing account of Henry's exploits among overseers, wild hunters, and the like, in the "piny woods," without saying: "I never heard anything that deserved to be called by the name of oratory, compared with his"—"we could not have got along in the Revolution without him"—"he produced our unanimity"—"he was a man of enlarged views"—"he was a truly great man."[2]

That Mr. Jefferson favored Mr. Crawford's election over

---

[1] The Republicans were accused of being adherents of France—the *cookery* of Monticello was French!

[2] These were, in substance, his habitual expressions in regard to Mr. Henry. The conversation which we have quoted from Mr. Trist's Memoranda (vol. i. p. 40), was but a sample of hundreds of conversations with his family and with others in their hearing.

General Jackson is certain. The main reasons have been stated in the letter last quoted. It is true that with all his attempts to maintain neutrality, he did not invariably avoid expressions which indicated his views. A good many persons can recollect the local excitement produced by his declaring to some one in conversation, that it was " poor policy to select a cock for a sailor, or a goose for a fighter." Nor is it impossible that he retained certain disagreeable recollections of Jackson's course on Burr's trial. Burr, on his first western journey, had thoroughly insinuated himself into the General's good graces. The latter detested Wilkinson. His likes and dislikes were vehement, and he came on to Richmond to flame and fulminate against the principal witness, the prosecution, and finally against the Administration. He is reported to have expressed himself much more vigorously than elegantly on the occasion![1] Mr. Jefferson did not, perhaps, sufficiently understand how far twenty years had tamed the early fires of that great man's character. But it would be most extraordinary that, to a known and very decided political opponent, like Mr. Webster, he should express himself with a severity towards a Republican candidate, that those most absolutely in his confidence never heard him employ.

Not a shadow of intentional misrepresentation is here imputed to Mr. Webster. His statements are regarded as rapid outline jottings, made, probably, only for private reference, but however made, giving the *sum* of the *impressions* the writer formed of Mr. Jefferson's opinions and feelings, rather than an actual report of his words.

The remark in the last quoted letter that the writer (long a resident of Monticello), never saw an expression of anger or impatience on Mr. Jefferson's face, recalls to mind two anecdotes. Older members of his family *had* seen such expressions on his face, and they remembered and related them as marvels. The first occasion was serious—the second ludicrous. Martha Jefferson used to say that once when travelling with her father,

---

[1] It should in justice to General Jackson be remarked, that he subsequently changed his views of Burr's character—that on coming to the Presidency he substantially turned his back on him—though Burr and his friends claimed that he had been materially instrumental in bringing Jackson forward for the Presidency. Burr's agency in the latter consisted in being one of the first, possibly the first, to name the General for that office. But there never was a moment after Burr's return from Europe, when his efforts in favor of any man's elevation to a popular office would not have proved damaging.

they came to a ferry, and found the two boatmen engaged in a violent quarrel. They took the travellers on board, however, and rowed silently to the middle of the stream, when chancing to catch each other's eyes, the contention at once broke out afresh. They ceased to use their oars or to steer the boat, which drifted swiftly towards some dangerous rapids. Mr. Jefferson spoke to them calmly, and then sternly, but they paid no attention to him. Martha said that her father suddenly started up with " a face like a lion," and with a hand over each of the boatmen, bade them, " in tones of thunder," to row for their lives or he would pitch them into the stream. They did pull for their lives, occasionally stealing a fearful glance upward at the form which remained rigid and immovable above them until they reached the shore.

On the other occasion, Mr. Jefferson directed one of his servants to take a horse and go to the Charlottesville post-office for his letters and papers. The boy replied that there was not a horse out of use but those belonging to the carriage. "Go, then," said Mr. Jefferson, " and tell Jupiter [the colored coachman] to lend you one of his horses." The boy soon returned, saying "old Jupe" sent back word that nobody could have *his* horses for that business. Mr. Jefferson looked amused, and told the boy to go again to Jupiter and tell him that the case was urgent, as he was expecting important letters. The sable Olympian, however, replied flatly that " neither of his horses should go for anybody." " Tell Jupiter to come here," said his master, evidently in a passion. The pampered coachman soon arrived to meet a look and hear a tone never before or afterwards witnessed at Monticello—never witnessed by any member of Mr. Jefferson's family, except by Martha in the boat. Jupiter at once prudently took in a good deal of sail, but he firmly declared that he must not be expected to keep the carriage horses in the desired condition, if they were to be "ridden round by boys." Mr. Jefferson admitted this, but he told his coachman that he had better never again take quite so blunt a method of " telling his mind." And here the matter ended.

Jefferson's correspondence in 1824 contains, we believe, but one expression in regard to the Presidential candidates. It appears in a letter (October 13th) to Mr. Rush, the American minister in England. He wrote:

" The *éclat* of this [Lafayette's] visit has almost merged the Presidential question, which nothing scarcely is said in our papers. That question will lie ultimately tween Crawford and Adams; but, as at the same time, the vote of the people will so distracted by subordinate candidates, that possibly they may make no rction, and let it go to the House of Representatives. There, it is thought, awford's chance is best."

And he added:

" We have nothing else interesting before the public. Of the two questions of a tariff and public improvements, the former, perhaps, is not yet at rest, and the tter will excite boisterous discussions. It happens that both these measures fall with the Western interests, and it is their secession from the agricultural ates which gives such strength to the manufacturing and consolidating parties, on ese two questions. The latter is the most dreaded, because thought to amount a determination in the Federal Government to assume all powers non-enumerated well as enumerated in the Constitution, and by giving a loose to construction, ake the text say whatever will relieve them from the bridle of the States. These difficulties for your day; I shall give them the slip."

It had been arranged that the University should be opened n the 1st of February, 1825. But when that period came, iree of the professors had not arrived from England. Jefferson vinced great uneasiness. He wrote Cabell, January 11th, iat he was " dreadfully nonplussed." Then came intelligence f a desolating Atlantic storm, in which shipping had greatly nffered, and his anxiety for the safety of these gentlemen reached painful point. He subsequently learned from Cabell, how-ver, that they were safe in an English port (Plymouth), on the th of December, and this good news, he said, " raised him from he dead, for he was almost ready to give up the ship." Ano-her of his letters, February 20th, states that the professors have rrived, and that they " excite strong presumptions that they iave been judiciously selected." The opening of the University zas then announced for the 7th of March, but it did not take .lace until April.

His expectations in regard to the professors, were fully satis-ied on his first acquaintance with those gentlemen; and he iever, subsequently, had occasion to change his mind.[1] His

[1] He wrote the Honorable J. Evelyn Denison, M.P. (of England), November 9th, 1825: It has been peculiarly fortunate that the Professors brought from abroad were as appy selections as could have been hoped, as well for their qualifications in science as orrectness and amiableness of character;" and to Mr. Giles, December 26th: " Our iniversity has been most fortunate in the five professors procured from England. A ner selection could not have been made. Besides their being of a grade of science which as left little superior behind, the correctness of their moral character, their accommo

personal relations with them became most agreeable. They were regularly invited to Monticello three times a week, and each understood that if his inclination carried him there oftener, his welcome would be always cordial.

Professor Dunglison—the present well-known Doctor Dunglison of Philadelphia—subsequently, but while the facts remained fresh in his memory, wrote an account of his journey to Charlottesville, and of his observations after his arrival. These memoranda were made *currente calamo*, merely for the gratification of a near and dear relative. But as they contained the only particular account of Mr. Jefferson's last illness drawn up by his medical attendant, an application for the facts, made under the sanction of Mr. Jefferson's family, scarcely admitted of a refusal—and having opened these private records to us, Dr. Dunglison kindly permitted us to further select at our discretion any passages which would throw light on other parts of our subject. The extracts which follow are given in the order of their occurrence, though they were often widely separated by intervening matter and topics.

After mentioning that he and his wife were welcomed to Richmond, by Mr. Jefferson's son-in-law, ex-Governor Randolph (then in the Legislature), and by Thomas Jefferson Randolph who had been dispatched to Richmond, by his grandfather, to meet the travellers and make suitable arrangements for their journey to Charlottesville, Dr. Dunglison proceeds to say :

"Soon afterwards [the arrival at Charlottesville] the venerable ex-President presented himself, and welcomed us with that dignity and kindness for which he was celebrated. He was then eighty-two years old, with his intellectual powers unshaken by age, and the physical man so active that he rode to and from Monticello, and took exercise on foot with all the activity of one twenty or thirty years younger. He sympathized with us on the discomforts of our long voyage, and on the disagreeable journey we must have passed over the Virginia roads ; and depicted to us the great distress he had felt lest we had been lost at sea—for he had almost given us up when my letter arrived with the joyful intelligence we were safe.

*   *   *   *   *   *

"The houses [the professors' houses or "pavilions" of the University] were much better finished than we had expected to find them, and would have been far more commodious had Mr. Jefferson consulted his excellent and competent daughter, Mrs.

dating dispositions, and zeal for the prosperity of the institution, leave us nothing to wish. I verily believe that as high a degree of education can now be obtained here, as in the country they left."

Randolph, in regard to the interior arrangements, instead of planning the aichitectural exterior first, and leaving the interior to shift for itself. Closets would have interfered with the symmetry of the rooms or passages, and hence there were none in most of the houses; and the only one which was furnished with a closet, it was told as an anecdote of Mr. Jefferson, that not suspecting it, according to his general arrangements, he opened the door and walked into it in his way out of the pavilion!

"He was fond of architecture, and anxious that the rotunda, and the different pavilions should present specimens of the various orders; and although from the necessity of building them of brick and wood, the effect was greatly diminished, it was, on the whole, agreeable. The heavy cornices in the interior of the rooms, of the Palladian style, were however anything but pleasing. Undoubtedly, too, the desire for having everything architecturally correct, according to his taste, induced him, in more cases than I have mentioned, to sacrifice convenience. He could not but admit the anomaly of having windows arranged as in modern habitations, but further than this it was difficult to induce him to go, and when I consulted him in regard to a distinct building for anatomical purposes, which he agreed to, he at the same time told me that he must choose the position, and the architectural arrangement externally, whilst all the interior arrangements should be left to me.

*   *   *   *   *   *

"As I have before remarked, the opening of the University, which had been fixed for the 1st of February, was postponed, on account of our late arrival in the country, until the 1st of April, when it took place. All the professors except the incumbent of the Law chair, were on the spot; and the faculty consisted of Mr. Long, Professor of Ancient Languages; Mr. Key, Professor of Mathematics; Mr. Bonnycastle, Professor of Natural Philosophy; Dr. Blaetterman, Professor of Modern Languages; Dr. Emmet, Professor of Chemistry; Mr. Tucker,[1] Professor of Moral Philosophy; and Dr. Dunglison, Professor of Medicine. All the professors were foreigners; for Dr. Emmet was born in Ireland, and Mr. Tucker in the Island of Bermuda.

*   *   *   *   *   *

"The fact of all the professors being foreigners, it might be imagined would be unfavorable to discipline, and might lead the disorderly to rebel against the authorities of the University. It is but justice, however, to a highly numerous body of generous young gentlemen to say, that during the whole period of my residence at the University, which amounted to nine years, no single act came to my knowledge of insubordination from that cause; whilst ample evidence was afforded of their great respect for those who had left their homes, and were zealously engaged in instructing them. Mr. Jefferson was, however, severely criticised for having gone abroad for Professors.[2]   *   *   *   *   *

"Not long after my arrival at the University, Mr. Jefferson found it necessary to consult me in regard to a condition of great irritability of the bladder, under which he had suffered for some time, and which inconvenienced him greatly. . . Few perhaps attain that advanced age without suffering more or less from diseases of the urinary organs. On examining the urethra, I found the prostatic portion was affected with stricture, accompanied, and apparently produced by enlargement

[1] Author of the Life of Jefferson.
[2] The "Philadelphia Journal of the Medical and Physical Sciences," edited by Dr. N. Chapman, at the time the most prominent medical journal in the United States, expressed great indignation on the subject.

of the prostate gland. [After describing the remedies and their favorable effects, the memoranda continue.]

"Mr. Jefferson was considered to have but little faith in physic: and has often told me that he would rather trust to the unaided, or rather uninterfered with, efforts of nature than to physicians in general. 'It is not,' he was wont to observe, 'to physic that I object so much as to physicians.' Occasionally, too, he would speak jocularly, especially to the unprofessional, of medical practice; and on one occasion gave offence, when most assuredly, if the same thing had been said to me, no offence would have been taken. In the presence of Dr. Everett, afterwards Private Secretary to Mr. Monroe, ... he remarked, ·that whenever he saw three physicians together, he looked up to discover whether there was not a turkey buzzard in the neighborhood.[1] The annoyance of the doctor, I am told, was manifest. To me, when it was recounted, it seemed a harmless jest.

"But whatever may have been Mr. Jefferson's notions of physic and physicians, it is but justice to say that he was one of the most attentive and respectful of patients. He bore suffering inflicted upon him for remedial purposes with fortitude; and in my visits, showed me, by memoranda, the regularity with which he had taken the prescribed remedies at the appointed times.

*   *   *   *   *

"His daughter Mrs. Randolph, or one of the grand-daughters, took the head of the table; he himself sat near the other end, and almost always some visitors were present. The pilgrimage to Monticello was a favorite one with him who aspired to the rank of the patriot and the philanthropist; but it was too often undertaken from idle curiosity, and could not, under such circumstances, have afforded pleasure to, whilst it entailed unrequited expense on its distinguished proprietor. More than once, indeed, the annoyance has been the subject of regretful animadversion. Monticello, like Montpellier, the seat of Mr. Madison, was some miles distant from any tavern, and hence, without sufficient consideration, the traveller not only availed himself of the hospitality of the ex-Presidents, but inflicted upon them the expenses of his quadrupeds. On one occasion at Montpellier, where my wife and myself were paying a visit to Mr. and Mrs. Madison, no fewer than nine horses were entertained during the night; and in reply to some observation which the circumstance engendered, Mr. Madison remarked, that whilst he was delighted with the society of the owners, he confessed he had not so much feeling for the horses.

"Sitting one evening in the porch of Monticello, two gigs drove up, each containing a gentleman and a lady. It appeared to me to be evidently the desire of the party to be invited to stay the night. One of the gentlemen came up to the porch and saluted Mr. Jefferson, stating that they claimed the privilege of American citizens in paying their respects to the President, and inspecting Monticello. Mr. Jefferson received them with marked politeness, and told them they were at liberty to look at everything around, but as they did not receive an invitation to spend the night, they left in the dusk and returned to Charlottesville. Mr. Jefferson, on that occasion, could scarcely avoid an expression of impatience at the repeated though complimentary intrusions to which he was exposed.[2]

---

[1] To understand the point of this remark, it may be necessary to inform some Northern readers that this well-known Southern bird (*Cathartes aura* of Temminck and Bonaparte—*Vultur aura* of Wilson) feeds on carrion, disabled animals, etc.! It is the scavenger of Southern cities.

[2] This seems to us obviously an account of the same incident, in which another eye-witness (Professor Tucker) describes Mr. Jefferson as "coldly replying" to his visitor that "he did not know what privilege he alluded to"—and then as "showing no dispo-

"In Mr. Jefferson's embarrassed circumstances in the evening of life, the immense influx of visitors could not fail to be attended with much inconvenience. *I had the curiosity to ask Mrs. Randolph what was the largest number of persons for whom she been called upon unexpectedly to prepare accommodations for the night, and she replied fifty!* In a country like our own, there is a curiosity to know personally those who have been called to fill the highest office in the Republic, and he who has attained this eminence must have formed a number of acquaintances who are eager to visit him in his retirement, so that when his salary as the first officer of the State ceases, the duties belonging to it do not cease simultaneously; and I confess I have no sympathy with the feeling of economy, political or social, which denies to the ex-President a retiring allowance, which may enable him to pass the remainder of his days in that useful and dignified hospitality which seems to be demanded by the citizens, of one who has presided over them.

    *   *   *   *   *   *

"At all times dignified, and by no means easy of approach to all,[1] he was generally communicative to those on whom he could rely; in his own house he was occasionally free in his speech, even to imprudence, to those of whom he did not know enough to be satisfied that an improper use might be made of his candor. As an example of this I recollect a person from Rhode Island visiting the University, and being introduced to Mr. Jefferson by one of my colleagues. The person did not impress me favorably; and when I rode up to Monticello, I found no better impression had been made by him on Mr. Jefferson and Mrs. Randolph. His *adhesiveness* was such that he had occupied the valuable time of Mr. Jefferson the whole morning, and staid to dinner, and during the conversation Mr. Jefferson was apprehensive that he had said something which might have been misunderstood and be incorrectly repeated. He therefore asked me to find the gentleman, if he had not left Charlottesville, and request him to pay another visit to Monticello. He had left, however, when I returned, but I never discovered he had abused the frankness of Mr. Jefferson. Mr. Jefferson took the occasion of saying to me how cautious his friends ought to be in regard to the persons they introduced to him. It would have been singular if, in the numerous visitors, some had not been found to narrate

---

sition to relieve him" from his obvious embarrassment, "or to encourage his probable purpose of visiting the interior of the mansion," whereupon, after a short pause, says Mr. Tucker, the speaker "withdrew in disappointment, and the carriages immediately descended the mountain." Professor Tucker says in the same paragraph, that "Mr. Jefferson was as remarkable for the general urbanity of his manners, and his good temper, as for his hospitality." Conceding the great accuracy of this writer generally in stating facts, and his utter indisposition to misrepresent Mr. Jefferson, still we cannot doubt that Dr. Dunglison's version is the correct one. Did the urbane, good-tempered, and hospitable Jefferson so suddenly resent an intrusion of every-day occurrence, as, in the presence of the guests of his dinner-table, to sharply repulse a party from even entering his house, and that, too, when the party was composed in part of *ladies*? To misremember an "expression of impatience," made in the hearing of two or three familiar friends after these free-and-easy guests had got out of hearing, into an expression made *to* the spokesman of the party, would be the most natural thing in the world. And this we have no doubt is the fact. The matter is of very trifling importance, and is only mentioned because those who knew Mr. Jefferson more than ten times as long and far more familiarly than *either* of the above writers, are fully satisfied that he never could have been guilty of the rudeness or harshness which a casual misrecollection imputes to him.

   [1] Dr. Dunglison (as he informs us personally) does not here mean that it was difficult for any person, of whatever degree, to respectfully approach or address Mr. Jefferson— but that very few felt disposed, or found it practicable, to assume anything like *familiarity* with him.

the private conversations held with such men as Jefferson and Madison, yet they were few ; and one of them,[1]   •   •   •   •
            •   •   •   •   •

"In the summer of 1825, the monotonous life of the college was broken in upon by the arrival of General Lafayette, to take leave of his distinguished friend Mr. Jefferson, preparatory to his return to France. A dinner was given to him in the rotunda, by the professors and students, at which Mr. Madison and Mr. Monroe were present, but Mr. Jefferson's indisposition prevented him from attending. 'The meeting at Monticello' says· M. Levasseur, the Secretary to General Lafayette during his journey, in his ' *Lafayette in America in* 1824 *and* 1825,' vol. ii. p. 245, of three men, who, by their successive elevation to the supreme magistracy of the state, had given to their country twenty-four years of prosperity and glory, and who still offered it the example of private virtues, was a sufficiently strong inducement to make us wish to stay there a longer time ; but indispensable duties recalled General Lafayette to Washington, and he was obliged to take leave of his friends. I shall not attempt to depict the sadness which prevailed at this cruel separation, which had none of the alleviation which is usually felt by youth ; for in this instance the individuals who bade farewell, had all passed through a long career, and the immensity of the ocean would still add to the difficulties of a reunion.

"M. Levasseur has evidently confounded this banquet with that given by the inhabitants of Charlottesville, the year preceding, during the first visit of Lafayette to Mr. Jefferson. At that period, there were neither professors nor students, as the institution was not opened until six months afterwards. 'Everything,' says M. Levasseur (vol. i. p. 220), 'had been prepared at Charlottesville, by the citizens and students, to give a worthy reception to Lafayette. The sight of the nation's guest, seated at the patriotic banquet, between Jefferson and Madison, excited in those present an enthusiasm, which expressed itself in enlivening sallies of wit and humor. Mr. Madison, who had arrived that day at Charlottesville to attend this meeting, was especially remarkable for the originality of his expressions, and the delicacy of his allusions. Before leaving the table, he gave a toast ' To liberty—with virtue for her guest, and gratitude for the feast,' which was received with rapturous applause.

"The same enthusiasm prevailed at the dinner given in the rotunda. One of the toasts proposed by an officer of the institution, I believe, was an example of forcing a metaphor to the full extent of its capability ; 'The apple of our heart's eye—Lafayette.' [2]

"In referring to Mr. Jefferson's bodily condition at this period, Mr. Tucker has the following remarks, Life of Jefferson, vol. ii., p. 478 :

---

[1] Left with a *carte blanche* to make a selection from confidential memoranda, without submitting that selection to the author, we have felt it due to him to abstain from any personal details liable to give offence in any quarter.

[2] Attorney-General Wirt wrote to his wife on the 20th of August, 1825 : " We had a great time to-day. I dined by invitation with the Marquis at the University, and was placed at his right hand ; and I, too, was toasted. They wanted me to make a speech. but I am *principled* against it. So I merely expressed my thanks for the unexpected honor they had done me ; told them that, although a public speaker by profession, I had not been accustomed to speak in my own cause, and begged them, in lieu of a speech. to accept a toast—which I gave them. Lafayette, who had been toasted, had merely returned thanks in so many words, and given his toast ; but my friend, Monroe, who was also there, had, upon being called out in his turn, made a speech—and not one of his best. I was thought to have made a great escape."—*Kennedy's Memoirs of William Wirt*, vol. ii. p. 177.

[Here follows an extract from Professor Tucker's work, mentioning his disease, etc. ; that a severer attack of it recurred in August ; that General Lafayette, on his second visit, found him on a couch in the drawing-room, suffering acute pain, and much changed from the preceding year ; that the General "manifested a good deal of solicitude for his friend—had conferences in regard to his health with Dr. Dunglison, and having learnt that certain preparations, useful in his disease, could be obtained better in Paris than elsewhere, he remembered the fact, and as soon as he returned, sent a supply which would have been sufficient for twenty patients." Having made this quotation from Mr. Tucker, Dr. Dunglison resumes:]

"The preparations referred to by Mr. Tucker were elastic gum catheters. Soon after Lafayette's return to France, he wrote to Mr. Randolph, stating that he had sent a small *caisse* as a present. What this could be puzzled us not a little. When it arrived, which was some time after the death of Mr. Jefferson, it proved to be a case of nearly one hundred elastic gum catheters.

"The announcement of Mr. Jefferson's decease gave occasion to another letter [from Lafayette,] in which, after expressing his grief at the loss of his old friend, he asked Mrs. Randolph to inform me how much he sympathized with me at the sad, although by him, not unexpected event.

"From the Life of General Lafayette, by M. Jules Cloquet, M.D., it appears those instruments were selected by him. 'Some years ago,' he remarks, 'Lafayette instructed me to choose for him some surgical instruments which he wished to present to President Jefferson, at the period of his last illness. When I handed him the box containing them, he thanked me with his usual kindness, and added: What think you of my friend's health? His situation causes me the greatest anxiety. Why can I not send him, with this box, not only the instruments he requires, but your experience and your guiding hand? At that period he little foresaw that one day he himself would be attacked by a similar malady, and that all my care would be ineffectual to preserve his life.' (Recollections of the Private Life of General Lafayette, by M. Jules Cloquet, M.D.)

*   *   *   *   *   *

"In the framing of a code of laws for the government of the University, Mr. Jefferson—for he was their chief author—was under the erroneous impression that more might be done with the students, by an appeal to their patriotism and honor, than by positive punishment; but whilst it may be admitted as a general rule that certainty of punishment is more effective than severity, and that the best spirits amongst a high-minded body of young gentlemen may be ruled and governed by such feelings as those invoked by Mr. Jefferson, the result proved, that all were not thus influenced, and that in many cases, separation from the University was indispensable. It was fancifully believed by that distinguished personage, that the students themselves might be induced to form a part of the government, to constitute a court for the trial of minor offences, and to inflict punishment on a delinquent colleague; and farther, that their coöperation might react beneficially in the prevention of transgressions. The scheme had a Republican appearance, and was favorably thought of by the Rector and Board of Visitors. In the first printed copy of the enactments of the institution (1825) is the following :

"'The major punishments of expulsion from the University, temporary suspension of attendance there, or interdiction of residence or appearance within its precincts, shall be decreed by the Professors themselves. Minor cases may be referred to a board of six censors, to be named by the Faculty, from among the most discreet of the students, whose duty it shall be, sitting as a board, to inquire into the facts,

propose the minor punishments which they think proportioned to the offence, and
to make report thereof to the Professors for their approbation, or their commutation
of the penalty, if it be beyond the grade of the offence. These censors shall hold
their offices until the end of the session of their appointment, if not sooner revoked
by the Faculty.'

"During the very first session of the University, events occurred to exhibit the
insufficiency of any enactment of the kind, and accordingly in the next edition
of the 'Enactments,' published in 1827, it was stricken out. So long indeed, as I
have elsewhere remarked (see article on 'College Instruction and Discipline' in the
American Quarterly Review for June, 1831, p. 294), as the *esprit de corps* or *Burschenschaft* prevails amongst students, which inculcates that it is a stigma of the deepest
hue to give testimony against a fellow student, it is vain to expect any coöperation
in the discipline of the institution from them. This 'loose principle in the ethics
of schoolboy combinations,' as it was termed by Mr. Jefferson, has, indeed, led to
numerous and serious evils. It has been a great cause of the combinations formed
in resistance to the lawful authorities, of intemperate addresses at the instigation of
some unworthy member, and of repeated scenes of commotion and violence. It is
rare for a youth to hesitate to depose in a court of justice, touching an offence
against the municipal laws of his country, committed by a brother-student. The
youth, and the people at large, are, indeed, distinguished for their ready attention
to the calls of justice. Yet it is esteemed the depth of dishonor to testify when
called upon by the college authorities, against the grossest violation not only of
collegiate but of municipal law ; as if it could be less honorable to give the same
testimony before one tribunal than the other ; or as if the morality of the act differed in the two cases.

"The fallacy of placing any reliance on appeals to reason and to sense of propriety on the part of the students, and the evils of this *Burschenschaft*, were apparent before the termination of the first session. Offences of a disturbing character
were committed, and when the offenders were detected they were first admonished,
and then mildly punished ; until, at length, riot and disorder occurred, which could
no longer be tolerated. 'Nightly disorders' (says Professor Tucker) 'were habitual with the students, until passing from step to step, they reached a point of riot
and excess, to which the forbearance of the Professors could no longer extend,
when the students considered their rights violated, and openly resisted the authority
of the Faculty. This happened in October, immediately before the annual meeting of the Visitors. The subject was laid before them by the Faculty. More deep
mortification, more poignant distress, could not be felt than was experienced by Mr.
Jefferson. The following day he came down with the other Visitors from Monticello, which was their head-quarters, summoned the students into their presence,
and they were addressed in short speeches by himself, Mr. Madison, and Chapman
Johnson. The object of these addresses was, not merely to produce in the young
men a disposition to obey the laws, and return to their studies, but to induce the
principal rioters to give up their names. The address of these men—the two first
venerable by their years, their services, and their authority—could not be resisted.
The offenders came forward, one by one, and confessed their agency. Among those
who thus almost redeemed their past error, by this manly course, was one of his
own nephews.[1] The shock which Mr. Jefferson felt when he, for the first time, discovered that the efforts of the last ten years of his life had been foiled, and put in

---

[1] This should be grand-nephews.

jeopardy by one of his family, was more than his own patience could endure, and he could not forbear from using, for the first time, the language of indignation and reproach. Some of the offenders, among whom was his nephew, were expelled by the Faculty ; and others were more lightly punished. Their offensive memorial was withdrawn, the exercises of the University were resumed, and under a system liberal without being lax, a degree of order and regularity has been progressively increasing, and is supposed to be now nowhere exceeded.' "

We will here drop Dr. Dunglison's Memoranda for a time.

It ought to be added to a preceding remark, that Mr. Jefferson's kindly social attentions to the members of the University were not confined to its officers. As often as once a week, a number of students were invited to dine with him. He sometimes, perhaps generally, ate apart on such occasions, as he could hear nothing amidst the clatter of a joyous company, and he wished to be no impediment to the enjoyment of others. But before and after the meal, he attentively devoted himself to his young guests.

CHAPTER XIII.

1825—1826.

AMONG the distinguished visitors to the University the first year of its establishment, were Duke Bernhard of Saxe-Weimar Eisenach; Mr. Stanley, now Lord Derby; the Honorable J. Evelyn Denison, M.P.; Mr. Stuart Wortley, and others. It is probable that most, if not all of these gentlemen were drawn to Charlottesville by a desire to visit Monticello.

Mr. Wirt made his last visit to Mr. Jefferson in August, 1825. The accomplished author of Wirt's Memoirs, Mr. Kennedy, says of this visit: "The meeting, we believe, was of

nelancholy concern to the Attorney-General.   It was the visit
.f a pilgrim, not to an empty shrine, but to an ancient hearth-
tone, where the friend of his youth yet inhabited, and where
nany vivid memories yet lingered to bring back the images of
he past, now saddened by the thought that the brittle chain of
. great life was soon to be broken, and with it, almost every
ur viving association which gave interest to the place.[1]

The Duke of Saxe-Weimar left the following account of his
:isit to Monticello, in his published " Travels in North America
n 1825 and 1826 :"

" The University is situated on a hill in a very healthy situation, and there is a
:ery fine view of the Blue Ridge. President Jefferson invited us to a family dinner;
)ut as in Charlottesville there is but a single hackney coach, and this being absent,
re were obliged to go the three miles to Monticello on foot.

" We went by a pathway, through well cultivated and inclosed fields, crossed a
:reek named Rivanna, passing on a trunk of a tree, cut in a rough shape, and with-
)ut rails ; then ascended a steep hill overgrown with wood, and came on its top, to
Mr. Jefferson's house, which is in an open space, walled round with bricks, forming
ın oblong, whose shorter sides are rounded ; on each of the longer sides are portals
)f four columns.

" The unsuccessful waiting for a carriage, and our long walk, caused such a
kelay, that we found the company at table when we entered; but Mr. Jefferson
:ame very kindly to meet us, forced us to take our seats, and ordered dinner to be
erved up anew.   He was an old man of eighty-six years of age, of tall stature,
)lain appearance, and long, white hair.

" In conversation, he was very lively, and his spirits, as also his hearing and sight,
eemed not to have decreased at all, with his advancing age.   I found in him a
nan who retained his faculties remarkably well in his old age, and one would have
aken him for a man of sixty.   He asked me what I had seen in Virginia.   I
:ulogized all the places that I was certain would meet with his approbation, and he
eemed very much pleased.   The company at the table consisted of the family of
ı is daughter, Mrs. Randolph, and of that of the Professor of Mathematics at the

[1] Mr. Kennedy says in a note on the same page : " The writer of this memoir visited
Monticello within a few weeks after the period referred to in the text.   I was accom-
)anied by a friend, and had a letter of introduction from Mr. Wirt.   I had never seen
ir. Jefferson.   It was a hot day in July when we reached the top of the mountain, and
:ntered the spacious hall of the mansion.   We presented the letter to a lady of the
amily.   Mr. Jefferson had been very ill with a recent attack of his malady, and there-
'ore excused himself from receiving company.   There was a large glass door which
)pened upon the hall and separated Mr. Jefferson's apartments from it.   Whilst we sat
n this hall, a tall, attenuated figure, slightly stooping forward, and exhibiting a coun-
enance filled with an expression of pain, slowly walked across the space visible through
he glass door.   It was Mr. Jefferson.   He was dressed in a costume long out of fashion
—smallclothes, a waistcoat with flaps, and, as it struck us, in the brief view we had,
ome remnants of embroidery.   The silence of the footfall, the venerable figure, the old
:ostume, and the short space in which that image glided past the glass door, made a
:trange and mysterious impression upon us.   It was all I ever saw of the sage of Mon-
kcello."
The hastiness of Mr. Kennedy's view betrayed him into some errors.   Mr. Jefferson
rore no embroidery.   The smallclothes had given place to pantaloons when he was
ibout seventy years old ; and with characteristic utilitarianism he had immediately
rondered that he had not discovered their superior convenience before.

University, an Englishman and his wife. I turned the conversation to the subject of the University, and observed that this was the favorite topic with Mr. Jefferson; he entertained very sanguine hopes as to the flourishing state of the University in future, and believed that it, and the Harvard University, near Boston, would in a very short time be the only institutions, where the youth of the United States would receive a truly classical and solid education. After dinner we intended to take our leave, in order to return to Charlottesville, but Mr. Jefferson would not consent to it. He pressed us to remain for the night at his house. The evening was spent by the fire; a great deal was said about travels, and objects of natural history; the fine arts were also introduced, of which Mr. Jefferson was a great admirer. He spoke also of his travels in France, and the country on the Rhine, where he was very much pleased. His description of Virginia is the best proof what an admirer he is of the beauties of Nature. He told us that it was only eight months since he could not ride on horseback; otherwise he rode every day to visit the surrounding country; he entertained, however, hopes of being able to re-commence, the next spring, his favorite exercise. Between nine and ten o'clock in the evening, the company broke up, and a handsome room was assigned to me.

"The next morning I took a walk round the house and admired the beautiful panorama which this spot presents. On the left I saw the Blue Ridge, and between them and Monticello are smaller hills. Charlottesville and the University lay at my feet; before me, the valley of the Rivanna River, which farther on makes its junction with the James River, and on my right was the flat part of Virginia, the extent of which is lost in distance; behind me was a towering hill which limited the sight. The interior of the house was plain, and the furniture somewhat of an old fashion. In the entrance was a marble stove with Mr. Jefferson's bust, by Ceracchi. In the room hung several copies of the celebrated pictures of the Italian school, views of Monticello, Mount Vernon, the principal buildings in Washington, and Harper's Ferry; there were also an oil painting and an engraving of the Natural Bridge, views of Niagara by Vanderlin, a sketch of the large picture by Trumbull, representing the Surrender at Yorktown, and a pen drawing of Hector's Departure, by Benjamin West, presented by him to General Kosciusko; finally, several portraits of Mr. Jefferson, among which, the best was that in profile, by Stuart. In the saloon, there were two busts, one of Napoleon, as First Consul, and another of the Emperor Alexander. Mr. Jefferson admired Napoleon's military tactics, but did not love him. After breakfast, which we took with the family, we bid the respectable old man farewell, and set out upon our return to Charlottesville.

"Mr. Jefferson tendered us the use of his carriage, but I declined, as I preferred walking in a fine and cool morning." Vol. i., p. 197, et seq.

The observing reader will note a number of trifling errors in this description, and in one or two instances an amusing tone of complaisance. But amiable Duke Bernhard does not take credit to himself for resolutely insisting, contrary to the protestations of Mrs. Randolph, that the cold meats be returned to the dinner table for him, precisely as they left it, and then of feeding from them with a relish which offered the best compliment to the housekeeping. Anxious to please, sensible and downright, he left a favorable impression on the mind of Mr. Jefferson, and every member of his family.[1] His Travels contain more serious errors in regard to the University, but these do not call for attention here.

We will return to Mr. Jefferson's correspondence. He wrote to Mr. Short, January 8th, 1825, a letter (commenting on some published statements of H. G. Otis and R. G. Harper) which will be read with curiosity by those who wish to know whether he preserved to the last the views so often expressed, during earlier political conflicts, in regard to the aims of the leaders of the two great American parties. His letter is cool, argumentative, and from the citations it contains was evidently written with deliberation. As unhesitatingly as twenty-five years earlier he asserts, on the evidence of his own ears, that Hamilton, Adams, and other great Federal leaders, were monarchists in theory, and again distinctly carries the idea that a portion of those leaders were monarchists in their *aims*. He again says, that " the true history of that conflict of parties " will never be understood, until " by the death of the actors in it the hoards of their letters shall be broken up and given to the world." He again prophesies that " time will in the end produce the truth." But he admits that " after all " these divisions were not to be wondered at—that under one name or another they have everywhere existed in the human heart—that they have exhibited themselves in every country " where not suppressed by the rod of despotism."

Edward Livingston forwarded to Mr. Jefferson, in March, a portion of his celebrated civil code of the State of Louisiana, requesting him to examine its provisions, weigh their bearings on each other in all their parts, their harmony with reason and nature, and their adaptation to the habits and sentiments of those for whom they were prepared. The latter, March 25th, declined this honorable task, but expressed great admiration of the

---

[1] Wirt wrote to his wife from Baltimore, October 30th, 1825: . . . "I dined yesterday with the Duke of Saxe-Weimar, at Mr. Oliver's. He is about a head taller than myself, with a nose *retroussé* and features a good deal like ——'s, not fair and auburn-haired, however, like ——, but with a sallow complexion, and dark hair; no redundant fat, but brawny, muscular, and of herculean strength. He is about thirty-five years old, and looks like a Russian, or one of those gigantic Cossacks. I dare say he makes a magnificent figure in uniform. He speaks English tolerably well; yet, he has that apparent dullness of apprehension which always accompanies a defective knowledge of a language, and which renders it rather up-hill work to talk with him."—*Kennedy's Memoirs of Wirt*, vol. ii. p. 178.

Code, declaring to Mr. Livingston that "it would certainly arrange his name with the sages of antiquity."

In a letter to ———,[1] October 25th, he gave a fuller course of ancient and modern reading for young persons, than we remember to have seen elsewhere in his writings; and it is interspersed with highly characteristic remarks. In answer to a letter from J. Evelyn Denison, he strongly commended the taste then reviving in England " for the recovery of the Anglo-Saxon dialect "—and also the publication of the existing " county dialects of England," which he said " would restore to our language all its shades of variation." To Lewis M. Wiss, November 27th, he made an explanation of the plan of dry-docks, recommended during his Presidency. This will be found far more accessible to those desiring to know the outlines of that plan, than the official records which contain them.

An application having been made to Mr. Jefferson to prepare a letter of advice for the future guidance of a little namesake, whose parents resided in Washington, he sent the following:

THOMAS JEFFERSON TO THOMAS JEFFERSON SMITH.

This letter will, to you, be as one from the dead. The writer will be in the grave before you can weigh its counsels. Your affectionate and excellent father has requested that I would address to you something which might possibly have a favorable influence on the course of life you have to run, and I too, as a namesake, feel an interest in that course. Few words will be necessary, with good dispositions on your part. Adore God. Reverence and cherish your parents. Love your neighbor as yourself, and your country more than yourself. Be just. Be true. Murmur not at the ways of Providence. So shall the life into which you have entered, be the portal to one of eternal and ineffable bliss. And if to the dead it is permitted to care for the things of this world, every action of your life will be under my regard. Farewell.

MONTICELLO, *February* 21, 1825.

THE PORTRAIT OF A GOOD MAN BY THE MOST SUBLIME OF POETS, FOR YOUR IMITATION.

Lord, who's the happy man that may to thy blest courts repair;
Not stranger-like to visit them, but to inhabit there?
'Tis he whose every thought and deed by rules of virtue moves;
Whose generous tongue disdains to speak the thing his heart disproves.
Who never did a slander forge, his neighbor's fame to wound;
Nor hearken to a false report, by malice whispered round.

[1] Name not given. See Congress edition of his Works, vol. vii. p. 411.

Who vice in all its pomp and power, can treat with just neglect ;
And piety, though clothed in rags, religiously respect.
Who to his plighted vows and trust has ever firmly stood ;
And though he promise to his loss, he makes his promise good.
Whose soul in usury disdains his treasure to employ ;
Whom no rewards can ever bribe the guiltless to destroy.
The man, who, by this steady course, has happiness insur'd,
When earth's foundations shake, shall stand, by Providence secur'd.

A DECALOGUE OF CANONS FOR OBSERVATION IN PRACTICAL LIFE.

1. Never put off till to-morrow what you can do to-day.
2. Never trouble another for what you can do yourself.
3. Never spend your money before you have it.
4. Never buy what you do not want, because it is cheap; it will be dear to you.
5. Pride costs us more than hunger, thirst, and cold.
6. We never repent of having eaten too little.
7. Nothing is troublesome that we do willingly.
8. How much pain have cost us the evils which have never happened.
9. Take things always by their smooth handle.
10. When angry, count ten, before you speak; if very angry, an hundred.

When President J. Q. Adams's first message to Congress ap-
ared, in December, Mr. Jefferson was deeply and painfully
armed at its tenor. He wrote to Mr. Madison, December 24th:

"I have for some time considered the question of internal improvement as
erate. The torrent of general opinion sets so strongly in favor of it as to be
istible. And I suppose that even the opposition in Congress will herafter be
le and formal, unless something can be done which may give a gleam of en-
ragement to our friends, or alarm their opponents in their fancied security. I
n from Richmond that those who think with us there, are in a state of perfect
aay, not knowing what to do or what to propose."

He said the representative of his county (Mr. Gordon) had
icited his advice, and that if Mr. Madison had not thought of
ything in this emergency, he would propose to him a line of
ion, which in the apparent hesitation exhibited by their
ponents, might prove "a bolt shot critically" to "decide the
itest by its effect on the less bold." It might "break the
stern coalition, by offering the same thing in a different form.
would be viewed with favor in contrast with the Georgia
position and fear of strengthening that. It would be an ex-
ple of a temperate mode of opposition in future and similar
ies. It would delay the measure a year at least. It would
e them the chance of better times and of intervening acci-
its; and in no way place them in a worse than their present

position." This measure consisted in the passage by the Legislature of Virginia of a solemn "Declaration and Protest," a proposed draft for which he inclosed to Mr. Madison.

This, after very temperately reciting the conditions of the federal compact, declared:

"But the federal branch has assumed in some cases, and claimed in others, a right of enlarging its own powers by constructions, inferences, and indefinite deductions from those directly given, which this Assembly does declare to be usurpations of the powers retained to the independent branches, mere interpolations into the compact, and direct infractions of it.

"They claim, for example, and have commenced the exercise of a right to construct roads, open canals, and effect other internal improvements within the territories and jurisdictions exclusively belonging to the several States, which this Assembly does declare has not been given to that branch by the constitutional compact, but remains to each State among its domestic and unalienated powers, exercisable within itself and by its domestic authorities alone.

"This Assembly does further disavow, and declare to be most false and unfounded, the doctrine that the compact, in authorizing its federal branch to lay and collect taxes, duties, imposts, and excises, to pay the debts and provide for the common defence and general welfare of the United States, has given them thereby a power to do whatever *they* may think, or pretend, would promote the general welfare, which construction would make that, of itself, a complete government, without limitation of powers; but that the plain sense and obvious meaning was, that they might levy the taxes necessary to provide for the general welfare, by the various acts of power therein specified and delegated to them, and by no others."

But in consideration of the feelings and interests of other states, " and as a further pledge of the sincere and cordial attachment of the Commonwealth of Virginia to the union of the whole," it concluded with the following proposed enactment:

"We therefore do enact, and be it enacted by the General Assembly of Virginia, that all citizens of this commonwealth, and persons and authorities within the same, shall pay full obedience at all times to the acts which may be passed by the Congress of the United States, the object of which shall be the construction of post roads, making canals of navigation, and maintaining the same, in any part of the United States, in like manner as if the said acts were, *totidem verbis*, passed by the Legislature of this commonwealth."

This proposition was not adopted. Immediately afterwards occurred that correspondence between Jefferson and Governor Giles of Virginia, in relation to Mr. Adams's political conduct in 1808–9, which has already been noticed. In discussing what steps were necessary to resist what he believed to be usurpations of the National Government in respect to internal improvements, Mr. Jefferson wrote the Governor:

e we, then, *to stand to our arms*, with the hot-headed Georgian? No. That
the last resource, not to be thought of until much longer and greater
;a. If every infraction of a compact of so many parties is to be resisted at
a dissolution of it, none can ever be formed which would last one year.
t have patience and longer endurance then with our brethren while under
; give them time for reflection and experience of consequences; keep our-
a situation to profit by the chapter of accidents; and separate from our
ons only, when the sole alternatives left, are the dissolution of our Union
m, or submission to a government without limitation of powers. Between
o evils, when we must make a choice, there can be no hesitation. But in
nwhile, the States should be watchful to note every material usurpation on
hts; to denounce them as they occur in the most peremptory terms; to
tgainst them as wrongs to which our present submission shall be considered,
cknowledgments or precedents of right, but as a temporary yielding to the
il, until their accumulation shall overweigh that of separation. I would go
her, and give to the federal member, by a regular amendment of the Con-
, a right to make roads and canals of intercommunication between the
roviding sufficiently against corrupt practices in Congress (log-rolling, etc.),
iring that the federal proportion of each State of the moneys so employed,
in works within the State, or elsewhere with its consent, and with a due
jurisdiction. This is the course which I think safest and best as yet."

e year 1826 opened gloomily on Mr. Jefferson. His pecu-
lifficulties had now reached their climax. While stagger-
ider the load of his own debts, he had suffered a loss by
ing, which, as he remarked, gave him the *coup de grâce*.
ote Cabell, January 20th:

r grandson, Thomas J. Randolph, attends the Legislature on a subject of
importance to my future happiness. My own debts were considerable, and
as added to them of $20,000 by indorsement for a friend. My application
egislature is for permission to dispose of property for payment in a way
ringing a fair price for it, may pay my debts, and leave a living for myself
ld age, and leave something for my family. Their consent is necessary. It
re no man, and few sessions pass without similar exercises of the same power
discretion. But I refer you to my grandson for particular explanations. I
just myself; and if it should appear so to you, I am sure your friendship as
justice will induce you to pay to it the attention which you may think the
l justify. To me it is almost a question of life and death." [1]

s request to the Legislature was for permission to dispose
property by a lottery. He drew up a paper on the sub-
hich was only intended to be shown to a few friends in the
, but has been published since his death, in both editions
Works, for the explanations of his views which it contains.

· this, and some subsequent correspondence between Jefferson and Cabell, not
d in the published Works of the former, see their correspondence in the History
niversity.

In this paper he assumed that lotteries are not immoral *per se*. He said if games of chance were immoral, then the pursuits of industry were immoral, for they were all subject to chance. He continued :

"These, then, are games of chance. Yet, so far from being immoral, they are indispensable to the existence of man, and every one has a natural right to choose for his pursuit such one of them as he thinks most likely to furnish him subsistence. Almost all these pursuits of chance produce something useful to society. But there are some which produce nothing, and endanger the wellbeing of the individuals engaged in them, or of others depending on them. Such are games with cards, dice, billiards, etc. And although the pursuit of them is a matter of natural right, yet society, perceiving the irresistible bent of some of its members to pursue them, and the ruin produced by them to the families depending on these individuals, consider it as a case of insanity, *quoad hoc*, step in to protect the family and the party himself, as in other cases of insanity, infancy, imbecility, etc., and suppress the pursuit altogether, and the natural right of following it. There are some other games of chance, useful on certain occasions, and injurious only when carried beyond their useful bounds. Such are insurances, lotteries, raffles, etc. These they do not suppress, but take their regulation under their own discretion. The insurance of ships on voyages is a vocation of chance, yet useful, and the right to exercise it therefore is left free. So of houses against fire, doubtful debts, the continuance of a particular life, and similar cases. Money is wanting for a useful undertaking, as a school, etc., for which a direct tax would be disapproved. It is raised therefore by a lottery, wherein the tax is laid on the willing only, that is to say, on those who can risk the price of a ticket without sensible injury, for the possibility of a higher prize. An article of property insusceptible of division at all, or not without great diminution of its worth, is sometimes of so large value as that no purchaser can be found, while the owner owes debts, has no other means of payment, and his creditors no other chance of obtaining it, but by its sale at a full and fair price. The lottery is here a salutary instrument for disposing of it, where many run small risks for the chance of obtaining a high prize. In this way, the great estate of the late Colonel Byrd (in 1756) was made competent to pay his debts, which, had the whole been brought into the market at once, would have overdone the demand, would have sold at half or quarter the value, and sacrificed the creditors, half or three-fourths of whom would have lost their debts. This method of selling was formerly very much resorted to, until it was thought to nourish too much a spirit of hazard. The Legislature were therefore induced, not to suppress it altogether, but to take it under their own special regulation. This they did, for the first time, by their act of 1769, c. 17, before which time, every person exercised the right freely ; and since which time, it is made lawful but when approved and authorized by a special act of the Legislature."

He then cited a great number of cases in which the Legislature had authorized sales by lottery for public and private purposes, since 1776. Some of these were yet in operation. The instances between 1782 and 1820 were not less than seventy. Lotteries for a long time furnished a part of the standing revenue the State. They had been resorted to for the benefit of ᵘlleges, Academies, Grammar and Charity Schools—for internal ᵢprovements of every kind—for the aid of religious societies, ᵈ to build churches—for private benevolent societies—for ᵌemasons—for sufferers by fire—for the erection of a paper ᵢll—for raising money to enable a person to complete his ᵒgraphical work—for enabling another to complete a literary ᵒrk, etc., etc.

After mentioning that lands could not then be sold for more ᵃn a third or fourth of their former value, and that to be pro᷍cted against a fatal sacrifice was the object of his application, ᵢ proceeded to state the considerations on which he thought he ᵢght have as good a claim to this protection as others who had ᵤceived it. He enumerated the offices he had filled, some of ᵉ prominent services he had performed, and then said : " Will ᵇe objected, that although not evil in itself, it may as a pre᷍dent lead to evil ? But let those who shall quote the preced᷍ᵢt, bring their case within the same measure. Have they, as ᵗhis case, devoted three score years and one of their lives, ᵤinterruptedly, to the service of their country ?" [1]

Mr. Jefferson spoke more plainly in this private paper of the ᵢportance of his public services than perhaps on any other ᵓcasion of his life.

A few of Mr. Jefferson's friends, consisting of leading mem᷍ᵣs of the Legislature, and the judges of the Court of Appeals, ᵉt together twice at Richmond, to consider the above applica᷍ᵓn. The judges unanimously favored the plan. Some of his ᵢends, however, could not reconcile themselves to the lottery ᵃture ; and Cabell therefore proposed in lieu of it, that a bill ᵒuld be brought forward to loan Mr. Jefferson $80,000 from ᵉ public treasury, free of interest, for the remainder of his life. ᵑt others feared this precedent would be still less acceptable, ᵢd it was at length unanimously decided to bring forward and ᵖport a bill establishing the lottery.

[1] While the soundness or unsoundness of his views on this subject is left to the ᵈgment of every reader, it is proper to remark that lotteries were then common in ᵃt of the States of the Union. Some of the most useful institutions now in the United ᵗᵉˢ were founded in part on funds obtained by this method.
Since writing the above, we have seen it stated in the newspapers that lotteries are ᵣ (1857) common in France for ecclesiastical and religious objects—that one was ᵉᵑtly drawn, for example, to purchase the holy hill of Fourvière and to build a sanc᷍ry thereon. Lotteries are still openly permitted in some of the American States, ᵢ continue to be indirectly resorted to in others, at charity fairs, etc.

Towards the close of January the House of Delegates, by a decisive vote, refused a pending application for a grant of money to the University. To add to Mr. Jefferson's mortification, two letters appeared in a Richmond paper, over the signature of an "American Citizen," describing a visit to Monticello, and narrating a conversation with Mr. Jefferson, in which he was represented as, in effect, saying that he had purposely kept the Legislature in the dark, in regard to the anticipated cost of the University, for the purpose of more easily obtaining each succeeding grant. In a letter to Cabell, February 7th, he indignantly disavowed the construction put upon his language. He said, "he could not express the pain which this unfaithful version and betrayment of private conversation had given him."[1]

As soon as he learned the failure of the University grant, he directed the Proctor to suspend every expense that was not absolutely necessary, and as quietly set himself to work to adapt every arrangement to the new situation of things, as if nothing had happened.

It would seem that Cabell wrote to him, February 2d, a letter which has not been published, in which he expressed apprehensions that Mr. Jefferson's own application (to be allowed to sell his property by lottery) would fail. The latter replied calmly and resignedly,—and he cut off all of Cabell's propositions for anything in the nature of a pecuniary *donation* by the Legislature.

"I had hoped [he said] the length and character of my services might have prevented the fear in the Legislature of the indulgence asked being quoted as a precedent in future cases. But I find no fault with their strict adherence to a rule generally useful, although relaxable in some cases, under their discretion, of which they are the proper judges. If it can be yielded in my case, I can save the house of Monticello and a farm adjoining, to end my days in, and bury my bones. If not, I must sell house and all here, and carry my family to Bedford, where I have not even a log hut to put my head into.[2] In any case I wish nothing from the Treasury. The pecuniary compensations I have received for my services, from time to time, have been fully to my own satisfaction."

[1] For this letter, see History of the University, p. 365. The statements of an "American Citizen" arose from Mr. Jefferson's jocularly illustrating the repeated calls of the University on the public purse by telling a story of old "Commodore" O'Brien, of Revolutionary and Barbary memories. The commodore brought a demand against the Government for certain services or losses, and it was paid. He then presented a new claim. A friend asked him why he did not include this in the former one? The veteran coolly demanded in return, whether his questioner had ever seen anybody attempt to cram *two* hot potatoes down another's throat at the same time?

[2] The dwelling-house built there had gone out of his possession.

The next day he wrote a deeply interesting letter to his oldest grandson, which has not been hitherto published.

To THOMAS J. RANDOLPH.

MONTICELLO, *February* 8, '26.

MY DEAR JEFFERSON:

I duly received your affectionate letter of the 3d, and perceive there are greater doubts than I had apprehended, whether the Legislature will indulge my request to them. It is a part of my mortification to perceive that I had so far over-valued myself as to have counted on it with too much confidence. I see in the failure of this hope, a deadly blast of all my peace of mind, during my remaining days. You kindly encourage me to keep up my spirits; but oppressed with disease, debility, age, and embarrassed affairs, this is difficult. For myself I should not regard a prostration of fortune, but I am overwhelmed at the prospect of the situation in which I may leave my family. My dear and beloved daughter, the cherished companion of my early life, and nurse of my age, and her children, rendered as dear to me as if my own from having lived with me from their cradle, left in a comfortless situation, hold up to me nothing but future gloom; and I should not care were life to end with the line I am writing, were it not that in the unhappy state of mind which your father's misfortunes have brought upon him, I may yet be of some avail to the family. Their affectionate devotion to me makes a willingness to endure life a duty, as long as it can be of any use to them. Yourself, particularly, dear Jefferson, I consider as the greatest of the godsends which heaven has granted to me. Without you, what could I do under the difficulties now environing me? These have been produced, in some degree, by my own unskillful management, and devoting my time to the service of my country, but much also by the unfortunate fluctuation in the value of our money, and the long continued depression of farming business. But for these last I am confident my debts might be paid, leaving me Monticello and the Bedford estate; but where there are no bidders, property, however great, is no resource for the payment of debts; all may go for little or nothing. Perhaps, however, even in this case, I may have no right to complain, as these misfortunes have been held back for my last days, when few remain to me. I duly acknowledge that I have gone through a long life, with fewer circumstances of affliction than are the lot of most men—uninterrupted health—a competence for every reasonable want—usefulness to my fellow-citizens—a good portion of their esteem—no complaint against the world which has sufficiently honored me, and above all, a family which has blessed me by their affections, and never by their conduct given me a moment's pain—and should this, my last request, be granted, I may yet close with a cloudless sun a long and serene day of life. Be assured, my dear Jefferson, that I have a just sense of the part you have contributed to this, and that I bear you unmeasured affection.

TH. JEFFERSON.

In a letter to Cabell, February 14th, he spoke in as business-like a tone as usual of the affairs of the University, and but a single trace of smothered feeling breaks the calm tenor of the letter. After again and again expressing his gratitude for the efforts of his friends, he closed thus: "Thanks to you all, and warm and affectionate acknowledgments. I count on nothing now. I am taught to know my standard, and have to meet with no further disappointment."

Cabell wrote on the 15th that he had no doubt the lottery bill would pass, " but not without a large minority." With the devotion of a friend and the tact of a gentleman, he added: " We have a wayward house to deal with, but I hope you will not suffer these things to depress you; for *we* are to be injured by them, not yourself." He then asked Mr. Jefferson to make alterations, solve doubts, and " say what was to be done," in the various educational bills before the House, as usual.

On the 17th, Mr. Jefferson wrote to Mr. Madison, and after giving a particular account of matters at the University, since the defeat of the appropriation, he thus alluded to his own affairs :

" You will have seen in the newspapers some proceedings in the Legislature, which have cost me much mortification. My own debts had become considerable, but not beyond the effect of some lopping of property, which would have been little felt, when our friend **** gave me the *coup de grâce*. Ever since that, I have been paying twelve hundred dollars a year interest on his debt, which, with my own, was absorbing so much of my annual income, as that the maintenance of my family was making deep and rapid inroads on my capital, and had already done it. Still, sales at a fair price would leave me competently provided. Had crops and prices for several years been such as to maintain a steady competition of substantial bidders at market, all would have been safe. But the long succession of years of stunted crops, of reduced prices, the general prostration of the farming business, under levies for the support of manufactures, etc., with the calamitous fluctuations of value in our paper medium, have kept agriculture in a state of abject depression, which has peopled the western States by silently breaking up those on the Atlantic, and glutted the land market, while it drew off its bidders. In such a state of things, property has lost its character of being a resource for debts. Highland and Bedford, which, in the days of our plethory, sold readily for from fifty to one hundred dollars the acre (and such sales were many then), would not now sell for more than from ten to twenty dollars, or one-quarter or one-fifth of its former price. Reflecting on these things, the practice occurred to me, of selling, on fair valuation, and by way of lottery, often resorted to before the Revolution to effect large sales, and still in constant usage in every State for individual as well as corporation purposes. If it is permitted in my case, my lands here alone, with the mills, etc., will pay everything, and will leave me Monticello and a farm free. If refused, I must sell everything here, perhaps considerably in Bedford, move thither with my family, where I have not even a log hut to put my head into, and whether ground for burial, will depend on the depredations which, under the form of sales, shall have been committed on my property. The question, then, with me was *utrum horum ?* But why afflict you with these details? Indeed, I cannot tell, unless pains are lessened by communication with a friend. The friendship which has subsisted between us, now half a century, and the harmony of our political principles and pursuits, have been sources of constant happiness to me through that long period. And if I remove beyond the reach of attentions to the University, or beyond the bourne of life itself, as I soon must, it is a comfort to leave that institution under your care, and an assurance that it will not be wanting. It has also been a great solace to me, to believe that you are engaged in vindicating to posterity the course we have pursued for preserving to them, in all their purity, the blessings of self-government, which we had assisted, too, in acquiring for them. If ever the earth has beheld a system of administration conducted with a single and steadfast eye to the general interest and happiness of those committed to it, one which, protected by truth, can never know reproach, it is that to which our lives have been devoted. To myself you have been a pillar of support through life. Take care of me when dead, and be assured that I shall leave with you my last affections."

The close is touching. It was written when Mr. Jefferson was conscious that the great change of which he spoke was swiftly approaching. He was probably not without a strong premonition that he was writing to Madison for the last time.

The friend who gave Mr. Jefferson the "*coup de grâce*," by bringing on him the payment of $20,000 as an indorser, was Governor Wilson C. Nicholas, and it happened in 1819. Nobody questioned the integrity of the latter. He sunk under the pressure of those disastrous times[1] which carried down so many other Virginia landholders.

The following narrative appertains in part to scenes from which good taste usually excludes the public eye. If, in throwing them open, we are adjudged to have overstepped the bounds of a delicate propriety, then all we can say is that we have mistaken what is due equally to Jefferson and to Wilson Cary Nicholas. A daughter of the latter had married a grandson of Mr. Jefferson, and with her husband lived on a portion of the Monticello estate. It was the custom of all the female members of Mr. Jefferson's family, living in his vicinity, on returning home, after an absence extending beyond a day or two, to first go to Monticello. It was a sort of regulation imposed by his affection, and which, we need not say, was joyfully acquiesced in. The grandson's wife just mentioned, was absent when she became apprised of her father's bankruptcy. She knew the loss Mr. Jefferson would incur, and was conscious it would prove fatal to him, in a pecuniary point of view. To go back and meet as usual him on whom her father had brought such a cala-

[1] See Colonel Benton's description of them at page 329 of this volume.

mity in his old age, was a painful trial, but it was of course encountered. After her arrival she chose not to disturb him until his dinner hour. An economist in minutes, he did not usually leave his study until the second dinner bell was rung. On this occasion, he came out at the first, and asked "has not **** come?" She heard his voice and flew to meet him. Instead of the usual hearty hand-shake and kiss, he folded her in his arms. His smile was radiant. He conversed with animation during dinner. Neither then, nor on any subsequent occasion, did he ever by a word or look make her aware that he was even conscious of the misfortune her father had brought upon him.

The next time Mr. Jefferson set out for Bedford, after Governor Nicholas's failure, on reaching the turning-off road to the residence of the latter, he said to one of his family: "I ought not to stop; I have not time; but it would be cruel to pass him." He met Nicholas as if nothing unusual had occurred. He showed no depression, and did not make an equal exposure of his feelings, by feigning extraordinary cheerfulness. Nicholas subsequently came to visit his daughter and her husband. He was preparing to endure the ordeal of again entering the mansion *he* had consigned to the speedy ownership of strangers. Mr. Jefferson got the start of him. Hearing that Nicholas was at Tufton, he immediately mounted his horse and rode thither. Madison and Monroe were sent for to meet him at Monticello. In the loftiest period of his prosperity, as the head of an ancient, powerful and talented family,—as the Administration leader in Congress—as the Governor of Virginia,—his reception could not have been more distinguished. Governor Nicholas died in the arms of the children we have mentioned. In his last hours, he declared with unspeakable emotion that Mr. Jefferson had never by a word, by a look, or in any other way, *made any allusion to his loss by him!*[1]

A lady visitor at Monticello, whose familiarity with the family entitled her, she thought, to use some freedoms, began on one occasion to indulge in unfavorable comments on Nicholas's imprudence in suffering his debt to fall on Mr. Jefferson. The latter immediately and effectually interrupted her by remarking

---

[1] It is scarcely necessary to say that the preceding facts were derived from the lips of the surviving actors in the scenes described.

gently but gravely, that he "had the highest opinion of Governor Nicholas, and felt the deepest sympathy for his misfortunes."

On the 20th of February, the zealous and faithful Cabell joyfully wrote from the Senate Chamber, that the lottery bill as received from the House of Delegates had been committed at 12 o'clock—that he had asked leave for the committee to sit during the session of the House—that they reported at one o'clock—that the bill passed "instanter"—that the vote stood ayes thirteen, nays four—that two of the minority "were carried off by their aversion to lotteries"—that the passage of the bill would have been communicated by special message, had not the House of Delegates adjourned on account of the death of a member. Five commissioners to value the property, were named in the bill. They were all exactly the proper persons for the situation, namely, friends of Mr. Jefferson, but men whose character gave ample assurance that the trust confided to them would be discharged both honestly and intelligently.

Mr. Jefferson had done injustice to the representatives of Virginia when he wrote Cabell that he "had been taught to know his standard." The legislature contained men who represented many interests which he had prostrated, many feelings and opinions with which he had placed himself in rude collision. Entail, primogeniture, hierarchy, family consequence and lastly Federalism had sunk under his assaults. Powerful local interests, influential institutions, strong class jealousies, were now temporarily arrayed against him, on account of his efforts for the University. "Scurvy politicians" could find a pretence for opposing his wishes in a harmless jest. He was known to be sinking rapidly into a debility which would unnerve the irresistible arm and tongue, and prevent him from waging any more conflicts, or avenging any more injuries. Yet a majority of the Legislature overcame their strong aversion to a practice which was becoming obsolete, and to a principle which they justly considered objectionable, to gratify his last request. The maternal heart of Virginia never failed to respond to the appeal of this honored and favored son.

He had better proofs of this even, than were furnished by the Legislative vote. While the bill was before the General Assembly, a public meeting was called at Richmond to approve of its

objects.   The attendance was numerous and embraced all
parties and sects.   Meetings were promptly called in other
counties.   As a specimen of their expressions, we quote the following, adopted by the citizens of Nelson County, June 26th:

"The undersigned citizens of Nelson County, concurring cordially in the views
lately expressed by their fellow-citizens, at the seat of government, and heartily sympathizing in the sentiments of grateful respect, and affectionate regard recently
evinced both there and elsewhere, for their countryman Thomas Jefferson, cannot disguise the sincere satisfaction which they derive from the prospect of a general coöperation to relieve this ancient and distinguished patriot.   The important
services for which we are indebted to Mr. Jefferson, from the days of his youth,
when he drew upon himself the resentment of Dunmore, to the present time, when,
at the close of a long life he is laboring to enlighten the nation which he has contributed to make free, place him in the highest rank of national benefactors, and
eminently entitle him to the character of the people's friend.   Whether considered
as the servant of the State or of the United States; whether regarded as an advocate or a statesman; whether as a patriot, a legislator, a philosopher, or a friend of
liberty and republican government, he is the unquestioned ornament of his country,
and unites in himself every title to our respect, our veneration and gratitude.   His
services are written in the hearts of a grateful people; they are identified with the
fundamental institutions of his country; they entitle him to "the fairest page of
faithful history;" and will be remembered as long as reason and science are respected on earth.   Profoundly impressed with these sentiments, the undersigned
citizens of Nelson County consider it compatible with neither the national character,
nor with the gratitude of the Republic, that this aged patriot should be deprived of
his estate, or abridged in his comforts at the close of a long life so ably spent in
the service of his country.   Therefore,

" *Resolved*—That the resolutions relative to Thomas Jefferson, recently adopted by
the citizens of Richmond and Manchester, meet the cordial approbation of the
undersigned citizens of Nelson County, etc."

The lottery scheme did not afford the kind or degree of aid
which the aroused public feeling pronounced befitting: individuals and newspapers hotly denounced the idea of suffering any
portion of Mr. Jefferson's estate to be taken from him to pay
debts, the amount of which they averred his countrymen owed
to him a hundred-fold.   This seemed to be the universal sentiment.   From all parts of the Union came proffers of assistance.
The Mayor of New York, Philip Hone, sent Mr. Jefferson
$8,500 raised without an effort; in like manner $5,000 were sent
from Philadelphia, $3,000 from Baltimore, and a thousand or two
from other places.   These were but first contributions, without
system or exertion, and, ostensibly, only the promises of greater
ones behind.

Under such circumstances the lottery project was of course suspended. Mr. Jefferson had the inexpressible gratification of believing that his debts would be paid—that his hearth-stone would descend to his children—that his family would be left independent. Happily, he died in that delusion. Those who knew how determinedly he had refused to accept, under any circumstances or in any form, a donation from the State, had felt some interest to know how he would receive the proposal to have his debts paid by a popular subscription. Instead of wounding, it gratified his feelings. It struck him in the light of a purely filial offering. " I have spent three times as much money and given my whole life to my countrymen," he declared, "and now they nobly come forward, in the only way they can, to repay me and save an old servant from being turned like a dog out of doors." " No cent of this," he exclaimed, " is wrung from the tax-payer—it is the pure and unsolicited offering of love." These feelings " closed with a cloudless sun a long and serene day of life."

There is no doubt that after the severe relapse which he suffered in the middle of February, 1826, Mr. Jefferson was fully conscious that his days and hours were numbered. Henceforth he scarcely spoke of his health, at home, and entered into no particulars with correspondents. What was more significant, he attempted to keep from the knowledge of his family the existence of a chronic diarrhœa which obstinately withstood all remedies, and which was steadily and surely sapping the remains of his great strength. He succeeded in this concealment until the assistance which his tottering steps required to get about the house necessarily revealed the secret. In March, he began to set his house in order, to die. On the 16th, he made his will, writing the whole with his own hand, and the next day appended a codicil of nearly equal length also written with his own hand.[1] His necessary directions on this occasion first apprised his oldest grandson of his expectations of speedy death. From the other members of his family he yet concealed them.

His family well remember the incidents of the closing scene. They treasured in their memories every look, every word, every incident. After his fresh attack in February, they left him alone as little as possible. He retained his life-long reluctance to

---

[1] For the Will, see APPENDIX, No. 33.

be helped, and to have any other person watching over his safety. As an example of this, he continued to ride a little on his favorite horse to within three weeks of his death, when he was so weak that he could not possibly mount him, except by getting *down* from one of the terraces into the saddle; yet, even then, he would not permit a servant to follow him.

Old Eagle, like his master, was well stricken in years, but he retained the fire and almost the swiftness of the monarch bird whose name he bore. It was a sight to see him brought out curvetting from the stable for his master's ride. If the latter was not quite ready, a hook and staple in a Persian willow, marked Eagle's place in the mean time; and there he stood with his ears back on his arched neck, pawing and stamping the ground with fiery impatience. But when led to the terrace to be mounted, he stood as immovable as a statue; and when the reins were disposed in the crippled hands—as ineffectual as an infant's to curb his strength—he moved off with slow and stately gravity, as if perfectly conscious of the necessity of discretion in his movements. But Eagle had his one fault. If suddenly and very severely frightened, he would whirl about to fly with a suddenness which no firmness of seat was proof against. He thus once (when an antlered deer suddenly started up from behind a pile of brush immediately in his path) threw Mr. Jefferson, when greatly stronger than now. On a recent occasion, when the latter was riding down into a ford on Moore's Creek, where the bank was rather steep, the fore feet of the horse stuck in a new-formed bank of mud, and Mr. Jefferson was pitched over his head into the stream. His broken left arm was in a sling, his right wrist without strength, the water high, and he would have been drowned had he not in falling clung to the bridle, or grasped it, while Eagle was extricating himself, and thus been dragged ashore.

These circumstances, and Mr. Jefferson's increasing debility, made his continued solitary rides sources of great apprehension to his family; and Mrs. Randolph finally besought him to allow himself to be accompanied by Burwell. His reply was that he had "helped himself" from childhood—that he had daily mused and conversed with nature alone—that the presence of a servant annoyed him—that it was too late to change the habits of a long life—that he would give up his rides if his family desired it, for his health was past remedy or preservation—but that if he rode, t must be *alone*.

Besides arranging his own affairs for his decease, in the early part of 1826, he continued to watch keenly and even minutely over the concerns of the University. Some traces of this will be found in his published letters to Professor Emmet; but he was generally consulted and gave his advice orally. His letters of the year exhibit the unclouded vigor of his faculties. His family, however, noticed that his memory, which had been failing for several years, occasionally betrayed him into manifest errors. The following letter is included in neither edition of his writings:

MONTICELLO, *May* 20, '26.

DEAR SIR:

The subject of your letter of April 20, is one on which I do not permit myself to express an opinion, but when time, place, and occasion may give it some favorable effect. A good cause is often injured more by ill-timed efforts of its friends than by the arguments of its enemies. Persuasion, perseverance, and patience are the best advocates on questions depending on the will of others. The revolution in public opinion which this cause requires, is not to be expected in a day, or perhaps in an age; but time, which outlives all things, will outlive this evil also. My sentiments have been forty years before the public. Had I repeated them forty times, they would only have become the more stale and threadbare. Although I shall not live to see them consummated, they will not die with me; but living or dying, they will ever be in my most fervent prayer. This is written for yourself and not for the public, in compliance with your request of two lines of sentiment on the subject. Accept the assurance of my good will and respect.

TH. JEFFERSON.[1]

MR. JAMES HEATON, *Middletown, Butler County, Ohio.*

Mr. Jefferson's last reading was principally the Bible, Æschylus, Sophocles, and Euripides. The majesty of Æschylus, the ripe art of Sophocles, the exhaustless invention of Euripides, now came back to him in more than their pristine grandeur and beauty; and in the Bible he found flights of sublimity more magnificent than in these, coupled with a philosophy to which the Grecian was imperfect, narrow, and base. No sentiment did he express oftener than his contempt for all moral systems compared with that of Christ.

---

[1] This reminds us that we have been repeatedly requested, while preparing these volumes, to furnish a connected view of Mr. Jefferson's opinions on the subject of slavery, slavery limitation, emancipation, etc. Originally believing that such a summary would necessarily fall within the plan of the work, we promised to furnish it in these pages. As it was not decided ultimately to pursue an analogous course in regard to other prominent topics of Mr. Jefferson's life and opinions, the promised explanation will be placed in the Appendix. See APPENDIX, No. 34.

While in this feeble condition, Browere, an artist, came from New York to take a cast in plaster of the head of Mr. Jefferson. The latter was exceedingly reluctant to have it done—and his family felt still more opposed to it. But Mr. Jefferson finally consented, saying that he could not find it in his heart to refuse a man so trifling a favor, who had come so far. He was placed on his back on a sofa, one of his hands grasping a chair which stood in front. Not dreaming of any danger, his family could not bear to see him with the plaster over his face, and therefore were not present; and his faithful Burwell was the only person besides the artist in the room. There was some defect in the arrangements made to permit his breathing, and Mr. Jefferson came near suffocation. He was too weak to rise or to relieve himself, and his feeble struggles were unnoticed or unheeded by his Parrhasius. The sufferer finally bethought himself of the chair on which his hand rested. He raised it as far as he was able and struck it on the floor. Burwell became conscious of his situation, and sprang furiously forward. The artist shattered his cast in an instant. The family now reached the room, and Browere looked as if he thought their arrival most opportune, for though Burwell was supporting his master in his arms, the fierce glare of his African eye boded danger. Browere was permitted to pick up his fragments of plaster and carry them off—and whether he ever put them together to represent features emaciated with age and debility, and writhing in suffocation, we are not informed.

Mr. Jefferson's deportment to his family was touching. He evidently made an effort to keep up their spirits. He was as gentle as a child, but conversed with such vigor and animation that they would have often cheated themselves with the belief that months, if not years of life were in store for him, and that he himself was in no expectation of speedy death—had they not witnessed the infant-like debility of his powerful frame, and had they not, occasionally, when they looked suddenly at him, caught resting on themselves that riveted and intensely loving gaze, which showed but too plainly that his thoughts were on a rapidly approaching parting. And as he folded each in his arms, as they separated for the night, there was a fervor in his kiss and gaze that declared as audibly as words, that he felt the farewell might prove a final one.

leclined to allow any member of his family to remain
n during the night, until very near his death. To the
declined the attendance of any of its female members,
he aware that the library door was left ajar to enable
steal round silently through the darkness to hover
s bed. He even required the servants that watched
n, to have their pallets in his room, so they could sleep
the night.

Jefferson and the other surviving signers of the Decla-
f Independence, were invited by the Mayor of Wash-
General Weightman, to attend the celebration of the
anniversary of American Independence in the federal
he following was Mr. Jefferson's reply, and it was his
er :

To Mr. Weightman.

Monticello, June 24, 1826.

Sir :

kind invitation I received from you, on the part of the citizens of the
ashington, to be present with them at their celebration of the fiftieth
y of American Independence, as one of the surviving signers of an
pregnant with our own, and the fate of the world, is most flattering to
d heightened by the honorable accompaniment proposed for the comfort
journey. It adds sensibly to the sufferings of sickness, to be deprived by
rsonal participation in the rejoicings of that day. But acquiescence is a
r circumstances not placed among those we are permitted to control.   I
leed, with peculiar delight, have met and exchanged there congratulations
with the small band, the remnant of that host of worthies, who joined with
day, in the bold and doubtful election we were to make for our country,
ubmission or the sword; and to have enjoyed with them the consolatory
our fellow-citizens, after half a century of experience and prosperity, con-
pprove the choice we made. May it be to the world, what I believe
(to some parts sooner, to others later, but finally to all), the signal of
nen to burst the chains under which monkish ignorance and superstition
aded them to bind themselves, and to assume the blessings and security
rernment. That form which we have substituted, restores the free right
ounded exercise of reason and freedom of opinion. All eyes are opened,
g, to the rights of man.   The general spread of the light of science has
id open to every view the palpable truth, that the mass of mankind has
orn with saddles on their backs, nor a favored few booted and spurred,
ide them legitimately, by the grace of God. These are grounds of hope
. For ourselves, let the annual return of this day, forever refresh our
ns of these rights, and an undiminished devotion to them.
ask permission here to express the pleasure with which I should have
dent neighbors of the city of Washington and its vicinities, with whom
o many years of a pleasing social intercourse ; an intercourse which so
ved the anxieties of the public cares, and left impressions so deeply
in my affections, as never to be forgotten. With my regret that ill

health forbids me the gratification of an acceptance, be pleased to receive for your-self, and those for whom you write, the assurance of my highest respect and friendly attachments. TH. JEFFERSON.

John Adams and Thomas Jefferson were summoned to a greater, and we would fain hope, a still more joyful meeting of ancient friends and comrades on that day. The national anniversary being the first semi-centennial one, seemed in the popular mind, to mark a distinctive epoch, and it was celebrated everywhere with unusual festivity and splendor. At fifty minutes past meridian, on that day, Jefferson died. At the moment, thousands of patriotic orations were being pronounced, in which his name figured second to none. Thousands of popular assemblies had listened that day to the great Declaration drafted by his hand. Bells were ringing, and cannons booming in every town and hamlet of our country. Aged men, clad in their holiday attire, were gathered in knots, discoursing of the sword and pen of America—of Washington and Jefferson. Nor was lion-hearted John Adams, Franklin, and others, forgotten. Young men and maidens were collected in happy parties ; some repairing to favorite retreats—some filling boats surmounted by gay streamers, on our lakes and rivers—some visiting stern old Revolutionary battle-fields. Even the little children were celebrating the day by waving miniature flags, firing miniature cannon, and dragging together, with shrill glee, the materials for the evening bonfire. The spirit of the great leader and lover of his kind appropriately ascended amidst the jubilant and noisy commotion of a nation's happiness. Thus would he have chosen to die.

Hundreds and hundreds of miles away, John Adams's last sands were running out. The very sky reëchoed the long exultant shouts as his characteristic toast was read at Quincy—" Independence for ever." He lingered behind Jefferson, and his last words, uttered in the failing articulation of the dying, were: " THOMAS JEFFERSON STILL SURVIVES." [1] All that was mortal of Jefferson had ceased to live when these words were spoken. Were they the less true ?

The following accounts include all the reliable particulars of Mr. Jefferson's death. The first is contained in a letter from his oldest grandson, Colonel T. J. Randolph.

[1] Life of John Adams, by his grandson, C. F. Adams, p. 636.

To Henry S. Randall.

Ŀ Sir:

* * * * * * *

Mr. Jefferson had suffered for several years before his death, from a
rhœa, which he concealed from his family, lest it might give them uneasiness.
aware of it, I was surprised, in conversation with him, in March, 1826, to hear
in speaking of an event likely to occur about midsummer, say doubtingly, that
right live to that time. About the middle of June, hearing that he had sent for
physician, Dr. Dunglison, of the University of Virginia, I went immediately to
iim,[1] and found him out in his public rooms. Before leaving the house, he sent
rvant to me, to come to his room, whereupon he handed me a paper, which he
ed me to examine, remarking, "don't delay, there is no time to be lost." He
nally declined, but would only have his servants sleeping near him : being
urbed only at nine, twelve, and four o'clock in the night, he needed little nursing.
oming uneasy about him, I entered his room, unobserved, to pass the night.
ing round inadvertently to assist him, he chided me, saying that being actively
loyed all day, I needed repose. On my replying that it was more agreeable to
o be with him, he acquiesced, and I did not leave him again. A day or two
·, my brother-in-law (Mr. Trist) was admitted. His servants, ourselves, and the
tor became his sole nurses. My mother sat with him during the day, but he
ld not permit her to sit up at night. His family had to decline for him
erous tenders of service, from kind and affectionate friends and neighbors,
ing and seeing that it would excite him to conversation injurious to him in his
k condition. He suffered no pain, but gradually sunk from debility. His mind
always clear—it never wandered. He conversed freely, and gave directions as
is private affairs. His manner was that of a person going on a necessary jour-
—evincing neither satisfaction nor regret. He remarked upon the tendency of
nind to recur back to the scenes of the Revolution. Many incidents he would
:e, in his usual cheerful manner, insensibly diverting my mind from his dying
ɓition. He remarked that the curtains of his bed had been purchased from the
cargo that arrived after the peace of 1782. Upon my expressing the opinion,
ɔne occasion, that he was somewhat better, he turned to me, and said, "do not
ɲine for a moment that I feel the smallest solicitude about the result ; I am like
ld watch, with a pinion worn out here, and a wheel there, until it can go no
er." On another occasion, when he was unusually ill, he observed to the Doc-
"A few hours more, Doctor, and it will be all over." Upon being suddenly
sed from sleep, by a noise in the room, he asked if he had heard the name of
Hatch mentioned—the minister whose church he attended. On my replying in
negative, he observed, as he turned over, " I have no objection to see him, as a
. and good neighbor." The impression made upon my mind at the moment was,
his religious opinions having been formed upon mature study and reflection,
ad no doubts upon his mind, and therefore did not desire the attendance of a
ɡyman ; I have never since doubted the correctness of the impression then
n. His parting interview with the different members of his family, was calm
composed ; impressing admonitions upon them, the cardinal points of which

---

Colonel Randolph lived on the estate, but in a separate house, at some distance from
icello.

were to pursue virtue, be true and truthful. My youngest brother, in his eighth year, seeming not to comprehend the scene, he turned to me with a smile and said, "George does not understand what all this means." He would speculate upon the person who would succeed him as Rector of the University of Virginia, and concluded that Mr. Madison would be appointed. With all the deep pathos of exalted friendship he spoke of his purity, his virtues, his wisdom, his learning, and his great abilities. The friendship of these great men was of an extraordinary character—they had been born, lived, and died within twenty-five miles of each other—they visited frequently through their whole lives. At twenty-three years old, Mr. Jefferson had been consulted on Mr. Madison's course of study—he then fifteen. Thus commenced a friendship as remarkable for its duration as it was for the fidelity and warmth of its feelings. The admiration of each for the wisdom, abilities, and purity of the other was unlimited. Their habit of reliance upon mutual counsel, equalled the sincerity of their affection, and the devotion of their esteem.

In speaking of the calumnies which his enemies had uttered against his public and private character, with such unmitigated and untiring bitterness, he said, that he had not considered them as abusing him; they had never known *him*. They had created an imaginary being clothed with odious attributes, to whom they had given his name; and it was against that creature of their imaginations they had levelled their anathemas.

On Monday, the third of July, his slumbers were evidently those of approaching dissolution; he slept until evening, when upon awaking he seemed to imagine it was morning, and remarked, that he had slept all night without being disturbed—"This is the fourth of July." He soon sunk again into sleep, and on being aroused at nine, to take his medicine, he remarked in a clear distinct voice, "No, Doctor, nothing more." The omission of the dose of laudanum administered every night during his illness, caused his slumbers to be disturbed and dreamy; he sat up in his sleep and went through all the forms of writing; spoke of the Committee of Safety, saying it ought to be warned. As twelve o'clock at night approached, we anxiously desired that his death should be hallowed by the Anniversary of Independence. At fifteen minutes before twelve we stood noting the minute hand of the watch, hoping a few minutes of prolonged life. At four A. M. he called the servants in attendance, with a strong and clear voice, perfectly conscious of his wants. He did not speak again. About ten he fixed his eyes intently upon me, indicating some want, which most painfully, I could not understand, until his attached servant, Burwell, observed that his head was not so much elevated as he usually desired it, for his habit was to lie with it very much elevated. Upon restoring it to its usual position, he seemed satisfied. About eleven, again fixing his eyes upon me, and moving his lips, I applied a wet sponge to his mouth, which he sucked and appeared to relish—this was the last evidence he gave of consciousness. He ceased to breathe, without a struggle, fifty minutes past meridian—July 4th, 1826. I closed his eyes with my own hands. He was at all times, during his illness, perfectly assured of his approaching end, his mind ever clear, and at no moment did he evince the least solicitude about the result; he was as calm and composed as when in health. He died a pure and good man. It is for others to speak of his greatness. He desired that his interment should be private, without parade, and our wish was to comply with his request, and no notice of the hour of interment, or invitations were issued. His body was borne privately from his dwelling, by his family and servants, but his neighbors and friends anxious to pay the last tribute of respect and affection to one whom they had loved and honored, waited for it in crowds at the grave."

The day was rainy, or the crowds would have been greater. The burial service of the Episcopal Church was read over Mr. Jefferson's remains by his friend, the Rev. Mr. Hatch, the clergyman of the parish.

In his narrative, Colonel Randolph alludes to three other persons as having been much of the time with Mr. Jefferson, near the period of his decease. These were Mr. Jefferson's daughter Mrs. Randolph, Mr. Trist, and Dr. Dunglison, Mrs. Randolph left no written account of the scene. On the 2d of July, Mr. Jefferson handed her a little casket. On opening it after his death, she found a paper on which he had written the lines of Moore, commencing:

> " It is not the tear at this moment shed,
>   When the cold turf has just been lain o'er him "—

On the same was written:

> " Heu ! quanto minus est cum reliquis versari quam tui meminisse."

There is also a touching tribute to his daughter, declaring that while he " goes to his fathers," " the last pang of life " is in parting from her—that " two seraphs " " long shrouded in death " (meaning doubtless his wife and younger daughter) " await him "—that he will " bear them her love." [1]

Mr. Trist's recollections of the closing scene coincide too closely with Colonel Randolph's in all material particulars, to require their transcription. In a few points he goes into more minute details. He says it was the call of his friend, Mr. Garret, Bursar of the University, and the whispered inquiry of a member of the family at the door, to know whether he should be admitted to the room, that Mr. Jefferson had mistaken for a similar

---

[1] We have seen all these souvenirs. Copies of them are before us. Mrs. Randolph shrunk from their exposure, except to the eye of the most intimate friendship. A rumor that an accident, or rather a well-intentioned indiscretion, had made them public, gave her much pain. It seemed to her a drawing aside of the veil from domestic scenes, from which delicacy should exclude the observation of all strangers. Mrs. Randolph has long reposed in death. We will not violate her living wishes. Why should we? Is anything wanting to prove Mr. Jefferson's paternal tenderness, or his high and fixed belief in Heaven!

Perhaps we have already said more of these souvenirs than would have accorded with Mrs. Randolph's wishes. If so, on us must rest the sole responsibility. In this, as in all parallel cases, we have acted with no limitation but our own sense of propriety. With confidence, with perhaps too much confidence, have all the possible materials of full biography been placed in our hands. If there shall be error on either side in using them, we have preferred that it be on the side of unreserve.

inquiry in relation to the Rev. Mr. Hatch. Mr. Trist drew the same inference from Mr. Jefferson's remark on that occasion, that Mr. Randolph did.

Mr. Trist thus more fully gives the particulars of what appears to have been an inquiry instead of a remark; and he places the event later in the evening :

> During the night of the 3d, as I sat on the sofa, close to his pillow, my eyes were constantly turning from his face to the clock in the corner,[1] the hands of which, it seemed to me, never would reach the point at which I wished to see them. . . . . . It wanted yet an hour or more of that moment, when his head turning toward me he whispered inquiringly, " This is the Fourth ?" Alas ! not yet. But I could not bear to say so, and took no notice of the inquiry. " This is the Fourth ?" he repeated. Thus pressed, repugnant as it was to me to deceive him, I nodded assent. " Ah," he murmured, as an expression came over his countenance, which said, " just as I wished."

When the dying man rose in his couch and imagined himself dispatching messages to the Revolutionary Committee of Safety, Mr. Trist remarks that he " used his hands as if writing on a tablet held in the left," and that his words were : " Warn the Committee to be on the alert."

A letter from Mr. Trist to the husband of another of Mr. Jefferson's grand-daughters, dated, " His bedside, July 4th, 1826, 9.15, A.M.," lies before us. Written from the room of death, it possesses interest, though it but repeats what has been already recorded :

> " There is no longer any doubt, unless one chance to a hundred thousand, or a million, may be ground for doubt. He has been dying since yesterday morning ; and until twelve o'clock last night, we were in momentary fear that he would not live, as he desired, to see his own glorious Fourth. It has come at last ; and he is still alive, if we can apply the word to one who is all but dead. He has been to the last, the same calm, clear-minded, amiable philosopher.
>
> From the first, he considered his case desperate : he knew the truth that the machine was worn out in some of its essential parts, and therefore could not go on. Yet, for the satisfaction of his family, he determined from the beginning to do everything and anything the Doctor recommended. This determination he adhered to with his wonted inflexibility."

>   *   *   *   *   *   · *   *   *   *

> " He has not aroused from his lethargy now for several hours : his pulse is barely perceptible to the nicest touch ; and his extremities have the clamminess of death. You will be too late ; yet I hope you'll be on your way before this reaches B———."

---

[1] This, an astronomical clock, was purchased at the sale of Mr. Jefferson's effects, by his family, for the purpose of presenting it to Dr. Dunglison ; and it is now in the possession of the latter gentleman.

he presence of E—— and C—— is of *inexpressible* importance to mother. I need
ot say more, nor attempt to depict her situation. They (mother and the girls) are
illy aware of his condition, and have been told to consider him as already gone.

Yours affectionately,

P.S.—Thus far (three quarters past eleven, A. M.) he has suffered no pain from
eginning to end.

In the parting interview with the female members of his
amily, Mr. Jefferson, besides general admonitions (the tenor of
rhich coresponded with those contained in his letter to Thomas
efferson Smith '), addressed them affectionate words of encou-
agement and practical advice, adapted to their several situa-
ions.   In this he did not even pass over a young great-grand-
hild (Ellen Bankhead), but exhorted her to diligently persevere
a her studies, "for they would help make life valuable to her."
Ie gently but audibly murmured : " Lord, now lettest thou thy
ervant depart in peace." '

We will now take up Dr. Dunglison's Memoranda, at the
oint where we left them.   Perhaps we should first, in justice to
his faithful family physician, mention the fact that Mr. Jeffer-
on was importuned by a Philadelphia friend who called on him,
nd who was alarmed at his condition, to send for the celebrated
)r. Physic of that city.   His reply was, " I have got a Dr.
?hysic of my own—I have entire confidence in Dr. Dunglison."
No other physician was called in.

DR. DUNGLISON'S MEMORANDA, RESUMED.

" In the spring of 1826 the health of Mr. Jefferson became more impaired ; his
nutrition fell off and at the approach of summer he was troubled with diarrhœa, to
rhich he had been liable for some years—ever since, as he believed, he had
esorted to the Virginia Springs, especially the White Sulphur, and had freely used
he waters externally for an eruption . . . which did not yield readily to the
rdinary remedies.   I had prescribed for this affection early in June, and he had
mproved somewhat ; but on the 24th of that month, he wrote me the last note I
eceived from him, begging me to visit him, as he was not so well.   This note was
erhaps the last he penned.   On the same day, however, he wrote an excellent let-
er to General Weightman, in reply to an invitation to celebrate, in Washington,
he fiftieth anniversary of the Declaration of Independence, which he declined on
he ground of indisposition.   This, Professor Tucker says was probably his last let-
er.   It had all the striking characteristics of his vigorous and unfaded intellect.

' See ante, p. 524.
' Some describer of Mr. Jefferson's death (we think Mr. Wirt) erroneously mentions
:hat he uttered this prayer of Simeon in Latin.

"The tone of the note I received from him satisfied me of the propriety of visiting him immediately, and having mentioned the circumstance to Mr. Tucker, he proposed to accompany me. I immediately saw that the affection was making a decided impression upon his bodily powers; and, as Mr. Tucker has properly remarked in his life of this distinguished individual, was apprehensive that the attack would prove fatal. Nor did Mr. Jefferson himself indulge any other opinion. From this time his strength gradually diminished and he had to remain in bed. The evacuations became less numerous, but it was manifest that his powers were failing.

     *   *   *   *   *   *   *

"Until the 2d and 3d of July, he spoke freely of his approaching death; made all his arrangments with his grandson, Mr. Randolph, in regard to his private affairs; and expressed his anxiety for the prosperity of the University and his confidence in the exertion in its behalf of Mr. Madison and the other Visitors. He repeatedly, too, mentioned his obligation to me for my attention to him. During the last week of his existence I remained at Monticello; and one of the last remarks he made was to me. In the course of the day and night of the 2d of July, he was affected with stupor, with intervals of wakefulness and consciousness; but on the 3d, the stupor became almost permanent. About seven o'clock of the evening of that day, he awoke, and seeing me staying at his bedside exclaimed, 'Ah! Doctor, are you still there?' in a voice, however, that was husky and indistinct. He then asked, 'Is it the Fourth?' to which I replied, 'It soon will be.'[1] These were the last words I heard him utter.   *   *   . *   *   *   *

"Until towards the middle of the day—the 4th,—he remained in the same state, or nearly so; wholly unconscious to everything that was passing around him. His circulation was gradually, however, becoming more languid; and for some hours prior to dissolution, the pulse at the wrist was imperceptible. About one o'clock he ceased to exist.

"The opportunities I had of witnessing the private life of Mr. Jefferson were numerous. It was impossible for any one to be more amiable in his domestic relations; it was delightful to observe the devoted and respectful attention that was paid him by all the family. In the neighborhood too he was greatly revered.[2] Perhaps, however, according to the all-wise remark, that no one is a prophet in his own country, he had more personal detractors there partly owing to difference in political sentiments which are apt to engender so much unworthy acrimony of feeling, but still more, perhaps, owing to the views which he was supposed to possess on the subject of religion; yet it was well known that he did not withhold his aid when a church had to be established in the neighborhood, and that he subscribed largely to the Episcopal church erected in Charlottesville. After his death much sectarian intolerance was exhibited owing to the publication of certain of his letters, in which he animadverted on the Presbyterians more especially; yet there could not have been a more unfounded assertion than that of a Philadelphia Episcopal divine,[3] . . . that Mr. Jefferson's memory was detested in Charlottesville and the vicinity. It is due,

---

[1] Dr. Dunglison, like Mr. Trist, understood this to be a *question*, and it will be observed they vary as to who answered it. We should remark that the three accounts of the eye and ear witnesses we draw from, were written years apart, and without either having seen the statements of the other.

[2] For a letter of Dr. Dunglison, more fully describing his impressions of Mr. Jefferson's character, see APPENDIX, No. 35.

[3] The reader is requested to suspend his judgment on the divine for further developments

also, to that illustrious individual to say, that in all my intercourse with him I never heard an observation that savored, in the slightest degree, of impiety. His religious belief harmonized more closely with that of the Unitarians than of any other denomination, but it was liberal and untrammelled by sectarian feelings and prejudices. It is not easy to find more sound advice, more appropriately expressed, than in the letter which he wrote to Thomas Jefferson Smith, dated February 21st, 1825. . .

"On the last day of the fatal illness of his grand-daughter who had married Mr. Bankhead . . . Mr. Jefferson was present in the adjoining apartment, and when the announcement was made by me, that but little hope remained, that she was, indeed, past hope, it is impossible to imagine more poignant distress than was exhibited by him. He shed tears; and abandoned himself to every evidence of intense grief.

"It was beautiful, too, to witness the deference that was paid by Mr. Jefferson and Mr. Madison to each other's opinions. When as Secretary, and as Chairman of the Faculty, I had to consult one of them, it was a common interrogatory, What did the other say of the matter? If possible, Mr. Madison gave indications of a greater intensity of this feeling, and seemed to think that everything emanating from his ancient associate must be correct. In a letter which Mr. Jefferson wrote to Mr. Madison a few months only before he died (February 17th, 1826) he thus charmingly expresses himself. [Here follows the conclusion of the letter given at p. 582, commencing at the words, "The friendship which has subsisted between us," etc.]

"It is somewhat singular, however, that about the very time this letter must have been penned, Mr. Jefferson should have declared at table in my presence, that he had no desire for posthumous reputation, nor could he well understand how any one could be anxious for it. I was surprised at the time to hear the sentiment expressed. The prospect of future rewards and punishments is confessedly one of the greatest incentives to correctness of conduct, and the transmitting of a good name to posterity must enter largely into the consideration of the good as one of those future rewards, and such could scarcely fail to have been the feeling of Mr. Jefferson when he asked Mr. Madison to take care of him when dead. Some paradox may have been involved in the remark which it is not easy to unravel.[1]

When Jefferson asked Madison to "take care of him when dead" the context shows that he was speaking of a vindication, which he supposed the former was preparing, of the aims and

---

[1] Mr. Jefferson's declaration on this occasion of his comparative estimate of posthumous reputation is distinctly corroborated in a letter to Madison, quoted in Vol. 2. p. 257, of this work; and we do not remember a conflicting assertion or hint in all his writings.

His thirst for contemporaneous reputation has been thought uncommonly strong, on account of a class of remarks which are to be found in his correspondence. He attached a very high value to the *approbation*, the *esteem*, and the *love* of his countrymen, and especially of his neighbors. This would be a natural, if not an inevitable result of his estimate of mankind—of the spirit of all of his political theories. But that he had any craving desire for contemporaneous glory or renown—any stronger feeling in that direction than such men as Washington, Franklin, or Samuel Adams—is not in our judgment deducible either from his writings or the tenor of his life. No democratic statesman ever escapes such imputations if he practises on his own theories—but those readiest to bring the charge, those who affect such a contempt for mankind, are generally found, in practice, quite as anxious to secure the world's plaudits and honors.

course of the early Republican party—of the "system of administration" pursued by the Presidents who belonged to that
party.   He uniformly expressed the belief that these had been
grossly misrepresented by the prominent historical writers who
had thus far appeared.   He had prepared some testimony on the
subject himself;[1] and he expected Madison would combine *all*
the proofs into a full vindication.   It was his *cause* which he
wished "taken care of," and himself only as a part of, or an instrument in, that cause.   Mr. Madison understood the request as
here explained.   How little he supposed Mr. Jefferson stood in
need either of public panegyric or defence will appear from the
following letter :

MR. MADISON TO N. P. TRIST.

MONTPELLIER, *July* 6, 1826.

DEAR SIR:

I have just received yours of the 4th. A few lines from Dr. Dunglison had prepared me for such a communication ; and I never doubted that the last scene of our
illustrious friend would be worthy of the life which it closed. Long as this has
been spared to his country and to those who loved him, a few years more were to
have been desired for the sake of both. But we are more than consoled for the
loss by the gain to him, and by the assurance that he lives and will live in the memory and gratitude of the wise and good, as a luminary of science, as a votary of
liberty, as a model of patriotism, and as a benefactor of the human kind. In these
characters I have known him, and not less in the virtues and charms of social life,
for a period of fifty years, during which there was not an interruption or diminution of
mutual confidence and cordial friendship, for a single moment, in a single instance.
What I feel, therefore now, need not, I should say, cannot be expressed. If there be
any possible way in which I can *usefully* give evidence of it, do not fail to afford me
the opportunity.[2] I indulge a hope that the unforeseen event will not be permitted
to impair *any* of the beneficial measures which were in progress, or in prospect. It cannot be unknown that the anxieties of the deceased were for others, not for himself.

Accept, my dear sir, my best wishes for yourself and for all with whom we sympathize : in which Mrs. Madison most sincerely joins.

JAMES MADISON.

Letters of the tenor of the preceding poured in upon Mr.
Jefferson's family from all quarters.   We shall present extracts
from but one other, and that only out of justice to the writer.
It was addressed to Mr. Trist, July 12, by Hon. Dabney

---

[1] In his Ana.
[2] Mr. Madison was understood to mean this for a delicately worded offer to contribute
his aid and influence to further any present or contemplated measure for the relief of
Jefferson's estate.

Carr, one of the Judges of the Court of Appeals of Virginia. The original is before us, and it appears to be tear-stained:

"The loss of Mr. Jefferson [writes Judge Carr] is one over which the whole world will mourn. He was one of those ornaments and benefactors of the human race, whose death forms an epoch, and creates a sensation throughout the whole circle of civilized man. But that feeling is nothing to what those feel who are connected with him by blood, and bound to him by gratitude for a thousand favors. To me he has been more than a father, and I have ever loved and reverenced him with my whole heart. . . . . Taken as a whole, history presents nothing so grand, so beautiful, so peculiarly felicitous in all the great points, as the life and character of Thomas Jefferson." [1]

These expressions were not confined to private sources. The death of Jefferson and Adams under ordinary circumstances, would have attracted much notice. They were the last of the Presidents who had been prime actors in the Revolution—the only ones who had signed the Declaration of Independence. Jefferson had always been an unbounded favorite with a vast majority of his countrymen. John Adams was again beginning to be properly understood. His great earlier services were remembered, and his death extinguished the smouldering fires of partisan prejudice. When it became known that they had both died on the same day, and that day the *fiftieth* anniversary of the Declaration of Independence, it fell on the public ear as something Providential and awful. It seemed as if Heaven itself had interfered to specially honor the exit of these aged and illustrious patriots.

The voice of sorrow, but of triumphal sorrow, broke forth over the land. Newspapers everywhere exhibited the marks of national mourning. Public edifices were draped with the badges of death. Every American vessel wore her flag at half mast. Minute guns were fired from our ships of war and fortresses. There were, perhaps, no cities and few villages of any considerable size which did not exhibit some public ceremonials in honor of the dead. A great number of funeral orations were

---

[1] The writer, Judge Carr, was the son of Mr. Jefferson's early friend of the same name, and of Mr. Jefferson's sister Martha. It was this widowed sister and her *children* that Mr. Jefferson was accused of defrauding out of their property, by "the Rev. Cotton Mather Smith of Shena," and others. The Rev. Mr. Smith declared the charge "could be proven." We have already said that any of the Carrs would have laid down their lives for their generous uncle. We have thought it proper to let one of the family speak for himself over the grave of his benefactor

pronounced before vast audiences by individuals who were chosen by their fellow-citizens to perform that honorable duty. The best talents of the nation, irrespective of creed or party, were devoted to this labor of love.[1]

---

[1] An octavo volume of selections from these orations has been published. The authors quoted are we believe the following and in the following order: "Tyler, Cushing, Cambreling, Samuel Smith, Sheldon Smith, Sergeant, Duer, P. Sprague, Shaw, Knapp, Webster, J. Sprague, Turner, Grundy, Johnson, Thornton, Wilkins, and Wirt." This list omits Everett, Biddle, and many others.

CHAPTER XIV.

1826—1848.

MR. JEFFERSON was a public professor of his belief in the Christian religion. In all his most important early State papers, such as his Summary View of the Rights of British America, his portion of the Declaration made by Congress on the Causes of taking up Arms, the Declaration of Independence, the draft of a Constitution for Virginia, etc., there are more or less pointed recognitions of God and Providence. In his two Inaugural Addresses as President of the United States, and in many of his annual messages he makes the same recognitions—clothes them on several occasions in the most explicit language—substantially avows the God of his faith to be the God of revelation—declares his belief in the efficacy of prayer, and the duty of ascriptions of praise to the Author of all mercies—and speaks of the Chris tian religion as professed in his country as a benign religion, evincing the favor of Heaven.[1]

Had his wishes been consulted, the symbol borne on our national seal would have contained our public profession of Christianity as a nation.[2]

There is nothing in his writings or in the history of his life to show that his public declarations were insincere, or thrown out for mere effect.[3] On the contrary, his most confidential writings sustain his public professions, and advance beyond them into the avowal of a belief in a future state of rewards and punishments.[4]

[1] The following passages are from his first Inaugural Address: . . . "enlightened by a benign religion, professed, indeed, and practised in various form, yet all of them including honesty, truth, temperance, gratitude, and the love of man; acknowledging and adoring an overruling Providence, which by all its dispensations proves that it delights in the happiness of man here and his greater happiness hereafter: with all these blessings, what more is necessary to make us a happy and prosperous people? . . . And may that Infinite Power which rules the destinies of the universe lead our counsels to what is best, and give them a favorable issue for your peace and prosperity."
From his first Annual Message, December 8th, 1801:
"While we devoutly return thanks to the beneficent Being who has been pleased to breathe into them the spirit of conciliation and forgiveness, we are bound with peculiar gratitude to be thankful to him that our own peace has been preserved through so perilous a season, and ourselves permitted quietly to cultivate the earth, and to practise and improve those arts which tend to increase our comforts."
From his second Annual Message, December 15th, 1802:
"When we assemble together, fellow citizens, to consider the state of our beloved country, our just attentions are first drawn to those pleasing circumstances which mark the goodness of that Being from whose favor they flow, and the large measure of thankfulness we owe for his bounty. Another year has come around, and finds us still blessed with peace and friendship abroad; law, order, and religion, at home."
From his third Annual Message, October 17th, 1803:
"While we regret the miseries in which we see others involved, let us bow with gratitude to that kind Providence which, inspiring with wisdom and moderation our late legislative counsels while placed under the urgency of the greatest wrongs, guarded us from hastily entering into the sanguinary contest, and left us only to look on and to pity its ravages."
In his fourth Annual Message, (November 8th, 1804) transmitted to Congress near the time of the Presidential election—and while the Federalists were denouncing Mr. Jefferson as an atheist, a foe to the Christian religion, etc., we think no reference occurs to God or Christianity.
In his second inaugural address, March 4th, 1805, he said:
"I shall need, too, the favor of that Being in whose hands we are, who led our forefathers, as Israel of old, from their native land, and planted them in a country flowing with all the necessaries and comforts of life; who has covered our infancy with his providence, and our riper years with his wisdom and power; and to whose goodness I ask you to join with me in supplications, that he will so enlighten the minds of your servants, guide their councils, and prosper their measures, that whatsoever they do, shall result in your good, and shall secure you the peace, friendship and approbation of all nations."
It cannot be necessary to follow these quotations further.
[2] See vol. 1, p. 192.
[3] We find him once, like John Adams and Hamilton, advocating a *fast* day for popular effect—he in the Revolution, they in later partisan conflicts. This is all;—nor does it in any way conflict with the declaration in the text.
[4] This is implied in his letter to Dr. Benjamin Waterhouse, June 26th, 1822. And if the inference needed any support it will be found in the fact that while he repeatedly dissents from doctrines imputed to Christ, he nowhere in his writings dissents from this one, which he enumerates as a cardinal doctrine of the Saviour and as "tending to the happiness of man." The letter to Waterhouse will be found in Randolph's edition of his Works, vol. iv. p. 349; in the Congress edition, vol. vii. p. 252.

He contributed freely to the erection of Christian churches, gave money to Bible societies and other religious objects, and was a liberal and regular contributor to the support of the clergy. Letters of his are extant which show him urging, with respectful delicacy, the acceptance of extra and unsolicited contributions, on the pastor of his parish, on occasions of extra expense to the latter, such as the building of a house, the meeting of an ecclesiastical convention at Charlottesville, etc. In these letters he assumes that he is only performing a duty, and pleasantly compares it to the discharge of a special service, by a feudal inferior to his liege lord, on those extraordinary occasions when it was required by the feudal law.

He attended church with as much regularity as most of the members of the congregation—sometimes going alone on horseback, when his family remained at home. He generally attended the Episcopal Church, and when he did so, always carried his prayer-book,[1] and joined in the responses and prayers of the congregation. He was baptized into the Episcopal Church in his infancy; he was married by one of its clergymen; his wife lived and died a member of it; his children were baptized into it, and when married were married according to its rites; its burial services were read over those of them who preceded him to the grave, over his wife, and finally over himself.

No person ever heard him utter a word of profanity, and those who met him most familiarly through periods of acquaintance extending from two or three to twenty or thirty years, declare that they never heard a word of impiety, or any scoff at religion, from his lips. Among his numerous familiar acquaintances, we have not found one whose testimony is different—or who entertained any doubts of the strict justice, sincerity, truthfulness, and exemplariness of his personal character.

A letter from Mr. Jefferson to his oldest daughter, has been given in these pages,[2] in which occurred the following passage:

"A promise made to a friend some years ago, but executed only lately, has placed my religious creed on paper. I have thought it just that my family by possessing this, should be able to estimate the libels published against me on this, as on

[1] The well worn copy he carried in his pocket when he rode to church is in the possession of his youngest grandson—the 15th Psalm copied on a blank leaf in his own hand, in a different version from the one we have seen him usually quoting.

[2] See ante, p. 45.

every other possible subject. I have written to Philadelphia for Dr. Priestley's History of the Corruptions of Christianity, which I will send you, and recommend to an attentive perusal, because it establishes the ground-work of my view of this subject."

The "religious creed on paper" here mentioned was the "Syllabus" etc., appended to the following letter to Doctor Rush:

TO DOCTOR BENJAMIN RUSH.

WASHINGTON, *April* 21, 1803.

DEAR SIR:

In some of the delightful conversations with you, in the evenings of 1798-99, and which served as an anodyne to the afflictions of the crisis through which our country was then laboring, the Christian religion was sometimes our topic; and I then promised you, that one day or other, I would give you my views of it. They are the result of a life of inquiry and reflection, and very different from that anti-Christian system imputed to me by those who know nothing of my opinions. To the corruptions of Christianity I am indeed opposed; but not to the genuine precepts of Jesus himself. I am a Christian, in the only sense in which he wished any one to be; sincerely attached to his doctrines, in preference to all others; ascribing to himself every *human* excellence; and believing he never claimed any other. At the short intervals since these conversations, when I could justifiably abstract my mind from public affairs, the subject has been under my contemplation. But the more I considered it, the more it expanded beyond the measure of either my time or information. In the moment of my late departure from Monticello, I received from Doctor Priestley, his little treatise of "Socrates and Jesus compared." This being a section of the general view I had taken of the field, it became a subject of reflection while on the road, and unoccupied otherwise. The result was, to arrange in my mind a syllabus, or outline of such an estimate of the comparative merits of Christianity, as I wished to see executed by some one of more leisure and information for the task, than myself. This I now send you, as the only discharge of my promise I can probably ever execute. And in confiding it to you, I know it will not be exposed to the malignant perversions of those who make every word from me a text for new misrepresentations and calumnies. I am moreover averse to the communication of my religious tenets to the public; because it would countenance the presumption of those who have endeavored to draw them before that tribunal, and to seduce public opinion to erect itself into that inquisition over the rights of conscience, which the laws have so justly proscribed. It behooves every man who values liberty of conscience for himself, to resist invasions of it in the case of others; or their case may, by change of circumstances, become his own. It behooves him, too, in his own case, to give no example of concession, betraying the common right of independent opinion, by answering questions of faith, which the laws have left between God and himself. Accept my affectionate salutations.

Syllabus of an Estimate of the Merit of the Doctrines of Jesus, compared with those of others.

In a comparative view of the Ethics of the enlightened nations of antiquity, of the Jews and of Jesus, no notice should be taken of the corruptions of reason among the ancients, to wit, the idolatry and superstition of the vulgar, nor of the corruptions of Christianity by the learned among its professors.

Let a just view be taken of the moral principles inculcated by the most esteemed of the sects of ancient philosophy, or of their individuals; particularly Pythagoras, Socrates, Epicurus, Cicero, Epictetus, Seneca, Antoninus.

I. Philosophers. 1. Their precepts related chiefly to ourselves, and the government of those passions which, unrestrained, would disturb our tranquillity of mind.[1] In this branch of philosophy they were really great.

2. In developing our duties to others, they were short and defective. They embraced, indeed, the circles of kindred and friends, and inculcated patriotism, or the love of our country in the aggregate, as a primary obligation: towards our neighbors and countrymen they taught justice, but scarcely viewed them as within the circle of benevolence. Still less have they inculcated peace, charity, and love to our fellow-men, or embraced with benevolence the whole family of mankind.

II. Jews. 1. Their system was Deism; that is, the belief in one only God. But their ideas of him and of his attributes were degrading and injurious.

2. Their Ethics were not only imperfect, but often irreconcilable with the sound dictates of reason and morality, as they respect intercourse with those around us; and repulsive and anti-social, as respecting other nations. They needed reformation, therefore, in an eminent degree.

III. Jesus. In this state of things among the Jews, Jesus appeared. His parentage was obscure; his condition poor; his education null; his natural endowments great; his life correct and innocent: he was meek, benevolent, patient, firm, disinterested, and of the sublimest eloquence.

The disadvantages under which his doctrines appear are remarkable.

1. Like Socrates and Epictetus, he wrote nothing himself.

2. But he had not, like them, a Xenophon or an Arrian to write for him. I name not Plato, who only used the name of Socrates to cover the whimsies of his own brain. On the contrary, all the learned of his country, entrenched in its power and riches, were opposed to him, lest his labors should undermine their advantages; and the committing to writing of his life and doctrines fell on unlettered and ignorant men; who wrote, too, from memory, and not till long after the transactions had passed.

3. According to the ordinary fate of those who attempt to enlighten and reform mankind, he fell an early victim to the jealousy and combination of the altar and the throne, at about thirty-three years of age, his reason having not yet attained the *maximum* of its energy, nor the course of his preaching, which was but of three years at most, presented occasions for developing a complete system of morals.

4. Hence the doctrines which he really delivered were defective as a whole, and fragments only of what he did deliver have come to us mutilated, misstated, and often unintelligible.

5. They have been still more disfigured by the corruptions of schismatizing fol

---

[1] To explain, I will exhibit the heads of Seneca's and Cicero's philosophical works, the most extensive of any we have received from the ancients. Of ten heads in Seneca, seven relate to ourselves, viz. *de irâ consolatio, de tranquillitate, de constantiâ sapientis, de otio sapientis, de vitâ beatâ, de brevitate vitæ;* two relate to others, *de clementia, de beneficiis;* and one relates to the government of the world, *de providentiâ.* Of eleven tracts of Cicero, five respect ourselves, viz. *de finibus, Tusculana, academica, paradoxa, de senectute:* one, *de officiis,* relates partly to ourselves, partly to others: one, *de amicitiâ,* relates to others: and four are on different subjects, to wit, *de naturâ deorum, de divinatione, de fato,* and *somnium Scipionis.*

lowers, who have found an interest in sophisticating and perverting the simple doctrines he taught, by engrafting on them the mysticisms of a Grecian sophist, frittering them into subtleties, and obscuring them with jargon, until they have caused good men to reject the whole in disgust, and to view Jesus himself as an impostor.

Notwithstanding these disadvantages, a system of morals is presented to us, which, if filled up in the style and spirit of the rich fragments he left us, would be the most perfect and sublime that has ever been taught by man.

The question of his being a member of the Godhead, or in direct communication with it, claimed for him by some of his followers, and denied by others, is foreign to the present view, which is merely an estimate of the intrinsic merits of his doctrines.

1. He corrected the Deism of the Jews, confirming them in their belief of one only God, and giving them juster notions of his attributes and government.

2. His moral doctrines, relating to kindred and friends, were more pure and perfect than those of the most correct of the philosophers, and greatly more so than those of the Jews; and they went far beyond both in inculcating universal philanthropy not only to kindred and friends, to neighbors and countrymen, but to all mankind, gathering all into one family, under the bonds of love, charity, peace, common wants and common aids. A development of this head will evince the peculiar superiority of the system of Jesus over all others.

3. The precepts of philosophy, and of the Hebrew code, laid hold of actions only. He pushed his scrutinies into the heart of man; erected his tribunal in the region of his thoughts, and purified the waters at the fountain head.

4. He taught, emphatically, the doctrines of a future state, which was either doubted, or disbelieved by the Jews; and wielded it with efficacy, as an important incentive, supplementary to the other motives to moral conduct.

Jefferson did not assent to all of Priestley's leading views. He wrote to John Adams, August 22d, 1813:

"You are right in supposing, in one of yours, that I had not read much of Priestley's Predestination, his no-soul system, or his controversy with Horsley. But I have read his Corruptions of Christianity, and Early Opinions of Jesus, over and over again; and I rest on them, and on Middleton's writings, especially his letters from Rome, and to Waterland, as the basis of my own faith. These writings have never been answered, nor can be answered, by quoting historical proofs, as they have done. For these facts, therefore, I cling to their learning, so much superior to my own."

And to the same, January 24th, 1814:

"I think with you that Priestley, in his comparison of the doctrines of philosophy and revelation, did not do justice to the undertaking. But he felt himself pressed by the hand of death."

He wrote the Rev. Mr. Whittemore, June 5th, 1822, that he had "never permitted himself to meditate a specified creed"— that those "formulas had been the bane and ruin of the Christian

Church ;" but to Dr. Waterhouse, to the Rev. Dr. Sparks, and other Unitarians, he signified a sufficient general concurrence in what he understood to be their system of faith, to feel no antagonism to it ; and, on the contrary, a wish to see it spread over the land.[1]

Mr. Jefferson never *published*, nor wrote with a view to publication, any attack on the religious faith, or on the character of any sect.

In his correspondence, published after his death, there are letters on religious topics which may be classed under three general heads. The first were in answer to inquiries concerning his religious opinions, or to arguments or publications against his supposed opinions, sent to him by religious people. His replies were always, in substance, that he sought to know no other person's creed—that he preferred to confine his own to his own bosom—that he supposed there were different roads to the same good end—that he accounted that religion good which produced good fruits, etc.

The second class of his answers were to Unitarians. To these, as already said, while rejecting any " specified creed," he sometimes expressed a general concurrence in their views. But when his permission was asked to publish any of these replies, he uniformly refused it.

The third class were directed to a very limited number of peculiarly intimate friends—men of mature years and ripened opinions—men invariably, whose views were as wide from the prevailing standards as his own—men fond of this kind of disquisition, and who it is believed in every instance had invited it with him. These individuals were Dr. Rush, John Adams, and William Short; and perhaps Dr. Cooper and one or two other persons are, to some extent, to be included in the number. To these individuals he wrote with the freedom of thought and strength of language habitual to him in confidential epistolary communication. Thus as an anti-Calvinist he spoke of Calvin and his doctrines—as a Unitarian, of the doctrine of the Trinity, as a Humanitarian, of the mission of Christ, etc. etc., in terms which now strike painfully on the ears of those whose views are opposed to his own. His speculations on various subjects take a bold range in thought and language. His denunciations of particular sects, and of the clergy, are severe, and in

[1] See letters to Waterhouse, June 26th, and July 19th, 1822.

various instances unquestionably unmerited. Much of all of this, had it been published by him, would have been inexcusably aggressive on the beliefs and feelings of others.

Mr. Jefferson was neither a proselyter nor a system-founder in theology, and consequently having given a pretty full outline of his beliefs (far fuller than would have been given but for special circumstances already named), we regard it as no part of our duty to attempt to follow him through the whole range of his particular opinions and speculations ; and still less do we propose to cull out and array for connected perusal every word that would be offensive to persons of a different belief.

Every one, of course, is entitled to form his own opinions as to the truth or error of Mr. Jefferson's views, but in taking his *language* as a criterion of his feelings and even of his ideas, justice demands that a few considerations be kept distinctly in view. First, his habitual freedom and strength of expression. Second, that his language was confidential. Third, that the controversial language of any period can only be fairly judged by the customs and the spirit of that period.[1] Fourth, that his remarks were not addressed to opponents whose feelings they would injure, to the young or the unsettled whose sentiments they could influence, or to any person whatever with a view of propagandism. Fifth, that he had received peculiar provocations to anger, prejudice, and acerbity of tone, by attacks on his public and private character from the clergy of particular denominations.[2]

Mr. Jefferson declared[3] that "he never attempted to make a convert, nor wished to change another's creed." His oldest grandson writes us :

[1] No man, for example, would now think of culling out all the harsh and disrespectful expressions used towards opposing sects, or opinions, by Calvin, Luther, and Knox, judging these by the standards of the present day, and then presenting them as fair expositions of the characters, feelings, and beliefs of the men. No one need to be told that it is but yesterday, as it were, since sects which now freely concede each other's orthodoxy, and which work harmoniously together in the Christian field, imprisoned, exiled, and put to death each other's members, and shook kingdoms with their religious wars. In this they represented the civilization of their day and generation. In religion as in politics, the opening of the present century had not witnessed any general advent of toleration in feeling, or respectfulness of language in controversy. Priestley, though his character was defended by such men as Dr. Parr, Robert Hall, and Lord Brougham, was persecuted, mobbed, and driven out of England. A wide-spread and bitter contest between the Congregationalists and Unitarians was going on in our country among the descendants of the crew of the Mayflower, and in sight of "Pilgrim Rock." The denunciations, the insinuations, the ridicule, etc., freely thrown out, are in the recollections of all aged men who lived within the theatre of the dispute. Nay, it would be difficult to find an aged man who had not heard nearly as severe language employed by disputants whose theological differences were infinitely smaller than those which exist between the Trinitarian and the Unitarian.

[2] See vol. i. p. 491, *et seq.* ; and vol. ii. p. 567, 568 ; and Appendix No. 18.

[3] See letter to Mrs. M. Harrison Smith, August 5th, 1816.

"Of his peculiar religious opinions his family know no more than the world. If asked by one of them his opinion on any religious subject, his uniform reply was that it was a subject each was bound to study assiduously for himself, unbiased by the opinions of others; it was a matter solely of conscience; after thorough investigation they were responsible for the righteousness, but not the rightfulness of their opinions; that the expression of his opinion might influence theirs, and he would not give it." [1]

All of Mr. Jefferson's grandchildren concur in this statement. One of them informs us that on asking him his reasons for withholding his religious views, he answered: "If I inform you of mine, they will influence yours—I will not take the responsibility of directing any one's judgment on this subject."

The paper which he gave his oldest daughter in 1803 to enable his family "to estimate the libels published against him," on the subject of religion, was intended for the eye of those who were, at the time, small children. It was seen by none of his grandchildren during his life; and he survived for twenty-three years. During that period not a view contained in it was pressed upon one of them—indeed they remained in ignorance that most of the views it contained were his.[2] They were aware that towards the close of his life he occasionally cut short all further inquiries or remarks tending towards discussion on the subject of religion from some of his old friends, by saying that he was a Unitarian—and that was about all they knew of any peculiar *doctrine* entertained by him. They heard him habitually speak reverently of God, the Saviour, and the great truths of Christianity.

It remains to us to state the closing up of Mr. Jefferson's pecuniary affairs. The plan of paying his debts by a subscription very naturally dropped at his death. The amount of money which had been already contributed in this way was greatly overestimated by the public. And it is probable that most persons thought his heirs could still successfully resort to the lottery if it should become necessary. Mr. Jefferson's executor attempted to dispose of the lottery scheme, but the feelings which

[1] The entire letter containing this, and many other passages previously quoted, will be found in APPENDIX, No. 36.
[2] After Dr. Rush's death, Mr. Jefferson wrote to Dr. Rush's family requesting the return of the Syllabus, etc., a request which was at once complied with. He never showed it to more than two or three other persons, two of whom were John Adams and William Short.

at first would have made it salable had now died away. The thing had become a mere matter of business; and as a matter of business, an investment was more desirable . in a lottery where the prizes were payable in money. Friends were willing to purchase tickets; but it was found that without taxing them too severely, a sufficient number would not be disposed of.

The executor took the only course that was left to him. The greater portion of the personal property was sold in January 1827, at a very great sacrifice; and the remainder in 1828. Owing to the depression of real estate in the market, the lands were not sold until 1829—and the sacrifice on these was still more severe. For example, a farm sold for six dollars an acre that in 1856 was readily marketable at forty dollars an acre. Another sold for ten dollars an acre which was bought back by the husband of one of Mr. Jefferson's descendants, in 1855, at forty dollars an acre. Bedford lands sold at from three to nine dollars an acre, which were subsequently worth from twenty to thirty; and the falling off was nearly as great compared with previous prices at various periods.

The proceeds of the sales did not fully meet the debts—but the executor paid all the remaining ones, besides making the manumissions[1] and carrying out the minor bequests of the will.

When some general knowledge of these facts became public —when it became known that Monticello had gone, or must go out of the hands of Mr. Jefferson's family, and that his only child was left without any independent provision, another exhibition of public feeling took place. The Legislatures of South Carolina and Louisiana promptly voted her $10,000 each—and the stocks they created for the purpose, sold for $21,800. Other plans were started in other States, which, had they been carried out, would have embraced a liberal provision for Mr. Jefferson's descendants. But, as is usual on such occasions, the people in each locality obtained exaggerated impressions of what was doing in others, and slackened their own exertions until the feeling that prompted them died away. That feeling was not any-

---

[1] It will be seen by reference to the will, that Burwell (so often named in these pages), was among those manumitted. His half-brother Wormley, was not formally manumitted, for reasons which it is needless here to state: but his manumission, in case he should desire it, was orally recommended to Mrs. Randolph. At her request, he received his freedom.

where kept alive for a moment by solicitations from those who were interested in the result.

Mr. Jefferson left, at his decease, the following descendants: his daughter Martha, wife of Thomas Mann Randolph, and her ten children:—1. Thomas Jefferson Randolph, intermarried with Jane Nicholas, daughter of Wilson Cary Nicholas, and their six children: 2. Ellen Wayles Randolph, wife of Joseph Coolidge of Boston, and one child: 3. Virginia Jefferson Randolph, wife of Nicholas P. Trist, and one child: 4. Cornelia Jefferson Randolph: 5. Mary Jefferson Randolph: 6. James Madison Randolph: 7. Benjamin Franklin Randolph: 8. Meriwether Lewis Randolph: 9. Septimia Anne Cary Randolph: 10. George Wythe Randolph.

The only surviving issue of Mr. Jefferson's second daughter, Maria, and her husband, John Wayles Eppes, was Francis Eppes. Francis Eppes was intermarried with Mary Elizabeth Cleland Randolph, daughter of Thomas Eston Randolph, and had two children.

By a deceased granddaughter, Anne Cary Randolph, daughter of Thomas Mann and Martha (Jefferson) Randolph, and intermarried with Charles Lewis Bankhead, Mr. Jefferson had four other great-grandchildren.

Of the grandchildren surviving at his death, but two are now (1857) deceased, namely, James Madison Randolph, and Meriwether Lewis Randolph. The number of his great-grandchildren has largely increased.

It has been mentioned that after Mr. Jefferson's death, in a private drawer were found various souvenirs of his wife and deceased children. In the same receptacle were some epitaphs, and a rough pen-and-ink sketch of a monument for himself. It was to be an obelisk of granite, eight feet high, and to bear the following inscription:

HERE WAS BURIED

THOMAS JEFFERSON,

AUTHOR

OF THE DECLARATION OF

AMERICAN INDEPENDENCE,

OF

THE STATUTE OF VIRGINIA,

FOR RELIGIOUS FREEDOM, AND

FATHER OF THE UNIVERSITY

OF VIRGINIA.

The inscription for the base was:

BORN APRIL 2D,

1743, O. S.

DIED   *   *   *   *

His wishes were carried out,[1] the blank in the last line being filled with " July 4th, 1826."

Governor Thomas Mann Randolph died on the 20th day of June, 1828. At some period before, he was riding on horseback near nightfall, on a wet cold day, when he overtook an aged man thinly clad, and apparently suffering. They were remote from any dwelling. Randolph unsolicited unbuckled his cloak, threw it on the old man, and rode on. He had a number of miles to go, and the exposure proved fatal to him. The gloom and misanthropy which had clouded his later years broke away at his dying couch. He expired at peace with all the world, and invoking blessings on every member of his family.

Mrs. Randolph died on the 10th of October, 1836. Her health had not been quite as good as usual during the autumn, but its condition excited no uneasiness, and she was preparing to make a long journey to visit one of her daughters. She was subject to severe attacks of sick-headache, and was suffering from one of these without appearing unusually ill until a few moments before her death. In the efforts produced by the nausea, a small blood-vessel was ruptured in her head, and she expired almost instantly in the arms of her children.

Three years after Mr. Jefferson's death (in 1829), appeared the first edition of his writings, published by his grandson who was the legatee of the papers.[2]

In 1848, Congress appropriated twenty thousand dollars for the purchase of Mr. Jefferson's manuscripts of a public character, and six thousand for printing and publishing them " under

---

[1] His monument is in the centre of a close group of graves, which are covered with horizontal tablets of white marble, on a level with the ground. His wife lies on one side of him, his youngest daughter on the other, Mrs. Randolph at right angles at the head of these, and Governor Randolph at their feet. The grave of Dabney Carr (the elder) is a yard or two off.

[2] These reopened wounds, and furnished new grounds of attack. Nowhere was this warfare more rancorously prosecuted than by a few persons in Charlottesville. For a circumstance which this led to, and for a decisive expression of the feelings of the people of Albemarle on the subject, see APPENDIX No. 37.

the authority of the joint committee on the Library, the whole or any part thereof to be printed as the said committee might direct." The Library committee employed Professor Henry A. Washington of Virginia to edit the papers. This, which we have generally mentioned as the Congress Edition of Mr. Jefferson's Works, was published in nine volumes octavo in 1853 and 1854.

The most cursory reader of this biography cannot fail to see how much we must have been indebted for personal information and details to Mr. Jefferson's family in a great many instances where no express acknowledgments have been made. Accordingly, without suggestion from them or from any other quarter, we feel desirous to say that in no instance have that family evinced an inclination to re-open or wage any controversies through these pages. Where personal circumstances have required their explanations, their information has stopped at the boundaries of necessary defence. While we make no apology for the truth in whatever form we have presented it, we are not willing that others incur any portion of what is our own proper and sole responsibility.[1]

[1] For an important correction in regard to Patrick Henry, see APPENDIX No. 38. Should other errors of fact or omissions be discovered before the completion of the work, they will be included in same Appendix.

APPENDIX.

———◆———

Six Letters from Mr. Jefferson to his Brother-in-Law, Francis Eppes, in 1775.

PHILADELPHIA, *June 26th,* 1775.

DEAR SIR: You will before this have heard that the war is now heartily entered into, without a prospect of accommodation but through the effectual interposition of arms. General Gage has received considerable reinforcements, though not to the whole amount of what was expected. There has lately been an action at the outlet of the town of Boston. The particulars we have not yet been able to get with certainty; the event, however, was considerably in our favor as to the numbers killed. Our account says we had between 40 and 70 killed, and 140 wounded. The enemy has certainly 500 wounded and the same account supposes that number killed; but judging from the proportion of wounded and slain on our part, they should not have perhaps above two hundred killed. This happened on Saturday, and on Monday, when the express came away, the provincials had begun to make another attack. Washington set out from here on Friday last as generalissimo of all the provincial troops in North America. Ward and Lee are appointed major-generals and Gates adjutant. We are exceedingly anxious till we hear of their arrival at Boston, as it is evident to every one that the provincial encampment is the most injudicious that can possibly be conceived. For the sole purpose of covering two small towns near Boston they have encamped so near the line of the ministerial army that the sentries may converse. Gage, too, being well fortified, is in little danger of an attack from them; while their situation is such that he may attack them when he pleases, and if he is unsuccessful, they cannot pursue him a foot scarcely, on account of the ships and floating batteries bearing on the Neck of Boston. If no evil arises from this till General Washington arrives, we may expect to hear of his withdrawing the provincial troops to a greater distance. The Congress have directed 20,000 men to be raised, and hope by a vigorous campaign to dispose our enemies to treaty. Governor Carleton has been spiriting up the Canadian Indians to fall on our back settlements; but this we hope will be prevented. Governor Skeene, appointed to take charge of the fortresses on the lakes, was intercepted here, and as we had already taken possession of those fortifications and provided a governor, there was no occasion for him to proceed. He is now, therefore, our prisoner. My best affections attend Mrs. Eppes and family. I am, dear sir,

Your friend and servant,
TH. JEFFERSON.

FRANCIS EPPES, Esq.,
At the Forest, Charles City.

PHILADELPHIA, *July 4th*, 1775.

DEAR SIR: Since my last, nothing new has happened. Our accounts of the battle of Charleston have become clear, and greatly to our satisfaction. Contrary to what usually happens, the first accounts were below truth; it is now certain that the regulars have had between 1200 and 1400 killed and wounded in that engagement, and that of these 500 are killed. Major Pitcairn is among the slain, at which everybody rejoices, as he was the commanding officer at Lexington, was the first who fired his own piece there and gave the command to fire. On our part were killed between 60 and 70, and about 150 wounded. Among those killed was a Dr. Warren, a man who seems to have been immensely valued in the North. The New Englanders are fitting out light vessels of war, by which it is hoped we shall not only clear the seas and bays here of everything below the size of a ship of war, but that they will visit the coasts of Europe and distress the British trade in every part of the world. The adventurous genius and intrepidity of those people is amazing. They are now intent on burning Boston as a hive which gives cover to regulars; and none are more bent on it than the very people who come out of it and whose whole prosperity lies there. This however, if done at all, it is thought better to defer till the cold season is coming on, as it would then lay them under irremediable distress. Powder seems now to be our only difficulty, and towards getting plenty of that nothing is wanting but saltpetre. If we can weather out this campaign, I hope that we shall be able to have a plenty made for another. Nothing is requisite but to set about it, as every colony has materials, but more especially Virginia and Maryland. My compliments most affectionately to Mrs. Eppes. Mr. and Mrs. Skipwith, I expect, have left you. Adieu.

TH. JEFFERSON.

FRANCIS EPPES, Esq.,
In Charles City County, Virginia.

PHILADELPHIA, *Oct.* 10th, 1775.

DEAR SIR: I wrote to Patty [Mrs. Jefferson] on my arrival here, and there being then nothing new in the political way, I inclosed her letter under a blank cover to you. Since that we have received from England news of much importance, which coming through many channels we believe may be confidently relied on. Both the ministerial and provincial accounts of the battle of Bunker's Hill had got to England. The ministry were determined to push the war with vigor, a measure in which they were fixed by the defeat of the Spaniards by the Moors. Ninety brass cannon were embarked from the Tower, and may be hourly expected either at N. York or Boston. Two thousand troops were to sail from Ireland about the 25th Sept.; these we have reason to believe are destined for N. York. Commodore Shuldam was to sail about the same time with a great number of frigates and small vessels of war, to be distributed among the middle colonies. He comes at the express and earnest intercessions of Ld. Dunmore, and the plan is to lay waste all the plantations on our river sides. Of this we gave immediate notice to our Committee of Safety ʃ an express whom we dispatched hence last Friday, that if any defence could be ⸱ovided on the rivers by fortifications or small vessels it might be done immedi- ely. In the spring, 10,000 men more are to come over. They are to be procured ʃ taking away two-thirds of the garrison at Gibraltar (who are to be replaced by ⸱me Hessians), by 2,000 Highlanders and 5,000 Roman Catholics, whom they pro- ⸱se to raise in Ireland. Instead of the Roman Catholics, however, some of our ⸱counts say foreigners are to be sent. Their plan is this. They are to take pos- ⸱ssion of New York and Albany, keeping up a communication between them by ⸱eans of their vessels. Between Albany and St. John's, they propose also to keep ⸱pen the communication, and again between St. John's, Quebec, and Boston. By ⸱iis means they expect Gage, Tryon, and Carleton may distress us on every side, ⸱cting in concert with one another. By means of Hudson's River, they expect to ⸱ut off all correspondence between the northern and southern rivers. Gage was ⸱ppointed Governor-General of all America; but Sir Jeffery Amherst consented fterwards to come over, so that Gage is to be recalled; but it is believed Amherst ⸱ill not come till the spring; in the meantime Howe will have the command. The ⸱oöperation of the Canadians is taken for granted in all the ministerial schemes. ʃe hope, therefore, they will all be dislocated by the events in that quarter. For ⸱n account of these I must refer you to Patty. My warmest affections attend Mrs. ⸱ppes. Adieu.

TH. JEFFERSON.

ʃ⸱ FRANCIS EPPES, in Charles City County, Virginia.
  To be sent by the Williamsburgh post.

PHILADELPHIA, Oct. 24, 1775.

DEAR SIR: Since my last, we have nothing new from England or from the amps at either Cambridge or St. John's. Our eyes are turned to the latter place ⸱ith no little anxiety, the weather having been uncommonly bad for troops in that ⸱uarter, exposed to the inclemencies of the sky without any protection. Carleton ⸱ retired to Quebec, and though it does not appear he has any intimation of Arnold's ⸱xpedition, yet we hear he has embodied 1,100 men to be on his guard. A small ⸱essel was the other day cast away on the Jersey shore (she was one of the trans- ⸱orts which had some time ago brought over troops to Boston), on board of which ⸱ere a captain, with his subordinate officers and marines, amounting to 23 in all, ⸱nd also a Duncan Campbell, who was going to recruit men at New York for Gene- ⸱al Gage, he having some time before undertaken the same business in the same ⸱lace, and actually carried off 60 men. The marines and their officers were all taken ⸱mmediately, except their captain and the recruiting gentleman; these pushed off ⸱n a little boat, and coasted it to Long Island, where they got on board a sloop ⸱hich was to have sailed in an hour, when the party sent after them came upon ⸱hem. They were brought to this city this morning, the marines having been here ⸱ome time. Our good old Speaker died the night before last. For the particulars ⸱f that melancholy event I must refer you to Patty. My affections attend Mrs ⸱ppes. Adieu.

TH. JEFFERSON.

  To MR. FRANCIS EPPES,
⸱t the Forest, in Charles City County, Virginia.

PHILADELPHIA, *Nov.* 7, 1775.

DEAR SIR: We have no late intelligence here except of the surrender of Chambly, with 90 prisoners of war, 6½ tons of powder, 150 stands of arms, and some other small matters. The acquisition of this powder, we hope, has before this made us masters of St. John's, on which Montreal and the upper parts of St. Lawrence will of course be ours. The fate of Arnold's expedition we know not as yet. We have had some disagreeable accounts of internal commotions in South Carolina. I have never received the scrip of a pen from any mortal in Virginia since I left it, nor been able by any inquiries I could make to hear of my family. I had hoped that when Mrs. Byrd came I should have heard something of them; but she could tell me nothing about them. The suspense under which I am is too terrible to be endured. If anything has happened, for God's sake let me know it. My best affections to Mrs. Eppes. Adieu.

TH. JEFFERSON.

To MR. FRANCIS EPPES,
　At the Forest, Charles City.

————

PHILADELPHIA, *Nov.* 21st, 1775.

DEAR SIR: After sealing my last letter to you, we received an account of the capture of St. John's, which I wrote on the letter. What I then gave you was a true account of that matter. We consider this as having determined the fate of Canada. A committee of Congress is gone to improve circumstances, so as to bring the Canadians into our Union. We have accounts of Arnold as late as October 11. All well and in fine spirits. We cannot help hoping him in possession of Quebec, as we know Carleton to be absent in the neighborhood of Montreal. Our armed vessels to the northward have taken some of the ships coming with provisions from Ireland to Boston. By the intercepted letters we have a confirmation that they will have an army of four or five and twenty thousands there by the spring, but they will be raw-teagues. 3,000 are lately arrived there. I have written to Patty a proposition to keep yourselves at a distance from the alarms of Ld. Dunmore. To her, therefore, for want of time, I must refer you, and shall hope to meet you as proposed. I am, dear Sir, with my best affections to Mrs. Eppes,

Your friend and servant,

TH. JEFFERSON.

FRANCIS EPPES, Esq.,
　At the Forest, Charles City.

————

APPENDIX NO. II.—Vol. I., p. 190.

The Mecklenburg Declaration of Independence.

The following is a copy of this paper as it was first published in the Raleigh (N. C.) Register, April 30th, 1819. The phrases coinciding with those of the National Declaration of Independence are placed in italics:

20th *May*, 1775.

" That whosoever directly or indirectly abetted, or in any way, form, or manner, countenanced the unchartered and dangerous invasion of our rights, as claimed by is an enemy to this country, to America, and to the *inherent and* * life* of man.

the citizens of Mecklenburg county, do hereby *dissolve the political* *ties connected* us to the mother country, and hereby *absolve* ourselves *iance to the British crown*, and abjure *all political connection*, con- *ciation* with that nation, who have wantonly trampled on our rights and inhumanly shed the blood of American patriots at Lexington.

do hereby declare ourselves a *free and independent* people; *are, and* *to be*, a sovereign and self-governing association, under the control ther than that of our God, and the general government of the Congress; nance of which independence, we solemnly *pledge to each other*, our ation, *our lives, our fortunes, and our* most *sacred honor*.

we now acknowledge the existence and control of no law or legal r military, within this county, we do hereby ordain and adopt as a all, each, and every of our former laws; wherein, nevertheless, the it Britain never can be considered as holding rights, privileges, immu- ority therein.

is further decreed, that all, each, and every military officer in this eby reinstated in his former command and authority, he acting con- hese regulations. And that every member present of this delegation th be a civil officer, viz., a justice of the peace, in the character of a in, to issue process, hear, and determine all matters of controversy, aid adopted laws; and to preserve peace, union, and harmony in said) use every exertion to spread the love of country and fire of freedom merica, until a more general and organized government be established ie.

"ABRAHAM ALEXANDER, Chairman.

NITT ALEXANDER, Secretary."

iothing at all noticeable in most of these coincidences. Any man his own such collocations of words as "free and independent," "all ection," etc., in 1776, or at any time before or since, without the impu- riarism. In fact, the whole matter, *so far as Mr. Jefferson is con-* not be entitled to a moment's notice, had not a train of subsequent given a degree of factitious notoriety to his connection with it.

blication of the paper in the Raleigh Register in 1819, it was copied o the Essex Register, in Massachusetts, and John Adams inclosed a June 22d) to Mr. Jefferson, with some remarks from which we select

:

t possible that this paper should have been concealed from me to this : been communicated to me in the time of it, I know, if you do not would have been printed in every whig newspaper upon the continent. it if I had possessed it, I would have made the hall of Congress echo ith it fifteen months before your Declaration of Independence. What int, malicious, short-sighted, crapulous mass is Tom Paine's "Common nparison with this paper. Had I known it, I would have commented the day you entered Congress till the fourth of July, 1776. The

"Inherent and" were connected with the others in Mr. Jefferson's draft, but were

genuine sense of America at that moment was never so well expressed before or since."

This use of, and consequent claim of priority to, expressions in the national Declaration of Independence, and something in the *tone* of Mr. Adams's inconsistent[1] and not very delicate critique imparted, perhaps, a portion of its liveliness to the following reply from Mr. Jefferson (July 9th):

"But what has attracted my peculiar notice, is the paper from Mecklenburg county, of North Carolina, published in the Essex Register, which you were so kind as to inclose in your last, of June the 22d. And you seem to think it genuine. I believe it spurious. I deem it to be a very unjustifiable quiz, like that of the volcano, so minutely related to us as having broken out in North Carolina, some half dozen years ago, in that part of the country, and perhaps in that very county of Mecklenburg, for I do not remember its precise locality. If this paper be really taken from the Raleigh Register, as quoted, I wonder it should have escaped Ritchie, who culls what is good from every paper, as the bee from every flower; and the National Intelligencer, too, which is edited by a North Carolinian: and that the fire should blaze out all at once in Essex, one thousand miles from where the spark is said to have fallen. But if really taken from the Raleigh Register, who is the narrator, and is the name subscribed real, or is it as fictitious as the paper itself? It appeals, too, to an original book, which is burnt, to Mr. Alexander, who is dead, to a joint letter from Caswell, Hughes, and Hooper, all dead, to a copy sent to the dead Caswell, and another sent to Dr. Williamson, now probably dead, whose memory did not recollect, in the history he has written of North Carolina, this gigantic step of its county of Mecklenburg. Horry, too, is silent in his history of Marion, whose scene of action was the country bordering on Mecklenburg. Ramsay, Marshall, Jones, Girardin, Wirt, historians of the adjacent States, all silent. When Mr. Henry's resolutions, far short of independence, flew like lightning through every paper, and kindled both sides of the Atlantic, this flaming declaration of the same date, of the independence of Mecklenburg county, of North Carolina, absolving it from the British allegiance, and abjuring all political connection with that nation, although sent to Congress, too, is never heard of. It is not known even a twelvemonth after, when a similar proposition is first made in that body. Armed with this bold example, would not you have addressed our timid brethren in peals of thunder, on their tardy fears? Would not every advocate of independence have rung the glories of Mecklenburg county, in North Carolina, in the ears of the doubting Dickinson and others, who hung so heavily on us? Yet the example of independent Mecklenburgh county, in North Carolina, was never once quoted. The paper speaks, too, of the continued exertions of their delegation (Caswell, Hooper, Hughes) 'in the cause of liberty and independence.' Now you remember as well as I do, that we had not a greater tory in Congress than Hooper; that Hughes was very wavering, sometimes firm, sometimes feeble, according as the day was clear or cloudy; that Caswell, indeed, was a good whig, and kept these gentlemen to the notch, while he was present; but that he left us soon, and their line of conduct became then uncertain until Penn came, who fixed Hughes and the vote of the State. I must not be understood as suggesting any doubtfulness in the State of North Carolina. No State was more fixed or forward. Nor do I affirm, positively,

---

[1] After reading Mr. Adams's phrase about the "genuine sense of America at that moment," the reader is requested to turn to his declarations in Vol. I. pp. 123–125, *et seq.*

paper is a fabrication; because the proof of a negative can only be pre-
e. But I shall believe it such until positive and solemn proof of its authen-
) produced. And if the name of McNitt be real, and not a part of the
on, it needs a vindication by the production of such proof. For the present,
e an unbeliever in the apocryphal gospel."

e was much in the facts and arguments of this letter which could not then
ered, and which never has been shaken by testimony since discovered. But
have been more politic in its author to confine himself to a simple denial
g seen the Mecklenburg paper (if he thought that necessary), and leave
set "things even." When his communication came before the world, it
ed the genuineness of a paper which had come to be regarded with peculiar
on throughout a State. His manner of referring to the North Carolina
s in Congress was unfortunate, granting all the facts asserted by him to be
he term "Tory" applied to Hooper grated harshly on the public ear,
sed by familiar use to specially apply that designation to the American loy-
Some petty critics, too, considered or affected to consider his questioning
enticity of certain names or signatures as an impeachment of the veracity
individuals who actually bore those names or affixed those signatures!
these various causes together, a statement of facts which he had intended
s defence of the *originality* and priority of the National Declaration of Inde-
e, was construed in some quarters to be an aggressive attack on the authen-
another and scarcely less venerated instrument.
controversy on the subject commenced at the period when the publication
Vorks had reöpened so many wounds—when all the interests, public and
he had ever offended, were banded together afresh to hunt down and over-
s reputation. It was a moment when the dead lion could be kicked with
impunity by the merest ass. Acrimonious replies to his "insulting *attack*"
Mecklenburg Declaration, and "on the State of North Carolina," rapidly
from newspaper articles into pamphlets, and from pamphlets into books.
I not here notice the contents of any of these.
e was, however, an entirely different class of objectors to Mr. Jefferson's
ons. They were prominent and highly respectable citizens of North Caro-
o believed the Mecklenburg Declaration a genuine document, and therefore
idably anxious in justice to their State and in justice to the individuals who
rt in making that Declaration, to collect and perpetuate the proofs of its
icity. Accordingly, the Legislature of the State very properly took up the
1831, and published in a pamphlet (commonly mentioned as "the State
et"), a mass of testimony which had been collected, intended to prove, first,
Declaration of Independence was made by representatives of the County of
iburg in May, 1775, and, second, that the paper first published in the
Register, April 30th, 1819, was a copy of that identical Declaration.
first fact—or rather the fact that a paper was adopted which the witnesses
poraneously considered a Declaration of Independence—was as satisfactorily
hed as could well be done, after such a lapse of time, by oral evidence.
ms perfectly credible survivors who participated in or witnessed the scene,
ly affirmed that a Declaration was made, and that they understood it to be a
tion of Independence. And we shall see that documentary evidence subse-
sustained these recollections.
t the newly discovered paper was a copy or record of the manifesto thus

remembered, several witnesses felt as positive as it would be practicable to feel in respect to the identity of a document which they had heard read but once [1] so many years before. A part of their certificates was made in 1819 and a part in 1830—so that the recollections of those who testified nearest the event, were required to stretch back forty-four years, and those of the others fifty-five years.

The internal and external evidences of authenticity connected with the paper itself, were as follows. A copy of it was found among the papers of John McNitt Alexander, signed by himself as secretary wholly or mostly in his own hand-writing.[2] He was a man of the highest respectability of character, and the idea that he would have forged the document could not be entertained. It was "mentioned on file" of the paper "that a copy of the proceedings was sent to Hugh Williamson, in New York, then writing a history of North Carolina, and that a copy was sent to William R. Davie." After Davie's death, a copy (or part of a copy[3]) was found among his papers, in the handwriting of John McNitt, Alexander. Hon. Montfort Stokes, Governor of North Carolina, declared (in 1831) that he saw a copy in Hugh Williamson's possession in 1793. Finally, the Rev. Humphrey Hunter published an autobiography in 1827, in which he stated that he was present when the Mecklenburg Declaration was made, and he gives Mr. Alexander's copy of the *body* of that paper.[4]

But Mr. John McNitt Alexander set forth no claim that the copy preserved by himself was the original record of the Declaration (or proceedings) or a copy made from such original. His manuscript concluded thus:

"It may be worthy of notice here to observe that the foregoing statement, though fundamentally correct, YET MAY NOT LITERALLY CORRESPOND WITH THE ORIGINAL RECORD OF THE TRANSACTIONS OF SAID DELEGATION AND COURT OF ENQUIRY, AS ALL THOSE RECORDS AND PAPERS WERE BURNT WITH THE HOUSE, ON APRIL 6TH, 1800; but previous to that time of 1800, a full copy of said records, at the request of Doctor Hugh Williamson, then of New York, but formerly a representative in Congress from this State, was forwarded to him by Col. Wm. Polk, in order that those early transactions might fill their proper place in a history of this State, then writing by said Doctor Williams, in New York.

"Certified, *to the best of my recollection and belief*, this 3d day of September, 1800, by

"J. McN. ALEXANDER.[5]

"*Mecklenburg County, N. C.*"

In a History of North Carolina, published in 1829, by Judge Martin, a North Carolina gentleman of the highest respectability, appears another version of the Mecklenburg declaration or resolutions. The document is as follows:

"*Resolved*, That whosover directly or indirectly abets, or in any way, form, or manner, countenances the invasion of our rights, as attempted by the Parliament

---

[1] We think none of the witnesses mention having heard it read but once, and then from the steps of the courthouse, as a public proclamation. The point, however, is of no consequence, whether they heard it once or a dozen times.

[2] We are informed by one who has often seen Mr. Alexander's manuscripts on this subject, that they exhibit a diversity of hand-writing, frequent interlineations, erasures, etc. Whether this applies to the resolutions themselves we are not specially apprised, but *suppose* our informant intended such application.

[3] It is generally stated to have been a copy, but we observe that the North Carolina University Magazine says that the Davie copy consisted of the last two resolutions "found on a mutilated manuscript" [see May No., 1853, p. 170].

[4] We are not aware, however, that he ever pretended that he obtained his copy when the Declaration was made. And no such contemporaneous document of Mr. Hunter has met the eyes of Governor Swain or the other eminent North Carolina investigators of the subject.

[5] University Magazine for May, 1853, p. 175. We find the name Williamson written Williams, as above, where it occurs the second time in this copy.

' Great Britain, is an enemy to this country, to America, and the rights of
an.

"*Resolved*, That we, the citizens of Mecklenburg County, do hereby dissolve the
litical bands which have connected us with the mother country, and absolve our-
lves from all allegiance to the British Crown, abjuring all political connection with
ation that has wantonly trampled on our rights and liberties, and inhumanly shed
e innocent blood of Americans at Lexington.

"*Resolved*, That we do hereby declare ourselves a free and independent people;
at we are, and of right ought to be, a sovereign and self-governing people, under
e power of God and the General Congress; to the maintenance of which independ-
nce, we solemnly pledge to each other our mutual coöperation, our lives, our for-
nes, and our most sacred honor.

"*Resolved*, That we hereby order and adopt, as rules of conduct, all and each of
r former laws, and the crown of Great Britain cannot be considered hereafter as
lding any rights, privileges, or immunities among us.

"*Resolved*, That all officers, both civil and military, in this county, be entitled to
ercise the same powers and authorities as heretofore: that every member of this
legation shall henceforth be a civil officer, and exercise the powers of a Justice of
e Peace, issue process, hear and determine controversies, according to law, pre-
rve peace, union and harmony in the country, and use every exertion to spread the
re of liberty and of country, until a more general and better organized system of
vernment be established.

"*Resolved*, That a copy of these resolutions be transmitted, by express, to the
esident of the Continental Congress assembled in Philadelphia, to be laid before
at body."

There are different accounts of the origin of this paper, but none that we have
m pretend to say from whom, or under what circumstances Judge Martin obtained

A writer in the North Carolina University Magazine, obviously well informed in
the facts, and familiar with all the *documents* pertaining to the subject, says:
Although inquiry was made of Judge Martin, it is not known whence he obtained
is paper. . . . His copy is evidently a polished edition of the Davie [Alexan-
r] copy—polished, because its guardians knew that this was not an extract from
iginal records, and therefore felt no particular reverence for it." [1]

The next phase of this curious affair is, that Colonel Peter Force, of Washington,
he indefatigable compiler of the American Archives), discovered in an English pe-
dical, a proclamation issued by Martin, then royal governor of North Carolina, on
e 8th August, 1775, from which he copied the following extract: "And whereas,
have also seen a most infamous publication in the Cape Fear Mercury, importing
be resolves of a set of people, styling themselves a committee for the county of
cklenburg, most traitorously declaring the entire dissolution of the laws, govern-
nt, and constitution of this country, and setting up a system of rule and regula-
n, repugnant to the laws and subversive of his Majesty's government," etc. [2]

This established beyond question two facts—that resolutions of an analogous
nor to those given from memory by J. McN. Alexander, were adopted by a "com-
ittee for the county of Mecklenburg" (the same body or authority to whom Alex-
der assigned the passage of the resolutions), and that the resolutions were contem-
raneously *published* in a *newspaper* printed in the same State.

[1] See University Magazine for May, 1853, pp. 170, 175.
[2] Martin's original proclamation-book was discovered a few months after this, and it contained
e proclamation thus quoted by Colonel Force.

remembered, several witnesses felt as positive a
respect to the identity of a document which they
years before. A part of their certificates was n
that the recollections of those who testified ne
stretch back forty-four years, and those of the ot

The internal and external evidences of autl
itself, were as follows. A copy of it was found
Alexander, signed by himself as secretary wholly
He was a man of the highest respectability of ch
have forged the document could not be enter
of the paper "that a copy of the proceeding
York, then writing a history of North Caro'
R. Davie." After Davie's death, a copy (
papers, in the handwriting of John M
Governor of North Carolina, declared
liamson's possession in 1793. Final
autobiography in 1827, in which he
Declaration was made, and he giv

But Mr. John McNitt Alexan
himself was the original record
from such original. His man;

"It may be worthy of
though fundamentally corr
NAL RECORD OF THE TRANS   e ch
THOSE RECORDS AND PAP   resoluti
previous to that time (a New Yor
Hugh Williamson, th   ., 1775; and ir
from this State, was   nern States. Tl
transactions might
said Doctor Willi   "C

mittee of the County met, a
Address presented to His 1
the American Colonies are

"*Beckle*   ve that all Laws and Comm

In a H   y of the King or Parliament, ar
rolina p   tion of these Colonies for the
lenbur   for the exigencies of this Coun
"   er and necessary to pass the follow
ma   Commissions, civil and military, b
               these Colonies, are null and void, a
               y wholly suspended.
               the Provincial Congress of each Pro
               ntal Congress, is invested with all 1
               spective Provinces, and that no othe
               xist, at this time, in any of these Col
               That as all former laws are now suspended i

President of the University of North Carolina.
delivered before the Historical Society of the Ur
Field Book of the Revolution, vol. ii. p. 623, note.

' judge it necessary, for the better preservation of
' regulations for the internal government of the
'a by the Congress.

     do meet on a certain day appointed by
'nto nine Companies, to wit: eight in
choose a Colonel and other mili-
ral powers by virtue of this
nd former Constitution of

'ministration of jus-
'iscreet freehold-
id determine
sum of twenty
in of forty shillings;
onvention of the select
a shall have power to exam-
etit larceny.

en, do jointly and together choose
wo persons properly qualified to act as
execution of their office.

. any persons to either of these select men, he
ae Constable, commanding him to bring the aggres-
ower said complaint.

een select men thus appointed, do meet every third Thurs-
, July, and October, at the Courthouse in Charlotte, to hear
matters of controversy for sums exceeding forty shillings, also
of felony, to commit the person or persons convicted thereof
until the Provincial Congress shall provide and establish laws
ceeding in all such cases.

ese eighteen select men, thus convened, do choose a clerk to record
of said Convention; and that said clerk, upon the application of
persons aggrieved, do issue his warrant to one of the constables of
which the offender belongs, directing said Constable to summons
offender to appear before the Convention at their next sitting, to
said complaint.

That any person making complaint upon oath to the Clerk or any mem-
Convention, that he has reason to suspect that any person or persons
him in a sum above forty shillings, intend clandestinely to withdraw
County without paying such debt, the Clerk or such member shall issue his
the Constable commanding him to take said person or persons into safe
until the next sitting of the Convention.

b. That when a debtor for a sum below forty shillings shall abscond and
e County, the warrant granted as aforesaid shall extend to any goods or
of said debtor as may be found, and such goods or chattels be seized and
custody by the Constable for the space of thirty days; in which time, if the
fail to return and discharge the debt, the Constable shall return the warrant
of the select men of the Company, where the goods are found, who shall issue
to the Constable to sell such part of said goods as shall amount to the sum
at when the debt exceeds forty shillings, the return shall be made to the
tion, who shall issue orders for sale.

A search was at once set on foot to discover the contemporaneous publication—none taking so active a part in the investigation as the Hon. David L. Swain, ex-Governor of North Carolina.[1] At length Dr. Joseph Johnson, of South Carolina, discovered in the Charleston Library, a copy of the "South Carolina Gazette and Country Journal," dated "Tuesday, June 13th, 1775," in which were the long-lost resolutions.

Governor Swain, in a published address, says:[2]

"Shortly subsequent to the discovery of Governor Martin's proclamation, Jared Sparks, while engaged in historical investigations in London, found in the State paper office, an original letter from Governor Martin to Lord Dartmouth, dated 'North Carolina, Fort Johnson, 30th June, 1775,' from which he copied the following paragraph: 'The resolves of the committee of Mecklenburg, which your Lordship will find in the enclosed *newspaper*, surpass all the horrid and treasonable publications that the inflammatory spirits of this continent have yet produced. . . . A copy of these resolutions, I am informed, was sent off by express to the Congress of Philadelphia, as soon as they were passed by the committee.' Mr. Sparks states that the newspaper alluded to, unfortunately, could not be found in the office."

Mr. Lossing, however, states,[3] it is presumed on Mr. Bancroft's authority, that the latter, then American Minister at London, had, before receiving intelligence of Dr. Johnson's discovery in the Charleston Library, found a copy of the same newspaper containing the Mecklenburg resolutions, which had been forwarded to Lord Dartmouth by Sir James Wright, then Governor of Georgia, with a letter in which he said: "By the inclosed paper your lordship will see the extraordinary resolves of the people of Charlottetown, in Mecklenburg county; and I should not be surprised if the same should be done everywhere else."

This rendered the identification of the resolutions complete. Colonel Force subsequently found copies of them in the New York Journal of June 29th, 1775; in the Massachusetts Spy of July 12th, 1775; and in other contemporaneous newspapers of the northern and southern States. The following is a copy of these resolutions:

"CHARLOTTETOWN, MECKLENBURG COUNTY,
May 31, 1775.

"This day the Committee of the County met, and passed the following Resolves:

"Whereas, by an Address presented to His Majesty by both Houses of Parliament in February last, the American Colonies are declared to be in a state of actual rebellion; we conceive that all Laws and Commissions confirmed by, or derived from, the authority of the King or Parliament, are annulled and vacated, and the former civil Constitution of these Colonies for the present wholly suspended. To provide in some degree for the exigencies of this County, in the present alarming period, we deem it proper and necessary to pass the following Resolves, viz.:

"1st. That all Commissions, civil and military, heretofore granted by the Crown, to be exercised in these Colonies, are null and void, and the Constitution of each particular Colony wholly suspended.

"2d. That the Provincial Congress of each Province, under the direction of the great Continental Congress, is invested with all legislative and executive powers within their respective Provinces, and that no other legislative or executive power does, or can exist, at this time, in any of these Colonies.

"3d. That as all former laws are now suspended in this Province, and the Congress

---

[1] Now President of the University of North Carolina.
[2] Lecture delivered before the Historical Society of the University of N. Carolina, April 1, 1853.
[3] See Field Book of the Revolution, vol. ii. p. 623, note.

have not yet provided others, we judge it necessary, for the better preservation of good order, to form certain rules and regulations for the internal government of the County, until laws shall be provided for us by the Congress.

"4th. That the inhabitants of this County do meet on a certain day appointed by this Committee, and having formed themselves into nine Companies, to wit: eight in the County, and one in the Town of Charlotte, do choose a Colonel and other military officers, who shall hold and exercise their several powers by virtue of this choice, and independent of the Crown of Great Britain and former Constitution of this Province.

"5th. That for the better preservation of the peace, and administration of justice, each of those companies do choose from their own body two discreet freeholders, who shall be empowered each by himself and singly, to decide and determine all matters of controversy arising within said Company, under the sum of twenty shillings; and jointly and together all controversies under the sum of forty shillings; yet so as that their decisions may admit of appeal to the Convention of the select men of the County; and also, that any one of these men shall have power to examine and commit to confinement persons accused of petit larceny.

"6th. That those two select men thus chosen, do jointly and together choose from the body of their particular company, two persons properly qualified to act as constables, who may assist them in the execution of their office.

"7th. That upon the complaint of any persons to either of these select men, he do issue his warrant, directed to the Constable, commanding him to bring the aggressor before him or them, to answer said complaint.

"8th. That these eighteen select men thus appointed, do meet every third Thursday in January, April, July, and October, at the Courthouse in Charlotte, to hear and determine all matters of controversy for sums exceeding forty shillings, also appeals; and in case of felony, to commit the person or persons convicted thereof to close confinement, until the Provincial Congress shall provide and establish laws and modes of proceeding in all such cases.

"9th. That these eighteen select men, thus convened, do choose a clerk to record the transactions of said Convention; and that said clerk, upon the application of any person or persons aggrieved, do issue his warrant to one of the constables of the Company to which the offender belongs, directing said Constable to summons and warn said offender to appear before the Convention at their next sitting, to answer the aforesaid complaint.

"10th. That any person making complaint upon oath to the Clerk or any member of the Convention, that he has reason to suspect that any person or persons indebted to him in a sum above forty shillings, intend clandestinely to withdraw from the County without paying such debt, the Clerk or such member shall issue his warrant to the Constable commanding him to take said person or persons into safe custody, until the next sitting of the Convention.

"11th. That when a debtor for a sum below forty shillings shall abscond and leave the County, the warrant granted as aforesaid shall extend to any goods or chattels of said debtor as may be found, and such goods or chattels be seized and held in custody by the Constable for the space of thirty days; in which time, if the debtor fail to return and discharge the debt, the Constable shall return the warrant to one of the select men of the Company, where the goods are found, who shall issue orders to the Constable to sell such part of said goods as shall amount to the sum due; that when the debt exceeds forty shillings, the return shall be made to the Convention, who shall issue orders for sale.

"12th. That all receivers and collectors of quit-rents, public and county taxes, do pay the same into the hands of the chairman of this Committee, to be by them disbursed, as the public exigencies may require; and that such receivers and collectors proceed no further in their office, until they be approved of by, and have given to this Committee good and sufficient security for a faithful return of such moneys when collected.

"13th. That the Committee be accountable to the County for the application of all moneys received from such public officers.

"14th. That all these officers hold their commissions during the pleasure of their several constituents.

"15th. That this Committee will sustain all damages that hereafter may accrue to all or any of these officers thus appointed and thus acting, on account of their obedience and conformity to these Resolves.

"16th. That whatsoever person shall hereafter receive a Commission from the Crown, or attempt to exercise any such Commission heretofore received, shall be deemed an enemy to his country; and upon information being made to the Captain of the Company in which he resides, the said Company shall cause him to be apprehended, and conveyed before the two select men of the said Company, who, upon proof of the fact, shall commit him, the said offender, to safe custody until the next sitting of the Committee, who shall deal with him as prudence may direct.

"17th. That any person refusing to yield obedience to the above Resolves shall be considered equally criminal, and liable to the same punishment as the offenders last above mentioned.

"18th. That these Resolves be in full force and virtue until instructions from the Provincial Congress, regulating the jurisprudence of the Province, shall provide otherwise, or the legislative body of Great Britain resign its unjust and arbitrary pretensions with respect to America.

"19th. That the eight militia companies in the County provide themselves with proper arms and accoutrements, and hold themselves in readiness to execute the commands and directions of the General Congress of this Province and of this Committee.

"20th. That the Committee appoint Colonel Thomas Polk and Dr. Joseph Kennedy to purchase 300 lbs. of powder, 600 lbs. of lead, and 1000 flints for the use of the militia of this County, and deposit the same in such place as the Committee may hereafter direct.

"Signed by order of the Committee,

"EPHRAIM BREVARD,

"Clerk of Committee." [1]

This document, it will be observed, is dated eleven days later than Mr. Alexander's copy of the resolutions, and this has given rise to the hypothesis that two separate declarations or manifestos of independence were issued by the Mecklenburg Committee—the one on the 20th, and the other on the 31st of the same month.

In favor of this view is the testimony of some of the witnesses published by the North Carolina Legislature in the "State pamphlet." But out of nearly twenty of these persons less than half mention the date of the meeting, and among those who omit it are Captain Jack, who bore the resolutions to Congress, and John Davidson, the last surviving member of the Committee who issued the manifestos. Of those who name the date of the 20th, nearly all add something which shows that they felt

[1] We take our copy of this paper from N. C. University Magazine, May, 1858.

the uncertainty which we should expect credible men to feel in testifying to such a fact after the lapse of half a century. Thus General Graham says, " as well as he can recollect after the lapse of fifty-five years." George Graham, William Hutchinson, Jonas Clark, and Robert Robinson (all inhabitants of Mecklenburg county) say " to the best of their recollection and belief." Rev. H. Hunter rests his recollection on a circumstance which, by his own showing, would bring the date of the declaration nearer to the 31st than the 20th—but on neither day. None of the witnesses remember *two* declarations. One of them (John Simeson) states that the resolutions contained an order that Colonel Polk, John Phifer, and Joseph Kennedy should secure military stores, etc. The resolutions of the 31st contain such an order to Colonel Polk and Joseph Kennedy; those of the 20th contain nothing of the kind. The North Carolina University Magazine says (while enumerating the arguments of objectors to the resolutions of the 20th), " We have not the letters which asked for the recollections of these gentlemen [the witnesses whose testimony is given in the State pamphlet]. Perhaps they contained leading questions and suggested dates, events, names, etc., etc." There is a more general, and it seems to us a very obvious solution, however, which puts the fairness not only of the witnesses but of the questioners beyond necessary suspicion. When these interrogatories were made and answered, there was no controversy as to the precise date of the Mecklenburg resolutions. The real question then was, were such resolutions passed a year or more anterior to the National Declaration of Independence. If so, all parties then naturally took it for granted that Mr. Alexander's copy gave the correct date.

It is not necessary to comment on the degree of actual identification which a particular paper can derive from recollections of so old date, and drawn out under such circumstances, as those given in the testimony published in the North Carolina State pamphlet, with a single exception. That exception is the declaration of Governor Montfort Stokes, already mentioned, that in 1793 he saw a copy of the resolutions of the 20th, in the hands of Dr. Williamson.

Governor Stokes was a man of the highest integrity and honor, and we have a manuscript letter lying before us from one who knew him intimately, saying that he had a remarkably retentive memory. His testimony is certainly important in one view. It puts the good faith of John McNitt Alexander beyond all reasonable suspicion. But Governor Stokes's recollections are *thirty-eight* years old. He, like the other witnesses, was aware of no issue as to *the* paper, provided it could be shown that *a* paper of similar tenor was a genuine record of proceedings in Mecklenburg in May, 1775. But if it could be shown that Governor Stokes's memory was so remarkably retentive as to preserve for thirty-eight years the *precise words* of the document, does not his testimony prove too much? It proves that a document was, *ipsissima verba*, a copy of another, when the maker of it claimed no such thing—when *he* only claimed that it contained the same substance.[1]

The intrinsic evidence furnished by the two manifestos would of itself be conclusive on the question under discussion. We shall only rapidly allude to a few of the most prominent of these.

1. Both documents, if genuine records, give the resolutions of the same representative body, publicly assembled to act, and vested with unlimited authority. The resolutions of May 31st are conceded on all sides to be genuine records. If those of the 20th also are, it follows:

2. That the Mecklenburg committee at the first-named date, after a public

---

[1] Of course this remark respecting Governor Stokes's testimony, would apply equally to the evidence of all the witnesses who testify to the identity of the papers.

discussion and two days sitting,[1] formally abrogated the British laws then in force in the county, vacated the offices held under the crown, and filled them by their own authority, organized a government, and made public proclamation of this fact before assembled thousands—and then met, eleven days afterward (*functus officio* so far as the *same acts* of sovereign authority were concerned) and did the whole thing over again! On the second occasion they abrogated laws which had been *eleven days* abrogated—vacated offices which had been eleven days vacated, and filled by a new appointment—and again organized an entire new government! No reasons for this unprecedented and anomalous second action are given; nor is the previous action even alluded to in the records kept on the occasion.

3. A cloud of witnesses remember the first proceedings (and some have thought, even the exact *language* and *date* of the manifesto then adopted), and have utterly forgotten the second proceedings, an account of which was contemporaneously printed and published in their State. And not the remotest contemporaneous allusion to those of the 20th, publicly proclaimed to assembled thousands, can be found in the newspapers which published those of the 31st.

4. The first document declares independence unconditionally—the second until "the legislative body of great Britain resign its unjust and arbitrary pretensions with respect to America." Did the committee, after incurring all the danger, recede to any extent from their previous action?

5. The reasons assigned for independence in the two documents are not the same. Those in the resolutions of the 31st, conform better to circumstances known to have existed in Mecklenburg and to have operated on the minds of many of the most decided whigs.[2]

6. The civil organizations effected, as already hinted, by the two manifestoes, were different. By the first, all military officers who acquiesced in the proceedings were reinstated, and the committee declared *themselves* justices of the peace. By the second, without any reference being made to these new appointments, or any reasons assigned for, or mention made of vacating *them*, new elections were ordered, for filling all military and civil offices by a popular vote.

7. It has already been seen that John Simeson testifies to occurrences recorded in the second and not in the first resolutions. Indeed, it is believed that a critical analysis of *all* the testimony in the State pamphlet, considered in reference to facts now settled, would almost establish the conclusion, without other evidence, that the witnesses were speaking of events which took place later than May 20th. But we shall not stop to enter upon such an analysis.

8. It is claimed in all the accounts of both meetings, that Dr. Ephraim Brevard drafted the resolutions. Passing over the other discrepancies, there is a manifest and utter difference in their literary style. Did Doctor Brevard's whole style change in eleven days? He is admitted on all sides to have been a graduate of Princeton— an elegant scholar—a man of talents. Did he who wrote with such nice propriety, both of construction and language, on the 31st, eleven days earlier, deliberately prepare for public proclamation a document of transcendent importance, into which he introduced such phraseology as an "*unchartered* invasion," an invasion "*as claimed* by Great Britain," "it is further *decreed*," etc., etc.—such a constructed

---

[1] It appears from Mr. Alexander's manuscript accompanying his resolutions, and by the statements of the witnesses, that the meeting was for two days.

[2] They had taken oaths during the Regulation troubles not to bear arms against his Majesty's government. It is in proof that this topic was discussed when the manifesto of Independence was under consideration, and that it was determined that inasmuch as his Majesty had declared the people out of his protection, allegiance ceased, and that their oaths were no longer binding. The resolutions of the 31st are obviously drawn to meet this view.

sentence as that which forms the fourth Alexander resolution—such an extravagant and bungling imitation throughout of the tautologies of legal instruments? And how happened he in the second paper to omit those collocations of words which were afterwards thought fine enough to be *borrowed* into the national Declaration of Independence!

9. And how came Dr. Brevard's style on the 20th, so unlike his own, to bear such a striking resemblance to J. McN. Alexander's; to exhibit the same method of frequently presenting several verbs and nouns to express the same action or thing; to give some of the same peculiar words; to present the same ambitious, forcible, but inaccurate diction; and in a word, to have the same *ring* throughout.[1]

The brave and true old man was graduated among battles and stirring events, instead of the classic halls of Princeton. He gave his recollections honestly, but he confounded the proceedings of different meetings, and his memory unconsciously blended the familiar phrases of a later declaration with that of Mecklenburg.

It is difficult for us, however, to believe that such a man would have fancied that he had been the secretary of a meeting on such a momentous *subject*, without some foundation for the belief. We are inclined to *conjecture* that there was a *popular meeting* at Charlottetown on the 19th and 20th of May, where discussion was had on the subject of independence, and probably some more or less explicit understanding arrived at, which became the basis of the committee's action on the 31st. If so, we make no doubt that J. McN. Alexander was secretary of that meeting. He probably, in that case, recorded the proceedings, and among them some resolution or resolutions in regard to the propriety of throwing off the British yoke. It would be more natural to suppose that such a popular expression preceded the all-important and decisive action of the committee, than to suppose the latter acted without such an expression. The same men figured in both meetings. The Polks, the Alexanders, the Brevards, the Balches, the Averys, the Grahams, the Kennons, the Morrisons, etc.—all the leaders of the unflinching Scotch Whigs of Mecklenburg—were on the ground, and advocated their views. It was in attempting to remember the records of that meeting, destroyed by fire, that John McN. Alexander, then an old man, fell into the errors we have named. Is this not a reasonable—the most reasonable—*conjecture!*

We have been favored by Mr. Bancroft with an inspection of the proof-sheets of his forthcoming volume of the History of the United States, where allusion is made to the Mecklenburg Declaration of Independence. It is known that he has carefully

[1] For example, Mr. Alexander writes:

"Conformably to these principles, Colonel Thomas Polk, through solicitation, issued an order to each captain's company in the County of Mecklenburg (then comprising the present County of Cabarrus), directing each militia company to elect two persons, and delegate to them ample power to devise ways and means to aid and assist their suffering brethren in Boston, and also generally to adopt measures to extricate themselves from the impending storm, and to secure unimpaired their *inalienable* rights, privileges, and liberties, from the dominant grasp of British imposition and tyranny.

"In conformity to said order, on the nineteenth of May, 1775, the said delegation met in Charlotte, vested with unlimited powers; at which time official news by express arrived of the battle of Lexington on that day of the preceding month. Every delegate felt the value and importance of the prize, and the awful and solemn crisis which had arrived; every bosom swelled with indignation at the malice, inveteracy, and insatiable revenge developed in the late attack at Lexington. The universal sentiment was: let us not flatter ourselves that popular harangues or resolves, that popular vapor will avert the storm, or vanquish our common enemy; let us deliberate; let us calculate the issue—the probable result; and then let us act with energy, as brethren leagued to preserve our property, our lives, and, what is still more endearing, the liberties of America.

*   *   *   *   *

"A number of by-laws were also added, merely to protect the *association* from confusion, and to regulate their general conduct as citizens. After sitting in the court-house all night, neither sleepy, hungry, nor fatigued, and after discussing every paragraph, they were all passed, sanctioned, and *decreed* unanimously, about two o'clock, A. M , May 20th.

and specially investigated the subject. He makes no allusion to any other meeting or declaration than that of 31st of May.

Those who wish a fuller and much more convincing exposition of this subject than has here been given, will receive it when a recent lecture, delivered by Dr Grigsby, at Richmond, shall be published.

APPENDIX NO. III.—Vol. I., p. 193.

Three Letters from Mr. Jefferson to Francis Eppes, between the Declaration of Independence and the resignation of his seat.

PHILADELPHIA, *July* 15th, 1776.

DEAR SIR: Yours of the 3d inst. came to hand to-day. I wish I could be better satisfied on the point of Patty's recovery. I had not heard from her at all for two posts before, and no letter from herself now. I wish it were in my power to return by way of the Forest, as you think it will be impracticable for Mrs. Eppes to travel to the mountains. However, it will be late in August before I can get home, and our Convention will call me down early in October. Till that time, therefore, I must defer the hope of seeing Mrs. Eppes and yourself. Admiral Howe is himself arrived at New York, and two or three vessels, supposed to be of his fleet, were coming in. The whole is expected daily.

Washington's numbers are greatly increased, but we do not know them exactly. I imagine he must have from 30 to 35,000 by this time. The enemy the other day ordered two of their men-of-war to hoist anchor and push by our batteries up the Hudson River. Both wind and tide were very fair. They passed all the batteries with ease, and, as far as is known, without receiving material damage; though there was an incessant fire kept up on them. This experiment of theirs, I suppose, is a prelude to the passage of their whole fleet, and seems to indicate an intention of landing above New York. I imagine General Washington, finding he cannot prevent their going up the river, will prepare to amuse them wherever they shall go.

Our army from Canada is now at Crown Point, but still one half down with the smallpox. You ask about Arnold's behavior at the Cedars. It was this. The scoundrel, Major Butterfield, having surrendered three hundred and ninety men, in a fort with twenty or thirty days' provision, and ammunition enough, to about forty regulars, one hundred Canadians, and five hundred Indians, before he had lost a single man—and Maj. Sherburne, who was coming to the relief of the fort with one hundred men, having, after bravely engaging the enemy an hour and forty minutes, killing twenty of them and losing twelve of his own, been surrounded by them, and taken prisoners also—Gen. Arnold appeared on the opposite side of the river and prepared to attack them. His numbers I know not, but believe they were about equal to the enemy. Capt. Foster, commander of the king's troops, sent over a flag to him, proposing an exchange of prisoners for as many of the king's in our possession, and, moreover, informed Arnold that if he should attack, the Indians would put every man of the prisoners to death. Arnold refused, called a council of war, and, it being now in the night, it was determined to attack next morning. A second flag came over ; he again refused, though in an excruciating situation, as he saw the en emy were in earnest about killing the prisoners. His men, too, began to be importunate for the recovery of their fellow-soldiers. A third flag came, the men grew more clamorous, and Arnold, now almost raving with rage and compassion, was obliged to consent to the exchange and six days suspension of hostilities, Foster declaring he had not boats to deliver them in less time. However, he did deliver them so much sooner as that before the six days were expired, himself and party had fled out of all reach. Arnold then retired to Montreal. You have long before this heard of Gén. Thompson's defeat. The truth of that matter has never appeared till lately. You will see it in the public papers. No men on earth ever behaved better than ours did. The enemy behaved dastardly. Col. Allen (who was in the engagement) assured me this day, that such was the situation of our men, half way up to the thighs in mud for several hours, that five hundred men of spirit must have taken the whole; yet the enemy were repulsed several times, and our people had time to extricate themselves and come off. It is believed the enemy suffered considerably. The above account of Arnold's affair you may rely on, as I was one of a committee appointed to inquire into the whole of that matter, and have it from those who were in the whole transaction, and were taken prisoners.

My sincere affections to Mrs. Eppes, and adieu,

TH. JEFFERSON.

FRANCIS EPPES, Esq.
    In Charles City.

————

PHILADELPHIA, *July* 23, 1776.

DEAR SIR: We have nothing new here now but from the southward. The successes there I hope will prove valuable here, by giving new spirit to our people. The ill successes in Canada had depressed the minds of many; when we shall hear the last of them I know not; everybody had supposed Crown Point would be a certain stand for them, but they have retreated from that to Ticonderoga, against everything which in my eye wears the shape of reason. When I wrote you last, we were deceived in General Washington's numbers. By a return which came to hand a day or two after, he then had but 15,000 effective men. His reinforcements have come in pretty well since. The flying camp in the Jerseys under General Mercer begins to form, but not as fast as exigencies require. The Congress have, therefore, been obliged to send for two of our battalions from Virginia. I hope that country is perfectly safe now; and if it is, it seemed hardly right that she should not contribute a man to an army of 40,000, and an army too on which was to depend the decision of all our rights. Lord Howe's fleet has not yet arrived. The first division sailed five days before he did, but report says it was scattered by a storm. This seems probable, as Lord Howe had a long passage. The two other divisions were not sailed when he came away. I do not expect his army will be here and fit for action till the middle or last of August; in the meantime, if Mercer's camp could be formed with the expedition it merits, it might be possible to attack the present force from the Jersey side of Staten Island, and get rid of that beforehand; the militia go in freely, considering they leave their harvest to rot in the field.

I have received no letter this week, which lays me under great anxiety. I shall leave this place about the 11th of next month. Give my love to Mrs. Eppes, and tell her that when both you and Patty fail to write to me, I think I shall not be unreasonable in insisting she shall. I am, dear sir,

Yours affectionately,

TH. JEFFERSON.

To FRANCIS EPPES, Esq.

PHILADELPHIA, *Aug.* 9*th*, 1776.

DEAR SIR: As Col. Harrison was about to have some things packed, I set out upon the execution of your glass commission, and was surprised to find that the whole glass stores of the city could not make out anything like what you desired. I therefore did what I thought would be best, imagining you wanted the number you mentioned at any event, and that not being able to get them of that form, you would take them of any other. I therefore got 4 pint cans, 10s.; 2 quart do. 8s.; and 6 half-pint tumblers, 6s., all of double flint. So that there still remains in my hands £4 16s., Pennsylva curr*cy*.

Your teckle is not yet come. It seems the man who had promised to sell it to the gentleman I employed to get it, now raises some difficulties either to get off others which he calls the set, or to enhance the price. However, the gentleman still expects it, and I am after him every day for it. Our galleys at New York have had a smart engagement with the men-of-war which went up the river; it is believed the enemy suffered a good deal. The galleys are much injured, though we lost but two men. The commander writes us word he retired, that he might go and give them another drubbing, which in plain English meant, I suppose, that he was obliged to retire. Gen. Washington commends the behavior of the men much. They lay pretty close to the enemy, and two of the galleys were exposed to the broadside of their ships almost the whole time. The damage done them proves they were in a warm situation. Madison (of the college) and one Johnson, of Augusta, were coming passengers in the New York packet; they were attacked by one of our armed vessels, and nothing but the intervention of night prevented the packet being taken. She is arrived at New York, and they permitted to come home. In a letter by them, we have intelligence that the French ministry is changed, the pacific men turned out, and those who are for war, with the Duke de Choiseul at their head, are taken in. We have also the king's speech on the prorogation of parliament, declaring he will see it out with us to the bitter end.

The South Carolina army with Clinton Sr., arrived at Staten Island last week, one of their transports, with 5 companies of Highlanders, having first fallen into General Lee's hands. They now make Lord Howe 12,000 strong. With this force he is preparing to attack. He is embarking his cannon; has launched 8 galleys, and formed his men-of-war into line of battle. From these circumstances, it is believed the attack of New York will be within three or four days. They expect with the utmost confidence to carry it, as they consider our army but as a rude undisciplined rabble. I hope they will find it a Bunker's Hill rabble. Notwithstanding these appearances of attack, there are some who believe, and with appearance of reason, that these measures are taken by the enemy to secure themselves and not to attack us. A little time will shew. General Arnold (a fine sailor) has undertaken to command our fleet on the lakes. The enemy are fortifying Oswego, and I believe our army there, when recovered from their sickness, will find they have lost a good campaign, though they have had no battle of moment.

My love to Mrs. Eppes. I hope my letter by last post got there time enough to stay Patty with her awhile longer. Adieu.

TH. JEFFERSON.

FRANCIS EPPES, Esq.,
    At the Forest,
By favor of Col. Harrison.

APPENDIX NO. IV.—Vol. I. p. 232.

Bradshaw's Supposititious Epitaph.

Mr. Trist's Memoranda proceed as follows:

" The epitaph on Bradshaw, written on a narrow slip of thin paper, was a fine specimen. This has gone to France, through Gen. La Fayette, for M. De Lyon, a young friend of his who accompanied him on his triumphal visit to our country, and was with him at Monticello. De Lyon (who afterwards did his part in the 'three days') having expressed an earnest desire to possess a piece of Mr. J.'s MS., I had promised to make his wish known at some suitable moment. But, having postponed doing so until too late, and being struck with the appropriateness of this epitaph as a present for a pupil of La Fayette (and, through him, to the mind of 'Young France'), I asked and obtained Mr. Randolph's consent to its receiving that destination.

" 'Tis evident, that the motto which we find on one of Mr. J.'s seals was taken from this epitaph, which, as we see from the note appended thereto, was supposed to be one of Dr. Franklin's *spirit-stirring* inspirations."

1776.

" The following inscription was made out, three years ago, on the cannon, near which the ashes of President Bradshaw were lodged, on the top of a high hill near Martha Bay, in Jamaica, to avoid the rage against the Regicides exhibited at the Restoration :

Stranger!
Ere thou pass, contemplate this cannon, nor regardless be told
That near its base lies deposited
the Dust of
JOHN BRADSHAW:
Who, nobly superior to all selfish regards,
Despising alike the pageantry of courtly splendour,
The blast of calumny, and the terrors of royal vengeance,
presided in the illustrious band
of Heroes and Patriots
who fairly and openly adjudged
CHARLES STUART,
Tyrant of England,
To a public and exemplary death:
Thereby presenting to the amazed world,
And transmitting down through applauding ages,
The most glorious example
Of unshaken virtue, love of freedom, and impartial justice,
Ever exhibited in the blood-stained theatre of human actions.
Oh Reader!
Pass not on, till thou hast blest his memory,
And never—never forget,
That REBELLION TO TYRANTS IS OBEDIENCE TO GOD.

"From many circumstances, there is reason to believe there does not exist any such inscription as the above, and that it was written by Dr. Franklin, in whose hands it was first seen. [This note was evidently a remark by Mr. J. himself.]"

APPENDIX NO. V.—Vol. I., p. 388.

Two Letters from Mr. Jefferson to Francis Eppes, in 1783.

PHILADELPHIA, *Jan.* 14, 1783.

DEAR SIR: You will hardly expect to receive a letter from me at this place, and of so late a date. Yet I have apprehensions of being here ten days or a fortnight longer, for though ready myself, some time since, the vessel in which I go is not ready. Yesterday's post brought no mail from Virginia. I was not disappointed in this, as I was pretty certain that under expectation of my being gone you did not write. I had entertained some hope of meeting a letter from you on my first arrival here, but suppose the same idea of its not coming in time prevented it, so that at present I have no hope of hearing again, while on this side water, from yourself and family and those dear little ones I have left with you. We have heard nothing since my .ast from which the length of my absence may be conjectured. The last authentic advices were of the 14th of October, but the affair of Gibraltar happened just then, and the negotiation was in such a state that what had passed between the negotiators was at that time under submission to the British court for their approbation or disavowal. How far this would be influenced by their good fortune at Gibraltar is the question which the next advices must certainly solve. Since I came here there has been sold the Westover copy of Catesby's History of Carolina. It was held near a twelvemonth at twelve guineas, and at last sold for ten. This seems to fix what should be given for Mr. Bolling's copy, if you can induce him to let me have it, which I am very anxious for. Perhaps it would be a temptation to offer that the ten guineas should be paid to Mr. Ross's agent at Nantes, where he could lay them out and send the articles to Mr. Bolling. His draft shall be paid on sight in Paris. Perhaps you had better effect this by making the proposition to Mrs. Bolling. Of this your knowledge of the family will enable you to judge. Be so good as to present me most affectionately to Mrs. Eppes, Mr. and Mrs. Skipwith, and the two families, and believe me to be, with very great sincerity, dear sir,

Your friend and servant,

TH. JEFFERSON.

PHILADELPHIA, *March* 4, 1783.

DEAR SIR: In my last, from Baltimore, I informed you that my voyage to Europe was at least suspended till further intelligence should be received. I returned to this place about four or five days ago, that I might be on the spot to act as shall be ultimately concluded by Congress. Though nothing since has come to us, we consider the event of peace as certain and speedy. The hearing nothing is a proof of this. The French minister, the British at New York, and Congress, are equally uninformed. This would not have been the case had the conferences for peace broken off, as has been pretended, or had they become languid. The packets and dispatch vessels are detained, doubtless, on a daily expectation of sending something more definitive than the signing of preliminaries. Capt. Barney is lying at L'Orient with the Washington, a dispatch vessel of Congress, ready to bring the advices from our plenipotentiaries. From these circumstances, you will judge that I expect every hour to receive permission to return home. I shall be here but a very few days after this shall be received, and expect to be myself the bearer of the first intelligence to you. There is nothing new here. I hope by the next post to receive a letter from you, though after near three months' absence without having ever heard a word of my dear little ones, I shall receive your letter with fear and trembling, lest any accident should have happened. This dread, I hope, will be removed. Patsy is well. I hope Mrs. Eppes has recovered better health. If my prayers would be a medicine, she should have them with more fervor than they were ever offered for myself. Present my love to her and the little ones, and whenever you have an opportunity, be so good as to let Mr. and Mrs. Skipwith know that I remember them with affection. I am, dear sir,

Your sincere friend,

Th. Jefferson.

Francis Eppes, Esq.,
    Eppington, (near Richmond.)

APPENDIX NO. VI.—Vol. I., p. 400.

Synopsis of Jefferson's Draft of Instructions for our Foreign Ministers, in 1784.

1. EACH party to have the right to carry and sell its own merchandise in its own bottoms in the ports of the other, and from thence to purchase and carry the merchandise of the other, paying, in both cases, only such duties as are paid by the most favored nation.

2. The United States to be allowed direct intercourse on the same conditions with the American possessions (or certain free ports in them) of European nations; or each to carry their own merchandise in their own bottoms to the other.

3. In all such treaties, the United States to be considered as one nation, upon the principles of the federal compact.

4. That "it be proposed, but not indispensably required," that in case of war, merchants of one country residing in the other, have nine months to collect their debts, and the privilege of carrying off their entire effects: that all unarmed fishermen, cultivators of the earth, artisans or manufacturers, peaceably following their employments, shall not be molested by the armed force of the enemy, and all things necessarily taken from them, paid for: that merchants and traders be allowed to pass freely: that all privateering be abolished.

5. That merchandise hitherto denominated contraband be no longer subject to confiscation, but that it be liable to be detained by the captor, on paying for such detention, or appropriated by him, on his paying its current value at its place of destination. If other nations will not consent to discontinue confiscation, to obtain its limitation to articles actually contraband, and a stipulation that when these are delivered up, vessels shall be allowed to proceed with the rest of their cargoes.

6. That where either of the contracting parties are at war with a third power, all goods not contraband, belonging to the subjects of such third power, and shipped in

the bottoms of the contracting party not engaged in the war, shall pass free [in other words, "free ships to make free goods."] Blockades only to exist where the assailing power shall have taken such a station as to expose to imminent danger ships sailing in or out of the blockaded port; no neutral to be stopped without a material and well-grounded cause, and prompt indemnification to be rendered when causelessly stopped.

7. No stipulations to be made for aliens to hold real property in the United States, but when an alien is heir to such property, he to be allowed a reasonable time to sell and withdraw the proceeds of the same.

8. Treaties to be made for a term not exceeding ten years.

9. Ministers to be allowed to extend treaties to fifteen years with nations insisting thereon. [Other provisions follow of no general interest.]

Mr. Jefferson only shares with Dr. Franklin the credit of the novel provisions here proposed to be engrafted into the code of international law. In a letter written but a short period before his death (to J. Q. Adams, March 30, 1826), he declared that the proposed stipulations in regard to privateering, blockades, contraband, and freedom of the fisheries, had before been suggested by Dr. Franklin, and that he (Jefferson) "happened only to have been the inserter of them in the first public act which gave [them] the formal sanction of a public authority."

———— ••• ————

APPENDIX NO. VII.—Vol. I., p. 415.

Mr. Jefferson to Francis Eppes.

PARIS, *Feb. 5, 1785.*

DEAR SIR: By the Marquis Fayette, which arrived here the 26th of Jan., I received yours of Sept. 16th, informing me of the illness of our children, and at the same time one from Dr. Currie, of Nov. 20th, mentioning its fatal termination. It is in vain to endeavor to describe the situation of my mind; it would pour balm neither into your wounds nor mine; I will therefore pass on from the subject. I wrote you by the last packet, of Jan. 13th, on the subject of the money which had been voted me by the Assembly. I find now, by your letter, that it cannot be reserved for the purpose I had in contemplation, and therefore wish you to call for and apply it as shall be most requisite, should Mr. Madison not have used it as I offered to him. When I look over the list of my debts as they stood at my departure from Virginia, and consider that Key has had the crop of 1783, and by this time that of 1784, I cannot but hope that with the aid abovementioned from the treasury, all very urging claims may be satisfied. I have a lot in Richmond, by the waterside, bought of Col. Byrd, to the sale of which I should have no objection; the purchaser undertaking to obtain the title from Mr. Carter, which has never yet been completely done. Europe presents nothing new. We are still hanging between peace and war, as heretofore, unable to conjecture which will take place. The depredations of the piratical States on our commerce is the most interesting circumstance to us. This can only be prevented by war or tribute. If the latter, it will not be light. Mr. Short is here, and well. Patsy enjoys perfect health; but I cannot recover mine. I am, however, so much better than I have been that I hope soon to be well. Perhaps this gloomy and damp climate may disappoint my hopes. Present me affectionately to Mrs. Eppes, who will kiss my dear, dear Polly for me—Oh! could I do it myself! Give our love, also, to the children, and be assured of the sincerity with which I am, dear sir,

Your affectionate friend and servant,
TH. JEFFERSON.

P. S.—I must beg the favor of you never to send a letter by any conveyance but the French packet. If your letters leave Richmond by the first of the month, addressed to the care of Neill Jamieson, in New York, they will reach that in time to come by the packet of that month; and we are sure of receiving them, submitting only to their being privately read by the postmaster, as is the case in every country in Europe; should there at any time be anything which ought not to be read by any other, it will be necessary to desire Mr. Jamieson to confide it to some passenger who will put it into my own hand. By the French packet I shall receive your letters in seven weeks from their date.

FRANCIS EPPES, Esq.

APPENDIX NO. VIII.—VOL. I. p. 544.

Jefferson to Madison, on the question, "Can one generation of men bind another?"

PARIS, *September 6th,* 1789.

*   *   *   *   *   *   *

The question, whether one generation of men has a right to bind another, seems never to have been started either on this or our side of the water. Yet it is a question of such consequences as not only to merit decision, but place also among the fundamental principles of every government. The course of reflection in which we are immersed here, on the elementary principles of society, has presented this question to my mind; and that no such obligation can be so transmitted, I think very capable of proof. I set out on this ground, which I suppose to be self-evident, that the *earth belongs in usufruct to the living;* that the dead have neither powers nor rights over it. The portion occupied by any individual ceases to be his when himself ceases to be, and reverts to the society. If the society has formed no rules for the appropriation of its lands in severalty, it will be taken by the first occupants, and these will generally be the wife and children of the decedent. If they have formed rules of appropriation, those rules may give it to the wife and children, or to some one of them, or to the legatee of the deceased. So they may give it to his creditor. But the child, the legatee or creditor, takes it, not by natural right, but by a law of the society of which he is a member, and to which he is subject. Then, no man can, by *natural right,* oblige the lands he occupied, or the persons who succeed him in that occupation, to the payment of debts contracted by him. For if he could, he might during his own life, eat up the usufruct of the lands for several generations to come; and then the lands would belong to the dead, and not to the living, which is the reverse of our principle.

What is true of every member of the society, individually, is true of them all collectively; since the rights of the whole can be no more than the sum of the rights of the individuals. To keep our ideas clear when applying them to a multitude, let us suppose a whole generation of men to be born on the same day, to attain mature age on the same day, and to die on the same day, leaving a succeeding generation in the moment of attaining their mature age, all together. Let the ripe age be supposed of twenty-one years, and their period of life thirty-four years more, that being the average term given by the bills of mortality to persons of twenty-one years of age. Each successive generation would, in this way, come and go off the stage at a fixed moment, as individuals do now. Then I say, the earth belongs to each of these generations during its course, fully and in its own right. The second generation receives it clear of the debts and incumbrances of the first, the third of the second, and so on. For if the first could charge it with a debt, then the earth would belong to the dead and not to the living generation. Then, no generation can contract debts greater than may be paid during the course of its own existence. At twenty-one years of age, they may bind themselves and their lands for thirty-four years to come; at twenty-two, for thirty-three; at twenty-three, for thirty-two; and at fifty-four, for one year only; because these are the terms of life which remain to them at the respective epochs. But a material difference must be noted, between the succession of an individual and that of a whole generation. Individuals are parts only of a society, subject to the laws of the whole. These laws may appropriate the portion of land occupied by a decedent, to his creditor rather than to any other, or to his child, on condition he satisfies the creditor. But when a whole generation, that is, the whole society, dies, as in the case we have supposed, and another generation or society succeeds, this forms a whole, and there is no superior who can give their territory to a third society, who may have lent money to their predecessors, beyond their faculties of paying.

What is true of generations succeeding one another at fixed epochs, as has been supposed for clearer conception, is true for those renewed daily, as in the actual course of nature. As a majority of the contracting generation will continue in being thirty-four years, and a new majority will then come into possession, the former may extend their engagements to that term, and no longer. The conclusion, then, is, that neither the representatives of a nation, nor the whole nation itself assembled, can validly engage debts beyond what they may pay in their own time, that is to say, within thirty-four years from the date of the engagement.

To render this conclusion palpable, suppose that Louis the XIV. and XV. had contracted debts in the name of the French nation, to the amount of ten thousand milliards, and that the whole had been contracted in Holland. The interest of this sum would be five hundred milliards, which is the whole rent-roll or net proceeds of the territory of France. Must the present generation of men have retired from the territory in which nature produces them, and ceded it to the Dutch creditors? No; they have the same rights over the soil on which they were produced, as the preceding generations had. They derive these rights not from them, but from nature. They, then, and their soil are, by nature, clear of the debts of their predecessors. To present this in another point of view, suppose Louis XV. and his cotemporary generation, had said to the money-lenders of Holland, "Give us money, that we may eat, drink, and be merry in our day; and on condition you will demand no interest till the end of thirty-four years, you shall then, forever after, receive an annual interest of fifteen per cent." The money is lent on these conditions, is divided among the people, eaten, drunk, and squandered. Would the present generation be obliged to apply the produce of the earth and of their labor, to replace their dissipations? Not at all.

I suppose that the received opinion, that the public debts of one generation de-

·olve on the next, has been suggested by our seeing, habitually, in private life, that ¹e who succeeds to lands is required to pay the debts of his predecessor; without ·onsidering that this requisition is municipal only; not moral, flowing from the will ·f the society, which has found it convenient to appropriate the lands of a decedent ¹n the condition of a payment of his debts: but that between society and society, ¹r generation and generation, there is no municipal obligation, no umpire but the ¹aw of nature.

The interest of the national debt of France being, in fact, but a two-thousandth ¹art of its rent-roll, the payment of it is practicable enough; and so becomes a ¹uestion merely of honor or of expediency. But with respect to future debts, would ¹t not be wise and just for that nation to declare in the constitution they are form-¹ng, that neither the legislature nor the nation itself, can validly contract more debt ¹han they may pay within their own age, or within the term of thirty-four years? ¹nd that all future contracts shall be deemed void, as to what shall remain unpaid ¹t the end of thirty-four years? This would put the lenders, and ¹he borrowers also, on their guard. By reducing, too, the faculty of borrowing ¹ithin its natural limits, it would bridle the spirit of war, to which too free a course ¹as been procured by the inattention of money lenders to this law of nature, that ¹ucceeding generations are not responsible for the preceding.

On similar ground it may be proved, that no society can make a perpetual con-¹titution, or even a perpetual law. The earth belongs always to the living genera-¹ion: they may manage it, then, and what proceeds from it, as they please, during ¹heir usufruct. They are masters, too, of their own persons, and consequently may ¹overn them as they please. But persons and property make the sum of the objects ¹f government. The constitution and the laws of their predecessors are extin-¹uished then, in their natural course, with those whose will gave them being. This ¹ould preserve that being, till it ceased to be itself, and no longer. Every constitu-¹ion, then, and every law, naturally expires at the end of thirty-four years. If it be ¹nforced longer, it is an act of force, and not of right. It may be said, that the ¹ucceeding generation exercising, in fact, the power of repeal, this leaves them as ¹ree as if the constitution or law had been expressly limited to thirty-four years only. In the first place, this objection admits the right, in proposing an equivalent. But the power of repeal is not an equivalent. It might be, indeed, if every form of government were so perfectly contrived, that the will of the majority could always be obtained, fairly and without impediment. But this is true of no form. The people cannot assemble themselves; their representation is unequal and vicious. Various checks are opposed to every legislative proposition. Factions get possession of the public councils, bribery corrupts them, personal interests lead them astray from the general interests of their constituents; and other impediments arise, so as to prove to every practical man, that a law of limited duration is much more man-ageable than one which needs a repeal.

This principle, that the earth belongs to the living and not to the dead, is of very extensive application and consequences in every country, and most especially in France. It enters into the resolution of the questions, whether the nation may change the descent of lands holden in tail; whether they may change the appro-priation of lands given anciently to the church, to hospitals, colleges, orders of chi valry, and otherwise in perpetuity; whether they may abolish the charges and privileges attached on lands, including the whole catalogue, ecclesiastical and feudal it goes to hereditary offices, authorities and jurisdictions, to hereditary orders, dis-tinctions and appellations, to perpetual monopolies in commerce, the arts or sciences, with a long train of *et ceteras;* and it renders the question of reimbursement a question of generosity and not of right. In all these cases, the legislature of the day could authorize such appropriations and establishments for their own time, but no longer; and the present holders, even where they or their ancestors have purchased, are in the case of *bona fide* purchasers of what the seller had no right to convey.   *   *   *   *   *   *

Madison's reply.[1]

NEW YORK, *February* 4, 1790.

DEAR SIR: Your favor of January 9th, inclosing one of September last, did not get to hand till a few days ago. The idea which the latter evolves is a great one, and suggests many interesting reflections to legislators, particularly when contracting and providing for public debts. Whether it can be received in the extent to which your reasonings carry it, is a question which I ought to turn more in my thoughts than I have yet been able to do, before I should be justified in making up a full opinion on it. My first thoughts lead me to view the doctrine as not in *all respects* compatible with the course of human affairs. I will endeavor to sketch the grounds of my skepticism.

"As the earth belongs to the living, not to the dead, a living generation can bind itself only : in every society the will of the majority binds the whole : according to the laws of mortality, a majority of those ripe for the exercise of their will, do not live beyond the term of 19 years : to this term, then, is limited the validity of every act of the society; nor can any act be continued beyond this term, without an *express* declaration of the public will." This I understand to be the outline of the argument.

The acts of a political society may be divided into three classes :

1. The fundamental constitution of the government.

2. Laws involving some stipulation, which renders them irrevocable at the will of the legislature.

3. Laws involving no such irrevocable quality.

1. However applicable in theory the doctrine may be to a constitution, it seems liable, in practice, to some weighty objections.

Would not a government ceasing of necessity at the end of a given term, unless prolonged by some constitutional act, previous to its expiration, be too subject to the casualty and consequences of an interregnum ?

Would not a government so often revised, become too mutable and novel to retain that share of prejudice in its favor, which is a salutary aid to the most rational government ?

Would not such a periodical revision engender pernicious factions, that might not otherwise come into existence, and agitate the public mind more frequently and more violently than might be expedient ?

2. In the second class of acts involving stipulations, must not exceptions, at least, to the doctrine be admitted ?

If the earth be the gift of *nature* to the living, their title can extend to the earth in its *natural* state only. The *improvements* made by the dead form a debt against the living, who take the benefit of them. This debt cannot be otherwise discharged than by a proportionate obedience to the will of the authors of the improvements.

---

[1] We are indebted to Professor Tucker's Life of Jefferson (vol. i., p. 292), for this letter. Professor Tucker received it from Mr. Madison.

But a case less liable to be controverted may perhaps be stated. Debts may be incurred with a direct view to the interest of the unborn, as well as of the living. Such are debts for repelling a conquest, the evils of which descend through many generations. Debts may be incurred principally for the benefit of posterity; such, perhaps, is the debt incurred by the United States. In these instances, the debt might not be dischargeable within the term of 19 years.

There seems then to be some foundation in the nature of things, in the relation which one generation bears to another, for the *descent* of obligations from one to another. Equity may require it. Mutual good may be promoted by it; and all that seems indispensable in stating the account between the dead and the living, is to see that the debts against the latter do not exceed the advances made by the former. Few of the incumbrances entailed on nations by their predecessors, would bear a liquidation even on this principle.

3. Objections to the doctrine, as applied to the third class of acts, must be merely practical. But in that view alone they appear to be material.

Unless such temporary laws should be kept in force by acts regularly anticipating their expiration, all the rights depending on positive laws, that is, most of the rights of property, would become absolutely defunct, and the most violent struggles ensue between the parties interested in reviving, and those interested in reforming the antecedent state of property. Nor does it seem improbable that such an event might be suffered to take place. The checks and difficulties opposed to the passage of laws, which render the power of repeal inferior to an opportunity to reject, as a security against oppression, would have rendered the latter an insecure provision against anarchy. Add to this, that the very possibility of an event so hazardous to the rights of property could not but depreciate its value; that the approach of the crisis would increase the effect; that the frequent return of periods, superseding all the obligations depending on antecedent laws and usages must, by weakening the sense of them, coöperate with motives to licentiousness already too powerful; and that the general uncertainty and vicissitudes of such a state of things would, on one side, discourage every useful effort of steady industry, pursued under the sanction of existing laws, and on the other, give an immediate advantage to the more sagacious over the less sagacious part of society.

I can find no relief from such embarrassments but in the received doctrine that a *tacit* assent may be given to established governments and laws, and that this assent is to be inferred from the omission of an express revocation. It seems more practicable to remedy by well constituted governments, the pestilent operation of this doctrine, in the unlimited sense in which it is at present received, than it is to find a remedy for the evils necessarily springing from an unlimited admission of the contrary doctrine.

Is it not doubtful whether it be possible to exclude wholly the idea of an implied or tacit assent, without subverting the very foundation of civil society?

On what principle is it that the voice of the majority binds the minority?

It does not result, I conceive, from a law of nature, but from compact founded on utility.

A greater proportion might be required by the fundamental constitution of society, if under any particular circumstances it were judged eligible. Prior, therefore, to the establishment of this principle, *unanimity* was necessary; and rigid theory accordingly presupposes the assent of every individual to the rule which subjects the minority to the will of the majority. If this assent cannot be given tacitly, or be not implied where no positive evidence forbids, no person born in society could, on attaining ripe age, be bound by any acts of the majority, and either an unanimous renewal of every law would be necessary, as often as a new member should be added to the society, or the express consent of every new member be obtained to the rule by which the majority decides for the whole.

If these observations be not misapplied, it follows that a limitation of the validity of all acts, to the computed life of a generation establishing them, is in some cases, not required by theory, and, in others, not consistent with practice. They are not meant, however, to impeach either the utility of the principle, as applied to the cases you have particularly in view, or the general importance of it in the eye of the philosophical legislator. On the contrary, it would give me singular pleasure to see it first announced to the world in a law of the United States, and always kept in view as a salutary restraint on living generations, from *unjust* and *unnecessary* burdens on their successors. This is a pleasure, however, which I have no hope of enjoying. It is so much easier to descry the little difficulties immediately incident to every great plan, than to comprehend its general and remote benefits, that further light must be added to the councils of our country, before many truths which are seen through the medium of philosophy, become visible to the naked eye of the ordinary politician.

APPENDIX NO. IX.—Vol. I., p. 573.

Mr. Madison's Explanations in regard to his Report of Hamilton's and Morris's Speeches in the Federal Convention.

The following extract from Mr. Trist's memoranda perhaps contains no absolutely new matter, unless it is the fact (which we do not now remember to have seen elsewhere stated) that Madison showed his report of Morris's speech to the maker. But it fills out more fully and clearly the explanations given in the Madison papers in regard to Hamilton's speeches, and to what took place between Madison and Hamilton in respect to them.

MONTPELLIER, *Sept. 27th,* 1834.

"*Hamilton's Life* (the forthcoming volumes) I (N. P. T.) mentioned to Mr. M., without telling him the *source*, what I had heard with regard to the bearing of the work upon him. His report of Hamilton's speech (in the convention which formed the Constitution), of which report I knew Mr. M. had furnished a copy to the son of A. H., was to be proved to be incorrect, and he was to be represented as having deserted Colonel Hamilton. Mr. M., 'I can't believe it.' Thereupon, I (N. P. T.) told him that my information as to the bearing of the forthcoming book upon him, came from the son of Colonel Hamilton himself—the son engaged in writing the life of his father, who had had a conversation on the subject with Professor Tucker of the University of Virginia, who has just returned from a trip to New York. Professor Tucker had mentioned it to Professor Davies, and the latter to me. I added, what I had heard, that there was nothing like unkind feeling towards him Mr. Madison) manifested by young Mr. Hamilton, but the reverse. Such, however, was to be the complexion of the work as to himself.

"Mr. M., 'Sorry for it.' After a pause: 'I can't conceive on what ground the fidelity of my report of Colonel H.'s speech can be impugned, unless it should proceed from the error of confounding together his *first* speech and his *second*. The first, I reported at length. It was a very able and methodical one, containing a lucid exposition of his views: *views which he made no secret of at the time or subsequently*, particularly with persons on a footing of the ordinary confidence among gentlemen thrown into political relations with each other on subjects of great moment. The *second* speech was little else than a repetition of the other, or parts of the other, with amplifications. *That* I did not report, for the reason just stated, and because he had told me of his intention to write it out himself, and had promised me a copy. The promised copy he never gave me; whether he ever executed his intention to write it out, even, I don't know. Yates has blended these two speeches together in his account of the proceedings.'

"I (N. P. T.) here reminded Mr. Madison of his having given me, some years ago, an account of these speeches, and those of others (of which I made a memorandum at the time, which is among my papers in Washington), and his having told me that he read to Colonel Hamilton and to Governeur Morris his reports of their speeches. That Col. H. acknowledged the accuracy of his, suggesting only one or two verbal alterations, and that G. M. laughed and said ' yes, it is all right.'

" Mr. M., ' Yes, Governeur Morris's speech was a very extravagant one. It displayed his usual talent, and also, in a striking degree, his usual fondness for saying things and advancing doctrines that no one else would. At the moment, he was not perhaps himself conscious how far he went; and when the thing *stared him in the face* (this was Mr. M.'s exact expression), as written down by me, it caused him to laugh, while he acknowledged its truth.'

" Mr. M., ' As to the other branch of the subject, I deserted Colonel Hamilton, or rather Colonel H. deserted me ; in a word, the divergence between us took place —from his wishing to *administration*, or rather to administer the Government (these were Mr. M.'s very words), into what he thought it ought to be ; while, on my part, I endeavored to make it conform to the Constitution as understood by the Convention that produced and recommended it, and particularly by the State conventions that *adopted* it.' "

APPENDIX NO. X.—Vol. II., p. 114.

Thomas Jefferson to Francis Eppes, Esq., Eppington.

PHILADELPHIA, *Apr. 7th,* 1793.

DEAR SIR: According to the information contained in my letter of March 17th, Jack now sets out for Virginia. The circumstances which have determined the moment of his departure have been the commencement of a term at William & Mary, should you accede to the proposition of his going there, and my relinquishing my house here and retiring to a small one in the country with only three rooms, and from whence I shall hold myself in readiness to take my departure for Monticello the first moment I can do it with due respect to myself. I can give you the most consoling assurances as to Jack's temper, prudence, and excellent dispositions. On these points I can say with truth everything a parent would wish to hear. As far, too, as his backwardness would ever give me an opportunity of judging, I can pronounce a very favorable verdict on his talents, in which I have been entirely confirmed by those who have had better opportunities of judging as having had better opportunities of unreserved conversations with him. After all, the talent for speaking is yet untried, and can only be tried at the moot courts at the college, which I propose for his next object.

My papers being packed for removal, I am not able to look to your last letter; but I think you say in it that, instead of money, we are to receive from Cary's executor only bonds of 6, 9, and 12 months. This being the case of an execution, I do not well understand it: however I will solicit your attention to it, on my behalf, to avail me of this resource for any sum of money which it may yield, and as early as it can be yielded (I mean my proportion only), for a disappointment from another quarter in Virginia has so far abridged the provision I had made for winding up my affairs here, as that it will fall considerably short, and will really distress me, and perhaps subject me to mortification. We may now give credit to the information that war is declared between France and England. If you have not sold your wheat, the moment will be favorable, but it should not be over-passed, as the purchases will of course cease as soon as the chance ceases of getting them to Europe before their harvest. I hope they will let us work in peace to feed them during the continuance of their follies. Present me most affectionately to Mrs. Eppes and the family, as also to our friends at Hors du Monde, when an occasion offers, and believe me to be most sincerely, dear sir,

Your friend and servant,
TH. JEFFERSON.

APPENDIX NO. XI.—Vol. II. p. 201.

Giuseppe Ceracchi, Washington's Bust, etc.

Ceracchi made a characteristic exit from a scene where he had met little besides buffets. He entered with fiery vehemence into the project of an Italian Republic in 1799. Compelled to leave his country, he went to Paris, and there received a commission to execute a bust of the first Consul, Bonaparte. Among the young artists of the French capital, he soon formed political affiliations, which induced him to enter into a conspiracy to take away the life of the Consul, whom he regarded as the oppressor of Italy. He was arrested and interposed no defence before the court which tried him, answering the questions put to him only in monosyllables. In February, 1801, he marched undauntedly to the guillotine. In respect to the further history of Washington's bust, Mrs. Randolph's manuscript contains the following :

"Mr. Madison thought it had been bought by Messrs. Viar and Jaudennes, the Spanish commissioners, and by them carried to —— [Spain?]; but Burrows, who executed the monument for the General's mother in Fredericksburg, says that a son of Mr. Howard, of Baltimore, bought it, and that Mr. Howard gave it to Burrows upon condition that he would place it upon the top of the old lady's monument. He told Mr. Madison that he had it, and meant of course to place it there."

Whether General Washington was displeased with the bust as a work of art, as a likeness, or because Ceracchi offered it to him (as in the case of Jefferson) as a gift, or because it was executed, and a price affixed to it, without previous order, we are wholly unable to say, and can but dimly conjecture.

In 1792, Cerracchi addressed duplicate letters to Governor George Clinton, of New York, a bass-relief of whom was to be placed on the National Monument. Both of the letters are before us. We present a copy, in the writer's very imperfect English and spelling, thinking it will possess a melancholy interest to lovers of art.

EXCELLENCY,

Give me live to testify my recollection for the honor I had to be acquainted with your Excellency, and beg the favor to send me your bust in clay I had the pleasure to model, in order to introduce your portrait in the basso rilievos of the National Monument, which according to the decree of Congress, in the year 1783, is to be expressed five military deeds in which General Washington was present, and with Genl. Washington other eminent caracters most naturaly be introduced.

Congress will probably in this session take up again this business, and carry a resolution in favor of it, but in this case I am in nead of your valuable influence in persuading som of your friends, members of the State of New York, which are contrary to this monument because Genl. Washington is yet alive. The greatest ancient nations erected monuments to their Heros while living in order to produce emulation.

Congress at that time when passed the decree show the [word illegible—looks like "true"] intention of erecting directeley the monument, but the skarsety of mony prevented it then (to be brought in execution; now this difficulty is over, and hope the Hon. gentlemen will be persuaded that the honor to which are gelos was gaged in the 1783). [1]

If your Excellency shall be pleased to honor me with an order, I beg to be directed to Mr. Alexorphius, in Amsterdam, and he will send it to me at Rome, where I shall be in October.

I beg live to present my respectful compliments to your Lady and Docters, while with a perfect estime and respect, I am

of your Excellency,

The most ob. ser.

J. CERACCHI.[2]

APPENDIX NO. XII.—VOL. II. p. 219.

Ceremonials practised in the first Administration.

Colonel Hamilton proposed what we believe constituted the basis of the more important official ceremonials which were adopted. The following was his communication to President Washington on the subject:

[1] The words in parenthesis in duplicate but not in draft. There are other disagreements in language and spelling.
[2] In both copies, he gives the initial as J. (for Joseph) instead of the initial of the Italian Giuseppe.

May 5, 1789.

Sir: In conformity to the intimation you were pleased to honor me with on . . . . . evening last, I have reflected upon the etiquette proper to be observed by the President, and now submit the ideas which have occurred to me on the subject.

The public good requires, as a primary object, that the dignity of the office should be supported.

Whatever is essential to this ought to be pursued, though at the risk of partial or momentary dissatisfaction. But care will be necessary to avoid extensive disgust or discontent. Men's minds are prepared for a pretty high tone in the demeanor of the Executive, but I doubt whether for so high a tone as in the abstract might be desirable. The notions of equality are yet, in my opinion, too general and too strong to admit of such a distance being placed between the President and other branches of the government as might even be consistent with a due proportion. The following plan will, I think, steer clear of extremes, and involve no very material inconveniences.

1. The President to have a levee once a week for receiving visits; an hour to be fixed at which it shall be understood that he will appear, and consequently that the visitors are to be previously assembled.

The President to remain half an hour, in which time he may converse cursorily on indifferent subjects, with such persons as shall invite his attention, and at the end of that half hour disappear. Some regulation will be hereafter necessary to designate those who may visit.

A mode of introduction through particular officers will be indispensable. No visits to be returned.

2. The President to accept no invitations, and to give formal entertainments only twice or four times a year, the anniversaries of important events in the Revolution. If twice, the day of the declaration of independence, and that of the inauguration of the President, which completed the organization of the Constitution, to be preferred; if four times, the day of the treaty of alliance with France, and that of the definitive treaty with Britain to be added. The members of the two houses of the Legislature; principal officers of the government; foreign ministers and other distinguished strangers only to be invited. The numbers form, in my mind, an objection; but there may be separate tables in separate rooms. This is practised in some European courts. I see no other method in which foreign ministers can, with propriety, be included in any attentions of the table which the President may think fit to pay.

3. The President, on the levee days, either by himself or some gentleman of his household, to give informal invitations to family dinners on the days of invitation. Not more than six or eight to be invited at a time, and the matter to be confined essentially to members of the legislature and other official characters. The President never to remain long at the table.

I think it probable that the last article will not correspond with the ideas of most of those with whom your excellency may converse; but, on pretty mature reflection, I believe it will be necessary to remove the idea of too immense an inequality, which I fear would excite dissatisfaction and cabal. The thing may be so managed as neither to occasion much waste of time nor to infringe on dignity.

It is an important point to consider what persons may have access to your excellency on business. The heads of departments will, of course, have this privilege. Foreign ministers of some descriptions will also be entitled to it. In Europe,

I am informed, ambassadors only have direct access to the chief-magistrate. Something very near what prevails there would, in my opinion, be right. The distinction of rank between diplomatic characters requires attention, and the door of access ought not to be too wide to that class of persons. I have thought that the members of the Senate should also have a right of *individual* access on matters relative to the *public administration.* In England and France peers of the realm have this right. We have none such in this country, but I believe that it will be satisfactory to the people to know that there is some body of men in the State who have a right of continual communication with the President. It will be considered a safeguard against secret combinations to deceive him.

I have also asked myself, will not the Representatives expect the same privilege, and be offended if they are not allowed to participate with the Senate? There is sufficient danger of this to merit consideration. But there is a reason for the distinction in the Constitution. The Senate are coupled with the President in certain executive functions, treaties, and appointments. This makes them in a degree his constitutional counsellors, and gives them a *peculiar* claim to the right of access. On the whole, I think the discrimination will be proper and may be hazarded.

I have chosen this method of communication because I understood your excellency that it would be most convenient to you. The unstudied and unceremonious manner of it will, I hope, not render it the less acceptable. And if, in the execution of your commands, at any time, I consult frankness and simplicity more than ceremony or profession, I flatter myself you will not on that account distrust the sincerity of my cordial wishes for your personal happiness, and the success of your Administration. I have the honor to be, with the highest respect,

Your excellency's most obedient and humble servant.

Levees.

The "Levees" are thus described in "Griswold's Republican Court:"

"Respectable citizens and strangers, properly introduced, were seen by the President every other Tuesday, between the hours of three or four in the afternoon. The receptions were in the dining-room, on the first floor, in the back part of the house. At three o'clock, all the chairs having been removed, the door was opened, and the President, usually surrounded by the members of his Cabinet or other distinguished men, was seen by the approaching visitor standing before the fireplace, his hair powdered and gathered behind in a silk bag, coat and breeches of plain black velvet, white or pearl-colored vest, yellow gloves, a cocked hat in his hand, silver knee and shoe-buckles, and a long sword, with a finely wrought and glittering steel hilt, the coat worn over it, and its scabbard of polished white leather. On these occasions he never shook hands, even with his most intimate friends. The name of every one was distinctly announced, and he rarely forgot that of a person who had been once introduced to him. The visitor was received with a dignified bow, and passed on to another part of the room. At a quarter past three, the door was closed, the gentlemen present moved into a circle, and he proceeded, beginning at his right hand, to exchange a few words with each. When the circuit was completed, he resumed his first position, and the visitors approached him in succession, bowed, and retired."

The well known Col. William L. Stone, of New York, gave the following picture of the levees:

"They were numerously attended by all that was fashionable, elegant, and refined in society; but there were no places for the intrusion of the rabble in

crowds, or for the mere coarse and boisterous partisan—the vulgar electioneerer—
or the impudent place-hunter—with boots, and frock-coats or round-abouts, or with
patched knees, and holes at both elbows. On the contrary, they were select, and
more courtly than have been given by any of his successors.   .   .   .   .

None were admitted to the levees but those who had either a right by official station to be there, or were entitled to the privilege by established merit and character;
and full dress was required of all."

President's Speech.

Mr. Griswold says, in his Republican Court:

"In going to the Senate he [General Washington] used the chariot with six
horses. All his servants were white, and wore liveries of white cloth, trimmed
with scarlet or orange."   .   .   .   .   "The state coach was the
finest carriage in the city. It was usually drawn by four horses, but when it conveyed the President to Federal Hall, always by six. The body was in the shape
of a hemisphere, and it was cream-colored, and ornamented with cupids, supporting
festoons, and with borderings of flowers around the panels."

Richard Rush describes with animation the spectacle witnessed by him when a
boy, of General Washington proceeding in his carriage, with his servants in "glowing livery," followed by his secretaries and others in other carriages, slowly proceeding through a lane, formed through the congregated thousands of spectators, to
open Congress with a speech; and Mr. Rush continues:

"Washington got out of his carriage, and, slowly crossing the pavement,
ascended the steps of the edifice, upon the upper platform of which he paused, and
turning half round, looked in the direction of a carriage which had followed the lead
of his own. Thus he stood for a minute, distinctly seen by everybody. He stood in
all his civic dignity and moral grandeur, erect, serene, majestic. His costume was
a full suit of black velvet; his hair, in itself blanched by time, powdered to snowy
whiteness, a dress-sword by his side, and his hat held in his hand. Thus he stood,
in silence; and what moments those were!"

He waited for his secretaries, who got out of a chariot "decorated like his own."
The secretary ascended the steps and handed him a paper, "probably a copy of the
speech he was to deliver;" both entered the building, and then the crowd "sent up
huzzas, loud, long, earnest and enthusiastic."

Answer of the Houses.

On the Houses agreeing to their addresses, they proceeded in a procession of
carriages to the Presidential mansion, and delivered them to the President.

Birth Days.

The President's birth days were celebrated with many imposing ceremonies,
closing with a magnificent ball. We have observed no particular description of the
ceremonials. Some glimpses of the forms practised at the balls appear in Jefferson's Ana.

The President Walking.

Mr. Griswold gives the following among other recollections of Mrs. Wallace of
Philadelphia—a lady, he remarks, of distinguished rank and "eminent for whatever was beautiful and noble in her sex." Her house was opposite General Washington's. She said:

"It was the General's custom, frequently, when the day was fine, to come out to walk, attended by his secretaries, Mr. Lear and Major William Jackson—one on each side. He always crossed directly over from his own door to the sunny side of the street, and walked down. He was dressed in black, and all three wore cocked hats. She never observed them conversing; she often wondered and watched, as a child, to see if any of the party spoke, but never could perceive that anything was said. It was understood that the aids were kept at regal distance."

The President Travelling.

On his Eastern tour (October, 1790), says Griswold, he travelled "in his own chariot, drawn by four Virginian bays, and accompanied by two of his secretaries, Tobias Lear and Major Jackson, on horseback." In his Southern tour, in 1791, he used six horses. In these journeys he was escorted from place to place by military companies and civic processions.

· Mrs. Washington.

Mr. Griswold says, "During the Revolution, Mrs. Washington had remained as much as possible with the Chief. At the close of each campaign an aid-de-camp repaired to Mount Vernon, to escort her, and her arrival in camp, in a plain chariot, with postillions in white and scarlet liveries, was always an occasion of general happiness," etc.

About a month after the election of her husband to the Presidency, "she set out for New York, in her private carriage, with a small escort on horseback." Troops of dragoons, the President of the Senate, and Speaker of the General Assembly of Pennsylvania, with a numerous cavalcade of citizens, met her ten miles from Philadelphia "with the honors due to the Commander-in-chief." Other processions met her at Gray's ferry, and she entered the city amidst the pealing of bells, the roar of cannon, and the "cheering shouts of an immense concourse of joyous people." As she approached New York, similar demonstrations awaited her. Her receptions were as stately as the President's. Colonel Stone remarks:

"Proud of her husband's exalted fame, and jealous of the honors due, not only to his own lofty character, but to the dignified station to which a grateful country had called him, Mrs. Washington was careful in her drawing-rooms to exact those courtesies to which she knew he was entitled, as well on account of personal merit, as of official consideration."

It was her custom, says Griswold, "to return visits on the third day, and she always thus returned Mrs. Binney's: a footman would run over, knock loudly, and announce Mrs. Washington, who would then come over with Mr. Lear."

Here we have a spice of politics: "When," says the same writer, "this sort of people ['Democrats'] came into fashion during the French Revolution, full grown, she cherished against them an intensity of dislike which made it quite impossible for even the most amiable of that patriotic class to regard her with any affection whatever."

Again: "With what feelings the excellent woman regarded these Democrats is shown in an anecdote of the same period [1794]. She was a severe disciplinarian, and Nelly Custis was not often permitted by her to be idle or to follow her own caprices. The young girl was compelled to practise at the harpsichord four or five hours every day; and one morning, when she should have been playing, her grandmother entered the room, remarking that she had not heard her music, and also that she had observed some person going out, whose name she would much like to know. Nelly was silent, and suddenly her attention was arrested by a blemish on he wall, which had been newly painted a delicate cream color. 'Ah it was no

Federalist!' she exclaimed, looking at the spot, just above a settee; 'none but a filthy Democrat would mark a place with his good-for-nothing head in that manner.'"

We think there is a good deal of exaggeration in these latter statements. The narrator was probably misinformed, and possibly he also unconsciously allowed his own views of "Democrats" (disclosed on every page of the Republican Court) to somewhat color his anecdotes. We know at least that there was one "Democrat" whom Mrs. Washington always treated with the dignity befitting her own position, with the grace of her sex, and with the cordiality of a friend. We know that she did this through and after her husband's presidency, to the last day of his life and after his death. That "Democrat" was Mr. Jefferson. We think posterity should be slow to believe that a wife who has never been accused of being unworthy of the Father of his Country, would allow herself to speak of the Republican party as "filthy Democrats." There is not a remote probability that she ever did anything of the kind.

APPENDIX NO. XIII.—Vol. II. p. 284.

From John Adams to Elbridge Gerry.

PHILADELPHIA, *May* 30, 1797.

DEAR SIR : I have just received your favors of 28th May, No. 6 and No. 7, with a copy of No. 3. This last I had rec⁴ before.

I had no share in the recall of Monroe, and, therefore, am not responsible for the reasons of it. But I have heard such reports of his own language in France at his own table, and the language of those whom he entertained and countenanced, and of his correspondences with Bache, Beckley, etc., and his communications through the Aurora, that I wonder not at his recall. His speech at his audience of leave is a base, false, and servile thing. Indeed, it was *Randolph* who appointed him. He was, in Senate, as dull, heavy, and stupid a fellow as he could be consistently with malignity and inveteracy perpetual. A more unfit piece of wood to make a Mercury could not have been culled from the whole forest. It is improper for me to delineate the system of speculation and the persons concerned in it. Members of Congress, collectors of customs, consuls, secretaries, and ministers, etc., etc., etc., are suspected of such a mystery of it, as I shudder to think of. How far Monroe was directly or indirectly concerned in it, I know not. But he was the friend and idol, and apparently the centre of the whole group. How is it that Hitchbourne has become so rich? How is it that so many others, have rolled in wealth in Philadelphia and New York, without any visible means. These were confidential correspondents and intimate acquaintances of Monroe. I know not that he is entitled to any hearing, as there is no accusation. But I doubt extremely his inclination to ask for hearings or inquiries. He will have hearings enough of his friends, and certificates enough of French politicians and American speculators I doubt not —as many as Silas Deane had.

The want of *principle* in so many of our citizens, which you mention, is awfully ominous to our elective government. Want of principle seems to be a recommendation to popularity and influence. The avarice and ambition which you and I have witnessed for these thirty years, is too deeply rooted in the hearts and education and examples of our people ever to be eradicated, and it will make of all our elections only a species of lucrative speculation, and, consequently, scenes of turbulence, corruption, and confusion, of which foreign nations will avail themselves in the future as the French did in the last.

That there is a strong anti-Gallican party so far as to oppose an undue influence of France, I know. There are some who are anti-Gallican because they think the French, a false, deceitful, treacherous people. There are others anti-Gallican because they hate Atheism, Deism, and debauchery. There are others anti-Gallican, because at present so many of the French profess to be democrats, sans-culottes, and disorganizers. As to anti-Gallicans because the French are republicans, I don't know any such; indeed, I don't know any anti-Gallicans who believe the French to be republicans or capable of a republican government—any more than a snowball can exist a whole week in the streets of Philadelphia, under a burning sun of August or September. There are many who believe the French republican system cannot endure, and I am one of these. There are many who believe that our republican system cannot last long, for the very reason you mention, the want of principle. I am not one of these—though our cities are corrupt, our country is not, and I believe our republican plan may last a good while. But it will not, if French influence as well as English is not resisted. That there are persons principled against republicanism, I suppose is true—but they are altogether among the class of old tories as far as I know, and are very few in number, and of no influence at all in the State. There may be others besides my Parson Wibirt, who think a hereditary King and House of Lords, with a good House of Commons the best form of government—but he is the only whig that I know of who professes this faith. I doubt not old C. J. Chew may be of the same opinion—and am told Dr. Nesbit, of Dickinson College, is also—and these are all I have heard of—indeed, some of the Quakers may be of this sect. But there is nothing to fear from these numbers or characters. The real danger is in the universal avarice and ambition of the people, which may make all the best men sick and weary of the perpetual anxiety, which electioneering projects and exertions occasion.

I wish you could have come on to Philadelphia. But the six children were excuse enough. Blessings on them and their parents. So says Mrs. A. as well as

JOHN ADAMS.

MR. GERRY.

The foregoing letter is accurately copied from the original autograph letter of Mr. Adams in my possession.

GEO. M. CONARROE.
PHILADELPHIA, June 17, 1856.

For MR. RANDALL.

APPENDIX NO. XIV.—Vol. II. p. 316.

Mr. Madison's Suppressed Correspondence.—Mr. Trist to Henry S. Randall.

PHILADELPHIA, ———, 1854.

Mr. Randall's query about Mr. Madison's letters returned to him, is answered by the following extracts from James Madison to N. P. Trist:

" MONTPELLIER, *June* 12, 1827.

" I have not made a thorough examination of the chasms in my letters to Mr Jefferson *returned by him;* among those acknowledged in his to me, and not in the *bundle returned by him,* I find:

in 1799— 4
    1800— 6
    1802— 6
    1803— 6
    1804—11
    1805— 8
    1806— 4
    1807—10
    1808— 8 perhaps more
    1814— 2
    1817— 2
    1818— 1

" It is quite possible that among the missing letters there were some of a nature more proper to be destroyed than preserved.[1]

" If there be any letters from me between 1783 and 1799, I shall be particularly glad to know the dates and subjects of them.

" In a letter to Mr. Jefferson of Jan. 22d, 1786, a printed proposition in the House of Delegates for giving commercial powers to Congress is referred to as inclosed in the letter; but was not in it when returned. The proposition as printed is stated in the letter to have been referred to a committee, and to have then received the alterations noted with the pen. This is the proposition referred to in the 1st vol. of the Laws of the U. S., page 53, and printed there as it was materially altered in committee of the whole, and not as it was originally made. It is more probable that the document was not preserved than that it was separated from the letter and is now to be found on the files of Mr. J. Should it, however, be there, I would wish a sight of it.

" Is there among the letters of Mr. J. to Mr. Adams senior, one dated December 28, 1796? The reason for the question I will explain when I see you."

[" The foregoing," says Mr. Trist, " led to a request for the return of the letters (which I had found), a request made orally to Mr. Jefferson Randolph through me, and acceded to by him. He was the bearer of the letters to Mr. M., as is seen by the following :"]

---

[1] Note by N. P. Trist.

" This shows what was his reason for wishing to repossess himself of his letters. Had the request been made to *me,* knowing . . . what must be his principal motive, at least, I should have hesitated long—and probably decided against their delivery, save with the condition annexed of retaining copies But, I was on the occasion a mere channel of a request, and it did not accord with my views of good faith towards Mr. M., as his chosen channel for a request, to proffer my opinion. I limited myself strictly to my capacity of channel."

"MONTPELLIER, *Feb.* 4, 1823.

" Since mine of the 26th ult., which I hope got safely to hand, I have received
yours of the 29th, since which, that of the 30th, with the bundle of letters, has been
handed to me by Mr. Randolph. I am very sorry for the trouble it cost you to
take advantage of that conveyance. I return, as you desire, the extracts you made
from some of the letters. I return also the copies of two letters, inclosed in yours
of the 1st instant, just brought by the mail, though not desired ; [1] making of one
of them, however, an extract only, by lopping from it a paragraph irrelative to the
subject."

APPENDIX NO. XV.—Vol. II. p. 356.

*The Forrest letter, and the comments of Mr. Adams's biographer.—John Adams to
Uriah Forrest.*

PHILADELPHIA, 28 *June*, 1797.

DEAR SIR : I received yesterday your favor of the 23d, and am very much
obliged to you for it. The paper inclosed in it is a serious thing. It will be a
motive, in addition to many others, to be upon my guard. It is evidence of a mind
soured, yet seeking for popularity, and eaten to a honey-comb with ambition, yet
weak, confused, uninformed, and ignorant. I have been long convinced that this
ambition is so inconsiderate as to be capable of going great lengths. I shall carefully keep the secret, as far as it may compromise characters and names.   .   .   .

To this letter Mr. Adams's biographer and annotator subjoins the following
explanation in a note :

" General Forrest had communicated to Mr. Adams, from memory, having heard
it read, the substance of one of the many letters circulated at this time by Mr. Jefferson, under the strongest injunctions that no copy should be allowed to be taken.
It is worth while to contrast the opinion here expressed of Mr. J. with the uneasiness
felt by Mr. Hamilton and his friends lest Mr. Adams should be *led* by that gentleman. Fortunate would it have been for all the parties, if the idea of *leading* Mr.
Adams had not been always uppermost in their minds !" (Adams's Works,
vol. viii. p. 547.)

The italics are those of the annotator. When we first came to a particular
examination of this subject, we were persuaded that the above application of the
harsh remarks of the Forrest letter to Jefferson was an inadvertent error, on the
part of Mr. Adams's biographer. We, therefore, addressed Mr. Charles Francis
Adams a letter stating these impressions, the facts and reasonings on which they
were based, and then proceeded to say :

" If Mr. Forrest's letter does not name or indicate Mr. Jefferson, you can judge
what weight the suggestions I have made ought to have on your mind ; and should
they lead you to a train of inquiries that should satisfy you that my solution of the

---

[1] Note by N. P. Trist.
" He here uses ' desired ' in the sense of *requested*. I did *desire* (wish) it. But I deemed it
indelicate to express the wish. Good faith forbid that I should retain copies without his consent.
Delicacy forbid that I should ask this consent. Such a request from me, under the circumstances,
might be unpleasant to him, as presenting an alternative, both horns of which would be disagreeable. I therefore inclosed the copies, leaving him to infer my wish, and leaving him free also to
acknowledge the inference or not, as might be most agreeable to him. As to the ' extracts ' I had
made, their nature was such as to preclude all hesitation in asking to be intrusted with them."

affair is the correct one—or that yours was erroneous—I make no doubt that it will give you profound pleasure to enable me at once, in my work, to correct your mistake on your authority.

"If, on the other hand, you should be satisfied that you are not in error as to facts or dates, I venture to solicit from you such a reference as will enable me to ascertain where those clandestinely circulated letters of Mr. Jefferson, or any of them, bearing date anterior to Forrest's letter, and which (presumably) contain attacks of some kind on Mr. Adams, are to be found. I venture on this liberty, because I am writing a Life of Mr. Jefferson under the full sanction of his family—because I am peculiarly anxious to trace accurately and justly to both parties, the relations which existed between him and John Adams—and because you are the sole authority I know of entitled to notice, that he wrote or secretly circulated letters up to May [June] 23d, 1797 (the date, I believe, of Forrest's letter), which it would be presumed could draw out such remarks as Mr. Adams makes to Mr. Forrest—and which, *therefore*, would be wholly at variance with other letters which Mr. Jefferson was *contemporaneously* writing to such men as Madison and Gerry, *not without the expectation, in some instances, that they would be shown to Mr. Adams!* [1]

"When your note appended to the Forrest letter was first read by myself, and many other friends of Mr. Jefferson, we deeply lamented, sir, that any feeling of forbearance or delicacy towards Mr. Jefferson should have prevented you from giving the Forrest letter, and some of the 'many' of Mr. Jefferson, corresponding with the one described in it, which you aver were then secretly circulating. Neither the family nor friends of Mr. Jefferson claim, by any means, that he was perfect. But they are content that he take the full blame of every misdeed that it can be shown he committed. They ask simply justice and no mercy for him."

＊　　＊　　＊　　＊　　＊　　＊　　＊　　＊　　＊

Mr. Adams's Answer.

To Henry S. Randall, Esq., Cortland Village, N. Y.

Boston, 18th *November*, 1855.

Dear Sir: You stand in no need of apology for the letter you were kind enough to address to me on the 13th. I am happy to receive suggestions from every quarter which may tend to insure greater correctness in matters of history. My observation of the errors committed by others, as well as those into which I fall myself in spite of all my anxiety to be accurate, leads me to be little inclined to be positive about anything. If I have made mistakes, I am very ready, on consideration, to repair them.

With respect to all the persons whose action I cannot help touching upon in my work, my rule has been never to do so without deliberation, and perfect calmness. Aware of my duty to tell the truth, I have tried to do so without acrimony, and without feeling. So far as Mr. Jefferson is concerned, I am very sure I entertain no unfriendly sentiment—for, although he at times did great injury to John Adams, at others he repaired it more generously than some did nearer home. It is not, therefore, with the smallest personal bias that I proceed to the analysis of his character. What I shall say of him in the forthcoming volume may not be correct, but I will answer, that it shall be free from every unworthy or illiberal motive.

---

[1] This remark was written under a misapprehension in regard to dates. The friendly letter intended to be shown to Mr. Adams, which we had in mind, was addressed to Elbridge Gerry, May 18th, 1797. Mr. Adams's communications to Congress *two days afterwards*, converted Jefferson into an open, decided, and sometimes censorious opponent.

In this spirit I approach a reëxamination of my note on the 547th page of the th volume, to which you call my attention, and compare it with my authority. .nd here I must say that I am obliged to you for drawing my attention to two rrors that shall be at once corrected on the plates. The first is typographical, and 1ust have occurred to you. I mean the *date* of the letter of J. A. to General For- ɔst. It should be the 28th of June and not the 20th.

The second error is in that part of my note which says that General Forrest had nly *heard* Mr. Jefferson's letter read. I find, on examination, that he says he read . over twice, and immediately committed his impressions of it to paper.

Further than this I see no mistake—and you will perceive that the correction 1akes the case stronger than I stated it rather than weaker.

You are mistaken in supposing that the feeling which the communication of this ɔtter occasioned in Mr. Adams grew out of any personal attack it made upon him. t was the disingenuous representation of the policy he was recommending which oused him—perhaps not more so than is common with men under strong party ias, but aggravated by the injunctions of secresy with which it was accompanied.

I do not feel as if I ought to communicate more of General Forrest's own letter han the facts it contains. The letter was written by "the Vice-President" to Mr. '. Fitzhugh, dated the 4th of June, 1797. Mr. Fitzhugh was a Democrat, but a elative of Forrest. The letter had been shown to several Democrats, but only to one 'ederalist besides General Forrest.

The statement respecting Mr. Jefferson's injunctions that no copy should be taken ɔf his letter to his correspondents, is taken from the abstracts of the letter itself rhich fully sustains it. If you possess a copy of that letter, which I presume you 1ust, you have it in your power to publish it, and thus leave the world to judge of he justice of my grandfather's commentary. If found too harsh, I shall not defend 1im.

While I am about it, permit me to express my regret that the publication made ɔf Mr. Jefferson's works had not likewise been intrusted to you. I mean the last ɔne in nine volumes. It swarms with typographical errors.

I am, very truly, your obedient servant,

C. F. ADAMS.

It does not appear from this that President Adams learned that more than one etter concerning himself or his Administration was "circulated at that time [June, 1797] by Mr. Jefferson under the strongest injunctions that no copy should be 1llowed to be taken;" and it does appear that this *one* letter contained no "personal 1ttack" on President Adams. Of its "disingenuous representations" (even as nterpreted through the "impressions" of an individual who wrote down from 1emory the substance of a private letter for the purpose of communicating it to the 1ubject of its animadversions),[1] the public are not allowed to judge. The letter is in 1either edition of Mr. Jefferson's works, and if it had been preserved among his 1anuscripts, we should naturally expect to find it in the Congress edition. That 1r. Jefferson went into more confidential or more dangerous disclosures or repre- ɔentations to Mr. Peregrine Fitzhugh at that critical moment, than he did to Madison

---

[1] It is possible Forrest obtained Fitzhugh's permission to make the communication, but we have 10 proof or assertion of that fact, and the contrary would be inferred on several grounds. 1. Fitz- 1ugh was a gentleman of character, and would not, therefore, be likely to intentionally betray the ɔontents of a private letter to the very individual whose conduct was censured in it. 2. He was 1olitically and personally friendly to Mr. Jefferson, and was not politically friendly to Mr. Adams. 1. See Jefferson's subsequent letter to him given in the text.

and others, would scarcely be expected from the degree of intimacy which existed between them. We think in all of Jefferson's published correspondence there are but two or three letters addressed to Fitzhugh. And, unless we are very much mistaken, that of June 4th, 1797, was, in the opinion of Fitzhugh himself, very grossly misrepresented by the " impressions " of those whom he had permitted to read it. We infer so from the following passages contained in a subsequent letter to him from Jefferson :

" PHILADELPHIA, *February* 23, 1798.

" DEAR SIR :—I have yet to acknowledge your last favor, which I received at Monticello, and, therefore, cannot now refer to the date. The *perversion of the expressions* of a former *letter to you which you mention to have been made* in the newspapers, I had not till then heard of. Yet the spirit of it was not new. I have been for some time used as the property of the newspapers, a fair mark for every man's dirt." .   .   .   .

APPENDIX No. XVI.—VOL. II. p. 369.

The Mazzei Letter and Pickering's Charges—Jefferson to Martin Van Buren.

MONTICELLO, *June* 29th, 1824.

DEAR SIR : I have to thank you for Mr. Pickering's elaborate philippic against Mr. Adams, Gerry, Smith and myself; and I have delayed the acknowledgment until I could read it and make some observations on it.

I could not have believed, that for so many years, and to such a period of advanced age, he could have nourished passions so vehement and viperous. It appears, that for thirty years past, he has been industriously collecting materials for vituperating the characters he had marked for his hatred ; some of whom, certainly, if enmities towards him had ever existed, had forgotten them all, or buried them in the grave with themselves. As to myself, there never had been anything personal between us—nothing but the general opposition of party sentiment ; and our personal intercourse had been that of urbanity, as himself says. But it seems he has been all this time brooding over an enmity which I had never felt, and that, with respect to myself as well as others, he has been writing far and near, and in every direction, to get hold of original letters where he could, copies where he could not, certificates and journals, catching at every gossiping story he could hear of in any quarter, supplying by suspicions what he could find nowhere else, and then arguing on this motley farrago, as if established on gospel evidence. And while expressing his wonder, that " at the age of eighty-eight, the strong passions of Mr. Adams should not have cooled ;" that, on the contrary, " they had acquired the mastery of his soul," (p. 100) ; that " where these were enlisted, no reliance could be placed on his statements," (p. 104) ; the facility and little truth with which he could represent facts and occurrences, concerning persons who were the objects of his hatred (p. 3) ; that " he is capable of making the grossest misrepresentations, and, from detached facts, and often from bare suspicions, of drawing unwarrantable inferences, if suited to his purpose at the instant " (p. 174) ; while making such charges, I say, on Mr. Adams, instead of his " *ecce homo* " (p. 100) ; how justly might we say to him, "*mutato nomine, de te fabula narratur.*" For the assiduity and industry he has employed in his benevolent researches after matter of crimination against us, I refer to his pages 13, 14, 34, 36, 46, 71, 79, 90 bis, 92, 93 bis, 101 ter, 104, 116, 118, 141, 143, 146, 150, 151, 153, 168, 171, 172. That Mr. Adams's strictures on him, written and printed, should have excited some notice on his part, was not perhaps to be wondered at. But the sufficiency of his motive for the large attack on me may be more questionable. He says (p. 4), " of Mr. Jefferson I should have said nothing, but for his letter to Mr. Adams, of October the 12th, 1823." Now the object of that letter was to soothe the feelings of a friend, wounded by a publication which I thought an "outrage on private confidence." Not a word or allusion in it respecting Mr. Pickering, nor was it suspected that it would draw forth his pen in justification of this infidelity, which he has, however, undertaken in the course of his pamphlet, but more particularly in its conclusion.

He arraigns me on two grounds: my actions and my motives. The very actions, however, which he arraigns, have been such as the great majority of my fellow-citizens have approved. The approbation of Mr. Pickering, and of those who thought with him, I had no right to expect. My motives he chooses to ascribe to hypocrisy, to ambition, and a passion for popularity. Of these the world must judge between us. It is no office of his or mine. To that tribunal I have ever submitted my actions and motives, without ransacking the Union for certificates, letters, journals, and gossiping tales, to justify myself and weary them. Nor shall I do this on the present occasion, but leave still to them these antiquated party diatribes, now newly revamped and paraded, as if they had not been already a thousand times repeated, refuted, and adjudged against him, by the nation itself. If no action is to be deemed virtuous for which malice can imagine a sinister motive, then there never was a virtuous action; no, not even in the life of our Saviour himself. But he has taught us to judge the tree by its fruit, and to leave motives to Him who can alone see into them.

But whilst I leave to its fate the libel of Mr. Pickering, with the thousands of others like it, to which I have given no other answer than a steady course of similar action, there are two facts or fancies of his which I must set to rights. The one respects Mr. Adams, the other myself. He observes that my letter of October the 12th, 1823, acknowledges the receipt of one from Mr. Adams, of September the 18th, which, having been written a few days after Cunningham's publication, he says was no doubt written to apologize to me for the pointed reproaches he had uttered against me in his confidential letters to Cunningham. And thus having " no doubt" of his conjecture, he considers it as proven, goes on to suppose the contents of the letter (19, 22), makes it place Mr. Adams at my feet, suing for pardon, and continues to rant upon it, as an undoubted fact. Now, I do most solemnly declare, that so far from being a letter of apology, as Mr. Pickering so undoubtedly assumes, there was not a word or allusion in it respecting Cunningham's publication.

The other allegation, respecting myself, is equally false. In page 34, he quotes Doctor Stuart as having, twenty years ago, informed him that General Washington, "when he became a private citizen," called me to account for expressions in a letter to Mazzei, requiring, in a tone of unusual severity, an explanation of that letter. He adds, of himself, "in what manner the latter humbled himself and appeased the just resentment of Washington, will never be known, as some time after his death the correspondence was not to be found, and a diary for an important period of his presidency was also missing." The diary being of transactions during his presidency, the letter to Mazzei not known here until some time *after he became a*

VOL. III.—39

private citizen, and the pretended correspondence of course after that, I know not why this lost diary and supposed correspondence are brought together here, unless for insinuations worthy of the letter itself. The correspondence could not be found, indeed, because it had never existed. I do affirm that there never passed a word, written or verbal, directly or indirectly, between General Washington and myself on the subject of that letter. He would never have degraded himself so far as to take to himself the imputation in that letter on the "Samsons in combat." The whole story is a fabrication, and I defy the framers of it, and all mankind, to produce a scrip of a pen between General Washington and myself on the subject, or any other evidence more worthy of credit than the suspicions, suppositions, and presumptions of the two persons here quoting and quoted for it. With Doctor Stuart I had not much acquaintance. I supposed him to be an honest man, knew him to be a very weak one, and, like Mr. Pickering, very prone to antipathies, boiling with party passions, and, under the dominion of these, readily welcoming fancies for facts. But come the story from whomsoever it might, it is an unqualified falsehood.

This letter to Mazzei has been a precious theme of crimination for Federal malice. It was a long letter of business, in which was inserted a single paragraph only of political information as to the state of our country. In this information there was not one word which would not then have been, or would not now be approved by every Republican in the United States, looking back to those times, as you will see by a faithful copy now inclosed of the whole of what that letter said on the subject of the United States, or of its government. This paragraph, extracted and translated, got into a Paris paper at a time when the persons in power there were laboring under very general disfavor, and their friends were eager to catch even at straws to buoy them up. To them, therefore, I have always imputed the interpolation of an entire paragraph additional to mine, which makes me charge my own country with ingratitude and injustice to France. There was not a word in my letter respecting France, or any of the proceedings or relations between this country and that. Yet this interpolated paragraph has been the burden of Federal calumny, has been constantly quoted by them, made the subject of unceasing and virulent abuse, and is still quoted, as you see, by Mr. Pickering, page 33, as if it were genuine, and really written by me. And even Judge Marshall makes history descend from its dignity, and the ermine from its sanctity, to exaggerate, to record, and to sanction this forgery. In the very last note of his book, he says, "a letter from Mr. Jefferson to Mr. Mazzei, an Italian, was published in Florence, and re-published in the Moniteur, with very severe strictures on the conduct of the United States." And instead of the letter itself, he copies what he says are the remarks of the editor, which are an exaggerated commentary on the fabricated paragraph itself, and silently leaves to his reader to make the ready inference that these were the sentiments of the letter. Proof is the duty of the affirmative side. A negative cannot be possibly proved. But, in defect of impossible proof of what was not in the original letter, I have its press-copy still in my possession. It has been shown to several, and is open to any one who wishes to see it. I have presumed only, that the interpolation was done in Paris. But I never saw the letter in either its Italian or French dress, and it may have been done here, with the commentary handed down to posterity by the judge. The genuine paragraph, re-translated through Italian and French into English, as it appeared here in a Federal paper, besides the mutilated hue which these translations and retranslations of it produced, generally gave a mistranslation of a single word, which entirely perverted its meaning, and made it a pliant and fertile text of misrepresentation of my political principles. The original, speaking of an Anglican, monarchical and aristocratical party, which had sprung up since he had left us, states their object to be "to draw over us the substance, as they had already done the *forms* of the British Government." Now the " forms " here meant, were the levees, birthdays, the pompous cavalcade to the state-house on the meeting of Congress, the formal speech from the throne, the procession of Congress in a body to reecho the speech in an answer, etc. etc. But the translator here, by substituting *form* in the singular number, for *forms* in the plural, made it mean the frame or organization of our Government, or its form of legislative, executive and judiciary authorities, coördinate and independent; to which *form* it was to be inferred that I was an enemy. In this sense they always quoted it, and in this sense Mr. Pickering still quotes it, pages 34, 35, 38, and countenances the inference. Now General Washington perfectly understood what I meant by these forms, as they were frequent subjects of conversation between us. When, on my return from Europe, I joined the Government in March, 1790, at New York, I was much astonished, indeed, at the mimicry I found established of royal forms and ceremonies, and more alarmed at the unexpected phenomenon, by the monarchical sentiments I heard expressed and openly maintained in every company, and among others by the high members of the Government, executive and judiciary (General Washington alone excepted), and by a great part of the legislature, save only some members who had been of the old Congress, and a very few of recent introduction. I took occasion, at various times, of expressing to General Washington my disappointment at these symptoms of a change of principle, and that I thought them encouraged by the forms and ceremonies which I found prevailing, not at all in character with the simplicity of republican government, and looking as if wishfully to those of European courts. His general explanations to me were, that when he arrived at New York to enter on the executive administration of the new government, he observed to those who were to assist him, that placed as he was in an office entirely new to him, unacquainted with the forms and ceremonies of other governments, still less apprised of those which might be properly established here, and himself perfectly indifferent to all forms, he wished them to consider and prescribe what they should be ; and the task was assigned particularly to General Knox, a man of parade, and to Colonel Humphreys, who had resided some time at a foreign court. They, he said, were the authors of the present regulations and that others were proposed so highly strained that he absolutely rejected them. Attentive to the difference of opinion prevailing on this subject, when the term of his second election arrived, he called the Heads of Departments together, observed to them the situation in which he had been at the commencement of the government, the advice he had taken and the course he had observed in compliance with it ; that a proper occasion had now arrived of revising that course, of correcting it in any particulars not approved in experience ; and he desired us to consult together, agree on any changes we should think for the better, and that he should willingly conform to what we should advise. We met at my office. Hamilton and myself agreed at once that there was too much ceremony for the character of our Government, and particularly, that the parade of the installation at New York ought not to be copied on the present occasion, that the President should desire the Chief Justice to attend him at his chambers, that he should administer the oath of office to him in the presence of the higher officers of the Government, and that the certificate of the fact should be delivered to the Secretary of State to be recorded. Randolph and Knox differed from us, the latter vehemently ; they thought it not advisable to change any of the established forms, and we authorized Randolph to report our opinions to the President. As these opinions were divided, and no positive advice given as to any change, no change was made. Thus the forms which I had censured in my letter to Mazzei were perfectly understood by General Washington, and were those which he himself but barely tolerated. He had furnished me a proper occasion for proposing their reformation, and my opinion not prevailing, he knew I could not have meant any part of the censure for him.

Mr. Pickering quotes, too (page 34), the expression in the letter, of " the men who were Samsons in the field, and Solomons in the council, but who had had their heads shorn by the harlot England ;" or, as expressed in the re-translation, "the men who were Solomons in council, and Samsons in combat, but whose hair had been cut off by the whore England." Now this expression also was perfectly understood by General Washington. He knew that I meant it for the Cincinnati generally, and that from what had passed between us at the commencement of that institution, I could not mean to include him. When the first meeting was called for its establishment, I was a member of the Congress then sitting at Annapolis. General Washington wrote to me, asking my opinion on that proposition, and the course, if any, which I thought Congress would observe respecting it. I wrote him frankly my own disapprobation of it ; that I found the members of Congress generally of the same sentiment; that I thought they would take no express notice of it, but that in all appointments of trust, honor, or profit, they would silently pass by all candidates of that order, and give an uniform preference to others. On his way to the first meeting in Philadelphia, which I think was in the spring of 1784, he called on me at Annapolis. It was a little after candle-light, and he sat with me till after midnight, conversing, almost exclusively, on that subject. While he was feelingly indulgent to the motives which might induce the officers to promote it, he concurred with me entirely in condemning it ; and when I expressed an idea that if the hereditary quality were suppressed, the institution might perhaps be indulged during the lives of the officers now living, and who had actually served; " No," he said, " not a fibre of it ought to be left, to be an eye-sore to the public, a ground of dissatisfaction, and a line of separation between them and their country ;" and he left me with a determination to use all his influence for its entire suppression. On his return from the meeting, he called on me again, and related to me the course the thing had taken. He said, that, from the beginning, he had used every endeavor to prevail on the officers to renounce the project altogether, urging the many considerations which would render it odious to their fellow-citizens, and disreputable and injurious to themselves ; that he had at length prevailed on most of the old officers to reject it, although with great and warm opposition from others, and especially the younger ones, among whom he named Colonel W. S. Smith as particularly intemperate. But that in this state of things, when he thought the question safe, and the meeting drawing to a close, Major L'Enfant arrived from France with a bundle of eagles, for which he had been sent there, with letters from the French officers who had served in America, praying for admission into the order, and a solemn act of their king permitting them to wear its ensign. This, he said, changed the face of matters at once, produced an entire revolution of sentiment, and turned the torrent so strongly in an opposite direction, that it could be no longer withstood: all he could then obtain, was a suppression of the hereditary quality. He added, that it was the French applications, and respect for the approbation of the king, which saved the establishment in its modified and temporary form. Disapproving thus of the institution as much as I did, and conscious that I knew him to do so, he could never suppose that I meant to include him among the Samsons in the field, whose object was to draw

form, as they made the letter say, of the British Government, and espe-
istocratic member, an hereditary House of Lords. Add to this, that the
g, " that two out of the three branches of legislature were against us," was
 exception of him ; it being well known that the majorities in the two
f Senate and Representatives were the very instruments which carried, in
to the old and real Republicans, the measures which were the subjects of
ion in this letter. General Washington, then, understanding perfectly
•hom I meant to designate, in both phrases, and that they could not have
tion or view to himself, could find in neither any cause of offence to him-
herefore neither needed, nor ever asked any explanation of them from
it even been otherwise, they must know very little of General Washing-
iould believe to be within the laws of his character, what Doctor Stuart
ave imputed to him. Be this, however, as it may, the story is infamously
ery article of it. My last parting with General Washington was at the
•n of Mr. Adams, in March, 1797, and was warmly affectionate; and I
any reason to believe any change on his part, as there certainly was none
But one session of Congress intervened between that and his death, the
ing, in my passage to and from which, as it happened to be not conve-
ll on him, I never had another opportunity; and as to the cessation of
ence observed during that short interval, no particular circumstance
or epistolary communication, and both of us were too much oppressed
writing, to trouble, either the other, with a letter about nothing.
ith is, that the Federalists, pretending to be the exclusive friends of
ashington, have ever done what they could to sink his character, by
eirs on it, and by representing as the enemy of Republicans him, who,
 is best entitled to the appellation of the Father of that republic which
endeavoring to subvert, and the Republicans to maintain. They cannot
iuse the elections proclaimed the truth, that the great body of the
proved the Republican measures. General Washington was himself
i friend to the republican principles of our Constitution. His faith,
. its duration, might not have been as confident as mine; but he repeated to me, that he was determined it should have a fair chance for suc-
hat he would lose the last drop of his blood in its support, against any
hich might be made to change it from its republican form. He made
irations the oftener, because he knew my suspicions that Hamilton had
s, and he wished to quiet my jealousies on this subject. For Hamilton
•wed that he considered the British Constitution, with all the corrup-
s administration, as the most perfect model of government which had
devised by the wit of man, professing, however, at the same time, that
•f this country was so fundamentally republican, that it would be vision-
k of introducing monarchy here, and that, therefore, it was the duty of
trators to conduct it on the principles their constituents had elected.
. Washington, after the retirement of his first Cabinet, and the compo-
is second, entirely Federal, and at the head of which was Mr. Pickering
d no opportunity of hearing both sides of any question. His measures,
ly, took more the hue of the party in whose hands he was. These
rere certainly not approved by the Republicans ; yet were they not im-
m, but to the counsellors around him ; and his prudence so far restrained
sioned course and bias, that no act of strong mark, during the remainder
inistration, excited much dissatisfaction. He lived too short a time after

and too much withdrawn from information, to correct the views into which he had been deluded; and the continued assiduities of the party drew him into the vortex of their intemperate career; separated him still farther from his real friends, and excited him to actions and expressions of dissatisfaction, which grieved them, but could not loosen their affections from him. They would not suffer the temporary aberration to weigh against the immeasurable merits of his life; and, although they tumbled his seducers from their places, they preserved his memory embalmed in their hearts, with undiminished love and devotion; and there it forever will remain embalmed, in entire oblivion of every temporary thing which might cloud the glories of his splendid life. It is vain, then, for Mr. Pickering and his friends to endeavor to falsify his character, by representing him as an enemy to Republicans and republican principles, and as exclusively the friend of those who were so; and had he lived longer, he would have returned to his ancient and unbiased opinions, would have replaced his confidence in those whom the people approved and supported, and would have seen that they were only restoring and acting on the principles of his own first Administration.

I find, my dear sir, that I have written you a very long letter, or rather a history. The civility of having sent me a copy of Mr. Pickering's diatribe, would scarcely justify its address to you. I do not publish these things, because my rule of life has been never to harass the public with fendings and provings of personal slanders; and least of all would I descend into the arena of slander with such a champion as Mr. Pickering. I have ever trusted to the justice and consideration of my fellow-citizens, and have no reason to repent it, or to change my course. At this time of life, too, tranquillity is the *summum bonum*. But although I decline all newspaper controversy, yet when falsehoods have been advanced, within the knowledge of no one so much as myself, I have sometimes deposited a contradiction in the hands of a friend, which, if worth preservation, may, when I am no more, nor those whom I might offend, throw light on history, and recall that into the path of truth. And if of no other value, the present communication may amuse you with anecdotes not known to every one.

I had meant to have added some views on the amalgamation of parties, to which your favor of the 8th has some allusion; an amalgamation of name, but not of principle. Tories are tories still, by whatever name they may be called. But my letter is already too unmercifully long, and I close it here with assurances of my great esteem and respectful consideration. TH. JEFFERSON.

This contains a manifest error in the statement that the declaration (in the Mazzei letter) that "two out of the three branches of legislature" were against the Republicans, was an "obvious exception" of General Washington. What makes the error more remarkable is, that the same *sentence* from which Mr. Jefferson thus quotes, contained the express affirmation, "against us are *the Executive*."[1] And did anybody know better than he, had he stopped to consider, that in the first session of the fourth Congress (1795-6) the Republicans were in the ascendency in the House, and that every page of the published journals of Congress would afford decisive evidence of that fact?

When Jefferson wrote to Mazzei, in 1796, he unquestionably meant what *he said*, that two branches of Congress were against the Republicans, and that one of these branches was the *Executive*. All the members of the Cabinet (Pickering, Wolcott,

---

[1] And he forwarded to Mr. Van Buren, a copy of the Mazzei letter containing this sentence.

d Lee) were decided Federalists. In the introduction to his Ana, and in
other places in his writings, Jefferson particularly and distinctly declares
d as a necessary consequence, under the Cabinet arrangements then pre-
the Executive department was practically in the hands of the Federal
, he declares so, a little further on, in the same letter to Mr. Van Buren.
ferson, just as uniformly where he mentions General Washington's
pinions, asserts that his principles were different from those of his
binet—that at heart he was a Republican—that he was "true to his
charge," etc.

s that he had always mentally, or by direct affirmation, made this
" of General Washington, Mr. Jefferson, with too little attention, was
o the error we have seen in the letter to Mr. Van Buren.

ibits one of those *momentary* aberrations of memory which would be
arkable, were they not so common among persons of advanced years.
n corrects his own error, two paragraphs later, by describing the
ical composition of the "Executive," "after the retirement of his
n's] first Cabinet," and consequently its political composition at the
the Mazzei letter was written.

another statement in the letter to Van Buren, which might at first
to involve an error, viz., that in which after mentioning his *affectionate*
General Washington in 1797, he proceeds to aver that he "never had
to believe any change" on Washington's part, as "there certainly was
is own. On the other hand, the introduction to the Ana contains this
'Understanding, moreover, that I disapproved of that [Jay's] treaty,
ily nourished with falsehoods by a malignant neighbor of mine, who
to be his correspondent, he had become alienated from myself *person-*
n the Republican body generally of his fellow-citizens," etc.

Jefferson expresses the opinion that there was no "change" on Wash-
t, he referred to *personal* feelings, for two paragraphs later, he distinctly
olitical alienations between Washington and the Republican party, and
ly alluded to *such* alienations between Washington and himself. In the
oted from the Ana, the word "personally" manifestly has the sense of
, as opposed to *generally* in the next clause. Otherwise, Jefferson must
od as meaning to declare that Washington was *personally* alienated from
ilican body generally of his fellow citizens"—in other words, from the
of the American people. This would be a preposterous interpretation !

r in regard to the "Executive," which a glance at the *adjoining words*
sentence would have served to correct, reminds us to make a remark
not recollect to have thrown out quite fully enough in the text of these
t has been mentioned that Mr. Jefferson's memory failed perceptibly for
ree or four years of his life; but it was not so much a settling of the
etfulness over all events in proportion to their importance or remoteness
occasional forgetfulnesses or rather aberrations of memory in regard to
r one or two, points in a subject of which his general recollections were
od. We have seen another distinct instance of this in his letters to.
?5, in regard to J. Q. Adams's disclosures, etc., in 1808-9, and one or
examples could be specified. He was painfully conscious of his liability
these errors of memory, and guarded against them jealously in writing.
are so very few; and it is fortunate that not one of them relates to a
overted point, or raises a vapor of doubt as to what constituted the
ions or belief of the writer on any point.

APPENDIX NO. XVII.—Vol. II. p. 451.

Jefferson's Draft of Kentucky Resolutions of 1798.

1. *Resolved,* That the several States composing the United States of America, are not united on the principle of unlimited submission to their General Government; but that by a compact under the style and title of a Constitution for the United States, and of amendments thereto, they constituted a General Government for special purposes—delegated to that Government certain definite powers, reserving each State to itself, the residuary mass of right to their own self-government; and that whensoever the General Government assumes undelegated powers, its acts are unauthoritative, void, and of no force; that to this compact each State acceded as a State, and is an integral party, its co-States forming, as to itself, the other party; that the Government created by this compact was not made the exclusive or final judge of the extent of the powers delegated to itself; since that would have made its discretion, and not the Constitution, the measure of its powers; but that, as in all other cases of compact among powers having no common judge, each party has an equal right to judge for itself, as well of infractions as of the mode and measure of redress.

2. *Resolved,* That the Constitution of the United States, having delegated to Congress a power to punish treason, counterfeiting the securities and current coin of the United States, piracies, and felonies committed on the high seas, and offences against the law of nations, and no other crimes whatsoever; and it being true, as a general principle, and one of the amendments to the Constitution having also declared, that "the powers not delegated to the United States by the Constitution, nor prohibited by it to the States, are reserved to the States respectively, or to the people," therefore the act of Congress, passed on the 14th day of July, 1798, and intituled "An Act in addition to the act intituled An Act for the punishment of certain crimes against the United States," as also the act passed by them on the — day of June, 1798, intituled "An Act to punish frauds committed on the bank of the United States" (and all their other acts which assume to create, define, or punish crimes, other than those so enumerated in the Constitution), are altogether void, and of no force; and that the power to create, define, and punish such other crimes is reserved, and, of right, appertains solely and exclusively to the respective States, each within its own territory.

3. *Resolved,* That it is true as a general principle, and is also expressly declared by one of the amendments to the Constitution, that "the powers not delegated to the United States by the Constitution, nor prohibited by it to the States, are reserved to the States respectively, or to the people;" and that no power over the freedom of religion, freedom of speech, or freedom of the press being delegated to the United States by the Constitution, nor prohibited by it to the States, all lawful powers respecting the same did of right remain, and were reserved to the States or the people; that thus was manifested their determination to retain to themselves the right of judging how far the licentiousness of speech and of the press may be abridged without lessening their useful freedom, and how far those abuses which cannot be separated from their use, should be tolerated, rather than the use be destroyed. And thus also they guarded against all abridgment by the United States

of the freedom of religious opinions and exercises, and retained to themselves the right of protecting the same, as this State, by a law passed on the general demand of its citizens, had already protected them from all human restraint or interference. And that, in addition to this general principle and express declaration, another and more special provision has been made by one of the amendments to the Constitution, which expressly declares, that "Congress shall make no law respecting an establishment of religion, or prohibiting the free exercise thereof, or abridging the freedom of speech or of the press;" thereby guarding in the same sentence, and under the same words, the freedom of religion, of speech, and of the press; insomuch that whatever violated either, throws down the sanctuary which covers the others, and that libels, falsehood, and defamation, equally with heresy and false religion, are withheld from the cognizance of Federal tribunals. That, therefore, the Act of Congress of the United States, passed on the 14th day of July, 1798, intituled "An Act in addition to the act intituled ' An Act for the punishment of certain crimes against the United States,' " which does abridge the freedom of the press, is not law, but is altogether void, and of no force.

4. *Resolved*, That alien friends are under the jurisdiction and protection of the laws of the State wherein they are; that no power over them has been delegated to the United States, nor prohibited to the individual States, distinct from their power over citizens. And it being true as a general principle, and one of the amendments to the Constitution having also declared, that "the powers not delegated to the United States by the Constitution, nor prohibited by it to the States, are reserved to the States respectively, or to the people," the act of the Congress of the United States, passed on the — day of July, 1798, entitled "An Act concerning aliens," which assumes powers over alien friends, not delegated by the Constitution, is not law, but is altogether void, and of no force.

5. *Resolved*, That in addition to the general principle as well as the express declaration, that powers not delegated are reserved, another and more special provision, inserted in the Constitution from abundant caution, has declared that "the migration or importation of such persons as any of the States now existing shall think proper to admit, shall not be prohibited by the Congress prior to the year 1808;" that this commonwealth does admit the migration of alien friends, described as the subject of the said act concerning aliens; that a provision against prohibiting their migration is a provision against all acts equivalent thereto, or it would be nugatory; that to remove them when migrated, is equivalent to a prohibition of their migration, and is, therefore, contrary to the said provision of the Constitution, and void.

6. *Resolved*, That the imprisonment of a person under the protection of the laws of this commonwealth, on his failure to obey the simple *order* of the President to depart out of the United States, as is undertaken by said act intituled "An Act concerning aliens," is contrary to the Constitution, one amendment to which has provided that "no person shall be deprived of liberty without due process of law;" and that another having provided that "in all criminal prosecutions, the accused shall enjoy the right to public trial by an impartial jury, to be informed of the nature and cause of the accusation, to be confronted with the witnesses against him, to have compulsory process for obtaining witnesses in his favor, and to have the assistance of counsel for his defence," the same act undertaking to authorize the President to remove a person out of the United States, who is under the protection of the law, on his own suspicion, without accusation, without jury, without public trial, without confrontation of the witnesses against him, without hearing witnesses

in his favor, without defence, without counsel, is contrary to the provision also of the Constitution, is therefore not law, but utterly void, and of no force; that transferring the power of judging any person, who is under the protection of the laws, from the courts to the President of the United States, as is undertaken by the same act concerning aliens, is against the article of the Constitution which provides that "the judicial power of the United States shall be vested in courts, the judges of which shall hold their offices during good behavior;" and that the said act is void for that reason also. And it is further to be noted, that this transfer of judiciary power is to that magistrate of the General Government who already possesses all the Executive, and a negative on all Legislative powers.

7. *Resolved,* That the construction applied by the General Government (as is evidenced by sundry of their proceedings) to those parts of the Constitution of the United States which delegate to Congress a power "to lay and collect taxes, duties, imports, and excises, to pay the debts, and provide for the common defence and general welfare of the United States," and "to make all laws which shall be necessary and proper for carrying into execution the powers vested by the Constitution in the government of the United States, or in any department or officer thereof," goes to the destruction of all limits prescribed to their power by the Constitution; that words meant by the instrument to be subsidiary only to the execution of limited powers, ought not to be so construed as themselves to give unlimited powers, nor a part to be so taken as to destroy the whole residue of that instrument; that the proceedings of the General Government under color of these articles, will be a fit and necessary subject of revisal and correction, at a time of greater tranquillity, while those specified in the preceding resolutions call for immediate redress.

8th. *Resolved,* That a committee of conference and correspondence be appointed, who shall have in charge to communicate the preceding resolutions to the Legislatures of the several States; to assure them that this commonwealth continues in the same esteem of their friendship and union which it has manifested from that moment at which a common danger first suggested a common union: that it considers union, for specified national purposes, and particularly to those specified in their late federal compact, to be friendly to the peace, happiness, and prosperity of all the States: that faithful to that compact, according to the plain intent and meaning in which it was understood and acceded to by the several parties, it is sincerely anxious for its preservation: that it does also believe, that to take from the States all the powers of self-government and transfer them to a general and consolidated government, without regard to the special delegations and reservations solemnly agreed to in that compact, is not for the peace, happiness or prosperity of these States; and that, therefore, this commonwealth is determined, as it doubts not its co-States are, to submit to undelegated, and consequently unlimited powers in no man, or body of men on earth: that in cases of an abuse of the delegated powers, the members of the General Government, being chosen by the people, a change by the people would be the constitutional remedy; but where powers are assumed which have not been delegated, a nullification of the act is the rightful remedy: that every State has a natural right in cases not within the compact (*casus non foederis*) to nullify of their own authority all assumptions of power by others within their limits: that without this right, they would be under the dominion, absolute and unlimited, of whosoever might exercise this right of judgment for them: that, nevertheless, this commonwealth, from motives of regard and respect for its co-States, has wished to communicate with them on the subject: that with them alone it is proper to communicate, they alone being parties to the compact, and solely authorized to judge in the last resort of the powers exercised under it, Congress being not a party, but merely the creature of the compact, and subject as to its assumptions of power to the final judgment of those by whom and for whose use itself and its powers were all created and modified : that if the acts before specified should stand, these conclusions would flow from them ; that the General Government may place any act they think proper on the list of crimes, and punish it themselves whether enumerated or not enumerated by the Constitution as cognizable by them : that they may transfer its cognizance to the President, or any other person, who may himself be the accuser, counsel, judge and jury, whose *suspicions* may be the evidence, his *order* the sentence, his *officer* the executioner, and his breast the sole record of the transaction : that a very numerous and valuable description of the inhabitants of these States being, by this precedent, reduced, as outlaws, to the absolute dominion of one man, and the barrier of the Constitution thus swept away from us all, no rampart now remains against the passions and the powers of a majority in Congress to protect from a like exportation, or other more grievous punishment, the minority of the same body, the legislatures, judges, governors and counsellors of the States, nor their other peaceable inhabitants, who may venture to reclaim the constitutional rights and liberties of the States and people, or who for other causes, good or bad, may be obnoxious to the views, or marked by the suspicions of the President, or be thought dangerous to his or their election, or other interests, public or personal : that the friendless alien has, indeed, been selected as the safest subject of a first experiment ; but the citizen will soon follow, or rather has already followed, for already has a sedition act marked him as its prey : that these and successive acts of the same character, unless arrested at the threshold, necessarily drive these States into revolution and blood, and will furnish new calumnies against republican government, and new pretexts for those who wish it to be believed that man cannot be governed but by a rod of iron : that it would be a dangerous delusion were a confidence in the men of our choice to silence our fears for the safety of our rights : that confidence is everywhere the parent of despotism—free government is founded in jealousy, and not in confidence ; it is jealousy and not confidence which prescribes limited constitutions, to bind down those whom we are obliged to trust with power : that our Constitution has accordingly fixed the limits to which, and no further, our confidence may go ; and let the honest advocate of confidence read the Alien and Sedition Acts, and say if the Constitution has not been wise in fixing limits to the government it created, and whether we should be wise in destroying those limits. Let him say what the government is, if it be not a tyranny, which the men of our choice have conferred on our President, and the President of our choice has assented to, and accepted over the friendly strangers to whom the mild spirit of our country and its laws have pledged hospitality and protection : that the men of our choice have more respected the bare *suspicions* of the President, than the solid right of innocence, the claims of justification, the sacred force of truth, and the forms and substance of law and justice. In questions of power, then, let no more be heard of confidence in man, but bind him down from mischief by the chains of the Constitution. That this commonwealth does, therefore, call on its co-States for an expression of their sentiments on the acts concerning aliens, and for the punishment of certain crimes hereinbefore specified, plainly declaring whether these acts are or are not authorized by the federal compact. And it doubts not that their sense will be so announced as to prove their attachment unaltered to limited government, whether general or particular. And that the rights and liberties of their co-States will be exposed to no dangers by remaining embarked in a common bottom with their own

That they will concur with this commonwealth in considering the said acts as so palpably against the Constitution as to amount to an undisguised declaration that that compact is not meant to be the measure of the powers of the General Government, but that it will proceed in the exercise over these States, of all powers whatsoever: that they will view this as seizing the rights of the States, and consolidating them in the hands of the General Government, with the power assumed to bind the States (not merely as the cases made federal (*casus fœderis*), but) in all cases whatsoever, by laws made, not with their consent, but by others against their consent : that this would be to surrender the form of government we have chosen, and live under one deriving its powers from its own will, and not from our authority ; and that the co-States, recurring to their natural right in cases not made federal, will concur in declaring these acts void, and of no force, and will each take measures of its own for providing that neither these acts, nor any others of the General Government not plainly and intentionally authorized by the Constitution, shall be exercised within their respective territories.

9th. *Resolved*, That the said committee be authorized to communicate by writing or personal conferences, at any times or places whatever, with any person or persons who may be appointed by any one or more co-States to correspond or confer with them ; and that they lay their proceedings before the next session of Assembly.

APPENDIX NO. XVIII.—Vol. II., p. 568.

Rev. Dr. Mason's Pamphlet on Jefferson's Religious Views, etc., issued during the Election of 1800.

Dr. Mason published this pamphlet in September, entitling it " The Voice of Warning to Christians on the Ensuing Election ;" and that it was not intended as a fugitive production, would be implied from the fact that it was included in his Works published by his son in 1849.

Dr. Mason informs his readers that the belief of Mr. Jefferson's infidelity had for years been uniform and strong, but that now, " happily for truth and for us, Mr. Jefferson had *written* and he had *printed*." He then assumes that Mr. Jefferson has avowed his infidelity in his Notes on Virginia in various ways, which he proceeds to specify.

The first regards the Deluge. Mr. Jefferson argued in the Notes against a general deluge having taken place, from the fact that all the contents of the atmosphere measured by weight, were they water, would cover the globe but thirty-five feet deep, or raise the ocean but fifty-two and a half feet above its present level. He therefore supposed that any deluge must have been partial and local. [He made no allusion to the Mosaic account, but was discussing the geological question whether the marine shells found in high mountains, and particularly those of South America, could be accounted for, as claimed by many, among the effects of a universal deluge.]

Dr. Mason makes an important admission :

" Mr. Jefferson's concession of the probability of deluges within certain limits, does not rank him with those great and good men who have supposed the deluge to be partial, because his argument concludes against the Scriptural narrative, even upon that supposition. He will not admit his partial deluges to rise above fifty-two and a half feet above the level of the ocean."

Mr. Jefferson had *said* nothing of the kind here imputed to him; and it will hardly do to infer that because he argued that the contents of the atmosphere would raise the *whole* ocean but fifty-two and a half feet, that they would not produce a " partial " deluge a hundred, a thousand, or ten thousand times that depth.

The geological argument grows amusing. Dr. Mason quotes and italicizes Mr. Jefferson's words as follows:

" A second opinion has been entertained, which is, that, in times anterior to the records either of history or tradition, the bed of the ocean, the principal residence of the shelled tribe, has, by some great convulsion of nature, been heaved to the heights at which we now find shells and other remains of marine animals. *The favorers of this opinion do well to suppose the great events on which it rests to have taken place beyond all the eras of history; for within these, certainly none such are to be found;* and we may venture to say further, that no fact has taken place, either in our own days, or in the thousands of years recorded in history, which proves the existence of any natural agents, within or without the bowels of the earth, of force sufficient to heave to the height of 15,000 feet, such masses as the Andes."

Dr. Mason pronounces this a " sneer at the Scripture itself," a " malignant sarcasm," an " oblique stroke at the Bible." He calls Mr. Jefferson " a profane philosopher," " an infidel," and other hard names. " It is thus," he exclaims, " Christians, that a man, whom you are expected to elevate to the chief magistracy, insults yourselves and your Bible."

Mr. Jefferson was arguing against the now adopted theory of *upheaval*; that is, that mountains had been raised from the beds of the ocean by volcanic or other dynamic agencies, operating from the interior of the earth; and he said the geologists who favored *this* theory did well to suppose such events took place beyond all the eras of history. Doctor Mason appears to have mistaken this for an attack·on the Mosaic declaration that " the same day were all the *fountains* of the great deep broken up !"

Passing over some other cosmic criticisms, about as profound, we find the reverend gentleman quoting the following sentence from the Notes on Virginia, a part of it placed in capitals, thus : " Those who labor in the fields are the chosen people of God, IF EVER HE HAD A CHOSEN PEOPLE."

Dr. Mason asks how Christian ears relish this "profane babbling," and he ranks it among other " affronts to the oracles of God." A writer, in our recollection, said : " Washington was great, if there ever was a great man." Was this writer to be understood as denying that there ever was a great man, or simply as using a familiar and purely idiomatic form of expression, to give strength to his affirmation ?

Dr. Mason quotes Mr. Jefferson as saying : " The legitimate powers of government extend only to such acts as are injurious to others. But it does me no injury for my neighbor to say there are twenty gods or no God. It neither picks my pocket nor breaks my leg." The meaning and peculiar phraseology of this sentence are sufficiently explained in vol. i. pp. 370, 371 of this work. Dr. Mason pronounced it a preaching of "atheism."

He declared that Mazzei told a Reverend Dr. Smith that on once expressing his surprise at the ruinous condition of a church to Jefferson, the latter replied : " It is good enough for him who was born in a manger !" Dr. Mason said some of

Mr. Jefferson's friends "have been desperate enough to challenge this anecdote as a calumny fabricated for electioneering purposes." But he declared he had himself heard it from the Rev. Mr. Smith, and he thought Mazzei would not have been guilty of "trumping up a deliberate lie," etc. etc.

Dr. Mason thought all these things proved Jefferson to be a confirmed infidel, but if anything was wanting to establish this, it would be shown by "his solicitude for wresting the Bible from the hands of their children—his notoriously unchristian character—his disregard of all the evidences of divine worship—his utter and open contempt of the Lord's day, inasmuch as to receive on it a public entertainment." Lastly, he pronounced Jefferson "a man who wrote against the truths of God's Word—who made not even a profession of Christianity—who was without Sabbaths—without the sanctuary—without so much as a decent external respect for the faith and worship of Christians."

Since the above was written, we find in the newspapers the following extract from the Rev. Dr. Sprague's "Annals of the American Pulpit." Some friendly describer of Dr. Mason, who appears to imagine that the Republican party proposed "an alliance with Napoleon Bonaparte," gives the following characteristic picture of the times:

"There is another sermon of which I retain a distinct remembrance, and to which I advert, partly because I regard it as one of Dr. Mason's greatest efforts, and partly because it serves to illustrate a feature of character for which he was distinguished above most men: I refer to his fearless disregard of consequences in the discharge of what he deemed a public duty. The sermon was preached upon a fast day, and at a time of extreme political excitement. Personal violence had been threatened in case he denounced, as he had before done, the proposed alliance with France. I myself remember to have heard a young lawyer and a violent partisan declare that 'if the Doctor dared to repeat the thing, even the horns of the altar should not protect him, for he would himself be one of the first to pull him out of the pulpit.' When the fast-day arrived, a large audience assembled, expecting to hear a sermon 'to the times.' The Doctor chose for his text, Ezekiel ii., 3, and the whole chapter was read in his most impressive manner. Near the close of his discourse, he broke forth into a solemn and impassioned apostrophe to Deity in nearly these words: 'Send us, if Thou wilt, murrain upon our cattle, a famine upon our land, cleanness of teeth in our borders; send us pestilence to waste our cities; send us, if it please Thee, the sword to bathe itself in the blood of our sons; but spare us, Lord God Most Merciful, spare us that curse—most dreadful of all curses—an alliance with Napoleon Bonaparte!' As he uttered these startling sentences, the blood gushed from his nostrils; he unconsciously put his handkerchief to his face, and the next instant made a gesture which looked as if he were designedly waving it before the audience like a bloody and symbolic flag. You can fancy better than I can describe the impression which this incident, coupled with the awful apostrophe, made upon the crowded assembly. Next day I asked the young lawyer why he did not proceed, as he had promised, to pull the Doctor from the pulpit. 'Why,' said he, 'I was perfectly horror-struck when he wound up that terrible apostrophe by waving his bloody handkerchief.'"

No doubt is intended here to be expressed that Dr. Mason was a well-meaning, devout, and within the limits of his profession, signally able man. Indeed, it is on account of his character, his talents, his erudition and high distinction, that we have chosen his as a more striking illustration of that clerical warfare on Jefferson, of which the "bloody flag" was truly "symbolic."

APPENDIX NO. XIX.—Vol. II. p. 612.

Deposition of J. A. Bayard.

The deposition of James A. Bayard, sworn and examined on the twenty——— day of ———, in the year of our Lord one thousand eight hundred and five, at Wilmington, in the State of Delaware, by virtue of a commission issuing out of the supreme court of judicature in the State of New York, to John Vaughn, directed for the examination of the said James A. Bayard, in a cause there depending between Aaron Burr, plaintiff, and James Cheetham, defendant, on the part and behalf of the defendant.

1st. To the first interrogatory this deponent answers and says: As a member of the House of Representatives, I paid a visit of ceremony to the plaintiff on the 4th of March, in the year one thousand eight hundred and one, and was introduced to him. I had no acquaintance with him before that period. I had no knowledge of the defendant but what was derived from his general reputation before the last session of Congress, when a personal acquaintance commenced upon my becoming a member of the Senate.

2d. To the second interrogatory this deponent saith: I was.

3d. To the third interrogatory this deponent saith: There was an equality of electoral votes for Mr. Jefferson and Mr. Burr, and the choice of one of them, did, of consequence, devolve on the House of Representatives.

4th. To the fourth interrogatory this deponent saith: The House, resolved into States, balloted for a President a number of times—the exact number is not at present in my recollection—before a choice was made. The frequency of balloting was occasioned by the preference given by the Federal side of the House to Mr Burr. With the exception of Mr. Huger, of South Carolina, I recollect no Federal member, who did not concur in the general course of balloting for Mr. Burr. I cannot name each member. The Federal members, at that time, composed a majority of the House, though not of the States. Their names can be ascertained by the Journals of the House of Representatives.

5th. To the fifth interrogatory this deponent saith: I know of no measures but those of argument and persuasion which were used to secure the election of Mr. Burr to the Presidency. Several gentlemen of the Federal party doubted the practicability of electing Mr. Burr, and the policy of attempting it. Before the election came on, there were several meetings of the party to consider the subject. It was frequently debated; and most of the gentlemen who had adopted a decided opinion in favor of his election, employed their influence and address to convince those who doubted, of the propriety of the measure. I cannot tell whether Mr. Burr was acquainted with what passed at our meetings. But I neither knew nor heard of any letter being written to him on the subject. He never informed me, nor have I reason to believe, further than inference from the open professions, and public course pursued by the Federal party, that he was apprised that an attempt would be made to secure his election.

6. To the sixth interrogatory the deponent saith: Mr. Burr, or any person on his behalf, never did communicate to me in writing, or otherwise, nor to any other

persons of which I have any knowledge, that any measures had been suggested, or would be pursued, to secure his election. Preceding the day of the election, in the course of the session, the Federal members of Congress had a number of general meetings, the professed and sole purpose of which was to consider the propriety of giving their support to the election of Mr. Burr. The general sentiment of the party was strongly in his favor. Mr. Huger, I think, could not be brought to vote for him. Mr. Craik and Mr. Baer, of Maryland, and myself, were those who acquiesced with the greatest difficulty and hesitation. I did not believe Mr. Burr could be elected, and thought it vain to make the attempt. But I was chiefly influenced by the current of public sentiment, which I thought it neither safe nor politic to counteract. It was, however, determined by the party, without consulting Mr. Burr, to make the experiment, whether he could be elected. Mr. Ogden never was authorized nor requested by me nor any member of the House to my knowledge, to call upon Mr. Burr, and to make any propositions to him of any kind or nature. I remember Mr. Ogden's being at Washington, while the election was depending. I spent one or two evenings in his company at Stiller's hotel, in small parties, and we recalled an acquaintance of very early life, which had been suspended by a separation of eighteen or twenty years. I spent not a moment with Mr. Ogden in private. It was reported that he was an agent for Mr. Burr, or it was understood that he was in possession of declarations of Mr. Burr, that he would serve as President if elected. I never questioned him on the subject. Although I considered Mr. Burr personally better qualified to fill the office of President than Mr. Jefferson, yet for a reason above suggested, I felt no anxiety for his election, and I presumed if Mr. Ogden came on any errand from Mr. Burr, or was desirous of making any disclosure relative to his election, he would do it without any application from me. But Mr. Ogden or any other person never did make any communication to me from Mr. Burr, nor do I remember having any conversation with him relative to the election. I never had any communication directly or indirectly with Mr. Burr in relation to his election to the Presidency. I was one of those who thought from the beginning that the election of Mr. Burr was not practicable. The sentiment was freely and openly expressed. I remember it was generally said by those who wished a perseverance in the opposition to Mr. Jefferson, that several Democratic States were more disposed to vote for Mr. Burr than for Mr. Jefferson. That out of complaisance to the known intention of the party they would vote a decent length of time for Mr. Jefferson, and as soon as they could excuse themselves by the imperious situation of affairs, would give their votes for Mr. Burr, the man they really preferred. The States relied upon for this change were New York, New Jersey, Vermont and Tennessee. I never, however, understood that any assurance to this effect came from Mr. Burr. Early in the election it was reported that Mr. Edward Livingston, the Representative of the city of New York, was the confidential agent of Mr. Burr, and that Mr. Burr had committed himself entirely to the discretion of Mr. Livingston, having agreed to adopt all his acts. I took an occasion to sound Mr. Livingston on the subject, and intimated that, having it in my power to terminate the contest, I should do so, unless he could give me some assurance that we might calculate upon a change in the votes of some of the members of his party. Mr. Livingston stated that he felt no great concern as to the event of the election, but he disclaimed any agency from Mr. Burr, or any connection with him on the subject, and any knowledge of Mr. Burr's designing to coöperate in support of his election.

7th. The deponent answering that part of the seventh interrogatory, which relates to letters received from the late Alexander Hamilton, says: I did receive, in the course of the winter of 1801, several letters from General Hamilton upon the subject of the election, but the name of David A. Ogden is not mentioned in any of them. The general design and effect of these letters was to persuade me to vote for Mr. Jefferson, and not for Mr. Burr. The letters contain very strong reasons and a very earnest opinion against the election of Mr. Burr. In answer to the residue of the same interrogatory, the deponent saith: I repeat that I know of no means used to promote the election of Mr. Burr, but persuasion. I am wholly ignorant of what the plaintiff was apprised of in relation to the election, as I had no communication with him, directly or indirectly; and as to the expectation of a change of votes from Mr. Jefferson to Mr. Burr, I never knew of a better ground for it than the opinions and calculations of a number of members.

8th. In answer to the eighth interrogatory, the deponent saith: I know of nothing which, in my opinion, can be of service to the defendant in the cause.

To the interrogatory on the part of the plaintiff, the deponent answers: Having yielded with Messrs Craik and Baer, of Maryland, to the strong desire of the great body of the party with whom we usually acted, and agreed to vote for Mr. Burr, and those gentlemen and myself being governed by the same views and motives, we pledged ourselves to each other to pursue the same line of conduct, and act together. We felt that some concession was due to the judgment of a great majority of our political friends, who differed from us in opinion, but we determined that no consideration should make us lose sight for a moment of the necessity of a President being chosen. We, therefore, resolved that as soon as it was fairly ascertained that Mr. Burr could not be elected, to give our votes to Mr. Jefferson. General Morris, of Vermont, shortly after acceded to this arrangement. The result of the ballot of the States had uniformly been eight States for Mr. Jefferson, six for Mr. Burr, and two divided. Mr. Jefferson wanted the vote of one State only; those three gentlemen belonged to the divided States, I held the vote of the State of Delaware; it was, therefore, in the power of either of us to terminate the election. Those gentlemen knowing the strong interest of my State to have a President, and knowing the sincerity of my determination to make one, left it to me to fix the time when the opposition should cease, and to make terms, if any could be accomplished, with the friends of Mr. Jefferson. I took pains to disclose this state of things in such a manner, that it might be known to the friends of Mr. Burr, and to those gentlemen who were believed to be most disposed to change their votes in his favor. I repeatedly stated to many gentlemen with whom I was acting, that it was a vain thing to protract the election, as it had become manifest that Mr. Burr would not assist us; and as we could do nothing without his aid, I expected, under these circumstances, if there were any latent engines at work in Mr. Burr's favor, the plan of operations would be disclosed to me. But, although I had the power, and threatened to terminate the election, I had not even an intimation from any friend of Mr. Burr's, that it would be desirable to them to protract it. I never did discover that Mr. Burr used the least influence to promote the object we had in view. And being completely persuaded that Mr. Burr would not coöperate with us, I determined to end the contest by voting for Mr. Jefferson. I publicly announced the intention which I designed to carry into effect the next day. In the morning of the day there was a general meeting of the party, where it was generally admitted that Mr. Burr could not be elected; but some thought it was better to persist in our vote, and to go without a President rather than to elect Mr. Jefferson. The greater number, however, wished the election terminated, and a

VOL. III.—40

President made; and, in the course of the day, the manner was settled, which was afterwards adopted, to end the business.

Mr. Burr, probably, might have put an end sooner to the election, by coming forward and declaring that he would not serve, if chosen; but I have no reason to believe, and never did think, that he interfered, even to the point of personal influence, to obstruct the election of Mr. Jefferson, or to promote his own.

APPENDIX NO. XX.—Vol. II. p. 639.

Sketch of the Life of General Smith.

General Samuel Smith, an officer of the Revolution, was born in Carlisle, Penn., on the 27th July, 1752. His grandfather, of the same name, was a large landed proprietor in Lancaster county, and having disposed of his estates, removed to Carlisle. There, in conjunction with his only son, John, he engaged, successfully, in mercantile pursuits. The latter was repeatedly elected a member of the legislature of Pennsylvania.

In 1760, his father having retired from business, he removed to Baltimore, finding the sphere of Carlisle too limited for his enterprises. Here, with his energy and sound judgment, he not only rapidly added to his capital, but contributed largely in giving a more invigorating impulse to the commerce of that town. It is not too much to say, that he, with several gentlemen of like character, who emigrated from Pennsylvania about the same time, were the founders of the commercial prosperity of Baltimore. He was a member of the convention, which, in 1776, framed the first, if not the best constitution that Maryland has enjoyed. Charles Carroll, of Carrollton, said: " I have John Smith on my committee for shaping the Senate, and it will be the safeguard of liberty and order."

Mr. Smith was, for several years, a member of the legislature, under the new constitution, and during nearly the whole of the war, was chairman of the Committee of Ways and Means, in the House of Delegates. Noted for his sound judgment and devoted patriotism, he was not the less distinguished for his probity, piety, and great simplicity of habits.

General Smith obtained the rudiments of his education at Carlisle, then he was a pupil in a school in Baltimore, and afterwards at another in Elkton. But, at a very early age, he was recalled, to enter his father's counting-house. In this situation he continued until 1771, when his father sent him in one of his own vessels to Europe. Whilst abroad, he travelled through Italy, Spain, Portugal, France, and England. Soon after his return, he became a partner in his father's mercantile house. On his voyage home, Major André was his companion, and a sincere friendship existed between them until the unhappy death of the latter.

Participating in the general feeling, that a resort to arms could alone secure the liberties of his country, he at an early period joined a volunteer company. This was the school in which he acquired such military knowledge as he possessed. In January, 1776, Smallwood's regiment was raised for the defence of the State. In this he had conferred on him the rank of captain. The regiment was soon after taken into the service of Congress, and marched in July to Long Island. It did eminent service, in the memorable battle there, losing one-third of its men, and being the last to quit the field. He was alike distinguished at Harlaem, and White Plains, where Captain Smith was slightly wounded. On the harassing retreat through New Jersey, it, in conjunction with the Delaware battalion, covered the rear, and was the last of the army that crossed the river to the Pennsylvania shore.

He was then, December, 1776, greeted with a major's commission, and ordered to Baltimore, on the recruiting service. When the seven Maryland regiments were embodied, in 1777, he received the commission of Lieutenant-Colonel of the fourth regiment, there being but a brief interval between the two commissions.

He was with his regiment at the attack on Staten Island, and in the hapless affair of the Brandywine. Immediately after this, he was detached by Gen. Washington, to the defence of Fort Mifflin. In this naked and exposed work, of mud and palisades, he maintained himself, under a continued fire from the land batteries and shipping of the enemy, from 26th September to the 11th November. On that day, he was so severely wounded as to make it necessary to remove him to the Jersey shore. For this gallant defence, Congress voted him thanks and an elegant sword. Not entirely recovered from the effects of his wound, he yet took part in all the sufferings of Valley Forge. From thence he was again ordered to Baltimore, on the recruiting service, and joining the army early in the spring, took an active part in the battle of Monmouth.

He went into the army a man of fortune. After a service of three and a half years he was reduced to poverty, by means of the suspension of commerce, continental money, the worthlessness of shipping property, and hopeless country debts. These causes brought his father's commercial business to a ruinous end, whilst they drove Colonel Smith to the painful necessity of resigning his commission. He did not, however, refrain absolutely from military duties. The command of a militia regiment was conferred on him, with which he continued to do duty, when its service was required, until the end of the war.

A few years after the peace, he was elected to the Legislature of Maryland, where he remained until he was chosen a member of Congress, in 1792. In that body, either in the House or in the Senate, he continued until 1833, having served forty years, in the national councils, with an interval of but six weeks during that long period.

When Mr. Jefferson was forming his first Cabinet, he tendered to Gen. Smith the Secretaryship of the Navy, and most urgently pressed it on him. He felt himself, however, constrained to decline the honor from considerations entirely private, and connected with his commercial house. He nevertheless, consented to serve, and did so, until the post was filled by Mr. Robert Smith, it having previously to the acceptance of it by the latter, been offered to Mr. Langdon, and to Mr. William Jones of Philadelphia.

On all important occasions, connected with mercantile or financial matters, he was consulted by the administrations of Jefferson, Madison, Monroe, Adams and Jackson, and he very frequently gave his opinions in writing. He was repeatedly chosen Vice-President pro tem. of the Senate, and generally was at the head of its Committee on Finance, as, in the House, he had been usually Chairman of the Committee of Ways and Means.

As a brigadier-general of militia, he commanded the Maryland Contingent on the Western Insurrection, known as the "Whisky Expedition," and as major-general of the same description of troops, he commanded in the defence of Baltimore in the war of 1812.

The knowledge he had acquired at Fort Mifflin, admirably adapted him to the task now imposed on him. As was the former, in 1777, so was Baltimore in 1812, wholly defenceless, with the exception of a miserable fort, having neither a bomb-proof magazine or a casemate to protect the men. Everything was to be done, and that too, on a brief notice; yet, with the hearty coöperation of his fellow-citizens, of all classes, whether in money, labor, supplies, counsel, or subordination, he succeeded in placing the city in as strong an attitude of resistance, as under the circumstances could well be. It suffices to say in this brief memoir, that the enemy, flushed with his triumph at Washington, was repulsed from Baltimore. This signal success, was as grateful to the patriot heart, as it was honorable to the commander and his gallant followers. It may be remarked that so untiring was his energy, and so wary his arrangements, that not an assailable point was left unprotected.

In his 83d year, a committee of his fellow citizens called on him at his country residence in the summer of 1835, to put down a fearful mob which had possession of the city, and was setting all law at defiance. With his native diffidence he expressed the belief that he had been forgotten, and did not possess the influence ascribed to him, by the committee. However, he immediately entered their carriage, and drove to the city.

He found a number of people collected at the Exchange, and soon after he was introduced, a series of resolutions was offered to the meeting. He at once rose up and said: "Resolutions!—we want no resolutions; let us have arms, and those who are ready to use them, follow me!" The result was, that from the moment, the mob may have been deemed as quelled. Before six o'clock of the evening of that day, every prominent point of the city was under the protection of armed men, and such artillery and cavalry as could be brought out. So intense was the feeling of gratitude, that he was elected Mayor, almost by acclamation. He continued in that office until a few months before his death. This event took place on the 22d of April, 1839.

Baltimore gave him a public funeral, which was attended by all the authorities, civil and military, as well as by the President of the United States, and his Cabinet. He retained his mental and physical faculties to the hour of his decease.

It may be added, that Col. Benton, who knew him well, having served with him many years in the Senate, has portrayed his character with masterly skill and signal justness. In the 2d vol. of his Thirty Years in the U. S. Senate, he says of Gen. Smith: "He was thoroughly a business member, under all the aspects of the character; intelligent, well informed, attentive, upright; a very effective speaker, without pretending to oratory; well read, but all his reading subordinate to common sense and practical views; . . . . . was particularly skilled in matters of finance and commerce, to which his clear head, and practical knowledge, lent light and order, in the midst of the most intricate statements. . . . . Patriotism, honor, and integrity were his eminent characteristics, and utilitarian the turn of his mind, and beneficial results the object of his labors. . . . He was a working member; and worked diligently, judiciously, and honestly, for the public good." In adverting to his services to Baltimore, Col. Benton adds: "As having defended her, both in the war of the Revolution, and in that of 1812; and as having made her welfare and prosperity a special object of his care, in all the situations of his life, both public and private."

The above sketch was drawn up at our request by an authorized hand; and we have presented it without any alterations. The following letters are published in neither edition of Mr. Jefferson's works:

WASHINGTON, *March* 9, 1801.

DEAR SIR: By the time you receive this, you will have been at home long enough, I hope, to take a view of the possibilities, and of the arrangements, which may enable you so to dispose of your private affairs, as to take a share in those of the public, and give us your aid as Secretary of the Navy; if you can be added to the Administration I am forming, it will constitute a mass so entirely possessed of the public confidence that I shall fear nothing. There is nothing to which a nation is not equal where it pours all its energies and zeal into the hands of those to whom they confide the direction of their force. You will bring us the benefit of adding in a considerable degree, the acquiescence at least of the leaders who have hitherto opposed us; your geographical situation, too, is peculiarly advantageous, as it will favor the policy of drawing our naval resources towards the centre, from which their benefits and protection may be extended equally to all the parts; but what renders it a matter not only of desire to us, but permit me to say, of more duty in you, is, that if you refuse, where are we to find a substitute? You know that the knowledge of naval matters in this country is confined entirely to persons who are under other absolutely disqualifying circumstances. Let me then, my dear sir, entreat you to join in conducting the affairs of our country, and to prove by consequences, that the views they entertained in the change of their servants are not to be without effect; in short, if you refuse, I must abandon, from necessity, what I have been so falsely charged of doing from choice—the expectation of procuring to our country such benefits as may compensate the expenses of their Navy. I hope, therefore, you will accede to the proposition. Everything shall be yielded which may accommodate it to your affairs. Let me hear from you favorably and soon. Accept assurances of my high and friendly consideration and esteem.

TH. JEFFERSON.

GEN. SAM'L SMITH.

WASHINGTON, *March* 18, 1801.

DEAR SIR: The circumstance of my intended departure induces me to press the promised answer to my last letter at the first possible moment, because whatever it be, some important measures must be adopted relative to the Navy before I can go away. In the wished for event of your acceptance, it would seem necessary you should be with us for three or four days to form those leading determinations which the laws and existing circumstances require respecting the Navy. In hopes, therefore, of hearing from you soon, as well as favorably, I tender you assurances of my high and affectionate esteem.

TH. JEFFERSON.

GEN. SAM'L SMITH.

WASHINGTON, *March*, 24, 1801.

DEAR SIR: I have to acknowledge the receipt of your favor of the 20th. The appointment of Secretary of the Navy was immediately, on receipt of your letter declining it, proposed to Mr. Jones of Philadelphia. I cannot have an answer from him till the night of the 26th, but I have great reason to expect a negative. In that case, I will gladly, for the public, accept your offer to undertake it for a time; besides, that it will comprehend important operations to be immediately carried into effect, it will give us time to look out for a successor. I mention it now in hopes that in the moment you receive notice from me of Mr. Jones's refusal, if it takes place, you may be so good as to be in readiness to come here for a few days. If I receive Jones's refusal on Thursday night, you shall hear from me Friday night, and may be here, I hope, yourself on Saturday night.   Sunday and Monday will probably suffice for the first decisions necessary, so that I may get away on Tuesday, which now becomes very urgent.

I inclose you the answer to the address you forwarded me.   Though these expressions of good will from my fellow-citizens cannot but be grateful to me, yet I would rather relinquish the gratification, and see republican self-respect prevail over movements of the heart, too capable of misleading the person to whom they are addressed.   However, their will, not mine, be done.

Be pleased to present my respects to Mrs. Smith, and to accept yourself, assurances of my high consideration and esteem.

TH. JEFFERSON.

GEN. SAM'L SMITH.

———

WASHINGTON, March 26, 1801.

DEAR SIR: According to what I had augured, I have this moment received Mr. Jones's refusal of the Secretaryship of the Navy.   In mine of two days ago, I mentioned to you this fear, and that in that event I must avail the public of your kind offer to accept the office for awhile.   I now take the liberty of repeating my request that you will be so good as to come on, on Saturday, that we may have a consultation on the measures immediately to be taken.   The urgency arises not only from the state of sufferance in which the department is, but from the necessity of my departure immediately, lest the assembling of our Administration at the time agreed on should be delayed, which would be very injurious to the public.   Accept assurances of my great respect and esteem.

TH. JEFFERSON.

GEN. S. SMITH.

———

WASHINGTON, July 9, 1801.

DEAR SIR: After the trouble you have been so good as to take with the Navy Department, and the complete disposition you have made of everything in it which was pressing, it is impossible for me to press anything further; on the contrary, it becomes my duty as a public officer to return you thanks in the name of our country for the useful services you have rendered, and the disinterested footing on which they have been rendered.   You have done for us gratis, what the emoluments of office have not yet been sufficient to induce others to undertake, and it is with equal truth and pleasure I testify that you have deserved well of your country. Mr. Langdon having ultimately declined, I must look into some other line of profession for a Secretary; and by this mail propose the office to your brother, Mr. Robert Smith.   It is not on his reading in Coke Littleton, that I am induced to this proposition, though that also will be of value in our Administration; but from a confidence that he must, from his infancy, have been so familiarized with naval things, that he will be perfectly competent to select proper agents and to judge of their conduct.   Let me beseech you, my dear sir, to give us the benefit of your influence with him, to prevail on his acceptance.   You can give him the necessary information as to the state of the office, and what it is like to be; and I hope, through your intercession and his patriotism, that this is the last time the commonwealth will have to knock at the door of its children to find one who will accept of one of its highest trusts. Accept yourself assurances of my constant and affectionate esteem and respect.

TH. JEFFERSON.

GEN SAM'L SMITH.

APPENDIX NO. XXI.—Vol. III. p. 253.

Gallatin's remarks on Vice-Presidential Nomination of 1804.

In Mr. Trist's Memoranda occurs the following record of a conversation which took place between himself and Mr. Gallatin, April 21st, 1829 :

" The custom [said Mr. Gallatin] was becoming established for the Vice-President to succeed to the Presidency ; the only exception had been in the case of Mr. Burr, who ' killed himself.' Under these circumstances it occurred to John Smith (perhaps N. P. T. is mistaken in the Christian name), an excellent man and very good friend of mine, to bring forward Governor Clinton. Governor Clinton was confessedly one of the most weighty characters in the Union ; but he had, thus far, confined himself altogether to his own State ; he had never aspired, nor did he now aspire, to federal office ; moreover, the age at which he was arriving, in a great measure, precluded a change of theatre. Still, he must needs be brought forward. Smith, considerably to my surprise, enlisted Wilson C. Nicholas in the plan. I called their attention to the standing of Governor Clinton, to the customary title to the presidency which had already, in some measure, become attached to the Vice-Presidency ; and pointed out that, if their intention was not to elevate Governor C. to the Presidency (which 'twas not), they must be cautious how they dealt with him. He was no man of straw, whom they could put up and take down, to suit their purposes. These admonitions had not the desired effect. At that time the caucus system was in full force. There was a party opposed to Smith's scheme, at the head of them John Randolph and Macon (' who were the leaders of the H. Reps.' N. P. T. thinks he said), who went into the caucus intending to set up old Langdon (N. P. T. thinks was the name), of Massachusetts ; the sort of man that the purposes of the party required. To their utter dismay, they found themselves in a minority, and Clinton was nominated. Macon swore he would never attend another caucus, and this was the origin of his enmity to them. When the period came, the party did not take up Clinton for President, and my anticipations were verified. The whole Clinton family and influence broke off."

Mr. Trist is undoubtedly correct in the name of John Smith, who was, at the time, a senator in Congress from New York. So, too, of Mr. Langdon, except that he was from New Hampshire instead of Massachusetts. Nicholas swore (or stated) on Burr's trial, that he himself was active in behalf of Clinton's nomination to the Vice-Presidency, and that fact is otherwise notorious. But the " whole Clinton family and influence " did *not* " break off," in consequence of George Clinton's not being " taken up," for President. That *he* felt sore on the subject is certain. But that he understood De Witt Clinton to be a supporter of Mr. Madison in the election of 1808, we have the evidence of his own hand, in manuscript letters. Do Witt Clinton was a senator in the New York Legislature, and before taking his seat in the session of 1807–8 (says Hammond in the Political History of New York), " renounced his *opposition to the Embargo laws,* and professed his approbation of the measures of the General Administration." On the 31st of January, 1809, he introduced resolutions in the New York Legislature approving of the Administration, and pledging the State of New York to its support. In his speech on the occasion, he denounced the measures in Massachusetts to prevent the Embargo from being enforced—charged the opposition there with pursuing measures tending to a dissolution of the Union—and applying to them a line from Milton, declared they thought it

" Better to reign in Hell than serve in Heaven."

APPENDIX No. XXII.—Vol. III. p. 301.

Memorial.

To the honorable the Senate and House of Representatives of the United States of America in Congress assembled, the Memorial of the subscribers, merchants and others, inhabitants of the city of New York, respectfully showeth :

That your memorialists feel, in common with the rest of their fellow-citizens, an anxious solicitude for the honor and interests of their country, and an equal determination to assert and maintain them.

That your memorialists believe that a continuation of the restrictive measures now in operation will produce all the benefits, while it prevents the calamities of war. That when the British ministry become convinced that a trade with the United States cannot be renewed, but by the repeal of the orders in council, the distress of their merchants and manufacturers, and their inability to support their armies in Spain and Portugal, will probably compel them to that measure.

Your memorialists beg leave to remark that such effects are even now visible; and it may be reasonably hoped that a continuance of the Embargo and non-importation laws, a few months beyond the fourth day of July next, will effect a complete and bloodless triumph of our rights.

Your memorialists, therefore, respectfully solicit of your honorable body the passage of a law continuing the Embargo, and giving to the President of the United States power to discontinue the whole of the restrictive system, on the rescinding of the British orders in council.

The conduct of France in burning our ships, in sequestering our property entering her ports, expecting protection in consequence of the promised repeal of the Berlin and Milan decrees, and the delay in completing a treaty with the American minister, has excited great sensations; and we hope and trust will call forth from your honorable body such retaliatory measures as may be best calculated to procure justice.

John Jacob Astor,	John T. Lawrence,	Amasa Jackson,
Samuel Adams,	Joseph W. Totten,	William J. Robinson,
Howland & Grinnel,	Isaac Schermerhorn,	Joseph Strong,
E. Slosson,	Alexander Ruden,	Abraham J. Hallet,
Israel Gibbs,	Joseph Otis,	Joshua Jones,
Isaac Clason,	Lewis Hartman,	Frederic Giraud, jr.,
John Slidell,	Garret Storm,	Robert Roberts,
John K. Townsend,	George Bement,	John Crookes.
Andrew Ogden & Co.,	S. A. Rich,	Hugh M'Cormick,
Thomas Storm,	Abraham Smith,	John Depeyster,
Amos Butler,	Thomas H. Smith, jr.,	Gilbert Haight,
Ebenezer Burrill,	Andrew Foster,	James Lovett,
Isaac Heyr,	Jacob Barker,	Leffert Lefferts,
Ralph Bulkley,	William Lovett,	Augustus Wynkoop,
Samuel Bell,	William Edgar, jun.	John W. Gale,
John F. Delaplaine,	Samuel Stillwell,	Thomas Rich,
Peter Stagg,	Jacob P. Giraud,	Samuel Marshall,
David Taylor,	John Hone,	Elbert Herring.
William Adee,	John Kane,	

New York, *June 1st*, 1812.

APPENDIX NO. XXIII.—Vol. III. p. 350.

Three Letters from Mr. Jefferson to a grand-daughter when a young child.

WASHINGTON, *April 3,* '08.

MY DEAR CORNELIA: I have owed you a letter two months, but have had nothing to write about, till last night I found in a newspaper the four lines which I now inclose you: and as you are learning to write, they will be a good lesson to convince you of the importance of minding your stops in writing. I allow you a day to find out yourself how to read these lines, so as to make them true. If you cannot do it in that time, you may call in assistance. At the same time, I will give you four other lines, which I learnt when I was but a little older than you, and I still remember.

> I've seen the sea all in a blaze of fire
> I've seen a house high as the moon and higher
> I've seen the sun at twelve o'clock at night
> I've seen the man who saw this wondrous sight."

All this is true, whatever you may think of it at first reading. I mentioned in my letter of last week to Ellen, that I was under an attack of periodical headache. This is the 10th day. It has been very moderate, and yesterday did not last more than three hours. Tell your mamma that I fear I shall not get away as soon as I expected. Congress has spent the last five days without employing a single hour in the business necessary to be finished. Kiss her for me, and all the sisterhood. To Jefferson I give my hand, to your papa my affectionate salutations. You have always my love.

TH. JEFFERSON.

P. S.—April 5. I have kept my letter open till to-day, and am able to say now, that my headache for the last two days has been scarcely sensible.

———

WASHINGTON, *Dec. 26,* '08.

I congratulate you, my dear Cornelia, on having acquired the valuable art of writing. How delightful to be enabled by it to converse with an absent friend, as if present! To this we are indebted for all our reading; because it must be written before we can read it. To this we are indebted for the Iliad, the Æneid, the Columbiad, Henriad, Dunciad, and now, for the most glorious poem of all, the Terrapiniad, which I now inclose you. This sublime poem consigns to everlasting fame the greatest achievement in war ever known to ancient or modern times: in the battle of David and Goliath, the disparity between the combatants was nothing in comparison to our case. I rejoice that you have learnt to write, for another reason; for as that is done with a goose-quill, you now know the value of a goose, and of course you will assist Ellen in taking care of the half-dozen very fine grey geese which I shall send by Davy. But as to this, I must refer to your mamma to decide whether they will be safest at Edgehill or at Monticello till I return home, and to give orders accordingly. I received letters a few days ago from Mr. Bankhead and Anne. They are well. I had expected a visit from Jefferson at Christmas, had there been a sufficient intermission in his lectures. But I suppose there was not, as he is not come. Remember me affectionately to your papa and mamma, and kiss Ellen and all the children for me.

TH. JEFFERSON.

P. S.—Since writing the above, I have a letter from Mr. Peale informing me that Jefferson is well, and saying the best things of him.

———

MONTICELLO, June 3, '11.

MY DEAR CORNELIA: I have lately received a copy of Miss Edgeworth's Moral Tales, which seeming better suited to your years than to mine, I inclose you the first volume. The other two shall follow as soon as your mamma has read them. They are to make a part of your library. I have not looked into them, preferring to receive their character from you, after you shall have read them. Your family of silk-worms is reduced to a single individual. That is now spinning his broach.[1] To encourage Virginia and Mary to take care of it, I tell them that as soon as they can get wedding-gowns from this spinner, they shall be married. I propose the same to you ; that, in order to hasten its work, you may hasten home ; for we all wish much to see you, and to express in person, rather than by letter, the assurance of our affectionate love.

TH. JEFFERSON.

P. S.—The girls desire me to add a postscript, to inform you that Mrs. Higginbotham has just given them new dolls.

———

APPENDIX NO. XXIV.—VOL. III., p. 363.

Disunion feelings in New England.

A strong disunion feeling manifested itself in New England, as early as 1796, during General Washington's Administration. A carefully-written series of papers, said at the time to be prepared by an association of individuals of the highest position and influence, appeared in a leading Connecticut newspaper (the Hartford Courant), over the signature of Pelham, urging a dissolution of the confederacy. The tenor and spirit of these articles will be sufficiently understood from the following extracts :

"The Northern States can subsist as a nation, as a Republic, without any connection with the Southern. It cannot be contested, that if the Southern States were possessed of the same political ideas, an union would still be more desirable than a separation. But when it becomes a serious question, whether we shall give up our government, or part with the States south of the Potomac, no man north of that river, whose heart is not thoroughly democratic, can hesitate what decision to make."

    *   *   *   *   *   *   *   *

"I shall in future papers consider some of the great events which will lead to a

---

[1] The name given by slaves, and probably generally, in common conversation in Virginia to a spool.

separation of the United States; show the importance of retaining their present Constitution, even at the expense of a separation; endeavor to prove the impossibility of an union for any long period in future, both from the moral and political habits of the citizens of the Southern States; and finally examine carefully to see whether we have not already approached the era when they must be divided."

   •   •   •   •   •   •   •   •

"Negroes are, in all respects, except in regard to life and death, the cattle of the citizens of the Southern States. If they were good for food, the probability is, that even the power of destroying their lives would be enjoyed by their owners, as fully as it is over the lives of their cattle. It cannot be, that their laws prohibit the owners from killing their slaves, because those slaves are human beings, or because it is a moral evil to destroy them. If that were the case, how can they justify their being treated, in all other respects, *like brutes!* for it is in this point of view alone that negroes in the Southern States are considered in fact as different from cattle. They are bought and sold—they are fed or kept hungry—they are clothed or reduced to nakedness—they are beaten, turned out to the fury of the elements, and torn from their dearest connections, with as little remorse as if they were beasts of the field."

The election of John Adams quieted these feelings for a period; and so rapid and general was the popular defection from the Federalists, on Jefferson's accession —so hopeless were the leaders of finding any followers—that disunion slept until the acquisition of Louisiana. We have already recorded that the younger Adams, when President (October 21st, 1828), declared publicly that a disunion party existed in New England at the period of the Embargo, and had existed there "for several years"—that he knew this from "unequivocal evidence." On the 26th of November following, Harrison Gray Otis, and twelve other prominent Federal gentlemen of Massachusetts, in a public letter, asked Mr. Adams to furnish "a full and precise statement of the facts and evidence relating to this accusation," solemnly declaring "that they had never known nor suspected that the party which prevailed in Massachusetts in the year 1808, or any other party in that State, ever entertained the design to produce a dissolution of the Union, or the establishment of a separate confederation."

President Adams replied, December 30th, 1828:

"This design had been formed in the winter of 1803 and '4, immediately after, and as a consequence of the acquisition of Louisiana. . . . . This plan was so far matured, that the proposal had been made to an individual to permit himself, at the proper time, to be placed at the head of the military movements, which it was foreseen would be necessary for carrying it into execution. . . . . That project, I repeat, had gone to the length of fixing upon a military leader for its execution; and although the circumstances of the times never admitted of its execution, nor even of its full development, I had yet no doubt in 1808 and 1809, and have no doubt at this time, that it is the key of all the great movements of these leaders of the Federal party in New England, from that time forward, till its final catastrophe in the Hartford Convention. . . . . The annexation of Louisiana to the Union was believed to be unconstitutional, but it produced no excitement to resistance among the people. Its beneficial consequences to the whole Union were soon felt, and took away all possibility of holding it up, as the labarum of a political religion of disunion. The projected separation met with other disasters, and slumbered till the attack of the Leopard on the Chesapeake, followed by the Orders in Council of 11th November, 1807, led to the Embargo of the 22d December of that year. . . . .

This was precisely the period at which the Governor of Nova Scotia was giving to his correspondent in Massachusetts, the friendly warning from the British Government of the revolutionizing and conquering plan of France, which was communicated to me, and of which I apprised Mr. Jefferson. The Embargo, in the meantime, had been laid, and had saved most of our vessels and seamen from the grasp of British cruisers. . . . . The question of the constitutionality of the Embargo was solemnly argued before the District Court of the United States at Salem; and although the decision of the judge was in its favor, it continued to be argued to the juries; and even when silenced before them, was, in the distemper of the times, so infectious, that the juries themselves habitually acquitted those charged with the violation of that law. . . . . I forbear to pursue the narrative. The two postulates for disunion were nearly consummated. The interposition of a kind Providence, restoring peace to our country and to the world, averted the most deplorable of catastrophes, and turning over to the receptacle of things lost upon earth, the adjourned convention from Hartford to Boston, extinguished (by the mercy of Heaven, may it be forever!) the projected New England confederacy.

     •   •   •   •   •   •   •   •

"It is not improbable that at some future day, a sense of solemn duty to my country, may require of me to disclose the evidence which I do possess, and for which you call. But of that day the selection must be at my own judgment, and it may be delayed till I myself shall have gone to answer for the testimony I may bear before the tribunal of your God and mine. Should a disclosure of names even then be made by me, it will, if possible, be made with such reserve as tenderness to the feelings of the living, and to the families and friends of the dead, may admonish."

Mr. Adams wrote Governor William Plumer, of New Hampshire, December 31st, 1828:

"Much of my information, at the time, was collected from Mr. Tracy, the Senator from Connecticut, who disapproved the project, but was, I believe, made acquainted with it in all its particulars. I think, though I am not sure, that it was he who named to me the writer of the plan by which the separation was to be effected, with three alternatives of boundary. 1. If possible, the Potomac. 2. The Susquehanna. 3. The Hudson. That is, the Northern confederacy was to extend, if it should be found practicable, so as to include Maryland. This was the maximum. The Hudson, that is, New England and a part of New York, was the minimum. The Susquehanna, or Pennsylvania, was the middle term." (See Life of William Plumer.)

The following extract, from a pamphlet written by himself in 1829, was subsequently communicated by Mr. Adams to Plumer. It gives the particulars of a visit made by Adams to Rufus King, April 8, 1804:

"I found there sitting, Mr. Timothy Pickering, who, shortly after I went in, took leave and withdrew. Mr. King said to me, 'Colonel Pickering has been talking to me about a project they have for a separation of the States, and a Northern confederacy; and he has also been this day talking of it with General Hamilton. Have you heard anything of it at Washington?' I said I had—much—but not from Colonel Pickering. [Adams and Pickering, though colleagues, were not friends.] 'Well,' said Mr. King, 'I disapprove entirely of this project; and so I have told him; and so, I am happy to tell you, does General Hamilton.'"

On seeing the denials of Otis and others, Governor Plumer, who was a Federal U. S. Senator from New Hampshire at the time of the acquisition of Louisiana (1803-4), addressed a letter to Mr. Adams, in which he declared that he (Plumer) was a disunionist at that period—"in favor of forming a separate government in New England "—that he was consulted on such a plan by Federal members of Congress from New England—but that on returning home, he found a great majority of the well-informed Federalists of his State entirely opposed to the project—and from "partial and limited inquiries," he concluded a nearly similar state of things existed in Massachusetts. He consented to have his letter to Mr. Adams containing these statements published.

Neither Governor Plumer's high personal character nor veracity was ever, we believe, questioned before or after this publication. Both are acknowledged in an article discussing this very subject in the North American Review, of October, 1856, written obviously under strong partialities for the accused parties.

In a life of Governor Plumer, by his son, various extracts are given from his contemporaneous journals and correspondence, exhibiting special and definite particulars of the plan of disunion, and of interviews in reference to it with its projectors and favorers. We have not found this biography readily accessible, and we shall quote extracts from it which we find in the article in the North American Review.

Under date of November 23d, 1806, Plumer mentions in his journal, that in the winter of 1804, Timothy Pickering, James Hillhouse and himself dined with Aaron Burr; that Hillhouse "unequivocally declared that it was his opinion that the United States would soon form two distinct and separate governments;" that "Mr. Burr conversed very freely" on the subject; "and the impression made on his [Plumer's] mind was, that he not only thought such an event would take place, but that it was necessary it should." Plumer adds: "to that opinion I was myself then a convert;" and then follows this characteristic touch of Burr: "Yet, on returning to my lodgings, after critically analyzing his words, there was nothing in them that necessarily implied his approbation of Mr. Hillhouse's observations. Perhaps no man's language was ever so apparently explicit and at the same time so covert and indefinite." The record of this conversation will remind the reader of General Eaton's testimony on the trial of Burr, that he (Eaton) "opened" to certain representatives of Connecticut, "the projects of Colonel Burr" for separating the Union, etc., during the winter of 1805-6; and that "they did not seem much alarmed." It will also remind the reader of a good many attempts on that trial and since, to laugh down Eaton's testimony on the ground of the utter absurdity of believing that a disunion project could at that time have possibly existed.

Plumer says, February 6th, 1809: "When the late Samuel Hunt intimated to me the necessity of receding from the Union, he observed that the work must commence in the State legislatures; so that those who acted should be supported by State laws. This, he said, was the opinion of ———, of Uriah Tracy, and of many others." Plumer wrote Oliver Peabody, January 19th, 1804: "What do you wish your senators and representatives to do here? We have no part in Jefferson, and no inheritance in Virginia. Shall we return to our homes, sit under our own vines and fig trees, and be separate from the slaveholders?" The Rev. Jedediah Morse, of Massachusetts, wrote Plumer, February 3d, 1804: "If we were peaceably severed from the rest of the United States, with perhaps some other States joined to us, and left to manage our own affairs in our own way, I think we should do much better than we now do." Plumer replied, March 10th: "I hope the time is not far distant when the people east of the North River will manage their own affairs in their own way, without being embarrassed by regulations from Virginia, and that the sound part will be separate from the corrupt"

On seeing Hillhouse's denial of Mr. Adams's statements in 1828, Plumer made the following entry in his journal:

"There is no circumstance in these publications that surprises me so much as the letter of James Hillhouse. I recollect, and am certain, that on returning early one evening from dining with Aaron Burr, this same Mr. Hillhouse, after saying to me that New England had no influence in the Government, added in an animated tone, 'The Eastern States must and will dissolve the Union, and form a separate government of their own; and the sooner they do this the better.' I think the first man who mentioned the subject of dismemberment to me was Samuel Hunt, a representative from New Hampshire. He conversed with me often and long upon the subject. But there was no man with whom I conversed so often, so fully and freely as with Roger Griswold. He was, without doubt or hesitation, decidedly in favor of dissolving the Union, and establishing a Northern confederacy. He thought it might be effected peaceably, without a resort to arms; and entered into a particular detail of the mode of effecting it. Next to Griswold, Uriah Tracy conversed most freely and fully upon this subject. It was he who informed me that General Hamilton had consented to attend a meeting of select Federalists at Boston, in the autumn of 1804. I do not recollect that he said Hamilton was in favor of the measure; but I know he said Hamilton had consented to attend. Tracy said the day for meeting was not appointed; nor were the persons who were to attend selected; but that I should be notified of the time, and invited to attend. It was Tracy who, in the session of 1804–5, informed me that the death of Hamilton had prevented the meeting in Boston; but, he added, the plan of separation is not abandoned. The three men last named, Tracy, Griswold, and Hunt, were the men with whom I principally conversed on that subject.

"One day, in the session of 1804–5, I distinctly recollect walking, about two hours, with Timothy Pickering, round the northerly and easterly lines of the City of Washington: and in that walk no other person accompanied us. I perfectly recollect his conversing with me at that time, as if he were desirous of saying something to me, which he hesitated to communicate. His manner made such a strong and deep impression on my mind, that I shall never forget it. At length he said, that he thought the United States were too large, and their interests too variant, for the Union to continue long; and that New England, New York, and perhaps Pennsylvania, might and ought to form a separate government. He then paused, and looking me fully in the face, awaited my reply. I simply asked him, if the division of the States was not the object which General Washington most pathetically warned the people to oppose? He said 'Yes; the fear of it was a ghost that for a long time haunted the imagination of that old gentleman.' I do not recollect that he afterwards mentioned to me the subject of dismemberment."

Of Hunt, Plumer, under date of July 31, 1831, says: "His object was to divide the United States into two separate independent governments; the States easterly of Maryland to unite and form a government more energetic, and more favorable to commerce than the one which then existed. To effect this object, he corresponded with a considerable number of influential Federalists in various States.'

Under date of June 4, 1840, Plumer says: "That Tracy told him in the winter of 1804, 'That he was in favor of the Northern States withdrawing from the Union.'"

Plumer's biographer (his son) calls attention to a significant fact. Timothy Pickering was alive when this controversy occurred in regard to the former existence of a disunion party in New England. Every one understood that _he was_ specially implicated by those charges. He did not deny them. Much as Mr. Pickering loved controversy—deeply as he hated the Adamses—he suffered the charge made by John Quincy Adams to go without a public denial. He probably understood that *his* denial of complicity would call out too many *proofs.*

APPENDIX NO. XXV.—Vol. III., p. 366.

Governor Coles' Visit to Mr. Adams.

PHILADELPHIA, *May* 11, 1857.

DEAR SIR:

*   *   *   *   *   *   *   *   *

I will now, without further explanation, comply with your request, by stating some of the facts you allude to as having heard from me, and which are mentioned in Mr. Jefferson's letter to Dr. Rush, of Dec. 5th, 1811. In the summer of 1811, while secretary to President Madison, I, accompanied by my brother John, made a tour through the Northern States, and took letters of introduction from the President to many of the most distinguished men of that section of the Union—among others, to ex-President John Adams, with whom we spent the greater part of two days, and were treated by him and his wife with great civility and kindness. Mr. Adams talked very freely of men and things, and detailed many highly interesting facts in the history of our country, and particularly of his own Administration, and of incidents connected with the Presidential election of 1800. This, and his knowledge of my being a neighbor and intimate with Mr. Jefferson, led him to converse freely, and by the nature of his remarks to open the door to expose his grievances, and to invite explanations of the causes of them. He complained, and mentioned several instances in which he thought he had reason to complain, of Mr. Jefferson's treatment of him. I told him I could not reconcile what he had heard of Mr. Jefferson's language, and conduct to him, with what I had heard him repeatedly say, and that, too, to friends who were politically opposed to Mr. Adams. Upon repeating some of the complimentary remarks thus made by Mr. Jefferson, Mr. Adams not only seemed, but expressed himself highly pleased. In our speaking of Mr. Jefferson's conduct, a remark of Mr. Adams seemed to elicit, and render it appropriate, in illustration of his course, for me to give Mr. Jefferson's account of the first interview they had after Mr. Adams had lost his election to the Presidency in 1800. I told him I had heard Mr. Jefferson say, that during the time of Mr. Adams's being President, and he Vice-President, in despite of party excitement, he regularly called on the President, and had his visits as Vice-President returned, and from time to time dined with President Adams, and when thus mingling together no one could see anything but the most civil and gracious conduct displayed by both. In the correctness of this, Mr. Adams concurred. I then told him at the first meeting of Congress after the election of 1800, Mr. Jefferson said, knowing Mr. Adams's sensitiveness, and wishing to do nothing to arouse it, he deliberated much as to the proper time for making his usual call on the President; fearing if he called very soon, it might have the appearance of exulting over him, and if, on the other hand, he delayed it any longer than Mr. Adams thought was usual, his sensitive feelings might construe it into a slight, or the turning a cold shoulder to him, in consequence of his having lost his election. When, finally, he concluded the proper time had arrived, he called on the President, and found him alone. But the first glimpse of him convinced Mr. Jefferson he had come too soon. Mr. Adams advanced to him in a hurried and agitated step, and with a tremulous voice, said, " You have turned me out, you have turned me out!" Mr. Jefferson replied in a mild and collected manner, " I have not turned you out, Mr. Adams, and am glad to avail myself of this occasion to show I have not, and to explain my views on this subject. In consequence," he said, " of a division of opinion existing among our fellow-citizens, as to the proper constitution of our political institutions, and of the wisdom and propriety of certain measures which had been adopted by our Government, that portion of our citizens who approved and advocated one class of these opinions and measures, selected you as their candidate for the Presidency, and their opponents selected me." If Mr. Adams or himself had not been in existence, or for any other cause had not been selected, other persons would have been selected in their places, and thus the contest would have been carried on, and with the same result, except that the party which supported Mr. Adams would have been defeated by a greater majority, as it was known that, but for Mr. Adams, his party would have carried their unpopular measures much further than they did. " You will see from this," said Mr. Jefferson, " that the late contest was not one of a personal character, between John Adams and Thomas Jefferson, but between the advocates and opponents of certain political opinions and measures, and, therefore, should produce no unkind feelings between the two men who happened to be placed at the head of the two parties." After these and other details, which the deep interest Mr. Adams evinced induced me to give, of which the above is but an outline, Mr. Jefferson said Mr. Adams became composed, and they took their seats, and talked on the usual topics of a morning visit. When I finished my narrative, Mr. Adams said if I had been present and witnessed the scene, I could not have given a more accurate account of what passed—and promptly added, " Mr. Jefferson said I was sensitive, did he? Well, I was sensitive. But I never heard before that Mr. Jefferson had given a second thought as to the proper time for making the particular visit described."

In the course of the many long conversations I had with Mr. Adams, he displayed, in general, kind feelings to Mr. Jefferson, and an exalted admiration of his character, and appreciation of his services to his country, as well during the Revolution as subsequently ; frequently making complimentary allusions to them, and displaying friendly feelings for him, in such expressions as " I always loved Jefferson, and still love him ;" expressing in strong terms his disapprobation and mortification at the course pursued by some of his (Adams's) friends in their scurrilous abuse of Mr. Jefferson, etc., etc. Mr. Jefferson's letter to Dr. Rush, above referred to, shows I communicated to him what passed of an interesting nature during my visit to Mr. Adams, and how instrumental it was in reviving the long-suspended correspondence between these two great men of 1776.

*   *   *   *   *   *   *   *

As I am tired of writing, and fear you are of reading, I will conclude by renewing assurances of my high respect and sincere regard.

EDWARD COLES.

HENRY S. RANDALL, Esq., Cortland Village.

APPENDIX NO. XXVI.—Vol. III. p. 401.

Jefferson's Delineation of Washington.

Doctor Walter Jones, of Virginia, had written an able essay on parties in the United States, and he proposed to prepare another. In respect to one of the topics of this essay, he expressed the doubt to Jefferson which is answered in the following letter :

Monticello, January 2d, 1814.

• • • • • • • • •

· You say that in taking General Washington on your shoulders, to bear him harmless through the federal coalition, you encounter a perilous topic. I do not think so. You have given the genuine history of the course of his mind through the trying scenes in which it was engaged, and of the seductions by which it was deceived, but not depraved. I think I knew General Washington intimately and thoroughly ; and were I called on to delineate his character, it should be in terms like these.

His mind was great and powerful, without being of the very first order ; his penetration strong, though not so acute as that of a Newton, Bacon, or Locke ; and as far as he saw, no judgment was ever sounder. It was slow in operation, being little aided by invention or imagination, but sure in conclusion. Hence the common remark of his officers, of the advantage he derived from councils of war, where hearing all suggestions, he selected whatever was best ; and certainly no general ever planned his battles more judiciously. But if deranged during the course of the action, if any member of his plan was dislocated by sudden circumstances, he was slow in a re-adjustment. The consequence was, that he often failed in the field, and rarely against an enemy in station, as at Boston and York. He was incapable of fear, meeting personal dangers with the calmest unconcern. Perhaps the strongest feature in his character was prudence, never acting until every circumstance, every consideration, was maturely weighed ; refraining if he saw a doubt, but, when once decided, going through with his purpose, whatever obstacles opposed. His integrity was most pure, his justice the most inflexible I have ever known, no motives of interest or consanguinity, of friendship or hatred, being able to bias his decision. He was, indeed, in every sense of the words, a wise, a good, and a great man. His temper was naturally irritable and high-toned ; but reflection and resolution had obtained a firm and habitual ascendency over it. If ever, however, it broke its bonds, he was most tremendous in his wrath. In his expenses he was honorable, but exact ; liberal in contributions to whatever promised utility ; but frowning and unyielding on all visionary projects, and all unworthy calls on his charity. His heart was not warm in its affections ; but he exactly calculated every man's value, and gave him a solid esteem proportioned to it. His person, you know, was fine, his stature exactly what one would wish, his deportment easy, erect and noble ; the best horseman of his age, and the most graceful figure that could be seen on horseback. Although, in the circle of his friends, where he might be unreserved with safety, he took a free share in conversation, his colloquial talents were not above mediocrity, possessing neither copiousness of ideas, nor fluency of words. In public, when called on for a sudden opinion, he was unready, short, and embarrassed. Yet he wrote readily, rather diffusely, in an easy and correct style. This he had acquired by conversation with the world, for his education was merely reading, writing, and common arithmetic, to which he added surveying at a later day. His time was employed in action chiefly, reading little, and that only in agriculture and English history. His correspondence became necessarily extensive, and, with journalizing his agricultural proceedings, occupied most of his leisure hours within doors. On the whole, his character was, in its mass, perfect, in nothing bad, in few points indifferent; and it may truly be said, that never did nature and fortune combine more perfectly to make a man great, and to place him in the same constellation with whatever worthies have merited from man an everlasting remembrance. For his was the singular destiny and merit, of leading the armies of his country successfully through an arduous war, for the establishment of its independence; of conducting its councils through the birth of a government, new in its forms and principles, until it had settled down into a quiet and orderly train; and of scrupulously obeying the laws through the whole of his career, civil and military, of which the history of the world furnishes no other example.

How, then, can it be perilous for you to take such a man on your shoulders? I am satisfied the great body of Republicans think of him as I do. We were, indeed, dissatisfied with him on his ratification of the British treaty. But this was short lived. We knew his honesty, the wiles with which he was encompassed, and that age had already begun to relax the firmness of his purposes; and I am convinced he is more deeply seated in the love and gratitude of the Republicans, than in the Pharisaical homage of the federal Monarchists. For he was no Monarchist from preference of his judgment. The soundness of that gave him correct views of the rights of man, and his severe justice devoted him to them. He has often declared to me that he considered our new Constitution as an experiment on the practicability of republican government, and with what dose of liberty man could be trusted for his own good; that he was determined the experiment should have a fair trial, and would lose the last drop of his blood in support of it. And these declarations he repeated to me the oftener and more pointedly, because he knew my suspicions of Colonel Hamilton's views, and probably had heard from him the same declarations which I had, to wit, "that the British constitution, with its unequal representation, corruption, and other existing abuses, was the most perfect Government which had ever been established on earth, and that a reformation of those abuses would make it an impracticable Government." I do believe that General Washington had not a firm confidence in the durability of our Government. He was naturally distrustful of men, and inclined to gloomy apprehensions; and I was ever persuaded that a belief that we must at length end in something like a British constitution, had some weight in his adoption of the ceremonies of levees, birth-days, pompous meetings with Congress, and other forms of the same character, calculated to prepare us gradually for a change which he believed possible, and to let it come on with as little shock as might be to the public mind.

These are my opinions of General Washington, which I would vouch at the judgment-seat of God, having been formed on an acquaintance of thirty years. I served with him in the Virginia Legislature from 1769 to the Revolutionary war, and again, a short time in Congress, until he left us to take command of the army. During the war and after it we corresponded occasionally, and in the four years of my continuance in the office of Secretary of State, our intercourse was daily, confidential and cordial. After I retired from that office, great and malignant pains were taken by our federal Monarchists, and not entirely without effect, to make him view me as a theorist, holding French principles of government, which would lead infallibly to licentiousness and anarchy. And to this he listened the more easily, from my known disapprobation of the British treaty. I never saw him afterwards, or these malignant insinuations should have been dissipated before his just judgment, as mists before the sun. I felt on his death, with my countrymen, that " verily a great man hath fallen this day in Israel."

More time and recollection would enable me to add many other traits of his character; but why add them to you, who knew him well? And I cannot justify to myself a longer detention of your paper.

Vale, proprieque tuum, me esse tibi persuadeas.

TH. JEFFERSON.

------------◆------------

APPENDIX NO. XXVII.—VOL. III. p. 406.

Jefferson to Edward Coles on Slavery, etc.

MONTICELLO, *Aug.* 25, 1814.

DEAR SIR: Your favor of July 31 was duly received, and was read with peculiar pleasure. The sentiments breathed through the whole, do honor both to the head and heart of the writer. Mine, on the subject of the slavery of negroes, have long since been in possession of the public, and time has only served to give them stronger proof. The love of justice and the love of country plead equally the cause of these people, and it is a mortal reproach to us that they should have pleaded so long in vain, and should have produced not a single effort, nay, I fear, not much serious willingness to relieve them and ourselves, from our present condition of moral and political reprobation.

From those in a former generation, who were in the fullness of age when I came into public life, which was while our controversy with England was on paper only, I soon saw that nothing was to be hoped. Nursed and educated in the daily habit of seeing the degraded condition, both bodily and mental, of those unfortunate beings, not reflecting that that degradation was very much the work of themselves and their fathers, few minds had yet doubted but that they were as legitimate subjects of property as their horses or cattle. The quiet and monotonous course of colonial life had been disturbed by no alarm, and little reflection on the value of liberty. And when an alarm was taken at an enterprise of their own, it was not easy to carry them the whole length of the principles which they invoked for themselves.

In the first or second session of the legislature, after I became a member, I drew to this subject the attention of Colonel Bland, one of the oldest, ablest, and most respected members, and he undertook to move for certain moderate extensions of the protection of the laws to these people. I seconded his motion, and, as a younger member, was more spared in the debate; but he was denounced as an enemy to his country, and was treated with the greatest indecorum. From an early stage of our Revolution, other and more distant duties were assigned to me, so that from that time till my return from Europe, in 1789, and I may say, till I returned to reside at home in 1809, I had little opportunity of knowing the progress of public sentiment here on this subject.

I had always hoped that the younger generation, receiving their early impressions after the flame of liberty had been kindled in every breast, and had become, as it were, the vital spirit of every American, that the generous temperament of youth, analogous to the motion of their blood, and above the suggestions of avarice, would have sympathized with oppression wherever found, and proved their love of liberty beyond their own share of it. But my intercourse with them, since my return, has not been sufficient to ascertain that they had made towards this point the progress I had hoped.

Your solitary but welcome voice is the first which has brought this sound to my ear; and I have considered the general silence which prevails on this subject, as indicating an apathy unfavorable to every hope. Yet the hour of emancipation is advancing in the march of time. It will come; and whether brought on by the generous energy of our own minds, or by the bloody process of St. Domingo, excited and conducted by the power of our present enemy, if once stationed permanently within our country, and offering asylum and arms to the oppressed, is a leaf of our history not yet turned over.

As to the method by which this difficult work is to be effected, if permitted to be done by ourselves, I have seen no proposition so expedient, on the whole, as that of emancipation of those born after a given day, and of their education and expatriation at a proper age. This would give time for a gradual extinction of that species of labor, and substitution of another, and lessen the severity of the shock, which an operation so fundamental cannot fail to produce. The idea of emancipating the whole at once, the old as well as the young, and retaining them here, is of those only who have not the guide of either knowledge or experience on the subject. For men, probably of any color, but of this color we know, brought up from their infancy without necessity for thought or forecast, are by their habits rendered as incapable as children of taking care of themselves, and are extinguished promptly wherever industry is necessary for raising the young. In the meantime, they are pests in society by their idleness, and the depredations to which this leads them. Their amalgamation with the other color produces a degradation to which no lover of his country, no lover of excellence in the human character, can innocently consent.

I am sensible of the partialities with which you have looked towards me as the person who should undertake this salutary but arduous work. But this, my dear sir, is like bidding old Priam to buckle on the armor of Hector—" *trementibus ævo humeris et inutile ferrumcingi.*" No, I have outlived the generation with which mutual labors and perils begat mutual confidence and influence. This enterprise is for the young—for those who can follow it up, and bear it through to its consummation.

It shall have all my prayers, and these are the only weapons of an old man. But, in the meantime, are you right in abandoning this property, and your country with it? I think not. My opinion has ever been that, until more can be done for them, we should endeavor, with those whom fortune has thrown on our hands, to feed and clothe them well, protect them from ill usage, require such reasonable labor only as is performed voluntarily by freemen, and be led by no repugnance to abdicate them, and our duties to them. The laws do not permit us to turn them loose, if that were for their good; and to commute them for other property, is to commit them to those whose usage of them we cannot control.

I hope, then, my dear sir, you will reconcile yourself to your country and its unfortunate condition ; that you will not lessen its stock of sound disposition, by withdrawing your portion from the mass. That, on the contrary, you will come forward in the public councils, become the missionary of this doctrine, truly Christian, insinuate and inculcate it, softly but steadily, through the medium of writing and conversation, associate others in your labors, and, when the phalanx is formed, bring on and press the proposition perseveringly, until its accomplishment.

It is an encouraging observation that no good measure was ever proposed which, if duly pursued, failed to prevail in the end. We have a proof of this in the history of the endeavors, in the British Parliament, to suppress that very trade which brought this evil on us. And you will be supported by the religious precept, "Be not wearied in well doing." That your success may be as speedy and as complete as it will be honorable and immortal consolation to yourself, I shall as fervently and sincerely pray, as I assure you of my great friendship and respect.

TH. JEFFERSON.

APPENDIX NO. XXVIII.—Vol. III., p. 411.

Proceedings in Massachusetts in 1814.

The first factious proceedings in Massachusetts in 1814, arose on the imprisonment of some British officers in the jails of that State. The circumstances were as follows: A number of our Irish-born soldiers (twenty-three we think) captured by the British at Queenston, were sent to England avowedly to be tried for *treason.* The President ordered an equal number of British prisoners into close confinement, to await the same punishment which should be inflicted on the former. Thereupon General Prevost imprisoned a double number of American officers, and declared that if the retaliation continued, he would not spare the American cities and villages. The President again made an even retaliation. Prevost next ordered *all* his prisoners into confinement, and the United States authorities did the same.

Some British officers were, by the orders of the Commissary-General, sent to the jail in Worcester, Massachusetts, under the Act of that State of 1790, which placed its jails at the service of the United States Government. A strong sympathy for these prisoners immediately manifested itself among the ultra-Federalists. A plan for their escape was concocted by citizens of Massachusetts, who assisted them to secure their keeper and break jail. Five were retaken, but four made good their flight. The Boston Daily Advertiser rejoiced over the escape of these "gallant officers whom Mr. Madison desired to answer for the lives of self-acknowledged traitors."

The Legislature promptly (February 7th, 1814) repealed the act of 1790, so far as it applied to the confinement of prisoners by other United States authorities beside the judiciary, and it ordered all prisoners in the State jails, "committed under the Executive authority of the United States," to be discharged within thirty days.

A memorial was addressed to the same Legislature, praying that a remonstrance be sent to Congress—that State laws be enacted against searches and seizures under the then existing Embargo law—and that delegates be appointed by the Legislature to meet other similarly appointed delegates "for the purpose of devising proper measures to procure the united efforts of the *commercial States* to obtain such amendments or explanations of the Constitution as would secure them from future evils."

A joint committee reported on this memorial, February 16th, declaring that remonstrances to Congress had already been too long resorted to—that the State laws were now adequate to prevent searches and seizures—and approving of the proposed convention of States. But inasmuch as a new Legislature was to be immediately elected and to assemble in May, the committee recommended that definitive action be deferred for its consideration. The language of the report was highly denunciatory and threatening towards the national Government. In regard to the war, for example, it said:

"We believe that-this war, so fertile in calamities, and so threatening in its consequences, has been waged' with the worst possible views, and carried on in the worst possible manner, forming a union of wickedness and weakness which defies, for a parallel, the annals of the world," etc.

And in regard to the Embargo:

"A power to regulate commerce is abused when employed to destroy it, and a voluntary abuse of power *sanctions the right of resistance* as much as a direct and palpable usurpation."

The approval of a call for a convention of only a part of the States to *change the Constitution*, could not be regarded otherwise than as an express sanction of disunion—and it alarmed that small body of Federalists who were neither disunionists nor so far swept away by the excitement of the times as not to see to what end the measure tended.

Of this class was Samuel Dexter, who had been Secretary of War, and subsequently Secretary of the Treasury during President John Adams's Administration. He was the ablest lawyer in New England, and had very few equals in the Union. His private character was irreproachable—his sincerity and earnestness as a politician unquestionable. He had gone with his party against the Embargo, the war, and all the principal measures of Jefferson's and Madison's administrations. He had even succeeded in convincing himself that the Embargo was unconstitutional—thus proving the strength of his party prejudices and fealty. But Mr. Dexter was not a disunionist, and when the initiatory step of disunion received a legislative sanction, he shrunk back. He published a letter, in which he appealed to his fellow-citizens to pause, and in the strongest terms pointed out the impolicy of dissolving the Union. He declared that the Eastern and Southern States "were made for each other," and that "a man and a woman might as reasonably quarrel on account of the difference of their formation." He avowed his continued opposition to commercial restrictions and war, but contended that as the war had been constitutionally declared, acquiescence was far preferable to disunion and civil war.

The Republicans thereupon nominated Dexter for Governor, hoping to draw off enough Federalists to defeat Strong, the ultra-Federal or disunion candidate. John Adams, who throughout the gathering storm had stood by his *whole* country as resolutely as in the Revolution, and a few other such men, voted for Dexter; but the heat and fury of local excitement and delusion may be estimated by the fact, that Strong's majority (March, 1814) was as large as it had been in the preceding election over the Republican candidate. This, however, was but trifling, so evenly were parties divided.

The new Legislature met in May. The Governor's speech and the replies of the houses took the usual tone, but the repeal of the new Embargo and the supposed

Increased prospects of peace, on account of the abdication of Napoleon, were thought to ·all for another delay in assembling a convention of the New England States.

The insulting conditions demanded by Great Britain of the American commis-s.oners sent to treat for peace, roused anew the war spirit of the middle and Southern States, and when the Massachusetts Legislature again convened in autumn, the prospect of speedy adjustment had apparently entirely subsided. Thereupon Otis's report from the joint committee (October 8th, 1814) was introduced, the Hartford Convention called, and an act passed to raise a State army, as mentioned in the text.

APPENDIX NO. XXIX.—VOL. III., p. 429.

Jefferson to Samuel Kercheval on the Constitution of Virginia.

MONTICELLO, July 12, 1816.

SIR: I duly received your favor of June the 13th, with the copy of the letters on the calling a convention, on which you are pleased to ask my opinion. I have not been in the habit of mysterious reserve on any subject, nor of buttoning up my opinions within my own doublet. On the contrary, while in public service especially, I thought the public entitled to frankness, and intimately to know whom they employed. But I am now retired: I resign myself, as a passenger, with confidence to those at present at the helm, and ask but for rest, peace and good will. The question you propose, on equal representation, has become a party one, in which I wish to take no public share. Yet, if it be asked for your own satisfaction only, and not to be quoted before the public, I have no motive to withhold it, and the less from you, as it coincides with your own. At the birth of our republic, I committed that opinion to the world, in the draught of a constitution annexed to the Notes on Virginia, in which a provision was inserted for a representation permanently equal. The infancy of the subject at that moment, and our inexperience of self-government, occasioned gross departures in that draught from genuine republican canons. In truth, the abuses of monarchy had so much filled all the space of political contemplation, that we imagined everything republican which was not monarchy. We had not yet penetrated to the mother principle, that " governments are republican only in proportion as they embody the will of their people, and execute it." Hence, our first constitutions had really no leading principle in them. But experience and reflection have but more and more confirmed me in the particular importance of the equal representation then proposed. On that point, then, I am entirely in sentiment with your letters; and only lament that a copy-right of your pamphlet prevents their appearance in the newspapers, where alone they would be generally read, and produce general effect. The present vacancy, too, of other matter, would give them place in every paper, and bring the question home to every man's conscience.

But inequality of representation in both Houses of our Legislature, is not the only republican heresy in this first essay of our revolutionary patriots at forming a constitution. For let it be agreed that a government is republican in proportion as every member composing it has his equal voice in the direction of its concerns (not. indeed in person, which would be impracticable beyond the limits of a city, or small township, but) by representatives chosen by himself, and responsible to him at short periods, and let us bring to the test of this canon every branch of our constitution.

In the Legislature, the House of Representatives is chosen by less than half the people, and not at all in proportion to those who do choose. The Senate are still more disproportionate, and for long terms of irresponsibility. In the Executive, the Governor is entirely independent of the choice of the people, and of their control; his council equally so, and at best but a fifth wheel to a wagon. In the Judiciary, the judges of the highest courts are dependent on none but themselves. In England, where judges were named and removable at the will of an hereditary executive, from which branch most misrule was feared, and has flowed, it was a great point gained, by fixing them for life, to make them independent of that executive. But in a government founded on the public will, this principle operates in an opposite direction, and against that will. There, too, they were still removable on a concurrence of the executive and legislative branches. But we have made them independent of the nation itself. They are irremovable, but by their own body, for any depravities of conduct, and even by their own body for the imbecilities of dotage. The justices of the inferior courts are self-chosen, are for life, and perpetuate their own body in succession forever, so that a faction once possessing themselves of the bench of a county, can never be broken up, but hold their county in chains, forever indissoluble. Yet these justices are the real executive as well as judiciary, in all our minor and most ordinary concerns. They tax us at will; fill the office of sheriff, the most important of all the executive officers of the county; name nearly all our military leaders, which leaders, once named, are removable but by themselves. The juries, our judges of all fact, and of law when they choose it, are not selected by the people, nor amenable to them. They are chosen by an officer named by the court and executive. Chosen, did I say? Picked up by the sheriff from the loungings of the court-yard, after everything respectable has retired from it. Where then is our republicanism to be found? Not in our Constitution certainly, but merely in the spirit of our people. That would oblige even a despot to govern us republicanly. Owing to this spirit, and to nothing in the form of our Constitution, all things have gone well. But this fact, so triumphantly misquoted by the enemies of reformation, is not the fruit of our Constitution, but has prevailed in spite of it. Our functionaries have done well, because generally honest men. If any were not so, they feared to show it.

But it will be said, it is easier to find faults than to amend them. I do not think their amendment so difficult as is pretended. Only lay down true principles, and adhere to them inflexibly. Do not be frightened into their surrender by the alarms of the timid, or the croakings of wealth against the ascendency of the people. If experience be called for, appeal to that of our fifteen or twenty governments for forty years, and show me where the people have done half the mischief in these forty years, that a single despot would have done in a single year; or show half the riots and rebellions, the crimes and the punishments, which have taken place in any single nation, under kingly government, during the same period. The true foundation of republican government is the equal right of every citizen, in his person and property, and in their management. Try by this, as a tally, every provision of our Constitution, and see if it hangs directly on the will of the people. Reduce your Legislature to a convenient number for full, but orderly discussion. Let every man who fights or pays, exercise his just and equal right in their election. Submit them to approbation or rejection at short intervals. Let the Executive be chosen in the same way, and for the same term, by those whose agent he is to be; and leave no screen of a council behind which to skulk from responsibility. It has been thought that the people are not competent electors of judges *learned in the law*. But I do not know that this is true, and, if doubtful, we should follow principle. In this, as in many other elections, they would be guided by reputation, which would not err oftener, perhaps, than the present mode of appointment. In one State of the Union, at least, it has been long tried, and with the most satisfactory success. The judges of Connecticut have been chosen by the people every six months, for nearly two centuries, and I believe there has hardly ever been an instance of change; so powerful is the curb of incessant responsibility. If prejudice, however, derived from a monarchical institution, is still to prevail against the vital elective principle of our own, and if the existing example among ourselves of periodical election of judges by the people be still mistrusted, let us at least not adopt the evil, and reject the good of the English precedent; let us retain amovability on the concurrence of the executive and legislative branches, and nomination by the Executive alone. Nomination to office is an Executive function. To give it to the Legislature, as we do, is a violation of the principle of the separation of powers. It swerves the members from correctness, by temptations to intrigue for office themselves, and to a corrupt barter of votes; and destroys responsibility by dividing it among a multitude. By leaving nomination in its proper place, among Executive functions, the principle of the distribution of power is preserved, and responsibility weighs with its heaviest force on a single head.

The organization of our county administrations may be thought more difficult. But follow principle, and the knot unties itself. Divide the counties into wards of such size as that every citizen can attend when called on, and act in person. Ascribe to them the government of their wards in all things relating to themselves exclusively. A justice, chosen by themselves, in each; a constable, a military company, a patrol, a school; the care of their own poor, their own portion of the public roads; the choice of one or more jurors to serve in some court, and the delivery, within their own wards, of their own votes for all elective officers of higher sphere, will relieve the county administration of nearly all its business, will have it better done, and by making every citizen an acting member of the government, and in the offices nearest and most interesting to him, will attach him by his strongest feelings to the independence of his country, and its republican constitution. The justices thus chosen by every ward would constitute the county court, would do its judiciary business, direct roads and bridges, levy county and poor rates, and administer all the matters of common interest to the whole county. These wards, called townships in New England, are the vital principle of their governments, and have proved themselves the wisest invention ever devised by the wit of man for the perfect exercise of self-government, and for its preservation.[1] We should thus marshal our Government into, 1. The general Federal republic, for all concerns foreign and federal; 2. That of the State, for what relates to our own citizens exclusively; 3. The county republics, for the duties and concerns of the county; and, 4. The ward republics, for the small, and yet numerous and interesting concerns of the neighborhood: and in government, as well as in every other business of life, it is by division and subdivision of duties alone, that all matters, great and small, can be managed to perfection.

[1] He wrote J. C. Cabell, Feb 2d, 1816: "How powerfully did we feel the energy of this organization in the case of embargo! I felt the foundations of the Government shaken under my feet by the New England townships. There was not an individual in their States whose body was not thrown with all its momentum into actio , and although the whole of the other States were known to be in favor of the measure, yet the organization of this little selfish minority enabled it to overrule the Union. What would the unwieldy counties of the middle, the South, and the West do?

And the whole is cemented by giving to every citizen, personally, a part in the administration of the public affairs.

The sum of these amendments is: 1. General suffrage; 2. Equal representation in the Legislature; 3. An Executive chosen by the people; 4. Judges elective or amovable; 5. Justices, jurors, and sheriffs elective; 6. Ward divisions; and, 7. Periodical amendments of the Constitution.

I have thrown out these, as loose heads of amendment for consideration and correction; and their object is to secure self-government by the republicanism of our Constitution, as well as by the spirit of the people; and to nourish and perpetuate that spirit. I am not among those who fear the people. They, and not the rich, are our dependence for continued freedom. And to preserve their independence, we must not let our rulers load us with perpetual debt. We must make our election between *economy and liberty*, or *profusion and servitude*. If we run into such debts, as that we must be taxed in our meat and in our drink, in our necessaries and our comforts, in our labors and our amusements, for our callings and our creeds, as the people of England are, our people, like them, must come to labor sixteen hours in the twenty-four, give the earnings of fifteen of these to the Government for their debts and their daily expenses; and the sixteenth being insufficient to afford us bread, we must live, as they now do, on oatmeal and potatoes; have no time to think, no means of calling the mismanagers to account; but be glad to obtain subsistence by hiring ourselves to rivet their chains on the necks of our fellow-sufferers. Our land-holders, too, like theirs, retaining indeed the title and stewardship of estates called theirs, but held really in trust for the treasury, must wander, like theirs, in foreign countries, and be contented with penury, obscurity, exile, and the glory of the nation. This example reads to us the salutary lesson that private fortunes are destroyed by public as well as by private extravagance. And this is the tendency of all human governments. A departure from principle in one instance becomes a precedent for a second; that second for a third; and so on, till the bulk of the society is reduced to be mere automatons of misery, to have no sensibilities left but for sinning and suffering. Then begins, indeed, the *bellum omnium in omnia*, which some philosophers observing to be so general in this world, have mistaken it for the natural, instead of the abusive state of man. And the fore-horse of this frightful team is public debt. Taxation follows that, and in its train, wretchedness and oppression.

Some men look at constitutions with sanctimonious reverence, and deem them like the ark of the covenant, too sacred to be touched. They ascribe to the men of the preceding age a wisdom more than human, and suppose what they did to be beyond amendment. I knew that age well: I belonged to it, and labored with it. It deserved well of its country. It was very like the present, but without the experience of the present; and forty years of experience in government is worth a century of book-reading: and this they would say themselves, were they to rise from the dead. I am certainly not an advocate for frequent and untried changes in laws and constitutions. I think moderate imperfections had better be borne with; because, when once known, we accommodate ourselves to them, and find practical means of correcting their ill effects. But I know also, that laws and institutions must go hand in hand with the progress of the human mind. As that becomes more developed, more enlightened, as new discoveries are made, new truths disclosed, and manners and opinions change with the change of circumstances, institutions must advance also, and keep pace with the times. We might as well require a man to wear still the coat which fitted him when a boy, as civilized society to remain ever under the regimen of their barbarous ancestors. It is this preposterous idea which has lately deluged Europe in blood. Their monarchs, instead of wisely yielding to the gradual changes of circumstances, of favoring progressive accommodation to progressive improvement, have clung to old abuses, entrenched themselves behind steady habits, and obliged their subjects to seek through blood and violence rash and ruinous innovations, which, had they been referred to the peaceful deliberations and collected wisdom of the nation, would have been put into acceptable and salutary forms. Let us follow no such examples, nor weakly believe that one generation is not as capable as another of taking care of itself, and of ordering its own affairs. Let us, as our sister States have done, avail ourselves of our reason and experience, to correct the crude essays of our first and unexperienced, although wise, virtuous, and well-meaning councils. And lastly, let us provide in our Constitutition for its revision at stated periods. What these periods should be, Nature herself indicates. By the European tables of mortality, of the adults living at any one moment of time, a majority will be dead in about nineteen years. At the end of that period, then, a new majority is come into place; or in other words, a new generation. Each generation is as independent of the one preceding, as that was of all which had gone before. It has, then, like them, a right to choose for itself the form of government it believes most promotive of its own happiness; consequently, to accommodate to the circumstances in which it finds itself, that received from its predecessors; and it is for the peace and good of mankind, that a solemn opportunity of doing this every nineteen or twenty years, should be provided by the Constitution; so that it may be handed on, with periodical repairs, from generation to generation, to the end of time, if anything human can so long endure. It is now forty years since the constitution of Virginia was formed. The same tables inform us, that, within that period, two thirds of the adults then living are now dead. Have, then, the remaining third, even if they had the wish, the right to hold in obedience to their will, and to laws heretofore made by them, the other two-thirds, who, with themselves, compose the present mass of adults? If they have not, who has? The dead? But the dead have no rights. They are nothing; and nothing cannot own something. Where there is no substance, there can be no accident. This corporeal globe, and everything upon it, belong to its present corporeal inhabitants, during their generation. They alone have a right to direct what is the concern of themselves alone, and to declare the law of that direction; and this declaration can only be made by their majority. That majority, then, has a right to depute representatives to a convention, and to make the Constitution what they think will be best for themselves. But how collect their voice? This is the real difficulty. If invited by private authority to county or district meetings, these divisions are so large that few will attend; and their voice will be imperfectly, or falsely pronounced. Here, then, would be one of the advantages of the ward divisions I have proposed. The mayor of every ward, on a question like the present, would call his ward together, take the simple yea or nay of its members, convey these to the county court, who would hand on those of all its wards to the proper general authority; and the voice of the whole people would be thus fairly, fully, and peaceably expressed, discussed, and decided by the common reason of the society. If this avenue be shut to the call of suffrance, it will make itself heard through that of force, and we shall go on, as other nations are doing, in the endless circle of oppression, rebellion, reformation; and oppression, rebellion, reformation, again; and so on, forever.

These, sir, are my opinions of the governments we see among men, and of the principles by which alone we may prevent our own from falling into the same dreadful track. I have given them at greater length than your letter called for. But I cannot say things by halves; and I confide them to your honor, so to use them as to preserve me from the gridiron of the public papers. If you shall approve and enforce them, as you have done that of equal representation, they may do some good. If not, keep them to yourself as the effusions of withered age, and useless time. I shall, with not the less truth, assure you of my great respect and consideration.

TH. JEFFERSON.

To John Taylor.

MONTICELLO, July 21, 1816.

DEAR SIR: Yours of the 10th is received, and I have to acknowledge a copious supply of the turnip seed requested. Besides taking care myself, I shall endeavor again to commit it to the repository of the neighborhood, generally found to be the best precaution against losing a good thing. I will add a word on the political part of our letters. I believe we do not differ on either of the points you suppose. On education, certainly not; of which the proofs are my bill for the diffusion of knowledge, proposed near forty years ago, and my uniform endeavors, to this day, to get our counties divided into wards, one of the principal objects of which is, the establishment of a primary school in each. But education not being a branch of municipal government, but, like the other arts and sciences, an accident only, I did not place it, with election, as a fundamental member in the structure of government. Nor, I believe, do we differ as to the county courts. I acknowledge the value of this institution; that it is in truth our principal executive and judiciary, and that it does much for little *pecuniary* reward. It is their self-appointment I wish to correct: to find some means of breaking up a cabal, when such a one gets possession of the bench. When this takes place, it becomes the most afflicting of tyrannies, because its powers are so various, and exercised on everything most immediately around us. And how many instances have you and I known of these monopolies of county administration! I knew a county in which a particular family (a numerous one) got possession of the bench, and for a whole generation never admitted a man on it who was not of its clan or connection. I know a county now of one thousand and five hundred militia, of which sixty are Federalists. Its court is of thirty members, of whom twenty are Federalists (every third man of the sect). There are large and populous districts in it, without a justice, because without a Federalist for appointment: the militia are as disproportionably under Federal officers. And there is no authority on earth which can break up this junto, short of a general convention. The remaining one thousand four hundred and forty, free, fighting, and paying citizens, are governed by men neither of their choice nor confidence, and without a hope of relief. They are certainly excluded from the blessings of a free government for life, and indefinitely, for aught the Constitution has provided. This solecism may be called anything but republican, and ought undoubtedly to be corrected. I salute you with constant friendship and respect.

TH. JEFFERSON.

To Samuel Kercheval.

MONTICELLO, September 5, 1816.

SIR: Your letter of August the 16th is just received. That which I wrote to you under the address of H. Tompkinson, was intended for the author of the pamphlet you were so kind as to send me, and therefore, in your hands, found its true destination. But I must beseech you, sir, not to admit a possibility of its being published. Many good people will revolt from its doctrines, and my wish is to offend nobody; to leave to those who are to live under it, the settlement of their own Constitution, and to pass in peace the remainder of my time. If those opinions are sound, they will occur to others, and will prevail by their own weight, without the aid of names. I am glad to see that the Staunton meeting has rejected the idea of a limited convention. The article, however, nearest my heart, is the division of the counties into wards. These will be pure and elementary republics, the sum of all which, taken together, composes the State, and will make of the whole a true democracy as to the business of the wards, which is that of nearest and daily concern. The affairs of the larger sections, of counties, of States, and of the Union, not admitting personal transaction by the people, will be delegated to agents elected by themselves; and representation will thus be substituted, where personal action becomes impracticable. Yet, even over these representative organs, should they become corrupt and perverted, the division into wards constituting the people, in their wards, a regularly organized power, enables them by that organization to crush, regularly and peaceably, the usurpations of their unfaithful agents, and rescues them from the dreadful necessity of doing it insurrectionally. In this way we shall be as republican as a large society can be; and secure the continuance of purity in our Government, by the salutary, peaceable, and regular control of the people. No other depositories of power have ever yet been found, which did not end in converting to their own profit the earnings of those committed to their charge. George the III., in execution of the trust confided to him, has, within his own day, loaded the inhabitants of Great Britain with debts equal to the whole fee-simple value of their island, and, under pretext of governing it, has alienated its whole soil to creditors who could lend money to be lavished on priests, pensions, plunder and perpetual war. This would not have been so, had the people retained organized means of acting on their agents. In this example, then, let us read a lesson for ourselves, and not " go, and do likewise."

Since writing my letter of July the 12th, I have been told, that on the question of equal representation, our fellow-citizens in some sections of the State claim peremptorily a right of representation for their slaves. Principle will, in this, as in most other cases, open the way for us to correct conclusion. Were our State a pure democracy, in which all its inhabitants should meet together to transact all their business, there would yet be excluded from their deliberations, 1. Infants, until arrived at years of discretion. 2. Women, who, to prevent depravation of morals and ambiguity of issue, could not mix promiscuously in the public meetings of men. 3. Slaves, from whom the unfortunate state of things with us takes away the rights of will and of property. Those then who have no will could be permitted to exercise none in the popular assembly; and of course, could delegate none to an agent in a representative assembly. The business, in the first case, would be done by qualified citizens only; and in the second, by the representatives of qualified citizens only. It is true, that in the general Constitution, our State is allowed a larger representation on account of its slaves. But every one knows, that that Constitution was a matter of compromise; a capitulation between conflicting interests and opinions. In truth, the condition of different descriptions of inhabitants in any country is a matter of municipal arrangement, of which no foreign country has a right to take notice. All its inhabitants are men as to them. Thus, in the New England States, none have the powers of citizens but those whom they call *freemen;* and none are *freemen* until admitted by a vote of the freemen of the town. Yet, in the General Government, these non-freemen are counted in their quantum of representation and of taxation. So, slaves with us have no powers as citizens; yet, in representation in the General Government, they count in the proportion of three to five; and so also in taxation. Whether this is equal, is not here the question. It is a capitulation of discordant sentiments and circumstances, and is obligatory on that ground. But this view shows there is no inconsistency in claiming representation for them from the other States, and refusing it within our own. Accept the renewal of assurances of my respect.

                                                         TH. JEFFERSON.

———————•◆•———————

APPENDIX NO. XXX.—VOL. III. p. 452.

Mr. Jefferson's Selections from the New Testament.

The following is the original collection of English texts made in 1803 (mentioned in letters to John Adams, October 13th, 1813; to Charles Thompson, January 9th, 1816; to Mr. Vanderkemp, April 25th, 1816, etc.); and which is also sometimes mentioned as Mr. Jefferson's collection for the Indians.

The Philosophy of Jesus of Nazareth.

Extracted from the account of his life and doctrines as given by Matthew, Mark, Luke, and John. Being an abridgment of the New Testament for the use of the Indians, unembarrassed with matters of fact or faith beyond the level of their comprehensions.

A table of the texts extracted from the Gospels, of the order in which they are arranged into sections, and the heads of each section.

§ I.—Luke ii. 1–7, 21, 22, 39–49, 51, 52. } History of Jesus.
        iii. 23–38.

  II.—Matt. x. 5–31, 42. Precepts for the Priesthood.

 III.—Luke xxii. 24–27. } Preachers to be humble.
        John xiii. 4–17.

 IV.—John x. 1–16.
       Luke xi. 52. } False teachers.
        xii. 13, 15.

  V.—John xiii. 34, 35. Disciples should love one another.

 VI.—Matt. xiii. 24–30, 36–43. Parable of the tares. Man not to judge for
                                              God.

VII.—Matt. xx. 1–16. Parable of the laborers.

VIII.—Mark ii. 15–17. } Physicians care for the sick. Parable of the lost
        Matt. xviii. 10, 11. } sheep. The lost piece of silver. The prodigal
        Luke xv. 3–32. } son.

 IX.—John viii. 1–11.
       Matt. xviii. 15–17. } The duty of mutual forgiveness and forbearance.
       Luke xiii. 6–9.

  X.—Matt. v. 1–10, 19–48.
        vi. 1–34. } The sermon on the mount.
        vii. 1–27.

XI.—Matt. xix. 13–24, 29, 30. } General moral precepts.
           xxii. 35–40.

XII.—Matt. xii. 1–5, 11, 12. } The Sabbath.
     Luke xiv. 1–6.

XIII.—   xi. 37–48. } Deeds and not ceremonies avail.
     Matt. xv. 1–9.

XIV.—   10–20. } Words the fruit of the heart.
       xii. 33–37.

XV.—   xiii. 1–9, 18–29. Parable of the sower.

XVI.—Luke vii. 36–47. } The will for the deed.
     Mark xii. 41–44.

XVII.—Matt. xi. 28–30. General exhortation.

XVIII.—Luke x. 25–37. Parable of the Samaritan, true benevolence.

XIX.—Matt. xxiii. 1–33. } Humility, pride, hypocrisy.
     Luke xviii. 9–14.

         xiv. 7–11. } Pharisaism.
     Matt. xviii. 1–6.

XX.—Luke xvi. 19–31. Dives and Lazarus. ⎫
     Matt. xxii. 1–14. The wedding supper. ⎬ God no respecter of persons.
         xii. 46–50. ⎪
         viii. 11. ⎭

XXI.—Luke xiii. 1–5. Misfortune no proof of sin.

XXII.—   xiv. 26–33. Prudence and firmness to duty.

XXIII.—   xvi. 1–13. Parable of the unjust steward, worldly wisdom.

XXIV.—   xviii. 1–8. Parable of the unjust judge.

XXV.—Matt. xxi. 33–41. Parable of the unjust husbandmen and their lord.

XXVI.—Luke xvii. 7–10. Mere justice no praise.

XXVII.—   xiv. 12–14. The merit of disinterested good.

XXVIII.—Matt. xxi. 28–31. Acts better than professions.

XXIX.—   xxii. 15–22. Submission to magistrates.

XXX.—   xix. 3–12. The bond of marriage.

XXXI.—   xxv. 14–30. The duty of improving our talent.

XXXII.—Luke xii. 16–21. Vain calculations of life.

XXXIII.—Matt. xxv. 1–13. } Watch and be ready.
      Luke xii. 35–48.

XXXIV.—John xii. 24, 25. A future life.

XXXV.—Matt. xxii. 23–32. The resurrection.

XXXVI.—   xxv. 31–46. The last judgment.

XXXVII.—   xiii. 31–33, 44, 52. The kingdom of heaven.

XXXVIII.—John iv. 24. God.

XXXIX.—John xviii. 12, 13 ; Matt. xxvi. 49, 50 ; John xviii. 4, 5, 8. ⎫
       Matt. xxvi. 55 ; John xviii. 12 ; Matt. xxvi. 57. ⎪
       John xviii. 19–23 ; Matt. xxvi. 59–62 ; Luke xxii. 67, 68, 70. ⎪ Death of
       Mark xiv. 60, 64 ; Luke xxiii. 1–3 ; John xviii. 36. ⎬ Jesus.
       Luke xxiii. 4–23 ; Matt. xxvii. 24, 25 ; Luke xxiii. 23, 24. ⎪
       Matt. xxvii. 26 ; John xix. 16 ; Luke xxiii. 33, 34. ⎪
       John xix. 25–27 ; Matt. xxvii. 46 ; John xix. 28–30. ⎭

The second collection is contained in a handsome octavo, bound in morocco, and, as already said, labelled on the back " Morals of Jesus." We copied its entire list of contents, and for greater accuracy, compared our copy with the original as read by a member of Colonel Randolph's family. The title page is in Mr. Jefferson's handwriting, and is as follows:

"THE

LIFE AND MORALS

OF

JESUS OF NAZARETH,

EXTRACTED TEXTUALLY

FROM THE GOSPELS

IN

GREEK, LATIN,

FRENCH AND ENGLISH."

Between the next two pages are pasted two printed maps, the first " *Loca terra Sanctæ quorum sit mentio in Evangeliis* "—the other, "*Tabula Geographica ad acta Apost.*" Then, on each left hand page, in parallel columns, are the Greek and Latin text, and on the right, the corresponding French and English text.

An index is pasted into the beginning of the book, of which the following is a copy:

A TABLE

Of the texts from the Evangelists employed in this narrative, and of the order of their arrangement.

PAGE	
1	Luke ii. 1–7 : Joseph and Mary go to Bethlehem, where Jesus is born.
	21, 39: He is circumcised and named, and they return to Naza-reth.
2	40, 42–48, 51, 52 : At 12 years of age he accompanies his parents to Jerusalem and returns.
	L. iii. 1, 2; Mk. i. 4 ; Mt. iii. 4, 5, 6 : John baptizes in Jordan.
	Mt. iii. 13 : Jesus is baptized. L. iii. 23 : At 30 years of age.
3	J. ii. 12–16 : Drives the traders out of the temple.
	J. iii. 22 ; Mt. iv. 12 ; Mk. vi. 17–28 : He baptizes, but retires into Gali-lee on the death of John.
4	Mk. i. 21, 22 : He teaches in the Synagogue.
5	Mt. xii. 1–5, 9–12 ; Mk. ii. 27 ; Mt. xii. 14, 15 : Explains the Sabbath.
	L. vi. 12–17 : Call of his disciples.
6	Mt. v. 1–12 ; L. vi. 24, 25, 26 ; Mt. v. 13–47 : L. vi. 34, 35, 36 ; Mt. vi.
to	1–34 ; vii. 1, 2 ; L. vi. 38 ; Mt. vii. 3–20 ; xii. 35, 36, 37 ; vii. 24–29:
15	The sermon on the mount.
	Mt. viii. 1 ; Mk. vi. 6 ; Mt. xi. 28, 29, 30 : Exhorts.
16	L. vii. 36–46 : A woman anointeth him.
17	Mk. iii. 31–35 ; L. xii. 1–7, 13–15 : Precepts.
18	L. xii. 16–21 : Parable of the rich man.
20	22–48, 54–59 ; L. xiii. 1–5 : Precepts.
21	L. xiii. 6–9 : Parable of the fig tree.
22	L. xi. 37–46, 52, 53, 54 : Precepts.

PAGE	
23	Mt. xiii. 1–9; Mk. iv. 10; Mt. xiii. 18–23: Parable of the sower.
24, 25	Mk. iv. 21, 22, 23: Precepts. Mt. xiii. 24–30, 36–52: Parable of the tares.
26, 27	Mk. iv. 26–34; L. ix. 57–62; L. v. 27–29;[1] Mk. ii. 15–17: Precepts.
	L. v. 36–39: Parable of new wine in old bottles.
28	Mt. xiii. 53–57: A prophet hath no honor in his own country.
29	Mt. ix. 36; Mk. vi. 7; Mt. x. 5, 6, 9–18, 23, 26–31, Mk. vi. 12, 30: Mission instructions, return of apostles.
30, 31	J. vii. 1; Mk. vii. 1–5, 14–24; Mt. xviii. 1–4, 7–9, 12–17, 21–35: Precepts.
32, 33	Mt. xviii. 23–35: Parable of the wicked servant.
34	L. x. 1–8, 10–12: Mission of the seventy.
35	J. vii. 2–16, 19–26, 32, 43–53: The feast of the tabernacles.
36	J. viii. 1–11: The woman taken in adultery.
37	J. ix. 1, 2, 3: To be born blind no proof of sin.
	J. x. 1–5, 11–14, 16: The good shepherd.
38	L. x. 25–37: Love God and thy neighbor; parable of the Samaritan.
39	L. xi. 1–13: Form of prayer.
40	L. xiv. 1–6: The Sabbath.
41	7–24: The bidden to a feast.
42	28–32: Precepts.
43, 44	L. xv. 1–32: Parables of the lost sheep and prodigal son.
45	L. xvi. 1–15: Parable of the unjust steward.
46	18–31: Parable of Lazarus.
47, 48	L. xvii. 1–4, 7–10, 20, 26–36: Precepts to be always ready.
49	L. xviii. 1–14: Parables of the widow and judge, the pharisee and publican.
50, 51	L. x. 38–42; Mt. xix. 1–26: Precepts.
52	Mt. xx. 1–16: Parable of the laborers in the vineyard.
53, 54	L. xix. 1–28: Zaccheus, and the parable of the talents.
55, 56	Mt. xxi. 1–3, 6–8, 10; J. xii. 19–24; Mt. xxi. 17: Goes to Jerusalem and Bethany.
	Mk. xi. 12, 15–19: the traders cast out from the temple.
	Mk. xi. 27; Mt. xxi. 27–31: Parable of the two sons.
57	Mt. xxi. 33; Mk. xii. 1–9; Mt. xxi. 45, 46: Parable of the vineyard and husbandman.
58	Mt. xxii. 1–14: Parable of the king and wedding.
59	15–33: Tribute, marriage, resurrection.
60	Mk. xii. 28–31; Mt. xxii. 40; Mk. xii. 32, 33: The two commandments.
61, 62	Mt. xxiii. 1–33: Precepts, pride, hypocrisy, swearing.
63	Mk. xii. 41–44: The widow's mite.
64	Mt. xxiv. 1, 2, 16–21, 32, 33, 36–39, 40–44: Jerusalem and the day of judgment.
	45–51: The faithful and wise servant.
65	Mt. xxv. 1–13: Parable of the ten virgins.
66	14–30: Parable of the talents.
67, 68	L. xxi. 34–36; Mt. xxv. 31–46: The day of judgment.
69	Mk. xiv. 1–8: A woman anointeth him.

[1] A part of verse 29 is quoted thus: "And Levi made him a great feast in his own house; and 1b."

PAGE.

70, 71	Mt. xxvi. 14-16 : Judas undertakes to point out Jesus.
	17-20 ; L. xxii. 24-27 ; J. xiii. 2, 4-17, 21-26, 31, 34, 35;
72	Mt. xxvi. 31, 33 ; L. xxii. 33, 34; Mt. xxvi. 35-45 : Precepts to his disciples, washes their feet, trouble of mind and prayer.
73	J. xviii. 1-3 ; Mt. xxvi. 48-50 : Judas conducts the officers to Jesus.
74	J. xviii. 4-8 ; Mt. xxvi. 50-52 ; 55, 56 ; Mk. xiv. 51, 52 ; Mt. xxvi. 57 ;
75	J. xviii. 15, 16, 17, 18 ; J. xviii. 25, 26, 27 ; Mt. xxvi. 75 ; J. xviii. 19-23 ; Mk. xiv. 55-61 ; L. xxii. 67, 68, 70 ; Mk. xiv. 63-65 : He is arrested and carried before Caiphas, the high-priest, and is condemned.
76	J. xviii. 28-31, 33-38 ; L. xxiii. 5 ; Mt. xxvii. 13 : Is then carried to Pilate.
77	L. xxiii. 6-12 : Who sends him to Herod.
78	L. xxiii. 13-16 ; Mt. xxvii. 15-23, 26 : Receives him back, scourges and delivers him to execution.
79, 80	Mt. xxvii. 27, 29-31, 3-8 ; L. xxiii. 26-32 ; J. xix. 17-24 ; Mt. xxvii.
81	39-43 ; L. xxiii. 39-41, 34 ; J. xix. 25-27 ; Mt. xxvii. 46-50, 55, 56 : His crucifixion, death, and burial.
	J. xix. 31-34, 38-42 ; Mt. xxvii. 60 : His burial.

APPENDIX NO. XXXI.—Vol. III., p. 475.

Mr. Jefferson's Reply to the Charge of Overdrawing his Accounts.

In a letter to Messrs Ritchie & Gooch (May 13th) Mr. Jefferson replied to a charge brought against him by a writer in the newspapers, over the signature of " A Native Virginian," of having overdrawn $1,148 of public money in the settlement of his account as Minister to France. In settling that account with the Government in 1792 (a pressure of business on the public accounting officers prevented them from taking it up earlier), a balance of $888 67, was found to be due from him, and was immediately paid. When the accounts of the United States bankers in Amsterdam (Willinks, Van Staphorsts & Hubbard) were subsequently received, it appeared that a bill of 2,800 florins Banco, credited to the Government in Mr. Jefferson's account as drawn by him to the order of Grand & Co., on the above bankers, had never been paid by them. Their accounts contained no notice of it. The auditor of the Treasury apprised Mr. Jefferson of this fact (in 1804), and consequently, that the 2,800 florins " stood at his debit only as a *provisional* charge." The latter allowed the matter to remain in this situation until 1809, when, making a final settlement of his official accounts with the Government, and twenty years having now elapsed without anything being heard of the bill drawn on the Amsterdam bankers, he accepted back its amount, declining, however, to receive interest. The auditor made a memorandum of the facts, and had it at any time subsequently appeared that Willinks, Van Staphorsts & Hubbard had actually paid the order, the overpayment to Mr. Jefferson by the Government would at once have been made apparent and capable of being remedied. But the Dutch bankers *never* brought any such bill into their account with our Government. It is therefore certain that the account was accurately settled, in this particular, as between the United States Government and Mr. Jefferson. If anybody suffered it was Willinks, Van Staphorsts & Hubbard, and purely by their own fault, in neglecting to charge the amount of a bill of exchange paid by them. This is not a very common oversight among bankers. Nor did they ever put forward a hint that such an oversight had occurred—though the matter was once or twice publicly discussed in the newspapers of the United States. Neither did Grand & Co., in their account against the United States, nor in their private account against Mr. Jefferson, ever notice such a bill.

Mr. Jefferson gives the following solution of the affair in his letters to Ritchie and Gooch:

"Turning to my pocket diary, I find that on the 21st day of October, 1789, the date of this bill, I was at Cowes in England, on my return to the United States. The entry in my diary is in these words: '1789, October 21st. Sent to Grand & Co., letter of credit on Willinks, Van Staphorsts & Hubbard, for 2,800 florins Banco. And I immediately credited it in my account with the United States in the following words: '1789, October 21. By my bill on Willinks, Van Staphorsts & Hubbard, in favor of Grand & Co., for 2,800 florins, equal to 6,250 livres 18 sous.' My account having been kept in livres and sous of France, the auditor settled this sum at the current exchange, making it $1,148. This bill, drawn at Cowes in England, had to pass through London to Paris by the English and French mails, in which passage it was lost, by some unknown accident, to which it was the more exposed in the French mail, by the confusion then prevailing; for it was exactly at the time that martial law was proclaimed at Paris, the country all up in arms, and executions by the mobs were daily perpetrating through town and country. However this may have been, the bill never got to the hands of Grand & Co., was never, of course, forwarded by them to the bankers of Amsterdam, nor anything more ever heard of it."

Turning to this "pocket diary," (which we have so repeatedly quoted as Mr. Jefferson's "pocket account-book") we observe that he arrived at Cowes "at half-past two in the morning" on the 9th of October; and running our eye over intervening entries, drawn out with the rigorous precision so often mentioned, down to October 21st, we find the following entry verbatim and literatim (the contractions apparently made to compress it into a single line): "21. Sent to Grand & Co., letter of credit on Will., V. Staph. & Hub., for 2,800 f. Bo."

"A Native Virginian" returned to the charge, taking the ground that Mr. Jefferson had at all events received the money twice, first of Grand & Co., on the sale or negotiation of the bill in Europe, and a second time from the Treasury. The first assertion he endeavored to sustain by quoting the following entry as if from Mr. Jefferson's account rendered to the Treasury, "*By cash received of Grand* for bill on Willinks &c." The words in italics were an interpolation or forgery, ventured on by this "psuedo Native Virginian," as Mr. Jefferson conjectures, from a sufficient familiarity with the Treasury department to know that the original account was destroyed in the Register's office, when the British burnt the public offices in 1814. But, unfortunately for this writer's ingenuity, Mr. Jefferson had retained a *press-copy* of that account, and he *now* tendered it to public inspection. Besides, he pertinently asked how he could have received money of Grand, when he was in England and Grand in France. The bill might, certainly, have been negotiated in England. Mr. Jefferson says that it never was so negotiated—that it was not drawn to raise money in the market—that it was inclosed to Grand & Co. in a letter for a particular purpose. His assailant did not claim that the bill was sold in England or to any one besides Grand & Co. But what if this claim had been made? Was there any proof of it? And whoever the bill was sold to, would it not have gone ultimately to the drawees, Messrs. Willinks, Van Staphorsts & Hubbard, and been by them cashed and charged to the American Government—or dishonored and then returned back by the holders to the original drawer?

Some other points were raised by a Native Virginian, but they are not entitled to notice.

APPENDIX NO. XXXII.—Vol. III. p. 502.

Jefferson and Henry Lee.

Henry Lee wrote to Mr. Jefferson, May 3d, 1826, that he was preparing a new edition of the Memoirs, etc., of his father, General Henry Lee—that he found "the account given of Arnold's invasion was not favorable to his [Jefferson's] foresight or energy"—and he offered to embody, or give literally, in notes to the work, any explanations the latter "might choose to furnish him with," should they appear satisfactory to his (Lee's) judgment. (Lee's Memoirs, etc., 2d edition, p. 203.)

On the 9th of the same month, without waiting for an answer to the above, he again wrote to Mr. Jefferson, "that under the circumstances in which the Governors of States and the Continental Officers were placed, it was reasonable to suppose that, however correct the former may have been, the opinions of the latter would be unfavorable to them." He said, "he had little doubt, if Jefferson had been the 'military chieftain,' and Green the regulated statesman—the *élève* of Montesquieu and Locke—that Green would have occasioned the same strictures which were actually applied to Jefferson." The letter contained much more in the same courteous strain. (Lee's Memoirs, p. 204.)

Mr. Jefferson replied to the first letter May 15th, 1826, giving that unanswerable defence of his administration, as Governor of Virginia, at the period of Arnold's invasion, which is published (without any address) in the Congress edition of his works, at vol. vii., p. 414. It is not given in Randolph's edition.

On the 30th of May, Jefferson replied to a letter from Lee of May 25th (not published), in which the latter had proposed to make a visit to Monticello. He said, "He should be happy to receive him at the time he mentioned, or at any other, if any other should be more convenient to Mr. Lee."

The visit was made during Mr. Jefferson's last illness, and Mr. Lee sent an account of what he saw to the Richmond Enquirer, containing some fanciful embellishments—all, however, we believe, drawn up in a tone of admiration towards Mr. Jefferson.

In 1827, Lee's edition of his father's Memoirs was published. He made no alterations in their text, in regard to Arnold's invasion of Virginia,[1] but he subjoined, in notes, his full correspondence with Mr. Jefferson on that subject, and he stated, that the "eloquent justification" of the latter "appeared to be directed

---

[1] The first edition is not before us. But the editor states in the "advertisement," at the opening of the volume, that he has not "ventured to alter" the text, except in regard "to such obvious mistakes as to dates, names, and places, as could not affect the identity of the composition," and in regard to a particular emendation which is specified.

against severer strictures than those to be found in the Memoirs *which applied rather to the inefficiency of the government of Virginia, at the time, than to the particular Executive magistrate.*"

Thus he not only vindicated Mr. Jefferson on his own judgment, but attempted to exonerate him from all the *individual* censure inflicted by General Lee.

In his conversations and letters of this period, Henry Lee avowed the most unbounded admiration of Mr. Jefferson's character, talents, and public services.

In 1829, Randolph's edition of Jefferson's Works was published. It contained Jefferson's strictures on General Henry Lee's personal and political conduct on various occasions, and also (in a letter to Colonel Monroe, January 1st, 1815) the following animadversion on General Lee's Memoirs: "Although the Legislature, who were personally intimate with both the means and measures, acquitted me with justice and thanks, yet General Lee has put all these imputations among the romances of his historical novel, for the amusement of credulous and uninquisitive readers."

Henry Lee, the son, took offence at these strictures. He appears to have thought that the editor of Mr Jefferson's Works *was* bound to "venture to alter the text," or either omit or explain away by notes, what probably Mr. Jefferson's editor did not believe truth or justice required to be obliterated. Or else, he was fired by finding evidences that Jefferson, as well as his father, had felt resentments, and expressed them—that he had retaliated to the extent of warmly declaring his indignation, where he conceived himself both privately and publicly wronged. Accordingly, the younger Lee, in 1832, published "Observations on the writings of Thomas Jefferson, with particular reference to the attacks they contain on the Memory of the late General Lee," etc.

Had this work defended General Lee with warmth, and retorted with severity on Mr. Jefferson, in respect to the issues which he himself had raised (or any related ones), nobody, under the circumstances, would have condemned the feelings, however much they might have dissented from the conclusions of an offended son. But when the latter went back to attack Mr. Jefferson's private character, in regard to transactions of old date and themes of old controversy—to rake together and revive Callender's scurrilities—he placed himself in that unfortunate predicament in which a witness never fails to stand who avows *enthusiastic* admiration until he quarrels, and then suddenly remembers that the subject of his overtures and caresses has always been infamous!

We shall leave Henry Lee's representations and acts, prior to 1829, to answer his later ones. Their comparative credibility needs no other illustrations than are to be drawn from the tenor of Mr. Jefferson's life, and from the feelings and presumed motives of Mr. Lee on these two different occasions.

Perhaps justice to Mr. Jefferson requires that we state more fully than we have done in the text the grounds on which he pronounced the Memoirs, etc., of General Lee a "historical novel." In doing this, we shall not discuss the *merits* of any of the controversies between the two men.

General Lee's Memoirs were written in 1809. No claim was put forward in them that they were founded on memoranda or journals kept by the writer while he was engaged in the Southern campaigns. The contrary was admitted.

In regard to the events of Arnold's invasion of Virginia, General Lee had no personal knowledge or recollections, as he was absent from the State at the time.

He gave the statements of none of the distinguished officers who commanded in Virginia, at the time, to confirm his own.

His opportunities for investigating historic facts in relation to that period are' therefore, presumed to have been the same with those of any other individual of the same research and capacity, whether in or out of military life.

Between the close of the war of the Revolution and the period of writing his Memoirs, he had been engaged in almost unceasing political hostilities against Jefferson. The latter accused him of attempting to produce a personal alienation between himself and Washington (see vol. ii. p. 298). Lee was in Congress when the struggle took place to elect Jefferson and Burr, in 1801, and was understood to be foremost amongst those who urged "desperate measures" to prevent Jefferson's success (see vol. ii. p. 608). He was thenceforth left out of political life, by the ascendency of Jefferson's political friends in Virginia. After eight years of this exclusion, and after a train of circumstances not calculated to soften his asperities of feeling, he wrote the "Memoirs."

Jefferson *considered* himself treated in them, with gross, and a sou. of cunning injustice—for the author, while producing his *effect* on the mind of the reader, abstained from those explicit and tangible asseverations which could be met and overthrown by well-settled facts. Under these circumstances, he pronounced the work a "historical novel."

———

Deeply reluctant to carry anything which seemed to savor of mere personal discussion into the limits of aggression, we had ultimately resolved to add nothing to the above explanations. But since the preceding remarks were penned, we have seen the statement put forth in a literary work of great general liberality and candor, that the charges of Henry Lee (the younger) against Jefferson have never been "directly answered." This remark is undeniably true. It is equally true that Callender's charges were never directly answered. Even witnesses of moral respectability, who sincerely believed what they wrote, were never directly answered, so far as we know, when they descended into petty or dirty personal allegations.[1] And, what is more, they probably never will be directly answered. If it was not held necessary by any friend of Mr. Jefferson contemporaneously to descend into the dirt to prove *negatives*, when a party in our country religiously believed the author of the Declaration of Independence was an incarnate demon who had no claims to honor or honesty, who spat upon the Bible, who lived in an African brothel, etc., etc., it probably will not be held necessary to do so now, when Mr. Jefferson's character is so well understood, that (as we remarked in the preface) not a candidate for civil office dare rise before any popular constituency within the American Republic and insult his memory.

Whenever, Henry Lee's "vial of rage"—as it is termed in a MS. letter of Mr. Madison, a copy of which lies before us—confines itself to the region of pure argument (as, for example, in his attempt to show that the Declaration of Independence was not much of a production, after all), it is of course entitled to all the weight which the same reasoning would possess by whomsoever uttered. But when he approaches the field of assertion, inference, conjecture, explanation, or conclusion, we are entitled to examine the motives and character of the assailant.

On the motives of Mr. Lee, sufficient light would be thrown already, if we had substantiated by facts our assertion of his sudden change, under the circumstances recorded, from a vehement admiration to a viperous hate of Mr. Jefferson's charac-

———

[1] Unless casually or incidentally, merely to illustrate the credulity or credibility of the witness, or the spirit of the times.

ter. It occurring to us that tangible evidence might exist, on this head, which it would be proper to make public, we addressed the gentleman on whom principally devolved the charge of entertaining Mr. Lee, during his visit to Monticello. He remembered having received letters from Mr. Lee, and on search found two, copies of which he placed at our disposal. The first was as follows:

Henry Lee to N. P. Trist.

DEAR SIR: You are probably aware that my late visit to Monticello grew out of a correspondence I had the honor to hold with Mr. Jefferson, and was intended to verify and illustrate the principal public facts to which that correspondence related. You are but too well acquainted with the melancholy cause of my disappointment, and that Providence had already determined to seal those hallowed lips from which I was to receive inspiration. Now that the illustrious patriot has ceased to live among the sons of men, and has attained a stage of existence as immortal as his own glory, a sentiment of more awful reverence and still more pious attachment devotes me to his memory, than actuated me towards his person and character. The utmost justice I am determined to do him, in the case produced by the republication of my father's Memoirs (now in the press), and to that end must publish our correspondence, as my letters will illustrate his, and his will vindicate him better than anything that I could possibly compose. His principal letter is in answer to two of mine, one of the 3d and one of the 9th of May last. Of that of the 9th, I retained a copy—or rather composed one from memory; of that of the 3d, I have no copy. The object of this letter is to get a copy of it, and I am sure it will not be asking too much of your politeness, to request that you obtain the consent of Mrs. Randolph, and send me by mail either a copy or the original, as you please. I understand Mr. J. was very careful of his papers, and hope there will be no difficulty in finding this. It will be esteemed the best fortune that ever befell me to find myself able to justify in the least this best of patriots and wisest of men—a man who entered every walk of politics and philosophy, and in all was foremost.

That I may express further my sentiments towards him, I beg leave to inclose for your perusal a rough sketch of a general order, which, at the request of a military friend, I prepared the other day. The news of Mr. Adams's death arriving, rendered it inexecutable and useless, and I had no wish to blend the two names.

With the most exalted esteem for Mr. Jefferson's daughter—more to be honored than either of Epamimondas's—and sincere respect for yourself,

I remain, dear sir,

Your very obedient and very humble servt.,

H. LEE.

WASHINGTON, 20th *July*, 1826.

MR. TRIST, Monticello.

The General-in-Chief has received, through the Department of War, the following order of the President: [Here follows order.]

"The event thus announced to the army overspreads the nation with sorrow. The Republic mourns its second founder, Liberty her most ardent advocate ; philosophy her great disciple, and learning her munificent friend. The author of the Declaration of Independence—the leader of our second Revolution—the founder of Louisiana—the sage of Monticello—the beloved and venerated THOMAS JEFFERSON is no more. 'Full of years, and full of honors,' the day of his death was that of his own and of his country's greatest glory.

" His were conquests—the conquests of truth over error—of reason over prejudice—of wisdom over violence—victories of the mind!—triumphs of patriotism and philanthropy.

"The army of the United States, consecrated to freedom and science and the service of the country, will feel peculiar and melancholy pride in obeying this order of the President, and in paying solemn honors to the memory of a man, whose sublime genius, extensive capacity, and splendid acquirements were unceasingly exerted through a long life, first, for the good of his country, and next for the good of mankind."

[The above is copied from the original, now in my possession ; said original being the paper inclosed in H. Lee's letter to me, dated, "Washington, 20th July, 1826."

PHILADELPHIA, *April* 4th, 1858.   N. P. TRIST.]

The other letter is very curious, but as it would not, strictly speaking, throw any further light on the only point which the foregoing was presented to illustrate, we shall not here transcribe it.

The character of the individual who has made himself witness and judge, in respect to the public and private life of Thomas Jefferson, has been passed upon in a high quarter, and under circumstances which admit of no pretence that political or personal prejudices influenced the verdict. When General Jackson was a candidate for the Presidency, in 1827 and 1828, Henry Lee labored and wrote for him with vehement energy, and with his customary ability. We could give on his own authority, did we suppose it called for, a striking specimen of his sharp electioneering tactics. He gave out that he was writing a life of General Jackson. He was a brilliant man in his address. He had borne a major's commission in the army of the United States, in the war of 1812. He represented a family which had been as distinguished for its talents, patriotism, and influence as any in the United States, and which yet had most honored and worthy representatives. Jackson knew him in these phases, and on his election promptly commissioned him Consul-General for the United States, for the City and Kingdom of Algiers, in the place of Mr. Shaler, resigned.

Lee's nomination was transmitted to the Senate of the United States, January 22d, 1830, and on the 10th of February, referred to the Committee on Foreign Relations. On the 8th of March, Mr. Tazewell, of Virginia, by direction of the Committee, moved " that the Committee of Foreign Relations *to whom was referred the nomination of Henry Lee, as Consul*," etc., "*be empowered to send for persons.*" The Senate adjourned while this motion was under consideration. On the resumption of its consideration, March 10th, it was ordered, on motion of Mr. McKinley, that it lie on the table. The Senate then took up the nomination and rejected it *unanimously*. On motion of Mr. Burnet, seconded by one fifth of the senators present, the yeas and nays were ordered, and they stood : yeas, none; nays, forty-six.[1] Comment is unnecessary.

[1] Those who voted against confirmation were: Messrs Adams, of Miss.; Barnard, of Pa.; Barton, of Mo.; Benton, of Mo.; Bell, of N. H.; Bibb, of Ky.; Brown, of N. C ; Burnet, of O.; Chambers, of Md ; Chase, of Vt.; Clayton, of Del.; Dickinson, of N. J.; Dudley, of N. Y.; Ellis, of Miss ; Foot, of Con.; Frelinghuysen, of N J ; Grundy, of Ten.; Hayne, of S. C.; Hendricks, of Ia ; Holmes, of Me ; Iredell, of N C.; Johnston, of La.; Kane, of Ill ; King, of Ala.; Knight, of R. I ; Livingston, of La ; McLean, of Ill ; McKinley, of Ala ; Marks, of Pa ; Naudain, of Del.; Robbins, of R I ; Rowan, of Ky ; Ruggles, of O.; Sanford, of N. Y ; Seymour, of Vt.; Silsbee, of Class ; Smith, of Md.; Smith, of S. C.; Sprague, of Me.; Tazewell, of Va ; Troup, of Ga.; Tyler, of Va ; Webster, of Mass ; White, of Ten ; Willey, of Con.; Woodbury, of N. H.—46.
Absent, Forsyth of Ga., and Noble, of Ia.

APPENDIX NO. XXXIII.—Vol. III., p. 537.

Mr. Jefferson's Will.

I, Thomas Jefferson, of Monticello, in Albermarle, being of sound mind, and in my ordinary state of health, make my last will and testament, in manner and form as follows:

I give to my grandson, Francis Eppes, son of my dear deceased daughter, Mary Eppes, in fee simple, all that part of my lands at Poplar Forest, lying west of the following lines, to wit: beginning at Radford's upper corner, near the double branches of Bear Creek and the public road, and running thence in a straight line to the fork of my private road, near the barn; thence along that private road (as it was changed in 1817), to its crossing of the main branch of North Tomahawk Creek; and from that crossing, in a direct line over the main ridge which divides the North and South Tomahawk, to the South Tomahawk, at the confluence of two branches where the old road to the Waterlick crossed it, and from that confluence up the northernmost branch (which separates McDaniel's and Perry's fields), to its source; and thence by the shortest line to my western boundary. And having, in a former correspondence with my deceased son-in-law, John W. Eppes, contemplated laying off for him, with remainder to my grandson, Francis, a certain portion in the southern part of my lands in Bedford and Campbell, which I afterwards found to be generally more indifferent than I had supposed, and therefore determined to change its location for the better; now, to remove all doubt, if any could arise on a purpose merely voluntary and unexecuted, I hereby declare that what I have herein given to my said grandson Francis, is instead of, and not additional, to what I had formerly contemplated. I subject all my other property to the payment of my debts in the first place. Considering the insolvent state of the affairs of my friend and son-in-law, Thomas Mann Randolph, and that what will remain of my property will be the only resource against the want in which his family would otherwise be left, it must be his wish, as it is my duty, to guard that resource against all liability for his debts, engagements, or purposes whatsoever, and to preclude the rights, powers, and authorities over it, which might result to him by operation of law, and which might, independently of his will, bring it within the power of his creditors, I do hereby devise and bequeath all the residue of my property, real and personal, in possession or in action, whether held in my own right, or in that of my dear deceased wife, according to the powers vested in me by deed of settlement for that purpose, to my grandson, Thomas J. Randolph, and my friends, Nicholas P. Trist, and Alexander Garret, and their heirs, during the life of my said son-in-law, Thomas M. Randolph, to be held and administered by them, in trust, for the sole and separate use and behoof of my dear daughter, Martha Randolph, and her heirs; and, aware of the nice and difficult distinction of the law in these cases, I will further explain by saying, that I understand and intend the effect of these limitations to be, that the legal estate and actual occupation shall be vested in my said trustees, and held by them in base fee, determinable on the death of my said son-in-law, and the remainder during the same time be vested in my said daughter and her heirs, and of course disposable by her last will, and that at the death of my said son-in-law, the particular estate of the trustees shall be determined, and the remainder, in legal estate, possession, and use, become vested in my said daughter and her heirs, in absolute property forever. In consequence of the variety and indescribableness of the articles of property within the house of Monticello, and the difficulty of inventorying and appraising them separately and specifically, and its inutility, I dispense with having them inventoried and appraised; and it is my will that my executors be not held to give any security for the administration of my estate. I appoint my grandson, Thomas Jefferson Randolph, my sole executor, during his life, and after his death, I constitute executors, my friends, Nicholas P. Trist and Alexander Garret, joining to them my daughter, Martha Randolph, after the death of my said son-in-law, Thomas M. Randolph. Lastly, I revoke all former wills by me heretofore made; and in witness that this is my will, I have written the whole, with my own hand, on two pages, and have subscribed my name to each of them, this sixteenth day of March, one thousand eight hundred and twenty-six.

TH. JEFFERSON.

I, Thomas Jefferson, of Monticello, in Albemarle, make and add the following codicil to my will, controlling the same so far as its provisions go:

I recommend to my daughter, Martha Randolph, the maintenance and care of my well-beloved sister, Anne Scott, and trust confidently that from affection to her, as well as for my sake, she will never let her want a comfort. I have made no specific provision for the comfortable maintenance of my son-in-law, Thomas M. Randolph, because of the difficulty and uncertainty of devising terms which shall vest any beneficial interest in him, which the law will not transfer to the benefit of his creditors, to the destitution of my daughter and her family, and disablement of her to supply him; whereas, property placed under the exclusive control of my daughter and her independent will, as if she were a *feme sole*, considering the relation in which she stands both to him and his children, will be a certain resource against want for all.

I give to my friend, James Madison, of Montpellier, my gold-mounted walking staff of animal horn, as a token of the cordial and affectionate friendship which for nearly now an half century, has united us in the same principles and pursuits of what we have deemed for the greatest good of our country.

I give to the University of Virginia, my library, except such particular books only, and of the same edition, as it may already possess, when this legacy shall take effect; the rest of my said library, remaining after those given to the University shall have been taken out, I give to my two grandsons-in-law, Nicholas P. Trist and Joseph Coolidge. To my grandson, Thomas Jefferson Randolph, I give my silver watch in preference of the golden one, because of its superior excellence, my papers of business going of course to him, as my executor, all others of a literary or other character I give to him as of his own property.

I give a gold watch to each of my grandchildren, who shall not have already received one from me, to be purchased and delivered by my executor to my grandsons at the age of twenty-one, and grand-daughters at that of sixteen.

I give to my good, affectionate, and faithful servant, Burwell, his freedom, and the sum of three hundred dollars, to buy necessaries to commence his trade of painter and glazier, or to use otherwise, as he pleases.

I give also to my good servants, John Hemings and Joe Fosset, their freedom, at the end of one year after my death; and to each of them respectively, all the tools of their respective shops or callings; and it is my will that a comfortable log-house be built for each of the three servants so emancipated, on some part of my lands convenient to them with respect to the residence of their wives, and to Charlottesville, and the University, where they will be mostly employed, and reasonably convenient also to the interests of the proprietor of the lands, of which houses I give the use of one, with a curtilage of an acre to each, during his life, or personal occupation thereof.

I give also to John Hemings the service of his two apprentices, Madison and Eston Hemings, until their respective ages of twenty-one years, at which period, respectively, I give them their freedom; and I humbly and earnestly request of the Legislature of Virginia a confirmation of the bequest of freedom to these servants, with permission to remain in this State, where their families and connections are, as an additional instance of the favor, of which I have received so many other manifestations, in the course of my life, and for which I now give them my last, solemn, and dutiful thanks.

In testimony that this is a codicil to my will of yesterday's date, and that it is to modify so far the provisions of that will, I have written it all with my own hand in two pages, to each of which I subscribe my name, this seventeenth day of March, one thousand eight hundred and twenty-six.

TH. JEFFERSON

APPENDIX NO. XXXIV.—Vol. III., p. 539.

Mr. Jefferson's Views on Slavery, etc.

Putting all his declarations in regard to African Slavery, emancipation, colonization, etc., together, he appears to have entertained the following views:

1. He was wholly opposed to slavery on *all* grounds, and desired its abolition.

2. He was opposed to emancipating the body of slaves at once, and retaining them in the United States. He thought this course would prove fatal to them, and destructive to the whites.

3. He was opposed to general emancipation, except as accompanied by colonization, and preceded by sufficient mental and industrial training to enable the emancicated slaves to take care of themselves as separate political communities. He was also opposed to "abandoning" them, as he termed it, in individual cases, where they did not possess a similar preparation for freedom.

4. He believed no preparation would render it expedient to admit them to the full rights of citizenship, by making them a part of the electoral body; and on the other hand, he considered their retention in the State as a permanently distinct, and inferior free caste, as fraught with insuperable evils and dangers.

5. He believed that emancipation should be gradual for the interest of both races; that it would be practicable only in regard to *post nati* (after-born); that actual property had been lawfully vested in slaves, and could not be lawfully taken from its possessors without compensation.

6. He was opposed to interference with slave-institutions by those living outside of Slave States, either by legislation or agitation—considering it unwarranted by the spirit of the Constitution, and calculated to defeat emancipation.

7. He considered constant slavery denunciation and agitation by inhabitants of Slave States, as also calculated to defeat emancipation, and that "persuasion, per

severance, and patience, were the best advocates on questions depending on the will of others."

8. He was in favor (in 1784) of introducing a provision into the Ordinance for organizing the Northwestern Territory, prohibiting the existence of slavery after the year 1800, in either the temporary or permanent governments formed therefrom.

9. He was opposed (in 1819, 1820, and 1821) to Congress making slavery inhibition a condition of the admission of Missouri into the Union—to refusing admission to that State, because it asked it with a constitution sanctioning slavery—to the 'Missouri Compromise," or the establishment of a geographical line between free and slave territory westward of Missouri. On the contrary, he believed that Congress had no power to regulate the conditions of the different descriptions of men composing a State—that it was expedient to let slavery spread into the States which desired it—that the emigration of slavery into the States formed out of French Louisiana, would not increase the number of slaves, while the comparatively small interests that States and individuals would thus be brought to hold in it would strongly tend to emancipation.

———

We have been repeatedly asked to give such information as we might possess from public and private sources, whether Mr. Jefferson "was consistent in his views," whether "he ever changed his views" on any of the great questions connected with slavery. His "consistency" is a matter of opinion, and we propose to confine ourselves strictly to facts. If his views underwent any "change," he did not appear to be himself conscious of it. He habitually, in conversation, referred his desire to prohibit the introduction of slavery into the Northwestern Territory, in 1784, to the fact, that the slave trade was not then prohibited, and that unless a slavery inhibition, understood to be permanent, was ingrafted into the ordinance for the government of that territory,[1] an immense importation of slaves would take place into it from Africa, thus correspondingly increasing the aggregate number in the United States.

When the Ordinance of the Northwestern Territory was moved by him in Congress, the Articles of Confederation were the only constitution possessed by the United States. These articles did not give the General Government any powers to govern territories. They did not recognize the existence of any territories apart from, and not under the jurisdiction of States. By the formal acceptance of the cession of the Northwest Territory from Virginia, the United States admitted the previous title, and, of consequence, received just such a title as Virginia conveyed. As this contained no restrictive condition, there arose no occasion for the General Government to show that it felt itself bound by the terms of the cession; but, in a precisely analogous case, that of North Carolina, whose title to her territories was derived from the same fountain-head, and rested on the same general basis with that of Virginia, the General Government directly and expressly acknowledged the validity of an annexed condition,[2] and acted upon it, when subsequently setting up temporary and permanent governments in that territory.

---

[1] Now embracing the States of Ohio, Indiana, Illinois, Michigan, and Wisconsin.
[2] North Carolina, in December 1789, ceded her western territory (Tennessee) to the United States, subject to the condition "that no regulation made, or to be made, by Congress, should tend to emancipate slaves" therein. Congress, in an Act passed April 2d, 1790, recited the entire North Carolina deed of cession, and affixed its acceptance, thus virtually making every word of that instrument a part or condition of the acceptance. On the 29th of May, the same year, it passed an "Act for the Government of the Territory of the United States south of the River Ohio," by which it erected a temporary government "similar to that which was then exercised in the territory northwest of the Ohio, except so far as was otherwise provided in the *condition expressed* in an act of

The deed by which Virginia ceded the Northwestern Territory to the United States, was signed by Mr. Jefferson—and as he was entirely the leading member of the Virginia delegation in Congress at the time, we must suppose that this important paper was at least drawn up under his supervision, or received his full assent. There is, in fact, little doubt that he drafted it. By this instrument, Virginia conveyed to the United States "ALL her right, title, and claim as well of SOIL AS OF JURISDICTION" to the Northwestern Territory.

Virginia thus granted all the sovereignty which she had possessed AS A STATE over this territory, and consequently the right to govern by the appointment of civil officers, the enactment of laws, and municipal regulations of every description. This would necessarily include the establishment or the abolition of slavery.

In 1788, and before the purchase of French Louisiana, the United States Constitution superseded the Articles of Confederation. This instrument recognized territories, outside of the limits of States, as the common property and possessions of all the States, and it gave to Congress " power to dispose of and make all needful rules and regulations respecting the territory or other property belonging to the United States."

France, in 1803, ceded to the United States her right of soil in Louisiana, and a jurisdiction subject to certain conditions. The conditions were as follows:

" The inhabitants of the ceded territory shall be incorporated in the Union of the United States, and admitted as soon as possible, according to the principles of the federal Constitution, to the enjoyment of all the rights, advantages and immunities of citizens of the United States ; and, in the meantime, they shall be maintained and protected in the free enjoyment of their liberty, property, and the religion which they profess."

By the " principles of the federal Constitution," all new States were admitted on terms of complete equality with the original States in respect to their own internal jurisdiction and sovereignty. No man had then, or has since, pretended that Congress has the constitutional right to create, prohibit, or abolish slavery in any of the original States. And by the adoption of the federal Constitution the peculiar jurisdiction of Congress over *States* formed from the Northwestern Territory was terminated, and they became as free as the original States to legislate on any subject, irrespective of any conditions imposed on them in the Acts for their organization. But were this otherwise, the right of States erected *elsewhere* to enter the Union with a sovereignty as absolute and unshackled as that of the original States, was guaranteed by the Constitution, and in the case of French Louisiana, was additionally guaranteed by the treaty of cession.

Having thus rapidly sketched an outline of the positions which we believe Mr. Jefferson occupied in 1784 and in 1819-21—which *he* regarded as consistent with each other—we leave the subject to the judgment of the reader.

Congress of the present session [that of April 2], entitled 'An Act to accept the claims of the State of North Carolina to a certain district of *western* territory.'" And Tennessee was admitted as a State June 1st, 1796, without any interference with the original condition expressed in the North Carolina cession.

APPENDIX NO. XXXV.—Vol. III., p. 548.

Dr. Dunglison's recollections of Mr. Jefferson.

PHILADELPHIA, *June 1st*, 1856.

MY DEAR SIR:

*   *   *   *   *   *   *

His [Mr. Jefferson's] philanthropy was actual and active. It embraced, I believe, the whole globe. His desire was to see all people prosperous and happy—all *peoples*, I may say. He did not like the *government* of England; was careful to separate it from the people. He certainly had no objection to Englishmen as such: on the contrary, his kind feelings towards them were exhibited with frankness and sincerity. I never knew him express a hatred towards political opponents of distinction. He would declare what he considered the malign influence they were exerting. His correspondence and excellent feeling to the last, with the elder Adams, sufficiently exhibited that differences in political sentiment did not exclude a warm appreciation of the man.

You ask me what where his private virtues that appeared conspicuous to all acquaintances? . . . . He was kind, courteous, hospitable to all; sincerely attached to the excellent family that were clustered around him; sympathizing with them in their pleasures, deeply distressed in their afflictions. I mentioned to you the scene I witnessed on the approaching death of a grand-daughter, Mrs. Bankhead. I knew nothing of any private vice of any kind, and never heard from him a loose or indecorous speech. I would say in your own language, that he was always in my observation "peculiarly decorous, modest, and decent in all things."

As to his "personal characteristics;" he was of commanding aspect, dignified, and would have been striking to any one not knowing in whose presence and company he was. He was, as I before remarked, courteous. His expression—as I recollect it—was pleasing, intellectual, contemplative. He was tall and thin—nothing, as far as I recollect, marked about the head. I do not speak *phrenologically*, the results of my observation having shown, that no satisfactory inference can be drawn from its *details*. Of the minute expression of eyes, mouth, etc., I cannot speak well from recollection, but as a whole, I liked his countenance much.

In his general knowledge, he appeared to me to be accurate and precise. His examinations of any subject that engaged his attention for the time, were full. I *never* knew him loose and inaccurate; but I am writing, you know, of him as he was to the best of my recollection, and after a lapse of upwards of thirty years, and ought, therefore, to give my conclusions with becoming caution.

As a University officer, he was always pleasant to transact business with, was invariably kind and respectful, but had generally formed his own opinions on questions, and did not abandon them easily. The first regulations of the University, which were mainly, I believe, his work, were the results of his reflections, but did not act well; and had to be abandoned—some of them, I know, with great reluctance on his part. He had a great respect for men of science and letters, and was always glad to do them honor; had a horror of superficial knowledge, as seen in his desire to get the best informed men for professors, no matter from what country they came; and would have delighted to patronize talent and learning united with worth wherever he found it.

To sum up. I had the most exalted opinion of him. I believed him essentially a philanthropist, anxious for the greatest good to the greatest number; a distinguished patriot, whose love of country was not limited by any considerations of self; who was eminently virtuous, with fixed and honorable principles of action not to be trammelled by any unworthy considerations; and whose reputation must shine brighter and brighter, as he is more and more justly judged and estimated.

* * * * * *

I am, my dear sir, faithfully yours,

ROBLEY DUNGLISON.

H. S. RANDALL, Esq.

APPENDIX NO. XXXVI.—VOL. III., p. 561.

Thomas Jefferson Randolph to Henry S. Randall.

DEAR SIR: In compliance with your request, I have committed to paper my reminiscences of Mr. Jefferson, as they, still green and fresh in my memory, have occurred to me. I was thirty-four years old when he died. My mother was his eldest and, for the last twenty-two years of his life, his only child; she lived with him from her birth to his death, except in his absence on public service, at Philadelphia and Washington; having lost her mother at ten years old, she was his inseparable companion until her marriage; he had sought to supply her loss with all the watchful solicitude of a mother's tenderness; her children were to him as the younger members of his family, having lived with him from their infancy. I being fifteen years older than my brothers, the duty devolved on me to place myself in the breach of his pecuniary embarrassments, and shield him, living and dead, from their practical effects. He never failed to comply with a pecuniary engagement; his creditors were all paid. It was unimportant to them whether they were paid from the proceeds of the sales of his property, or the sacrifices and toil of his descendants. I was more intimate with him than with any man I have ever known; his character invited such intimacy—soft and feminine in his affections to his family, he entered into and sympathized with all their feelings, winning them to paths of virtue by the soothing gentleness of his manner. His private apartments were open to me at all times, I saw him under all circumstances. While he lived, and since, I have reviewed with severe scrutiny those interviews, and I must say, that I never heard from him the expression of one thought, feeling or sentiment inconsistent with the highest moral standard, or the purest Christian charity in its most enlarged sense. His moral character was of the highest order, founded upon the purest and sternest models of antiquity, softened, chastened and developed by the influences of the all-pervading benevolence of the doctrines of Christ—which he had intensely and admiringly studied. As a proof of this, he left two codifications of the morals of Jesus—one for himself, and another for the Indians; the first of which I now possess, viz., a blank volume, red morocco, gilt, lettered on the back "The Morals of Jesus"—into which he pasted extracts in Greek, Latin, French and English, taken textually from the four Gospels, and so arranged that he could run his eye over the readings of the same verse in four languages. The boldness and self-confidence of his mind was the best guaranty of his truthfulness—he never uttered an untruth himself, or used duplicity, and he contemned it in others—no end, with him, could sanctify falsehood.

In his contemplative moments, his mind turned to religion, which he studied thoroughly. He had seen and read much of the abuses and perversions of Christianity; he abhorred those abuses and their authors, and denounced them without reserve. He was regular in his attendance on church, taking his prayer-book with him. He drew the plan of the Episcopal Church in Charlottesville—was one of the largest contributors to its erection, and contributed regularly to the support of its minister. I paid, after his death, his subscription of $200 to the erection of the Presbyterian church in the same village. A gentleman of some distinction calling on him, and expressing his disbelief in the truths of the Bible, his reply was, " Then, sir, you have studied it to little purpose." He was guilty of no profanity himself, and did not tolerate it in others—he detested impiety, and his favorite quotation for his young friends as a basis for their morals, was the xv. psalm of David. He did not permit cards in his house—he knew no game with them. Of his peculiar religious opinions, his family know no more than the world. If asked by one of them, his opinion on any religious subject, his uniform reply was, that it was a subject each was bound to study assiduously for himself, unbiased by the opinions of others—it was a matter solely of conscience; after thorough investigation, they were responsible for the righteousness, but not the rightfulness of their opinions; that the expression of his opinion might influence theirs, and he would not give it ! He held it to be an invasion of the freedom of religious opinion, to attempt to subject the opinions of any man to the ordeal of public judgment ; he would not submit to it in his own case, nor sanction it in another—he considered that religious opinions should be judged by the fruits they produced—if they produced good men, they must be good. My mother was educated in a convent—the best school of the day—in Paris; she took up a girlish desire to join the Catholic church, and wrote to her father to ask his permission. He called for her, took her home, and placed her in the gay society of the court of Louis XVI., where all such thoughts quickly vanished. His calling for her was the only intimation she ever had of the receipt of her letter, the subject was never alluded to by him.

His codification of the Morals of Jesus was not known to his family before his death, and they learnt from a letter addressed to a friend, that he was in the habit of reading nightly from it, before going to bed. His report as Rector of the Board of Visitors of the University of Virginia, to the Legislature, places in its proper view, his sense of the importance of religious instruction.

[Here follows this report as given in this volume, commencing at page 468.]

His family, by whom he was surrounded, and who saw him in all the unguarded privacy of private life, believed him to be the purest of men. His precepts were those of truth and virtue. "Be just, be true, love your neighbor as yourself, and your country more than yourself," were among his favorite maxims, and they recognized in him a truthful exemplar of the precepts he taught. He said he had left the government of his country "with hands as clean as they were empty." His family circle knew that with calm serenity he had left the theatre of life, with a conscience as unsullied as his life had been just and upright. The beauty of his character was exhibited in the bosom of his family, where he delighted to indulge in all the fervor and delicacy of feminine feeling. Upon his death, there were found carefully preserved in a little sanctum sanctorum, locks of hair and other memorials of his wife and the children he had lost, with words of fond endearment written in his own hand upon the envelopes of the little mementoes. Before he lost his taste for the violin,

In winter evenings, he would play on it, having his grandchildren dancing around him. In summer he would station them for their little races on the lawn—give the signal for the start—be the arbiter of the contest, and award the prizes.

His manner was dignified, reserved with strangers, but frank and cordial with his friends; his conversation cheerful, often sportive, and illustrated by anecdotes. He spoke only of the good qualities of men, which induced the belief that he knew little of them, but no one knew them better. I had formed this opinion, and on hearing him speak very favorably of men with defects known to myself, stated them to him, when he asked if I supposed he had not observed them, adding others not noted by me, and evincing much more accurate knowledge of the individual character than I possessed, observing, "My habit is to speak only of men's good qualities." When he believed that either men or measures were adverse to Republican institutions, he spoke of them with open and unqualified condemnation.

Standing himself on an elevated position, from his talents, education, fortune and political station, he was emphatically the friend of the working-man. On passing the home of a neighbor (Mr. Jesse Lewis), a blacksmith, remarkable for his probity, his integrity and his industry, and too wise, when past the meridian of life, to be ashamed to work at the trade that had made his fortune, he often remarked of him, "it is such men as that who constitute the wealth of a nation, not millionaires."

He never indulged in controversial conversation, because it often excited unpleasant feeling, and illustrated its inutility by the anecdote of two men who sat down candidly to discuss a subject, and each converted the other. His maxim was, that every man had a right to his own opinion on all subjects, and others were bound to respect that right; hence, in conversation, if any one expressed a decided opinion differing from his own, he made no reply, but changed the subject; he believed men could always find subjects enough to converse on, in which they agreed in opinion, omitting those upon which they differed; unreserved and candid himself, he was a listener, encouraging others to converse. His tact in the management of men was great; he inquiringly followed out adverse opinions to their results, leaving it to their friends to note the error into which it led them, taking up their doubts as important suggestions, never permitting a person to place himself upon the defensive, or if he did, changing the subject, so as not to fix him in a wrong opinion by controverting it. With men of fertile and ingenious minds, fond of suggesting objections to propositions stated, he would sometimes suggest the opposite of the conclusion to which he desired them to come, then assent to the force of their objections, and thus lead them to convert themselves. If information was sought, he gave it freely; if doubts were suggested, he explained them without reserve, never objecting to the scrutiny or canvass of his own opinions. As a public man, his friends complained that he spoke too freely, communicating more than they thought prudent. His powers of conversation were great, yet he always turned it to subjects most familiar to those with whom he conversed, whether laborer, mechanic or other; and if they displayed sound judgment and a knowledge of the subject, entered the information they gave, under appropriate heads, for reference, embodying thus a mass of facts upon the practical details of every-day life. His capacity to acquire knowledge was of the highest order; his application intense and untiring—his system and arrangement for the preservation of, and reference to the sources of his acquirements, most methodical and exact. The Hon. Littleton Waller Tazewell told me, that when a young man, his father being in the Senate, and Mr. Jefferson Vice-President, some case of impeachment coming on, he was sent with a note to Mr. Jefferson, asking some references to authorities on the subject. On the delivery of the note, he took a note-book from a drawer and instantly copied the references. On delivering them to his father, the latter observed he believed he had sent him chapter and verse for everything written on the subject. Of his voluminous correspondence, embracing upwards of forty thousand letters, written and received, and the private and public accounts of his whole life, he could in a moment lay his hand on any letter or receipt. Shortly after his death, Mr. Madison expressed to me the opinion, that Mr. Jefferson would be found to be the most learned man that had ever devoted so much time to public life. He was economical, exact, and methodical in his expenses and accounts. The account books, now in my possession, of his Maitre d'Hotel, at Paris and Washington, show the minutest details of household expenditure, and notes and figures in his own hand-writing, exhibit the closest personal inspection by himself, and a monthly analysis in a tabularized form of the expenditures in each item. His own numerous account books show the entry at the time, in his own hand, of each expenditure, however minute.

His manners were of that polished school of the Colonial Government, so remarkable in its day—under no circumstances violating any of those minor conventional observances which constitute the well-bred gentleman, courteous and considerate to all persons. On riding out with him, when a lad, we met a negro who bowed to us; he returned his bow, I did not; turning to me he asked, "do you permit a negro to be more of a gentleman than yourself?"

There was a little emulation endeavored to be excited among the older gentlemen of the neighborhood, in their gardening; and he who had peas first, announced his success by an invitation to the others to dine with him. A wealthy neighbor, without children, and fond of horticulture, generally triumphed. Mr. Jefferson, on one occasion had them first, and when his family reminded him that it was his right to invite the company, he replied "No, say nothing about it, it will be more agreeable to our friend to think that he never fails." In his person he was neat in the extreme. In early life, his dress, equipage, and appointments were fastidiously appropriate to his rank. As he grew old, although preserving his extreme neatness, his dress was plainer, and he was more indifferent to the appearance of his equipage. When at Paris, Philadelphia, and Washington, his furniture, table, servants, equipage and the *tout ensemble* of his establishment, were deemed highly appropriate to the position he held. He was a gentleman everywhere. On entering the Presidency, he determined not to have weekly levees, like his predecessors, and so announced. His political opponents determined that he should continue the custom. On the first levee day, he rode out at his usual hour of one o'clock, returning at three, and on entering the President's house, booted, whip in hand, soiled with his ride, found himself in a crowd of ladies and gentlemen, fashionably dressed for the occasion. He greeted them with all the ease and courtesy of expected guests that he had been prepared to receive, exhibiting not the slightest indication of annoyance. They never again tried the experiment. At home, he desired to live like his neighbors, in the plain hospitality of a Virginia gentleman. It was a source of continued and deep regret to him, that the number of strangers who visited him, kept his neighbors from him; he said, "he had to exchange the society of his friends and neighbors for those whom he had never seen before, and never expected to see again."

Mr. Jefferson's hair, when young, was of a reddish cast, sandy as he advanced in years—his eye, hazel—dying in his 84th year, he had not lost a tooth, or had one defective; his skin, thin, peeling from his face on exposure to the sun, and giving it a tettered appearance; the superficial veins so weak, as upon the slightest blow, to cause extensive suffusions of blood, in early life, upon standing to write for any length of time, bursting beneath the skin: it, however, gave him no inconvenience. His countenance was mild and benignant, and attractive to strangers. While President, returning on horseback from court, with company whom he had invited to dinner, and who were, all but one or two, riding ahead of him, on reaching a stream over which there was no bridge, a man asked him to take him up behind and carry him over. The gentlemen in the rear coming up just as Mr. Jefferson had put him down and rode on, asked the man how it happened that he had permitted the others to pass without asking them? He replied, "From their looks I did not like to ask them—the old gentleman looked as if he would do it, and I asked him." He was very much surprised to hear that he had ridden behind the President of the United States. Mr. Jefferson's stature was commanding, six feet two and a half inches in height, well formed, indicating strength, activity, and robust health; his carriage, erect; step firm and elastic, which he preserved to his death; his temper, naturally strong, under perfect control—his courage, cool and impassive—no one ever knew him exhibit trepidation—his moral courage of the highest order—his will, firm and inflexible—it was remarked of him that he never abandoned a plan, a principle, or a friend. A bold and fearless rider, you saw at a glance, from his easy and confident seat, that he was master of his horse, which was usually the fine blood horse of Virginia. The only impatience of temper he ever exhibited, was with his horse, which he subdued to his will by a fearless application of the whip, on the slightest manifestation of restiveness. He retained to the last his fondness for riding on horseback; he rode within three weeks of his death, when from disease, debility and age, he mounted with difficulty. He rode with confidence, and never permitted a servant to accompany him; he was fond of solitary rides and musing, and said that the presence of a servant annoyed him. He held in little esteem the education that made men ignorant and helpless as to the common necessities of life; and he exemplified it by an incident which occurred to a young gentleman returned from Europe, where he had been educated. On riding out with his companions, the strap of his girth broke, at the hole of the buckle; and they, perceiving it an accident easily remedied, rode on and left him. A plain man coming up and seeing that his horse had made a circular path in the road in his impatience to get on, asked if he could aid him? "Oh, sir," replied the young man, "if you could only assist me to get it up to the next hole." "Suppose you let it out a hole or two on the other side," said the man.

His habits were regular and systematic. He was a miser of his time, rose always at dawn, wrote and read until breakfast, breakfasted early, and dined from three to four—after breakfast read for half an hour in his public rooms or portico, in summer—visited his garden and workshops—returned to his writing and reading till one, when he rode on horseback to three or half past—dined, and gave the evening to his family and company—retired at nine, and to bed from ten to eleven. He said in his last illness, that the sun had not caught him in bed for fifty years. He always made his own fire. He drank water but once a day, a single glass, when he returned from his ride. He ate heartily, and much vegetable food, preferring French cookery, because it made the meats more tender. He never drank ardent spirits or strong wines—such was his aversion to ardent spirits that when, in his last illness, his physician desired him to use brandy as an astringent, he could not induce him to take it strong enough.

He inherited from his father 1,900 acres of land, and some negroes. He commenced the practice of the law soon after he came of age. When he married, in his

29th year, he had increased his estate to 5,000 acres, all paid for. His accounts show a receipt of $3,000 a year from his practice at the bar, and $2,000 from his farms, a large income at that day. The death of his father-in-law ensuing soon after his marriage, he acquired a large addition to his estate, but the share of debt which fell to him was £3,749 12s. He sold property immediately to pay it. The payments for this property were made in paper money, which he deposited in the loan office, and received it back again at a depreciation out to him, of one for forty. He sold again in 1785 and 1792, to discharge the debt, with its accumulated interest. This swept nearly half of his estate. He was absent from his estate, as Minister to France, Secretary of State, Vice-President and President from 1782 to 1809—27 years, with the exception of four years, from 1793 to 1797, which he devoted to his farms. He returned in his old age to be hunted down by the reputation he had won in the service of his country. Twelve years before his death, he remarked to me, in conversation, that if he lived long enough he would beggar his family—that the number of persons he was compelled to entertain would devour his estate; many bringing letters from his ancient friends, and all coming with respectful feelings, he could not shut his door in their faces. A heavy loss by indorsing for a friend in 1819, and the extreme depression in the value of property, when it became necessary to bring his into market, completed the catastrophe, and verified his anticipations.

[Here follows the account of Mr. Jefferson's last illness and death, commencing at page 543 of this volume, and it comprises the entire remaining portion of the letter.]

Very respectfully,

Th. J. Randolph.

APPENDIX NO. XXXVII. Vol. III. p. 564.

The Albemarle Resolutions vindicating Mr. Jefferson from Posthumous Slanders.

A distinguished clergyman of the Episcopal Church visited Charlottesville, in the spring of 1840, and circumstances threw him among the coterie, named in the text, so hostile to Mr. Jefferson.

He heard all the exploded tales of a life-time, brought out fresh—reaffirmed— "told with a cirumstance" against the latter. Accordingly, in a letter which was published in the Episcopal Recorder, in Philadelphia, he stated, in substance, that he found Mr. Jefferson's character was held in aversion in the neighborhood in which he lived and died—that he there heard more against it than he had ever heard before.

This publication found its way back to Charlottesville. The editor of the Whig paper (opposed to the party with which Mr. Jefferson had acted in politics) called public attention to it, and we think it was he who first suggested that a meeting of the citizens of the county be held on the subject. The proposal at once met favor. The high-minded men of the Whig party felt that it was time to vindicate their party, their county, and themselves from all suspicion of countenancing assaults on Mr. Jefferson's memory, which, however easily disproved, and contemptible where they were made, acquired a degree of importance in other places, because they purported to have the sanction of Mr. Jefferson's former *neighbors*. And it is for the latter reason solely, that we refer to these petty aggressions, and the rebuke they called forth.

The proposed meeting was held on the 18th of July, 1840. Much feeling was manifested—the Whig gentlemen of the county taking the lead in the proceedings. It was resolved to hold a subsequent meeting, and to appoint a committee of twenty-one to report thereat the sense of the county on the attacks made on Mr. Jefferson. The committee comprised the most distinguished gentlemen of Albemarle—leading and eminent men in different religious sects—persons who had held important offices, and who were known throughout the State, and, in some instances, throughout a much wider sphere, as civilians and politicians.

They were William C. Rives, Lucian Minor, Thomas Wood, Thomas W. Maury, Richmond Terrell, Isaac A. Coles, John T. Brown, John H. Craven, John Timberlake, Robert H. Carter, Allan W. Magruder, Gen. William F. Gordon, Col. Nimrod Bramham, Charles J. Merriwether, Col. Thomas Durrett, Walter Coles, Reuben Maury, Col. George W. Kinsolving, Thomas H. Brown, Richard Gamble, and Alonzo Gooch.

The proceedings of the adjourned meeting were thus contemporaneously published under the authority of its officers:

"At a very numerous meeting of the people of Albemarle, at their Court House in Charlottesville, on the 3d of August, 1840 (being court-day), held pursuant to the call made by a preliminary meeting of July 18th, in order to consider a recent publication in the (Philadelphia) Episcopal Recorder, reflecting upon Thomas Jefferson:

"The assembly was called to order by Gen. Wm. F. Gordon, who briefly recited the wrong done by the aforementioned publication to the memory of Mr. Jefferson, and to the people of his county, in ascribing to them feelings utterly at war with the reverence which they cherish for him, and suggested the tone and character of the vindication that became them. Then, on the motion of Gen. Gordon, Col. Bramham was called to the chair, and Mr. Lucian Minor appointed Secretary.

"Mr. William C. Rives, as Chairman of the Committee of 21, appointed at the preliminary meeting, then reported the following preamble and resolution, which were unanimously adopted by the meeting, viz.:

" The citizens of Albemarle, here assembled, have seen with deep and painful regret, certain strictures on the character and memory of Mr. Jefferson, contained in a letter of the *Reverend* ———, written from Charlottesville, under date of the 27th May last, and published in the Episcopal Recorder of the 13th June. Having been made parties, in some sort, to this posthumous disparagement of their illustrious countryman by the ascription of sentiments of peculiar 'aversion and want of respect for his name, to the very neighborhood in which he lived and died,' and where the writer alleges he found his *character* worse than even he, with the most unfavorable prepossessions, *ever conceived* it to be—they feel themselves called on by a solemn duty to the dead, to disavow for themselves all privity or participation in the sentiments here imputed. If Mr. Jefferson, like other men who have passed through long and busy lives, should have had the misfortune to create some individual enmities, it was hoped that even these had long since been silenced and disarmed at the sacred precincts of the tomb. But that there ever was, among the great body of his neighbors and countymen, any other sentiment towards him than one of professed gratitude for his services to the cause of American freedom, of an admiration (in which the whole world partook), of his character as one of the boldest and most sagacious champions of human rights, and of cordial respect for him in the relations of social life—no one, it is believed, who has had an opportunity of personally knowing the true state of the facts, will venture to assert.

"History, indeed, has preserved an emphatic and touching testimony borne to his merits, in these respects, by the body of his countymen, thirty-one years ago, in their address of welcome to him on his return among them, after his retirement from the Presidency. Who, among us, can have forgotten the eloquent and affecting appeal he then made, with the erectness of conscious integrity, to the '*triers of the vicinage*'—those who had been 'the eye-witnesses and observers' of his daily life! 'Of you, my neighbors,' he said, 'I may ask in the face of the world' —whose ox have I taken, or whom have I defrauded ? Whom have I oppressed, or from whose hand have I received a bribe to blind mine eyes therewith ?' The same testimony, which the people of Albemarle then zealously bore to the living citizen and statesman, we their descendants and successors, this day feel ourselves solemnly impelled by our duty to the dead, to reiterate and renew.

"In vindicating the memory of Mr. Jefferson from the injurious representations above referred to (representations originating, as we hope, in unintentional error on the part of Dr. ———), we are not to be considered as either justifying or criticising the opinions of Mr. Jefferson on the subject of our holy religion, with whose promises and precepts a faith, sacredly cherished, has indissolubly united the dearest hopes and interests of many of us. But this consideration does not, in our view, cancel the obligations of truth and candor, nor should it withhold the award of discriminative justice to a great public benefactor and patriot, who lived and died among us, and with the monuments of whose useful labors the history and archives of the nation, the Statute-book of Virginia, and the very face of our land, and especially our own portion of it, are profusely covered over.

"*Resolved*, therefore, that the foregoing declaration be adopted as an expression of the sense of this meeting, on the occasion which has brought us together; and that copies of it, together with this resolution, attested by the signatures of the President and Secretary of the meeting, be furnished for publication to the newspapers printed in this place, and in the City of Richmond.

"Attest,

"N. BRAMHAM, *Chairman.*

"LUCIAN MINOR, *Secretary.*"

We have struck out the name of the author of the letter published in the Episcopal Recorder, wherever it occurs in these proceedings. He acted in perfect good faith in the first instance, and has in the spirit of a Christian and a gentleman voluntarily and frankly made ample retraction and reparation for all unintentional error. His name is by far too conspicuous to be concealed from those who desire to trace it out; but we at least will not aid to place it before the world in what we regard as purely an adventitious and disagreeable connection.

The reverend gentleman placed in our hands the following paper :

To HENRY S. RANDALL.

"In any reference which you may make in your memoir of Mr. Jefferson to certain resolutions adopted at a meeting in Charlottesville, Virginia, in 1840, occasioned by the publication of a letter from me in the Episcopal Recorder in Philadelphia, permit me also to say :

"That in that letter I stated only the fact of my having heard in Charlottesville assertions more derogatory to the character of Mr. Jefferson than I had ever heard before; I did not repeat those assertions, nor express any judgment of their truth—I did suppose them to be true, however, and therefore made no reserve in referring to them. I have since become convinced that they were not true. And I must now consider it my duty to express my regret that I was led in any way to refer to them in a public communication, and to withdraw all responsibility for their future propagation, believing them now to be unfounded imputations upon the private character of Mr. Jefferson."

APPENDIX NO. XXXVIII.—Vol. III., p. 565.

Correction in regard to Patrick Henry's action on the question of Independence.

Partly from a letter addressed by General Charles Lee to Mr. Henry, and partly from an omission, which could not have been expected, in Wirt's Life of Henry (to say nothing of other earlier historical productions), we were led into the error which is corrected below by one of the most candid and accurate historical investigators and critics of our country. We need not say with what deep gratification we insert the correction.

Norfolk, Va., January 15, 1858.

My dear Sir: I have read the first volume of your Life of Jefferson with the deepest interest, but I would not have troubled you with a letter until I had read the forthcoming volumes, had I not seen an error into which you had fallen respecting Patrick Henry, which I hope it is not too late to correct. You speak of the backwardness of Henry in sustaining the measure of Independence in the Virginia Convention of May, 1776. You allude to the subject on three several occasions, and, for the sake of accuracy, I will quote your words. You say, rather doubtingly (vol. i. p. 128), "Would Wirt have claimed for Henry such a remarkable prescience in regard to the Declaration of Independence, had he known that a letter would one day see the light, which seems to conclusively show that Mr. Henry actually hesitated a little in regard to making that declaration when it was finally proposed?" This is an interrogative, but demands an answer unfavorable to Henry. But, in a note on the page quoted above, you say: "As Mr. Henry did not *oppose* the resolution of independence in the Convention, he probably did not allow the views expressed to General Lee to become public. But this, perhaps, explains why, *on this occasion of occasions*, Henry's 'supernatural voice' was not heard." And again, on page 141, you observe: "It might or might not have been foreseen that the 'supernatural voice' of the old popular leader in the Convention (Henry) would remain silent." You cite as your authority the letter of Gen. Charles Lee to Patrick Henry (Am. Archives, Fifth Series, vol. i., 96), dated May 7, 1776, in which Lee states the objections to an immediate declaration made by Henry in conversation the day before, and endeavors to refute them. With this letter I have been familiar since its publication, and I readily see how well adapted it is to lead astray. Yet, it does not, strictly speaking, authorize the assertion, or even an innuendo, that Henry was silent when the proposition of independence was about to be decided by the Virginia Convention. The statements of Lee in their utmost extent, merely show that *eight days before* the resolution of independence was adopted by the body, Henry had in private conversation with Lee urged some arguments against an immediate declaration, "before the pulse of France and Spain was felt." Henry well knew the ability of Lee and his familiarity with foreign topics, and, following his old and familiar habit of gathering intelligence, might very naturally urge objections derived from the temper of foreign powers in order to elicit the views and opinions of Lee. Strictly speaking, then, this letter of the 7th of May, referring wholly to a conversation held on the sixth, can prove nothing *conclusively* concerning what one of the parties actually said or did eight days later in a public body.

But, fortunately, we are not left to mere inferences from the letter of Gen. Lee on this subject. We have direct and positive testimony to prove that Henry, so far from being neutral or silent when the resolution instructing the delegates of Virginia in Congress to propose independence was discussed and decided in the Convention, he was its boldest and most eloquent advocate on the floor. We know from the express declaration of a member of the committee which drafted the Declaration of Rights and the first constitution of Virginia, and who was, at one time certainly, a mortal enemy of Henry, that the resolution of independence was drawn by Pendleton, was offered in committee by Gen. Nelson, and was "sustained against all opposition by Henry with that abounding energy and eloquence of which he was a master," and to which no writer has done more ample justice than yourself. Such was the testimony of Edmund Randolph, uttered four years after the death of Henry, in the hall of the House of Delegates in Richmond, over the corpse of Pendleton. (Virginia Gazette, Nov. 2d, 1803, in the library of Virginia.)

I cannot blame you for not knowing the contents of an old newspaper published more than half a century ago, of which but a single copy is in existence; and when I saw the error into which you had been led by the letter of Lee, I knew that no man living would more cordially desire to exonerate the memory of Henry than yourself. With great respect,

I am very truly yours,

HUGH B. GRIGSBY.

HENRY S. RANDALL, Esq.

An incident connected with the Declaration of Independence.

Some of the old painters were fond of introducing a homely or even a grotesque minor accessory into their stateliest pictures. Here is something of the kind without borrowing from imagination. The following is from a letter to us from a familiar visitor at Monticello, General J. Spear Smith, of Maryland: [1]

"Whilst the question of Independence was before Congress, it had its meetings near a livery stable. The members wore short breeches and silk stockings, and with handkerchief in hand, they were diligently employed in lashing the flies from their legs. So very vexatious was this annoyance, and to so great an impatience did it arouse the sufferers, that it hastened, if it did not aid, in inducing them to promptly affix their signatures to the great document, which gave birth to an empire republic.

"This anecdote I had from Mr. Jefferson, at Monticello, who seemed to enjoy it

------

[1] Son of Mr. Jefferson's life-long friend, General Samuel Smith, of Maryland.

very much, as well as to give great credit to the influence of the flies. He told it with much glee, and seemed to retain a vivid recollection of the severity of an attack, from which the only relief was signing the paper, and flying from the scene."

Jefferson's letters to Thomas Mann Randolph as N. R.

In vol. ii. p. 523, an extract is given from a letter from Mr. Jefferson to N. R., and it is mentioned in a note that "these initials occur here and again, where it would seem that the letters must have been addressed to his son-in-law, Colonel T. M. Randolph." Their second occurrence is in same volume, p. 601, and it is there suggested or intimated in a note that the "fictitious direction" may have been intended to guard against the suspected infidelities of the post.

We since learn that the letters were, as we supposed, written to Randolph, but that the direction was not "fictitious," as would appear in the Congress edition, where the letters only appear. Mr. Jefferson, in writing his son-in-law's initials, habitually combined them into an abbreviated character, which was mistaken for N. R.

John Adams's Correspondence.

The tenth volume of the "Life and Works of John Adams" was not received until after the completion of this Biography.

GENERAL INDEX.

ADAMS, JOHN, his description of Jefferson's first appearance in Congress, Vol. I. 113; he describes Jefferson's character as a member, 114; his views on reconciliation with England, 123–127; his statements in regard to preparation of Declaration of Independence, 165, 166; he is the great champion of the Declaration, 179; his speeches thereon, 180; his oratory, 181; compared with Franklin, 183; his inaccuracy in statement, 166; he questions originality of Declaration, 186; his unlucky claim, 187–189; inequalities of his character, 187: he is with Jefferson in France, 413; their personal relations, 182, 185; he invites Jefferson to London, 444; negotiations, 445; his description of his reception by public personages in England, 446, 447; with Jefferson visits Stratford-upon-Avon, Worcester, etc., 449, 450; Jefferson's private opinion of him, 464; Jefferson's letter to him on hereditary officers, 486; his comparisons between monarchical and popular government, 587; he is consulted by Washington on allowing Lord Dorchester's passage, and his answer, 621; Jefferson to, explaining his note to J. B. Smith, Vol. II. 4; Adams's reply, 5, 6; his defence of the American Constitutions, and discourses on Davila, 7, 8; he is reëlected Vice-President, 102; Jefferson to, 228; assigns reasons for the refusals to enter Washington's Cabinet, 247; his views of English feelings towards U. S., 261; his letter to Gerry on Monroe's recall and conduct, 283, 284; is a candidate for Presidency in 1796, 311; his election, 315; Jefferson willing to form a coalition with him, 320–328; his political views, 320–328; his jealousy of Hamilton, 323, 324; his account of his interview with Jefferson, 324, 325; his inclination to coalesce with the Republicans, 325–328; jealousies of him entertained by the Federal leaders, 327; declares the result of Presidential election in Senate, 332; proposes to send Jefferson or Madison minister to France, 334, 337; his inauguration as President, 336; his speech, 336, 337; his feelings towards France and England, 343; his critical period of entering office, 343, 344; danger of dismissing the existing Cabinet, 344; character of his Cabinet, 344, 345; excited by Cabinet against France and Jefferson, 346, 347; his vanity inflamed, 348; France dismisses Monroe with distinction, and refuses to receive Pinckney, 349; President convenes a special session of Congress, 349; his warlike speech, 349, 350; addresses of the houses, 350; action of Congress, 351, 352; his views on an English alliance, 381; on the "treachery of the common people," 381; his message to Congress, 381; consults his Cabinet on declaring war against France, etc., 381; warlike message, 382; Congress on fire, 382; Sprigg's resolutions, 383; the X Y Z dispatches, 384–387; effect on public mind, 387, 388; war measures in Congress, 388; aliens take flight, 388; war addresses pour upon the President, and his replies, 389; terrorism, 389; insults of England, 390, 391; rumors of a French invasion, 391; Marshall's return, and new war

THE END.

Printed in the United States
109560LV00005B/8/A

9 781432 635534